The Routledge Companion to Coopetition Strategies

As more and more strategic alliances are forged between competitors, a dedicated word has been coined to described this strategy: coopetition. Coopetition strategy research began in the early 1990s and has been steadily increasing; yet, a global overview of the field has been lacking.

This reference volume is the first to provide a comprehensive international survey of coopetition research. Organized thematically and written by the world's most-cited researchers in the field, it views the topic through the lens of a variety of disciplines including innovation, strategic management, operations management, and marketing.

This reference book is the definitive resource for researchers looking to understand the field of coopetition throughout business and management.

Anne-Sophie Fernandez is Associate Professor in Strategic Management at the University of Montpellier, France.

Paul Chiambaretto is Associate Professor in Marketing and Strategy at Montpellier Business School and Associate Researcher at École Polytechnique, France.

Frédéric Le Roy is Professor in Strategic Management at the University of Montpellier and Affiliate Professor at Montpellier Business School, France.

Wojciech Czakon is Professor in Strategic Management at Jagiellonian University in Kraków, Poland.

"Coopetition has emerged as a word, as a business practice, and as a field of academic research in recent years. Yet, much ambiguity and misunderstanding about the definition and implications of coopetition remain. *The Routledge Companion to Coopetition Strategies* put together by Anne-Sophie Fernandez, Paul Chiambaretto, Frédéric Le Roy, and Wojciech Czakon, who are among the first academics to have extensively investigated coopetition, is a clear, comprehensive, and much-needed contribution to the understanding of this new phenomenon."

Pierre Dussauge, Professor of Strategic Management, HEC Paris

"A book on coopetition has been much needed given the prevalence of this phenomenon and a growing body of research studying it. Fernandez and colleagues are expert guides in the coopetition safari helping the reader to understand the paradoxes of coopetition, comprehend what extant research has already been done, and discover exciting new research opportunities. The book is very well written and easy to read. I strongly recommend this book not only for seasoned scholars doing research on coopetition or PhD students getting inspired to study this research area, but also for faculty teaching strategic management, entrepreneurship, and marketing to graduate and undergraduate students."

Olga Bruyaka, Assistant Professor, University of West Virginia

"Fernandez, Chiambaretto, Le Roy, and Czakon invite us all on a safari into the wilds of coopetition research. With 37 thoughtful essays on multiple different aspects of coopetition, *The Routledge Companion to Coopetition Strategies* is a valuable resource for both academics and thoughtful practitioners on how to better understand and manage the inherent paradoxical tensions associated with simultaneous competition and collaboration."

Professor Tomi Laamanen, DSc (Strategy), DSc (Finance), Director and Chair of Strategic Management, Institute of Management, University of St. Gallen

The Routledge Companion to Coopetition Strategies

*Edited by Anne-Sophie Fernandez,
Paul Chiambaretto, Frédéric Le Roy,
and Wojciech Czakon*

Routledge
Taylor & Francis Group

LONDON AND NEW YORK

First published 2019
by Routledge
4 Park Square, Milton Park, Abingdon, Oxon OX14 4RN

and by Routledge
605 Third Avenue, New York, NY 10017

First issued in paperback 2022

Routledge is an imprint of the Taylor & Francis Group, an informa business

Publisher's Note
The publisher has gone to great lengths to ensure the quality of this reprint but points out that some imperfections in the original copies may be apparent.

British Library Cataloguing-in-Publication Data
A catalogue record for this book is available from the British Library

Library of Congress Cataloging-in-Publication Data
A catalog record has been requested for this book

ISBN 13: 978-1-03-247605-6 (pbk)
ISBN 13: 978-1-138-73689-4 (hbk)
ISBN 13: 978-1-315-18564-4 (ebk)

DOI: 10.4324/9781315185644

Typeset in Bembo
by Out of House Publishing

Contents

Contents

Figures

Tables

Contributors

Sascha Albers is Professor of International Management at the University of Antwerp, Belgium. His teaching, research, and consulting focuses on strategic management and inter-organizational design problems in international business contexts, particularly in the transportation industry. His research has been published in leading international management and logistics journals, such as the *Journal of Management* and the *International Journal of Physical Distribution and Logistics Management*. Professor Albers is a Research Fellow of the University of Cologne and has been a visiting lecturer and invited presenter at various universities and business schools in the US, Europe, Australia, and New Zealand.

Jamal Eddine Azzam is Associate Professor and Head of the Master's in Innovation Management at Toulouse School of Management (University of Toulouse 1 Capitole, France). He completed his PhD in Management Science at Nice-Sophia Antipolis University, where he also served as a lecturer and teaching assistant. He was an academic guest at ETH Zurich, TIMGROUP (Chair of Technology and Innovation Management) and lecturer at Aix-Marseille University. His research focuses on innovation and patent management, with a particular emphasis on capabilities and licensing in open innovation. He has published in journals such as *Management International* and *International Journal of Technology Management*.

Philippe Baumard is Professor of Organizational Theory and Strategy at the Conservatoire national des arts & métiers, Paris; Dean for Research at ESLSCA Business School, Paris; and Associate Researcher with École Polytechnique's Management Research Center. Philippe Baumard is the 2013 and 2014 laureate of the French BPI National Innovation awards for cybersecurity in the field of autonomous behavioral learning. He has authored ninety refereed journal articles and twelve books on corporate strategy, knowledge dynamics, coopetition, organizational failures, and innovation management.

Maria Bengtsson is Professor in Entrepreneurship at Umeå School of Business and Economics, Sweden. Her research is mainly focused on coopetition, the dynamics of inter-organizational relationships, and innovation. She has published books and articles in journals such as *Industrial Marketing Management*, *Scandinavian Journal of Management*, *Regional Studies* and *International Small Business Journal*.

Héloïse Berkowitz is Researcher at CNRS (UMR5303) and TSM-R. She has a PhD in management from École Polytechnique and she graduated from the Sorbonne in History; HEC Paris in the Programme Grande École; and the CEMS Alliance in International Management. She has been a visiting scholar at Columbia University and the Stanford Center for Ocean

Solutions, and is currently at Institut Barcelona d'Estudis Internacionals. Her research deals with transitions to sustainability, with a focus on sectoral governance and collective action among organizations (meta-organizations), in various empirical settings from natural resources to collaborative economy or ocean sustainability. Her work has been published in the *Academy of Management Review*, the *Journal of Business Ethics*, and *European Management Review*.

Ricarda B. Bouncken has been Chair Professor of Strategic Management and Organization, University of Bayreuth, Germany since 2009. From 2005 to 2009 she was Chair Professor at the University of Greifswald, and before that Professor of Planning and Innovation Management, Brandenburg Institute of Technology. She achieved her Habilitation from the University Lüneburg in 2002, and her PhD from the University of St. Gall, Switzerland in 1997. Her research centers on coopetition, strategies, organizational design, and the management of innovation, particularly between organizations. Recent research also focuses on new work-organization in collaborative workspaces among start-ups, corporates, and freelancers, partly as corporate venturing. She has authored more than 200 publications.

David Carfi is Researcher and Lecturer of Advanced Linear Algebra, Differential Geometry and Functional Analysis applied to Economics, Finance, Relativity and Quantum Mechanics at the University of California, Riverside. He is an expert on and lecturer in game theory, decision theories, and the Laurent Schwartz theory of distributions and applications. He has published several papers on coopetition in game theory with applications to various fields, and many books about game theory and related applications. He gives seminars about the relationship between mathematics and music and about algebraic structures in music composition. He is also a classic concert pianist and composer.

Hervé Chappert is Associate Professor at the University of Montpellier and a member of Montpellier Research Management (MRM). His fields of interest cover relational strategies and technological competition. He also works on standardization in the IT industry and on innovations and virtual environments. He has over twenty years of teaching experience in IT at undergraduate and postgraduate levels in the public sector and worked in the private sector as an IT consultant from 1986 to 2008. Hervé completed his first graduate degree in information systems management in 1990, a second graduate degree in management sciences in 1994, a master's degree in management sciences in 2008, and a PhD in management sciences in 2012. He is also a Microsoft-certified systems engineer (2000) and a certified Novell administrator (1997).

Tadhg Ryan Charleton is a Fulbright Scholar at the Department of Management, Pamplin College of Business, Virginia Tech, USA. He is also a PhD candidate in strategic management at the School of Business, Maynooth University, Ireland. Tadhg's research focuses on value creation through coopetition and the competitive dynamics of collaborative relationships. His work has received awards from national and international bodies including the Fulbright Commission, Enterprise Ireland, John F. Kennedy Fund, John & Pat Hume Awards, and the Irish Research Council.

Henry Chesbrough is currently Adjunct Professor and the faculty director of the Garwood Center for Corporate Innovation at the Haas School of Business at the University of California, Berkeley. He is recognized as the "father" of open innovation and has published many research papers and books, with more than 50,000 citations on Google Scholar.

Paul Chiambaretto is Associate Professor of Strategy and Marketing at Montpellier Business School and Associate Researcher at École Polytechnique. His main research topics are inter-organizational relationships (such as alliances, alliance portfolios, and coopetition) and branding strategies. He has developed a strong expertise on the air and rail transportation industries. His research has been published in ranked journals such as *Industrial Marketing Management, International Studies of Management and Organization, Long Range Planning, M@n@gement, Management International,* and many more. He has been a visiting researcher at several foreign institutions, such as the University of Oxford, Concordia University, and Umeå University.

Wojciech Czakon is Professor of Management at the Faculty of Management and Communication of the Jagiellonian University in Kraków, Poland. His research revolves around inter-organizational phenomena, strategies, and structures. In particular, coopetition at various levels of analysis and in various empirical settings has recently attracted his attention. For these studies he uses in-depth qualitative approaches, but also quantitative data analysis techniques. His lectures are dedicated to inter-organizational collaboration, strategic management, and research methodology. He has been Guest Editor of several journal special issues, and has organized workshops and conference tracks on coopetition. He is a Member of the Polish Academy of Sciences Committee for Management and Organization Science.

Katarzyna Czernek-Marszałek is Assistant Professor at the Faculty of Management, University of Economics in Katowice, Poland. Her research interests include entities' relations, especially collaboration, in tourism regions and their influence on tourism region development. In her research she uses management theories and also theories from heterodox economics (e.g., New Economic Sociology and institutional theories). For these studies she uses in-depth qualitative approaches, but also quantitative data analysis techniques, including quantitative tools of social network analysis. Her lectures are dedicated to international tourism and to regional and local aspects of tourism development, including inter-organizational collaboration and marketing in tourism.

Giovanni Battista Dagnino is Chair of Management and President of the MSc Program in Economics and Management at the University of Rome LUMSA, Palermo Campus, Italy. He held visiting positions in eleven universities and business schools throughout the world. He is known for his pioneering work on coopetition strategy, a management area he contributed to set off, and the management of temporary advantage. Other investigation concerns hubris-driven strategies, the relationship between strategy, governance and entrepreneurship and research methods in strategic management. He has authored/edited thirteen books and several articles in leading management journals.

Stefanie Dorn is a postdoc at the University of Cologne, Germany. She previously worked as a research and teaching associate at the Institute of Trade Fair Management and the Department of Business Policy and Logistics at the University of Cologne, where she also earned her PhD. During her PhD studies, Dorn visited the Coopetition Lab at the University of Montpellier. Her research focuses on coopetition between firms, especially on research problems regarding strategic management and organizational design of coopetition.

Hervé Dumez is Director of the Interdisciplinary Institute for Innovation (i3-CNRS) and of the Research Center in Management Studies of the École Polytechnique (i3-CRG). He has been a visiting professor at MIT and at the Stockholm School of Eonomics (SCORE). He has written more than sixty papers (*Academy of Management Review, Journal of Business Ethics, European Management Review, M@n@gement*) and ten books (among them, *Comprehensive Research. A methodological and epistemological introduction to qualitative research*, Copenhagen Business School Press, 2016).

Isabel Estrada is Assistant Professor at the Department of Innovation Management & Strategy, University of Groningen. She is also an associate fellow of the SOM Research Institute and a member of the VinCi Center of Expertise. Isabel teaches courses on organizational and collaborative innovation in different education programs (Master of Science, Research Master, and Executive Master). Her research focuses on collaborative innovation strategies, including Industry–University alliances, R&D consortia, and cooperation between competitors. Isabel has published several chapter books and articles in journals such as *Research Policy, Industrial Marketing Management, Journal of Knowledge Management, Journal of Small Business Management*, and *Innovation: Management, Policy and Practice*.

Anne-Sophie Fernandez is Associate Professor of Strategic Management at the University of Montpellier (Montpellier Management Institute) and a member of Montpellier Research in Management (MRM). She focuses on how competitors can successfully achieve common innovation projects. She has worked in both aerospace and the airline industry. She has already published several articles in ranked journals (*Industrial Marketing Management, British Journal of Management, Long Range Planning*) and has participated in the organization of special tracks in her area (AIMS, EURAM) and in the coordination of special issues of academic journals.

Robert J. Galavan holds the Chair in Strategic Management at the School of Business, Maynooth University. He was the founding Head of School and is a former Dean of the Faculty of Social Sciences. His research examines management and organizational cognition, conflict intervention, and competitive dynamics. Dr. Galavan has published several books, most recently as contributor and co-editor (and series co-editor) for *New Horizons on Managerial and Organizational Cognition: Uncertainty and Strategic Decision Making*, and previously *Strategy, Innovation and Change*, published by Oxford University Press. Dr. Galavan directs the MSc in Strategy and Innovation at Maynooth University and is co-founder and Academic Director of the Edward M. Kennedy Institute. He is a member of the Executive Council of the Irish Academy of Management and chairs the IAM Strategy SIG.

Johanna Gast is Assistant Professor at the Montpellier Business School (France), where she is member of Montpellier Research in Management (MRM). In June 2017, she received her doctoral degree from Lappeenranta University of Technology, Finland. Her research focuses on strategy, coopetition, entrepreneurship, family business, and innovation. Her work has been published widely in leading academic and professional journals such as the *Journal of Product Innovation Management, Small Business Economics, Journal of Small Business Management*, and *Review of Managerial Science*.

Devi R. Gnyawali is Department Head and R. B. Pamplin Professor of Management at the Department of Management, Pamplin College of Business, Virginia Tech, USA. He is also a member of the International Advisory Board at the Umeå School of Business and Economics in Sweden. Dr. Gnyawali's current research examines why and how firms engage in coopetition and what the implications are of such coopetition. His research also seeks to understand how firms acquire external resources possessed by their alliance partners, how they develop internal resources such as technology and shared knowledge, and how they leverage external and internal resources in order to innovate and enhance their competitive position. Dr. Gnyawali is Associate Editor of the *Journal of Management* and has served on the Editorial Board of the *Academy of Management Review* and *Journal of Management*. His research has been published in premier business journals and has won awards from national and international conferences and journals.

Arash Golnam is an Industrial Engineer by training. He completed his PhD in the Management of Technology at École Polytechnique Fédérale de Lausanne (EPFL), and holds a certificate of advanced studies in system dynamics from Worcester Polytechnic Institute. Besides his research activities at EPFL, where he currently works as a research scientist, he is an adjunct professor at Business School Lausanne and Webster University Geneva. His areas of teaching and research include systems modelling, system dynamics simulation, problem structuring, and organizational decision making.

Aleksios (Alex) Gotsopoulos is Assistant Professor of Management at the SKK Graduate School of Business in Seoul, Korea. His research focuses on the emergence of new industries, particularly on first-mover (dis)advantages, the evolution and influence of categories in emerging industries, and the dynamics of legitimacy, competition and coopetition. Alex's research has appeared in the *Strategic Management Journal*, the *Academy of Management Journal*, and the *Academy of Management Review*, and has been featured in outlets such as the *Wall Street Journal* and *Inc.com*.

Călin Gurău is Professor of Marketing at Montpellier Business School, France. His present research interests are focused on marketing strategies for high-technology firms, entrepreneurial marketing, and sustainable development. He has published more than fifty papers in internationally refereed journals, such as *Industrial Marketing Management, International Marketing Review, Journal of Consumer Marketing, Journal of Marketing Communications*, and many more.

Marcus Holgersson is Associate Professor at the Department of Technology Management and Economics at Chalmers University of Technology. His research focuses on the strategic management and economics of innovation, technology, and intellectual property. He has previously held visiting positions at UC Berkeley, the University of Gothenburg, and Stanford University.

Wolfgang Hora holds a Diploma in Business and Economics from the Johannes Kepler University Linz, Austria. Besides his current work as a Research and Teaching Assistant at the University of Liechtenstein, he works as an independent management consultant specialized in the development of digitalisation concepts for SMEs.

Pia Hurmelinna-Laukkanen is Professor of Marketing, especially International Business, at the Oulu Business School, University of Oulu, and Adjunct Professor of Knowledge Management at the Lappeenranta University of Technology, School of Business and Management. Most of her research has involved innovation management and appropriability issues, including the examination of different knowledge protection and value capturing mechanisms. She has published over sixty refereed articles in journals such as the *Journal of Product Innovation Management, Industrial and Corporate Change, Industrial Marketing Management, R&D Management*, and *Technovation*. Her practical business experience comes, for example, from board membership and company-funded research.

Alain Jeunemaitre is Director of Research at the Interdisciplinary Institute for Innovation (i3-CNRS) and Professor Chargé de Cours at the École Polytechnique. He has held associate research positions at the University of Oxford (SAID Business School, Regulatory Policy Institute Hertford College, Centre for Social Legal Studies, Wolfson College, Nuffield College) and LSE (Department of Management). He has worked for the European Commission (DGREN, SESAR JU) on Air Traffic Services and has co-written books with Hervé Dumez on regulation and globalization for *The Macmillan Press,* and in the academic journals *European Management Review* and *M@n@gement.*

Marlene Johansson is Assistant Professor in Entrepreneurship at Umeå School of Business and Economics, Sweden. Her current research interest is focused on coopetition, SMEs, innovation, and strategic alliance capabilities. She has published in journals such as the *International Small Business Journal*, the *IMP Journal*, and *European Business Review.*

Sören Kock is Professor of Management in the Department of Management and Organisation at Hanken School of Economics in Finland. His main research interests are coopetition, international entrepreneurship, and business networks. His research has been published in, among other scientific journals, *Industrial Marketing Management, International Small Business Journal, International Business Research, The Journal of Business and Industrial Marketing, European Journal of Marketing,* and *Competitiveness Review.*

Patrycja Klimas is Assistant Professor at the University of Economics in Katowice. As a researcher she conducts research focused on inter-organizational cooperation, coopetition, networking, co-creation, and innovativeness. Her research projects refer mainly to high-tech and creative industries, including aviation, the video game industry, entertainment, and tourism. She uses both qualitative and quantitative research methods while specialising in multivariate regression, structural equation modeling, and social network analysis. She is experienced in the implementation of research projects at the local, national, and European level. She is a member of the European Academy of Management.

Sascha Kraus is Professor in Entrepreneurship at ESCE Paris (France) as well as Visiting Professor at Lappeenranta University of Technology, Finland. He holds a doctorate in Social and Economic Sciences from Klagenfurt University, Austria, a PhD in Industrial Engineering and Management from Helsinki University of Technology, and a Habilitation (Venia Docendi) from Laapeenranta University of Technology, both in Finland.

Frank Lasch is Professor in Entrepreneurship at Montpellier Business School. He holds a joint PhD in Economic Geography (2002, University of Regensburg, Germany and University of Montpellier, France) and a French habilitation of supervising doctoral research in Management Science (2007, "HDR," University of Montpellier). His major topics of research are regional entrepreneurship, international entrepreneurship, inter-firm cooperation, types of entrepreneurs, outcomes of entrepreneurship, entry modes of entrepreneurship, and copreneurship. His research has been published in a variety of journals, including *Entrepreneurship Theory & Practice, Small Business Economics, International Small Business Journal, Entrepreneurship & Regional Development, Management Decision, International Journal of Entrepreneurship & Small Business, Journal of Asia Entrepreneurship and Sustainability,* among others.

Frédéric Le Roy is Professor in Strategic Management at the University of Montpellier (Montpellier Management Institute) and Montpellier Business School, France. He is head of the research group MRM-Strategic Management and head of the Coopetition Lab (hosted by the

Labex Entreprendre). He is also director of the Master of Science in Consulting in Management, Organization, and Strategy. He has published several books and many research articles in journals such as *Long Range Planning, British Journal of Management, European Management Review, Industrial Marketing Management, Small Business Economics,* and so on.

Benjamin Lehiany is a permanent Assistant Professor of Strategy and the Scientific Director of the MSc International Strategy and Influence at Skema Business School. He is also Research Associate at the Interdisciplinary Institute for Innovation (i3-CNRS) and *Maître de conference* at École Polytechnique, Paris. His fields of expertise are industrial strategy and competitive intelligence with a sectoral specialization in network industries (energy/telecoms/transportation). He has also worked as an independent consultant in the energy and transportation sectors. Dr. Lehiany holds a Master's degree from Toulouse School of Economics and a PhD in Management Science from École Polytechnique.

Eva-Lena Lundgren-Henriksson is Lecturer at the Department of Management and Organisation at Hanken School of Economics in Finland. Her current research focuses on coopetition, strategy-as-practice, strategic change, and sensemaking.

Marcello Mariani is Full Professor of Entrepreneurship and Management at the Henley Business School, University of Reading and member of the Henley Center for Entrepreneurship, the Academy of Management, and the European Institute for Advanced Studies in Management. After earning his PhD in Business Administration at the University of Bologna (Italy) and a postdoc at the University of Technology Sydney (Australia), he has been an academic faculty member of the University of Bologna and has acted as visiting professor at the Stern School of Business, New York University (USA) and a number of other universities. His research has been published in a wide range of highly ranked academic journals.

Anna Minà is Assistant Professor in Management at Kore University of Enna, Italy. She received her PhD in Business Economics and Management from the University of Catania, was a postdoctoral research fellow at the University of Rome "La Sapienza," and has held visiting positions at New York University and the Indian School of Business at Hyderabad. Her research interests cover coopetition strategy and the antecedents and consequences of corporate social irresponsibility. She has published in various international outlets, including *Academy of Management Perspectives, Journal of Business and Industrial Marketing,* and the *International Journal of Technology Management.*

Anne Mione is Full Professor at Montpellier University. She is affiliated to the Montpellier Research in Management research lab. She teaches strategic marketing, quality management, and strategy. Her main research relates to standards, certifications, and quality labels and she specifically observes the firm strategies in the emergence, diffusion, and competition between standards and rival networks. She has published a book on standardization strategies and now focuses on coopetition on standardization. She has also written articles in journals such as *M@n@gement, Management International, International Journal of Entrepreneurship and Small Business, Science Direct-TransTech Publications,* and the *Journal of Innovation Economics and Management.*

Malin H. Näsholm is Associate Professor in Management at Umeå School of Business and Economics, Sweden. She is currently doing research on coopetition for innovation, the management of coopetition, and the influence of individuals and their experiences. She has published in journals such as *Industrial Marketing Management* and the *Journal of Business Environment.*

André Nemeh is Assistant Professor in Strategic Management at Rennes School of Business (France) and a member of the Center of Technology and Innovation Management (CTim). His research focuses on c-oopetition strategy and its relationship with technological innovation. The European wireless telecommunication sector constitutes his main research field, an area in which he has published a number of articles.

Mahito Okura is Associate Professor in the Department of Social System Studies, Faculty of Contemporary Social Studies, Doshisha Women's College of Liberal Arts, Kyoto, Japan. He received his PhD from the Graduate School of Business Administration, Kobe University, Japan. His research interest is in risk management and insurance theory. One of his publications in coopetition studies is "Coopetitive strategies to limit the insurance fraud problem in Japan," in Giovanni Battista Dagnino and Elena Rocco (eds), *Coopetition Strategy: Theory, Experiments and Cases* (Routledge, 2009).

Tatbeeq Raza-Ullah is Assistant Professor at Umeå School of Business and Economics, Sweden. His research enquires into special types of inter-firm relationships that involve the competition–cooperation paradox, also known as coopetition, and further investigates the nature and role of tension, emotions, and managing capabilities in such relationships.

Paavo Ritala is Professor of Strategy and Innovation at the School of Business and Management, Lappeenranta University of Technology (LUT). His main research themes include collaborative innovation, knowledge sharing and protection, coopetition and platforms and ecosystems, as well as sustainable value creation. His research has been published in journals such as the *Journal of Product Innovation Management, Industrial and Corporate Change, Industrial Marketing Management, British Journal of Management*, and *Technovation*. He is also closely involved with business practice through company-funded research projects and executive and professional education programs, and in speaker and advisory roles.

Marc Robert is Associate Professor of Strategic Management and Economics at Montpellier Business School. He is a member of Montpellier Management Research (MRM). His research focuses both on coopetition strategies in innovation networks and management innovation. He has co-published many research articles in international and national peer review journals such as *International Studies of Management and Organization, International Journal of Entrepreneurship and Small Business*, and *Revue Française de Gestion*. He has also co-authored several book chapters for publishers such as Dunod Edition, EMS Edition, or Presses des Mines.

Thuy Séran is the holder of a PhD in Management Sciences, specializing in control, from the University of Montpellier. Thuy is also a graduate of the HEC Paris. After working for six years as an auditor at Ernst & Young, she is currently Associate Professor and Head of the higher university degree program in Accounting and Management at the University of Montpellier. Her main area of research is management accounting. Based on qualitative methodology, her studies analyze the cooperative bank network as a meta-organization. She also focuses on the governance aspect of banking information systems and the role of boundary objects in the organizational control system. With a team from the University of Montpellier, she is currently working on the theme of developing coopetitive strategies related to banking networks and emphasizes the specific types of management and key methods used in reducing internal tensions over coopetitive strategy within hybrid networks such as the French cooperative banks.

Gorica Tapandjieva is a PhD student in the Systemic Modeling Laboratory at the École Polytechnique Federale de Lausanne. Her main research interests include service strategy, service modeling, enterprise architecture, and systems thinking. In her PhD thesis, while conducting action research, she designs artifacts that facilitate an organization's transformation towards service-orientation.

David J. Teece is a US-based organizational theorist and Professor in Global Business and Director of the Tusher Center for the Management of Intellectual Capital at the Walter A. Haas School of Business, University of California, Berkeley. Teece is also the chairman and cofounder of Berkeley Research Group, an expert services and consulting firm headquartered in Emeryville, California. His areas of interest include corporate strategy, entrepreneurship, innovation, competition policy, and intellectual property. Teece is one of the most influential authors in the strategic management field. He is identified as being partially responsible for the dynamic capabilities perspective in strategic management and has more than 125,000 citations on Google Scholar.

Annika Tidström is a Professor at the Department of Management, University of Vaasa, Finland. Her research interests are related to business networks, industrial relationships, coopetition, tensions, and strategy-as-practice. She has published several articles in journals such as *Industrial Marketing Management, Journal of Business and Industrial Marketing, Journal of Purchasing and Supply Management,* and *Scandinavian Journal of Management.* Professor Tidström is an active member of the international coopetition research community and is also involved in the Industrial Marketing and Purchasing (IMP) group.

Vladimir Vanyushyn is Associate Professor at Umeå School of Business and Economics, Sweden. His research lies at the intersection of innovation and entrepreneurship and focuses primarily on inter-organizational collaboration for innovation development and internationalization. His papers on inter-organizational collaboration have appeared in journals such as *Industrial Marketing Management, Journal of Small Business Management, Environment and Planning C,* and *International Small Business Journal.*

Chander Velu is Assistant Professor at the Institute for Manufacturing (IfM) at the Department of Engineering, University of Cambridge. Prior to joining the IfM, he was a member of the faculty at Judge Business School, University of Cambridge. He has worked as a consultant with PricewaterhouseCoopers and Booz Allen & Hamilton in London. He is a Fellow of the Institute of Chartered Accountants in England and Wales. His research work focuses on marketing strategy and innovation, with a particular interest in business model innovation.

Jako Volschenk is Senior Lecturer in Strategy and Sustainability at the University of Stellenbosch Business School (USB), as well as on other Masters programs in South Africa, France, and Ukraine. He has worked with a number of South African and global institutions, including WWF, Nedbank, and USAID. He consults in the areas of strategy, environmental sustainability, and energy policy. Dr. Volschenk has furthermore published in the areas of coopetition, energy, and sustainability, as well as microfinance. He has supervised more than 100 Masters students in these areas. He holds a PhD in the area of coopetition.

Alain Wegmann has worked for fifteen years at Logitech in development (Switzerland, USA, and Taiwan), manufacturing (Taiwan) and marketing (USA). In 1997, he became Professor at École Polytechnique Fédérale de Lausanne (EPFL). He heads a laboratory that develops the systemic enterprise architecture method (SEAM), a method designed to work on business and IT alignment. SEAM is applied to define business and technical strategies, as well as business and IT services (ITIL-compatible). SEAM is applied for teaching and consulting (http://lams.epfl.ch/reference/seam).

Miriam Wilhelm is Associate Professor of International Business and Management at the Faculty of Economics and Business, University of Groningen, the Netherlands. She received her PhD from the Freie Universität Berlin, Germany. Her research interests include buyer–supplier relations, coopetition, and organizational paradoxes. Her research has been published in several top-tier journals, such as *Organization Science* and the *Journal of Operations Management*.

Introduction

Coopetition

From neologism to a new paradigm

Anne-Sophie Fernandez, Paul Chiambaretto,
Frédéric Le Roy, and Wojciech Czakon

Comfortably sitting on your sofa, you watch your favorite show on your Sony TV. Did you know that the screen is front of you was jointly developed by both Sony and Samsung, two rival firms in the consumer electronics industry (Gnyawali & Park, 2011)?

You are in Dubai on top of the tallest building in the world, the Burj Khalifa. Despite being very high in the sky, your smartphone receives a perfect signal. Did you know that the telecommunications network in the United Arab Emirates is the fruit of two competing giants of the satellite telecommunication industry, Airbus and Thales (Fernandez et al., 2014)?

You feel a bit dizzy. Since your doctor has diagnosed you with heart disease, you have to take a pill. On the package, you read Plavix. Did you know that this drug would not exist without the collaboration of two competing pharmaceutical companies, BMS and Sanofi (Bez et al., 2016)?

You are at a New York airport waiting to board your flight across the Atlantic Ocean. Did you know that when you buy a Delta Airlines ticket on an intercontinental flight, you have a more-than-fifty-percent chance of being on an Air France flight? Despite being strong competitors, Air France and Delta Airlines cooperate together to offer more flights and destinations, as well as reduced connecting times and the best possible experience during the flight (Chiambaretto & Fernandez, 2016).

You have just arrived at your hotel for a well-deserved holiday break. You decided to enjoy your holidays in Poland because you saw an advertisement in the subway back home. Did you know that competing hotels and theme parks in this region have decided to join forces to promote their region and make sure you visit, all while remaining in competition (Czakon & Czernek, 2016)?

These examples show that in many industries, competing firms rely heavily on collaboration with their direct rivals to better and faster achieve their objectives, to provide their customers with the utmost satisfaction, and to reach higher performance levels. To grasp this paradoxical combination of simultaneous cooperation and competition, several decades ago a specific term was coined: "coopetition." The neologism "coopetition," invented at the end of the twentieth century, results from the combination of "cooperation" and "competition." In the 1990s, Ray Noorda, the CEO of Novell, used this term to describe the firm's relationships, which were simultaneously cooperative and competitive with other firms in the IT industry (Brandenburger & Nalebuff, 1996).

In the early 2000s, the term was seized by academics, and coopetition became a concept. Since then, interest in coopetition has continued to grow in strategic management and beyond into other disciplines and sciences. Because they combine the benefits of both cooperation and competition, coopetition strategies are expected to help firms increase their chance of success in the marketplace. As a result, coopetition has become a new paradigm, a new way to analyze social and economic phenomena.

Coopetition has become a behavioral standard for most companies in most industries. Very diverse types of firms and organizations use it widely. Coopetition among large companies or even between smaller firms helps them to overcome their specific challenges. Furthermore, large firms may also collaborate with smaller competitors. However, coopetition is not only relevant for firms; NGOs, associations, and institutions rely on coopetition to reach their objectives. Coopetition is everywhere; it is not exclusive to one industry or one activity.

Coopetition offers various benefits to develop radical and incremental innovation (Bouncken & Kraus, 2013). However, new product development is far from the only activity in which competing firms can work together. Market share, productivity, and financial performance can all be improved through collaboration with carefully chosen and closely managed coopetition (Le Roy & Czakon, 2016). Coopetition relationships can be useful across many functions in the firm, such as marketing activities (Chiambaretto et al., 2016), logistics (Wilhelm, 2011), operations (Czernek et al., 2017), or management control (Graftona & Mundy, in press). All the functions of the firm can potentially be used to foster collaboration between competing firms. This is even truer in the current economy. New issues in globalization and digitalization have contributed to the creation of new business models based on coopetition (Ritala et al., 2014; Velu, 2016).

The need for a dedicated theory of coopetition

We argue that the only way of addressing contemporary challenges that is beneficial to all involved firms and to customers is coopetition. Traditional strategies, such as pure competition or pure collaboration, are widespread across industries; their potential has widely been captured, and thus, comparative advantages have eroded. Recent development of coopetition in various economic areas challenges scholars, first in strategic management. It is absolutely essential for researchers to understand this paradoxical phenomenon and explain how it can safely lead to the creation of superior performance. To address this theoretical challenge, researchers have tried to rely on traditional perspectives in strategic management, such as competitive advantage or collaborative advantage theory.

On the one hand, competitive advantage theory, first developed by Porter (1980), explained that the competitive advantage depends on the position of the firm in its industrial environment. A rigorous analysis of the industry combined with an analysis of the strategic groups and with the value chain of the firm will make it possible to identify the best strategy for the firm. Along a similar line, Barney (1986, 1991), with the resource-based view of the firm, explains that the creation or the control of strategic resources is key to the firm's success. Firms are invited to invest in the development of strategic resources in order to differentiate themselves from their competitors and to improve their performance.

While shifting attention from the external contingencies to the internal potential in a swift pendulum movement (Hoskinsson et al., 1999), both industry organization view and RBV face the same limitations. They conceive inter-organizational relationships exclusively through a competitive lens. They fail to incorporate collaborative relationships developed between different actors in an industry with substitutes, new entrants, or even with competitors. Firms also collaborate to actually develop the strategic resources they need to compete efficiently in the market. Consequently, competitive advantage theory is not comprehensive enough to capture the coopetition phenomenon.

On the other hand, collaborative advantage theory builds on sociological approaches to explain firm performance. From a social network perspective, firms are encouraged to develop strong collaborative ties with all members of the network. The position of the firm within the network determines its performance (Gulati et al., 2000). In a similar view, alliance theory presents alliances as the key for the success of firms (Dyer & Singh, 1998). Because firms cannot control all resources they need, they have to look for access to missing resources through alliances with partners (Gulati, 2007). The success of the firm thus relies on its ability to access "network resources" and its relational capabilities to maintain stable alliances. As a consequence, the social network and alliance theories analyze inter-organizational relationships only from a collaboration perspective. The theories neglect the competitive dimension that actually exists in any collaboration. Thus, collaborative advantage is relevant to understand coopetition, but it is not comprehensive enough and is thus inadequate to address coopetitive relationships.

As a result, both competitive advantage and collaborative advantage theories focus on only one side of the coin, either the competition or the cooperation, without considering interactions between them. By doing so, they fail to address tensions (Fernandez et al., 2014), to observe and incorporate balance (Bengtsson et al., 2016), to explain how this interaction of collaboration with competition can be understood by managers (Gnyawali & Park, 2009), and to propose how collaboration and competition interplay can be turned into successful management of coopetition (Le Roy & Czakon, 2016). As a consequence, established theories are not relevant enough to analyze the specifics of coopetition.

The emergence of a coopetition theory

Because of its paradoxical nature, coopetition invites scholars to analyze strategies, behaviors, and relationships from a dual perspective. The very nature of coopetition raises new, stimulating questions that need to be addressed by scholars. Considering the simultaneous combination of cooperation and competition, why do actors put themselves in such complexity when they have simpler alternatives? How do they address this complexity over time? What outcomes do they expect from these relationships? How do they manage potential risks? How do they capture the value created?

A dedicated theory of coopetition is needed to explain the success of firms involved simultaneously in cooperative and competitive relationships. Approaching cooperation and competition as two opposites of a continuum becomes nonsense. One of the theoretical challenges is to address both directions simultaneously, focusing on the interdependences between collaboration and competition. Building a new theory was the only option for academics to explain this new strategy. Studies, research articles, and books have flourished over recent years to understand this new strategic behavior.

Since the seminal work of Brandenburger and Nalebuff (1996), coopetition research continued to grow. As shown in Figure I.1, coopetition research has increased considerably over the last two decades. This extraordinary growth of publications on coopetition reflects a growing and sustained interest of scholars all over the world. In addition to this growth, we can notice a significant improvement of the ranking of the outlets. This publication upgrading demonstrates the recognition of coopetition as a real research topic by scholars. Looking deeper, we must highlight that these publications address a wide range and offer a large variety. Such diversity leads us to think that the coopetition concept appears as one of the richest and most inspiring concepts in strategic management. Recent publications highlight that coopetition pushes back

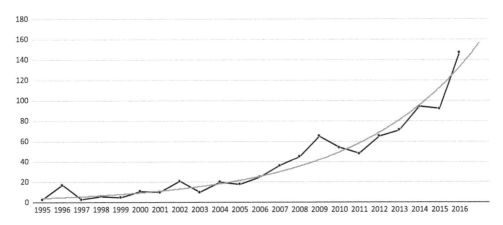

Figure I.1 Number of research articles with the word "coopetition" in the title

the traditional boundaries of strategic management. Indeed, coopetition is becoming insightful to other disciplines in management (Chiambaretto et al., 2016; Graftona & Mundy, in press).

The theory of coopetition is still a work in progress. Some systematic reviews show the richness, the youngness, and the diversity of this new field of research (Czakon et al., 2014; Dorn et al., 2016). Coopetitive frameworks used by scholars are based on established theory as game theory (Brandenburger & Nalebuff, 1996), resource-based view (Bengtsson & Kock, 2000), network theory (Sanou et al., 2016), or, more recently, cognition theory (Bengtsson et al., 2016), resource dependence theory (Chiambaretto & Fernandez, 2016), etc. There is not yet a coopetition theory as established as *transaction cost theory*, for example. Building a theory or some theories of coopetition is a great challenge for the future. Going into this challenge is a key to understanding contemporary and future strategies of the firm. The construction of this theory is still a work in progress. It does not start from zero, and it can be based on past coopetition studies—a journey described here as a safari.

Coopetition safari

Now that you are convinced of the interest of coopetition, you are willing to initiate or to pursue new investigations on coopetition. However, you might wonder: where should I start? What question should I address? Am I sure that this issue has not been addressed yet? How could I contribute to coopetition theory? *The Routledge Companion to Coopetition Strategies* will help you to find your way in the wild world of coopetition. We provide an exhaustive and structured overview of coopetition research since the birth of the concept. Therefore, this volume pursues a double objective. It will help to position your own research in the coopetition literature, and it will inspire you to conduct future studies on coopetition.

We invite you to join us for a safari into the coopetition world. Figure I.2 maps the path we will follow. We will discover, step by step, the six major questions about coopetition.

1. *How do we theorize coopetition?* First, it is important to understand the theoretical debates surrounding coopetition. Several theoretical approaches to coopetition are presented in the six chapters of this first part.
2. *Why do firms adopt coopetition?* After understanding the theoretical debates surrounding coopetition, six chapters will analyze the drivers, antecedents, and determinants explaining why firms adopt coopetition strategies.

3. *How can firms succeed in coopetition?* After understanding the drivers and antecedents of coopetition, seven chapters will develop insights about the implementation and the management of coopetition strategies.

4. *What can coopetition look like?* After acknowledging the implementation and the management of coopetition, we explore the morphology of coopetition through six chapters.

5. *What can we get from coopetition?* After studying the morphology of coopetition, we invite you to dig into its outcomes and implications.

6. *How can coopetition take us beyond strategy?* To end the overview of coopetition research, we would like to open new doors and to explore studies built on coopetition, but go beyond strategic management.

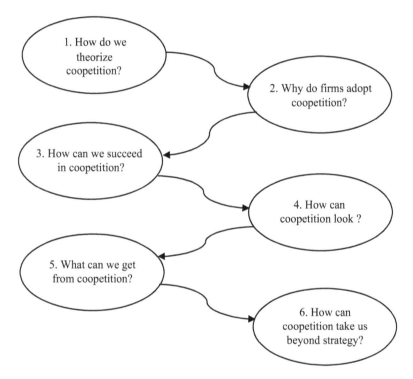

Figure I.2   Roadmap of the coopetition safari

Is it just the beginning?

After this exciting safari, you might wonder: is coopetition research over or should we keep investigating? So much has been done; there is not much more to examine. However, we believe this is just the beginning of coopetition research.

As each chapter notes, coopetition created disruption and a new school of thought. Previous studies provided insights into some of the major questions surrounding coopetition. However, all these contributions only represent the genesis of coopetition research such that most of the questions addressed are only partially answered. Many research directions require further investigation.

We, coopetition scholars, believe that coopetition is a promising research field, but contributions to this topic have only begun. We call for more research on coopetition and for more researchers to investigate the complexity and the challenges of coopetition relationships. Coopetition research already goes beyond the boundaries of strategic management to other management fields as marketing management (Chiambaretto et al., 2016) or accounting (Graftona & Mundy, in press). Furthermore, coopetition research is now a topic in economic science (Rey & Tirole, 2013), political science (Sack, 2011), and psychology (Landkammer & Sassenberg, 2016). Moreover, coopetition research escapes from social sciences to basic science! For instance, coopetition is now a concept used in biology (Khoury et al., 2014) and physics (Chu-Hui et al., 2017)!

Therefore, we can assume that *The Routledge Companion to Coopetition Strategies* gives access to studies that are just the beginning of a new upcoming coopetitive world!

The Routledge Companion to Coopetition Strategies outline

This book is structured in six parts that are related to the six major questions we identified on coopetition.

Part I. Coopetition Theory. First, it is important to understand the theoretical debates surrounding coopetition. Several theoretical approaches to coopetition are presented.

The first one is offered by Maria Bengtsson (Umeå University, Sweden), Sören Kock (Hanken School of Economics, Finland), and Eva-Lena Hundgren-Eriksson (Hanken School of Economics, Finland). They provide an overview of coopetition roots and argue that micro-level-oriented theories have major potential to advance future coopetition theory.

A second approach was developed by Tadhg Ryan Charleton (Maynooth University, Ireland), Devi R. Gnyawali (Virginia Tech, USA), and Robert Galavan (Maynooth University, Ireland). They combine insights from five important theories and illustrate how an integrative approach can generate a more systematic understanding of coopetition.

A third perspective was proposed by Frédéric Le Roy (University of Montpellier and Montpellier Business School, France), Anne-Sophie Fernandez (University of Montpellier, France), and Paul Chiambaretto (Montpellier Business School and École Polytechnique, France). They present a managerial theory of coopetition, arguing that management is one of the most important factors for coopetition to be a successful strategy.

A fourth approach was taken by Wojciech Czakon (Jagiellonian University, Poland). The author advocates that coopetition at the network level displays distinctive features and promising advantages compared to dyadic coopetition. He presents the main knowledge and invites further research.

In the fifth chapter, Paavo Ritala (Lappeenranta University of Technology, Finland) and Pia Humerlinna-Laukkanen (University of Oulu, Finland) develop a dynamic interplay model of value creation and appropriation in coopetition that examines the roles and relationships of these two processes.

The last chapter of the first section is written by Giovani Battista Dagnino (University of Catania, Italy) and Anna Mina (Kore University of Enna, Italy). They provide an overview of the four phases of coopetition research and offer some hints on its convergence on a few specific issues.

Part II. Coopetition Antecedents and Drivers. After understanding the theoretical debates surrounding coopetition, six chapters will analyze the drivers, antecedents, and determinants explaining why firms adopt coopetition strategies.

The first chapter, written by Wojciech Czakon (Jagiellonian University, Poland) and Katarzyna Czernek-Marszałek (University of Katowice, Poland), explains how different trust-building mechanisms encourage competitors to enter into two types of dyadic and network-collaborative relationships.

The second chapter, proposed by Frédéric Le Roy (University of Montpellier and Montpellier Business School, France), Frank Lasch (Montpellier Business School, France), and Marc Robert (Montpellier Business School, France), questions the best partner choice in an innovation network. They underline in which conditions a competitor is the best partner for innovation.

In a third chapter, Marcello Mariani (University of Reading, United Kingdom) exposes the role of policy makers and regulators in driving and affecting coopetition. The author shows that economic actors did not intentionally plan to coopete before the external institutional stakeholders created the conditions for the emergence of coopetition.

Fourth, Patrycja Klimas (University of Katowice, Poland) identifies organizational cultural features and cultural models that could drive coopetitive relationships in different industries.

Fifth, Anne Mione (University of Montpellier, France) introduces the context of standardization as an antecedent of coopetitive relationships. Interactions between standardization and coopetition are discussed.

Finally, Mahito Okura (Doshisha Women's College of Liberal Arts, Japan) and David Carfi (University of California, USA) explain the advantages of building on game theory to understand coopetition. They present some models and encourage further research.

Part III. Coopetition Tensions and Management. After understanding the drivers and antecedents of coopetition, seven chapters will develop insights about the implementation and the management of coopetition strategies.

The first chapter, written by Annika Tidström (University of Vaasa, Finland), highlights the tensions resulting from the combination of cooperation and competition. She encourages a dynamic, multi-level, and practice perspective to analyze the phenomenon.

In the second chapter, Anne-Sophie Fernandez (University of Montpellier, France) and Paul Chiambaretto (Montpellier Business School and École Polytechnique, France) study the specific tension related to simultaneously sharing and protecting information in coopetitive relationships. They analyze the resulting tensions and suggest ways to manage those efficiently in coopetitive projects.

Third, Isabel Estrada (University of Groningen, Netherlands) focuses her attention on knowledge management in coopetitive projects. Coopetitors need to share their knowledge with one another and, at the same time, protect their knowledge from one another. She highlights promising directions to advance the field.

Fourth, Eva-Lena Lundgren-Henriksson (Hanken School of Economics, Finland) and Sören Kock (Hanken School of Economics, Finland) study the place of individuals in coopetition. They discuss possible incorporation of the sensemaking perspective to analyze the interplay of discourses and emotions at the individual and collective levels.

In the fifth chapter, Anne-Sophie Fernandez (University of Montpellier, France) and Frédéric Le Roy (University of Montpellier and Montpellier Business School, France) reveal an original organizational design and a specific managerial principle to manage coopetition at the project level.

The sixth chapter, written by Tatbeeq Raza-Ullah (Umeå University, Sweden), Maria Bengtsson (Umeå University, Sweden), and Vladimir Vanyushyn (Umeå University, Sweden), develops the concept of coopetition capability. Coopetition capability helps managers to address coopetition paradox inherent to alliances between competitors and the resulting paradoxical tensions.

Finally, Stefanie Dorn (University of Cologne, Germany) and Sascha Albers (University of Antwerp, Belgium) propose an integrative multi-level approach to coopetition management. They highlight the interdependencies between these different levels.

Part IV. Coopetition at Different Levels. After acknowledging the implementation and the management of coopetition, we explore the morphology of coopetition through six chapters.

7

First, Philippe Baumard (CNAM, France) introduces some thoughts about the possible asymmetric gains when small and large firms coopete. He shows that the mismatch of scale between the partners can create dramatic levels of asymmetry.

In a second chapter, Paul Chiambaretto (Montpellier Business School and École Polytechnique, France) and Anne-Sophie Fernandez (University of Montpellier, France) adopt a portfolio perspective to analyze the evolution of coopetition. They show that the share of coopetition in an alliance portfolio tends to increase under high levels of uncertainty.

Third, Aleksios Gotsopoulos (Sungkyunkwan University, South Korea) shows that coopetition could occur in larger groups, involving larger size and more diverse resources. He encourages further research on coopetitive groups to grasp their dynamics.

Alain Wegmann (École Polytechnique Fédérale de Lausanne, Switzerland), Paavo Ritala (Lappeenranta University of Technology, Finland), Gorica Tapandjieva (École Polytechnique Fédérale de Lausanne, Switzerland), and Arash Golnam (École Polytechnique Fédérale de Lausanne, Switzerland) show in the fourth chapter that ecosystem is a useful concept for analyzing strategies in which competitors are also considered complementary partners.

In the fifth chapter, Heloise Berkowitz (CNRS-Toulouse School of Management, France) and Jamal Azzam (Toulouse School of Management, France) focus on the dynamics of coopetition in meta-organizations. They explore coopetition among actors who agree to license their patents through meta-organizational devices such as patent pools.

Finally, Alain Jeunemaitre (École Polytechnique, France), Hervé Dumez (École Polytechnique, France), and Benjamin Lehiany (SKEMA Business School and École Polytechnique, France) present coopetition as a multifaceted concept. They analyze how visuals substantiate the concept and how far visualization may explain it and recommend the use of specific templates.

Part V. Coopetition Outcomes and Implications. After studying the morphology of coopetition, we invite you to dig into its outcomes and implications.

We will take the first step with Johanna Gast (Montpellier Business School, France), Wolfang Hora (University of Liechtenstein, Liechtenstein), Ricarda Bouncken (Bayreuth University, Germany), and Sascha Kraus (ESCE, France) to explore the complicated relationship between coopetition and innovation. The authors analyzed quantitative contributions to present the debate on coopetition and innovation performance.

Then, André Nemeh (Rennes School of Business, France) presents a discussion about coopetition strategy and the first-mover advantage (FMA) perspective. He shows that different approaches to orchestration of resources will lead to different benefits/speeds of products' introduction for coopetitive NPD projects.

Third, Marcus Holgersson (Chalmers University of Technology, Sweden) offers a reflection on intellectual property management in technology-based coopetition. He designs a framework to analyze IP agreements in coopetition and shows that knowledge, technology, and IP can be protected to enable controlled sharing through licensing in coopetition.

In the fourth chapter, Paavo Ritala (Lappeenranta University of Technology, Finland) presents an overview of previous studies about coopetition and market performance. He reviews the existing evidence for key mechanisms, contingencies, and practical examples to explain how and why a firm's market performance is affected by its coopetition strategy.

Fifth, Jako Volschenk (University of Stellenbosch Business School, South Africa) discusses the different types of value that can be generated and captured in coopetition. He incorporates the stakeholder theory and the six capital models into an integrated typology of value creation in coopetition.

Lastly, Chandler Velu (University of Cambridge, United Kingdom) explores the relationship between business model design and coopetition-based strategies among competing firms. The chapter proposes a framework on how, when, and why business model innovation is required for coopetition-based strategies in order to contribute to competitive advantage.

Part VI. Coopetition Beyond Strategy. To end the overview of coopetition research, we would like to open new doors and to explore studies built on coopetition but that go beyond strategic management.

The first perspective is offered by David Teece (Berkeley Haas, USA). Considering that coopetition can take numerous forms, David Teece analyzes strategic aspects of these arrangements and discusses how the dynamic capabilities' framework addresses the fundamental issues of how coopetition arrangements are selected.

Second, a marketing approach to coopetition is proposed by Călin Gurău (Montpellier Business School, France), Paul Chiambaretto (Montpellier Business School and École Polytechnique, France), and Frédéric Le Roy (University of Montpellier and Montpellier Business School, France). After defining the concept of coopetitive marketing and its origins, the authors show the interest of investigating coopetition strategies through a marketing lens, such as pricing or branding policies.

In a third chapter, Thuy Seran (University of Montpellier, France) and Hervé Chappert (University of Montpellier) combine management accounting and strategy approaches to shed new light on coopetitive tension management. Based on Simon's levers of control, they design and discuss an integrative framework to efficiently manage coopetition at the network level.

Fourth, Miriam Wilhelm (University of Groningen, the Netherlands) opens a discussion between coopetition and supply chain management. She outlines the concept of vertical coopetition that occurs in buyer–supplier relations, and she demonstrates the value of applying a triadic perspective on vertical coopetition.

In the fifth chapter, Malin Näsholm (Umeå University, Sweden) and Maria Bengtsson (Umeå University, Sweden) adopt an entrepreneurship perspective on coopetition. They discuss the specificities of small firms that make coopetition important for their growth and success but also make them particularly vulnerable. They conclude on the capabilities required to make coopetition a successful strategy for SMEs.

Finally, Frédéric Le Roy (University of Montpellier and Montpellier Business School, France) and Henry Chesbrough (Berkeley Haas, USA) develop the concept of open coopetition, combining insights from both the open innovation and coopetition literatures. After defining the concept, they question the key success factors of open innovation based on collaboration with a competitor.

References

Barney, J. B. (1986). Types of competition and the theory of strategy: Toward an integrative framework. *Academy of Management Review*, 11(4), 791–800.

Barney, J. (1991). Firm resources and sustained competitive advantage. *Journal of Management*, 17(1), 99–120.

Bengtsson, M. & Kock, S. (2000). "Coopetition" in business networks—to cooperate and compete simultaneously. *Industrial Marketing Management*, 29(5), 411–426.

Bengtsson, M., Raza-Ullah, T., & Vanyushyn, V. (2016). The coopetition paradox and tension: The moderating role of coopetition capability. *Industrial Marketing Management*, 53, 19–30.

Bez, M., Le Roy, F., Gnyawali, D. Dameron, S. (2016). Open innovation between competitors: A 100 billion dollars case study in the pharmaceutical industry. *3th World Open Innovation Conference*, Barcelona, Spain.

Bouncken, R. B. & Kraus, S. (2013). Innovation in knowledge-intensive industries: The double-edged sword of coopetition. *Journal of Business Research*, 66(10), 2060–2070.

Brandenburger, A. M. & Nalebuff, B. J. (1996). *Co-opetition*. New York: Bantam Doubleday Dell Publishing Group.

Chiambaretto, P. & Fernandez, A.-S. (2016). The evolution of coopetitive and collaborative alliances in an alliance portfolio: The Air France case. *Industrial Marketing Management*, 57, 75–85.

Chiambaretto, P., Gurău, C., & Le Roy, F. (2016). Coopetitive branding: Definition, typology, benefits and risks. *Industrial Marketing Management*, 57, 86–96.

Chu-Hui, F, Dong, Y., Yi-Mou, L., & Jin-Hui W. (2017). Coopetition and manipulation of quantum correlations in Rydberg atoms. *Journal of Physics B: Atomic, Molecular and Optical Physics*, 50(11).

Czakon, W., Mucha-Kus, K., & Rogalski, M. (2014). Coopetition research landscape – A systematic littérature review 1997–2010. *Journal of Economics & Management*, 17, 121–150.

Czakon, W. & Czernek, K. (2016). The role of trust-building mechanisms in entering into network coopetition: The case of tourism networks in Poland. *Industrial Marketing Management*, 57, 64–74.

Czernek, K., Czakon, W., & Marszałek, P. (2017). Trust and formal contracts: Complements or substitutes? A study of tourism collaboration in Poland. *Journal of Destination Marketing & Management*, 6(4), 318–326.

Dorn, S., Schweiger, B., & Albers S. (2016). Levels, phases and themes of coopetition: A systematic literature review and research agenda. *European Management Journal*, 34 (5): 484–500.

Dyer, J. H. & Singh, H. (1998). The relational view: Cooperative strategy and sources of interorganizational competitive advantage. *Academy of Management Review*, 23(4), 660–679.

Fernandez, A.-S. & Chiambaretto, P. (2016). Managing tensions related to information in coopetition. *Industrial Marketing Management*, 53, 66–76.

Fernandez, A.-S., Le Roy, F., & Gnyawali, D. R. (2014). Sources and management of tension in co-opetition case evidence from telecommunications satellites manufacturing in Europe. *Industrial Marketing Management*, 43(2), 222–235.

Gnyawali, D. R. & Park, B.-J. R. (2009). Co-opetition and technological innovation in small and medium-sized enterprises: A multilevel conceptual model. *Journal of Small Business Management*, 47(3), 308–330.

Gnyawali, D. R. & Park, B.-J. R. (2011). Co-opetition between giants: Collaboration with competitors for technological innovation. *Research Policy*, 40(5), 650–663.

Graftona, J. & Mundy, J. (in press), Relational contracting and the myth of trust: Control in a co-opetitive setting. *Management Accounting Research*.

Gulati, R., Nohria, N., & Zaheer, A. (2000). Strategic networks. *Strategic Management Journal*, 203–215.

Gulati, R. (2007). *Managing Network Resources: Alliances, Affiliations, and other Relational Assets*. Oxford: Oxford University Press.

Hoskisson, R. E., Wan, W. P., Yiu, D., & Hitt, M. A. (1999). Theory and research in strategic management: Swings of a pendulum. *Journal of Management*, 25(3), 417–456.

Khoury, G. A., Liwo, A., Khatib, F., Zhou, H., Chopra, G., Bacardit, J., Bortot, L. O., Faccioli, R. A., Deng, X., He, Y., Krupa, P., Li, J., Mozolewska M. A., Sieradzan, A. K., Smadbeck, J., Wirecki, T., Cooper, S., Flatten, J., Xu, K., Baker, D., Cheng, J., Delbem, A. C. B., Floudos, C. A., Keasar, C., Levitt, M., Popović, Z., Scheraga, H. A., Skolnick, J., Crivelli, S. N., & Players, F. (2014). WeFold: A coopetition for protein structure prediction. *Proteins: Structure, Function, and Bioinformatics*, 82(9), 1850–1868.

Landkammer, F. & Sassenberg, K. (2016). Competing while cooperating with the same others: The consequences of conflicting demands in co-opetition. *Journal of Experimental Psychology: General*, 145(12), 1670–1686.

Le Roy, F. & Czakon, W. (2016). Managing coopetition: the missing link between strategy and performance. *Industrial Marketing Management*, 53, 3–6.

Porter, M. E. (1980). *Competitive Strategy: Techniques for Analyzing Industries and Competition*. New York: The Free Press.

Rey, P. & Tirole, J. (2013). Cooperation vs. collusion: How essentiality shapes co-opetition. *Working paper*, n°IDE-801, October 13, Toulouse School of Economics, Toulouse, France.

Ritala, P., Golnam, A., & Wegmann, A. (2014). Coopetition-based business models: The case of Amazon. com. *Industrial Marketing Management*, 43(2), 236–249.

Sack, D. (2011). Governance failures in integrated transport policy – on the mismatch of "co-opetition" in multi-level systems. *German Policy Studies*, 7(2), 43–70.

Sanou, H., Le Roy, F., & Gnyawali, D. (2016). How does centrality in coopetition network matter? Empirical investigation in the mobile telephone industry. *British Journal of Management*, 27, 143–160.

Velu, C. (2016). Evolutionary or revolutionary business model innovation through coopetition? The role of dominance in network markets. *Industrial Marketing Management*, 53, 124–135.

Wilhelm, M. M. (2011). Managing coopetition through horizontal supply chain relations: Linking dyadic and network levels of analysis. *Journal of Operations Management*, 29(7), 663–676.

Part I
Coopetition theory

1

Coopetition research

Rooting and future agendas

Maria Bengtsson, Sören Kock, and Eva-Lena Lundgren-Henriksson

Introduction

The former industrial logic—encompassing internal resources and a clean picture of the business environment—has largely been replaced by an industrial logic based on the ability to access external resources in a networked and shared economy. This has changed the previously clear anchorage of various activities within the boundaries of an organization, and made the roles of different firms (i.e., competitors, customers, and suppliers) unclear, which makes the understanding of new forms of business relationship and network contexts important. Research on coopetition had already acknowledged this change in the 1990s and has increased dramatically during the last fifteen years (Bengtsson & Raza-Ullah, 2016). It has even been argued to be a new paradigm for research that takes the changed character of today's business into account (Bengtsson et al., 2010; Yami et al., 2010).

Research on coopetition has been developed over almost three decades. Seminal work in the 1990s focused on the simultaneity of contradicting logics of cooperation and competition (Bengtsson & Kock, 1995, 1999; Gnyawali & Madhavan, 2001), different types of coopetition (Dowling et al., 1996; Lado et al., 1997), and coopetition strategies (Bengtsson & Kock, 2000; Brandenburger & Nalebuff, 1996). This work primarily provided conceptual attempts to broadly defined coopetition, its antecedents and outcomes, and capabilities or strategies needed to manage coopetition. Recent reviews of the field show that further recent research on coopetition has contributed extensively to the field's development by providing empirical examinations of coopetition focusing on more specific dimensions (Bengtsson et al., 2013; Bengtsson & Raza-Ullah, 2016; Bouncken et al., 2015; Gast et al., 2015; Gnyawali & Song, 2016). This suggests that the research field has reached a breaking point, and that it is time to reflect upon the past and present in terms of what has been accomplished, as well as to generate agendas for future research.

Coopetition research makes an essential contribution to the understanding of today's changing business environment, but the field of research is fragmented. The definitions and adopted theoretical perspectives are shattered, and the theory of coopetition research has been argued to suffer from incompleteness. Several scholars argue that the field is lacking coherence in the adoption of theories (Bengtsson et al., 2010), and that the lack of precision when it comes to adopting a general definition of coopetition has even been problematic, hindering further advancements of the field (Bengtsson et al., 2013; Gnyawali & Song, 2016). In this chapter, we will discuss the the rooting of coopetition and discuss the implications of the incongruence; we suggest that one solution could be to acknowledge that coopetition appears on many levels, and we also emphasize the multi-level character of the phenomenon, which has been underresearched.

Definitions and theoretical rooting of coopetition

We argue that coopetition is a business relationship, but in previous research the term "coopetition" has been used to describe many different things. Concepts such as coopetition strategy and coopetition advantages (Padula & Dagnino, 2007;Yamï et al., 2010), coopetition as practices (Dahl et al., 2016) and coopetition paradox (Bengtsson & Raza-Ullah, 2017; Gnyawali et al., 2016; Raza-Ullah, 2017), as well as coopetition mindsets (Gnyawali & Park, 2009) and coopetition business models (Ritala et al., 2014), have been born. These different conceptualizations bring in different theoretical perspectives on coopetition. It is important to further discuss the underlying assumptions and theoretical rooting of different concepts to detect what coopetition could be.

Network theory, research on competition dynamics, the resource-based view (RBV) and game theory are four important roots of coopetition research (dashed arrows in Figure 1.1.).This rooting has implications for how the phenomenon is depicted and understood. By tradition, relationships between buyers and sellers have been in focus when studying business networks, while relationships between competing companies have received less research attention within this research field (Ford & Håkansson, 2013).Actors are, according to network theory, embedded in relationships with other firms in order to gain access to needed resources (Kock, 1991). Håkansson and Snehota (2006) argue, in line with Richardson (1972), that "no business is an island," indicating that companies are involved in long-term relationships and that atomistic companies do not exist.The relationships in focus have mainly been cooperative relationships. In contrary, theories on competitive dynamics explain the interaction among competitors through firms' actions and responses, and pay little attention to the cooperation between firms (c.f. Chen, 1996; Smith et al., 1991). Inter-firm competition is explained by the structure of industry and the behavior of the firms, and emphasizes the repertoires of strategic actions that firms can use to achieve dominance and shape the market (c.f. Chen & Miller, 1994; Santos & Eisenhardt, 2009). Research on coopetition has developed by linking these two lines of research together.

Network researchers started to realize that "a firm must coordinate its management of horizontally and vertically directed network relationships in order to obtain a favorable and stable overall network position" (Elg & Johansson, 1996), and started to evoke the idea that it is not enough to only study relationships of cooperation; competition also plays a vital role in networks.The role of cooperation for dynamic coopetition was also stressed. Gnyawali and Madhavan (2001) provided an early attempt at further developing the theory on competitive dynamics by explaining competitive actions and responses with firms embedded in networks, aguing that "actors' purposeful actions [in competition] are embedded in concrete and enduring strategic relationships that impact those actions and their outcomes". More recently, Zang et al. (2010: 78) have extended this argument and propose that the presence of competition "is not limited to horizontal alliances but is contained in any type of alliances," implying that coopetition is involved in all relationships.

To acknowledge that cooperation and competition are equally important and coexistent challenges the previously clear distinction between actors with different roles in networks and industries. Traditional network theory assumes that the relations between a firm and its customers and suppliers are well-defined and that the roles of different actors in relation to a focal firm are clear. The definition of roles is nowadays difficult as roles are not as clear-cut as they used to be. A customer in one activity can at the same time be a competitor, supplier or partner in other activities. Moreover, different forms of direct and indirect competition and cooperation further blur roles and their definitions. Similarly, the definition of competitors was also once clear. All companies in the same industry are generally seen as competitors (Porter, 1980), indicating that all companies providing similar product solutions that satisfy similar customer needs are competitors. This definition has been nuanced by defining competitors as firms in the same strategic group that differ from other groups of firms in the same industry through strategic decisions.

The conceptualization of firms, based on their roles, as competitors, partners, suppliers, and so on is less relevant in present business practice as the same actors can compete and cooperate at the same time (Bengtsson & Kock, 1999, 2000). The concept of role-set, developed by Merton (1957), and the concept of role conflict, presented by Shenkar and Zeira (1992), have been suggested as useful means to solve this problem (Bengtsson & Kock, 2003). A firm can have at least five different roles—as buyer, supplier, competitor, collaborative partner, and complementary actor—that can be part of the role-set in a firm's relation to another firm. Thus, the activities performed within a relationship can enable or force actors to simultaneously take on many different roles, with conflicts or tension possibly arising between them. Ross and Robertson (2007) address this problem in a similar way, introducing the concept of compound relationships, suggesting that such relationships consist of many sub-relationships. However, we suggest that to capture coopetition relationships between firms we should abound the concept of roles when dyadic relations are discussed and instead talk about activities and the interactions related to them.

Based on the resource-based view (e.g., Barney, 1991; Peteraf, 1993) coopetition research focuses also on the firm specific advantages that can be obtained through coopetition. Cooperating with competitors becomes a quest for resources that would otherwise be inaccessible for firms (e.g., Bonel & Rocco, 2009; Gnyawali & Park, 2009) that in turn can be used to create and ameliorate a firm's competitive advantage. The firm's capability, based on its own resources and strength, to leverage externally accessed knowledge and resources is critical for the firm's appropriation of them for private gains. Finally, in line with research on dynamic competition, game theory emphasizes the dynamic aspects of interactions among firms, which in turn are linked to coopetition as strategy. Brandenburger and Nalebuff (1996) extend the pure competitive perspective of game theory and argue that "[the] firm can use game theory to achieve positive-sum gains by changing the players, the rules of the game, and the scope of the game" (Gnyawali & Park, 2009: 312). Positions and roles are argued to be important when coopetition strategies are developed. An actor's position in a business network helps in accessing new competitive capabilities and enhances the possibilities to attract new researches and relationships (Gnyawali & Madhavan, 2001). If we also acknowledge that a focal firm can have both direct relationships with a firm and, through this relationship, also have indirect relationships with other firms in the network it becomes important to understand the network context to be able to navigate in a business environment were there are multiple, continuously changing roles for different actors. It is more relevant to discuss roles and positions on the network level as firms on an aggregated level can be defined as mainly being a competitor, customer, or supplier within a specific industry or network. The dynamic aspects of coopetition put great demands not only on firms, but also on current research. Dynamic business models need to be developed that capture the dynamic interplay between actors in networks and that account for the continuously changing roles that different actors play.

The study of coopetition must still be regarded as a nascent field of research. Many empirical studies have been undertaken demonstrating the relevance of coopetition in business life and research (Bouncken et al., 2015; Gnyawali & Song, 2016); however, several challenges point to the need to widen the scope of the studies. For example, in order to understand the real dynamics of coopetition, focus needs to shift upwards, moving from studying one relationship to studying the network level (e.g., Czakon & Czernek, 2016). At the same time, we need to move downward, deeper analyzing the coopetitive activities, as well as different perceptions of these, between the individuals in organizations that are involved in coopetition. Put differently, we need to understand the origin and coping of tensions and conflicts at multiple levels that coopetition creates through the transfer and non-transfer of knowledge between organizations that are positioned as competitors but also cooperate with each other, as an outcome of getting access to resources that they do not themselves possess.

Emerging trends and a research agenda bringing together multiple levels

Research in coopetition needs to be improved to fully account for the multilevel nature of coopetition. Dyadic relationships, coopetition in networks and coopetition strategies have been explored in extensive research studies, but it is often not clearly stated whether it is coopetition in networks or dyadic relationships that the focus of a study (Bengtsson & Raza-Ullah, 2016). Recent research points at the importance of coopetition practice, tension and trust in coopetition, and coopetition mindsets that are all fundamentally related to individuals and what they think, feel, and do (Huy, 2010) in a situation of coopetition. Accordingly, theoretical approaches focusing on the micro-foundation of coopetition and the interplay between the individual, firm, inter-organizational and network level are needed, yet socio-psychological theories, and theories on organizational behavior, are less frequently addressed in the field. Few studies have investigated the link between the individual level and outcomes and developments of higher-level constructs, such as relational dynamics, strategy, or capabilities (Bengtsson & Kock, 2014; Bengtsson et al., 2016b; Gnyawali et al., 2016; Lundgren-Henriksson & Kock, 2016b; Park et al., 2014). We therefore believe that potential exists for filling these gaps by embracing and further developing the recently emergent trends in the field, as well as integrating these with the established theoretical roots (solid arrows in Figure 1.1). We will now discuss the emergent trends and how they can contribute to a future research agenda.

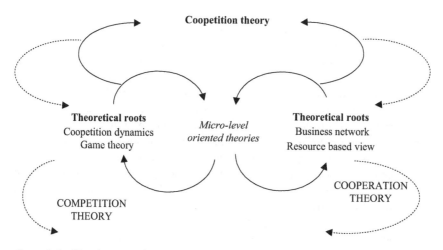

Figure 1.1 The theoretical roots of coopetition and future growth of the research field

Increased interest in the micro-foundation and the multilevel nature of coopetition

A general research trend in the coopetition field is a move toward individual and microlevel approaches to coopetition. This is, for example, manifested through conferences with special themes or tracks embracing the strategy-as-practice approach (e.g., the special track in the IMP conference in Kolding, Denmark in 2015 and the 6th Workshop on Coopetition Strategy in Umeå in 2013). An increased interest has, for example, been given to the discussion on managing coopetition tensions, i.e., the actual manifestation of coopetition paradoxes (Gnyawali et al., 2016; Raza-Ullah, 2017a) stemming from simultaneous cooperation and competition (Bengtsson et al., 2016b; Gnyawali et al., 2016; Le Roy & Czakon, 2016; Séran et al., 2016; Tidström, 2014). The interest in addressing micro-level mechanisms and drivers underlying coopetition formation and development, such as emotions and trust (Czernek & Czakon, 2016; Raza-Ullah et al., 2014; Raza-Ullah, 2017), as well as routines and practices (Dahl, 2014; Dahl et al., 2016; Lundgren-Henriksson & Kock, 2016a, 2016b), has also emerged. Closely related, but still in its infancy, is to approach coopetition strategies as emergent through practice (Mintzberg & Waters, 1985; Wittington 2007). Some studies have acknowledged the simultaneity of deliberate and emergent features of coopetition (Dahl et al., 2016; Mariani, 2007), signaling the need to acknowledge and investigate both intentional and unintentional features in order to fully understand developments and outcomes of coopetition strategies and relationships.

Another identified field of emergence is the application of institutional and stakeholder theories to coopetition (Akpinar & Vincze, 2016; Volschenk et al., 2016). This discussion has the potential to contribute to the research field by addressing the important issue of multiple actors' influence on the formation, development of dynamics, and outcomes of coopetition, both within and outside organizational boundaries (Kylänen & Rusko, 2011). For example, previous advances have shown that external institutional actors might influence the formation and development of coopetition strategies (Mariani, 2007; Tidström, 2014), and that the existence of conflicting goals within the organization might influence the development of the coopetition dynamics (Dahl, 2014). There has recently been a call for multilevel research looking deeper into the cognitive and behavioral dimensions of coopetition as well as the role of multiple actors in coopetition (Bengtsson & Kock, 2014; Bengtsson & Raza-Ullah, 2016; Fernandez et al., 2014; Gnyawali et al., 2016; Raza-Ullah et al., 2014; Tidström, 2014), particularly through the adoption of new theories (Bengtsson & Kock, 2014; Le Roy & Czakon, 2016).

A micro foundations approach could thus explain why different outcomes occur by focusing on how individuals and social processes across levels are interrelated (cf. Felin et al., 2012). We believe that the micro foundations approach could substantially complement the theoretical roots, increasing understanding of the relational dimension regarding how interrelated processes at multiple actor levels (Bengtsson et al., 2010) aggregate to changes in cooperation and competition (Dahl, 2014; Mattsson & Tidström, 2015), and accordingly in roles in business networks.

Integrating the emerging trends: Bridging the micro and macro levels

As previously stated by a number of scholars (e.g., Bengtsson & Kock, 2014; Bouncken et al., 2015), coopetition as a concept needs further clarification, both in terms of its key characteristics as well as its levels of analysis. Following the general trend particularly in strategic management, moving from process-based research towards practice and micro-level research (Whittington, 2007), we believe that scholars need to move beyond descriptive research, such as examining what processes and activities occur, as well as what is generated, to investigating in-depth how coopetition processes and activities form and develop in practice, as well as why these processes and activities take place.

We hence call for a stronger focus on how multiple actors—from the network to individual levels—influence, and are influenced by, coopetition. This would incorporate an extension of the goals and motives included in coopetition strategies from pure economic values to also include social ones (Lundgren-Henriksson & Kock, 2016a), as well as an extension of more stakeholders included in the coopetition picture (Chen & Miller, 2015). We believe that micro-level approaches to strategy and capabilities can assist in accomplishing this shift (Bengtsson et al., 2016a). What the strategy-as-practice approach particularly recognizes is the fact that strategic participation is driven by individual incentives, and that views of strategies do not necessarily converge across the organization (Jarzabkowski et al., 2007). When developing coopetition at inter- and intra-organizational levels, stipulated cooperative and competitive goals and activities in the beginning might not be realized, or new goals and activities might arise along the way, that might diverge (Dahl, 2014; Dahl et al., 2016). Accordingly, there might be stakeholders other than the direct coopeting parties, either intra-organizational or external (Whittington, 2006), with their own interests and goals to realize, which might influence the formation and development of coopetition in an intentional or unintentional manner (Akpinar & Vincze, 2016; Mariani, 2007; Volschenk et al., 2016).

We believe that the above-mentioned areas of advancement and emerging trends call for a redefinition of current ideas about coopetition, where the concept of paradox is developed further. Hence, we propose that coopetition should be defined as simultaneous intentional and unintentional cooperative and competitive interaction between multiple stakeholders at any level of analysis, which are driven by different interests and goals and that, subsequently, form a paradoxical relationship.

Extending the notion of coopetition capabilities

Finally, micro-level approaches can in particular contribute to the coopetition capability discussion. In order to combine the resources obtained at the network and inter-organizational levels with internal resources, as well as leverage from these (Bouncken & Kraus, 2013; Ritala 2012), firms engaging in coopetition must draw upon their capabilities (e.g., Ritala & Hurmelinna-Laukkanen, 2013). Coopetition researchers have accordingly proposed that the capability signifies support of both value creation in inter-competitor interactions and intra-organizational value appropriation activities in order to profit from coopetition (Gnyawali & Park 2009; Luo et al., 2006; Luo, 2007; Ritala & Hurmelinna-Laukkanen, 2009; Ritala & Tidström, 2014). Furthermore, coopetition capability also needs to embrace an ability to manage paradoxical tension and the cognitive difficulty and emotional ambivalence of which it consists (Raza-Ullah, 2017b).

We have also seen a recent increased interest in approaching coopetition capabilities as coping with tensions (Bengtsson et al., 2016b; Gnyawali et al., 2016; Le Roy & Fernandez, 2015; Raza-Ullah et al., 2014, Raza-Ullah, 2017a) at multiple levels, including the individual level, as well as from a cognitive point of view—as the individual ability to think paradoxically (Bengtsson et al., 2016b; Gnyawali et al., 2016). Furthermore, we also need the capability to manage ambivalent emotions as part of paradoxical tension (Raza-Ullah, 2017b). This interest coincides with recent research on micro foundations, where a "managerial cognitive capability" has been introduced that includes cognitive and psychological processes (Helfat & Peteraf, 2015: 832) to understanding macro-level constructs. The commonly held assumption in coopetition studies is that these capabilities are to be found in the minds of top managers (Luo, 2007; Peng & Bourne, 2009); yet, in-depth knowledge of this mindset is scarce (Fernandez et al., 2014). Recent research also shows that coopetition tensions occur at lower levels in organizations, and that a capability accordingly involves creating understandings of coopetition that are shared internally in the organization (Bengtsson et al., 2016b).

Applying a micro-level-oriented approach to coopetition capabilities could thus complement these insights, by approaching the strategic dimension of coopetition from a novel perspective. By going deeper into the psychological and cognitive dimensions (Bengtsson & Kock, 2014; Le Roy & Czakon, 2016) of both managers and employees when it comes to simultaneous cooperative and competitive interactions, knowledge of the nature and origin—as well as individual-level perceptions and coping—of tensions and role conflicts could therefore be increased. A micro foundations approach to coopetition (Gnyawali et al., 2016) would hence establish an explanatory link between aggregated coping of tensions at multiple actor levels, and more (Lindström & Polsa, 2016; Morris et al., 2007) or less (Bouncken & Kraus, 2013) beneficial coopetition strategy outcomes.

We have argued throughout this chapter that a more systematic integration of micro-level perspectives into coopetition research has potential to build a solid coopetition theory. We therefore hope that the suggested research agenda will inspire future research at the macro level, such as coopetition capabilities, dynamics, and strategies, by addressing emerging concepts in the field, such as emotions, cognition, and social processes, from the perspectives of multiple individuals.

References

Akpinar, M. & Vincze, Z. (2016). The dynamics of coopetition: A stakeholder view of the German automotive industry. *Industrial Marketing Management*, 57, 53–63.

Barney, J. B. (1991). Firm resources and sustained competitive advantage. *Journal of Management*, 17(1), 99–120.

Bengtsson, M., Eriksson, J., & Wincent, J. (2010). Co-opetition dynamics: An outline for further inquiry. *Competitiveness Review: An International Business Journal*, 20(2), 194–214.

Bengtsson, M. & Kock, S. (1995) Relationships among competitors in business networks – competition and cooperation in three Swedish industries. *Paper presented at the 13th Nordic Conference on Business Studies in Copenhagen, Denmark, August, 14–16.*

Bengtsson, M. & Kock, S. (1999). Cooperation and competition in relationships between competitors in business networks. *Journal of Business and Industrial Marketing*, 14(3), 178–193.

Bengtsson, M. & Kock, S. (2000). "Coopetition" in business networks – to cooperate and compete simultaneously. *Industrial Marketing Management*, 29(5), 411–426.

Bengtsson, M. & Kock, S. (2003) Tension in co-opetition. *Developments in Marketing Science* 26, 38–42

Bengtsson, M., Johansson, M., Näsholm, M., & Raza-Ullah, T. (2013). A systemic review of coopetition: Levels and effects on different levels. *Paper presented at the 13th EURAM Conference, Istanbul, Turkey, June 26–29.*

Bengtsson, M. & Kock, S. (2014). Coopetition – Quo vadis? Past accomplishments and future challenges. *Industrial Marketing Management*, 43(2), 180–188.

Bengtsson, M., Kock, S., Lundgren-Henriksson, E.-L., & Näsholm, M. (2016a). Coopetition research in theory and practice: Growing new theoretical, empirical, and methodological domains. *Industrial Marketing Management*, 57, 4–11.

Bengtsson, M. & Raza-Ullah, T. (2016). A systematic review of research on coopetition: Towards a multi-level understanding. *Industrial Marketing Management*, 57, 23–39.

Bengtsson, M. & Raza-Ullah, T. (2017). Paradox at a inter-firm level: A coopetition lens. In Lewis, M., Smith, W., Jarzabkowski P., & Langly, A. (Eds), *Oxford Handbook of Organizational Paradox: Approaches to Plurality, Tensions and Contradictions.*

Bengtsson, M., Raza-Ullah, T., & Vanyushyn, V. (2016b). The coopetition paradox and tension: The moderating role of coopetition capability. *Industrial Marketing Management*, 53, 19–30.

Bonel. E. & Rocco, E. (2009). Coopetition and business model change – A case-based framework of coopetition-driven effects. In Dagnino, G. B. & Rocco, E. (Eds), *Coopetition strategy – Theory, experiments and cases* (pp. 191–218). Oxon: Routledge.

Bouncken, R. B. & Kraus, S. (2013). Innovation in knowledge-intensive industries: The double-edged sword of coopetition. *Journal of Business Research,* 66(10), 2060–2070.

Bouncken, R. B., Gast, J., Kraus, S., & Bogers, M. (2015). Coopetition: A systematic review, synthesis, and future research directions. *Review of Managerial Science,* 9(3), 577–601.

Brandenburger, A. M. & Nalebuff, B. J. (1996). *Co-opetition.* New York: Bantam Doubleday Dell Publishing Group.

Chen, M.-J. (1996). Competitor analysis and interfirm rivalry: Toward a theoretical integration. *Academy of Management Review,* 21(1), 100–134.

Chen, M.-J. & Miller, D. (1994). Competitive attack, retaliation and performance: An expectancy–valence framework. *Strategic Management Journal,* 15(2), 85–102.

Chen, M.-J. & Miller, D. (2015). Reconceptualizing competitive dynamics: A multidimensional framework. *Strategic Management Journal,* 36(5), 758–775.

Czakon, W., & Czernek, K. (2016). The role of trust-building mechanisms in entering into network coopetition: The case of tourism networks in Poland. *Industrial Marketing Management,* 57, 64–74.

Czernek, K. & Czakon, W. (2016). Trust-building in tourist coopetition: The case of a Polish region. *Tourism Management,* 52, 380–394.

Dahl, J. (2014). Conceptualizing coopetition as a process: An outline of change in cooperative and competitive interactions. *Industrial Marketing Management,* 43(2), 272–279.

Dahl, J., Kock, S., & Lundgren-Henriksson, E.-L. (2016). Conceptualizing coopetition strategy as practice – A multilevel interpretative framework. *International Studies of Management and Organization,* 46(2–3), 94–109.

Dowling, M. J., Roering, W. D., Carlin, B. A., & Wisnieski, J. (1996). Multifaceted relationships under coopetition – Description and theory. *Journal of Management Inquiry,* 5(2), 155–167.

Elg, U., Johansson, U. (1996). Networking when national boundaries dissolve. European Journal of Marketing, 30(2), 61-74.

Felin, T., Foss, N. J., Heimeriks, K. H., & Madsen, T. L. (2012). Microfoundations of routines and capabilities: Individuals, processes, and structure. *Journal of Management Studies,* 49(8), 1351–1374.

Fernandez, A.-S., Le Roy, F., & Gnyawali, D. R. (2014). Sources and management of tension in coopetition case evidence from telecommunications satellites manufacturing in Europe. *Industrial Marketing Management,* 43(2), 222–235.

Ford, D. & Håkansson, H. (2013). Competition in business networks. *Industrial Marketing Management,* 42(7), 1017–1024.

Gast, J., Filser, M., Gundolf, K., & Kraus, S. (2015). Coopetition research: Towards a better understanding of past trends and future directions. *International Journal of Entrepreneurship and Small Business,* 24(4), 492–521.

Gnyawali, D. R., Madhavan, R., He, J., & Bengtsson, M. (2016). The competition-cooperation paradox in inter-firm relationships: A conceptual framework. *Industrial Marketing Management,* 53, 7–18.

Gnyawali, D. R. & Madhavan, R. (2001). Networks and competitive dynamics: A structural embeddedness perspective. *Academy of Management Review,* 26(3), 431–445.

Gnyawali, D. R. & Park, B.-J. (2009). Co-opetition and technological innovation in small and medium-sized enterprises: A multilevel conceptual model. *Journal of Small Business Management,* 47(3), 308–330.

Gnyawali, D. R. & Song, Y. (2016). Pursuit of rigor in research: Illustration from coopetition literature. *Industrial Marketing Management,* 57, 12–22.

Helfat, C. E. & Peteraf, M. A. (2015). Managerial cognitive capabilities and the microfoundations of dynamic capabilities. *Strategic Management Journal,* 36(6), 831–850.

Huy, Q. (2010) Emotions and strategic change. In Cameron, K. S. and Spreitzer, G. M. (Eds), *Handbook of Positive Organizational Psychology.* Oxford: Oxford University Press.

Håkansson, H. & Snehota, I. (2006). No business is an island: The network concept of business strategy. *Scandinavian Journal of Management,* 22(3), 256–270.

Jarzabkowski, P., Balogun, J., & Seidl, D. (2007). Strategizing: The challenges of a practice perspective. *Human Relations,* 60(1), 5–27.

Kock, S. (1991). A Strategic process for gaining external resources through long-lasting relationships – examples from two Finnish and two Swedish industrial firms. *Economy and Society no. 47, Swedish School of Economics and Business Administration,* Helsinki, Finland.

Kylänen, M. & Rusko, R. (2011). Unintentional coopetition in the service industries: The case of Pyhä-Luosto tourism destination in the Finnish Lapland. *European Management Journal*, 29(3), 193–205.

Lado, A. A., Boyd, N. G., & Hanlon, S. C. (1997). Competition, cooperation, and the search for economic rents: A syncretic model. *Academy of Management Review*, 22(1), 110–141.

Le Roy, F. & Czakon, W. (2016). Managing coopetition: The missing link between strategy and performance. *Industrial Marketing Management*, 53, 3–6.

Le Roy, F. & Fernandez, A-S. (2015). Managing coopetitive tensions at the working-group level: The rise of the coopetitive project team. *British Journal of Management*, 26(4), 671–688.

Lindström, T. & Polsa, P. (2016). Coopetition close to the customer – A case study of a small business network. *Industrial Marketing Management*, 53, 207–215.

Lundgren-Henriksson, E.-L. & Kock, S. (2016a). A sensemaking perspective on coopetition. *Industrial Marketing Management*, 57, 97–108.

Lundgren-Henriksson, E.-L. & Kock, S. (2016b). Coopetition in a headwind – The interplay of sensemaking, sensegiving, and middle managerial emotional response in coopetitive strategic change development. *Industrial Marketing Management*, 58, 20–34.

Luo, Y. (2007). A coopetition perspective of global competition. *Journal of World Business*, 42(2), 129–144.

Luo, X. M., Slotegraaf, R. J., & Pan, X. (2006). Cross-functional "coopetition": The simultaneous role of cooperation and competition within firms. *Journal of Marketing*, 70(2), 67–80.

Mariani, M. M. (2007). Coopetition as an emergent strategy: Empirical evidence from an Italian consortium of opera houses. *International Studies of Management and Organization*, 37(2), 97–126.

Mattsson, L.-G. & Tidström, A. (2015). Applying the principles of Yin-Yang to market dynamics. *Marketing Theory*, 15(3), 347–364.

Merton, R. K. (1957). The role-set: Problems in sociological theory. *The British Journal of Sociology*, 8(2), 106–120.

Mintzberg, H. & Waters, J. A. (1985). Of strategies, deliberate and emergent. *Strategic Management Journal*, 6(3), 257–272.

Morris, M. H., Koçak, A., & Özer, A. (2007). Coopetition as a small business strategy: Implications for performance. *Journal of Small Business Strategy*, 18(1), 35–55.

Park, B.-J., Srivastava, M. K., & Gnyawali, D. R. (2014). Walking the tight rope of coopetition: Impact of competition and cooperation intensities and balance on firm innovation performance. *Industrial Marketing Management*, 43(2), 210–221.

Padula, G. & Dagnino, G. B. (2007). Untangling the rise of coopetition – The intrusion of competition in a cooperative game structure. *International Studies of Management & Organization*, 37(2), 32–52.

Peng, T. J. A. & Bourne, M. (2009). The coexistence of competition and cooperation between networks: Implications from two Taiwanese healthcare networks. *British Journal of Management*, 20(3), 377–400.

Peteraf, M. (1993) The cornerstones of competitive advantage: A resource-based view. *Strategic Management Journal*, 14, 179–191.

Porter, M. E. (1980). *Competitive strategy*. New York: Free Press.

Raza-Ullah, T. (2017a) A Theory of Experienced Paradoxical Tension in Co-opetitive Alliances (Doctoral dissertation, Umeå Universitet).

Raza-Ullah, T. (2017b) The role of emotional ambivalence in coopetition alliances. Academy of Management Proceedings. *Paper presented at 77th Annual Meeting of the Academy of Management, Atlanta, August 4–8, 2017.*

Raza-Ullah, T., Bengtsson, M., & Kock, S. (2014). The coopetition paradox and tension in coopetition at multiple levels. *Industrial Marketing Management*, 43(2), 189–198.

Richardson, G. B. (1972). The organisation of industry. *The Economic Journal* 82, 883–896.

Ritala, P. (2012). Coopetition strategy – When is it successful? Empirical evidence on innovation and market performance. *British Journal of Management* 23(3), 307–324.

Ritala, P. & Hurmelinna-Laukkanen, P. (2009). What's in it for me? Creating and appropriating value in innovation-related coopetition. *Technovation*, 29(12), 819–828.

Ritala, P. & Hurmelinna-Laukkanen, P. (2013). Incremental and radical innovation in coopetition – The role of absorptive capacity and appropriability. *Journal of Product Innovation Management*, 30(1), 154–169.

Ritala, P., Golnam, A., & Wegmann, A. (2014). Coopetition-based business models: The case of Amazon.com. *Industrial Marketing Management*, 43(2), 236–249.

Ritala, P. & Tidström, A. (2014). Untangling the value-creation and value-appropriation elements of coopetition strategy: A longitudinal analysis on the firm and relational levels. *Scandinavian Journal of Management*, 30, 498–515.

Ross, W. T., Jr. & Robertson, D. C. (2007). Compound relationships between firms. *Journal of Marketing*, 71(3), 108–123.

Santos, F. M. & Eisenhardt, K. M. (2009). Constructing markets and shaping boundaries: Entrepreneurial power in nascent fields. *Academy of Management Journal*, 52(4): 643–671.

Séran, T., Pellegrin-Boucher, E., & Gurau, C. (2016). The management of coopetitive tensions within multi-unit organizations. *Industrial Marketing Management*, 53, 31–41.

Shenkar, O. & Zeira, Y. (1992). Role conflict and role ambiguity of chief executive officers in international joint ventures. *Journal of International Business Studies*, 55–75.

Smith, K. G., Grimm, C. M., Gannon, M. J., & Chen, M.-J. (1991). Organizational information processing, competitive responses, and performance in the U.S. domestic airline industry. *Academy of Management Journal*, 34(1), 60–85.

Tidström, A. (2014). Managing tensions in coopetition. *Industrial Marketing Management*, 43(2), 261–271.

Volschenk, J., Ungerer, M., & Smit, E. (2016). Creation and appropriation of socio-environmental value in coopetition. *Industrial Marketing Management*, 57, 109–118.

Whittington, R. (2006). Completing the practice turn in strategy research. *Organization Studies*, 27(5), 613–634.

Whittington, R. (2007). Strategy practice and strategy process: Family differences and the sociological eye. *Organization Studies*, 28(10), 1575–1586.

Yami, S., Castaldo, S., Dagnino, B., & Le Roy, F. (Eds) (2010). Introduction – Coopetition strategies: Towards a new form of inter-organizational dynamics? In Yami, S., Castaldo, S., Battista Dagnino, G., & Le Roy, F. (Eds), *Coopetition – Winning strategies for the 21st century* (pp. 1–16). Cheltenham; Northampton, MA: Edward Elgar.

Zhang, H. S., Shu, C. L., Jiang, X., & Malter, A. J. (2010). Managing knowledge for innovation: the role of cooperation, competition, and alliance nationality. *Journal of International Marketing*, 18(4), 74–94.

2

Theoretical perspectives of coopetition

Review and integration

Tadhg Ryan Charleton, Devi R. Gnyawali, and Robert J. Galavan

Introduction

Coopetition—simultaneous competition and cooperation among firms—has emerged as an important phenomenon within strategic management (Ansari, Garud, & Kumaraswamy, 2015; Bengtsson & Kock, 2000; Gnyawali, He, & Madhavan, 2006). It has garnered great interest in high-technology sectors where high R&D costs, rapid innovation, and short product life cycles (Gnyawali & Park, 2011) push firms to simultaneously pursue the benefits associated with competition (e.g., pressure to innovate) and those of cooperation (e.g., resource access) (Bengtsson & Kock, 2000; Gnyawali, Madhavan, He, & Bengtsson, 2016; Lado, Boyd, & Hanlon, 1997). Scholarly research on the topic has grown substantially and researchers have used various theories to examine the coopetition phenomenon. Two critical challenges have emerged with growth in the literature. First, wide variation in how and when theories are used (e.g., Bengtsson, Raza-Ullah, & Vanyushyn, 2016; Gnyawali & Park, 2009; Gnyawali & Song, 2016; Quintana-Garcia & Benavides-Velasco, 2004; Ritala & Hurmelinna-Laukkanen, 2009) has led to the fragmentation of explanations stemming from fundamentally different assumptions. As different theories focus on different aspects of the phenomenon, they have resulted in different hypotheses and contributed different, sometimes conflicting, insights to the coopetition literature. Second, fragmented use of different theories has led to incomplete insights that have inhibited the development of deeper understanding and novel explanations. The integration of explanations from multiple theories would likely help to develop richer insights.

Our chapter makes advancements in both regards. First, we lay out the current state of the literature concerning how important theoretical perspectives are used to explain coopetition. This is significant in two ways: it outlines the role of particular theories in explaining the phenomenon and helps researchers to develop a more rounded understanding of coopetition by building on the totality of explanations. Second, we illustrate how integrative efforts that draw from multiple theories can provide a deeper and more systematic understanding of coopetition. After illustrating the complementary role that two theoretical perspectives can play, we highlight potential benefits of more extensive integration. Taking the major concerns of transaction cost economics regarding coopetition as an example, we identify novel contingencies and explanations that emerge when insights from four other important perspectives are integrated.

Accordingly, we chart a path for future researchers to uncover novel, fine-grained explanations by integrating multiple theories.

Theoretical perspectives

"Theory is the answer to queries of why" (Sutton & Staw, 1995: 378) and good theory is important because it facilitates explanation (Whetten, 2009). Utilized appropriately, theory may delve into underlying processes to uncover fine-grained explanations and causal nuances as to why a phenomenon occurs in the way it does. In an emergent field like coopetition, theories are significant because they create bridges with existing research in other areas, thereby enhancing understanding of a phenomenon we know relatively little about.

Several theories have achieved prominence in strategic management for their ability to explain different aspects of firm behavior and performance. We focus on five that are relevant in explaining coopetition behavior and performance: the resource-based view, transaction cost economics, inter-firm network theory, game theory, and paradox theory. Figure 2.1 lays out key insights from each theory and summarizes novel explanations that emerge from their combination. The resource-based view and transaction cost perspectives illuminate factors that motivate firm-level behaviors, emphasizing value creation and cost minimization respectively. Inter-firm network theory offers a high-level perspective of how firms access advantages by working with one another. Game theory highlights how value can be created, divided, and potentially damaged when firms interact. Paradox theory illustrates how coopetition generates tensions through the concurrent and opposing forces of competition and cooperation. We begin with a brief description of the core ideas of each theory and then outline how they have been used in coopetition research. We proceed to illustrate how rich insights and novel explanations can emerge when multiple theories are integrated. The boxes in Figure 2.1 outline key points derived from individual perspectives while the linking statements highlight some opportunities for perspectives to be integrated.

The resource-based view

The resource-based view (RBV) assumes that differences in firm performance can be attributed to resource bundles. Superior performance is achieved when firms control rare, valuable, inimitable, and non-substitutable resources (Barney, 1991) that are heterogeneously distributed and not easily tradeable (Dierickx & Cool, 1989; Wernerfelt, 1984). When resource-based concerns lead firms to form partnerships, they are more likely to focus on resources that are strategically relevant (Das & Teng, 2000; Gulati, Lavie, & Madhavan 2011).

Competitors may possess highly relevant resources because they target similar customers and confront similar challenges (Dussauge, Garrette, & Mitchell, 2000; Gnyawali & Park, 2009:2011; Ritala & Hurmelinna-Laukkanen, 2009). Coopetition can therefore provide access to relevant and complementary resources (Bengtsson, Eriksson, & Wincent, 2010) and reduce the time and costs associated with internal development (Gnyawali & Park, 2009). Competitors can also combine homogeneous resources to achieve major projects that are risky to pursue alone (Garrette, Castañer, & Dussauge, 2009), economies of scale, or other cost-sharing objectives. If firms compete based on homogeneous resources, coopetition can protect them from other competitors or serve as a means by which the combined resource pool can be grown (Ingram & Qingyuan, 2008).

Their similarities mean that competitors also exhibit overlapping dominant logics, which suggests that potential exists for high relative absorptive capacity (e.g., Cohen & Levinthal, 1990;

Resource-based view

- Coopetition facilitates prompt access to valuable, rare, inimitable, and non-substitutable resources that may be time-consuming or difficult to develop alone.

- Overlapping interests create conditions where competitors can recognize, assimilate, and apply each other's valuable resources.

- Superior value creation in coopetition can occur through:
  - the contribution of highly specialized assets
  - capabilities and routines for sharing tacit knowledge
  - the combination of complementary and scarce resources

Structural network patterns determine access to external resources which enable competitive actions. Resource complementarity is determined by external resources as well as internal stocks.

Inter-firm networks

- Structural patterns within a coopetition network shape conduct and performance.

- Advantageous network positions lead to greater volume and diversity of competitive actions, and increased market performance.

Opportunistic tendencies may vary by network positioning.

Certain "coopetition capabilities" can generate superior benefits for coopetition partners.

Homogeneity among competitors' resource sets and environmental challenges may reduce the costs of high asset specificity and raise the productive value available from specific assets that are redeployed.

Transaction cost economics

- Opportunism and knowledge leakage in coopetition may raise search, monitoring, and contracting costs.

- Coordinating partially conflicting interests also incurs coordination costs.

Paradox theory

- The coopetition paradox manifests through dualities (alliance level) and contradictions (firm level).

- These lead to tensions that can be managed by paradox management capability.

- Rather than separating competition and cooperation, the coopetition paradox may be transcended by integrating both elements into a unified whole.

Where coopetition partners can retaliate outside the alliance, risks of opportunism and associated transaction costs may be less.

Game theory

- Cooperation between competitors can avoid mutually destructive outcomes.

- Positive-sum outcomes are available in certain contexts.

- Cooperation in some areas is an optimal outcome where there are repeated interactions.

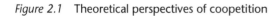

Figure 2.1   Theoretical perspectives of coopetition

Lane & Lubatkin, 1998). Absorptive capacity is often beneficial—it enables partners to identify, assimilate, and apply each other's new and valuable knowledge (Dussauge et al., 2000; Gnyawali & Park, 2009) and reduces associated learning barriers (Alvarez & Busenitz, 2001). This aids collaboration by facilitating tacit knowledge transfer, fueling rapid learning, and preserving causal ambiguity vis-à-vis firms outside the partnership. However, it also enables the capture and re-deployment of spillover knowledge and other resources. When absorptive capacity creates conditions for partners to misappropriate each other's resources, it can lead to suspicion and hostility in ways that are ultimately damaging to performance.

Transaction cost economics

Transaction cost economics (TCE) focuses on minimizing exchange costs by identifying the most efficient organizing form (Williamson, 1975, 1985). By analyzing how exchange attributes influence costs, TCE facilitates distinctions between activities that are most efficiently conducted within firm boundaries and those which are not (Teece, 1985). This has traditionally been defined as a dichotomous "make or buy" decision point. However, in response to industry developments, inter-firm cooperation has emerged as a hybrid governance form that sits between markets and internal hierarchies (Williamson, 1979, 1991). Hybrids balance the benefits of coordination offered by hierarchies with the greater incentive intensity offered by markets, while compromising the costs of bureaucracy (hierarchies) with those of controlling opportunism (markets) (Williamson, 1991). Inter-firm cooperation thus extends the traditional "make or buy" dichotomy to "make, buy, or ally."

When TCE is used to explain coopetition in the literature, the main focus is on increased costs that may emerge (Kogut, 1989; Park & Russo, 1996; Park & Ungson, 2001). From a TCE perspective, self-interest permeates all aspects of the analysis and supplants potential for joint or dyad-level congruencies. It is therefore argued that competitors' individualistic motivations bring higher risks of opportunism, while their relative absorptive capabilities increase the potency of such behaviors. As a result, firms must assume increased transaction safeguards to avoid knowledge costs (Park & Russo, 1996; Quintana-Garcia & Benavides-Velasco, 2004). In addition, coopetition partners have partially conflicting interests arising from sharing some common goals while simultaneously harboring competitive intent (Padula & Dagnino, 2007). Managing competitive and cooperative interests in tandem incurs coordination costs that may also make coopetition suboptimal relative to other organizing forms.

Inter-firm network theory

Though partnerships are often treated as dyadic alliances, "key precursors, processes, and outcomes associated with them can be defined and shaped by the social networks within which most firms are embedded" (Gulati, 1998: 295). A network, consisting of actors (nodes) and relationships among them (ties), emerges when multiple actors are connected through relationships with one another. In an inter-firm context, a network is an agglomeration of cooperative ties between firms. These ties act as conduits and facilitate the flow of assets, information, and status (Gnyawali & Madhavan, 2001) that are the core focus of network theory (Gimeno, 2004; Gulati, 1999; Jarillo, 1988) and bear significant implications for firm behavior and performance.

A coopetition network arises when a number of competitors engage in cooperative relationships with each other (Gnyawali et al., 2006). Advantageous positions are those that are central (with a large number of connections) and structurally autonomous (with many non-redundant ties) (Gnyawali et al., 2006; Sanou, Le Roy, & Gnyawali, 2016). The advantages that firms derive from these positions make them more likely to initiate a competitive action and less likely to experience retaliation (Gnyawali & Madhavan, 2001). Centrality is positively related to both volume (Gnyawali et al., 2006) and diversity (Sanou et al., 2016) of competitive actions, while autonomy is positively related to diversity (Gnyawali et al., 2006). In shaping firm behavior, structural patterns become a critical determinant of performance (Gulati, Nohria, & Zaheer 2000; Rowley, Behrens, & Krackhardt, 2000). For instance, by fueling an increased volume and diversity of actions, a large number of connections in a coopetition network can enhance market performance (Sanou et al., 2016), especially in dense networks (Andrevski, Brass, & Ferrier, 2016).

Game theory

Game theory offers a framework for rationalizing observed behavior when outcomes are partly dependent on another actor (Brandenburger & Stuart, 1996). In an inter-firm context, it highlights how interdependencies between firms mean that the actions of one can influence others (Axelrod, 1984; Teece, Pisano, & Shuen, 1997) and, in turn, manipulate value creation and capture (Ritala & Hurmelinna-Laukkanen, 2009). Though often focused on short-term "tit-for-tat" interactions, game theory also illustrates how the fates of individual actors are intertwined with the collective fate of the ecosystem within which they operate (Brandenburger & Nalebuff, 1996).

On one hand, game theory demonstrates how cooperation between competitors is a mechanism for avoiding mutually destructive outcomes. A Prisoner's Dilemma model illustrates that, even in fixed-sum environments, firms can diminish payoffs by overly aggressive or opportunistic acts (Quintana-Garcia & Benavides-Velasco, 2004; Ritala & Hurmelinna-Laukkanen, 2009). Game theoretic logic also suggests that cooperative norms between competitors in certain areas may be optimal in both one-off and repeated engagements. In one-off engagements, cooperative norms preserve mutual payoffs and maintain the firm's network reputation as a desirable collaborative partner (Gulati et al., 2000; Hill, 1990). In repeated engagements, noncooperation can incite retaliation and eliminate future opportunities to cooperate (Axelrod, 1984; Hill, 1990). As inter-firm cooperation is often an important performance driver, these effects may lead to inferior performance over time for non-cooperative firms (Hill, 1990).

On the other hand, a Stag Hunt model highlights how cooperation between competitors can create positive-sum outcomes where available (Quintana-Garcia & Benavides-Velasco, 2004). The stag hunt analogy illustrates how two hunters can work independently to each catch a hare, or collaborate to catch a deer. Naturally, a deer represents a bigger coup than two hares (Ritala & Hurmelinna-Laukkanen, 2009). In the same vein, coopetition presents opportunities for competitors to combine complementary and homogeneous resources in innovative ways to create a level of value that neither could manage alone (Bengtsson & Kock, 2000; Garrette et al., 2009; Gnyawali & Park, 2011).

Paradox theory

A paradox "denotes contradictory yet inter-related elements … that seem logical in isolation but absurd and irrational when appearing simultaneously" (Lewis, 2000: 760). A paradox is evident when contradictory elements exist simultaneously and persist over time (Smith & Lewis, 2011). Paradox researchers have explored how contradictory elements, such as competition and cooperation, can be attended to simultaneously (Smith & Lewis, 2011). Chen notes, "as the traditional yin-yang symbol suggests, opposites define and are defined by each other, so that it becomes impossible to conceptualize an idea without considering and incorporating its inverse." (2008: 198).

Paradox theory is relevant to the study of coopetition because competition and cooperation are contradictory, interdependent opposites that persist over time as firms engage in coopetition (Gnyawali et al., 2016; Raza-Ullah & Bengtsson, 2014). The resultant coopetition paradox manifests through incongruities at the alliance and firm levels. At the alliance level, dualities involve the simultaneous pursuit of seemingly opposite ends (e.g., value creation and value capture). At the firm level, there are partner-specific contradictions (e.g., the economic interests of the focal firm versus those of the coopetition partner) (Gnyawali et al., 2016). Both contradictions and dualities lead to tensions that must be managed (Fernandez, Le Roy, & Gnyawali, 2014). Early coopetition research suggests that individuals cannot simultaneously balance two conflicting logics and so competition and cooperation need to be separated rather than integrated (Bengtsson & Kock, 2000). This approach of separation is a predominantly Western approach involving avoidance or confrontation where the totality of the paradox becomes the sum of the parts. This contrasts with a more holistic Eastern approach, where a shift occurs from avoidance (separation) or confrontation (trade-off) to integration. Integration means that the totality of the paradox is not linearly determined by its components, and creates potential for the holism of the paradox to be understood and harnessed (Chen, 2008).

Paradoxical tensions from coopetition may be leveraged through a suite of unique coopetition capabilities (Bengtsson et al., 2016; Gnyawali et al., 2016). Three critical capabilities have been identified in the literature: analytical capability, executional capability (Gnyawali et al., 2016), and emotional capability (Raza-Ullah, 2017). Analytical capability facilitates an accurate and holistic understanding of the sources of tension and their interdependencies, while executional capability describes the development, implementation, and utilization of routines, and determines how productively the tension in a coopetition relationship can be managed (Gnyawali et al., 2016). Emotional capability refers to an ability to accept, understand, and regulate ambivalent emotions and their effects, stemming from opposing forces of competition and cooperation (Raza-Ullah, 2017).

An integrative approach

Despite valuable explanations offered by each theoretical perspective independently, a deeper understanding of coopetition requires integration of multiple perspectives. Good theories (those offering useful explanations) engage in systematic scrutiny of specific dimensions but, although narrow theoretical focus is necessary for fine-grained understanding, it naturally leaves less scope to understand other dimensions. It is therefore important to integrate multiple theories for a deep understanding of the totality of coopetition. For instance, joint outcomes from coopetition have been understood through theories like the RBV and game theory, but individual outcomes rely more heavily on TCE, inter-firm network theory, and paradox theory. Unravelling coopetition outcomes in their entirety, positive and negative, requires systematic analysis of both sets of outcomes. Similarly, different resources will exhibit unique influences on transaction costs (Madhok, 2002), which means that an appreciation of value creating resources is a pre-requisite for addressing concerns of TCE.

Despite the importance of integrating multiple perspectives, limited integrative efforts are found in the literature. We indicate two remedial approaches that researchers may pursue. We highlight how insights from two different perspectives—RBV and inter-firm networks—can be combined to provide deeper explanations (such as those suggested by linking statements in Figure 2.1). In addition, taking coopetition transaction costs as an example, we illustrate how integration of the four other perspectives outlined—RBV, inter-firm network theory, game theory, and paradox theory—can illuminate novel insights that challenge the current understanding of transaction costs in coopetition.

Integrating two theories: RBV and inter-firm network theory

Despite the traditional focus of resource-based theory on advantages arising from internal resources (Barney, 1991; Dierickx & Cool, 1989; Wernerfelt, 1984), an inter-firm networks perspective illuminates how external resources are also important (Gnyawali & Madhavan, 2001; Gnyawali et al., 2006). Where firms cannot meet resource requirements on their own, partnerships create opportunities for access to relevant resources (Cassiman, di Guardo, & Valentini, 2009; Dyer & Singh, 1998). By incorporating a networks perspective, resource accessibility, in addition to ownership or control, becomes a source of advantage (Lavie, 2006). Therefore, integrating the RBV and inter-firm network theories can offer a deeper understanding of advantages than either perspective in isolation.

First, network-based advantages are critically determined by resource characteristics. Network ties serve as conduits to enable resource flow between firms, and resource flow leads to resource asymmetries, which enable firms to carve out advantageous positions (Gnyawali & Madhavan, 2001). Advantage, however, is critically determined by the nature and quality of the resources available (Gulati et al., 2011). For instance, central actors—equipped to undertake a greater volume of competitive actions—are capable in this regard because of the resources they can access (Gnyawali et al., 2006). Central actors experience a higher volume and greater speed of resource access, while their resource superiority increases their tendency to seize the competitive initiative. This enables these firms to undertake more competitive actions, as well as more resource-intensive actions, while better information means that their efforts are more likely to generate a positive performance impact (Gnyawali & Madhavan, 2001).

Second, the availability of external resources means that complementarity or "fit" between partners' resource sets is not merely an outcome of their internal stocks. Instead, complementary potential also relies on the portfolios of external resources that each partner can access. An assessment of benefits available from a given partner's resources must consider not only how they complement internal resources, but also how they fit with the resource sets of other partners. For example, the advantages that Samsung can derive from accessing Philips' TV-development capabilities are immediately reduced once Samsung begins to cooperate with Sony, a firm with similar expertise. Network influences on resource advantages may also be illustrated at the relationship level—resource flows that fill structural holes can generate earlier access to higher-quality information and resources (Burt, 1992; Gnyawali & Madhavan, 2001) relative to those trickling down from more structurally autonomous actors.

Integrating multiple theories: New insights regarding coopetition transaction costs

Having illustrated how deeper appreciation can arise from the integration of two theories, we proceed to integrate multiple perspectives to generate new avenues for understanding coopetition transaction costs. As noted, the prevalent TCE view is that the risks and costs of opportunism mean that coopetition alliances experience higher costs (Park & Russo, 1996; Park & Ungson, 2001). Yet, this is at odds with industry evidence of benefits across a variety of sectors (e.g., Fernandez et al., 2014; Gnyawali & Park, 2011; Quintana-Garcia & Benavides-Velasco, 2004).

We integrate TCE with insights from other theories in order to reconcile such industry evidence with extant theory. Our analysis suggests that there may be transaction benefits, as well as costs, arising from coopetition.

First, TCE illuminates how exchange performance increases with investments in specialized assets (Parkhe, 1993) but a resource-based analysis suggests that the costs of such asset specialization may be lower in a coopetition exchange. In general, the more specialized an asset becomes, the lower its value in alternative uses and the more exposed the owner becomes to potential risks of hold-up from an opportunistic partner (Dyer, 1997; Williamson, 1991). However, driven by similarity in their resource bases (Baum & Mezias, 1992; Chen, 1996), coopetition partners' investments in specialized assets may not require the same level of departure from strategic resource goals as non-competitors. In addition to lower investments in specialized assets, partners may experience reduced risks. This occurs because competitors who are facing the same exogenous challenges (Gnyawali & Park, 2011; Ingram & Qingyuan, 2008; Peng, Pike, Yang, & Roos, 2012) can more efficiently identify other purposes for specialized assets that must be redeployed. Thus, both the level of additional investment required and the size of the hold-up risk may be reduced through coopetition. This may generate benefits such as superior opportunities for differentiation, rapid cycles of innovation, and the preservation of causal ambiguity (Dyer & Singh, 1998).

Second, game theory highlights how additional interactions between coopetition partners may generate less-costly safeguards against opportunism. Coopetition partners are characterized by some market commonality, technological rivalry, or resource overlap, in addition to cooperation. This means there are, at minimum, two points of contact: one cooperative and one competitive (Baum & Korn, 1996; Gimeno & Woo, 1996). Multiple and interdependent contacts bring additional opportunities for retaliation against opportunistic behavior (e.g., Axelrod, 1984; Heide & Miner, 1992; Kelley & Thibaut, 1978) which create a greater deterrent (Chen, 1996; Chen & MacMillan, 1992; Chen, Smith, & Grimm, 1992). Coopetition arrangements may therefore offer self-enforcing protection against opportunism without assuming the full and otherwise necessary costs of contracting, monitoring, and enforcement. Self-enforcing safeguards, such as interdependent interactions, are less costly than contractual safeguards, lowering transaction costs in coopetition and releasing more resources for productive, value creating purposes (Dyer & Singh, 1998).

Third, the literature suggests that a firm's network position influences its competitive market behavior (Gnyawali & Madhavan, 2001; Gnyawali et al., 2006; Sanou et al., 2016) and we argue that similar structural patterns may also influence competitive alliance behavior (i.e., opportunism). A partner who is a central actor in their network is not dependent on a small number of ties for accessing external resources and may experience greater volume and speed of resource access. They are less worried about competitive escalation with any single partner and, therefore, their increased likelihood of competitive actions in the market (Gnyawali et al., 2006; Sanou et al., 2016) may be mirrored by a greater tendency towards opportunism in coopetition. This is exacerbated in relationships between nonequivalent actors (e.g., Gnyawali & Madhavan, 2001) where "an actor's power to sanction an exchange partner depends on the extent of his ability to diffuse negative information … [to] potential future trading partners" (Stuart, 2003: 193). Thus, risks of opportunism may vary depending on partners' network positions.

Fourth, insights from paradox theory suggest that coordination costs arising from concurrent competition and cooperation can be offset through analytical and executional capabilities for understanding, managing, and leveraging sources of paradoxical tension in coopetition (Gnyawali et al., 2016). Both sets of capabilities contribute to limiting the costs associated with paradoxical tension. Analytical capabilities refer to partners' abilities to simultaneously hold the conflicting logics of competition and cooperation, to understand the competition–cooperation paradox, and to regulate tensions (Gnyawali et al., 2016). They enable partners to maintain tensions at acceptable levels (e.g., Lado et al., 1997; Park, Srivastava, & Gnyawali, 2014) through accurate assessments of the paradox. By appreciating its nature, partners can identify and manage sources of paradoxical tension, prioritize complexities, and forecast future tensions. Executional capabilities move from understanding tensions to designing and implementing actions to deal with them (Gnyawali et al., 2016). This involves developing routines, implementing processes that transform routines into capabilities, and timely utilization and refinement of routines and capabilities for specific purposes. The effect of executional capabilities occurs in three ways: effective management of joint relationships, creation of greater value from broader coopetition relationships (an experience-based capability where a firm incrementally becomes "better" at coopetition over time), and superior internal value creation (e.g., applying knowledge or technology in other areas). As a clear and expedited understanding of tensions facilitates better decisions about routines and processes required to leverage them, executional capabilities are enhanced by analytical capabilities and, in combination, both offer a "synthesis and integration" approach to tackling paradoxical tensions arising from coopetition (Gnyawali et al., 2016; Poole & van de Ven, 1989). Where both are utilized appropriately, coordination costs may be constrained.

Discussion and implications

Growth of coopetition research brings great promise but also significant challenges. We focused on two related issues: the variety of theories being used to explain coopetition and the lack of attempts to integrate insights from multiple perspectives. We began by laying out the main insights available through analysis of coopetition from five core perspectives. The resource-based view is used to explain how firms can create value through coopetition by combining complementary and homogeneous resources. Transaction cost economics highlights potential costs arising from risks of opportunism in coopetition and partners' partially conflicting interests. The inter-firm network perspective illuminates how firms may achieve advantages in a coopetition network when they have a large number of connections and a high level of non-redundant ties. Game theory demonstrates how cooperation among competitors could reduce mutually destructive outcomes and create greater value than a single competitor could manage alone, while cooperative norms in some areas may be beneficial in both one-off and repeated engagements. Paradox theory explains how contradictions and dualities, emerging from the conflicting logics of competition and cooperation, generate tension which requires unique capabilities to understand and manage. We subsequently illustrated the benefits of integrating multiple perspectives, initially focusing on the resource-based view and inter-firm networks, before proceeding to leverage each of four additional perspectives to illustrate how new explanations regarding coopetition transaction costs may be uncovered.

Our chapter offers two contributions to the literature. First, we have laid out extant coopetition explanations from five key theoretical perspectives. As noted, the variety with which theories are used to explain coopetition has generated incomplete and often conflicting insights within the literature. This often leads to hasty conclusions where one particular dimension of coopetition is overemphasized at the expense of others. By outlining the extent of knowledge from five core perspectives, our paper offers a more holistic explanation of the coopetition phenomenon than currently exists.

Second, we illustrated how integrating multiple theoretical perspectives can foster more systematic understanding of coopetition. At present, there is a dearth of research that integrates multiple theories to generate novel explanations. This is problematic because deep understanding of the nuances of coopetition requires the strengths and insights of multiple perspectives. By showing how multiple theories may be integrated to build rich insights, and outlining how researchers may seek similar opportunities in other areas, our paper charts a path for future researchers to generate deep and novel explanations.

It is important to note limitations of our analysis. The integrative insights we offer are intended to be illustrative and not exhaustive. Systematic consideration may uncover explanations that directly conflict with those we have laid out and we urge researchers to be rigorous in their examination. For example, the effectiveness of self-enforcing safeguards or cognitive capabilities may be highly contingent on the level of spatial separation between competitive and cooperative activities (e.g., Bengtsson & Kock, 2000; Gnyawali, He, & Madhavan, 2008).

Our analysis also spans several levels, from network to dyad to firm and intra-firm levels. We have been clear in terms of the key mechanisms and how they might work, but a multi-level consideration naturally constrains the depth to which any one level can be explored. However, that is not to say that any single theory is only relevant at one level. Certain theories are more relevant than others at particular levels but may also contribute insights elsewhere. Inter-firm network theory, for example, is most relevant at the aggregate network level but also informs firm-level behaviors (e.g., Gnyawali & Madhavan, 2001). Paradox theory is most relevant at firm and dyad levels (Gnyawali et al., 2016) but also contributes to transaction-level analysis. Other theories may follow similar patterns in their ability to uncover insights at multiple levels.

Good theory answers important questions of why (Sutton & Staw, 1995; Whetten, 2009) and, indeed, there are many "why" questions awaiting new and better answers in coopetition. Why do competitors cooperate or cooperators compete? Why might it be particularly beneficial/challenging? Why is performance enhanced/diminished by coopetition? Our chapter suggests that existing theories, when combined, can generate improved answers to some aspects of these "why" questions. If scholars opt to pursue a coopetition theory in the future, we encourage rigor in providing evidence that such a theory can offer answers to important "why" questions that extend above and beyond what can be achieve through existing theories.

Unsurprisingly, there are many other promising opportunities to introduce established theories in ways that enhance our understanding of coopetition. First, the literature suggests that competitors' relative absorptive capacity leaves them disproportionately well-equipped to identify, assimilate, and apply each other's new and valuable knowledge. This brings both benefits and challenges. To understand the underlying processes that may drive this capability, as well as potential outcomes, in-depth examination and integration of organizational learning theories will be helpful. Second, short product life cycles, rapid innovation, and high R&D costs contribute to the uptake of coopetition in high-tech industries (Gnyawali & Park, 2011). However, there may be more deep-rooted mechanisms at play that could be uncovered by incorporating theories of complexity or uncertainty. Third, the relationship between competitors' resources is something we highlight and a population ecology perspective (e.g., Hannan & Freeman, 1989) will be useful to more deeply understand how they develop and interact over time.

In summary, our chapter lays out the understanding of coopetition from five key theoretical perspectives and stresses the importance of integrating multiple theories to develop deeper analysis and build new explanations. We hope that our work can underpin robust future inquiries and spark innovative conceptual explanations.

References

Alvarez, S. A. & Busenitz L. W. (2001). The entrepreneurship of resource-based theory. *Journal of Management*, 27, 755–775.

Andrevski, G., Brass, D. J., & Ferrier, W. J. (2016). Alliance portfolio configurations and competitive action frequency. *Journal of Management*, 42, 811–837.

Ansari, S. S., Garud, R., & Kumaraswamy, A. (2015). The disruptor's dilemma: TiVo and the US television ecosystem. *Strategic Management Journal*, 37, 1829–1853.

Axelrod R. (1984). *The evolution of cooperation*. New York: Basic Books.

Barney, J. B. (1991). Firm resources and sustained competitive advantage. *Journal of Management*, 17, 99–120.

Baum, J. A. & Mezias, S. J. (1992). Localized competition and organizational failure in the Manhattan hotel industry, 1898–1990. *Administrative Science Quarterly*, 37, 580–604.

Baum, J. A. & Korn, H. J. (1996). Competitive dynamics of interfirm rivalry. *Academy of Management Journal*, 39, 255–291.

Bengtsson, M. & Kock, S. (2000). "Coopetition" in business networks—to cooperate and compete simultaneously. *Industrial Marketing Management*, 29, 411–426.

Bengtsson, M., Eriksson, J., & Wincent, J. (2010). Co-opetition dynamics—an outline for further inquiry. *Competitiveness Review*, 20, 194–214.

Bengtsson, M., Raza-Ullah, T., & Vanyushyn, V. (2016). The coopetition paradox and tension: The moderating role of coopetition capability. *Industrial Marketing Management*, 53, 19–30.

Brandenburger, A. M. & Nalebuff, B. J. (1996). *Co-opetition*. New York: Doubleday.

Brandenburger, A. M. & Stuart, H. W. (1996). Value-based business strategy. *Journal of Economics and Management Strategy*, 5, 5–24.

Burt, R. S. (1992). *Structural holes*. Cambridge, MA: Harvard University Press.

Cassiman, B., di Guardo, M. C., & Valentini, G. (2009). Organising R&D projects to profit from innovation: Insights from co-opetition. *Long Range Planning*, 42, 216–233.

Chen, M. J. (1996). Competitor analysis and interfirm rivalry: Toward a theoretical integration. *Academy of Management Review*, 21, 100–134.

Chen, M. J. (2008). Reconceptualizing the competition–cooperation relationship: A transparadox perspective. *Journal of Management Inquiry*, 17, 288–304.

Chen, M. J. & MacMillan, I. C. (1992). Nonresponse and delayed response to competitive moves: The roles of competitor dependence and action irreversibility. *Academy of Management Journal*, 35, 539–570.

Chen, M. J., Smith, K. G., & Grimm, C. M. (1992). Action characteristics as predictors of competitive responses. *Management Science*, 38, 439–455.

Cohen, W. M. & Levinthal, D. A. (1990). Absorptive capacity: A new perspective on learning and innovation. *Administrative Science Quarterly*, 35, 128–152.

Das, T. K. & Teng, B. S. (2000). Instabilities of strategic alliances: An internal tensions perspective. *Organization Science*, 11, 77–101.

Dierickx, I. & Cool, K. (1989). Asset stock accumulation and sustainability of competitive advantage. *Management Science*, 35, 1504–1511.

Dussauge, P., Garrette, B., & Mitchell, W. (2000). Learning from competing partners: Outcomes and durations of scale and link alliances in Europe, North America and Asia. *Strategic Management Journal*, 21, 99–126.

Dyer, J. H. (1997). Effective interfirm collaboration: How firms minimize transaction cost and maximize transaction value. *Strategic Management Journal*, 18, 535–556.

Dyer, J. H. & Singh, H. (1998). The relational view: Cooperative strategy and sources of interorganizational competitive advantage. *Academy of Management Review*, 23, 660–679.

Fernandez, A.-S., Le Roy, F., & Gnyawali, D. R. (2014). Sources and management of tension in coopetition case evidence from telecommunications satellites manufacturing in Europe. *Industrial Marketing Management*, 43, 222–235.

Garrette, B., Castañer, X., & Dussauge, P. (2009). Horizontal alliances as an alternative to autonomous production: Product expansion mode choice in the worldwide aircraft industry 1945–2000. *Strategic Management Journal*, 30, 885–894.

Gimeno, J. (2004). Competition within and between networks: The contingent effect of competitive embeddedness on alliance formation. *Academy of Management Journal*, 47, 820–842.

Gimeno, J. & Woo, C. Y. (1996). Hypercompetition in a multimarket environment: The role of strategic similarity and multimarket contact in competitive de-escalation. *Organization Science*, 7, 322–341.

Gnyawali, D. R., He, J., & Madhavan, R. (2008). Co-opetition: promises and challenges. In *21st Century Management: A Reference Handbook*, Wankel, C. (Ed.). London, UK: Sage, 386–398.

Gnyawali, D. R. & Madhavan R. (2001). Cooperative networks and competitive dynamics: A structural embeddedness perspective. *Academy of Management Review*, 26, 431–445.

Gnyawali, D. R. & Park B. J. (2011). Co-opetition between giants: Collaboration with competitors for technological innovation. *Research Policy*, 40, 650–663.

Gnyawali, D. R. & Park, B. J. (2009). Co-opetition and technological innovation in small and medium-sized enterprises: A multilevel conceptual model. *Journal of Small Business Management*, 47, 308–330.

Gnyawali, D. R. & Song, Y. (2016). Pursuit of rigor in research: Illustration from coopetition literature. *Industrial Marketing Management*, 57, 12–22.

Gnyawali, D. R., He, J., & Madhavan, R. (2006). Impact of co-opetition on firm competitive behavior: An empirical examination. *Journal of Management*, 32, 507–530.

Gnyawali, D. R., Madhavan, R., He, J., & Bengtsson, M. (2016). The competition–cooperation paradox in inter-firm relationships: A conceptual framework. *Industrial Marketing Management*, 53, 7–18.

Gulati, R. (1998). Alliances and networks. *Strategic Management Journal*, 19, 293–317.

Gulati, R. (1999). Network location and learning: the influence of network resources and firm capabilities on alliance formation. *Strategic Management Journal*, 20, 397–420.

Gulati, R., Lavie, D., & Madhavan R. (2011). How do networks matter? The performance effects of interorganizational networks. *Research in Organizational Behavior*, 31, 207–224.

Gulati, R., Nohria, N., & Zaheer, A. (2000). Strategic networks. *Strategic Management Journal*, 21, 203–215.

Hannan, M.T. & Freeman, J. (1989). *Organizational ecology*. Cambridge, MA: Harvard University Press.

Heide, J. B. & Miner, A. S. (1992). The shadow of the future: Effects of anticipated interaction and frequency of contact on buyer-seller cooperation. *Academy of Management Journal*, 35, 265–291.

Hill, C. W. (1990). Cooperation, opportunism, and the invisible hand: Implications for transaction cost theory. *Academy of Management Review*, 15, 500–513.

Ingram, P. & Qingyuan, L.Y. (2008). Structure, affect and identity as bases of organizational competition and cooperation. *Academy of Management Annals*, 2, 275–303.

Jarillo, J. C. (1988). On strategic networks. *Strategic Management Journal*, 9, 31–41.

Kelley, H. H. & Thibaut, J. W. (1978). *Interpersonal relations: A theory of interdependence*. New York: John Wiley & Sons.

Kogut, B. (1989). The stability of joint ventures: Reciprocity and competitive rivalry. *Journal of Industrial Economics*, 38, 183–198.

Lado, A. A., Boyd, N. G., & Hanlon, S. C. (1997). Competition, cooperation, and the search for economic rents: A syncretic model. *Academy of Management Review*, 22, 110–141.

Lane, P. J. & Lubatkin, M. (1998). Relative absorptive capacity and interorganizational learning. *Strategic Management Journal*, 19, 461–477.

Lavie, D. (2006). The competitive advantage of interconnected firms: An extension of the resource-based view. *Academy of Management Review*, 31, 638–658.

Lewis, M. W. (2000). Exploring paradox: Toward a more comprehensive guide. *Academy of Management Review*, 25, 760–776.

Madhok, A. (2002). Reassessing the fundamentals and beyond: Ronald Coase, the transaction cost and resource-based theories of the firm and the institutional structure of production. *Strategic Management Journal*, 23, 535–550.

Padula, G. & Dagnino, G. B. (2007). Untangling the rise of coopetition: the intrusion of competition in a cooperative game structure. *International Studies of Management & Organization*, 37, 32–52.

Park, B. J., Srivastava, M. K., & Gnyawali, D. R. (2014). Walking the tight rope of coopetition: Impact of competition and cooperation intensities and balance on firm innovation performance. *Industrial Marketing Management*, 43, 210–221.

Park, S. H. & Russo, M.V. (1996). When competition eclipses cooperation: An event history analysis of joint venture failure. *Management Science*, 42, 875–890.

Park, S. H. & Ungson, G. R. (2001). Interfirm rivalry and managerial complexity: A conceptual framework of alliance failure. *Organization Science*, 12, 37–53.

Parkhe, A. (1993). Strategic alliance structuring: A game theoretic and transaction cost examination of interfirm cooperation. *Academy of Management Journal*, 36, 794–829.

Peng, T. J. A., Pike, S., Yang, J. C. H., & Roos, G. (2012). Is cooperation with competitors a good idea? An example in practice. *British Journal of Management*, 23, 532–560.

Poole, M. S. & Van de Ven, A. H. (1989). Using paradox to build management and organization theories. *Academy of Management Review*, 14, 562–578.

Quintana-Garcia, C. & Benavides-Velasco, C. A. (2004). Cooperation, competition, and innovative capability: A panel data of European dedicated biotechnology firms. *Technovation*, 24, 927–938.

Raza-Ullah, T., Bengtsson, M., & Kock, S. (2014). The coopetition paradox and tension in coopetition at multiple levels. *Industrial Marketing Management*, 43, 189–198.

Raza-Ullah, T. (2017). *A Theory of Experienced Paradoxical Tension in Co-opetitive Alliances*. PhD Dissertation, Umeå University, Sweden.

Ritala, P. & Hurmelinna-Laukkanen, P. (2009). Whats in it for me? Creating and appropriating value in innovation-related coopetition. *Technovation*, 29, 819–828.

Rowley, T., Behrens, D., & Krackhardt, D. (2000). Redundant governance structures: An analysis of structural and relational embeddedness in the steel and semiconductor industries. *Strategic Management Journal*, 21, 369–386.

Sanou, F. H., Le Roy, F., & Gnyawali, D. R. (2016). How does centrality in coopetition networks matter? An empirical investigation in the mobile telephone industry. *British Journal of Management*, 27, 143–160.

Smith, W. K. & Lewis, M. W. (2011). Toward a theory of paradox: A dynamic equilibrium model of organizing. *Academy of Management Review*, 36, 381–403.

Stuart, T. (2003). Governing strategic alliances. In Buskens, V., Raub, W., & Snijders, C. (Eds), *The Governance of Relations in Markets and Organizations*, Connecticut: JAI, 189–208.

Sutton, R. I. & Staw, B. M. (1995). What theory is not. *Administrative Science Quarterly*, 40, 371–384.

Teece, D. J. (1985). Multinational enterprise, internal governance, and industrial organization. *American Economic Review*, 75, 233–238.

Teece, D. J., Pisano, G., & Shuen, A. (1997). Dynamic capabilities and strategic management. *Strategic Management Journal*, 18, 509–533.

Wernerfelt, B. (1984). A resource-based view of the firm. *Strategic Management Journal*, 5, 171–180.

Whetten, D. A. (2009). Modeling theoretic propositions. In *Designing Research for Publication*, Huff, A. S (Ed.). London, UK: Sage, 217–250.

Williamson O. E. (1985). *The Economic Institutions of Capitalism*. New York: The Free Press.

Williamson, O. E. (1975). *Markets and Hierarchies: Analysis and Antitrust Implications*. New York: The Free Press.

Williamson, O. E. (1979). Transaction-cost economics: The governance of contractual relations. *Journal of Law and Economics*, 22, 233–261.

Williamson, O. E. (1991). Comparative economic organization: The analysis of discrete structural alternatives. *Administrative Science Quarterly*, 36, 269–296.

3

From strategizing coopetition to managing coopetition

Frédéric Le Roy, Anne-Sophie Fernandez, and Paul Chiambaretto

Introduction

Since the seminal book by Brandenburger and Nalebuff (1996), coopetition has been the subject of an increasing amount of research. Publications on coopetition have been developed in numerous directions, making it difficult to form a complete synthesis (Bengtsson & Kock, 2014; Bengtsson & Raza-Ullah, 2016; Czakon et al., 2014; Dorn et al., 2016; Yami et al., 2010). A common agreement among coopetition scholars is that coopetition can lead to higher levels of performance. As a consequence, coopetition is not only a research topic but also a strategy leading to a higher performance level than other strategies. Firms that implement coopetition strategies, i.e., *strategizing* coopetition, should expect higher performance than firms that implement purely cooperative or purely competitive strategies (Brandenburger & Nalebuff, 1996; Lado et al., 1997).

The power of strategizing coopetition was first justified by *game theory* (Brandenburger & Nalebuff, 1996). In the Prisoner Dilemma, although counter-intuitive, the cooperative solution is still the best strategy. Another explanation of the relevance of strategizing coopetition is rooted in the *resource-based view theory* (Bengtsson & Kock, 1999). As competitors have specific and highly complementary resources, combining those resources leads to a high-performance level. Other theoretical lenses can be used to justify the power of coopetition, including the *network theory* (Gnyawali & Madhavan, 2001), the *resource dependence theory* (Chiambaretto & Fernandez, 2016), and the *dynamic capabilities theory* (Estrada et al., 2016).

However, from other theoretical perspectives, the link between coopetition strategies and performance may appear to be null or negative. For instance, according to the *transaction cost theory*, high levels of uncertainty lead to opportunism. As coopetition is characterized by high uncertainty, especially in radical innovation projects, coopetitors could be damaged by high-technology plunders and unintended spillover. Therefore, they must avoid coopetition strategies (Arranz & Arroyabe, 2008). In the same way, the *core competence theory* considers that coopetitors are engaged in a learning race that could be damaging for the loser (Hamel, 1991; Khanna et al., 1998).

To sum up, coopetition can be a win–win strategy but also a win–lose strategy. Therefore, strategizing coopetition is not enough to reach high levels of performance. Coopetitors should pay attention to the risk of plunder in coopetition relationships. This risk of plunder does not mean that coopetitors must end or refuse a coopetitive relationship, but rather that they must manage it properly to create the conditions of successful coopetition. To make coopetition a successful strategy, the key point is management. Management is the "missing link" between coopetition and performance (Le Roy & Czakon, 2016). In this way, the core hypothesis defended in this chapter is that coopetition strategy can have a positive, null or negative impact on performance depending on the quality of the coopetition management implemented.

Strategizing coopetition: A double-edged sword

Coopetition is a dual and paradoxical relationship, simultaneously combining collaboration to create value and competition to capture a higher share of the value jointly created (Peng et al., 2012; Ritala, 2012). The paradox generated by the simultaneity of competition and cooperation represents the essence of the concept of coopetition (Bengtsson & Kock, 2000; Raza-Ullah, Bengtsson, & Kock, 2014).

The idea of combining collaboration and competition instead of opposing them is new in the literature. *Economic theory* considers that collaboration means collusion and is not good for welfare. Thus, efficient competition implies the absence of collaboration between competitors. Conversely, coopetition considers that collaboration between competitors could be good for the consumer if and only if this collaboration does not mean the end of competition. Collaboration between competitors is better than pure competition as long as the competitors continue to compete (Jorde & Teece, 1990).

This original point of view still requires theoretical justification and empirical evidence. Coopetition as a successful strategy for companies was first legitimated using game theory (Brandenburger & Nalebuff, 1996). The well-known Prisoner Dilemma and the stag hunt game have been used to demonstrate the value of collaborating and competing at the same time (Ritala & Hurmelinna-Laukkanen, 2009). The coopetitive solution is counter-intuitive, and the actors will prefer a competitive solution. However, the coopetitive solution is the best one for them and leads to an optimal equilibrium.

Bengtsson & Kock (1999, 2000) built on the resource-based view (RBV) to justify the relevance of strategizing coopetition. The RBV explains why competitors are very good potential partners. Indeed, as they have similar and complementary resources, they can combine them to encourage economies of scale and learning (Gnyawali & Park, 2011; Ritala & Hurmelinna-Laukkanen, 2009). These arguments are consistent with the *capabilities-based view* (CBV) (Estrada et al., 2016). From the CBV perspective, the recombination of knowledge is critical to build dynamic capabilities (Helfat & Peteraf, 2003). More specifically, innovation capabilities emerge from the recombination of complementary knowledge (Kogut & Zander, 1992). For this reason, several scholars suggest that coopetition is one of the best ways to combine complementary knowledge and develop successful product innovation (Gnyawali & Park, 2009, 2011; Quintana-García & Benavides-Velasco, 2004; Ritala & Hurmelinna-Laukkanen, 2009).

Network theory provides arguments that align with the RBV and the CBV. It recommends that firms in the same industry, with different but complementary resources and capabilities, should collaborate deeply. Indeed, by collaborating not only at the dyadic level but also at the industry level, they can benefit from a broader knowledge base and become more performant (Gnyawali & Madhavan, 2001; Gnyawali et al., 2006). According to this approach, the challenge for a firm is to become the central actor in the coopetitive network (Sanou et al., 2016). The best strategy consists of being highly cooperative to become central in the network. This central position will give power to the focal firm, which will be able to become more aggressive and therefore more profitable. Following this approach, coopetition strategy is better than either a pure competition or a pure cooperation strategy (Le Roy & Sanou, 2014; Robert et al., 2018).

Game theory, RBV, CBV and network theory all lead to an optimistic view of coopetition, which becomes a better strategy than pure competition or pure collaboration. However, this optimistic view of coopetition is inconsistent with research built on *transaction cost theory* (TCT) (Arranz & Arroyabe, 2008; Park & Russo, 1996). The TCT considers that coopetition creates a high level of uncertainty, giving actors the incentive to behave opportunistically. Therefore, coopetitors cannot develop trustworthy relationships and cannot fully collaborate. According to this approach, coopetition is a particular type of cooperation in which trust is difficult to develop (Arranz & Arroyabe, 2008; Czakon & Czernek, 2016). As both coopetitors are aware of opportunistic risks, they are discouraged from pooling their core knowledge. Cooperation with competitors exposes the firm to undesired spillover that can be used by the coopetitor. Thus, firms are reluctant to collaborate openly, and it is difficult to develop the necessary level of trust for the success of common projects.

In the same way, the core competence theory considers that coopetition is a risky strategy in which coopetitors are involved in a learning race (Hamel, 1991). Cooperating with a competitor involves sharing knowledge, skills and resources. Without this sharing, the collaboration is useless. However, because the coopetitor is an opportunist by nature, it might use this knowledge for its own individual benefit rather than for common benefits. If there is a significant asymmetry of learning, coopetition becomes a win-lose strategy; i.e., one coopetitor is winning at the expense of the other (Baumard, 2010; Hamel et al., 1989).

The TCT and core competence theory lead to a pessimistic view of coopetition. On the one hand, because collaboration is not really possible between competitors, coopetition cannot have a positive effect. On the other hand, because of the high risks of opportunism, coopetition can be very damaging. Therefore, the coopetition effect should be null in the best situation and negative in the worst situation. Coopetition strategies should thus be avoided as much as possible.

To sum up, depending on the perspective adopted, strategizing coopetition can lead to different outcomes. According to game theory, the RBV, the CBV and network theory, the best partner is a competitor and coopetition is a powerful win–win strategy, even better than purely collaborative or purely competitive strategies. Conversely, the TCT and the core competence theory consider coopetition to be an inefficient, and in some extreme cases a potentially damaging, strategy. Coopetition is conceptualized as a win-lose strategy that firms should avoid.

Strategizing coopetition in and of itself is not sufficient to create a high level of performance. Thus, the decision for any firm is not whether to strategize coopetition, but rather how to successfully strategize coopetition. Our main idea in this chapter is that managing coopetition is the principal success factor in strategizing coopetition.

From strategizing coopetition to coopetitive tensions

By simultaneously combining two opposite behaviors (collaboration and competition), coopetition can be understood as a paradoxical strategy (De Rond & Bouchiki, 2004; Raza-Ullah et al., 2014; Smith & Lewis, 2011). The combination of collaborative and competitive behaviours contributes to the emergence of tensions at different levels: inter-organizational, intra-organizational and inter-individual (Bengtsson & Kock, 2000; Czakon, 2010; Fernandez et al., 2014; Le Roy & Fernandez, 2015; Luo et al., 2006; Padula & Dagnino, 2007). Tensions between cooperation and competition are driven by the conflict between generating shared benefits and capturing private benefits (Czakon, 2010; Khanna et al., 1998; Ritala & Tidström, 2014).

At the inter-organizational level, tension initially arises out of the dilemma between the creation of common value and the appropriation of private value (Ritala & Tidström, 2014; Gnyawali et al., 2016). After the knowledge creation phase, tensions arise between the distributive and integrative elements of knowledge appropriation (Oliver, 2004). Another type of coopetitive tension occurs based on the risks of transferring confidential information and the risks of technological imitation. Partners pool strategic resources to achieve their goals (Gnyawali & Park, 2009); however, at the same time, they must protect their core competences to remain strong competitors.

At the intra-organizational level, i.e., at the project level, coopetitive tensions are even more important because the implementation of coopetition strategies requires employees from competing parent firms to work together (Fernandez et al., 2014; Gnyawali & Park, 2011). The project level is thus crucial to an understanding of how intra-organizational tensions are managed.

One critical intra-organizational tension arises from the dilemma between sharing and protecting information (Fernandez et al., 2014; Fernandez & Chiambaretto, 2016; Levy et al., 2003). Partners in an alliance can easily learn from one another, especially if they are competitors (Baruch & Lin, 2012; Estrada et al., 2016; Khanna et al., 1998). Although partners must share information and knowledge to achieve the common goal of the collaboration (Gnyawali & Park, 2011; Mention, 2011), each partner must also protect the strategic core of its knowledge from its competitor because partners that operate in the same industry must develop unique skills (Baumard, 2010; Ritala et al., 2015). Information that is shared within a common collaborative project could potentially be used in a different market in which the partners compete. The competing partner could benefit by appropriating the shared information (Hurmelinna-Laukkanen & Olander, 2014).

In a coopetitive project in which partners could utilize shared information for their own purposes, the risk of opportunism and appropriation is particularly high (Baruch & Lin, 2012; Bouncken & Kraus, 2013; Hurmelinna-Laukkanen & Olander, 2014; Ritala & Hurmelinna-Laukkanen, 2009, 2013). Fernandez and Chiambaretto (2016) defined this coopetitive tension related to information as "the difference between a firm's need to share information to ensure the success of the common project and its need to limit information sharing to avoid informational spillovers into other markets."

Another critical tension occurs among the different business units (Luo et al., 2006). Managers involved in internal activities compete with colleagues involved in coopetitive activities to obtain human, technological and financial resources from the parent firm (Tsai, 2002).

At the inter-individual level, coopetitive tensions appear for a variety of reasons. Individuals face the dilemma of choosing between a single strategy and collaboration. In a purely collaborative project, a common identity is gradually created as individuals from different companies work together over time. In a coopetitive project, two firms' identities are mixed without being merged. The psychological equilibrium of the individuals involved can be disturbed (Gnyawali et al., 2008; Gnyawali et al., 2016; Raza-Ullah et al., 2014). Another source of tension relates to employees involved in activities developed with competitors. These employees face tensions when a current competitor becomes a partner or when a partner becomes a competitor (Gnyawali and Park, 2011; Raza-Ullah et al., 2014).

In a nutshell, there are substantial tensions in coopetition due to the competitive dimension of the coopetitive relationship. These tensions can be considered very damaging for the quality of the collaboration between coopetitors. They can create mistrust, mutual negative effects and unsolvable conflicts between coopetitors. However, they can also be considered the real source of coopetition success because they encourage coopetitors to find a way to transcend their paradoxical coopetitive relationship.

In this way of thinking, coopetition provides coopetitors with additional resources and competitive challenges to best use these resources. Coopetitive tensions stimulate firms and individuals to give the best of themselves and to go faster and further than pure competition or pure collaboration. Therefore, coopetitive tensions are considered more as a strength than a weakness of coopetition. In this perspective, reducing coopetitive tensions will lead to a decrease in competition and thus to an end of coopetition (Park et al., 2014). Consequently, companies must not attempt to reduce or eliminate these tensions but should instead manage them efficiently (Le Roy & Czakon, 2016). Instead of reducing competition or collaboration, firms should rather maintain a balance (Clarke-Hill et al., 2003). Relevant managerial tools are then required to reach and preserve this balance (Bengtsson et al., 2016; Chen et al., 2007; Chen, 2008).

When coopetitive tensions require the management of coopetition

Coopetition paradox belongs to a larger stream of literature dedicated to the management of paradoxes (Lewis, 2000; Smith & Lewis, 2011). In this literature, two contradictory approaches to managing paradoxical tensions are frequently debated. The first approach recommends paradox resolution by splitting opposite forces (Poole & Van de Ven, 1989). The second approach suggests that separation creates vicious cycles. Therefore, scholars in this second approach recommend accepting and transcending the paradox at both the individual and the organizational levels. Once the paradox is accepted, a resolution strategy should be implemented (Smith & Lewis, 2011; Smith & Tushman, 2005).

According to the paradox resolution approach, several coopetition scholars consider that the management of collaboration and the management of competition should be split to manage coopetitive tensions (Bengtsson & Kock, 2000; Dowling et al., 1996; Herzog, 2010). The separation can be functional or spatial. For instance, coopetitors can cooperate on one dimension of the value chain (i.e., R&D) while competing on another dimension (i.e., marketing activities), or coopetitors can cooperate in a given market while competing in another one.

However, other scholars have noted the limitations of this principle and recommended a more integrative approach (Chen, 2008; Oshri & Weeber, 2006). The main problem with the separation principle is the creation of internal conflict in the company between people dedicated to competition and people dedicated to collaboration (Pellegrin-Boucher et al., forthcoming). In line with the paradox acceptance approach, the integration principle requires individuals to understand their roles in a paradoxical context and to behave accordingly, following both logics simultaneously. Thus, the challenge for managers is to transcend the paradox, to simultaneously manage collaboration and competition, and to thereby optimize the benefits of coopetition (Luo, 2007).

The separation principle and the integration principle belong to two different and opposite schools of thought. In the first one, the basic idea is that individuals cannot integrate the paradox; therefore, the separation principle is needed and the only one to implement coopetition strategy. In the second school of thought, the separation principle is considered a negation of the paradoxical nature of coopetition. Companies can successfully manage coopetition if and only if individuals can develop a coopetitive mindset.

A third school of thought attempts to combine these two opposite approaches. Instead of opposing the separation and the integration principles, scholars suggest that both principles should be used simultaneously to efficiently manage coopetitive tensions (Fernandez et al., 2014; Fernandez & Chiambaretto, 2016; Séran et al., 2016). The separation principle is required at the organizational level. Competition and cooperation should be split between different levels of the value chain or between different products or markets. This separation is necessary to define a dominant role, either collaborative or competitive, for each activity within the firm. However, this single separation is not sufficient to efficiently manage multiple coopetitive tensions because they generate additional tensions within the organization at the individual level.

At the individual level, the integration of the coopetition paradox is necessary to manage coopetitive tensions. Indeed, the separation principle creates internal tensions within firms between those employees in charge of collaboration and those in charge of competition. The only way to control these tensions is to encourage people to understand the role of each employee in a coopetitive setting. The understanding of the coopetition paradox limits the tensions within the firm and allows individuals to adopt simultaneous cooperative and competitive behaviors with their coopetitors. The integration of the coopetition paradox by individuals is facilitated by the joint implementation of formal coordination (procedures, regular meetings, etc.) and informal coordination (social networks, social interaction, trust, etc.) (Séran et al., 2016).

The separation and the integration principles are complementary. Each principle has virtues and limits, and the combination of both principles compensates for their limits. For instance, Fernandez and Chiambaretto (2016) showed empirically how to combine both principles to manage tensions related to information at the project level. According to the separation principle, managers use formal control mechanisms, i.e., the information system, to share only the critical information required to achieve a project goal and to protect the non-critical information. Simultaneously, managers use informal control mechanisms to differentiate appropriable critical information from non-appropriable critical information, to transform one into the other. Such abilities developed by managers rely on a cognitive integration of the coopetition paradox. Thus, efficiently managing tensions related to information requires a combination of both the separation and integration principles.

Other empirical evidence is provided by Séran and colleagues (2016) in the banking sector. In this sector, coopetition relationships exist within multi-unit organizations, such as Crédit Agricole and Banque Populaire Caisse d'Epargne. Coopetitive tensions appear at the intra-organizational and inter-individual levels. Authors have shown that these tensions are efficiently managed by the implementation of a separation principle—independent banks, distinct brands and staff—and the implementation of an integration principle based on formal and informal coordination.

Opening the black box: Managing coopetition on a daily basis

The separation and integration principles are used together but at different levels. The separation principle is associated with the organizational design of the company, or at least within the business unit. Within this unit, certain projects are conducted with rivals and other projects are performed in pure competition with these rivals. The integration principle pertains to the individual level. People are more or less able to integrate the paradox of coopetition and adopt both a balanced mindset and behavior.

Between the organizational–design level and the individual level, an intermediary level is the working group dedicated to the common project with the competitor. At this working-group level, people from competing firms work together on a daily basis, sharing their knowledge, know-how, resources and competencies. Therefore, at this level, the value of coopetition is created, but the risks of plunder are at their highest. Consequently, this level is critical for coopetition success.

How should firms manage coopetition at this working-group level? Two previous studies are dedicated to this question. The first focuses on technology coopetition (Le Roy & Fernandez, 2015) and the second focuses on selling coopetition (Pellegrin-Boucher et al., 2018). Both each identify an additional principle: the co-management principle for technology coopetition and the arbitration principle for selling coopetition.

First, the co-management principle is required for technology coopetition (Le Roy & Fernandez, 2015). This co-management principle is implemented into the common team created by the coopetitors: the coopetitive project team. The co-management principle is based on peer logic. The coopetitive project team is managed via a dual managerial structure. Team members from competing firms are pooled and work together on a daily basis. Parent firms adopt an organizational design in which they equally share the decision-making process, thus managing the risk of opportunism. Therefore, power is balanced and symmetric in a horizontal collaboration. Although this redundancy in managerial functions may appear to be a waste of resources, it is essential to develop trust and to encourage necessary knowledge-sharing among team members (Fernandez et al., 2018; Le Roy & Fernandez, 2015).

Second, the arbitration principle is needed for selling coopetition (Pellegrin-Boucher et al., forthcoming). Selling coopetition relies on alliance managers, whose mission is to win calls for tenders by collaborating with competitors. This mission creates internal tensions between alliance managers and sales managers who may also apply for these calls for tenders alone. These tensions cannot be resolved by the separation and integration principles, and thus the hierarchy must rely on arbitration to address these internal conflicts.

Based on these previous studies, we propose a multi-level framework to analyze the management of coopetition strategies (Figure 3.1). The separation principle is relevant to managing coopetitive tensions at the organizational level, and the integration principle is appropriate for managing coopetitive tensions at the individual level. At the project level (R&D or sales project), the co-management principle is relevant in technology coopetition, whereas the arbitration principle is better suited for selling coopetition. These principles should be simultaneously combined and implemented to efficiently manage coopetitive tensions.

The importance of the combination of these principles was initially found in the space industry for technology coopetition (Le Roy & Fernandez, 2015) and in the ICT industry for selling coopetition (Pellegrin-Boucher et al., 2018). These high-tech industries are characterized by high levels of R&D costs, high levels of risk, high levels of knowledge, high market uncertainty, etc. All companies evolving in high-tech industries face similar issues. Thus, our framework could guide these companies to adopt coopetition strategies and to succeed in such environments. Further studies could confirm this assumption in other high-tech or low-tech industries. From this perspective, coopetition management is a new and stimulating research topic with significant potential for researchers and practitioners.

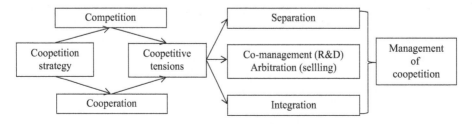

Figure 3.1 From coopetition strategy to coopetition management

Conclusion and research perspectives

In this chapter, we indicate that coopetition strategy can be a double-edged sword, representing either a win-win or a win-lose strategy. The positive or negative effect of strategizing coopetition clearly depends on the management of coopetition. Because coopetition simultaneously combines two contradictory logics, it creates tensions at several different levels: inter-organizational, intra-organizational and inter-individual. These tensions must be efficiently managed so that firms can benefit from coopetition. The question of relevant principles for managing coopetition is therefore the key question in coopetition research.

This question remains an open one and, thus far, three schools of thought can be distinguished. The first is based on the separation principle, the second on the integration principle and the third on a combination of the separation and integration principles. In this third school, some researchers explore more deeply at the working-group level and identify two other principles depending on the coopetition type: the co-management principle for technology coopetition and the arbitration principle for selling coopetition. Overall, successfully managing coopetition requires a combination of complementary principles: the separation principle at the business unit level; the co-management principle (for technology coopetition) or the arbitration principle (for selling coopetition) at the working-group level; and the integration principle at the individual level.

Coopetition remains more of an open field of research than a closed one. Research on managing coopetition remains scarce, and further research is needed in other industries to discuss the relevance of the preliminary results presented in this chapter. Is our framework relevant for companies in low-tech industries or for SMEs? Understanding and analyzing the management tools used in coopetition strategy in these circumstances is crucial.

As highlighted in this chapter, previous research remained focused on management principles. Once these management principles have been identified, it is necessary to delve further into the black box of coopetition. For instance, researchers should explore organizational designs used by firms at the working-group level. Le Roy and Fernandez (2015) identified the coopetitive project team. Do companies use organizational designs other than coopetitive project teams and why? One recent contribution suggests that a company can use another organizational design known as the separated-project team, based on the risks, costs and innovativeness of the project (Fernandez et al., 2018). Additional research is needed to reveal other organizational designs and to understand their drivers and implications. In particular, we must examine how companies manage their coopetition strategy when the coopetitive project involves more than two coopetitors.

Future studies should also focus on certain managerial aspects of coopetitive projects. For instance, the information systems used to achieve coopetitive projects represent an exciting research perspective. The pioneering work of Fernandez and Chiambaretto (2016) requires additional research to better understand how information is shared and protected by coopetitors. We also must further investigate the management control of coopetitive projects. Preliminary research shows that management control creates specific issues that can be more thoroughly investigated (Grafton & Mundy, 2017). The marketing management of coopetition represents another fascinating research perspective. Pellegrin-Boucher et al. (2018) suggest that managing the selling of coopetition involves a specific principle known as arbitration. Futures studies could examine the management of selling coopetition as well as marketing, distribution or branding coopetition (Chiambaretto et al., 2016). Managing coopetition in supply chains, purchasing and logistics is an entirely open question that should also be specifically examined.

To sum up, researchers have taken the first steps towards a broader understanding of coopetition management. Given that coopetition management is the key success factor in strategizing coopetition, further research on this topic is necessary.

References

Arranz, N. & Arroyabe, J. C. (2008). The choice of partners in R&D cooperation: An empirical analysis of Spanish firms. *Technovation*, 28, 88–100.

Baruch, Y. & Lin, C.-P. (2012). All for one, one for all: Coopetition and virtual team performance. *Technological Forecasting and Social Change*, 79(6), 1155–1168.

Baumard, P. (2010). Learning in Coopetitive Environments. In Yami, S., Castaldo, S., Dagnino, G. B., & Le Roy, F. (Eds), *Coopetition: winning strategies for the 21st century*. Cheltenham; Northampton, MA: Edward Elgar.

Bengtsson, M. & Kock, S. (2000). "Coopetition" in business networks—to cooperate and compete simultaneously. *Industrial Marketing Management*, 29(5), 411–426.

Bengtsson, M. & Kock, S. (2014). Coopetition—quo vadis? Past accomplishments and future challenges. *Industrial Marketing Management*, 43(2), 180–188.

Bengtsson, M. & Raza-Ullah, T. (2016). A systematic review of research on coopetition: Towards a multi-level understanding. *Industrial Marketing Management*, 57, 23–39.

Bengtsson, M., Raza-Ullah, T., & Vanyushyn, V. (2016). The coopetition paradox and tension: The moderating role of coopetition capability. *Industrial Marketing Management*, 53, 19–30.

Bonel, E. & Rocco, E. (2007). Coopeting to survive; surviving coopetition. *International Studies of Management & Organization*, 37(2), 70–96.

Bouncken, R. B. & Kraus, S. (2013). Innovation in knowledge-intensive industries: The double-edged sword of coopetition. *Journal of Business Research*, 66(10), 2060–2070.

Brandenburger, A. M. & Nalebuff, B. J. (1996). *Co-Opetition: A Revolutionary Mindset That Redefines Competition and Cooperation*. Doubleday: New York, 121.

Chen, M.-J. (2008). Reconceptualizing the competition-cooperation relationship: a transparadox perspective. *Journal of Management Inquiry*, 17(4), 288–304.

Chen, M.-J., Su, K.-H., & Tsai, W. (2007). Competitive tension: The awareness-motivation-capability perspective. *Academy of Management Journal*, 50(1), 101–118.

Chan, S. H., Kensinger, J. W., Keown, A. J., & Martin, J. D. (1997). Do strategic alliances create value? *Journal of Financial Economics*, 46, 199–221.

Chiambaretto P., Calin G., & Le Roy F. (2016). Coopetitive branding: Definition, typology, benefit and risks. *Industrial Marketing Management*, 57, 86–96.

Chiambaretto, P. & Fernandez, A.-S. (2016). The evolution of coopetitive and collaborative alliances in an alliance portfolio: The Air France case. *Industrial Marketing Management*, 57, 75–85.

Clarke-Hill, C., Li, H., & Davies, B. (2003). The paradox of co-operation and competition in strategic alliances: towards a multi-paradigm approach. *Management Research News*, 26(1), 1–20.

Czakon, W. & Czernek, K. (2016). The role of trust-building mechanisms in entering into network coopetition: The case of tourism networks in Poland. *Industrial Marketing Management*, 57, 64–74.

Czakon, W., Fernandez, A-S., & Minà, A. (2014). From paradox to practice: the rise of coopetition strategies. *International Journal of Business Environment*, 6(1), 1–10.

De Rond, M. & Bouchikhi, H. (2004). On the dialectics of strategic alliances. *Organization Science*, 15(1), 56–69.

Dorn, S., Schweiger, B., & Albers, S. (2016). Levels, phases and themes of coopetition: A systematic literature review and research agenda. *European Management Journal*, 34(5), 484–500.

Dowling, M. J., Roering, W. D., Carlin, B. A., & Wisnieski, J. (1996). Multifaceted relationships under coopetition description and theory. *Journal of Management Inquiry*, 5(2), 155–167.

Estrada, I., Faems, D., & de Faria, P. (2016). Coopetition and product innovation performance: The role of internal knowledge sharing mechanisms and formal knowledge protection mechanisms. *Industrial Marketing Management*, 53, 56–65.

Fernandez, A.-S. & Chiambaretto, P. (2016). Managing tensions related to information in coopetition. *Industrial Marketing Management*, 53, 66–76.

Fernandez, A.-S., Le Roy, F., & Gnyawali, D. R. (2014). Sources and management of tension in co-opetition case evidence from telecommunications satellites manufacturing in Europe. *Industrial Marketing Management*, 43(2), 222–235.

Fernandez, A.-S., Le Roy, F., Chiambaretto, P. (2018). Implementing the right project structure to achieve coopetitive innovation projects. *Long Range Planning*, 51(2), 384–405.

Gnyawali, D. R. & Madhavan, R. (2001). Networks and competitive dynamics: A structural embeddedness perspective. *Academy of Management Review*, 26(3), 431–445.

Gnyawali, D. R., He, J., & Madhavan, R. (2006). Impact of co-opetition on firm competitive behavior: An empirical examination. *Journal of Management*, 32, 507–530.

Gnyawali, D. R., He, J., & Madhavan, R. (2008). Co-opetition. Promises and challenges. *In 21st Century Management: A Reference Handbook*, Wankel, C. (Ed). London: Sage Publications, 386–398.

Gnyawali, D. R., Madhavan, R., He, J., & Bengtsson, M. (2016). The competition–cooperation paradox in inter-firm relationships: A conceptual framework. *Industrial Marketing Management*, 53, 7–18.

Gnyawali, D. R. & Park, B.-J. (2009). Co-opetition and technological innovation in Small and Medium-Sized Enterprises: a multilevel conceptual model. *Journal of Small Business Management*, 47(3), 308–330.

Gnyawali, D. R. & Park, B.-J. (2011). Co-opetition between giants: Collaboration with competitors for technological innovation. *Research Policy*, 40(5), 650–663.

Hamel, G. (1991). Competition for competence and inter-partner learning within international strategic alliances. *Strategic Management Journal*, 1, 83–103.

Hamel, G., Doz, Y. L., & Prahalad, C. K. (1989). Collaborate with your competitors – and win. *Harvard Business Review*, 67(1), 133–139.

Helfat, C. E. & Peteraf, M. A. (2003). The dynamic resource-based view: capability lifecycles. *Strategic Management Journal*, 24, 997–1010.

Herzog, T. (2010). Strategic management of coopetitive relationships in CoPS-related industries. In *Coopetition: winning strategies for the 21st century*, Yami, S., Castaldo, S., Dagnino, G. B., Le Roy, F. (Eds). Cheltenham; Northampton, MA: Edward Elgar.

Hurmelinna-Laukkanen, P. & Olander, H. (2014). Coping with rivals' absorptive capacity in innovation activities. *Technovation*, 34(1), 3–11.

Grafton, J. & Mundy, J. (2017), Relational contracting and the myth of trust: Control in a co-opetitive setting. *Management Accounting Research*, 36, 24–4.

Jorde, T. M. & Teece, D. J. (1990). Innovation and cooperation: implications for competition and antitrust. *Journal of Economic Perspectives*, 4(3), 75–96.

Khanna, T., Gulati, R., & Nohria, N. (1998). The dynamics of learning alliances: competition, cooperation, and relative scope. *Strategic Management Journal*, 19(3), 193–210.

Kim, J. & Parkhe, A. (2009). Competing and cooperating similarity in global strategic alliances: an exploratory examination. *British Journal of Management*, 20(3), 363–376.

Kogut, B. & Zander, U. (1992). Knowledge of the firm, combinative capabilities, and the replication of technology. *Organization Science*, 3, 383–397.

Lado, A. A., Boyd, N. G., & Hanlon, S. C. (1997). Competition, cooperation, and the search for economic rents: A syncretic model. *Academy of Management Review*, 22(1), 110–141.

Le Roy, F. & Czakon, W. (2016). Managing coopetition: the missing link between strategy and performance. *Industrial Marketing Management*, 53, 3–6.

Le Roy, F. & Sanou, F. H. (2014). Does Coopetition Strategy improve Market Performance: an Empirical Study in Mobile Phone Industry. *Journal of Economics and Management*, 17, 63–94.

Le Roy, F. & Fernandez, A.-S. (2015). Managing coopetitive tensions at the working-group level: the rise of the coopetitive project team. *British Journal of Management*, 26(4), 671–688.

Levy, M., Loebbecke, C., & Maier, R. (2003). SMEs, co-opetition and knowledge sharing: the role of information systems. *European Journal of Information Systems*, 12(1), 3–17.

Lewis, M. W. (2000). Exploring paradox: Toward a more comprehensive guide. *Academy of Management Review*, 25, 760–776.

Luo, X., Rindfleisch, A., & Tse, D. K. (2007). Working with rivals: the impact of competitor alliances on financial performance. *Journal of Marketing Research*, 44(1), 73–83.

Luo, X., Slotegraaf, R. J., & Pan, X. (2006). Cross-functional "coopetition": The simultaneous role of cooperation and competition within firms. *Journal of Marketing*, 70(2), 67–80.

Mention, A.-L. (2011). Co-operation and co-opetition as open innovation practices in the service sector: Which influence on innovation novelty? *Technovation*, 31(1), 44–53.

Oshri, I. & Weeber, C. (2006). Cooperation and competition standards-setting activities in the digitization era: The case of wireless information devices. *Technology Analysis & Strategic Management*, 18(2), 265–283.

Padula, G. & Dagnino, G. (2007). Untangling the rise of coopetition: The intrusion of competition in a cooperative game structure. *International Studies of Management and Organization*, 37(2), 32–52.

Park, B.-J. (Robert), Srivastava, M. K., & Gnyawali, D. R. (2014). Walking the tight rope of coopetition: Impact of competition and cooperation intensities and balance on firm innovation performance. *Industrial Marketing Management*, 43(2), 210–221.

Pellegrin-Boucher, E., Le Roy, F., & Gurău, C. (2018). Managing Selling Coopetition: a case study of the ERP industry. *European Management Review*, 15(1), 37–56.

Pellegrin-Boucher, E., Le Roy, F., & Gurău, C. (2013). Coopetitive strategies in the ICT sector: typology and stability. *Technology Analysis & Strategic Management*, 25(1), 71–89.

Peng, T.-J. A., Pike, S., Yang, J.C.-H., & Roos, G. (2012). Is Cooperation with competitors a good Idea? An example in practice. *British Journal of Management*, 23(4), 532–560.

Poole, M. S. & Van de Ven, A. H. (1989). Using paradox to build management and organization theories. *Academy of Management Review*, 14, 562–578.

Quintana-García, C. & Benavides-Velasco, C. A. (2004). Cooperation, competition, and innovative capability: a panel data of European dedicated biotechnology firms. *Technovation*, 24(12), 927–938.

Raza-Ullah, T., Bengtsson, M., & Kock, S. (2014). The coopetition paradox and tension in coopetition at multiple levels. *Industrial Marketing Management*, 43(2), 189–198.

Ritala, P. (2012). Coopetition Strategy – When is it successful? Empirical evidence on innovation and market performance. *British Journal of Management*, 23(3), 307–324.

Ritala, P. & Hurmelinna-Laukkanen, P. (2009). What is in it for me? Creating and appropriating value in innovation-related coopetition. *Technovation*, 29, 819–882

Ritala, P. & Hurmelinna-Laukkanen, P. (2013). Incremental and radical innovation in Coopetition—The role of absorptive capacity and appropriability. *Journal of Product Innovation Management*, 30(1), 154–169.

Ritala, P. & Tidström, A. (2014). Untangling the value-creation and value-appropriation elements of coopetition strategy: A longitudinal analysis on the firm and relational levels. *Scandinavian Journal of Management*, 30(4), 498–515.

Ritala, P., Olander, H., Michailova, S., & Husted, K. (2015). Knowledge sharing, knowledge leaking and relative innovation performance: An empirical study. *Technovation*, 35, 22–31.

Robert, M., Chiambaretto, P., Mira, B., & Le Roy, F. (2018). Better, Faster, Stronger: The impact of market-oriented coopetition on product commercial performance. *M@n@gement*, 21, 574–610.

Sanou, F. H., Le Roy, F., & Gnyawali, D. R. (2016). How does centrality in coopetition networks matter? An empirical investigation in the mobile telephone industry. *British Journal of Management*, 27, 143–160.

Séran, T., Pellegrin-Boucher, E., & Gurau, C. (2016). The management of coopetitive tensions within multi-unit organizations. *Industrial Marketing Management*, 53, 31–41.

Smith, W. K. & Lewis, M. (2011). Toward a theory of paradox: a dynamic equilibrium model of organizing. *Academy of Management Review*, 36(2), 381–403.

Tsai, W. (2002). Social structure of "coopetition" within a multiunit organization: Coordination, competition, and intraorganizational knowledge sharing. *Organization Science*, 13(2), 179–190.

Yami, S., Castaldo, S., Dagnino G. B., & Le Roy, F. (2010). *Coopetition winning strategies for the 21st century*. Cheltenham; Northampton, MA: Edward Elgar.

4

Network coopetition

Wojciech Czakon

Introduction

If collaboration between two rivals can dramatically improve their market position (Gnyawali & Park, 2009) and, if carefully managed, contribute to increasing the respective firms' performance (Fernandez et al., 2014), then collaboration between three and more partners unlocks the true potential of coopetition. The more actors involved in creating value, the more value that can be generated and appropriated. This chapter takes coopetition thinking back to its origins, rooted in the value net concept, which brings in various actors and establishes collaborative relationships along with competition among them (Brandenburger & Nalebuff, 1997). As opposed to a dyad, where tensions and paradoxes attract researchers' attention (Tidström, 2009), it is value creation potential that remains at the core of network coopetition. In order to unlock it, firms need to understand the value net scope, the nature of relationships linking actors together and the strategic challenges related to network coopetition entry, as well as common value generation and capture.

The value network and coopetition

Coopetition is an intriguing concept both for managers and academics, because it is difficult to conceive a simultaneously friendly and rivalrous relationship with a single partner. Significant attention has been attributed to this challenge, by conceptually positioning coopetition as one of four possible inter-firm relationships (Bengtsson & Kock, 2000), along with competition, collaboration and coexistence. This early proposition locates collaboration on some value chain activities, while competition takes place on others, so that the two opposing relational logics are separated. To date, theoretical contributions and empirical studies have provided solid grounds for understanding the paradoxical nature of coopetition (Czakon et al., 2014).

However, the introduction of coopetition into management literature has adopted a value net level of analysis (Brandenburger & Nalebuff, 1997). Scholars have recently underlined the need to shift beyond dyadic coopetition, in order to tap into the network level of analysis in coopetition studies (Gnywali et al., 2006; Pathak et al., 2014; Sanou et al., 2016; Wilhelm, 2011). Network coopetition refers to multiple actors' interactions involving various firms, covering the value net. It involves rivals, suppliers, customers and complementors in a joint effort to increase "the business pie," offering more value for appropriation by each individual actor (Brandenburger & Nalebuff, 1997). Collaboration rather than competition is in the best interests of each actor, as game theoretical models suggest (Okura, 2007). The baseline argument of coopetition is therefore connected more with the network level of analysis (Pathak et al., 2014), the collective effort to create value and the dynamics of value capture, rather than solely the paradoxical interplay of coopetition and collaboration at dyadic level.

Yet, coopetition research has seldom taken the network level of analysis. The inherent complexity of network coopetition requires a precise delimitation in order to adequately address the actors, structure and dynamics under scrutiny (Figure 4.1). Scholars have used two different concepts: the coopetitive network (Gnyawali et al., 2006), and the coopetition-in-supply network (Wilhelm, 2011).

A coopetitive network is a particular type of network within an industry, unique by the consequences of simultaneous collaboration and competition between its members (Sanou et al., 2016). Different from collaborative networks, coopetitive networks: entail the existence of competitive relationships among actors; are based on business needs rather than trust; and provide access to rival firms' resources. This unique type of network has been found to have emerged in the steel (Gnyawali et al., 2006) and mobile telecommunication (Sanou et al., 2016) industries.

Supply networks incorporate sets of individual and connected supply chains with links among them (Wilhelm, 2011). Inter-firm relations are established both vertically and horizontally. They involve pure collaboration, competition, co-existence or coopetition. The sourcing strategies of a focal firm create tensions at the horizontal level between respective suppliers. Tensions inherent to coopetition (Fernandez et al., 2014) manifest themselves in vertical relationships differently from horizontal relationships, but impact each other.

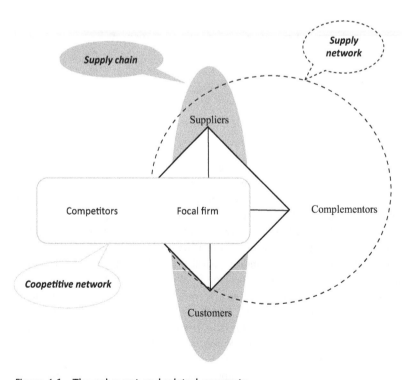

Figure 4.1 The value net and related concepts

Those two concepts have been introduced for specific purposes and therefore limit the scope of attention to emergent networks focused on resource access, or to sourcing network management (Figure 4.1). Interestingly the original concept of a value net is broader, both by the type of actors involved and by the general-purpose statement that is value creation. The inclusion of complementors into the value net goes beyond the scope of supply chain logic. Similarly, value creation can be decided by the customer, who assembles the final composition of offerings available in the value net; therefore, access to resources may reveal itself to be secondary to resource pooling through gathering relevant partners in a joint value creation process.

This chapter addresses distinct phenomena and challenges typical to network coopetition. If it is a clearly intentional strategy to collaborate with a specific actor, does network coopetition display more deliberate or more consequential features (Czakon, 2009)? How do firms nested in interdependent relationships choose their relationship-mix, resulting in the adoption of various coopetition strategies (Czakon & Rogalski, 2014)? Why do some firms enter network coopetition, while others do not (Czakon & Czernek, 2016)? What benefits does coopetition offer to all involved firms, beyond satisfying their individual needs (Czakon et al., 2016)?

Deliberate or emergent? Coopetition patterns within networks

Deliberate strategies have their corresponding alter egos, with several possible strategies in between. Emergence is seen as "patterns realized in spite of or in the absence of intentions" (Mintzberg & Waters, 1985), and encapsulates all behaviors, processes and resource allocations that have not been previously planned in a rational process (Figure 4.2.). Emergence captures the gap between what has been planned and what is actually being done, opening ways to a more dynamic understanding of strategy, where various factors interact in a long-term process. Coopetition strategies have been depicted as normative and deliberate (Le Roy & Czakon, 2016), similarly to competition and cooperation strategies, which are usually viewed as intentional, with generic options identified by scholars. Yet, their interplay in coopetition may instead be seen as an emergent process (Mariani, 2007). In this section, an overview of studies tackling network coopetition in banking, airlines and tourism sheds light on the various factors impacting coopetition adoption in order to better understand this dynamic process.

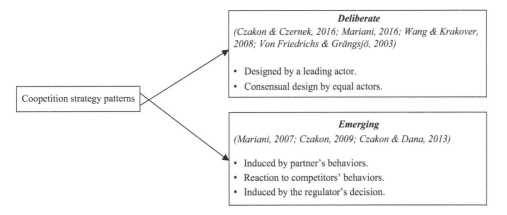

Figure 4.2 Network coopetition development patterns

A Polish banking franchise system study, focused on a medium-sized retail bank and its 460 franchisees, unveiled the emergence of competition between the franchisees and the franchisor (Czakon, 2009). The franchise network is centralized around the focal bank, and exploits a portfolio of standardized dyadic relationships designed by: 1) specifying goals; 2) defining the scope of respective actors' activities; 3) setting a governance structure; and 4) declaring partners' commitment specification.

Interfirm relationships are designed to last, so over time their assessment may lead to various changes (Ring & Van de Ven, 1994). When assessment reveals unsatisfactory results or processes, mutual adjustments are needed, otherwise the relationship is dissolved either by consensual decision or unilaterally. Franchisees were found to expect a fairer share of the business pie, and to demand collaboration process modifications, while the franchisor took a power position and demonstrated low flexibility by sticking to the initial agreement (Czakon, 2009). Consequently, three types of franchisee reactions have been identified: 1) acceptance of the initial conditions; 2) unilateral contract dissolution; and 3) unilateral rent seeking within and beyond the franchise network. Hence, competitive behaviors emerged within the collaborative setting of a franchise network.

A different process of network coopetition development, as a response to changes in the dominant strategies adopted by various firms, has been identified in a long-term study of the airlines industry (Czakon & Dana, 2013). Distinct phases in global airline industry development since deregulation in the late 1970s triggering major shakeouts of existing market rules have been identified (Czakon & Dana, 2013). Firms have adopted dyadic coopetition strategies as soon as market regulation has been relaxed. Next, dyadic coopetition portfolios appeared, mostly focused on marketing and sales. Finally, network alliance competition in the industry followed, competitive both towards other alliances and within the respective networks. Hence, coopetition has emerged from a path of innovation-imitation-covergence across the airline industry. After an innovative model is successfully implemented, actors compete for the best share in the value created. In sum, a collective effort to shape the industry so that it creates more value than before has driven network coopetition.

Network coopetition can also be adopted in a more deliberate process, organized by a leading actor with the consensual agreement of others. For instance, in tourism destinations, marketing coopetition may prove beneficial for involved actors by increasing the competitive advantage against other destinations (Wang & Krakover, 2008). Various interests are nested in a tourism destination, and firms are interdependent to a large extent. Collective problems require collective solutions, including cooperative marketing initiatives, public-private partnerships, intergovernmental coalitions and inter-sector planning (Selin & Chavez, 1995). While industry specific factors foster coopetition in tourism, destinations vary in the degree of cooperation between rivals. Two opposing logics of interaction have been identified: competition where tourist firms try to maximize their individual benefits without engaging in collective action, and collaboration where individual tourism businesses participate in collective action to achieve common goals (Wang & Krakover, 2008).

The development of a network coopetition project requires coordinated action. Dominated networks have been identified in which one central actor establishes a number of bilateral relationships with other, usually smaller companies (von Fredrichs Grängsjö, 2003). However, "equal partners' networks" formed by small and medium enterprises without a bigger focal firm are also equipped to cope with the strategic challenges local firms face, without the intervention of a dominant player (Della Corte & Aria, 2016). Starting with issue identification (Selin & Chavez, 1995), through network formation (Czakon & Czernek, 2016), to operations coordination (Mariani, 2016), the role of a network leader implementing a network design is crucial.

Relationship-mix: Coopetition strategies in networks

Coopetition can be a deliberate choice for some firms, while being an emerging strategy for other players of the same market (Czakon & Rogalski, 2014). The rationale for engaging in collaboration with rivals may therefore emerge from exogenous pressures such as customer demand or regulatory obligations, or inversely be driven by individual firms' strategies. Extant research focuses on the central or leading actor, whereas our understanding of other actors' strategies and foci in coopetition strategizing are largely absent from the literature.

Typically, firm-, relationship-, network- and industry-level factors combine to play a role in determining the likelihood of coopetition adoption, as proposed in a theoretical model for coopetition in innovation (Gnyawali & Park, 2009). Network coopetition appears to be complex, by the number of actors involved and their respective relationship and, a dynamic phenomenon, by the interactions (both collective and unilateral) that unfold over time. Hence, various coopetitive behaviors may be displayed on various markets. Prior research has used structural variables (Luo, 2004; Chin et al., 2008) in order to identify coopetition types depending on the intensity of collaboration and competition, or behavioral variables to develop a coopetition typology based on a firm's behavioral pattern (Lado et al., 1997).

The structural approach uses the relative strength of competition and collaboration to develop a relationship typology. Coopetition can be dominated by collaboration, or by competition, or display an equal strength of its components (Bengtsson & Kock, 2000). Furthermore, a matrix (Figure 4.3) of coopetition types has been developed (Luo, 2004) based on separate and orthogonal measurement of collaboration (high- or low-intensity) and competition (high- or low-intensity). As yet, moderate degrees of relationship intensity have not been identified.

The behavioral approach focuses on strategic behaviors of firms (Lado et al., 1997), an approach that avoids measurement issues. Firms display different profiles depending on their collaborative or competitive mix: monopolistic when firms are unwilling to both collaborate and compete; collaborative rent-seeking when they opt for partnering and leave completion beyond the scope of preferred behaviors; competitive rent-seeking when they opt for rivalry; and syncretic rent-seeking when collaborative and competitive behaviors are strongly manifested.

A study on the Polish electricity market recognised the development of the behavioral approach by identifying passive and active behaviors (Czakon & Rogalski, 2014). Passive collaboration reflects firms' mutual interactions that are mandatory by law, where a large partner

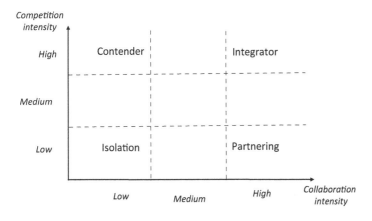

Figure 4.3   Relationship intensity-based coopetition matrix

cannot refuse to collaborate if asked to do so but is not seeking collaboration. Inversely, active collaboration refers to deliberate collaboration such as partnering agreements or market actions coordinated among firms. Similarly, passive competition refers to non-targeted marketing, sales promotion conducted in the media and sales to customers done only in reaction to their own requests. Finally, active competition encompasses sales activities of firms involving direct, intentional and aggressive sales aimed at specific customers. Evidence shows that firms display three distinct types of coopetitive behavior: passive coopetition, mixed coopetition or flexible coopetition. Interestingly, this study unveils that coopetition can be both active and passive. As a result, the matrix of possible coopetition types expands to nine, capturing passive, passive/active and fully active behaviors (Czakon & Rogalski, 2014). Hence, coopetition takes several forms, with many actors, and a mix of relationships is deliberately adopted by firms.

All in all, coopetition has so far revealed many manifestations, both from a typological perspective developed in early conceptual contributions and from an empirical perspective. Firms face the challenge of shaping their portfolio of relationships with relevant actors in their own environment.

Network coopetition entry: A leap of faith

Game-theoretical models suggest that collaboration with rivals is the best strategy for all involved parties (Brandenburger & Nalebuff, 1997). However, empirical applications of those models show that firms are reluctant in adopting coopetition, even if it came in connection with clear benefits (Okura, 2007).

Coopetition adoption likelihood models indicate several factors that may play a role in the process: those connected with either the industry, the firm or the dyad. Industry-specific factors are attributed with an interesting feature of impacting all industry players in a similar way, so that they shape the likelihood of coopetition adoption in a given industry (Gnyawali & Park, 2009). In order to explain the adoption of coopetition by a particular firm, scholars have referred to its strategic challenges: gaining access to valuable resources (Bengtsson & Kock, 2000), increasing the market, improving efficiency and strengthening the competitive position (Ritala et al., 2014). Coopetition appears to be instrumental in alleviating resource constraints and in achieving clear-cut strategic objectives by establishing collaboration with a purposefully selected partner. Therefore, dyadic factors are important in coopetition adoption because the partner is expected to provide complementary resources, similar resources, technological capabilities and pursue congruent strategic goals (Gnyawali & Park, 2009).

If industry-, dyad- and firm-level factors are in place, managers still need to adopt a mindset that allows collaboration with others, including rivals, in a shift of attention from the focal firm to the network (Brandenburger & Nalebuff, 1997). More generally, at a micro-fundamental level of analysis coopetition depends on the extent of: the understanding of private and common benefits, micro or macro ways of thinking, perceived levels of interdependence, perceived levels of complementarity, the personality of owners/managers, the availability of leadership, the locality of marketing activities and a focus on total experience by tourists (Wang, 2008).

Although the drivers for dyadic coopetition occurrence have been discussed in the literature, we lack insight into why firms would join coopetition networks. The dyad-formation decision is very different from network entry. One reason is that at dyadic level interactions connect parties knowledgeable of each other, while at network level the number of partners makes it very difficult to gather necessary information, update it and control the behaviors of others. While the role of control is attributed or taken by a leading actor, the scope of control of all other network members remains limited. Also, in multiparty settings harmful behaviors of one or several partners are more difficult to identify than in dyads, which may foster opportunism of some actors (Zeng & Chen, 2003). Additionally, the influence of a firm on the selection of other partners is limited (Czakon & Czernek, 2016). As a result, "swimming with sharks" (Katila et al., 2008) or "sleeping with the enemy" (Gnyawali & Park, 2009), referring to potential misbehavior and misappropriation of value, is magnified at network level.

Hence, network coopetition requires firms to place their trust in others. Perhaps the most challenging application of trust is related to competitors. This "leap of faith" complements rational calculation to predict partners' behavior-prediction (Kumar & Das, 2007). Researchers have identified trust as a coopetition success factor during the process (Chin et al., 2008), examined its relationship to innovation output (Bouncken & Fredrich, 2012) and suggested its critical role at the formation stage of multiparty coopetition (Wang, 2008).

Trust is more than a phenomenon that spontaneously emerges between individuals, but rather a dynamic process that can be influenced, shaped and purposefully used by managers (Bachmann, 2011). In business relationships trust develops in interrelated processes: calculative, capability assessment, intentions assessment, reputation and transference (Doney & Cannon, 1997). The application of a framework of trust-building processes to network coopetition formation reveals that they play various roles.

Difficulties related to the development of calculative, capability-based and intentionality-based trust in network coopetition have been empirically grounded (Czakon & Czernek, 2016). Indeed, identifying prospective benefits in network coopetition and gathering necessary information on the coopetition network is time-consuming and requires experience, analytical skills and information access. Consequently, the trust-building mechanisms usually associated with successful trust-building at dyadic level do not appear to have a positive impact, or any impact, in network settings (Czakon & Czernek, 2016).

By contrast, transference from public-sector institutions appears to be a strong trust-building mechanism, a sufficient condition to join network coopetition. More than inciting or pushing firms into coopetition (Kylänen & Mariani, 2014), public institutions are crucially important in establishing trust among actors. Public authorities are perceived as dedicated to common benefits, as opposed to private actors, who are instead focused on their own private benefits. Additionally, reputation has been found to be a strong trust-building mechanism, especially in small communities. It creates trust sufficient to engage into network coopetition with reputable actors.

Environment- and firm-level drivers fail to explain network coopetition formation. At network level, partner selection is not the key issue. Instead, the dilemma of accepting or turning down the opportunity to join a network is as a key challenge.

Common benefits in coopetition

The paradoxical nature of coopetition attracts all the more attention; normative theories clearly indicate it can be expected to yield benefits otherwise unavailable (Czakon, 2010). Scholars have therefore investigated the benefits that firms may achieve by engaging in coopetition.

Value creation involves synergies by integrating complementary and supplementary resources among competitors. Collaborating with competitors offers the unique advantage of similar positioning in the industry and understanding the customers, business logic and technologies, which fosters knowledge-sharing and available efficiency increases (Ritala & Tidström, 2014). Collaboration involves the process of combining and jointly exploiting resources held by many firms in order to synergistically generate more value than would be possible if the resources were kept separate (Dyer et al., 2008). Collaborating firms generate private benefits, which accrue to the individual firm within the alliance, and common benefits, which accrue collectively to all participants (Khanna et al., 1998).

An emerging thread of research focuses instead on identifying the benefits available to many involved parties through collaboration. "Benefits" refer to the process of value appropriation (Volschenk et al., 2016). Distinct types of benefits have been identified: private, common and public. Private benefits are those that a "firm can earn unilaterally by picking up skills from its partner and applying ... to its own operations in areas unrelated to the alliance activities" (Khanna et al., 1998). "Common benefits" refer to benefits that accrue collectively to all participants in the alliance, and can be captured by each partner of the cooperative relationship (Khanna et al., 1998). Interestingly, common benefits are both a collective benefit of all network coopetitors and a privately captured share (Volschenk et al., 2016). Public benefits are available in turn to society due to coopetitive network operations. These latter benefits are either released purposefully or cannot be effectively protected by the network coopetitors.

A study of the Polish energy balancing market addressed the question of common benefits and provided evidence that coopetition is indeed different from collusion (Czakon et al., 2016). In the energy market, each actor acts separately, and all collectively face the problem of the technical requirement of balancing energy supply and demand at any time, coupled with legal pressures from independent actors to achieve this objective, and a financial drive to balance the market at the lowest possible cost. Indeed, coopetition significantly decreases the balancing costs of all involved firms; this effect is not random, but is connected with the increasing number of coopetitors. Rivals have entered coopetitive relationships because of an inability to achieve efficiency increases alone; they have further developed the coopetition network in order to maximize available common benefits.

The classic competitive strategy argument is that increases in market power lead to lower supply prices. Such increases can be achieved by collectively acting with rivals. This view on collective action focuses on value appropriation, rather than on value creation. The study of the Polish energy balancing market coopetition shows how firms can generate cost reductions for all participants. The best choice is to collaborate with one's rival, as it has similar concerns, needs and capabilities. Such collaboration is value-adding, and not value-capturing, as it does not exert increased market power on actors outside the coopetition network. Interestingly, involved firms realized the benefit when they started to work together in small groups, and then expanded the network by including more and more actors. More than increasing individual efficiency, coopetition offers collective or common efficiency increases.

Conclusions

The network level of analysis reflects the normative, original meaning of the coopetition concept. Collaboration with various actors, despite conflicting interests or direct rivalry, may largely contribute to an increase in total available value. While directly alleviating resource access concerns, increasing market power and firms' efficiency (Ritala, 2012), network coopetition also generates common benefits, available to all involved parties (Czakon et al., 2016), and public benefits that accrue to society due to coopetitive relationships (Volschenk et al., 2016). At the network level of analysis, the emergence of additional value is more important as compared to dyads. Further research may address common benefits, public benefits and private capturing of those benefits. If cooperation is an efficient way of utilizing limited resources and coopetition a way of managing both competition and collaboration (Wang & Krakover, 2008), then sustainability calls for more attention. Common pool resources need careful governance in order to avoid overexploitation, opportunism or the pursuit of selfish interests at the expense of other actors. Further research in coopetition needs to address value networks as socio-ecological systems where sustainability plays a crucial role (Pathak et al., 2014).

Differently from a dyadic setting, where collaborating with a rival is largely deliberate, coopetition has also been revealed as an emergent strategy at network level. Deliberate network coopetition identified in supply chains appears to be much different from self-initiated and self-coordinated relations between suppliers that lack a moderating third party, and is more likely to be characterized by an equal distribution of power (Wilhelm, 2011).

Various pressures impact on the likelihood of collaboration between many rivals. Pressures may emerge within otherwise collaborative settings due to relational concerns (Czakon, 2010), or within clearly competitive settings due to common issues that are impossible to cope with alone (Czakon & Czernek, 2016). Long-term studies indicate that the pursuit of value appropriation induces airlines to enter into various dyadic and network relationships with rivals (Czakon & Dana, 2013).

Whenever firms decide to launch a network coopetition project, challenges that differ between partners need to be addressed. Trust is necessary to enter network collaboration with rivals, even if theoretical propositions suggest a dominant role of business needs over trust in a network setting (Gnyawali et al., 2006). Our current understanding of network coopetition antecedents is limited to theoretical propositions and qualitative studies. Propositions need quantitative testing in order for us to understand the process of network coopetition emergence, including industry specificity and cultural contingencies (Rusko, 2011).

How network coopetition receives a design, an architecture of relationships and a centralized management within emerging setting governance is clearly under-researched. Some emerging archetypes have been identified in supply network coopetition (Pathak et al., 2014), in horizontal coopetition (Czakon & Rogalski, 2014) or in coopetitive networks (Gnyawali et al., 2006), but other manifestations in different industry settings need to be identified. Coopetition is recognized as an industry-specific phenomenon, therefore it is necessary expand research on different industries in order to increase the generalizability of findings (Wilhelm, 2011) and to carry out industry comparisons (Rusko, 2011), including high-tech versus traditional industries (Sanou et al., 2016).

The distinctive assumption within the network stream of coopetition research is that vertical relationships impact horizontal relationships (Wilhelm, 2011), as much as indirect relationships impact direct relationships around a firm. Therefore, our understanding of network's dynamics requires a close scrutiny of network structural characteristics (Pathak et al., 2014) and coordination mechanisms (Wilhelm, 2011). Prior research on the role of network centrality (Gnyawali et al., 2006; Sanou et al., 2016) indicates a strong association between this structural variable and competitive aggressiveness. Expanding the scope of scrutiny may involve other structural variables, such as heterogeneity, density or size impact on coopetitive dynamics, firm behavior and performance. Interestingly, central actors who take the leading role in designing and exploiting network coopetition have been in focus (Sanou et al., 2016), while non-central and peripheral actors have received much less attention (Czakon & Czernek, 2016). Yet, our understanding of network coopetition cannot be comprehensive if the motives, behaviors and performance of non-central actors are left beyond the scope of scrutiny.

Network coopetition poses distinct methodological challenges due to its inherent complexity and dynamics. This thread of research refers to the original idea of value nets, which populate the landscape. Figure 4.1 clearly shows that extant research needs to address the whole value net. So far, researchers have been reducing the scope of attention and leaving some actors and respective relationships beyond scrutiny. Therefore typologies, process models and comprehensive models explaining behavior and performance of both the individual member and the whole network offer immense opportunities for future research.

References

Bachmann, R. (2011). At the crossroads: Future directions in trust research. *Journal of Trust Research*, 1(2), 203–213.

Bengtsson, M. & Kock, S. (2000). "Coopetition" in business Networks—to cooperate and compete simultaneously. *Industrial Marketing Management*, 29(5), 411–426.

Bouncken, R. B. & Fredrich, V. (2012). Coopetition: performance implications and management antecedents. *International Journal of Innovation Management*, 16(05), 1250028.

Brandenburger, A. M. & Nalebuff, B. J. (1997). *Co-Opetition: A revolution mindset that combines competition and cooperation: the game theory strategy that's changing the game of business.* Currency Double Day, New York.

Chin, K. S., Chan, B. L., & Lam, P. K. (2008). Identifying and prioritizing critical success factors for coopetition strategy. *Industrial Management & Data Systems*, 108(4), 437–454.

Czakon, W. (2009). Power asymmetries, flexibility and the propensity to coopete: an empirical investigation of SMEs' relationships with franchisors. *International Journal of Entrepreneurship and Small Business*, 8(1), 44–60.

Czakon, W. (2010). Emerging coopetition: an empirical investigation of coopetition as inter-organizational relationship instability. In Yami, S., Castaldo, S., Dagnino, G. B., & Le Roy, F. (Eds), *Coopetition: Winning Strategies for the 21st Century.* Cheltenham; Northampton, MA: Edward Elgar, pp. 58–72.

Czakon, W. & Dana, L. P. (2013). Coopetition at Work: how firms shaped the airline industry. *Journal of Social Management/Zeitschrift für Sozialmanagement*, 11(2).

Czakon, W., Fernandez, A. S., & Minà, A. (2014a). Editorial–From paradox to practice: the rise of coopetition strategies. *International Journal of Business Environment*, 6(1), 1–10.

Czakon, W., Mucha-Kuś, K., & Sołtysik, M. (2016). Coopetition strategy—what is in it for all? A study of common benefits in the Polish energy balancing market. *International Studies of Management & Organization*, 46(2–3), 80–93.

Czakon, W. & Rogalski, M. (2014). Coopetition typology revisited–a behavioural approach. *International Journal of Business Environment*, 6(1), 28–46.

Czakon, W. & Czernek, K. (2016). The role of trust-building mechanisms in entering into network coopetition: The case of tourism networks in Poland. *Industrial Marketing Management*, 57, 64–74.

Della Corte, V. & Aria, M. (2016). Coopetition and sustainable competitive advantage. The case of tourist destinations. *Tourism Management*, 54, 524–540.

Doney, P. M. & Cannon, J. P. (1997). An examination of the nature of trust in buyer-seller relationships. *The Journal of Marketing*, 35–51.

Dyer, J. H., Singh, H., & Kale, P. (2008). Splitting the pie: rent distribution in alliances and networks. *Managerial and Decision Economics*, 29(2–3), 137–148.

Fernandez, A. S., Le Roy, F., & Gnyawali, D. R. (2014). Sources and management of tension in co-opetition case evidence from telecommunications satellites manufacturing in Europe. *Industrial Marketing Management*, 43(2), 222–235.

Gnyawali, D. R., He, J., & Madhavan, R. (2006). Impact of co-opetition on firm competitive behavior: An empirical examination. *Journal of Management*, 32(4), 507–530.

Gnyawali, D. R. & Park, B. J. R. (2009). Co-opetition and technological innovation in small and medium-sized enterprises: A multilevel conceptual model. *Journal of Small Business Management*, 47(3), 308–330.

Katila, R., Rosenberger, J. D., & Eisenhardt, K. M. (2008). Swimming with sharks: Technology ventures, defense mechanisms and corporate relationships. *Administrative Science Quarterly*, 53(2), 295–332.

Khanna, T., Gulati, R., & Nohria, N. (1998). The dynamics of learning alliances: Competition, cooperation, and relative scope. *Strategic Management Journal*, 193–210.

Kumar, R. & Das, T. K. (2007). Interpartner legitimacy in the alliance development process. *Journal of Management Studies*, 44(8), 1425–1453.

Kylänen, M. & Rusko, R. (2011). Unintentional coopetition in the service industries: The case of Pyhä-Luosto tourism destination in the Finnish Lapland. *European Management Journal*, 29(3), 193–205.

Kylänen, M. & Mariani, M. M. (2014). The relevance of public-private partnerships in coopetition: Empirical evidence from the tourism sector. *International Journal of Business Environment* 5, 6(1), 106–125

Lado, A. A., Boyd, N. G., & Hanlon, S. C. (1997). Competition, cooperation, and the search for economic rents: a syncretic model. *Academy of Management Review*, 22(1), 110–141.

Le Roy, F. & Czakon, W. (2016). Managing coopetition: the missing link between strategy and performance. *Industrial Marketing Management*, 53, 3–6.

Luo, Y. (2004). A coopetition perspective of MNC–host government relations. *Journal of International Management*, 10(4), 431–451.

Mariani, M. M. (2007). Coopetition as an emergent strategy: Empirical evidence from an Italian consortium of opera houses. *International Studies of Management & Organization*, 37(2), 97–126.

Mariani, M. M. (2016). Coordination in inter-network co-opetitition: Evidence from the tourism sector. *Industrial Marketing Management*, 53, 103–123.

Mintzberg, H. & Waters, J. A. (1985). Of strategies, deliberate and emergent. *Strategic Management Journal*, 6(3), 257–272.

Nielsen, B. B. (2011). Trust in strategic alliances: Toward a co-evolutionary research model. *Journal of Trust Research*, 1(2), 159–176.

Okura, M. (2007). Coopetitive strategies of Japanese insurance firms a game-theory approach. *International Studies of Management & Organization*, 37(2), 53–69.

Pathak, S. D., Wu, Z., & Johnston, D. (2014). Toward a structural view of co-opetition in supply networks. *Journal of Operations Management*, 32(5), 254–267.

Ring, P. S. & Van de Ven, A. H. (1994). Developmental processes of cooperative interorganizational relationships. *Academy of Management Review*, 19(1), 90–118.

Ritala, P. (2012). Coopetition strategy—when is it successful? Empirical evidence on innovation and market performance. *British Journal of Management*, 23(3), 307–324.

Ritala, P. & Tidström, A. (2014). Untangling the value-creation and value-appropriation elements of coopetition strategy: A longitudinal analysis on the firm and relational levels. *Scandinavian Journal of Management*, 30(4), 498–515.

Ritala, P., Golnam, A., & Wegmann, A. (2014). Coopetition-based business models: The case of Amazon. com. *Industrial Marketing Management*, 43(2), 236–249.

Rusko, R. (2011). Exploring the concept of coopetition: A typology for the strategic moves of the Finnish forest industry. *Industrial Marketing Management*, 40(2), 311–320.

Sanou, F. H., Le Roy, F., & Gnyawali, D. R. (2016). How does centrality in coopetition networks matter? An empirical investigation in the mobile telephone industry. *British Journal of Management*, 27(1), 143–160.

Selin, S. & Chavez, D. (1995). Developing an evolutionary tourism partnership model. *Annals of Tourism Research*, 22(4), 844–856.

Tidström, A. (2009). Causes of conflict in intercompetitor cooperation. *Journal of Business & Industrial Marketing*, 24(7), 506–518.

Volschenk, J., Ungerer, M., & Smit, E. (2016). Creation and appropriation of socio-environmental value in coopetition. *Industrial Marketing Management*, 57, 109–118.

von Friedrichs Grängsjö, Y. (2003). Destination networking: Co-opetition in peripheral surroundings. *International Journal of Physical Distribution & Logistics Management*, 33(5), 427–448.

Wang, Y. (2008). Collaborative destination marketing understanding the dynamic process. *Journal of Travel Research*, 47(2), 151–166.

Wang, Y. & Krakover, S. (2008). Destination marketing: competition, cooperation or coopetition?. *International Journal of Contemporary Hospitality Management*, 20(2), 126–141.

Wilhelm, M. M. (2011). Managing coopetition through horizontal supply chain relations: Linking dyadic and network levels of analysis. *Journal of Operations Management*, 29(7), 663–676.

Zeng, M. & Chen, X. P. (2003). Achieving cooperation in multiparty alliances: A social dilemma approach to partnership management. *Academy of Management Review*, 28(4), 587–605.

5

Dynamics of coopetitive value creation and appropriation

Paavo Ritala and Pia Hurmelinna-Laukkanen

Introduction

Coopetition is a relationship in which competition and collaboration co-exist, constituting a persisting paradox (Gnyawali et al., 2016). This paradox invites numerous tensions, in particular those of value creation and value appropriation (for discussion, see Bouncken et al., 2018; Raza-Ullah et al., 2014; Ritala & Hurmelinna-Laukkanen, 2009; Volschenk et al., 2016). Such value-related analysis has been at the core of theorizing about coopetition ever since its seminal formulation (Brandenburger & Nalebuff, 1996), and these two concepts are broadly used to explain how value is created via coopetition relationships, and how this value is captured and divided.

Value creation and appropriation in coopetition—and their interplay—is a multifaceted issue. At the firm strategy level, coopetition provides additional means for individual companies to create value in collaboration with their competitors and to appropriate a share of that value themselves. Several case-based studies have shown how firms have adopted a coopetition strategy for these purposes. For instance, Ritala et al. (2014) show how Amazon.com developed business models that allowed the firm to collaborate with its competitors, to jointly create value via increasing online sales, and finally, to appropriate a margin of the growing markets. Similarly, the LCD TV market collaboration between Samsung Electronics and Sony Corporation demonstrates the challenges and opportunities of coopetition for value creation and appropriation (see Gnyawali & Park, 2011).

At the relationship and network levels, coopetition is seen as a particular context within which value is created and appropriated, creating a juxtaposition that has implications for the management and outcomes of the relationship (see, e.g., Bouncken et al., 2018; Fernandez et al., 2014; Fernandez & Chiambaretto, 2016). In coopetition relationships, value creation and appropriation are continuously adjusted, bargained and developed in an interactive process between the actors (Raza-Ullah, Begntsson, & Kock, 2014; Ritala & Tidström, 2014; Yami & Nemeh, 2014).

These processes also unfold over individual and collective levels of analysis. Value creation can happen partially within individual organizations, or it can be conducted via joint activities. Similarly, value can be appropriated jointly (e.g., via joint products and service sales) or individually, for example, by differentiating products and services under different brands among those involved in coopetition (Gnyawali & Park, 2011). Therefore, these processes are complex and multilevel, and further clarity of their interplay and dynamics is needed.

In order to improve our understanding of the important conceptual underpinnings of value creation and appropriation in coopetition, we first briefly discuss them within the general inter-organizational context. This is followed by a discussion of a "baseline model," which is the typically utilized logic across theoretical and empirical contributions. Following this, we introduce a more detailed conceptual model that describes how value creation and appropriation are interconnected over time, including feedback loops that explain the temporal dynamics. This model contributes to the coopetition literature by providing an overarching framework to explain how coopetition helps to create and appropriate value.

Value creation and appropriation in the inter-organizational context

In economics, *value* refers formally to the end customer's willingness to pay for a certain product, service, or offering (Brandenburger & Stuart, 1996). The important question for strategy research, then, is by whom and how can this value be created, and by whom and how can this value be appropriated? (See also Garcia-Castro & Aguilera, 2015.)

Value creation refers to the activities in the value chain that increase the end customer's willingness to pay (Bowman & Ambrosini, 2000; Brandenburger & Stuart, 1996). Firms engage in value creation when the profits generated by an activity exceed the input required (Lepak et al., 2007). Such added value contributions can include any activities that end up increasing the perceived value by those receiving it, from early-stage research and development to the provision of materials and resources and branding and marketing.

Inter-organizational relationships, such as alliances, networks, and ecosystems, provide opportunities to facilitate and advance value creation by providing chances to integrate complementary and supplementary resources and capabilities (Barringer & Harrison, 2000; Das & Teng, 2000). Regardless of the actual form of these relationships, the key logic for value creation is that more value is created jointly compared to the resources and capabilities being utilized in separation (Dyer & Singh, 1998).

However, the (jointly) created value is not worth much to its creators if it is not appropriated in the end (Arrow, 1962). In general, *value appropriation* can be defined as extracting profits in the marketplace (Teece, 1986; 1998). Value appropriation involves various activities, and several mechanisms have been identified that increase appropriability. Typically, these mechanisms relate to protecting valuable assets and creations (Alnuaimi & George, 2016; Hurmelinna-Laukkanen & Olander, 2014) and utilizing the mechanisms to regulate their exclusivity, free use, and controllability (Hurmelinna-Laukkanen, 2012; James et al., 2013). Value appropriation is also future-oriented. It is important also to recognize the potential to generate future profits based on previous value appropriation (Ahuja et al., 2013; Gans & Ryall, 2017).

In inter-organizational arrangements, value appropriation easily becomes a debated issue, as firms bargain over the division of value (Adegbesan & Higgins, 2011; Dyer et al., 2008). For instance, there may be firm-level concerns about others exploiting the assets that an actor provides for the collaborative activities (Heiman & Nickerson, 2004; Hurmelinna-Laukkanen & Olander, 2014). Likewise, it may not always be easy to decide how the jointly created outputs are going to be appropriated (see, e.g., James et al., 2013 on alternative strategies for value capture) and if an individual actor is able to secure its part (Dyer et al., 2008). However, appropriation can also be viewed at the relationship and network levels. Not only do organizations compete against each other for their share of value (Ritala & Hurmelinna-Laukkanen, 2009); networks also compete with other networks, which further changes the dynamics of appropriation (see Nätti et al., 2014). Coopetition context provides specific implications for value creation and appropriation, as discussed in the following.

Value creation and appropriation in coopetition: From a baseline model to dynamic interplay

In laying out the game-theoretic foundation for coopetition, Brandenburger & Nalebuff (1996) put forward the seminal quote:

> *Co-opetition means cooperating to create a bigger business "pie", while competing to divide it up*

Coopetition literature has built strongly on this idea, and much of the literature is based on the foundational assumption that coopetition allows firms to create more value together and, thus, there will be more for each actor to appropriate later on. Competing firms are seen to *collectively create value* together when this increases the "size of the pie" more than if firms would not engage in such activity. Such value might include economic and social benefits, larger markets, new knowledge and innovation, and so forth (for a discussion, see, e.g., Ritala & Hurmelinna-Laukkanen, 2009;Volschenk et al., 2016). *Value appropriation*, however, is considered an *individual activity* in which competitors try to capture a share of the created value. The "slice of the pie" among actors changes based on their own differentiation abilities, and on the appropriability mechanisms at the disposal of each actor (Gnyawali & Park, 2011; Ritala & Hurmelinna-Laukkanen, 2009). The competitive setting also means that the value appropriation phase is subject to more tensions than in relationships among non-competitors (see, e.g., Bouncken et al., 2018;Yami & Nemeh, 2014, for discussion). Figure 5.1 illustrates this baseline model.

As visualized in Figure 5.1, coopetition provides opportunities for creating more value than is available for individual actors (illustrated by a larger range of the collective gray area in contrast to the individual white and black circles). Furthermore, it is shown here that value appropriation often ends up being asymmetrical (illustrated in that the "black firm" appropriates a larger share of the value created). However, this is merely for illustration purposes, as value appropriation can also be more or less symmetrical, depending on the context and contingencies of the coopetition relationship, as well as the individual abilities and aspirations of the actors in appropriating the value.

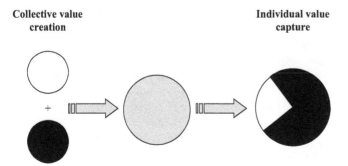

Figure 5.1 The baseline model of value creation and appropriation in coopetition

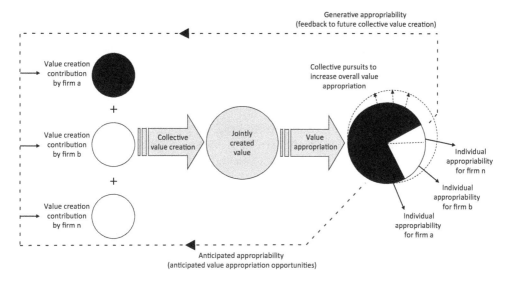

Figure 5.2 The extended model of value creation and appropriation in coopetition

For most purposes, this simplified model provides a good foundation for explaining value creation and appropriation processes in coopetition. Consider, for example, how collective R&D efforts by Sony and Samsung turn into firm-specific pursuits to capture profits from consumer markets (Gnyawali et al., 2011) or how the global automotive industry creates value by developing joint technology while later competing for market share in the end-product markets (Gwynne, 2009; Wilhelm, 2011).

However, we argue that the processes are often more complex than portrayed in the baseline model. At first sight, value creation and appropriation might look polarized among the elements of coopetition; that is, collaboration relates to value creation and competition to value appropriation. However, in reality, value is being created and appropriated by individual firms themselves and within the scope of the coopetition relationship (see, e.g., Ritala & Tidström, 2014). Value creation and appropriation in coopetition can be viewed as ongoing parallel processes that are mutually interconnected and dynamic, and that can be seen to affect each other over time (Bouncken et al., 2018; Yami & Nemeh, 2014). In this regard, the logic of coopetition, and especially the duality of value creation and appropriation, can be viewed from the paradox perspective, where they are portrayed as mutually interdependent, parallel, and continuous processes (Gnyawali et al., 2016).

In the remainder of this chapter, we develop an extended model that takes into account the parallel, interdependent, and dynamic nature of these processes, as shown in Figure 5.2.

Individual and collective value creation

The baseline model (Figure 5.1) gives an impression that the value creation side of coopetition is straightforward. Resources are combined to produce unique combinations and synergy. In this sense, competitors can utilize their joint background knowledge of markets and technologies to efficiently put together their existing resources (Ritala & Hurmelinna-Laukkanen, 2009).

However, at the firm level, contributing to value creation also means providing relevant resources to competitors, potentially leading to the emergence of coopetitive tensions in value creation (Bouncken et al., 2018). In the best case, the returns are high nevertheless. For instance, Ritala (2009) suggests that the competitive background between collaborating actors might enable them to create more value than is the case with non-competitors. Furthermore, Alnuaimi & George (2016) suggest that, in the long term, the immediate loss of knowledge to other actors can be recuperated by absorbing refined knowledge. It is shown in Figure 5.2 that collective alignment enables competitors to jointly create value beyond individual contributions, which can be divided by the same actors.

In the value creation phase, the coopetitors naturally assess the prospects of value appropriation in the future (Bouncken et al., 2018). We refer to this process as the *anticipated appropriability* (see Figure 5.2, feedback loop at the bottom). This term illustrates the temporal feedback component, which emerges as firms see the prospects for appropriating value from the coopetition relationship and are consequently motivated to provide inputs to mutual value creation. In essence, the incentive effect of anticipated appropriation suggests that the "shadow of the future" connects value appropriation and creation. The actual experience of increased appropriability can strengthen this link. On the negative side, the firms might see that their prospects for value appropriation are weak. This might lead to a risk of harming future developments due to overprotection and underinvestment in the firm's own development activity (Bouncken et al., 2018; Ritala & Hurmelinna-Laukkanen, 2009).

Individual and collective value appropriation

For actors to have incentives to engage in coopetition and joint value creation in the first place, a value appropriation trajectory needs to be in sight (Ritala & Hurmelinna-Laukkanen, 2009). As depicted on the right side of Figure 5.2, value appropriation is fundamentally based on individual aspirations, where each competitor aims to gain as big a share of the jointly created value as possible, following the pie-splitting logic of coopetition and alliances in general (Brandenburger & Nalebuff, 1996; Dyer et al., 2008).

However, at the same time, there are other dynamics to be considered: within alliances and networks, value appropriation often pursues to achieve fair allocation of the results (see, e.g., Adegbesan & Higgins, 2011; Dhanaraj & Parkhe, 2006) but also may extend to making sure that the value created benefits the actors within the coopetition networks rather than those outside (see Hurmelinna-Laukkanen et al., 2012). In this way, the value appropriation activity can be collective, and the companies involved in coopetition may well put joint effort into extending appropriation possibilities for all participants (see, e.g., Nätti et al., 2014; Ritala & Tidström, 2014). This is shown as the expanding value appropriation area on the right side of Figure 5.2.

Furthermore, the individual appropriability for different firms in coopetition is also affected by the governance form and other coordination mechanisms of the coopetition relationship. For instance, joint ventures and other equity-based arrangements typically provide a relatively clear contractual base for dividing the profits from alliances and partnerships. However, for non-equity alliances that rely on formal and relational contracts, the division of value is not as clear-cut (see, e.g., Contractor & Ra, 2002; Olander et al., 2010; Oxley, 1997). In those cases, the relational dynamics of coopetition and individual firms' efforts affect the individual share of the value appropriated more (see, e.g., Ritala & Tidström, 2014).

In the best cases, the increase in value appropriation at the relationship or network level means that the companies involved in coopetition benefit not only from the immediate profits but can also start a new cycle of value creation. The anticipated appropriability is not the only mechanism that can connect value appropriation to further value creation; as the willingness of end customers to pay results in increased profits, there are more resources to allocate to new value creation endeavors. In addition, the generated outputs can be turned into background assets for subsequent value creation (Alnuaimi & George, 2016). This *generative appropriability* (Ahuja et al., 2013) is a relevant feedback component between value appropriation and subsequent value creation (see Figure 5.2, feedback loop at the top).

Implications

Overall, our chapter provides several implications for coopetition research, practice, and policy, and outlines useful directions for future research. These implications are discussed next.

Research implications

Joint *value creation* is a central motivation for coopetition. In this chapter, we extended this logic further. In particular, we suggest that this activity is not solely collective, as is often depicted, but simultaneously takes place individually, with the potential to concurrently provide individual benefits (see also Alnuaimi & George, 2016). At the same time, negative outcomes may emerge if a firm's contribution is exploited by others, the value creation inputs are unequal, or if the firm becomes held captive by the coopetition activity, unable to pursue its own development trajectories.

Our model further suggests that *value appropriation* relates to individual pursuits to maximize the share of the value captured, as well as to collective efforts in this regard. The former aspect is well researched, while the latter has received less attention. Although distributing the outputs fairly among the actors and allowing individual value appropriation is relevant (Dhanaraj & Parkhe, 2006; Hurmelinna-Laukkanen et al., 2012), joint efforts for increasing overall value appropriation should be considered. From this perspective, the boundaries of appropriation can also be linked at the collective level, where competitors jointly improve the overall appropriation (e.g., Ritala & Tidström, 2014). In that case, value appropriation enhances the overall commercial exploitation and prevents valuable knowledge from leaking to rival networks or companies (Hurmelinna-Laukkanen et al., 2012; Hurmelinna-Laukkanen & Olander, 2014).

Following the definition of paradox (Gnyawali et al., 2016; Smith & Lewis, 2011), we perceive value creation and appropriation as interdependent forces that persist over time in coopetition relationships. This means that value creation and appropriation are interconnected in a *dynamic interplay with several feedback loops*. The developed framework (Figure 5.2) shows two feedback loops—*anticipated* and *generative appropriability*—that connect value creation and appropriation. The first relates to individual actors' anticipated value appropriation, which affects their motivations to provide inputs to the value creation, while the latter refers to the resources available for value creation that are generated over time through appropriation. Although the existence of generative appropriability (Ahuja et al., 2013) in particular has been acknowledged in literature (more and less implicitly), placing these feedback components explicitly within the coopetition context allows understanding of the dynamics that guide these activities.

Practical and policy implications

For coopetition practice, our model suggests that collective and individual aspirations need to be balanced throughout coopetitive relationships. For instance, the motivations to participate in value creation need to be examined actor by actor, and reflected against anticipated value appropriation prospects. Furthermore, free riding and opportunism need to be dealt with efficiently to maintain a collective and individual balance of inputs and captured value, in the short and long term.

In addition, important policy implications are related to collusive features of value creation and appropriation, which are often overlooked. In general, *value created* in coopetition is expected to benefit the actors involved and to spill over to the end customers. However, there are also situations where the value creation-appropriation connection generates negative market implications. One notable issue is that oligopolistic market features may emerge that diminish the actual value to end customers or suppliers. If coopetition affects appropriation in such a way that the bargaining power of downstream and/or upstream markets is too heavily restricted, a collusion problem emerges (see Pressey et al., 2014; Pressey & Vanharanta, 2016).

As competitors join forces in value creation, the number of alternative offerings might be limited, and some developments are unrealized. This outcome might relate to limited resources and attention, or to power relationships, where one firm sets the direction for other companies. When a coopetitive arrangement is formed, it may be that such a firm (or a group of firms) eventually directs the whole industry along a specific path (see Wiener & Saunders, 2014).

Collective forms of coopetitive *value appropriation* may be at least equally problematic. Different forms of cartels with price-fixing and dividing of markets may emerge from initially beneficial coopetition activities (Pressey & Vanharanta, 2016). In these instances, the value spilling over to end customers might be directly limited as collaborating competitors retain a larger part of it with increasing margins. The value appropriated might also be controlled indirectly as firms outside the coopetition get pushed aside.

This issue has been acknowledged by policy makers and regulators. Competition laws have been introduced to address these issues, such as Article 101(1) of the Treaty on the Functioning of the European Union (TFEU) prohibiting competition-restricting collaboration by competitors, accompanied by Article 101(3), which allows for joint value creation when the benefit goes to consumers. That is, as long as coopetitive value creation and value appropriation do not endanger the benefit of end customers, such activities are acceptable. In the best cases, the created value in coopetition is notable enough to benefit the involved competitors and the end customers, and healthy competition creates further differentiation, innovation, and market development.

Future research agenda

Value creation and appropriation—in addition to collaboration and competition—are probably the most decisive theoretical components that have been used to explain the coopetition phenomenon (Brandenburger & Nalebuff, 1996; Gnyawali et al., 2016; Raza-Ullah et al., 2014; Ritala & Hurmelinna-Laukkanen, 2009; Volschenk et al., 2016). In this chapter, we briefly outlined an integrative view of the state of the art in this regard and put forward a suggestion for a dynamic model of value creation and appropriation in coopetition. Even with the cumulating evidence in coopetition literature, there are yet-unexplored aspects, especially when we take the dynamic view suggested in the current study. This provides several avenues for further conceptual and empirical inquiry.

First, further studies could examine the interplay of value creation and appropriation. Based on the research discussed throughout this chapter, we know that value creation and appropriation affect each other and are often parallel processes, not just sequential (i.e., creation precedes appropriation). Examining the tensions arising from this parallel processing of partially contradictory logics could build on the strategic dualities and paradox research (e.g., as suggested by Gnyawali et al., 2016) in further explaining how firms in coopetition can cope with often opposing demands. This calls for firm-level inquiry where individual firms' abilities to cope with such a paradox are investigated, as well as alliance-, network-, and system-level examinations of value creation and appropriation dynamics in coopetition.

Second, the two feedback loops suggested in this study (generative appropriability and anticipated appropriability) provide opportunities for future research. For instance, how much do firms appreciate the value creation efforts in the present that have only uncertain appropriation prospects versus those with immediate ones? How do coopetitive dynamics affect this perception? For generative appropriability, how can firms in coopetition ensure that the value they appropriate can be used for future value creation in those relationships? To what extent does joint value appropriation facilitate continuity in coopetitive ties? Questions such as these call for longitudinal research designs where the process and outcomes of coopetition are examined, and the aforementioned and other links between creation and appropriation are distinguished.

Conclusion

Collective value creation has typically been seen to precede the individual value appropriation efforts in coopetition. We have argued that while this portrays many instances of coopetition, the reality is more multifaceted and there are more dynamics between and among these processes. The perspective described in this chapter suggests that instead of a linear view, a more dynamic model of value creation and appropriation is useful for capturing the temporal and inter-level dynamics of coopetition.

References

Adegbesan, J. A. & Higgins, M. J. (2011). The intra-alliance division of value created through collaboration. *Strategic Management Journal*, 32(2), 187–211.

Ahuja, G., Lampert C., & Novelli, E. (2013). The second face of appropriability: generative appropriability and its determinants. *Academy of Management Review*, 38(2), 248–269.

Alnuaimi, T. & George, G. (2016). Appropriability and the retrieval of knowledge after spillovers. *Strategic Management Journal*, 37(7), 1263–1279.

Arrow, K. (1962). Economic welfare and the allocation of resources for invention. In: *The Rate and Direction of Inventive Activity: Economic and Social Factors*. Nelson, R. (Ed.). New York: Princeton University Press: 609–625.

Barringer, B. R. & Harrison, J. S. (2000). Walking a tightrope: Creating value through interorganizational relationships. *Journal of Management*, 26(3), 367–403.

Bouncken, R., Fredrich, V., Ritala, P., & Kraus, S. (2018). Coopetition in new product development alliances: advantages and tensions for incremental and radical innovation. *British Journal of Management*, 29(3), 391–410.

Bowman, C. & Ambrosini, V. (2000). Value creation versus value capture: towards a coherent definition of value in strategy. *British Journal of Management*, 11(1), 1–15.

Brandenburger, A. M. & Nalebuff, B. J. (1996). *Co-opetition*. New York: Doubleday.

Brandenburger, A. M. & Stuart, H. W. (1996). Value-based business strategy. *Journal of Economics & Management Strategy*, 5(1), 5–24.

Contractor, F. J. & Ra, W. (2002). How knowledge attributes influence alliance governance choices: a theory development note. *Journal of International Management*, 8(1), 11–27.

Das, T. K. & Teng, B. S. (2000). A resource-based theory of strategic alliances. *Journal of Management*, 26(1), 31–61.

Dhanaraj, C. & Parkhe, A. (2006). Orchestrating innovation networks. *Academy of Management Review*, 31(3), 659–669.

Dyer, J. H. & Singh, H. (1998). The relational view: Cooperative strategy and sources of interorganizational competitive advantage. *Academy of Management Review*, 23(4), 660–679.

Dyer, J. H., Singh, H., & Kale, P. (2008). Splitting the pie: rent distribution in alliances and networks. *Managerial and Decision Economics*, 29(2–3), 137–148.

Fernandez, A.-S. & Chiambaretto, P. (2016). Managing tensions related to information in coopetition. *Industrial Marketing Management*, 53, 66–76.

Fernandez, A.-S., Le Roy, F., & Gnyawali, D. R. (2014). Sources and management of tension in co-opetition case evidence from telecommunications satellites manufacturing in Europe. *Industrial Marketing Management*, 43(2), 222–235.

Gans, J. & Ryall, M. D. (2017). Value capture theory: A strategic management review. *Strategic Management Journal*, 38(1), 17–41.

Garcia-Castro, R. & Aguilera, R. V. (2015). Incremental value creation and appropriation in a world with multiple stakeholders. *Strategic Management Journal*, 36(1), 137–147.

Gnyawali, D. R., Madhavan, R., He, J., & Bengtsson, M. (2016). The competition–cooperation paradox in inter-firm relationships: A conceptual framework. *Industrial Marketing Management*, 53, 7–18.

Gnyawali, D. R. & Park B.-J. R. (2011). Co-opetition between giants: Collaboration with competitors for technological innovation. *Research Policy*, 40(5), 650–663.

Gwynne, P. (2009). Automakers hope "coopetition" will map route to future sales. *Research Technology Management*, 52(2), 2.

Heiman, B. A. & Nickerson, J. A. (2004). Empirical evidence regarding the tension between knowledge sharing and knowledge expropriation in collaborations. *Managerial and Decision Economics*, 25(6–7), 401–420.

Hurmelinna-Laukkanen, P. (2012). Constituents and outcomes of absorptive capacity – Appropriability regime changing the game. *Management Decision*, 50(7), 1178–1199.

Hurmelinna-Laukkanen, P. & Olander, H. (2014). Coping with rivals' absorptive capacity in innovation activities. *Technovation*, 34(1), 3–11

Hurmelinna-Laukkanen, P., Olander, H. Blomqvist, K., & Panfilii, V. (2012). Orchestrating R&D networks: Absorptive capacity, network stability, and innovation appropriability. *European Management Journal*, 30(6), 552–563.

James, S. D., Leiblein, M. J., & Lu, S. (2013). How firms capture value from their innovations. *Journal of Management*, 39(5), 1123–1155.

Lepak, D. P., Smith, K. G., & Taylor, M. S. (2007). Value creation and value capture: A multilevel perspective. *Academy of Management Review*, 32(1), 180–194.

Nätti, S., Hurmelinna-Laukkanen, P., & Johnston, W. (2014). Absorptive capacity and network orchestration in innovation communities – Promoting service innovation. *Journal of Business & Industrial Marketing*, 29(2), 173–184.

Oxley, J. E. (1997). Appropriability hazards and governance in strategic alliances: A transaction cost approach. *The Journal of Law, Economics, and Organization*, 13(2), 387–409.

Pressey, A. D. & Vanharanta, M. (2016). Dark network tensions and illicit forbearance: Exploring paradox and instability in illegal cartels. *Industrial Marketing Management*, 55, 35–49.

Pressey, A. D., Vanharanta, M., & Gilchrist, A. J. (2014). Towards a typology of collusive industrial networks: Dark and shadow networks. *Industrial Marketing Management*, 43(8), 1435–1450.

Raza-Ullah, T., Bengtsson, M., & Kock, S. (2014). The coopetition paradox and tension in coopetition at multiple levels. *Industrial Marketing Management*, 43(2), 189–198.

Ritala, P. (2009). Is coopetition different from cooperation? The impact of market rivalry on value creation in alliances. *International Journal of Intellectual Property Management*, 3(1), 39–55.

Ritala, P., Golnam, A., & Wegmann, A. (2014). Coopetition-based business models: The case of Amazon. com. *Industrial Marketing Management*, 43(2), 236–249.

Ritala, P. & Hurmelinna-Laukkanen, P. (2009). What's in it for me? Creating and appropriating value in innovation-related coopetition. *Technovation*, 29(12), 819–828.

Ritala, P. & Tidström, A. (2014). Untangling the value-creation and value-appropriation elements of coopetition strategy: A longitudinal analysis on the firm and relational levels. *Scandinavian Journal of Management*, 30(4), 498–515.

Smith, W. K. & Lewis, M. W. (2011). Toward a theory of paradox: A dynamic equilibrium model of organizing. *Academy of Management Review*, 36(2), 381–403.

Teece, D. J. (1986). Profiting from technological innovation: implications for integration, collaboration, licensing and public policy. *Research Policy*, 15(6), 285–305.

Teece, D. J. (1998). Capturing value from knowledge assets: the new economy, markets for know-how, and intangible assets. *California Management Review*, 40(3), 55–79.

Yami, S. & Nemeh, A. (2014). Organizing coopetition for innovation: The case of wireless telecommunication sector in Europe. *Industrial Marketing Management*, 43(2), 250–260.

Volschenk, J., Ungerer, M., & Smit, E. (2016). Creation and appropriation of socio-environmental value in coopetition. *Industrial Marketing Management*, 57, 109–118.

Wiener, M. & Saunders, C. (2014). Forced coopetition in IT multi-sourcing. *The Journal of Strategic Information Systems*, 23(3), 210–225.

Wilhelm, M. M. (2011). Managing coopetition through horizontal supply chain relations: Linking dyadic and network levels of analysis. *Journal of Operations Management*, 29(7), 663–676.

6

The swinging pendulum of coopetition inquiry

Giovanni Battista Dagnino and Anna Minà

Introduction

Strategic management research has traditionally posited that firms are separate entities that compete with each other to achieve performances that are higher vis-à-vis their rivals. As separate entities, firms have conflicting interests and experiment a win-lose game in which the winner of the competition race will be only *one* (Dagnino, 2016).

Due to technological and market uncertainties that firms face in a hypercompetitive arena (Afuah, 2000), in the late 1980s the business world showed that firms increasingly tend to *cooperate* with suppliers, buyers, and/or partners that are also their major competitors (Dowling et al., 1996). However, while inter-firm relationships could "incorporate elements of both traditional competitive relationships and collaborative relationships" (Dowling et al., 1996: 155), for many years strategy research has seemingly been focused on polarized relationships that are either simply competitive or cooperative (Smith et al., 1995; Wu, 2014). Therefore, strategy inquiry has continued to look at competition and cooperation in a separate fashion and as alternative strategies.

Following the seminal contribution of Brandenburger and Nalebuff (1996), coopetition—epitomizing the simultaneous coexistence of cooperation and competition—has received increasing acknowledgment in the management realm. During the last decade, together with its remarkable and continuous diffusion in practice, coopetition research has experienced an impressive expansion. On the one hand, the proliferation of studies on coopetition characteristics and the various methods of inquiry that scholars have adopted (qualitative, quantitative, and mixed) are unambiguous signals of the vigor that this research area has progressively assumed. On the other hand, coopetition literature takes multiple theoretical angles and presents mixed empirical findings (Table 6.1 displays the most influential articles, book chapters, and conference papers on coopetition to date). Taken together, these conditions motivate the need to perform a critical overview of the coopetition literature.

By detecting the four main phases of coopetition development in the last two decades, this study aims to outline a reasoned understanding of existing coopetition studies. Specifically, we ask: how has coopetition literature evolved over time? And to what extent is coopetition literature converging on some specific issues? As anticipated, this overview is targeted at detecting

Table 6.1 The most influential articles, book chapters, and conference papers on coopetition

#/N.	Year	Authors	Journal/Book/Conference	Citations on Google Scholar
1.	1996	Dowling, Roering, Carlin, & Wisnieski (1996)	*Journal of Management Inquiry*	210
2.	1997	Nalebuff & Brandenburger (1997)	*Strategy & Leadership*	237
3.	1999	Loebecke, Van Fenema & Powell (1999)	*Acm Sigmis Database*	191
4.	2000	Bengtsson & Kock (2000)	*Industrial Marketing Management*	1621
5.	2002	Tsai (2002)	*Organization Science*	1895
6.	2002	Dagnino & Padula (2002); then published as Dagnino (2009)	*Innovative Research in Management, European Academy of Management (EURAM Conference Paper)* Book Chapter: Coopetition Strategy	550
7.	2003	Levy, Loebbecke, & Powell (2003)	*European Journal of Information Systems*	301
8.	2004	Zineldin (2004)	*Marketing Intelligence & Planning*	296
9.	2004	Luo (2004)	*Journal of International Management*	138
10.	2005	Luo (2005)	*Journal of World Business*	286
11.	2006	Luo, Slotegraaf, & Pan (2006)	*Journal of Marketing*	432
12.	2006	Gnyawali, He, & Madhavan (2006)	*Journal of Management*	341
13.	2007	Luo (2007)	*Journal of World Business*	417
14.	2007	Walley (2007)	*International Studies of Management & Organization*	323
15.	2007	Padula & Dagnino (2007)	*International Studies of Management & Organization*	304
16.	2007	Morris, Koçak, & Özer (2007)	*Journal of Small Business Strategy*	153
17.	2007	Mariani (2007)	*International Studies of Management & Organization*	145
18.	2007	Gurnani, Erkoc, & Luo (2007)	*European Journal of Operational Research*	121
19.	2008	Chin, Chan, & Lam (2008)	*Industrial Management & Data Systems*	199
20.	2008	Wang & Krakover (2008)	*International Journal of Contemporary Hospitality Management*	198
21.	2008	Eriksson (2008)	*Journal of Construction Engineering and Management*	126
22.	2009	Gnyawali & Park (2009)	*Journal of Small Business Management*	421
23.	2009	Ritala & Hurmelinna-Laukkanen (2009)	*Technovation*	263
24.	2009	Bakshi & Kleindorfer (2009)	*Production and Operations Management*	107
25.	2009	Cassiman, Di Guardo, & Valentini (2009)	*Long Range Planning*	103
26.	2010	Bengtsson, Eriksson, & Wincent (2010)	*Competitiveness Review: An International Business Journal*	176
27.	2011	Wilhelm (2011)	*Journal of Operations Management*	156

(continued)

Table 6.1 (Cont.)

#/N.	Year	Authors	Journal/Book/Conference	Citations on Google Scholar
28.	2011	Gnyawali & Park (2011)	*Research Policy*	365
29.	2011	Mention (2011)	*Technovation*	252
30.	2011	Li, Liu, & Liu, (2011)	*Journal of Operations Management*	113
31.	2011	Kylänen & Rusko (2011)	*European Management Journal*	93
32.	2011	Rusko (2011)	*Industrial Marketing Management*	92
33.	2012	Ritala (2012)	*British Journal of Management*	161
34.	2013	Ritala & Hurmelinna-Laukkanen (2013)	*Journal of Product Innovation Management*	194
35.	2013	Bouncken & Kraus (2013)	*Journal of Business Research*	129
36.	2014	Bengtsson & Kock (2014)	*Industrial Marketing Management*	184
37.	2014	Raza-Ullah, Bengtsson, & Kock (2014)	*Industrial Marketing Management*	97
38.	2014	Ritala, Golnam, & Wegmann (2014)	*Industrial Marketing Management*	89
39.	2014	Fernandez, Le Roy, & Gnyawali (2014)	*Industrial Marketing Management*	94
40.	2015	Bengtsson & Kock (2015)	*Book Chapter:* Creating and Delivering Value in Marketing	94
41.	2015	Bouncken, Gast, Kraus, & Bogers (2015)	*Review of Managerial Science*	78

Note: we selected papers located on Google Scholars by searching for "coopetition" or "co-opetition" in the title (15/09/2017). For papers published in the time frame spanning from 1996 to 2010 (from phase 1 to phase 3), we considered 100 citations as a cut-off. Since citations are biased by time elapsed from the time when articles were published, for papers published in the time frame spanning from 2011 to 2016 (phase 4), we considered 75 citations as a cut-off. We removed five articles that did not contribute to coopetition research.

the key phases in coopetition research and to suggest some hints on its convergence on few specific issues. In such a way, it will be possible to capture the critical aspects underlying the emergence of coopetition research as well as to disentangle its current theoretical and empirical advancements.

Drawing on Hoskisson et al. (1999), this chapter shows that the evolution of coopetition literature may be depicted through the metaphor of the "swing of a pendulum." Actually, it is possible to single out alternate phases in which the coopetition literature emphasizes the influx of *exogenous* aspects, such as the context and the interactions with actors in the choice of cooperating with rivals, with other phases in which the emphasis is instead on *endogenous* aspects, such as firms' internal resource deployment to manage the tensions underlying coopetitive relationships.

Research path

Our research path relates to performing a temporal analysis of the key articles contributing to the evolution of coopetition research. As anticipated earlier, to illustrate the path of evolution characterizing coopetition literature, we adopt the metaphor of the swing of a pendulum by drawing on Hoskisson et al. (1999). As known, the pendulum is a weight that is suspended from a fixed pivot so it can swing freely back and forth thanks to gravity. When the pendulum is sideways from its center position, it is exposed to a restoring force that will accelerate it back and report it to the center position. The restoring force and the pendulum's mass allow it to swing back and forth. Since the swing of a pendulum has typically been used to identify time periods and phases, we argue that it is helpful to portray the evolutionary path of coopetition literature in the last two decades by reframing the state of the art of coopetition studies through the metaphor of the swing of a pendulum. Specifically, by "decomposing time lines into distinct phases where there is continuity in activities within each phase and discontinuity at the frontiers" (Langley, 2010: 919), we partition the time scale of the bulk of coopetition literature into four distinct phases. This methodological choice allows us to extricate, for each phase, the continuities that conceptual and empirical coopetition studies share, as well as to unveil the discontinuities in issues (Langley & Truax, 1994).

The four phases we identify are reported as follows:

1. the *birth* phase: early development of coopetition (1996–2000);
2. the *childhood* phase: grasping the balance between competition and cooperation (2001–2005);
3. the *adolescence* phase: understanding benefits and pitfalls of coopetitive strategies (2006–2010);
4. the *younghood* phase: managing coopetitive tensions (2011–2016).

Figure 6.1 illustrates the key phases we have identified through the metaphor of the swing of a pendulum. As mentioned before, it understands them by using the two perspectives, looking respectively at the *endogenous* and *exogenous* sides of coopetition. The *endogenous* side of coopetition considers how firms organize themselves to deal with coopetition. It focuses on the role of firms' resources and the organizational structures firms can use to manage cooperation with their rivals. In a nutshell, the *endogenous* side takes into account the internal mechanisms firms develop to manage coopetition and achieve a coopetitive advantage.

The *exogenous* side of coopetition considers the relational aspects related to the role of the external contexts in which coopetition occurs, and the interactions occurring among coopetitive firms. In this vein, the focus rests on the context in which firms operate and the actions rivals develop, thereby affecting their performance. Authors pay particular attention to "the dependence between competitors due to structural conditions [that] can explain why competitors cooperate and also why they compete" (Bengtsson & Kock, 2000: 416). Starting in the next section, we will review the main studies epitomizing each phase and discuss the swing of the pendulum in coopetition research. Table 6.2 offers a synopsis of each phase of coopetition literature identified.

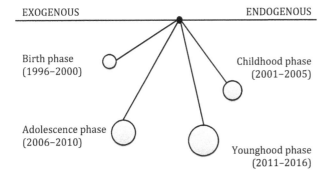

Figure 6.1   The swinging pendulum of coopetition research

Table 6.2 Synopsis of the four key phases in coopetition research

Phase	Side of Pendulum	Characteristic Traits	Prevalent Methodology	Influential Studies
Birth (1996–2000); early development of coopetition	Exogenous	Conceptualization of coopetition and recognizing the conditions supporting the emergence of coopetition; emphasis on contexts and actors involved	Theoretical development and few case studies	Brandenburger & Nalebuff, 1996; Dowling et al., 1996; Bengtsson & Kock, 2000
Childhood (2001–2005); grasping the balance between competition and cooperation	Endogenous	How firms organize themselves to develop a coopetition strategy	Case studies	Tsai, 2002; Luo, 2005, Dagnino & Padula, 2002
Adolescence (2006–2010); benefits and pitfalls of coopetitive strategies	Exogenous	Consequences of coopetitive strategies as concerns benefits and pitfalls of coopetitive strategies in different empirical settings	Case study; network analysis	Dagnino, 2009; Gnyawali et al., 2006; Gnyawali & Park, 2009
Younghood (2011–2016); managing coopetitive tension	Endogenous	Theorizing coopetition and finding new solutions to deal with coopetitive tensions as regards characteristics of industries and actors	Case study and econometric analysis	Bengtsson & Kock, 2014; Gnyawali & Park, 2011; Ritala, 2012, Park et al., 2014 Tidström, 2014

The birth phase: Early development of coopetition (1996–2000)

The early development phase encompasses coopetition studies published from 1996 to 2000, thereby recognizing as seminal the following pieces: Afuah (2000), Bengtsson and Kock (2000), Brandenburger and Nalebuff (1996), Carayannis and Alexander (1999), Carayannis and Roy (2000), and Dowling et al. (1996). Such contributions devote their attention to introducing the concept of coopetition and to digging deeper into the logic underlying the emergence of such a "new" strategy.

In this phase, there are three main theoretical lenses coopetition studies essentially takes: resource dependence theory, transaction cost economics, and game theory. Authors intend to unveil the nature and the kinds of inter-firm relationships that embrace competition and cooperation (Bengtsson & Kock, 2000; Dowling et al., 1996). Thus, they offer a preliminary sketch explaining why coopetition occurs, its antecedents, and the moves and countermoves firms should develop to manage coopetition. For instance, Dowling et al. (1996) identify the types of multifaceted relationships occurring under coopetition (i.e., buyers or sellers in "direct competition," buyers or sellers in "indirect competition," and partners in competition), and the strategic dilemma they present. Similarly, Bengtsson and Kock (2000) identify three types of coopetitive relationships (i.e., cooperation-dominated relationships, equal relationships, and competition-dominated relationships) based on the predominance of competition or cooperation over the other.

In unveiling the antecedents of coopetition, authors call attention to the *exogenous* dimensions of coopetition that are connected to industry concentration, munificence of resources, interconnectedness, opportunism, asset specificity, and so on (Dowling et al., 1996). Interestingly, Brandenburger and Nalebuff (1996) extend the analytical spectrum of previous cooperation research by defining the set of actions and responses that firms can deploy based on the pay-offs they can achieve through their choices. Furthermore, Afuah (2000: 388) argues that, "if a firm has come to depend on its coopetitor's capabilities, obsolescence of such capabilities can result in lower performance for the firm."

From a methodological point of view, it is worth noting that the bulk of the papers published in this initial phase are conceptual pieces. At this stage, it was important to acknowledge the complexity underlying coopetitive relationships in which "two diametrically different logics of interaction" take place (Bengtsson & Kock, 2000: 412), as well as to understand which aspects of competition and cooperation emerge, so as to identify the essential features of coopetition (Afuah, 2000; Bengtsson & Kock, 2000). On the other hand, empirical evidence is limited and is mainly aimed at providing insightful examples of coopetition (Bengtsson & Kock, 2000; Dowling et al., 1996).

From the viewpoint of competition/cooperation integration or separation, in this phase we see that, while studies favor the importance of considering competition and cooperation simultaneously, they inspect "how the division between the cooperative and the competitive part of the relationship can be made and to further scrutinize the advantages of coopetition" (Bengtsson & Kock, 2000: 412).

As Figure 6.1 shows, the pendulum is clearly located on the *exogenous* side, meaning that, despite the fact that interactions among rival firms are explored focusing on resources and capabilities endowment and deployment, authors particularly stress industry structure conditions that in turn push firms to cooperate with rivals (Bengtsson & Kock, 2000).

The childhood phase: Grasping the balance between competition and cooperation (2001–2005)

During the second evolutionary phase of coopetition research, here labeled the "childhood stage," we see an increased number of studies on coopetition. Scholars recognize the relevance of identifying novel, intriguing solutions to simultaneously combine and cope with competition and cooperation. For instance, Quintana-Garcia and Benavides-Velasco (2004) introduce a bouquet of alternative moves that firms may develop (i.e., unilateral cooperation, mutual cooperation, unilateral defection, and mutual defection), that might originate from blurring competition and cooperation.

Interestingly, in this phase most coopetition studies share the centrality of firms and how they should draw on their internal resources and capabilities to balance competition and cooperation, thereby achieving a coopetitive advantage over their rivals. In coopetitive relationships, "while competing with each other, business players also cooperate among themselves to acquire new knowledge from each other" (Tsai, 2002: 180). Therefore, in this phase the emphasis is on how firms organize themselves to balance the critical duality between cooperation—that informs the value creating process—and competition—that informs the value appropriation process (Luo, 2005). For instance, M'Chirgui (2005) underscores that players in the smart card industry need to cooperate with each other to face the technological and market uncertainty stemming from the industry. However, the focus rests on organizing firms' internal resources and capabilities, developing R&D activities to anticipate rival-partners moves, and promoting the technological standard. In this perspective, coopetition is "a powerful means of identifying new market opportunities and developing business conduct" (M'Chirgui, 2005: 933).

From a theoretical point of view, the resource-based view alters the prevalent perspective through which authors choose to investigate coopetition. From such a perspective, rival firms can decide to collaborate with each other if there is room for combining and recombining their similar and/or complementary resources and capabilities to shape rare, inimitable, and valuable synergies. Studies appear focused on exploring how competition and cooperation may impact knowledge sharing (Levy et al., 2003; Quintana-Garcia & Benavides-Velasco, 2004; Tsai, 2002). Given the emphasis on the resources needed to compete, authors explore coopetition in different kinds of firms, such as firms operating in high-tech industries (Carayannis & Alexander, 2001; M'Chirgui, 2005), firms of different sizes (Levy et al., 2003; Lin & Zhang, 2005), and firms operating in various geographies or having geographic diversification (Luo, 2005).

From the methodological point of view, the bulk of studies continue to present inductive case-based studies focusing on one central actor or on only few firms. At the same time, in this phase we start seeing a small amount of pieces adopting large-sample empirical methods that would allow the achievement of more generalizable results. Interestingly, considering the youth of the coopetition research area, in-depth case studies of single firms or industries are clearly favored in this phase. This condition occurs since case studies provide the opportunity to gather real-time data and conduct explorative investigation.

From the viewpoint of competition/cooperation integration or separation, we see that studies persist in approaching coopetition "as simultaneous, inclusive interdependence comprised of cooperation and competition as two interrelated but separate axes" (Luo, 2005: 73). In more detail, the subunits of the firm face "diverse issues and play diverse roles, giving rise to cooperation on some issues, projects, functions, or knowledge development and competition on other issues, projects, functions, or markets" (Luo, 2005: 73).

As Figure 6.1 shows, the pendulum of coopetition studies swings from the exogenous side further to the other extreme, the *endogenous* side. Authors call attention to firms' resources, capabilities, and organizational structures supporting coopetition and allowing firms to perform better than rivals. Hence, the orchestration of resources firms possess represents the crucial asset for adopting a coopetitive strategy.

The adolescence phase: Benefits and pitfalls of coopetitive strategies (2006–2010)

The phase of coopetition research spanning from 2006 to 2010 represents the "adolescence" of coopetition studies. In this phase, we observe a significant increase in the number of coopetitive studies published in journals as well as a few books dedicated to the key issue. Among them, we acknowledge the presence of chapter collections published specifically in two edited books (Dagnino, 2009; Yami et al., 2010).

In this third phase, we recognize the emergence of studies exploring coopetition among firms at various levels of analysis,[1] such as at inter-firm level (Bakshi & Kleindorfer, 2009; Venkatesh et al., 2006) and network level (Gnyawali et al., 2006; Peng & Bourne, 2009). These studies share emphasis on the *exogenous* side of coopetition, by stressing the impact of the international contexts (Luo, 2007; Luo & Rui, 2009) and, more generally, of industry factors (Gnyawali & Park, 2009; Watanabe et al., 2009). This condition applies to various environmental settings, such as the supply chain (Wu et al., 2010), knowledge-intensive industries

(Cassiman et al., 2009; Luo et al., 2006; Watanabe et al., 2009), the healthcare industry (Peng & Bourne, 2009), and interactions with external agents, such as institutions and governments (Dagnino & Mariani, 2010), affecting firms' abilities to achieve easier and/or earlier access to information and knowledge.

From a theoretical point of view, we notice that the majority of studies ground the firm's choice to collaborate with rivals on higher/lower transaction costs or on the threat of opportunistic behavior. Interestingly, some authors argue that the benefits stemming from cooperation with rivals depend on the higher costs related to the threat of a rival's opportunistic behavior that may be exerted during the coopetitive interaction to appropriate the value created (Ritala & Hurmelinna-Laukkanen, 2009). They draw on the resource-based theory to emphasize the relevance in high-tech industries of collaborating with rivals to generate knowledge and to become more innovative (Ritala & Urmelinna-Laukkanen, 2009). Finally, a few papers draw on game theory to explain the competitive factors emerging during interaction among rival firms (Wu et al., 2010).

From a methodological point of view, while some scholars (Cassiman at al., 2009; Dagnino & Mariani, 2010; Watanabe et al., 2009) carry on to adopt qualitative detailed case-study methodology to grasp how to manage the coopetition emerging among R&D projects to extract profit from innovation activities (Cassiman at al., 2009), or to develop new technologies (Watanabe et al., 2009), others use other methods, such as network analysis, to seize the impact of coopetition on rivals' competitive behavior (Gnyawali et al., 2006; Peng & Bourne, 2009).

From the viewpoint of competition/cooperation integration or separation, in this phase we observe that, to appreciate the essence of coopetition, studies generally acknowledge the relevance of digging deeper into the mechanisms underlying the integration of competition and cooperation (Dagnino, 2009). Specifically, by "making either the cooperation element or the competition element hidden" (Gnyawali et al., 2008: 395), Gnyawali et al. (2008) identify three guidelines to deal with coopetition: (a) spatial separation; (b) temporal separation, and (c) integration of competition and cooperation.

As Figure 6.1 shows, the pendulum of coopetition studies swings in this phase from the *endogenous* side to the other extreme, or the *exogenous* side. Authors call attention to the benefits and risks underlying the adoption of a coopetitive strategy, as well as on the impact of external factors on the firm's decision to collaborate with rivals and, therefore, to develop a coopetition strategy. Additionally, eclectic approaches to coopetition and the wide portfolio of methodologies present in this phase confirms that, between 2006 and 2010, coopetition literature has eventually reached its adolescence.

The younghood phase: Managing coopetitive tensions (2011–2016)

The period of research spanning from 2011 to 2016 represents, in our understanding, the "younghood" phase of coopetition studies. This phase is characterized by the continuous and remarkable growth of coopetition literature. The amount of papers published and special issues of academic journals produced (i.e., two issues of *Industrial Marketing Management* in 2014 and 2016, one issue of the *International Journal of Management and Organization* in 2014, one issue of the *International Journal of Business Environment* in 2014, and one issue of the *International Journal of Technology Management* in 2016) confirm the increasing consensus that the coopetition research area is actually experiencing in the management realm (Minà & Dagnino, 2016), as well as the growing interest of the management community in developing a robust academic debate on the key aspects of coopetition so as to tackle the open issues and foster future research (Bengtsson & Kock, 2014).

Articles published in this phase explore the management of competition and cooperation intensity, and the *balance* between them for achieving increased firm innovation and performance. Specifically, authors call for consideration of the management of coopetitive *tensions* emerging at various levels of analysis (Fernandez et al., 2014; Séran et al., 2016). In this line of reasoning, Tidström (2014) detects the key drivers of coopetitive tensions and identifies the approaches firms should adopt to deal with them. Actually, different styles of action can employ different approaches to managing coopetitive tensions, thereby producing different outcomes that can be mutually positive, mutually negative, or mixed for the parties involved (Tidström, 2014). This condition emphasizes the relevance of managing the competition-cooperation paradox emerging in coopetition (Bengtsson & Raza-Ullah, 2016; Czakon et al., 2014; Gnyawali et al., 2016; Raza-Ullah et al., 2014).

In addition, the fourth phase of coopetition studies shares the emphasis on the regained centrality of firms and the importance of digging deeper into the mechanisms of managing coopetition for achieving *coopetitive advantage*. Remarkably, some authors call attention to the effect of coopetition strategy on innovation and performance (Bouncken et al., 2016; Estrada et al., 2016; Park et al., 2014; Ritala, 2012; Ritala & Hurmelinna-Laukkanen, 2013; Wilhem, 2011).

From a theoretical point of view, the majority of studies take a resource-based view or transaction-cost-of-economics stance. Analyzing the actors involved in coopetition, authors observe that increased cooperation might develop concerns about opportunistic behavior (Sainio et al., 2012). This stream of study implicitly summons up Hamel's (1991) piece, according to which collaboration between competitors leads to the emergence of *learning races*. In this context, firms struggle against time to access and exploit their partner's knowledge faster than their partner can do the same in such a way that they can forsake the coopetitive relationship when they have obtained what they wanted. Such concerns are primarily rooted in the potential threat that partners may always act in an opportunistic fashion.

From a methodological point of view, in this phase we observe a notable increase in the amount of papers adopting quantitative methods. While the previous phases of coopetition research have been methodologically dominated primarily by cases studies, in the younghood phase, scores of studies present quantitative data-driven and longitudinal analyses. For instance, Wu (2014) analyzes 1499 Chinese firms operating in several industries to detect an inverted U-shaped relationship between coopetition and product innovation performance. Furthermore, using a sample of 627 manufacturing firms, Estrada et al. (2016) unveil the role of internal knowledge-sharing mechanisms and formal knowledge protection mechanisms in the relation between coopetition and innovation. Similarly, Bouncken et al. (2016) develop a survey-based study of 372 vertical alliances in the medical device industry to investigate how firms can enhance their product innovation pace in coopetitive alliances. Overall, since the adoption of econometric-based empirical methods allows the academic community to deal with more generalizable results, this condition also applies to coopetition research. However, interestingly enough in this phase, conceptual pieces and theoretical frameworks are still being developed (Bengtsson & Kock, 2014; Gnyawali et al., 2016; Mariani, 2016).

From the viewpoint of competition/cooperation integration or separation, since authors have begun to accept that coopetition is inherently betrothed by tensions arising from the simultaneous interaction of cooperative and competitive actions (Bengtsson & Kock, 2014), they fine-tune their research to the paradox of managing coopetition and the required analytical and execution capabilities to do so (Gnyawali et al., 2016).

As Figure 6.1 clearly shows, the pendulum of coopetition studies swings out from the *exogenous* side to the other extreme, or to the *endogenous* side. While in the previous phase—labeled the adolescence of coopetition—scholars tended to examine why and to what extent firms involved in coopetitive relationships were committed to cooperation to achieve their shared objectives, for the first time in this phase authors emphasize that "coopetitive tension is fundamentally an individual level construct, which is experienced and felt by managers that are carrying out the contradictory tasks of coopetition" (Bengtsson & Raza-Ullah, 2016: 12). Therefore, it appears crucial to explore the inner mechanisms that emerge when competition and cooperation occur simultaneously, as well as the ways through which firms should deal with them (Fernandez et al., 2014).

Conclusion

In this chapter, we have interpreted the evolution of coopetition literature through the metaphor of a swinging pendulum. The pendulum swings from the *exogenous* side, giving relevance to the characteristics of context and actors representing key antecedents and factors leading to cooperation with rivals and coopetition performance, to the *endogenous* side, focusing on how firms organize themselves and invest resources in dealing with coopetition. Specifically, we have seen that, from the birth phase of early development to the childhood phase, the pendulum swings from the *exogenous* side to the *endogenous* side of coopetition. Later on, during the adolescence phase, the pendulum swings back towards the *exogenous* side. Finally, in the younghood phase, the pendulum swings forward once more to the *exogenous* side of coopetition, in which the focus is on how to manage coopetitive tensions.

We believe that strategic management inquiry may benefit from an overview such as this one, integrating various insights from prior research. In fact, the comprehensive picture of the four-phased evolution of coopetition literature we have supplied in this chapter is to be seen as the backbone to shaping an intriguing introduction to the coopetition domain that may be of interest to a wide array of strategy scholars and students, who have developed or are developing awareness in coopetition and/or wish to join its exploration in the future.

Note

1   Interestingly, some authors have also explored coopetition among groups and among functions and strategic business units (Cassiman et al., 2009; Luo et al., 2006).

References

Afuah, A. (2000). How much do your "co-opetitors'" capabilities matter in the face of technological change? *Strategic Management Journal*, 21(3), 387–404.

Bakshi, N. & Kleindorfer, P. (2009). Co-opetition and investment for supply-chain resilience. *Production and Operations Management*, 18(6), 583–603.

Bengtsson, M., Eriksson, J., & Wincent, J. (2010). Co-opetition dynamics—an outline for further inquiry. *Competitiveness Review: An International Business Journal*, 20(2), 194–214.

Bengtsson, M. & Kock, S. (2000). "Coopetition" in business networks—to cooperate and compete simultaneously. *Industrial Marketing Management*, 29(5), 411–426.

Bengtsson, M. & Kock, S. (2014). Coopetition—Quo vadis? Past accomplishments and future challenges. *Industrial Marketing Management*, 43(2), 180–188.

Bengtsson, M. & Kock, S. (2015). Tension in Co-opetition. In Spott, H. E. (Ed.). *Creating and delivering value in marketing*. Cham: Springer, 38–42.

Bengtsson, M. & Raza-Ullah, T. (2016). A systematic review of research on coopetition: toward a multilevel understanding. *Industrial Marketing Management*, 57, 23–39.

Bouncken, R. B., Clauß, T., & Fredrich, V. (2016). Product innovation through coopetition in alliances: Singular or plural governance? *Industrial Marketing Management*, 53, 77–90.

Bouncken, R. B., Gast, J., Kraus, S., & Bogers, M. (2015). Coopetition: a systematic review, synthesis, and future research directions. *Review of Managerial Science*, 9(3), 577–601.

Bouncken, R. B. & Kraus, S. (2013). Innovation in knowledge-intensive industries: The double-edged sword of coopetition. *Journal of Business Research*, 66(10), 2060–2070.

Brandenburger, A. M. & Nalebuff, B. J. (1996). *Co-opetition*. New York: Doubleday.

Carayannis, E. G. & Alexander, J. (2001). Virtual, wireless mannah: a co-opetitive analysis of the broadband satellite industry. *Technovation*, 21(12), 759–766.

Carayannis, E. G. & Alexander, J. (1999). Winning by co-opeting in strategic government-university-industry R&D partnerships: the power of complex, dynamic knowledge networks. *The Journal of Technology Transfer*, 24(2), 197–210.

Carayannis, E. G. & Roy, R. I. S. (2000). Davids vs Goliaths in the small satellite industry:: the role of technological innovation dynamics in firm competitiveness. *Technovation*, 20(6), 287–297.

Cassiman, B., Di Guardo, M. C., & Valentini, G. (2009). Organising R&D projects to profit from innovation: Insights from co-opetition. *Long Range Planning*, 42(2), 216–233.

Chin, K. S., Chan, B. L., & Lam, P. K. (2008). Identifying and prioritizing critical success factors for coopetition strategy. *Industrial Management & Data Systems*, 108(4), 437–454.

Czakon, W., Fernandez, A. S., & Minà, A. (2014). Editorial–From paradox to practice: the rise of coopetition strategies. *International Journal of Business Environment*, 6(1), 1–10.

Dagnino, G. B. (2009). Introduction—coopetition strategy: a "path recognition" investigation approach. In Dagnino, G. B. & Rocco, E. (Eds), *Coopetition strategy: theory, experiments and cases*. New York: Routledge, 1–21.

Dagnino, G. B. (2016). Evolutionary lineage of the dominant paradigms in strategic management research. In Dagnino, G. B. & Cinici, M. C. (Eds), *Research Methods for Strategic Management*. New York: Routledge, 15–48.

Dagnino, G. B. & Mariani, M. M. (2010). Coopetitive value creation in entrepreneurial contexts: The case of AlmaCube. In Yami, S., Castaldo, S., Dagnino, B., & Le Roy, F. (Eds), *Coopetition: winning strategies for the 21st century*. Cheltenham, UK; Northampton, MA: Edward Elgar, 101–123.

Dagnino, G. B. & Padula, G. (2002). Coopetition strategy: a new kind of interfirm dynamics for value creation. In *Innovative Research in Management, European Academy of Management (EURAM)*, second annual conference, Stockholm, May (Vol. 9).

Dowling, M. J., Roering, W. D., Carlin, B. A., & Wisnieski, J. (1996). Multifaceted relationships under coopetition: Description and theory. *Journal of Management Inquiry*, 5(2), 155–167.

Eriksson, P. E. (2008). Procurement effects on coopetition in client-contractor relationships. *Journal of Construction Engineering and Management*, 134(2), 103–111.

Estrada, I., Faems, D., & de Faria, P. (2016). Coopetition and product innovation performance: The role of internal knowledge sharing mechanisms and formal knowledge protection mechanisms. *Industrial Marketing Management*, 53, 56–65.

Fernandez, A. S., Le Roy, F., & Gnyawali, D. R. (2014). Sources and management of tension in co-opetition case evidence from telecommunications satellites manufacturing in Europe. *Industrial Marketing Management*, 43(2), 222–235.

Gnyawali, D. R., He, J., & Madhavan, R. (2006). Impact of co-opetition on firm competitive behavior: An empirical examination. *Journal of Management*, 32(4), 507–530.

Gurnani, H., Erkoc, M., & Luo, Y. (2007). Impact of product pricing and timing of investment decisions on supply chain co-opetition. *European Journal of Operational Research*, 180(1), 228–248.

Gnyawali, D. R., He, J. & Madhavan, R. (2008). Co-opetition: Promises and challenges. *21st century management: A reference handbook*, 386–398.

Gnyawali, D. R., Madhavan, R., He, J., & Bengtsson, M. (2016). The competition–cooperation paradox in inter-firm relationships: A conceptual framework. *Industrial Marketing Management*, 53, 7–18.

Gnyawali, D. R. & Park, B. J. R. (2009). Co-opetition and technological innovation in small and medium-sized enterprises: A multilevel conceptual model. *Journal of Small Business Management*, 47(3), 308–330.

Gnyawali, D. R. & Park, B. J. R. (2011). Co-opetition between giants: Collaboration with competitors for technological innovation. *Research Policy*, 40(5), 650–663.

Hamel, G. (1991). Competition for competence and interpartner learning within international strategic alliances. *Strategic Management Journal*, 12(S1), 83–103.

Hoskisson, R. E., Hitt, M. A., Wan, W. P., & Yiu, D. (1999). Theory and research in strategic management: Swings of a pendulum. *Journal of Management*, 25(3), 417–456.

Kylänen, M. & Rusko, R. (2011). Unintentional coopetition in the service industries: The case of Pyhä-Luosto tourism destination in the Finnish Lapland. *European Management Journal*, 29(3), 193–205.

Langley, A. (2010) Temporal Bracketing. In Mills, A. J., Durepos, G., & Wiebe, E. (Eds). (2010). *Encyclopedia of case study research: L-Z; index* (Vol. 1). California: Sage.

Langley, A. & Truax, J. (1994). A process study of new technology adoption in smaller manufacturing firms. *Journal of Management Studies*, 31(5), 619–652.

Levy, M., Loebbecke, C., & Powell, P. (2003). SMEs, co-opetition and knowledge sharing: the role of information systems. *European Journal of Information Systems*, 12(1), 3–17.

Lin, C. Y. Y. & Zhang, J. (2005). Changing structures of SME Networks: Lessons from the publishing industry in Taiwan. *Long Range Planning*, 38(2), 145–162.

Li, Y., Liu, Y., & Liu, H. (2011). Co-opetition, distributor's entrepreneurial orientation and manufacturer's knowledge acquisition: Evidence from China. *Journal of Operations Management*, 29(1), 128–142.

Loebecke, C., Van Fenema, P. C., & Powell, P. (1999). Co-opetition and knowledge transfer. *ACM SIGMIS Database*, 30(2), 14–25.

Luo, Y. (2004). A coopetition perspective of MNC–host government relations. *Journal of International Management*, 10(4), 431–451.

Luo, Y. & Rui, H. (2009). An ambidexterity perspective toward multinational enterprises from emerging economies. *Academy of Management Perspectives*, 23(4), 49–70.

Luo, X., Slotegraaf, R. J., & Pan, X. (2006). Cross-functional "coopetition": The simultaneous role of cooperation and competition within firms. *Journal of Marketing*, 70(2), 67–80.

Luo, Y. (2005). Toward coopetition within a multinational enterprise: a perspective from foreign subsidiaries. *Journal of World Business*, 40(1), 71–90.

Luo, Y. (2007). A coopetition perspective of global competition. *Journal of World Business*, 42(2), 129–144.

M'Chirgui, Z. (2005). The economics of the smart card industry: towards coopetitive strategies. *Economics of Innovation and New Technology*, 14(6), 455–477.

Mariani, M. M. (2007). Coopetition as an emergent strategy: Empirical evidence from an Italian consortium of opera houses. *International Studies of Management & Organization*, 37(2), 97–126.

Mariani, M. M. (2016). Coordination in inter-network co-opetitition: Evidence from the tourism sector. *Industrial Marketing Management*, 53, 103–123.

Mention, A. L. (2011). Co-operation and co-opetition as open innovation practices in the service sector: Which influence on innovation novelty? *Technovation*, 31(1), 44–53.

Minà, A. & Dagnino, G. B. (2016). In search of coopetition consensus: shaping the collective identity of a relevant strategic management community. *International Journal of Technology Management*, 71(1–2), 123–154.

Morris, M. H., Koçak, A., & Özer, A. (2007). Coopetition as a small business strategy: Implications for performance. *Journal of Small Business Strategy*, 18(1), 35.

Nalebuff, B. J. & Brandenburger, A. M. (1997). Co-opetition: Competitive and cooperative business strategies for the digital economy. *Strategy & Leadership*, 25(6), 28–33.

Padula, G. & Dagnino, G. B. (2007). Untangling the rise of coopetition: the intrusion of competition in a cooperative game structure. *International Studies of Management & Organization*, 37(2), 32–52.

Park, B. J. R., Srivastava, M. K., & Gnyawali, D. R. (2014). Walking the tight rope of coopetition: Impact of competition and cooperation intensities and balance on firm innovation performance. *Industrial Marketing Management*, 43(2), 210–221.

Peng, T. J. A. & Bourne, M. (2009). The coexistence of competition and cooperation between networks: implications from two Taiwanese healthcare networks. *British Journal of Management*, 20(3), 377–400.

Quintana-Garcia, C. & Benavides-Velasco, C. A. (2004). Cooperation, competition, and innovative capability: a panel data of European dedicated biotechnology firms. *Technovation*, 24(12), 927–938.

Raza-Ullah, T., Bengtsson, M., & Kock, S. (2014). The coopetition paradox and tension in coopetition at multiple levels. *Industrial Marketing Management*, 43(2), 189–198.

Ritala, P. (2012). Coopetition strategy—when is it successful? Empirical evidence on innovation and market performance. *British Journal of Management*, 23(3), 307–324.

Ritala, P., Golnam, A., & Wegmann, A. (2014). Coopetition-based business models: The case of Amazon. com. *Industrial Marketing Management*, 43(2), 236–249.

Ritala, P. & Hurmelinna-Laukkanen, P. (2009). What's in it for me? Creating and appropriating value in innovation-related coopetition. *Technovation*, 29(12), 819–828.

Ritala, P. & Hurmelinna-Laukkanen, P. (2013). Incremental and radical innovation in coopetition—The role of absorptive capacity and appropriability. *Journal of Product Innovation Management*, 30(1), 154–169.

Rusko, R. (2011). Exploring the concept of coopetition: A typology for the strategic moves of the Finnish forest industry. *Industrial Marketing Management*, 40(2), 311–320.

Sainio, L. M., Ritala, P., & Hurmelinna-Laukkanen, P. (2012). Constituents of radical innovation—exploring the role of strategic orientations and market uncertainty. *Technovation*, 32(11), 591–599.

Séran, T., Pellegrin-Boucher, E., & Gurau, C. (2016). The management of coopetitive tensions within multi-unit organizations. *Industrial Marketing Management*, 53, 31–41.

Smith, K. G., Carroll, S. J., & Ashford, S. J. (1995). Intra-and interorganizational cooperation: Toward a research agenda. *Academy of Management Journal*, 38(1), 7–23.

Tidström, A. (2014). Managing tensions in coopetition. *Industrial Marketing Management*, 43(2), 261–271.

Tsai, W. (2002). Social structure of "coopetition" within a multiunit organization: Coordination, competition, and intraorganizational knowledge sharing. *Organization Science*, 13(2), 179–190.

Venkatesh, R., Chintagunta, P., & Mahajan, V. (2006). Research note—sole entrant, co-optor, or component supplier: Optimal end-product strategies for manufacturers of proprietary component brands. *Management Science*, 52(4), 613–622.

Walley, K. (2007). Coopetition: an introduction to the subject and an agenda for research. *International Studies of Management & Organization*, 37(2), 11–31.

Wang, Y. & Krakover, S. (2008). Destination marketing: competition, cooperation or coopetition? *International Journal of Contemporary Hospitality Management*, 20(2), 126–141.

Watanabe, C., Lei, S., & Ouchi, N. (2009). Fusing indigenous technology development and market learning for greater functionality development—an empirical analysis of the growth trajectory of Canon printers. *Technovation*, 29(4), 265–283.

Wilhelm, M. M. (2011). Managing coopetition through horizontal supply chain relations: Linking dyadic and network levels of analysis. *Journal of Operations Management*, 29(7), 663–676.

Wu, J. (2014). Cooperation with competitors and product innovation: Moderating effects of technological capability and alliances with universities. *Industrial Marketing Management*, 43(2), 199–209.

Wu, Z., Choi, T. Y., & Rungtusanatham, M. J. (2010). Supplier–supplier relationships in buyer–supplier–supplier triads: Implications for supplier performance. *Journal of Operations Management*, 28(2), 115–123.

Yami, S., Castaldo, S., Dagnino, B., & Le Roy, F. (Eds) (2010). *Coopetition: winning strategies for the 21st century*. Cheltenham, UK; Northampton, MA: Edward Elgar.

Zineldin, M. (2004). Co-opetition: the organisation of the future. *Marketing Intelligence & Planning*, 22(7), 780–790.

Part II
Coopetition antecedents and drivers

7

Trust in tourism dyadic and network coopetition

Wojciech Czakon and Katarzyna Czernek-Marszałek

Introduction

Coopetition research has so far explored the benefits sought by firms and the process of coopeting, leaving the reasons why some firms choose to enter this relationship, while others do not, relatively under-researched. In this chapter we focus on trust, a recognized antecedent of inter-firm relationship formation (Chin et al., 2008). In mutual interdependency situations and consequent mutual vulnerability to actions of others, the role of trust is particularly important (De Wever et al., 2005). While partnering in general exposed firms to risks relative to the misbehaviors of partners, coopetition adds to this exposure its intrinsic inter-firm rivalry. Should coopetition yield the benefits attributed to this strategy (Le Roy & Czakon, 2016), involved firms need to behave collaboratively and predictably. Trust resides between knowledge and unawareness about somebody, i.e., it is some kind of hypothesis about an actor's behavior (Simmel 1975, p. 396) and is perceived as a form of positive expectation regarding counterparts (Lewichi et al., 1998, p. 438). Trust understanding ranges from a behavior predictor to a positive and benevolent behavior expectation.

The bulk of trust literature has been focused on vertical relationships, leaving horizontal collaboration relatively under-researched (Morris et al., 2007). When a firm is involved in horizontal relationships, trust refers to both collaborative and competitive activities, captured in the coopetition concept. Within collaborative relationships, firms trust that their partners will share resources, communicate openly, meet deadlines, and display commitment, while at the same time refraining from acting opportunistically (Wang, 2008). Trust is a recognized building block of collaboration (Bouncken & Fredrich, 2012). However, competition in horizontal relationships requires firms to trust that partners will not engage in competitive actions that will strengthen them at the focal firm's expense (Le Roy & Czakon, 2016). Hence, trust in coopetition appears to be more complex than in vertical collaborative relationships; it plays a crucial role even before coopetition actually starts (Morris et al., 2007).

Through two studies of coopetition in a tourist destination in southern Poland we provide in-depth insights into how trust-building mechanisms impact on coopetition formation. By stratifying our results depending on the level of analysis— dyads and networks—we shed light on the differences between both types of coopetition and the role of trust in entering into each of them. We conclude that the relationship between trust-building mechanisms and each type of coopetition is quite complex.

Dyadic and network coopetition formation challenges

Most existing contributions acknowledge coopetition as a complex and dynamic phenomenon (Padula & Dagnino, 2007). Research suggest that the competitive and collaborative behaviors strongly impact each other (Mariani, 2007; Tidström, 2008). For instance, the upsurge of competition within a collaborative agreement alters the relationship and hampers its performance. Similarly, fostering collaboration within an otherwise-competitive relationship alters market structure and provides advantages to competitors. In turn, the complexity of coopetition stems from the number of actors involved, and from their respective relationships. Dyadic relationships expose actors to different contingencies and interdependencies as compared with multiple-actor network coopetition.

The differences between dyadic and network coopetition are particularly identifiable at the formation stage. By analogy to inter-organizational relationship formation, coopetition between two rivals follows "fit logic," in order to assess the extent to which two firms would cope better with the challenges they face (Czakon & Czernek, 2016). Indeed, competitors face the same challenges and have developed a similar resource base and expertise (Peng et al. 2012), which makes them particularly valuable partners. An in-depth study of collaborative alliances in the airline industry shows that rivals can be the second-best choice for those firms that desperately need a partner to respond to the challenges of an extreme environment (Chiambaretto & Fernandez, 2016). Indeed, competitors are aware of their rivals, motivated to confront, and capable of engaging in rivalry (Chen et al., 2007). As a result, the quest to identify the "best fit" with a rival results in identifying the "worst enemy." Collaboration with such a rival does not decrease the competitive tension (Le Roy & Czakon, 2016). Trust has therefore been identified as an essential element for building a coopetitive relationship (Chin et al. 2008).

Network coopetition poses quite different challenges to coopetition in dyads. Firms need to identify a common problem that can be solved through joint action (Wang, 2008). Interdependency recognition opens ways to finding a domain consensus necessary for collective action (Selin & Chavez, 1995). Based on domain recognition, the identification of fit among prospective actors is possible, and partner selection is actionable. However, while identifying complementarities and overlaps between two partners requires advanced managerial competencies, the same exercise for a larger number of partners increases the difficulty and inevitably creates overlaps, gaps, and tensions. Actors that occupy central positions in industry networks have been found to enjoy a structural advantage when engaging in coopetitive networks (Gnyawali et al., 2006), and are more able to deploy aggressive competitive actions (Sanou et al., 2016). Additionally, power relationships, the distribution of benefits, authority, and credibility emerge in network settings (Fyall et al., 2012). Extant literature attributes trust with the capacity to mitigate those concerns. Yet, trust is necessary at the formation stage in order to successfully make the "leap of faith" and enter into network coopetition.

Collaborating with rivals is a risky endeavor, and requires as much management (Le Roy & Czakon, 2016) as trust in partners (Czakon & Czernek, 2016; Czernek & Czakon, 2016). Trust is particularly important at the formation stage, where governance and management structures are not yet in place (Bouncken et al., 2015). Hence, trust-building can be viewed as a critical process in coopetition formation.

Trust-building mechanisms in coopetition formation

The concept of trust has a long-standing and popular use in interfirm relationships research. In the vast majority of studies it has been used as a homogeneous variable (Czernek & Czakon, 2016), helping involved actors to establish, maintain, and develop collaborative relationships.

Trust has been found to be a predictor for collaboration with competitors, along with commitment and mutual benefit, conceptualized as relationship dimensions (Morris, Koçak, & Ozer, 2007). A number of studies claim that trust is also key, or at least one of the most important determinants of collaboration, in the tourism sector (Grängsjö, 2006; Nunkoo et al., 2012; Nunkoo & Ramkisson 2011). The reason is that trust favors establishing collaboration, further impacting the collaboration process and outcomes. Researchers claim that "trust is the emotional basis of collaboration" or the "lubricant facilitating collaboration" (Sztompka, 1999).

The role of trust in developing (Morgan & Hunt, 1994) and sustaining relationships has solid theoretical and empirical foundations (Nielsen, 2011). The success of coopetitive relationships depends on how tensions among competitors are managed. Trust is seen as an important factor in alleviating tensions inherent to coopetitive relationships. Scholars attribute trust with the capacity to reduce the potential for tensions, i.e., even before they arise, and the capacity to alleviate tensions when trust is coupled with commitment (Tidström, 2009). Coopetition success has been found to depend on relational antecedents, demonstrating that high trust fosters success, especially if coupled with high dependence (Bouncken & Fredrich, 2012). A theoretical framework based on coopetition in in-depth destination marketing studies provides an even more comprehensive view on trust. It appears to be a precondition to collaboration, an outcome variable, and a success factor throughout the collaboration process (Wang & Fesenmaier, 2007).

However, researchers have seldom opened trust's black box in order to examine in detail its relationship with coopetition. Not much is known about its role in the formation phase of relationships (Bouncken et al., 2015), especially those among rivals. We encapsulate trust as a complex and heterogeneous result of various mechanisms, i.e., repeatable patterns of actions and responses activated in particular contexts or not, depending on conditions (Huang & Wilkinson, 2013). Several such mechanisms have been identified in the literature (Table 7.1). Each exposes a different source (McAllister, 1995) of a partner's behavior predictions, ranging from a purely rational calculation of costs and benefits associated with different behaviors, to expectations based on a positive perception of the partner as an individual.

Table 7.1 Trust-building mechanisms: Conceptual framework

No	Type of Trust	Reference	Trust-building Mechanism
1.	Calculative	Bachmann & Zaheer, 2008	Benefits of collaboration exceed costs of a partner's potential opportunistic behavior
2.	Reputation-based	Dolinger et al., 1997	Behaviors are relatively stable over time and can be a good predictor of future action
3.	Third-party legitimation	Dacin et al., 2007	Trust can be transferred from a more trusted individual to others
4.	Embeddedness-based trust	Buskens, 1998	Social networks act as bonds, deterring opportunism with social sanctions
5.	Partners' intentions assessment	Claro & Claro, 2008	Partners' intentions and motives analysis acts as behavior predictor
6.	Partners' capabilities assessment	Doney & Cannon, 1997	Partners' capabilities assessment acts as a mutual fit and behavior predictor
7.	Partners' personal predisposition	Hardin, 2006	Morality and personal features act as a behavior predictor
8.	Emotional bonds	McAllister, 1995	Friendship, kinship, etc. allow a firm to go beyond calculative trust

(Source: authors' own, based on the literature.)

Table 7.2 Trust-building mechanisms' roles in coopetition formation

Trust-building Mechanism	Dyad	Network
Calculative	Potential individual benefits exceeding costs are necessary to form coopetition	Potential costs exceeding benefits justify the decision not to enter coopetition
Reputation	Reputation is a necessary but not sufficient condition to start coopetition	Reputation stimulates coopetition entry
Capabilities assessment	Incorporated in reputation	Partners' capabilities assessment cannot build trust
Intentions assessment	Incorporated in reputation	Partners' intentions negatively impact coopetition entry decision
Third-party legitimation	Legitimating is not a relevant trust-building mechanism	Legitimation by a third party stimulates coopetition entry
Social embeddedness	Facilitates coopetition for local actors, hampers coopetition for outsiders	
Emotional bonds	Emotional bonds play a moderating role between calculative trust and coopetition formation	None identified

(Source: Czakon & Czernek, 2016; Czernek & Czakon, 2016.)

Our studies (Czakon & Czernek, 2016; Czernek & Czakon, 2016) show that trust develops differently in dyadic, as compared to network, coopetition, and that trust-building mechanisms play distinct roles in establishing coopetition (Table 7.2).

Calculative trust

Our respondents claimed that in each and every single case, economic calculation has been the basis for entering dyadic coopetition (Czernek & Czakon, 2016). In line with prior research, establishing a collaborative relationship with a competitor is instrumental in achieving utility for the focal firm (Morris et al., 2007). Our interviewees declared that they estimated their own benefits and costs of coopetition both in financial and nonfinancial terms. When the benefits of working with a particular rival were very clearly seen, trust developed easily. Thus, dyadic coopetition usually occurs in two situations: in everyday activities—for example, recommending other providers because of full accommodation and no possibility of serving customers; and in a situation of a common problem or opportunity—for example, the possibility of engaging in a development project. Coopetition is more easily initiated with a rival offering complementary services.

For network coopetition it revealed much more difficult to identify individually appropriable coopetition benefits, as compared to clear and measurable costs such as attendance or membership fees (Czakon & Czernek, 2016). While for the network leader the overall benefit of collective action may be clear, it is still necessary that potential members of the coopetitive network develop a shared vision of the problem domain (Selin & Chavez, 1995) followed by a clear definition of benefits and costs associated with collective action. Network coopetition benefits are mainly collective, show up usually in the long term, and are difficult to measure. The diversity and large number of partners make it very difficult to develop a benefit-based trust. Additionally, in some cases the willingness to collaborate with competitors was limited by the fear that a partner's benefits could be higher than a firm's own, or that a firm's own costs could be higher than those paid by its partners. Thus, despite theoretical suggestions that coopetitive networks are formed based on business needs rather than trust (Sanou et al., 2016) we find evidence that, given the difficulties in developing a clear calculation of benefits and costs, firms look for other sources of trust before making the decision to enter network coopetition.

Reputation-based trust

We identified many situations where trust in dyads came from the need to start or continue relations based on reputation (Czernek & Czakon, 2016). Good reputation coupled with clear benefits was enough to initiate coopetition, with no necessity for formal agreements. The reputation of a tourism business was important in recommending services to tourists by other entrepreneurs. Interviewees stressed the importance of an entrepreneur's reputation, because it translated into their own reputation. At the same time a care to maintain reputation also encouraged the counterpart to try to fulfill agreed commitments.

In network coopetition it reveals difficult to assess the reputation of each member of the partnership structure (Czakon & Czernek, 2016). However, the initiators of network coopetition were often able to select potential network members by assessing their reputation. Those initiators suggested that collaboration with providers with whom they had already collaborated was easier to start, and often was much more successful. Interestingly, those actors who joined different kinds of partnership initiatives often decided to do so because of trust in an initiator having a good reputation.

Intentions- and capabilities-based trust-building mechanisms

Two trust-building mechanisms, oriented at a partner's intentions or capabilities, revealed to be incorporated into a partner's perception by the focal firm, stemming either from experience or reputation derived from prior behaviors. These two mechanisms were not identified as distinct and relevant in dyadic coopetition (Czernek & Czakon, 2016).

For network coopetition it was difficult to develop trust based on intentions and competence assessments because the evaluation of partners appeared very challenging. Network coopetition typically involved from several to several-dozen partners, who often had no knowledge about one another (Czakon & Czernek, 2016). Inversely, the perception of intentions as selfish was a source of distrust, and did not encourage entry into coopetition.

Third-party legitimation-based trust

Interestingly, coopetition between two firms did not require third-party legitimization as actors relied on their own knowledge about potential partners (Czernek & Czakon, 2016).

However, this trust-building mechanism was identified in network coopetition. For actors intending to be members of a partnership structure, the lack of possibility to develop trust through the typical methods available in individual settings induced actors to rely on legitimization by a third party. Local government was often desired as the legitimizing third party (Czakon & Czernek, 2016). Its involvement is often substantiated by resource allocation: a legal seat, equipment, or a subsidy. This stimulates entrepreneurs to build trust towards potential partners and organizations as a whole, and to join a network.

Emotional bonds-based trust

We found that trust in dyads emerged from the need to assure one's own, as well as the benefits of a counterpart because of appreciation and care for a counterpart's prosperity when, for example, friendship is involved. However, this type of trust only strengthened the coopetition based on positive economic calculation of benefits and the costs of sustaining relations with the partner.

On the other hand, we did not find evidence of trust-building based on emotional bonds in networks; the number of partners often unknown before deciding to join a partnership structure made it virtually impossible (Czernek & Czakon, 2016).

We found no evidence that actors developed trust in others because of their morality, personal features, or character. However, it seems that living in a small environment, caring about one's own reputation, and being aware of one's own role in the business provided the actors with some knowledge about such features, and provided enough incentive for actors to try to remain reliable.

Trust based on social network embeddedness

In some cases trust stemmed from existing social networks. Strong social embeddedness helped to gain and transfer information among local society, which allowed trust to be built. However, the role of this mechanism was not only positive. The respondents who did not originally come from the region, or had only been citizens for a short time, often claimed that they were not embedded in dense social networks in which actors trusted only one another. This made potential dyadic collaboration more difficult to establish (Czernek & Czakon, 2016).

The role of trust based on social network embeddedness in coopetition was identified mainly in dyadic relations. However, actors who were not embedded in the local community had limited access to knowledge about potential forms of cooperation with competitors, which hampered their potential engagement in coopetition.

The complexity of trust's role in coopetition formation

Our research exemplifies the complexity of trust, which has sociological, psychological, and economic dimensions (Castaldo & Dagnino, 2009). It is in line with this work to present not only the complexity of the trust concept, but also its role as a moderating and mitigating factor in coopetition.

Firms enter coopetitive relationships when additional benefits from joint action are available (Brandenburger & Nalebuff, 1996). Our study extends this claim by showing that calculating counterparts' benefits breeds trust. The decision to establish coopetition does not rely only on the individual decision-maker's cost-benefits analysis, but also on how she/he perceives the counterparts' economic benefit. Benefit-based trust provides a strong basis for coopetition because it assures involved participants that collaboration is more beneficial to each party than acting opportunistically (Parkhe, 1993).

Our study of coopetition in a mountain tourism destination shows that emotions- and social embeddedness-based trust are not sufficient to initiate coopetition. Without clear benefits for its participants, the relationship would not be established, and if established would rapidly be dissolved. When firms perceive collaboration as beneficial, they look for partners they already know, are connected to by social ties, or with whom they have prior collaborative experience (Granovetter, 1985; Gulati, 1995). Our research shows that coopetition can be established through similar processes. Interestingly, business benefits appear in our study as primary, while social relationships impact the partner selection process. This suggests that emotions-based trust plays a moderating, neither direct nor autonomous role in the trust–coopetition relationship.

Reputation in turn appears as a condition for establishing dyadic coopetition and for the long-term collaborative climate of the community. Our empirical setting involves small communities, where any actor's prior behaviors are widely known. Therefore, a strong desire to preserve good reputation has been noticed. This reflects a propensity to collaborate in the future, even if at present the opportunities are not clear.

The different trust-building mechanisms often appeared together, strengthening one another. However, the use of only a few mechanisms in building trust between the same competitors did not promote the initiation of collaboration if it was not justified by individual economic profits. Also, trust proved to be a dynamic category during the whole process of collaboration. This permanent calculation allowed partners to decide whether to continue or end their collaboration.

Network coopetition data suggest a clearly different relationship with trust. Prior literature seldom differentiated trust between dyadic and network settings. Our study shows that actors underline a number of difficulties in developing benefits-based trust, in using emotions-based trust, and in assessing the motives or competencies of multiple participants in the value network. Interestingly, the assessment logic typically used for dyadic coopetition revealed difficult to perform in network settings. Data access, time, and possibly also the complexity of the task appeared prohibitive in our empirical setting (Czakon & Czernek, 2016). A crucial factor pointed out in our study is third-party legitimation. In establishing collaboration, trust towards an important actor can be transferred to other actors (Oliver, 1990) and to a collaborative project itself. Our study extends prior research by showing that in destination tourism this legitimating role is typically played by local authorities. Interestingly, other network leaders (that is, private businesses) do not enjoy the credibility of a public agent.

Moreover, our study suggests that reputation plays the double role of attracting to the coopetition network both participants to a reputable initiating actor, and reputed participants by the initiating actor (Czakon & Czernek, 2016). Therefore, reputation is a relevant source of trust and conditions the mere possibility of forming network coopetition. We believe that this effect is particularly strong in small communities. However, this mutual reputation attraction can reveal to be exclusive, by always involving the same actors over time. Despite the fact that our data generally display trust in a positive role, it can bring negative results as well. Actors from outside the municipality/region are often excluded from collaboration, even if it would be beneficial. Such a situation has been called over-embeddedness (McLoughlin & Horan, 2002; Rowley, 1997) in prior research, which links it to a number of drawbacks: limited innovativeness, opacity, or structural petrification.

All in all, some general propositions regarding the role of trust in coopetition in tourism can be formulated:

Proposition 1: Dyadic coopetition depends on other sources of trust than network coopetition.

> *Proposition 1a: Benefits-based trust is a condition of entering dyadic coopetition.*
> *Proposition 1b: Emotional trust and reputation-based trust strengthen the role of benefits-based trust in establishing dyadic coopetition.*
> *Proposition 1c: Third-party legitimation is a condition of network coopetition formation.*
> *Proposition 1d: In the absence of benefits, trust is not sufficient for coopetition.*
> *Proposition 1e: Dyadic coopetition is easier than network coopetition formation.*

Proposition 2: Reputation in small communities is important for long-term coopetition.

This last source of trust seems to be typical of small tourist municipalities such as those that we studied. Perhaps that was the reason why reputation was very often declared as a source of trust between competitors in the researched region.

Conclusions

This chapter presents how different trust-building mechanisms help competitors to enter into two types of collaborative relationships—dyads and networks. Those two types of coopetition rely on different trust-building mechanisms, and the same trust-building mechanism impacts dyadic and network coopetition in different ways.

Research on coopetition formation has clear managerial implications. In order to encourage competitors to enter dyadic or network cooperation, different trust-building mechanisms should be used. To encourage a firm to cooperate with one rival (dyadic coopetition), calculative trust is the most important. Thus, the focus should be on the potential benefits of such cooperation, which should be greater than its cost. Moreover, a belief needs to be developed that it is also in the partner's interest not to act opportunistically, i.e., that the cost of opportunistic behavior outweighs its potential benefits. To establish dyadic coopetition the role of partners' reputation, emotional bonds, and social embeddedness cannot be underestimated. Those trust-building mechanisms should therefore be treated by firms as strategic assets that are generated in combination with the perceived benefits of coopetition.

Regarding network coopetition, it is important to use third-party legitimation to encourage entities to join coopetitive networks. In tourist destinations this role can be played by local authorities, or some firm recognized in the local community. Also, partners' reputation—those being the leaders and potential or actual members of such a network—is very important in establishing network coopetition. Partners have to be aware that the benefits of such coopetition usually come in the long term, although its costs have to be borne immediately (calculation-based trust).

Our study breeds further inquiry into the role of trust in coopetition. A fine-grained analysis stratified by the level of coopetition can be followed by stratification by the scope of coopetition. Furthermore, studies focused on trust dynamics relative to the collaborative component versus the competitive component of coopetition may shed more light on trust complexity and dynamics.

Further research of trust's varying role throughout the coopetitive relationship life cycle is needed. Extant research indicates that trust mediates success (Morris et al., 2007), yet our understanding of the mechanisms of trust development, management, and the changing nature of its impact is shallow. Moreover, coopetition involves two different types of trust: one connected with the collaborative part of the relationship, and the other with the competitive part of the relationship. The interplay of those two distinct types of trust remains unclear. In a similar vein, high trust and high dependency have been found to increase coopetition success. However, trust-building mechanisms (Czernek & Czakon, 2016) that allow progress from low or moderate to high levels of trust remain under-researched.

Also, trust is seen as a relational factor impacting inter-firm relationships (Bouncken & Fredrich, 2012). Other relational factors, such as commitment (Morris et al., 2007), dependency, and power (Bouncken & Fredrich, 2012) have been found to interact with trust. Therefore, further research needs to bring the various relational factors into the scope of study in order to better understand trust dynamics and their impact on coopetition performance.

References

Bachmann, R. & Zaheer, A. (2008). Trust in interorganizational relations. In: S. Cropper, M. Ebers, C. Huxham, & P. S. Ring (Eds), *The Oxford Handbook of Inter-organizational Relations* (pp. 533–554). Oxford: Oxford University Press.

Bouncken, R. B. & Fredrich, V. (2012). Coopetition: Performance implications and management antecedents. *International Journal of Innovation Management*, 16(5), 1–28.

Bouncken, R. B., Gast, J., Kraus, S., & Bogers, M. (2015). Coopetition: a systematic review, synthesis, and future research directions. *Review of Managerial Science*, 9(3), 577–601.

Brandenburger, A. M. & Nalebuff, B. J. (1996). *Co-opetition*. New York: Doubleday Currency.

Buskens, V. (1998). The social structure of trust. *Social Networks*, 20(3), 265–289.

Castaldo, S. & Dagnino, G. (2009). Trust and coopetition: the strategic role of trust in interfirm coopetitive dynamics. In: G. Dagnino & E. Rocco (Eds). *Coopetition Strategy: Theory, Experiments and Cases* (pp. 74–100). USA: Routledge.

Chen, M. J., Su, K. H., & Tsai, W. (2007). Competitive tension: The awareness-motivation capability perspective. *Academy of Management Journal*, 50(1), 101–118.

Chiambaretto, P. & Fernandez, A. S. (2016). The evolution of coopetitive and collaborative alliances in an alliance portfolio: the Air France case. *Industrial Marketing Management*, 57, 75–85.

Chin, K. S., Chan, B. L., & Lam, P. K. (2008). Identifying and prioritizing critical success factors for coopetition strategy. *Industrial Management & Data Systems*, 108(4), 437–454.

Claro, D. P. (2008). Managing trust relationships: Calculative, affective, belief and performance. *Brazilian Administration Review*, 5(4), 289–303.

Czakon, W. & Czernek K. (2016). The role of trust-building mechanisms in entering into coopetition: The case of tourism networks in Poland. *Industrial Marketing Management*, 57, 64–74.

Czernek K. & Czakon W. (2016). Trust building processes in tourist coopetition: the case of a Polish region. *Tourism Management*, 52, 380–94.

Dacin, M. T., Oliver, C., & Roy, J. P. (2007). The legitimacy of strategic alliances: An institutional perspective. *Strategic Management Journal*, 28(2), 169–187.

De Wever, S., Martens, R., & Vandenbempt, K. (2005). The impact of trust on strategic resource acquisition through interorganizational networks: Towards a conceptual model. *Human Relations*, 58(12), 1523–1543.

Dollinger, M. J., Golden, P. A., & Saxton, T. (1997). The effect of reputation on the decision to joint venture. *Strategic Management Journal*, 18(2), 127–140.

Doney, P. M. & Cannon, J. P. (1997). An examination of the nature of trust in buyer-seller relationships. *Journal of Marketing*, 61, 35–51.

Fyall, A., Garrod, B., & Wang, Y. (2012). Destination collaboration: A critical review of theoretical approaches to a multi-dimensional phenomenon. *Journal of Destination Marketing & Management*, 1(1), 10–26.

Gnyawali, D. R., He, J., & Madhavan, R. (2006). Impact of co-opetition on firm competitive behavior: An empirical examination. *Journal of Management*, 32(4), 507–530.

Grängsjö, Y. v. F. (2006). Hotel networks and social capital in destination marketing. *International Journal of Service Industry Management*, 17(1), 58–75.

Granovetter, M. (1985). Economic action and social structure. The problem of embeddedness. *American Journal of Sociology*, 93(3), 481–510.

Gulati, R. (1995). Does familiarity breed trust? The implications of repeated ties for contractual choice in alliances. *Academy of Management Journal*, 38(1) 85–112.

Hardin, R. (2006). *Trust*. Cambridge: Polity Press.

Huang, Y. & Wilkinson, I. F. (2013). The dynamics and evolution of trust in business relationships. *Industrial Marketing Management*, 42(3), 455–465.

Hunt, R. (1937). Co-opetition. *Los Angeles Times*, Nov. 20, 4–9.

Le Roy, F. & Czakon, W. (2016), Managing coopetition: the missing link between strategy and performance. *Industrial Marketing Management*, 53, 3–6.

Lewichi R. J., McAllister, D. J., & Bies, R. J. (1998). Trust and distrust: New relationship and realities. *Academy of Management Review*, 23(3), 438–458.

Mariani, M. (2007). Coopetition as an emergent strategy. Empirical evidence from an Italian consortium of opera houses. *International Studies of Management & Organization*, 37(2), 97–126.

McAllister, D. J. (1995). Affect- and cognition-based trust as foundations for interpersonal cooperation in organizations. *Academy of Management Journal*, 38(1), 24–59.

McLoughlin, D. & Horan, C. (2012). Markets-as-networks: Notes on a unique understanding. *Journal of Business Research*, 55(7), 535–543.

Miles, M. B. & Huberman, A. M. (1994). *Qualitative Data Analysis: An Expanded Sourcebook*. California: Sage Publications.

Morgan, R. M. & Hunt, S. D. (1994). The commitment-trust theory of relationship marketing. *Journal of Marketing*, 58, 20–38.

Morris, M. H., Koçak, A., & Ozer, A. (2007). Coopetition as a small business strategy: implications for performance. *Journal of Small Business Strategy*, 18(1), 35–55.

Nielsen, B. B. (2011). Trust in strategic alliances: Toward a co-evolutionary research model. *Journal of Trust Research*, 1(2), 159–176.

Nunkoo, R., Ramkissoon, H., & Gursoy, D. (2012). Public trust in tourism institutions. *Annals of Tourism Research*, 39(3), 1538–1564.

Nunkoo R. & H. Ramkisson (2011), Power, trust, social exchange and community support. *Annals of Tourism Research*, 39(3), 1538–1564.

Oliver, C. (1990). Determinants of interorganizational relationships: Integration and future directions. *Academy of Management Review*, 15(2), 241–265.

Padula, G. & Dagnino, G. (2007), Untangling the rise of coopetition – the intrusion of competition into cooperative game structure. *International Studies of Management and Organization*, 37(2), 32–52.

Parkhe, A. (1993). Strategic alliance structuring: A game theoretic and transaction cost examination of interfirm cooperation. *Academy of Management Journal*, 36(4), 794–829.

Peng, T. J. A., Pike, S., Yang, J. C. H., & Roos, G. (2012). Is cooperation with competitors a good idea? An example in practice. *British Journal of Management*, 23(4), 532–560.

Rowley, T. J. (1997). Moving beyond dyadic ties: A network theory of stakeholder influences. *Academy of Management Review*, 22(4), 887–910.

Sanou, F. H., Le Roy, F., & Gnyawali, D. R. (2016). How does centrality in coopetition networks matter? An empirical investigation in the mobile telephone industry. *British Journal of Management*, 27(1), 143–160.

Selin, S. & Chavez, D. (1995). Developing an evolutionary tourism partnership model. *Annals of Tourism Research*, 22(4), 844–856.

Simmel, G. (1975). *Socjologia*. Warszawa: PWN.

Sztompka, P. (1999). *Trust. A Sociological Theory*. Cambridge: Cambridge University Press.

Tidström, A. (2008). Perspectives on coopetition on actor and operational levels. *Management Research*, 6(3), 207–218.

Tidström, A. (2009). Causes of conflict in intercompetitor cooperation. *Journal of Business & Industrial Marketing*, 24(7), 506–518.

Tidström, A. (2014). Managing tensions in coopetition. *Industrial Marketing Management*, 43(2), 261–271.

Wang, Y. (2008). Collaborative destination marketing understanding the dynamic process. *Journal of travel Research*, 47(2), 151–166.

Wang, Y. & Fesenmaier, D. R. (2007). Collaborative destination marketing: A case study of Elkhart county, Indiana. *Tourism Management*, 28(3), 863–875.

Yamagishi T. & Yamagishi, M. (1994). Trust and commitment in the United States and Japan. *Motivation and Emotion*, 18(2), 126–166.

8

Are competitors the best partners in innovation networks?

Frédéric Le Roy, Frank Lasch, and Marc Robert

Introduction

The literature highlights the relevance of cooperation in the development of innovative products (Belderbos et al., 2004; Fey & Birkinshaw, 2005; Cassiman & Veugelers, 2006; Chesbrough, 2006; Fey & Neyens et al., 2010; Nieto & Santamaria, 2007; Santamaria & Surroca, 2011; Tomlinson, 2010; Yami et al., 2010). Reaching such an objective, firm-level innovation strategy relies more and more on inter-organizational cooperation (Fey & Birkinshaw, 2005). Currently, we observe that product innovations result frequently from inter-firm cooperation, rather than being developed in "isolation" from single firms.

Here, cooperation partners range from public universities to customers, suppliers, competitors, and so on. The literature identifies three main partners in inter-organizational cooperation contexts (Yami et al., 2010): research institutions (public, such as universities, or private); partners that are not considered to be in competition for similar products, services, or markets, such as suppliers or clients (henceforth termed "non-competitors"); and, finally, firms in direct competition (henceforth termed "competitors"). But firms that seek to develop innovation face complexity and struggle to identify the best type of cooperation partner (and in consequence the best cooperation strategy). Entrepreneurs, managers, and other stakeholders consider cooperation with competitors much riskier than engaging with non-competitors. Several reasons lead to this perception, one of which is trust. Trust is often presented as a central dimension of interaction between partners and as essential for cooperation, but more difficult to establish and to maintain with a competitor as cooperation partner (Ritala & Hurmelinna-Laukkanen, 2009). In such a context of simultaneous cooperation and competition, coopetition—the sharing of information, knowledge, and resources—is particularly complex to organize, and trust an important moderator for effective coopetition management.

In consequence, when firms pursuing an innovation strategy engage in coopetition, negative effects of such a complex relationship and inherent difficulties in managing interactions or resource sharing should result in coopetition being less effective as compared to cooperation with non-competitors or more "neutral" partners, such as research institutions. But we see in the literature that most research conducted on inter-organizational cooperation (including coopetition specifically) has difficulty determining the better option in terms of cooperation partner choice.

Some find negative (or, at best, some) effects of coopetition on innovation; others find clearly positive effects of cooperation with non-competitors, including research institutions (Nieto & Santamaria, 2007; Santamaria and Surroca, 2011; Tomlinson, 2010). This leads to the general conclusion that inter-organizational cooperation with non-competitors is the better strategy for firms that seek to develop innovation. However, more and more evidence emerges to challenge this assumption and points to comparable (and positive) effects of both cooperation with non-competitors and coopetition (Belderbos et al., 2004; Neyens et al., 2010). Who is now the better innovation partner: a competitor, a non-competitor, a research institution? In the following we draw on recent empirical studies (Le Roy, Robert, & Lasch, 2016) to provide a more detailed understanding of the opportunities, risks, and challenges in the choice of a cooperation partner.

Inter-firm cooperation and innovation

Literature stresses the importance of inter-firm cooperation for economic performance of organizations in general and technological innovation in particular (Cassiman & Veugelers, 2006). Aside from tangible complementary assets, intangible resources such as knowledge or information exchange about new customer needs and novel techniques for the development of products and services are part of interactions between cooperating firms. In consequence, inter-firm cooperation is part of today's innovative firm strategy as it increases organizational flexibility, knowledge absorption, and learning capacity. Another advantage of inter-firm cooperation is the alleviation of complex coordination often observed in firms with high levels of hierarchy (Belderbos et al., 2004).

For innovative firms, innovation networks are a particularly interesting form of inter-firm cooperation (Belderbos et al., 2004; Brandenburger & Nalebuff, 1996; Neyens et al., 2010; Nieto & Santamaria, 2007; Tomlinson, 2010; Yami et al., 2010). In particular, network relations with heterogeneous partners increase the capacity of organizations to develop new, innovative products or services.

Further advantages of cooperation are a better management of uncertainty in today's rapidly changing economies and markets thanks to a higher (and thus more current and relevant) knowledge exchange between cooperating firms (Belderbos et al., 2004; Cassiman & Veugelers, 2006; Fey and Birkinshaw, 2005). Shared knowledge is central in innovation-driven and entrepreneurial economies to reach economies of scale. Such exchange of knowledge and resources creates synergy, facilitates organizational learning, and leads ultimately to new, complementary, assets. In the following, we will review the advantages and risks of cooperation by distinguishing between different cooperation partners in general (Section 1.1), and by including the dimension of competition in inter-firm relations, in particular (Section 1.2).

The absence of competition in inter-firm cooperation

We distinguish two completely different situations in inter-firm cooperation. In the first, on which we focus in this section, the firms engaged in cooperation are non-competitors or public/private research institutions, meaning they do not compete in the same markets. Here, the purpose of cooperation is to overcome resource scarcity and inability to independently create an innovative product or service by combining firm-specific competencies and resources. From a theoretical viewpoint, the literature describes the absence of competition as the central element for the necessary development of trust between cooperation partners. Trust helps engagement in cooperation, is necessary to sustain cooperation, and ultimately leads to intensified cooperation (Whitley, 2002). Inter-firm cooperation under such conditions is regarded as particularly effective in achieving common innovation projects because the firms involved share knowledge, information, competencies, skills, and other sets of resources in a spirit of trusting interaction with the objective to reach a common goal.

In the present section we define the absence of competition as an inter-organizational cooperation with a non-competing firm or a public/private research institution. Hereby, the cooperating firms also draw resources from their respective innovation networks, which bring additional technology-combining value to the cooperation. Two network types can be considered here. The first one is termed "upstream," as it covers value chain sections of the production phase. Typically, here, network partners are suppliers. Other upstream relations can be of commercial nature (transactional types) that can ultimately evolve into formalized inter-firm cooperation. An example for such a relation is the sharing of technology resources with universities. The second network type is termed "downstream" as it refers to the market (customer needs, product/service innovation opportunities, etc.). Both cooperation types, in the absence of competition, both upstream and downstream, are considered facilitators to step across the boundaries set between a firm and its environment (Chesbrough, 2006). Here mutual innovation flows are important and in consequence, whether aware of it or not, firms "outsource" innovation. At this point, cooperation also means managing innovation in an open innovation system.

In the following we highlight some differences between cooperating with upstream (suppliers, customers) and downstream cooperation partners. For further illustration, we summarize results from an empirical study (Le Roy et al., 2016).

Cooperation with suppliers and customers

The first "upstream" (or "vertical") cooperation partners of a firm are suppliers and customers. Reviewing the literature, at first glance the effects of upstream cooperation are relatively consistent across studies and conclude overall a positive impact on product innovation. Upstream cooperation positively influences: (i) the intention of a firm to introduce new products (Miotti & Sachwald, 2003); (ii) the likelihood of introducing new products (Arranz & Arroyabe, 2008); (iii) the ability to achieve high levels of novelty (Nieto and Santamaria, 2007); (iv) the general innovation performance of a firm (Neyens et al., 2010; Tomlinson, 2010); and (v) the frequency of product innovation (Santamaria & Surroca, 2011).

Overall, most studies conclude that cooperation with suppliers has higher effects as compared to cooperation with customers. Only, when we analyze suppliers and customers separately, the results are much more mixed. In the literature, we observe that the effects of cooperation with suppliers are much less straightforward than for cooperation with customers (Belderbos et al., 2004; Neyens et al., 2010; Nieto & Santamaria, 2007; Santamaria & Surroca, 2011; Tomlinson, 2010). Some conclude in positive effects, some in negative ones, others do not find any effects at all. In particular, negative or null effects are explained by asymmetric consequences of inter-firm cooperation: suppliers benefit more from cooperation as their products encounter higher levels of improvement as compared to those of the partner firm. However, improving the products of the supplier is potentially a good strategy for the partner firm to improve its own products—but the impact is not linear. Only if a firm has sufficient financial resources to fund both the innovation of its supplier and its own, upstream cooperation becomes relevant and results in positive effects. If financial resources are limited, allocating resources to improve the product of the supplier could lead to asymmetric benefits, as described above.

Cooperation with research institutions

The second type of cooperation, which we label "downstream" (or "vertical"), is often conducted with research institutions. In part, as a result of government actions, cooperation with research institutions has been growing very strongly in recent years. Such cooperation can take various forms, ranging from a simple attempt to capture knowledge informally to highly formalized cooperation (Monjon & Waelbroeck, 2003). The informal way is relevant for firms that focus on imitation of technology strategy to develop incremental innovations. In contrast, the formalization of cooperation seems a necessity for firms aiming to develop more radical innovation.

If we look at the outcomes of cooperation with research institutions, literature concludes generally on positive effects such as: (i) a higher ability to conduct innovation product research and development at technological frontiers (Miotti & Sachwald, 2003); (ii) a higher propensity for the development of patents (Miotti & Sachwald, 2003); (iii) a higher level of novelty in product innovation (Nieto & Santamaria, 2007); (iv) a positive effect on the growth of innovative sales per employee (Belderbos et al., 2004); and (v) performance of radical innovation (Neyens et al., 2010).

Similar to the "upstream"-type cooperation examples discussed above, while at first sight the literature finds overall consistent (and positive) effects of cooperation with research institutions, some evidence points to a more complex picture and reports negative effects on product innovation performance (Caloghirou et al., 2004; Monjon & Waelbroeck, 2003). This is explained by the fact that cooperation strategies with universities do not impact all involved actors in the same way (Mohen & Hoareau, 2003). In particular, firm size effects are to be considered in assessing the effects (or the value) of cooperating with research institutions. Large firms take often greater benefit from such cooperation than small ones. Having a more powerful economic imprint and legitimacy, they possess more resources to allocate to the formalization of contracts, the search for public funding and support, etc. Large firms obtain comparatively higher government support for patent development. In contrast, cooperation between small and medium-sized enterprises (SMEs) and public research institutions such as universities is less frequent, and in consequence benefits less from public support. This is one explanation why the effect on SME product innovation when cooperating with research institutions is lower as compared to large firms in cooperation (Mohen & Hoareau, 2003).

Main empirical findings for cooperation with non-competitors
We present here a summary of the main empirical findings of the literature on inter-organizational cooperation under absence of competition between partners. Focusing on innovation as one of the most important motives to engage in inter-firm cooperation, our review of the literature found, taken together, mostly positive effects when firms join to develop new innovative products or services (Table 8.1). We found evidence for both "upstream" (vertical) and "downstream" (horizontal) types of cooperation. Upstream cooperation was found to increase, for example, firm innovation performance (Tomlinson, 2010), frequency of product innovation (Santamaria & Surroca, 2011), novelty in innovation (Nieto & Santamaria (2007), and labor productivity (Belderbos et al., 2004). With respect to cooperation intensity over time, Neyens et al. (2010) found that occasional cooperation increases incremental innovation performance, while regular cooperation favors radical innovation performance. Similar results for downstream cooperation (with research institutions) were found (Kang & Kang, 2010) for product innovation in general, and in particular for labor productivity (Belderbos et al., 2004) and novelty (Nieto & Santamaria, 2007).

The presence of competition in inter-firm cooperation: Cooperation with competitors

The second situation of cooperation we consider is when firms cooperate but also compete, meaning they compete simultaneously in the same markets. Here, the firms engaged in cooperation are competitors. Termed coopetition, such a relationship involves firms that offer a similar

Table 8.1 Main findings of selected literature

Author(s)	Topic	Sample	Results
Miotti & Sachwald (2003)	Drivers and impact of cooperative R&D	CIS France (1994–1996)	Positive effect of vertical coop. on propensity to introduce new products; coop. with public institutions increase capability of high-end technological research, patents; no effect of coop. with rivals.
Belderbos, Carree, & Lokshin (2004)	R&D cooperation and performance	CIS Dutch (1996, 1998)	Positive effect of coop. with suppliers and competitors on labour productivity; positive effect of coop. with competitors and research institutes on of innovative sales per employee
Arranz & Arroyabee (2007)	Partner choice in R&D cooperation	CIS Spain 1997–1998	Positive effect of vertical coop. with clients and suppliers on the probability of sharing innovative products in turnover
Nieto & Santamaria (2007)	Coop. networks and innovation	Spanish firms	Positive effect of coop. with suppliers, customers, research institutions on novel innovation; positive effect of coop. with competitors
Tomlinson (2010)	Coop. ties and innovation performance	436 firms (UK)	Pos. effect of vertical cooperation on innovation performance; Some positive effects of coop. horizontal relationships
Neyens, Faems, & Sels (2010)	Continuous/ dis-continuous coop. on innovation performance	217 Finnish start-up firms	Pos. effect of discontinuous coop. with suppliers, customers and competitors on incr. innovation perf.; Pos. effect of continuous coop. with suppliers, customers, competitors, research institutes on radical innovation perf.
Kang & Kang (2010)	R&D coop. and product innovation	Korean Innovation Survey	Positive effect of R&D coop. with customers and universities on product innovation; inverted-U-shape relationship of R&D coop. with suppliers and customers on product innovation
Un, Cuervo-Cazurra,, & Asakawa (2010)	R&D cooperation and product innovation	Manu-facturing firms	Highest effect of R&D coop. with suppliers on product innovation, followed by coop. with universities; no effect of coop. with consumers; negative effect of coop. with competitors
Santamaria & Surroca (2011)	Impact of R&D cooperation on innovation	1300 Spanish firms	Vertical coop. increases frequency of product/process innovation, horizontal does not; horizontal coop. has no or negative effect on innovation outcomes

(Source: adapted and completed from Le Roy et al., 2016.)

product for the same type of customer or a similar market (Le Roy & Fernandez, 2015). It describes a paradoxical situation in the sense that (i) cooperation partners also compete; (ii) such organizational behavior, which oscillates between two contradictory elements (cooperation and competition), does not lead to lower levels of competition between the firms involved; and (iii) desired outcomes are beneficial to both partners (albeit in competition).

For these reasons, from a theoretical and practical perspective, coopetition challenges common-sense and habitual business practice. In the past, the protection of resources, knowledge, competencies, and skills kept within organizational boundaries has been considered a necessary condition for successful competition with rival firms. But in the current economy, we observe that cooperation between competitors is more and more common practice, in particular in innovation- and knowledge-intense industries. Paradoxically, in such contexts, the "best" cooperation partner is the one who develops similar or complementary products (often for the same market). In consequence, the "best" cooperation partner is the "worst" opponent and the most dangerous competitor, but in the end also the most attractive partner (Hamel et al., 1989; Hamel, 1991).

Compared to cooperation in the absence of competition, asymmetric risks are multiplied in coopetition, because such relationships can lead to strengthening a competitor and weakening a firm's own position (information, knowledge, resource leakages, etc.). This risk is omnipresent in coopetition and hard to avoid, as too-high protection barriers would affect collaborative work, endanger a common innovation project, and result in the failure of the cooperation with the competitor. In contrast, a firm that intends to speed up the common innovation process will be forced to increase the risk of "openness" *viz.* the transfer of resources and competencies (Pellegrin-Boucher et al., 2013).

If the risk of transferring resources and knowledge is of hypothetical order (and easy to control) in inter-firm cooperation in the absence of competition, it is real (and hard to control) in a context of coopetition. Naturally, competing with a rival firm tends to use the common knowledge created to improve a firm's own competitiveness. We normally expect that this difference between cooperation in situations of absence and of presence of competition should make coopetition less effective.

In a coopetition context, required elements that create the value of cooperation, such as trust and knowledge-sharing, are much more difficult to establish (Fernandez et al., 2014). Finding the right balance (Park et al., 2014) of knowledge exchange versus protection and trust versus caution appears to be more complex, risky, and could render cooperation less efficient. Therefore, common sense would expect that coopetition (as compared to inter-firm cooperation with non-competitors) should lead to lower innovation performance.

But surprisingly, we find little support for this assumption in literature. On the contrary, empirical studies investigating the effects of coopetition on outcomes of inter-organizational cooperation reveal a quite mixed picture. The first group argues that coopetition has negative (or at best, any) effects on cooperation (Nieto & Santamaria, 2007; Santamaria & Surroca, 2011). On the opposite, a second stream finds that coopetition has a much less negative effect on outcomes of cooperation such as innovation or firm growth than depicted by the first stream. Authors belonging to this line of thinking often find clearly measurable positive effects. Kang & Kang (2010), for example, observe inverted U-shaped effects when competing firms join together in R&D projects to develop new innovative products or services. Others find that coopetition is positive for the innovation performance in general of the involved partners (Tomlinson, 2010), the labor productivity of employees involved in coopetition-based projects (Belderbos et al., 2004), and Neyens et al. (2010) conclude that a link exists between coopetition intensity over time and the nature of innovation. Here, ongoing coopetition is found to be beneficial for radical innovation performance and occasional or disruptive coopetition leading to incremental innovations.

The contradictory nature of evidence on the effects of coopetition has resulted in a lively discussion about which measure to use to assess coopetition outcomes. In this debate, more and more of a distinction is made between incremental and radical innovation in order to better shape out the effects of coopetition on innovation. Using this lens, empirical evidence draws a fairly nuanced picture. Overall, literature points to the idea that coopetition is rather positive when the aim of the cooperation is incremental innovation. Or in other words, coopetition might be a cooperation strategy that is easier to manage when desired innovation levels are moderate (incremental). This is the argument of Nieto & Santamaria (2007); they conclude that cooperating with a competitor is incompatible when radical innovation is at the heart of the relationship. In line with this, Ritala & Sainio (2014) find a negative effect on technological radicalness, but a positive effect on business-model radicalness. While this stream of literature describes coopetition as a good strategy for incremental innovation, another stream claims the opposite. Again, distinguishing between different levels of innovation intensity (or quality), Bouncken & Kraus (2013) argue that coopetition is useful to achieve radical innovation (but dangerous for highly novel revolutionary innovation). Looking at time-related dimensions and the evolution of coopetitive relationships, Bouncken et al. (2017) observe positive effects on incremental innovation in the early stages of cooperation (pre-launch and launch phases), and some positive effects on radical innovation (but only in later stages, such as the launch phase).

Who is the best coopetition partner? A contingency approach

Cooperation partner type and location

In sum, the literature presents contradictory evidence of coopetition on (i) the outcomes of such a relationship (positive versus negative); and (ii) the nature of innovation as the most frequent aim of such a relationship (incremental versus radical innovation). While our understanding of coopetition as a good or a bad strategy (depending on specific contexts) is increasing, the question of who is the best partner in a competitive relationship remains to be further addressed.

To move in this direction and to shed more light on the crucial question of the best coopetition partner choice, we draw upon the literatures about cooperation in situations under the absence of competition (Section 1.1) and recent empirical work we conducted on the crossroad of the type of coopetition partner and the type of innovation. In the latter, we adopted a contingency approach by introducing new, contextual variables (geographical scope of cooperation/coopetition, type of partners, firm size).

The first study investigates effects of coopetition on innovation outcomes (radical versus incremental) by controlling for different types of cooperation partners. The second study refines the results by introducing firm size as a new dimension to advance our understanding of the coopetition process, the involved firms (partner choice), and innovation as an outcome of coopetition strategy. Taken together, we formulate recommendations for practitioners and policy.

In the following section, we summarize the main results of our analysis of coopetition strategies and their effects on innovation, by discriminating between the types of partner with whom such cooperation is established.

First, we look at inter-firm cooperation in situations of competition (coopetition) and the effects of simultaneous cooperation and competition on innovation (incremental versus radical). Here the primary focus was on the geographical scope of the partnership (location of the competitor). Overall, we find the following pattern (Table 8.2):

(i)   Coopetition, independent of the location of the competing firm, does not show any effect on incremental innovation;

Table 8.2 Cooperation depending on location and type of partner

	Radical Innovation	Incremental Innovation
Cooperation with competitors (location)		
In the same region	-	ns
In other regions of France	ns	ns
In Europe	+++	ns
In North America	+++	ns
In Asia	ns	ns
Cooperation with non-competitors (types)		
Firms of a company group network	ns	ns
Suppliers	-	ns
Customers	+++	+++
Private R&D	ns	ns
Public universities	+++	+++
Public R&D institutions	+	ns
Control variables		
Number of employees	+++	+++
Network membership	-	--
Company group membership	+	+++
Absorptive capacity	ns	ns
External technology/knowledge	ns	ns

(-/+) $p < 0.05$, (--/++) $p < 0.01$, (---/+++) $p < 0.001$.

(Source: adapted from Le Roy et al., 2016.)

(ii) We find some effects of coopetition on radical innovation, but only for international cooperation (North America and Europe).

Second, we look at inter-firm cooperation in the absence of competition and the effects on innovation (incremental versus radical). Here the primary focus was on the type of cooperation partner (networked firms, suppliers, customers, and research institutions). Overall, we find the following pattern (Table 8.2):

(i) Cooperation with customers has comparatively the greatest effect on both incremental and radical innovation;
(ii) Cooperation with public universities proves generally positive for both incremental and radical innovation;
(iii) Cooperation with research institutions (public and private) has no or little effect on both incremental and radical innovation;
(iv) Surprisingly, cooperation with suppliers reveals to be negative for radical innovation and has no effect on incremental innovation.

As a conclusion, the best choice of cooperation partner we identified in our sample is the following: if the objective of the cooperation is to achieve incremental innovation, the best partner choices are customers or public universities. If radical innovation is the aim, customers and universities also stand out as excellent cooperation partners. If cooperation is engaged with a competitor, only international partners in innovation-driven economies are relevant choices (North America and Europe, in our case).

Inter-firm cooperation and the effects of firm size

The findings of the first study underline the relevance of using a contingency approach by introducing new variables in the debate about value, opportunities, and risks of inter-firm cooperation (in presence of competition or not). We continue to advance our understanding of cooperation by using another, currently little-explored, context variable: firm size. Does firm size influence the relationship between cooperation/coopetition and innovation (Le Roy et al., 2015)? Current knowledge argues that coopetition could be a "double-edged sword," in particular for small firms (Bouncken & Fredrich, 2012). The reason for this view is the resource scarcity typical for small firms (Miller et al., 2007; van Gils & Zwart, 2009). Such firms try to overcome size-related constraints through cooperation to increase competitiveness, to create synergies and to obtain complementary resources (Eikebrokk & Olsen, 2007; Lechner & Leyronas, 2009). One risk of cooperating with a larger counter-partner is power asymmetry (Dussauge et al., 2000). According to this line of thinking, we suggest that effects of cooperation/coopetition are different across firm size (small versus large firms). Using a similar approach and the identical database as for our previous study, our main results are the following:

(i) Cooperation with customers has a positive effect on innovation both for small and large firms (the positive effect being stronger for small firms);
(ii) Cooperation with public research institutions and universities has a positive effect on innovation for large firms, but we find no measurable effects for small firms;
(iii) Cooperation with suppliers has no effect for large firms and a negative effect for small firms;
(iv) Coopetition has a positive effect on innovation for small firms, but we find no effects for large firms.

Taken together, our findings suggest that small firms benefit from cooperation when the cooperation partner is close to the market (customers, competitors). In contrast, we observe that public universities and suppliers are not a good choice for small firms. Large firms benefit from cooperation when the small firm is distant from the market. Overall, we present evidence for the assumption that effects of different types of partners on firm-level innovation differs across firm size.

Conclusion

We provide some new insights for the crucial question of who could be the most relevant innovation partner for inter-firm cooperation. But this question remains to be addressed further, and is still more or less "open." Reviewing the evidence of our latest empirical work, cooperation with non-competitors and/or research institutions appears to be the less risky and potentially the most fruitful. But again, our findings were not fully conclusive to definitively answer this question. For example, the literature stresses the importance of cooperating with customers; we could confirm this. But we found mixed argument for cooperating with universities, and more-than-controversial results for suppliers. Depending on the empirical design, the effects of cooperating with a competitor seem very risky at the least, damaging at the worst, but sometimes we find positive effects and sometimes we do not find any support at all for benefits or risks of coopetition.

However, introducing contingency variables improves our understanding of coopetition. The first one we used was the location of the competitor. In the French sample, cooperating with national competitors showed a negative effect, but international cooperation led to positive effects (in particular North American and European firms). The effects of coopetition also depended on firm size. Here, we identified that coopetition is a good strategy for small firms, but not for large ones.

Overall, from a methodological viewpoint, we recommend further use of the contingency approach to help firms identify the best cooperation partner. In particular, geographical location and firm size proved their usefulness. But other contingency variables measuring external factors should also have an effect (technological intensity, industry convergence, product type, market size, etc.). Some internal factors could also be important to study, such as internal R&D funding, openness to the cooperation partner, market power of firms engaged in cooperation/coopetition, etc. More research is needed to move into this direction and to replicate our work.

New research could investigate, for example, how partner choice impacts processes and outcomes of innovation. Intuitively, cooperation and competition are considered paradoxical situations, difficult to combine in order to create value. Therefore, two firms should engage in cooperation only if they are not competing in the same markets or for the same products. Considered the best cooperation partner choices are non-competitors (customers, suppliers, research institutions). But this view—dictated by common sense—does not match with examples of successful coopetition, such as the Samsung–Sony case (Gnyawali and Park, 2011). In consequence, we need to advance our understanding to be able to explain why cooperation with competitors can be so fruitful. In return, we also need to improve our knowledge to understand why cooperation in the absence of competition does not result in mutual benefits (and, in consequence, forces firms to seek cooperation with competitors).

According to conventional views, cooperation with non-competitors appears to be the less-risky strategy. Here, cooperation partners do not compete in the same markets, and should in consequence face no barriers for full cooperation. But as we have shown, this view does not resist empirical scrutiny. First, vertical cooperation partners possess different knowledge and skills that might not combine into sufficient opportunities to reach economies of scale (which are in general the result of the combination of similar or complementary assets). Second, different knowledge and skills limit the potential to exploit the opportunity of cross-fertilization. For successful cross-fertilization, combined knowledge and skills should be different, but not *too* different. If the differences are not significant, there is little chance that value-added creativity can be reached. If they are too strong, the combination of skills might prove difficult to obtain. This could explain the poor effects of cooperation with vertical partners (and little opportunity to take the full potential of cross-fertilization). This is also true for cooperation with public universities.

In contrast, coopetition as a specific type of inter-firm cooperation can lead to immense opportunities. The competing firms involved target the same market and possess similar knowledge, skills, "language" (organizational culture), technologies, etc. to fully exploit such opportunities. Theoretically, they can relatively easily cooperate to create scale effects. For example, if they have the same purchases in nature and processes, they can better obtain the most competitive prices in placing shared orders. In the same vein, R&D or production costs can be lowered through cooperation. Similar knowledge of competing firms also facilitates working together on an operational, everyday basis. They can combine their close (but not fully identical) knowledge to create new products or services and take full potential of cross-fertilization.

As a conclusion, if coopetition opportunities are high, coopetition risks are also high. Coopetition for innovation could result in spectacular success, as the Samsung–Sony case suggests (Gnyawali and Park, 2011), but creates at the same time an immense risk of knowledge and resource leakage (to be potentially exploited or not by the cooperating firm). This explains why in literature and in practice coopetition leads to sometimes positive and sometimes negative outcomes. The questions to be further addressed are the following: under which conditions does coopetition lead to powerful alliances and highly fruitful outcomes, and under which conditions is it dangerous for the involved firms? Under which conditions is cooperation a better strategy than coopetition (with non-competitors, research institutions, etc.)? For a deeper understanding of coopetition as a potentially powerful strategy, future research is called to address these questions.

References

Arranz, N. & Arroyabe, J. C. (2008). The choice of partners in R&D cooperation: An empirical analysis of Spanish firms. *Technovation*, 28, 88–100.

Belderbos, R., M. Carree, & B. Lokshin. (2004). Cooperative R&D and firm performance. *Research Policy* 33 (10): 1477–1492.

Belderbos, R., M. Carree, & B. Lokshin. (2006). Complementarity in R&D cooperation strategies. *Review of Industrial Organization* 28 (4): 401–426.

Bengtsson, M. & S. Kock. (1999). Cooperation and competition in relationships between competitors in business networks. *Journal of Business and Industrial Marketing* 14: 178–190.

Bengtsson, M. & S. Kock. (2000). Coopetition in business networks – to cooperate and compete simultaneously. *Industrial Marketing Management* 29: 411–426.

Bengtsson M. & S. Kock. (2014). Coopetition-Quo vadis? Past accomplishments and future challenges. *Industrial Marketing Management* 43 (2): 180–188.

Bouncken, R. B. & V. Fredrich. (2012). Coopetition: performance implications and management antecedents. *International Journal of Innovation Management* 16 (5): 12500.281–12500.2828.

Bouncken, R. B. & S. Kraus (2013). Innovation in knowledge-intensive industries: The double-edged sword of coopetition. *Journal of Business Research*, 66(10), 2060–2070.

Bouncken, R., Fredrich, V., Ritala, P., & S. Kraus (2017). Coopetition in new product development alliances – Advantages and tensions for incremental and radical innovation. *British Journal of Management*.

Brandenburger, A. & B. Nalebuff (1996). *Co-opetition*. New York: Doubleday.

Caloghirou, Y., Kastelli, I., & A. Tsakanikas. (2004). Internal capabilities and external knowledge sources: complements or substitutes for innovative performance? *Technovation*, 24(1): 29–39.

Cassiman, B. & R. Veugelers. (2006). In search of complementarity in innovation strategy: internal R&D and external knowledge acquisition. *Management Science* 52: 68–82.

Chesbrough, H. (2003). *Open Innovation: The New Imperative for Creating and Profiting from Technology*. Boston: Harvard Business School Press Books.

Chesbrough, H. (2006). *Open Business Models: How to Thrive in the New Innovation Landscape*. Boston: Harvard Business School Press Books.

Chesbrough, H. (2012). Open innovation. *Research Technology Management* 55: 20–27.

Chesbrough, H. & S. Brunswickerm. (2014). A fad or a phenomenon? The adoption of open innovation practices in large firms. *Research Technology Management* 57: 16–25.

Dussauge, P., Garrette, B., & W. Mitchell. (2000). Learning from competing partners: Outcome and durations of scale and link alliances in Europe, North America and Asia. *Strategic Management Journal* 21(2): 99–126.

Eikebrokk, T. R. & D. H. Olsen. (2007). An empirical investigation of competency factors affecting e-business success in European SMEs. *Information & Management* 44: 364–383.

Fernandez, A.-S., F. Le Roy, & D. Gnyawali. (2014). Sources and management of tension in coopetition case evidence from telecommunications satellites manufacturing in Europe. *Industrial Marketing Management* 43: 222–235.

Fey, C. F. & J. Birkinshaw. (2005). External sources of knowledge, governance mode, and R&D performance. *Journal of Management* 31: 597–621.

Gnyawali D. R., J. He, & R. Madhavan. (2008). Co-opetition: Promises and challenges. In C. Wankel (Ed.), *21st Century Management*. Thousand Oaks, CA, 386–398.

Gnyawali, D. R. & B. J. Park. (2011). Co-opetition between giants: Collaboration with competitors for technological innovation. *Research Policy* 40: 650–663.

Hamel, G. (1991). Competition for competence and inter-partner learning within international strategic alliances. *Strategic Management Journal* 12: 83–104.

Hamel, G., Y. Doz, & C. K. Prahalad. (1989). Collaborate with your competitors and win. *Harvard Business Review* 67: 133–139.

Kang, K. H. & J. Kang. (2010). Does partner type matter in R&D collaboration for product innovation? *Technology Analysis and Management* 22 (8): 945–959.

Kwanghui L., H. Chesbrough, & R. Yi. (2010). Open innovation and patterns of R&D competition. *International Journal of Technology Management* 52: 295–321.

Lechner C. & C. Leyronas. (2009). Small-business group formation as an entrepreneurial development model. *Entrepreneurship Theory and Practice* 33(3): 645–667.

Le Roy, F. & A.-S. Fernandez. (2015). Managing coopetitive tensions at the working-group level: The rise of the Coopetitive Project Team. *British Journal of Management* 26: 671–688.

Le Roy, F., M. Robert, & P. Chiambaretto. (2015). Size matters: When small and large firms look for the best partners to innovate. *EURAM 15th Conference*, Warsaw, Poland.

Le Roy, F., M. Robert, & F. Lasch. (2016). Choosing the best partner for product innovation: Talking to the enemy or to a friend? *International Studies of Management Organisation* 46: 136–158.

Miller, N. J., T. Besser, & A. Malshe. (2007). Strategic networking among small businesses in small US communities. *International Small Business Journal* 256: 631–665.

Miotti, L. & F. Sachwald. (2003). Co-operative R&D: why and with whom?: An integrated framework of analysis. *Research Policy*, 32(8): 1481–1499.

Mohen, P. & C. Hoareau. (2003). What type of enterprise forges close links with universities and government labs? Evidence from CIS 2. *Managerial and Decision Economics*, 24(2/3): 133–146.

Monjon S. & P. Waelbroeck. (2003). Assessing spillovers from universities to firms: evidence from French firm-level data. *International Journal of Industrial Organization*, 21(9): 1255–1270.

Neyens, I., D. Faems, & L. Sels. (2010). The impact of continuous and discontinuous alliance strategies on start-up innovation performance. *International Journal of Technology Management* 52: 392–410.

Nieto, M. J. & L. Santamaria. (2007). The importance of diverse collaborative networks for the novelty of product innovation. *Technovation* 27: 367–377.

Park, B. J. R., M. K. Srivastava, & D. R. Gnyawali. (2014). Walking the tight rope of coopetition: Impact of competition and cooperation intensities and balance on firm innovation performance. *Industrial Marketing Management* 43: 210–224.

Pellegrin-Boucher, E., F. Le Roy, & C. Gurau. (2013). Coopetitive strategies in the ICT sector: typology and stability. *Technology Analysis & Strategic Management* 25(1): 71–89.

Ritala, P. & L.-M. Sainio. (2014). Coopetition for radical innovation: technology, market and business-model perspectives. *Technology Analysis & Strategic Management*, 26(2): 155–169.

Ritala, P. & P. Hurmelinna-Laukkanen. (2009). What's in it for me? Creating and appropriating value in innovation related coopetition. *Technovation* 29: 819–828.

Santamaria, L. & J. Surroca. (2011). Matching the goals and impacts of R&D collaboration. *European Management Review* 8: 95–109.

Tomlinson, P. R. (2010). Co-operative ties and innovation: some new evidence for UK manufacturing. *Research Policy* 39: 762–775.

Tsai, K. H. (2009). Collaborative networks and product innovation performance: toward a contingency perspective. *Research Policy* 38 (5): 765–778.

Van Gils, A. & P. S. Zwart. (2009). Alliance formation motives in SMEs: An explorative conjoint analysis study. *International Small Business Journal* 27(1): 5–37.

West, J., A. Salter, W. Vanhaverbeke, & H. Chesbrough. (2014). Open innovation: The next decade. *Research Policy* 43(5): 805–811.

Whitley, R. (2002). Developing innovative competences: the role of institutional frameworks. *Industrial and Corporate Change* 11: 497–528.

Yami, S., S. Castaldo, G. B. Dagnino, F. Le Roy, & W. Czakon. (2010). Introduction – coopetition strategies: towards a new form of interorganizational dynamics? In *Coopetition: Winning Strategies for the 21st Century*, ed. S. Yami, S. Castaldo, G. B. Dagnino, and F. Le Roy (Eds) (1–16). Cheltenham, UK; Northampton, MA: Edward Elgar.

9

The role of policy makers and regulators in coopetition

Marcello Mariani

Introduction

Nowadays economic actors (individuals and organizations) are confronted with unprecedented levels of uncertainty and complexity stemming from an increasingly fast-changing and turbulent global environment. To address both uncertainty and complexity, they might decide to simultaneously compete and cooperate, thus engaging in a paradoxical relationship wherein "regardless of whether they are in horizontal or vertical relationships, [they are] simultaneously involved in cooperative and competitive interactions." (Bengtsson & Kock, 2014: 182).

The simultaneous pursuit of cooperation and competition, termed coopetition (Brandenburger & Nalebuff, 1996; Brandenburger & Stuart, 1996), is a challenging endeavor, which brings entrepreneurs and firms to juxtapose conflicting interests and common interests, and deal with the resulting tensions (Bengtsson & Kock, 2014; Fernandez et al., 2014).

Management scholars in a number of different disciplinary fields (including strategy, marketing, innovation management, supply chain management, operations, etc.) are closely studying coopetition, its multifaceted manifestations, and related issues in a number of different empirical settings and by leveraging a variety of theoretical lenses and methodological approaches. Accordingly, recent systematic literature reviews have shown an exponential growth in the number of scientific works pertaining to coopetition (Bengtsson et al., 2013; Czakon et al., 2014).

So far, a relatively limited amount of studies have dealt with how coopetition and coopetitive interactions are triggered, inhibited and affected by external institutional stakeholders (for a review see Bengtsson & Raza-Ullah, 2016). Among those, an even smaller part has addressed the role of policy makers and regulators in triggering and affecting coopetitive interactios. To this aim, this chapter is intended as a critical synthesis of selected research around the role played by policy makers and regulators in affecting coopetition. The critical overview, far from being a comprehensive literature review, builds mainly on the author's previous extensive work on the topic and on other relevant contributions. In the ensuing section, we provide a demarcation of the drivers of coopetition, with a focus on external drivers and especially external stakeholders. We enrich this discussion with a reflection on aspects related to intentionality versus unintentionality of the focal coopeting actors when policy makers or regulators shape an institutional environment that can promote, hinder or generally affect coopetition. In section three, we review the studies that have mostly dealt with the role of policy makers and regulators in triggering and affecting coopetition, and discuss and critically re-elaborate their findings in view of roles played and desired objectives. In the fourth section, we draw several conclusions and reflect on what we currently know (and do not know) about the role of policy makers and regulators in coopetition.

The role of intentionality and external stakeholders in driving coopetition

Intentional and unintended strategies

Strategy and strategizing can be either intentional or unintentional. While the mainstream strategy literature is concerned mostly with deliberate strategies, a minority of contributions have emphasized and theorized that the process of strategy formation can be characterized in some instances by a relative lack of intentionality (Mintzberg, 1978; Mintzberg & McHugh, 1985; Mintzberg & Waters 1982). In the footsteps of Mintzberg, strategy can be defined as "a pattern in a stream of decisions" (1978: 935). Accordingly, strategies can at first sight be clustered into two main groups: deliberate strategies (i.e., strategies that might be realized more or less as previously intended) and emergent strategies (i.e., strategies that might be realized differently and despite ex-ante intentions) (Mintzberg & Waters, 1985). In theory, a perfectly emergent strategy implies that there must be "order in the absence of intention" about it (Mintzberg & Waters, 1985: 2). However, the assumptions behind the perfectly emergent and perfectly deliberate strategies appear extreme and somehow rare, thus suggesting that both the purely emergent and deliberate strategies are the conceptual extremes of a continuum along which real strategies typically fall (Mintzberg & Waters, 1985).

In most of the literature dealing with coopetition, the units of analysis are typically the actors involved in the coopetitive relationship (focal coopeting actors) and there is an underlying assumption that coopetition is somehow deliberately planned by the coopeting actors due to the risks involved in cooperating with a competitor (Pellegrin-Boucher et al., 2013; Tidström, 2008).

However, in many real-world contexts, there are external factors (i.e., political, social, economic, and technological) and stakeholders (i.e., policy makers and regulators) that might set the scene for how economic actors engage in coopetitive interactions during the formation and the development stages of the strategy lifecycle. In certain situations, the very same rules of the game could be modified by regulatory changes (Czakon & Rogalski, 2014; Depeyre & Dumez, 2010; Mariani, 2007), over which individual economic actors have little or no control.

More specifically, a particular subset of external stakeholders, namely policy makers and regulatory agencies in an industry, can introduce new rules or modify the existing ones, thus affecting the way economic actors engage and coopete with each other. In other terms, coopetition is not always and necessarily a by-product of the choice of an economic agent (be it an entrepreneur or a firm), but might be an unintended and unintentional outcome (desired or not) of mandates of external institutional stakeholders (DiMaggio & Powell, 1983).

Until 2007, coopetition studies had not sufficiently addressed the aspect of intentionality. The strong assumption was (and still is, in many mainstream coopetitive analyses) that economic actors engaging in coopetitive interactions always act intentionally (Dagnino & Mariani, 2010). However, this is not necessarily the case, especially when external stakeholders such as policy makers and regulators induce an unintended strategic process that contributes to the establishment of coopetitive ties among economic actors. For instance, regulators can influence the institutional environment that might in turn trigger, inhibit, or affect coopetition.

In general, when coopetition is intentional, it can be because of external and/or internal drivers. Similarly, when coopetition is unintentional, it could be because of external and/or internal drivers. In the ensuing paragraph, we will succinctly describe the drivers of coopetition, with a focus on external drivers and, more specifically, external stakeholders.

Drivers of coopetition: A focus on external drivers

In the footsteps of Bengtsson and Raza-Ullah (2016) we can distinguish three partly over-lapping categories of coopetition drivers: internal, relation-specific, and external. Internal drivers include firms' goals, resources, and capabilities. Relation-specific drivers include partner features and relationship characteristics. External drivers encompass influential stakeholders, industrial features, and technological demands. For a complete and updated account of the articles dealing with internal, relation-specific, and external factors we refer to Bengtsson and Raza-Ullah (2016).

In what follows we focus on a few studies related to internal and external drivers, with an emphasis on external ones. Internal drivers encompass internal goals and capabilities, perceived vulnerability, and prospective strategies. They relate to organizational resources and capabil-ities (Gnyawali & Park, 2009), strategies (Luo, 2007), past experience of coopeting together (Mariani, 2016), and motives related to the improvement of performance (M'Chirgui, 2005). For instance, Gnyawali and Park (2009) underline that for competing SMEs it might be beneficial to cooperate because they can pool resources and capabilities to develop similar technologies in the same market. Luo (2007) suggests that cooperating with rivals might be a suitable strategy to penetrate into new markets. Mariani (2016) points out that past experience of collaboration and coopetition might induce even more coopetition. Based on a study of the smart card industry, M'Chirgui (2005) finds that coopetition can be driven by the quest for better performance.

External drivers include environmental conditions such as technological demand (Bengtsson et al., 2013; Bouncken & Kraus, 2013; Dai, 2008), industrial characteristics (Chen, 2014; Dowling et al., 1996; Ritala, 2012) and external stakeholders (Castaldo et al., 2010; Depeyre & Dumez, 2010; Ho & Ganesan, 2013; Mariani, 2007, Wang et al., 2010). Technological uncertainty and complexity have been found to be possible precursors of coopetitive relationships (Bouncken & Kraus, 2013; Dai, 2008), very much like the fact that different firms from different indus-tries have to progressively integrate their technological capabilities and skills to develop new technologies (Bengtsson et al. , 2013). Coopetitive interactions are also influenced by industrial characteristics including concentration and degree of regulation (Dowling et al., 1996), growth rates and level (Chen, 2014), and instability (Ritala, 2012). External stakeholders such as policy makers, regulators, independent mediators, interlocking directorates, and buyers can play a major role in coopetition formation and development. For instance, in the opera sector policy makers can trigger coopetition among previously cooperating organisations (Mariani, 2007). In the US defence industry, regulators such as antitrust authorities have been found to play an architectural role, by setting the rules governing the arrangements, interconnections, and interdependences of coopeting actors (Depeyre & Dumez, 2010). Mediators are relevant in vertical coopetition (Castaldo et al., 2010) where companies such as ACNielsen can link and separate coopeting actors (in this case the supplier and the retailers) for the benefit of a project. Policies granting public subsidies can shape coopetition as well (Wang et al., 2010). Coopetition between firms is also driven by interlocking directorates serving multiple corporate boards in a focal industry (Simoni & Caiazza, 2012). In a number of cases, strong buyers can generate a cooperative attitude among competing firms (Ho & Ganesan, 2013), especially when they operate in a monopsony (Depeyre & Dumez, 2010). In the following section, we review a selected number of coopetition studies dealing with the roles and objectives of a subset of external stakeholders able to trigger and affect coopetitive interactions: policy makers and regulators.

Policy makers and regulators and their roles and objectives in coopetition interactions

Policy makers and regulators are a particular subset of external stakeholders that have so far been studied with a certain degree of depth in coopetition literature. They are typically governmental public bodies external to inter-firm relationships and without a profit motive. They can mandate a higher or lower level of competition/cooperation than the status quo to pursue the following objectives:

1) avoid the formation of trusts, cartels, oligopolies, monopolies, collusion;
2) prevent a decline in firms' customer orientation;
3) rationalize public expenditure and streamline public subsidies;
4) ensure asset complementarity and the use of other firms' capabilities.

In what follows we synthesize the findings of selected research in the four aforementioned situations, with a focus on how firms and organisations in the industry typically adhere to the rules set up by the policy makers and regulators often before forming any coopetitive strategy. Afterwards they might shape coopetitive strategies that are not intentional but emergent.

Avoiding the formation of trusts, cartels, oligopolies, monopolies, and collusion

Policy makers and regulators might be concerned with a few industry characteristics such as concentration and might want to limit the formation of trusts, cartels, oligopolies, and monopolies through the introduction and enforcement of antitrust regulations or other rules. In this case, they will try to deter tacit or explicit collusion (Ouchi & Bolton, 1988; Telser, 1985; Williamson, 1985). Consequently, firms that were cooperating might be forced to increasingly compete and this could lead to the formation or modification of new/existing coopetitive interactions.

Depeyre and Dumez (2010) study the role played by the US defense regulators on the formation and modifications of coopetitive interactions over a forty-year time span. They argue that both the US Defence Department and regulators (i.e., antitrust authorities) have contributed to shape the fabric of the industry architecture, by setting the rules governing the coopetitive interconnections of the production firms supplying weapons to the US defense industry. They show that the regulators of the industry have affected coopetitive interactions between weapon suppliers at different moments in time by reducing the influence of the only customer (i.e., the Department of Defense (DoD)), operating since 1989 in a situation of monopsony.

They describe that over the period 1989–1999, competition between the military forces was dissolved as they were merged into a single monopsony under the DoD; moreover, the number of suppliers were reduced to two for every weapon system (i.e., fighters, submarines, bombers, etc.). In exchange, the government promised to financially support the reorganisation, which led to a wave of mergers and acquisitions (M&A). However, the M&A wave was ended in 1998 when the Antitrust Division of the Department of Justice prohibited the acquisition of Northrop Grumman by Lockheed Martin. This regulatory decision had structural effects: the new antitrust rules pushed many SMEs to quit the market that was left in the hands of several big vertically integrated primes (i.e., the winners of a tender). The DoD enforced a winner-takes-all rule among a very limited amount of primes and allied suppliers selected through a competitive process. Moreover, it oversaw that the tenders could be won by all of the (few) competing firms to avoid favoring collusive practices and a monopoly. However, firms had to cooperate as no prime could deal with the development of all the weapons subsystems. In the end, the DoD had encouraged concentration among a few big suppliers, vertically integrated, and highly specialised (Boeing, Lockheed Martin, etc.). Regarding the regulatory authorities, they influenced coopetitive interactions also from a behavioral point of view as they imposed "firewalls" minimising vertical cooperation within firms and generating vertical cooperation with competitors to maintain horizontal competition. This state of affairs, due to the structural change triggered by the antitrust authority, has been named by the authors "structural complementarity coopetition" (Depeyre and Dumez, 2010: 141).

Overall, the case illustrated by Depeyre and Dumez (2010) portrays the interplay between policy makers in the defence industry and anti-trust regulators in influencing structural conditions and firms' behavior regarding coopetitive interactions. Their findings clearly point to the idea that policy makers and regulators can drive and affect coopetition by laying down rules and enforcing them at different moments in time; thus, not only triggering coopetition but also affecting its evolution over time.

Interestingly, the activities of regulatory authorities and policy makers could lead to unexpected consequences. For instance, Czakon and Rogalski (2014) offer empirical evidence that coopetition might be emergent rather than deliberate. Based on an in-depth study of the Polish energy trade market, they investigate the motives and rationale for companies to enter into coopetition. Among the findings, they highlight that coopetition might be the consequence of changes of demand or the reaction to regulatory inducements. More specifically, since the reference regulator in the Polish electricity trade market is concerned about the formation of tacit or explicit collusion, its role is to promote coopetition that paradoxically and unintendedly forces competitors to collaborate with each other, thus creating the preconditions for coopetition.

Preventing a decline in firms' customer orientation

In situations of collusion (tacit or explicit), it has been shown that colluding firms might increase their profitability at the expense of customer orientation.

Rindfleisch and Moorman (2003) conduct a longitudinal study on competitor-dominated firm alliances and control for the presence of third parties such as antitrust authorities functioning as watchdog organisations, making sure that market operators do not engage in anticompetitive practices. They found that coopeting firms operating in a context where a government agency is monitoring them experienced structurally no descrease in customer orientation over the three-year study period, whereas firms operating in a context without such a watchdog organization recorded a sharp decrease over the same period.

The authors interpret their findings based on neoclassical economics speculations that competitor-dominated firm alliances might not damage customers if they are governed by a monitoring system of their activities and enforcement against anticompetitive practices. This is the reason why the inclusion of a neutral third party, such as a government agency, is seen as an effective solution against tacit or explicit collusion (Ouchi & Bolton, 1988; Teece, 1992; Telser, 1985; Williamson, 1985). In practice, this is the reason why governmental bodies such as the US Department of Justice (DoJ) have rendered most forms of horizontal cooperation in the aforementioned alliances subject to a high level of scrutiny—if not illegal. Moreover, in some instances the monitoring party can be deployed as a facilitator or a neutral judge to help solve disagreements and help build trust among companies (Scott, 2000).

Rationalizing public expenditure and streamlining public subsidies

Policy makers and regulators might be willing to rationalize an industry where the public sector is directing a substantial amount of financial resources (e.g., the defense industry, the publicly supported cultural sector, the national air transportation industry, the energy industry). By imposing higher levels of cooperation, policy makers and regulators might trigger coopetition among firms that were previously merely competing or might bring a shift in extant coopetitive interactions to cooperation-dominated coopetition.

For instance, Mariani (2007) conducts a longitudinal empirical investigation on a consortium of nearby opera companies in Italy and analyses how imposed inter-competitor cooperation is triggered and evolves over time. The case describes the key role of the Tuscany-region policy maker in triggering, through the imposition of cooperation, the emergence of inter-competitor cooperation among the three Italian opera houses of Livorno, Lucca, and Pisa. The multiple-case study is deployed to introduce the brand new concept of induced coopetition that can be described as "the transitory initiation stage of a coopetitive strategy life cycle where cooperation is imposed on competing organizations, and 'emergentness' prevails on (and anticipates) 'deliberateness'." (Mariani, 2007: 117).

The qualifying elements of induced coopetition are the imposition of cooperation on behalf of the policy maker and the incremental adoption of organizational solutions and stratagems (e.g., a common scenery set, a shared orchestra, etc.) enabling the creation of actual interfaces among competing organizations' value chains. Interestingly, the process is described as incremental in the sense that cooperation could originally happen on an individual activity, a portion of an activity, or even a single project, and then be extended to other activities and projects, thus commending one or more reconfigurations of the division of labor within the inter-organizational value chain (Porter, 1985). In their turn, incremental changes might prompt strategic learning based on activities and processes, which subsequently can potentially stimulate additional activity-based (Johnson et al., 2003; Whittington, 1996) cooperative strategies that can develop and consolidate trust among partners and support business processes reengineering within the interorganizational value chain.

The coopetitive attitudes of Italian opera companies are compared with those of other companies in Australia (Mariani, 2009) and Germany (Mariani, 2008) to find that cultural policy makers at different levels of government (federal, state, regional, citystate) are trying to impose cooperation between publicly subsidized opera houses with the aim of rationalising the opera productions on offer and obtaining better value for taxpayers' money. These topdown interventions carried out by the policy makers improved coordination among the individual opera houses involved, thus minimizing costs and gradually triggering something similar to a collective strategy (Astley & Fombrun, 1983). Induced coopetition was therefore also found to be relevant in the German context. Interestingly, in all the performing arts contexts analyzed, the policy maker was able to infuse fresh ideas and to minimize the dangers of overlapping knowledge and projects across organizations (Rindfleisch & Moorman, 2003).

By borrowing the concept of unintentional coopetition from Mariani (2007), Kylänen and Rusko (2011) study the Pyha-Luosto tourism destination (Finnish Lapland) and emphasize the formation of unintentional coopetitive interactions as the by-product of geographic proximity, co-location, and micro clusters as well as the role of public and semi-public organizations. They especially distinguish between two groups of organizations: those interested in strategic long-term development of the destinations (such as provinces, destination marketing organizations (DMO), municipalities, and larger firms) and those interested in the operational short-term profitability of the destinations (such as small firms and workers).

Strategic level (level of province, DMO, municipalities and the larger firms in the case; a longer time-frame)

		Cooperation	Coopetition	Competition
Operational level (level of single smaller firms or workers in the case; a shorter time-frame)	Cooperation	I Intentional cooperation	II Cooperation-based coopetition	III Unintentional coopetition: strategic level competition turns out to be cooperation in operational level
	Coopetition	IV Cooperation-based coopetition	V Intentional coopetition	VI Competition-based coopetition
	Competition	VII Unintentional coopetition: strategic-level cooperation turns out to be competition in operational level	VIII Competition based coopetition	IX Intentional competition

Source: (Kylanen and Rusko, 2011)

Figure 9.1 Different forms of intentional and unintentional coopetition in the context of interaction between strategic-level and operational-level viewpoints

Based on a matrix matching the strategic dimension on one hand and the operational dimension on the other (see Figure 9.1), they come up with two situations where unintentional coopetition occurs: 1) when strategic-level cooperation (cooperation going on between the province, DMO, municipality, and larger firms) turns out to be competition at the operational level; 2) when strategic-level competition turns out to be cooperation at the operational level.

Overall, Kylänen and Rusko (2011) confirm the findings of Mariani (2007, 2009) that public sector organizations might exert a very important effect in the way coopetition is formed and can actually change the "center of gravity" between competition and cooperation.

Mariani (2007, 2008, 2009) and Kylanen and Rusko (2011) highlight that changes triggered by external institutional stakeholders can generate learning opportunities for the actors involved in coopetitive interactions. For instance, Mariani (2009) underlines that induced coopetition is able to enhance strategic learning since it might activate cognitive processes leading managers to revise their mental models as they are forced to think about alternative ways of designing and managing interorganizational value chains, by implementing activity-based cooperation and forms of business process re-engineering.

While trust has been found to be a critical determinant for coopetition in the tourism sector (Czakon & Czernek, 2016), certainly the role of local policy makers in supporting collaboration between co-located highly interdependent competing tourism firms has been emphasized extensively (Kylänen & Mariani, 2012, 2014a, 2014b; Mariani, 2016; Wang & Krakover, 2008).

Rationalization objectives for policy makers have been found to play a major role not only in the cultural sector, but also in sectors as diverse as the defense, travel and tourism sectors.

In their longitudinal study, Depeyre and Dumez (2010) illustrate that during the Cold War period, US defense customers (i.e., the Navy, Air Force, Army, etc.) selected a prime supplier (i.e., the winner of the tender) and second-tier suppliers through a competitive process and imposed vertical cooperation between the prime and second-tier suppliers; the latter were often competitors of the former in other tenders and therefore coopetition emerged as a by-product of a governmental department's decisions that allowed regulation of the competitive processes. This first stage, labeled "imposed coopetition," was intended to improve the rationalization of a heavily publicly funded industry.

In their work on the Northern Italian tourism sector, Mariani and Giorgio (2017) found a strong trend of rationalization of subsidies for destination management organizations (DMOs) and tourism firms geographically close to each other and/or part of the same administrative area to attract tourist flows, increase tourism expenditure, and promote investments in the area. This allowed DMOs especially to pool and rationalize financial and non-financial resources (Mariani et al., 2014) to rebrand a wider region subsuming smaller areas.

Ensuring asset complementarity and the use of other firms' capabilities

In their work on the Polish energy sector, Czakon and Rogalski (2014) identify a second reason why companies start to coopete: the need to rationalize the activities by ensuring asset complementarity and the use of other firms' competencies through outsourcing.

Depeyre and Dumez (2010) note that in the third stage of the development of the US defense industry (after 1999), a major watershed event took place: the advent and consolidation of complex network-centric systems that demanded a strategic competitive mindset. More specifically, the complexity of weapon production transformed the production process into a system of systems that could be managed only by very few firms, which needed to shape alliances with each other to deliver the final output. The firm that manages to become the prime in this new situation has to demonstrate that its alliance with competitors could generate the production results and secure a monopolistic relationship with the DoD for a long time, likely obtaining a sustainable competitive advantage leveraging path-dependency and lock-in.

Conclusions: What we know and don't know about coopetition driven or affected by policy makers and regulators

In this concluding section we summarize what we know and what we would like to know about coopetition driven and affected by policy makers and regulators; recognizing that what we would like to know itself represents a challenging future research agenda.

Today we know that external stakeholders such as policy makers can not only set the scene for coopetitive interactions but can actually trigger coopetition and affect it once it has been formed. In many cases an external stakeholder (for instance, a policy maker or a regulatory agency) can mandate (higher levels of) cooperation or competition, thus paving the way for the formation of coopetitive interactions. As this situation was not deliberately planned ex-ante by the coopeting actors, clearly those actors have unintentionally entered coopetition, in some cases ultimately embracing induced coopetition (Mariani, 2007, 2008, 2009).

Unintentional coopetition can generate learning processes, leading managers to revise their cognitive models as they would need to think about different ways of designing inter-organizational value chains through the implementation of activity-based cooperation and forms of business process re-engineering.

Imposed coopetition can lead to a more effective distribution of tasks among coopetitive partners, as demonstrated by Depeyre and Dumez (2010) in the defense industry, Czakon and

Rogalski (2014) in the energy industry, Mariani (2007, 2008, 2009) in the publicly subsidized cultural sector, and Kylanen and Rusko (2011), Czakon and Czernek (2016), and Mariani (2016) in the tourism sector. Regardless of the specific mechanisms through which policy makers and regulators might trigger the formation of a coopetitive relationship, it is worthwhile noticing that at any given time a change of the rules might affect the coopetitive interactions and either strengthen or weaken the cooperative/competitive component that allows a coopetitive inter-action to exist. Overall, external stakeholders such as policy makers and regulators could inter-vene at different stages of a coopetitive strategy life cycle and might thus influence how economic actors (i.e., entrepreneurs and companies) coopete over time (Czakon, 2010; Depeyre & Dumez, 2010; Kylänen & Mariani, 2012, 2014a, 2014b; Mariani & Kylänen, 2014; Mariani, 2007, 2009; Mariani, 2016; Mariani & Giorgio, 2017).

While this is what we know at the moment of writing, much still remains on the table for further investigation. First, while policy makers' driven coopetition has been found to trigger learning processes, it has been hypothesized that strategic learning arising in an induced-coopetition context might be different from that taking place in a competitive or cooperative situation (Mariani, 2007, 2009). This hypothesis certainly needs further empirical validation and testing. Second, and related to the first point, it has been suggested that the coopetitive actors' enacted environment (Pfeffer & Salancick, 1978) could significantly change, thus triggering an intense modification in managerial mental models. This aspect also needs more empirical substantiation and might be further developed and validated with studies on other industries and contexts. Third, it would be relevant to refine the conceptualization of a specific subset of external stakeholders such as policy makers and regulators in coopetitive settings and track them over time in different empirical contexts, sectors, and industries. Fourth, and related to the third point, most of the extant research has focused on the implementation phase, while the aspect of how policy makers and regulators behave once coopetition has formed is somehow neglected. Consequently, it would be valuable to bridge this gap in order to understand if and to what extent policy makers and regulators help coopetitors manage their tensions.

From a methodological point of view, several advancements seem necessary. First, coopetition strategy scholars should devise appropriate methods to study how policy makers and regulators can drive coopetition. Often it is rather complicated to determine if coopetition (and induced/imposed coopetition in particular) is simply dictated by a single external stakeholder's interven-tion or adds to other conjoint external environmental factors. Second, and related to the first point, methods should be devised to disentangle the individual contribution of one external stakeholder from the cumulative contribution of two or more third parties to the initiation and development of a coopetitive relationship. Third, a process perspective might help address the role of policy makers and regulators in triggering and affecting coopetition changes over time. In the studies of Mariani (2007) and Depeyre and Dumez (2010) the architectural roles of the regulators and policy makers respond to changing environmental conditions (e.g., political, eco-nomic, and social conditions) that are translated into new or revised rules that affect how firms and organizations interact with each other and coopete. Accordingly, more emphasis should be given to a diachronic approach to the understanding of coopetition mandated or affected by policy makers and regulators, with an emphasis on longitudinal studies. Last, as already claimed by Mariani (2007, 2009) there is a need to shift the attention to the processes of coopetitive strategy formation, maintenance, and dissolution. This might be undertaken by embracing a theory of change (Dahl, 2014) and its related methods (Van de Ven & Poole, 2005); certainly this theoretical perspective and related methods might add value to extant longitudinal analyses and perhaps shed light on several aspects that still are underexplored.

References

Astley, W. G. & Fombrun, C. J. (1983). Collective strategy: Social ecology of organizational environments. *Academy of Management Review*, 8(4), 576–587.

Bengtsson, M. & Raza-Ullah, T. (2016). A systematic review of research on coopetition: Towards a multi-level understanding. *Industrial Marketing Management*, 57, 23–39.

Bengtsson, M., Johansson, M., Näsholm, M., & Raza-Ullah, T. (2013). A systematic review of coopetition, levels and effects at different levels. 13th EURAM Conference, Istanbul, Turkey, June 26–29.

Bengtsson, M. & Kock, S. (2014). Coopetition—Quo Vadis? Past accomplishments and future challenges. *Industrial marketing management*, 43(2), 180–188.

Bengtsson, M., Eriksson, J., & Wincent, J. (2010b). Co-opetition dynamics—an outline for further inquiry. *Competitiveness Review*, 20(2), 194–214.

Bengtsson, M., Eriksson, J., & Wincent, L. (2010a). New ideas for a new paradigm. In S. Yami, S. Castaldo, G. B. Dagnino, & F. Le Roy (Eds), *Coopetition: Winning Strategies for the 21st Century* (pp. 19–39). Cheltenham: Edward Elgar.

Bengtsson, M. & Kock, S. (2000). Coopetition in business networks—to cooperate and compete simultaneously. *Industrial Marketing Management*, 29(5), 411–425.

Bengtsson, M. & Kock, S. (1999). Cooperation and competition in relationships between competitors in business networks. *Journal of Business and Industrial Marketing*, 14, 178–190.

Bouncken, R. B. & Kraus, S. (2013). Innovation in knowledge-intensive industries: The double-edged sword of coopetition. *Journal of Business Research,* 66(10), 2060–2070.

Brandenburger, A. M. & Nalebuff, B. J. (1996). *Co-opetition.* New York: Doubleday.

Brandenburger, A. M. & Stuart, S. (1996). Value-based business strategy. *Journal of Economical Management Strategy*, 5(1), 5–14.

Castaldo, S., Möellering, G., Grosso, M., & Zerbini, F. (2010). Exploring how third-party organizations facilitate co-opetition management in buyer-seller relationships. In S. Yami, S. Castaldo, G. B. Dagnino, & F. Le Roy (Eds), *Coopetition: Winning Strategies for the 21st Century* (pp. 141–165). Cheltenham: Edward Elgar.

Chen, L.-T. (2014). Dynamic co-opetitive approach of a closed loop system with remanufacturing for deteriorating items in e-markets. *Journal of Manufacturing Systems*, 33(1), 166–176.

Czakon, W. & Czernek, K. (2016). The role of trust-building mechanisms in entering into network coopetition: The case of tourism networks in Poland. *Industrial Marketing Management*, 57, 64–74.

Czakon, W. & Rogalski, M. (2014). Coopetition typology revisited–a behavioural approach. *International Journal of Business Environment*, 6(1), 28–46.

Czakon, W., Mucha-Kuś, K., & Rogalski, M. (2014). Coopetition research landscape – A Systematic literature review 1997–2010. *Journal of Economics and Management*, 17, 122–150.

Czakon, W. (2010). Emerging coopetition: an empirical investigation of coopetition as interorganizational relationship instability. In S. Yami, S. Castaldo, G. B. Dagnino, & F. Le Roy (Eds), *Coopetition: Winning Strategies for the 21st Century* (pp. 58–73). Cheltenham: Edward Elgar.

Dagnino, G. B. & Mariani, M. M. (2010). Coopetitive value creation in entrepreneurial contexts: The case of AlmaCube. In S. Yami, S. Castaldo, G. B. Dagnino, & F. Le Roy (Eds), *Coopetition: Winning Strategies for the 21st Century* (pp. 101–123). Cheltenham: Edward Elgar.

Dahl, J. (2014). Conceptualizing coopetition as a process: An outline of change in cooperative and competitive interactions. *Industrial Marketing Management*, 43, 272–279.

Dai, L. (2008). Maximizing cooperation in a competitive environment. *Competition Forum*, 6(1), 63–74.

Depeyre, C. & Dumez, H. (2010). The role of architectural players in coopetition: the case of the US defense industry. In S. Yami, S. Castaldo, G. B. Dagnino, & F. Le Roy (Eds), *Coopetition: Winning Strategies for the 21st Century* (pp. 124–140). Cheltenham: Edward Elgar.

DiMaggio, P. J. & Powell, W. W. (1983). The iron cage revisited: Institutional isomorphism and collective rationality in organizational fields. *American Sociological Review*, 48(2), 147–160.

Dowling, M. J., Roering, W. D., Carlin, B. A., & Wisnieski, J. (1996). Multifaceted relationships under coopetition – Description and theory. *Journal of Management Inquiry*, 5(2), 155–167.

Fernandez, A. S., Le Roy, F. & Gnyawali, D. R. (2014). Sources and management of tension in co-opetition case evidence from telecommunications satellites manufacturing in Europe. *Industrial Marketing Management*, 43(2), 222–235.

Fjeldstad, Ø., Becerra, M., & Narayananc, S. (2004). Strategic action in network industries: an empirical analysis of the European mobile phone industry. *Scandinavian Journal of Management*, 20(1–2), 173–196.

Gnyawali, D. R. & Park, B. J. (2009). Co-opetition and technological innovation in small and medium-sized enterprises: A multilevel conceptual model. *Journal of Small Business Management*, 47(3), 308–330.

Ho, H. & Ganesan, S. (2013). Does knowledge base compatibility help or hurt knowledge sharing between suppliers in coopetition? The role of customer participation. *Journal of Marketing*, 77(6), 91–107.

Johnson, G., Melin, L., & Whittington, R. (2003). Micro-strategy and strategizing. Towards an activity-based view. *Journal of Management Studies*, 40(1), 3–22.

Kylänen, M. & Mariani, M. M. (2014b). Cooperative and coopetitive practices: Cases from the tourism industry. In M. M. Mariani, R. Baggio, D. Buhalis, & C. Longhi (Eds), *Tourism Management, Marketing and Development. Volume I: the Importance of Networks and ICTs* (pp. 149–178). New York: Palgrave.

Kylänen, M. & Mariani, M. M. (2014a). Unpacking the temporal dimension of coopetition in tourism destinations: evidence from Finnish and Italian theme parks. In R. Baggio, W. Czakon, & M. Mariani (Eds), *Managing Tourism in a Changing World: Issues and Cases* (pp. 61–74). London: Routledge.

Kylänen, M. & Mariani, M. M. (2012). Unpacking the temporal dimension of coopetition in tourism destinations: evidence from Finnish and Italian theme parks. *Anatolia: An International Journal of Tourism and Hospitality Research*, 23(1), 61–74.

Kylänen, M. & Rusko, R. (2011). Unintentional coopetition in the service industries: the case of Pyhä-Luosto tourism destination in the Finnish Lapland. *European Management Journal*, 29(3), 193–205.

Luo, Y. (2007). A coopetition perspective of global competition. *Journal of World Business*, 42(2), 129–144.

M'Chirgui, Z. (2005). The economics of the smart card industry: towards coopetive strategies. *Economics of Innovation and New Technology*, 14(6), 455–477.

Mariani, M. M. & Giorgio, L. (2017). The "Pink Night" festival revisited: Meta-events and the role of destination partnerships in staging event tourism. *Annals of Tourism Research*, 62, 89–109.

Mariani, M. (2016). Coordination in inter-network co-opetition: evidence from the tourism sector. *Industrial Marketing Management*, 53, 103–123.

Mariani, M. & Kylänen, M. (2014). The relevance of public-private partnerships in coopetition: Empirical evidence from the tourism sector. *International Journal of Business Environment*, 6(1), 106–125.

Mariani, M. M. (2009). Emergent coopetitive and cooperative strategies in inter-organizational relationships: empirical evidence from Australian and Italian operas. In G. B. Dagnino, & E. Rocco (Eds), *Coopetition strategy. Theory, experiments and cases* (pp. 166–190). London: Routledge.

Mariani, M. M. (2008). Induced coopetition and emergent cooperation: an international study on the opera houses sector. *Public*, 15, 1–6.

Mariani, M. M. (2007). Coopetition as an emergent strategy: Empirical evidence from an Italian consortium of opera houses. *International Studies of Management & Organization.* 37(2), 97–126.

Mariani, M. M, Buhalis, D. Longhi C., & Vitouladiti, O. (2014). Managing change in tourism destinations: Key issues and current trends. *Journal of Destination Marketing & Management*, 2, 269–272.

Mintzberg, H. (1978). Patterns in strategy formation. *Management Science*, 24(9), 934–948.

Mintzberg, H. & McHugh, H. (1985). Strategy formation in adhocracy. *Administrative Science Quarterly*, 30(2), 160–197.

Mintzberg, H. & Waters, W. J. (1982). Tracking strategy in an entrepreneurial firm. *Academy of Management Journal*, 25 (3), 465–499.

Mintzberg, H. & Waters, W. J. (1985). Of strategies, deliberate and emergent. *Strategic Management Journal*, 6(3), 257–272.

Ouchi, W. G. & Bolton, M. K. (1988). The logic of joint research and development. *California Management Review*, 30 (Spring), 9–33.

Pellegrin-Boucher, E., Le Roy, F., & Gurau, C. (2013). Coopetitive strategies in the ICT sector: typology and stability. *Technology Analysis & Strategic Management*, 25(1), 71–89.

Pfeffer, J. & Salancick, G. (1978). *The External Control of Organizations*. New York: Harper & Row.

Porter, M. (1985). *Competitive Advantage*. New York: Free Press.

Rindfleisch, A. & Moorman, C. (2003). Interfirm cooperation and customer orientation. *Journal of Marketing Research*, XL, 421–436.

Ritala, P. (2012). Coopetition strategy — when is it successful? Empirical evidence on innovation and market performance. *British Journal of Management*, 23(3), 307–324.

Scott, J. T. (2000). Strategic research partnerships: What have we learned. Working paper, Department of Economics, Dartmouth College.

Simoni, M. & Caiazza, R. (2012). Interlocks network structure as driving force of coopetition among Italian firms. *Corporate Governance: The International Journal of Business in Society*, 12(3), 319–336.

Teece, D. J. (1992). Competition, cooperation, and innovation: Organizational arrangements for regimes of rapid technological progress. *Journal of Economic Behavior and Organization*, 18, 1–25.

Telser, L. G. (1985). Cooperation, competition, and efficiency. *Journal of Law and Economics*, 28 (May), 271–291.

Tidström, A. (2008). Perspectives on coopetition on actor and operational levels. *Management Research*, 6(3), 207–217.

Van de Ven, A. H., & Poole, M. S. (2005). Alternative approaches for studying organizational change. *Organization Studies*, 26(9), 1377–1404.

Wang, R., Ji, J. H., & Ming, X. G. (2010). R&D partnership contract coordination of information goods supply chain in government subsidy. *International Journal of Computer Applications in Technology*, 37(3–4), 297–306.

Wang, Y. & Krakover, S. (2008). Destination marketing: competition, cooperation or coopetition? *International Journal of Contemporary Hospitality Management*, 20(2), 126–141.

Williamson O. E. (1985). *The Economic Institutions of Capitalism*. New York: The Free Press.

Whittington, R. (1996). Strategy as practice. *Long Range Planning*, 29(5), 731–735.

10
Organizational culture models of coopetitors

Patrycja Klimas

Introduction

Coopetition is understood as a relationship covering simultaneous cooperation and competition (Bengtsson & Kock, 2000; Gnyawali & Park, 2011; Luo et al., 2006; Luo, 2007). From that perspective, any sequential, alternating appearance of cooperation and competition should be seen as a coopetitive relationship (Czakon et al., 2014). The newest coopetition literature identifies five current research areas (Dorn et al., 2016): (1) the nature of the relationship; (2) governance and management; (3) the output of the relationship; (4) actors' characteristics; and (5) environmental characteristics. This chapter refers to the fourth area, namely coopetitors' characteristics and their cultural profile in particular. Exploration of this area is reasoned as our knowledge about contextual factors is limited, hence the development of full conceptualization of coopetition in different managerial settings is hampered (Bouncken et al., 2015). Furthermore, given the results of several literature reviews on coopetition, (Bengtsson et al., 2010; Bengtsson & Raza-Ullah, 2016; Czakon et al., 2014; Dorn et al., 2016; Gast et al., 2015), even if organizational culture was the subject of explorative research, it remains fragmentarily recognized in the field of coopetition. This is surprising, as cultural aspects were claimed to be insufficiently explored in the context of coopetition more than a decade ago (Rijamampianina & Carmichael, 2005).

Following Luo (2007), the partnering of competitor's needs: resource complementarity, goal compatibility, and respective cooperative culture, which ought to be based on shared values, philosophies, and assumptions. Similarly, Rijamampianina and Carmichael (2005) showed coopetitive relationships to be a function of cultural compatibility and strategic complementarity. In their proposition, it is possible to establish coopetition based on cultural compatibility, including centrality and visibility of cultural elements. Moreover, among the types of coopetitive relationships, there is a culturally based coopetition, which is characteristic for business rivals displaying similar strategic imperatives and compatible cultures (Rijamampianina & Carmichael, 2005). Finally, in research on collaborative networks, run from an organizational culture perspective, Srivastava and Banaji (2011) introduced the term of collaborative organizational culture, which emphasizes cross-boundary collaboration based on pro-cooperative beliefs, assumptions, and values.

The nuts and bolts of organizational culture

Organizational culture is understood as a set of beliefs, assumptions, artefacts, meanings, and perceptions (Denison, 1996; Hatch, 1993; Schein, 2010) shared by members of an organization (Cameron & Quinn, 2011; Naranjo-Valencia et al., 2010). As claimed by Denison (1996), organizational culture refers to the deep structure of an organization that is invisible and deeply rooted in values. However, when the above components of organizational culture are employed and take visible manifestations (e.g., behaviors, practices), they are considered to be more flexible, more psychological organizational features, namely the organizational climate.

In the current body of knowledge it is claimed that the exploration of organizational culture needs consideration of a wide range of aspects (Gregory et al., 2009; Maximini, 2015; Strese et al., 2016), for example, level of formalization, level of centralization, level of tolerance/avoidance of risks, degree of orientation on personal/impersonal relationships and communication, focus either on external or on internal environment, level of flexibility, level of control, or structure and strategic focus. All in all, there is no agreement about the structure and operationalization of this complex and latent construct; nonetheless, there are two general approaches to define the models of organizational culture. First, the models can be identified based on a set of specific features displayed by a particular company (see, for instance, Jarratt & O'Neill, 2002). Second, the model of culture adopted by the company may be identified using two differentiating and dichotomous continua; see Table 10.1.

Models of organizational culture suitable for coopetitors

Prior literature shows that there are differences in organizational cultures adopted by coopetitors (Strese et al., 2016). Likewise, their cultural models are different from the models of non-coopetitors operating in the same industry settings (Klimas, 2016). However, it still remains unclear *whether there is one perfect solution, namely the most suitable (characteristic) model of organizational culture for coopetitors*. However, if we take a closer look at the different models of organizational cultures identified by different scholars (Table 10.1), it would be possible to outline the models being potentially the most suitable for organizations interested in coopetition.

First, following differentiating continua proposed by Harrison in 1972 (Maximini, 2015), the most appropriate model of organizational culture for coopetitors seems to be the "task/achievement orientation" characteristic for organizations with low centralization and high formalization. Given the results of research carried out on German companies, the level of centralization negatively influences, while the level of formalization positively influences, coopetition performance (Strese et al., 2016). Additionally, explorative research on organizational culture models of coopetitors in the Polish aviation industry shows high levels of formalization expressed by an extensive system of norms, rules, and procedures as characteristic for coopetitors (Klimas, 2016).

Second, given actuality/possibility and personal/impersonal dichotomies considered by Schneider, it is possible to identify the general (independent from national culture or industry settings) models of organizational cultures (as cited by Maximini, 2015). These dichotomies take into account the commitment and fulfilment of staff in utilizing opportunities arising from the company's environment. Thus, the "competence" model based on impersonal relationships/communication and focused on the exploitation of future possibilities seems to be the most suitable for organizations interested in the adoption of coopetition. It seems to be the most rational, as coopetition is usually utilized by high-tech companies (Czakon et al., 2014) interested in radical innovation implemented on a global scale (Ritala & Hurmelinna-Laukkanen, 2013) and

Table 10.1 Brief summary of different organizational culture models

Author(s)	Year	Differentiating Continua	Models of Organizational Culture
Harrison	1972 (1897)	High/low formalization High/low centralization	Role orientation Task/achievement orientation; Person/support orientation power orientation
Schneider	1999	Actuality/possibility Personal/impersonal	Collaboration; control; competence; cultivation
Deal and Kennedy	2000	Fast/slow feedback High/low risk	Work hard/play hard; tough-guy/macho/s'ras; bet-your-company process
Iivari and Huisman	2007	Change/stability Internal focus/external focus	Group; developmental; rational; hierarchical; *balanced**
Cameron and Quinn	2011	Flexibility and discretion/ stability and control Internal focus and integration/ external focus and differentiation	clan; adhocracy; market hierarchy; *balanced**

* As indicated by Gregory, Harris, Armenakis, and Shook (2009), companies may adopt a balanced model of organizational culture if all CVF culture domains are strongly held by the company.

(Source: based on Cameron & Quinn, 2011; Maximini, 2015; Strese et al., 2016.)

operating in industries driven by innovation and technology pressures (Gnyawali & Park, 2009; 2011). Furthermore, as coopetition is tension-based (Fernandez et al., 2014) and contains the risk of opportunistic behaviors (Bengtsson et al., 2010), coopetitors do not trust each other (an atmosphere of distrust is typical; Gnyawali & Park, 2009) and thus use developed protection mechanisms (Klimas, 2016), which also favors the suitability of the "competence" model of organizational culture.[1]

Third, taking into account the two continua (labeled as marketplace factors) adopted by Deal and Kennedy in their organizational culture framework (Maximini, 2015), the "bet-your-company" cultural model (high risk and slow feedback) seems to be the most appropriate for coopetitors. Companies that adopt this model take a long view on values, development, and investment, but the speed of their reactions to environment changes is low, while the efforts that should be taken to get feedback about the efficiency of those actions are high. Given that coopetition is adopted due to high levels of uncertainty (Gnyawali & Park, 2011; Ritala, 2012), as well as the need for the development and introduction of radical innovation (Ritala & Hurmelinna-Laukkanen, 2013), this culture seems to be the most appropriate.

Fourth, among many different models of organizational culture, the most popular approach still remains the competing value framework (CVF) (Eckenhofer & Ershova, 2011; Gregory et al., 2009; Naranjo-Valencia et al., 2011). This model provides models of cultures that match the most important management theories about organizational success, organizational quality, organizational roles, leadership, and management skills (Cameron & Quinn, 2011). As shown in Table 10.1, CVF is based on two independent continua (Gregory et al., 2009): (1) flexibility and discretion/stability and control (evaluating the structural dimension of the organization and its culture); and (2) internal focus and integration/external focus and differentiation (assessing the strategic focus of the organization). Simultaneous consideration of these two continua (dimensions) allows distinction between four models of organizational culture, i.e., clan, adhocracy, hierarchy, and market.

Prior literature shows two models as characteristic for cooperating companies. Namely, "clan culture," which has been identified based on research on Austrian companies (Eckenhofer & Ershova, 2011), and the "adhocracy model" (also labeled the "developmental model" in terms of the typology provided by Ivari & Huisman in 2007; see Table 10.1), which has been shown as the most suitable for German organizations focused either on short-term and periodic interaction or longitudinal cooperation with both non-coopetitors and the greatest business rivals (Strese et al., 2016).

Summing up, there are different models of organizational culture that can be deliberately or inadvertently adopted by organizations interested in successful coopetition adoption. Nonetheless, in the context of coopetition, organizational culture still remains under-researched (Dorn et al., 2016; Klimas, 2016; Strese et al., 2016).

Research on cultural models of coopetitors in a nutshell

Comparison of prior studies on models of organizational cultures of coopetitors suggests that the model of organizational culture most suitable for coopetitors may be conditioned by external factors like industry or country. The results of two prior studies run in this area show that German manufacturers that maintain coopetitive relationships usually adopt the adhocracy model of organizational culture (flexibility and external focus; Strese et al., 2016), whereas Polish aviation coopetitors usually adopt the hierarchy model (stability and internal focus; Klimas, 2016). It is hard to confront the identified suitability of particular models of organizational cultures as both external factors—country/industry type—might be responsible for the results obtained. Therefore, to limit the contextual influence to one external factor we set the following research question: are there any models of organizational cultures that are shared by coopetitors functioning in the same country but in different industries?

The research aimed at answering the above question was explorative in nature and was focused on the development of our fragmentary knowledge about the existence of one specific model of organizational culture adopted by coopetitors.[2] Given that "there is no ideal instrument for cultural exploration" (Jung et al., 2009: 1087), in this study the competing values framework was adopted as the most popular one. Each model of organizational culture was assessed using two differentiating continua (Gregory et al., 2009): structural (from flexible to stable) and strategic (from external to internal focus). The measurement tool and the approach to data analysis were adopted from prior studies carried out on cultural facets of Polish aviation coopetitors.[3]

The comparative explorations were made in parallel for coopetitors operating in two different industry sectors: aviation and the video game industry (VGI). First and foremost, purposeful selection of these industries was reasoned as both of them are innovation-based, knowledge-intensive, classified as high-tech, and aimed at the production of complex and global products (Klimas, 2016; O'Donnell, 2012), while those industry characteristics are shown as the most favorable for coopetition occurrence (Gast et al., 2015; Gnyawali & Park, 2009; Luo, 2007; Ritala,

Table 10.2 Data-gathering in aviation and the video game industry

Industry	Aviation Industry in Poland	Video Game Industry in Poland
Time scope	2012–2013	2017
Industry size	Approximately 140—Report on Innovativeness of the Aviation Sector in Poland in 2010 ordered by the Polish Agency for Enterprise Development	Approximately 150 – The stat of Polish Video Games Sector. Report 2015 ordered by The Ministry of Culture and National Heritage.
Cooperation	Joint participation in national and international research projects—database provided by the Polish Agency of Information and Foreign Investments, Polish Agency for Enterprise Development, and Community Research and Development Information Service	Joint participation in national and international research projects—database provided by the National Centre for Research and Development, Ministry of Culture and National Heritage, and Community Research and Development Information Service
Competition	Direct competition in sales—manufacturing the same products and (or) delivering the same services according to information presented by databases of aviation networks	Direct competition in sales—development of free-to-play games in freemium model sold through App Store/Google Play Store
Identified coopetitors—targeted sample	35; invitation sent to all	74; invitation sent to all
Research sample	27	19

2012). In order to limit the influence of national context on models adopted by coopetitors, the scope of research was limited to Poland—see Table 10.2.

Specific models of organizational cultures of coopetitors in business practice

Given the average levels of particular cultural features (proxy for intensity of cultural characteristics), the differences among coopetitors from aviation and VGI identified using the share of coopetitors are confirmed—see Figure 10.1.

Coopetitors in VGI seem to be less stable and control-driven while they are more focused on dynamism and discretion than cooperating business rivals in aviation. Similarly, given the dichotomous cultural continua used in CVF the structural continuum seems to differentiate the industries more than the strategic approach. The difference in the intensity of cultural extrema considered on the structural continuum results from differences in the level of stability indicated by coopetitors in VGI and aviation while the level of flexibility is quite similar. Note, however, that flexible structure covers flexibility and dynamism. In the case of aviation the level of flexible structure results from the importance of flexibility but not from dynamism (Klimas, 2016). Last but not least, considering particular cultural features it was possible to identify the most- and the least-suitable models of organizational culture for coopetitors. As shown in Figure 10.2, the results are different in both the most- and the least-suitable cultural models for coopetitors from aviation and VGI.

As identified earlier (Klimas, 2016), the most-suitable model of organizational culture for coopetitors from the aviation industry is hierarchy, while the least-suitable model is adhocracy.

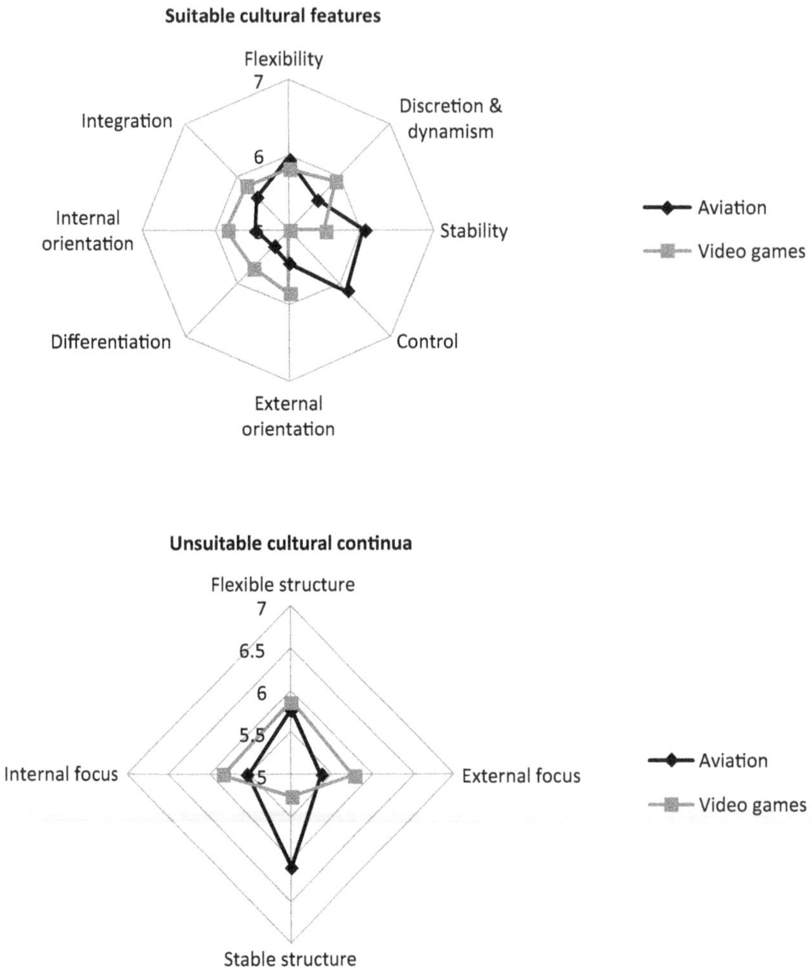

Figure 10.1 The level of cultural features and cultural continua suitable for coopetitors in the aviation and video game industries

Surprisingly, the cultural model that best matches the features of video game coopetitors is clan culture, whereas the market model is the least-suitable organizational culture. However, it's worth noting that in both industries the most-suitable organizational culture models assume internal focus while the least-suitable models assume concentration on the environment.

Summing up, the results of this explorative research suggest that *there is no specific model of organizational culture best-suited to all coopetitors regardless of the type of industry*. Furthermore, the results may suggest that coopetitors—regardless of the industry—adopt organizational cultures characterized by internal focus.

Conclusions and implications for both theory and further research

A bibliometric analysis of prior works shows that there are some coopetition-specific contexts influencing coopetitive relationships, while industry is one of the most often applied (Gast

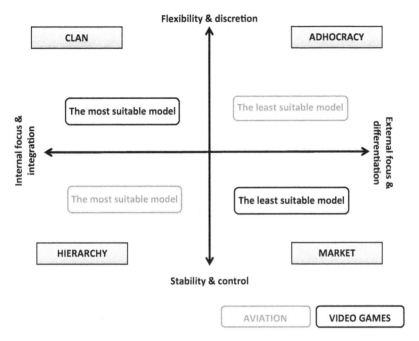

Figure 10.2 The most- and least-suitable models of organizational cultures for coopetitors in the aviation and video game industries

et al., 2015). Indeed, coopetition is expressed as an extremely industry-related phenomenon (Bouncken et al., 2015; Czakon et al., 2014; Dorn et al., 2016), while prior empirical efforts aimed at recognition of the cultural specificity of coopetitors was restricted to one industry (compare, e.g., Klimas, 2016; Strese et al., 2016), thus in order to improve the state of our knowledge it was reasoned to explore more deeply the specificity of cultural models of coopetitors without restricting the scope of research to one industry. Furthermore, to limit the risk of potential differences caused by national differences, including differences in national cultures, the research should be run in one country. Therefore, the exploration of the most suitable models of organizational culture for coopetitors focused on coopetitors operating in one country (Poland) but in two different industries: aviation and video games.

As indicated by Deal and Kennedy, the type of organizational culture model appropriate for any company is conditioned by external factors, including the level of competition, globalization, technological advancement, innovativeness, customer pressure, etc. (Maximini, 2015). This means that industry settings are more important than endogenous decisions about the nature of organizational culture adopted. Indeed, Naranjo-Valencia et al. (2010, 2011) pointed out that outcome-based environments privilege a market culture, creative surroundings are seen as appropriate for an adhocracy culture, the hierarchy model is the best solution in cases of a strict and formalized organizational culture, while in a much more loose, informal, and sociable context it is better to adopt clan culture. In the context of coopetition, a brief review of different typologies (see Table 10.1) of organizational culture models shows different models of culture suitable for companies interested in cooperation with business rivals. Moreover, the results of empirical investigation show that the most-suitable as well as the least-suitable models of organizational culture of coopetitors are different between considered industries.

First, the most suitable model of culture (following classification based on the CVF approach, developed by Cameron and Quinn in 2011) for coopetitors operating in the aviation there is hierarchy, while for those operating in VGI it is clan culture. In prior research, the hierarchy model has been indicated as a model with the lowest support for both the establishment and maintenance of inter-organizational cooperation (Eckenhofer & Ershova, 2011: 39). Important research on innovation and imitation strategies adopted by Spanish companies has shown that hierarchy promotes an imitation strategy inside clusters, while it also has a negative effect on innovation strategy (Naranjo-Valencia et al., 2011). Such findings seem to be contradictory to those obtained in this research. However, in the light of other results, the collaborative organizational culture can be based on formalized decision processes (Srivastava & Banaji, 2011); especially in cases of mature industries and manufacturing firms based on strategic resources, control cultures (actuality and impersonal dimensions) characterized by a great focus on hierarchy, predictability, and a longitudinal approach are the most successful and reasoned (Maximini, 2015).

Second, the most suitable model of culture for coopetitors operating in VGI is clan culture. Such result remain in line with prior studies showing this model to have been adopted by companies engaging in inter-organizational relationships, as a model that "supports the creation of solid networks the most" (Eckenhofer & Ershova, 2011: 38).

Third, the adhocracy model has been identified as the least suitable for aviation coopetitors, whereas market culture has been shown as the least suitable for cooperating business rivals in VGI. Given the lack of prior research focusing on the least-suitable models of organizational cultures for companies with a coopetitive approach, it was impossible to confront the results with any other empirical findings. However, it is worth noting that the explorative results suggest the differences in adequacy of adopted models of organizational culture to be conditioned by the type of industry. It is claimed that these differences may be explained by the following industry conditions: VGI is very fast-moving, especially due to the rapid expansion of mobile and "free-to-play" (F2P) games; aviation is conditioned by extensive safety regulations at global, European, and national level; the life cycles of products provided by those industries significantly differ—aircrafts are produced for four to five decades while games stay on the market for no longer than five to seven years (O'Donnell, 2012). Furthermore, as suggested by Klimas (2016), coopetitors in aviation pay attention to responsiveness and adaptiveness to external changes (flexibility), whereas they do not display a proactive and enterprising approach that results in the triggering of those changes (dynamism). This is the case as aviation is subordinated to safety and international regulations. Therefore, the majority of changes are induced by the institutional and political environment and companies must adapt to them as soon as possible. In other words, before change can be triggered by particular companies in a business practice, external approval must be assured by (usually global) policy makers. All in all, even though the most- and least-suitable models for coopetitors seem to be different, our findings confirm the preliminary assumptions about sectoral conditioning of cultural settings in the context of coopetition.

However, it should be noted that in both considered industries coopetitors seem to be more focused on internal issues and integration than on differentiation and external relationships, and the possibility of accessing resources and capabilities. This remains in contrast to findings on cross-functional coopetition showing adhocracy (developmental) culture as the most oriented on external cooperation, including cooperation with competitors (Strese et al., 2016). Simultaneously, such results may add to prior findings that show that the fear of a "lose-lose" situation (i.e., negative results of non-cooperating organizations) more often drives cooperation with business rivals than awareness and willingness of taking benefits from such cooperation (Liu, 2013: 91). Coopetitors may operate under enormous innovation, technological, and customer pressure leading them to cooperation with business rivals, even the closest ones. Hence, their awareness of coopetition-related risks (e.g., the asymmetry of information flows—Chai & Yang, 2011; a wide range of opportunistic behaviors—Bouncken & Kraus, 2013; value appropriation—Ritala & Tidström, 2014) limits their external focus and drives the development of extensive protection mechanisms. To conclude, it is argued there is no single most-suitable model of organizational culture for coopetitors, while the most appropriate cultural profile seems to depend on industrial settings.

This chapter confirms that coopetition is influenced not only by organizational-level, but also by environment- and industry-level factors (Gnyawali & Park, 2009). However, the focus here is on one organizational-level factor, namely organizational culture, considered in two different industry settings—hence, in the same national context. This national context, as well as the realization of research in only two industries, can be seen as a limitation.

However, this research was aimed at exploration, not at generalization. Thus, in further studies it would be valuable to consider the role of national cultures as they may be significant for coopetition strategy adoption, as they have not been investigated in a coopetition context so far. In fact, national context influences the models of organizational culture adopted, as national cultures do matter to organizations, while countries do differ in terms of cultural settings (Hofstede, 1981; Xiao & Tsui, 2007). Thus, it is suggested to run replication research on VGI or aviation (Klimas, 2016) outside of Poland, or on manufacturing companies outside of Germany (Strese et al., 2016) in order to compare the results. It would be interesting to run international or even global research on cultures adopted by coopetitors in industries characteristic for coopetition strategy adoption—those classified as high-tech, knowledge-intensive, or hyper-dynamic. Last but not least, to complete the cultural profile of coopetitors it would be good to run further research applying other differentiating continua (see Table 10.1) than those used in CVF.

Acknowledgment

The preparation of this paper was financially supported by the National Science Centre under the project titled: Co-creative relationships and innovativeness – the perspective of the video game industry (UMO-2013/11/D/HS4/04045).

Notes

1   Even though Schneider distinguished the "cooperation" model of organizational culture, which allows "fully utilizing one another as resources" (Schneider, 1999: 45; quoted by Maximini, 2015: 15), we consider it unsuitable for coopetitors as they still stay enemies (not friends) linked by both cooperative and competitive relationships at the same time.
2   The findings presented in this chapter are one of the results of two broader, separately run studies focused on organizational proximity in the aviation industry and co-creative relationships exploited by game developers. The same national scope and focus on organizational culture were the only joint aspects in those studies.
3   A detailed description of the research framework (including measurement method, survey questionnaire, methodology of data analysis) can be found in Klimas (2016).

References

Bengtsson, M. & Kock, S. (2000). "Coopetition" in business Networks—to cooperate and compete simultaneously. *Industrial Marketing Management*, 29(5), 411–426.
Bengtsson, M. & Raza-Ullah, T. (2016). A systematic review of research on coopetition: Toward a multilevel understanding. *Industrial Marketing Management*, 57, 23–39.

Bengtsson, M., Eriksson, J., & Wincent, J. (2010). Co-opetition dynamics–an outline for further inquiry. *Competitiveness Review: An International Business Journal*, 20(2), 194–214.

Bouncken, R. B., Gast, J., Kraus, S., & Bogers, M. (2015). Coopetition: a systematic review, synthesis, and future research directions. *Review of Managerial Science*, 9(3), 577–601.

Bouncken, R. B. & Kraus, S. (2013). Innovation in knowledge-intensive industries: the double-edged sword of coopetition. *Journal of Business Research*, 66(10), 2060–2070.

Cameron, K. S. & Quinn, R. E. (2011). *Diagnosing and Changing Organizational Culture: Based on the Competing Values*. San Francisco, CA: John Wiley & Sons.

Chai, Y. & Yang, F. (2011). Risk control of coopetition relationship: An exploratory case study on social networks "Guanxi" in a Chinese logistics services cluster. *International Journal of Interdisciplinary Social Sciences*, 6(3): 29–39.

Czakon, W., Mucha-Kuś, K., & Rogalski, M. (2014). Coopetition research landscape-a systematic literature review 1997–2010. *Journal of Economics & Management*, 17, 121.

Deal, T. & Kennedy, A. (2000). *Corporate Cultures: The Rites and Rituals of Corporate Life* (2000 Edition). New York: Basic Books.

Denison, D. R. (1996). What is the difference between organizational culture and organizational climate? A native's point of view on a decade of paradigm wars. *Academy of Management Review*, 21(3), 619–654.

Dorn, S., Schweiger, B., & Albers, S. (2016). Levels, phases and themes of coopetition: A systematic literature review and research agenda. *European Management Journal*, 34(5), 484–500.

Eckenhofer, E. & Ershova, M. (2011). Organizational culture as the driver of dense intra-organizational networks. *Journal of Competitiveness*, 3(2), 28–42.

Fernandez, A.-S., Le Roy, F., & Gnyawali, D. R. (2014). Sources and management of tension in co-opetition case evidence from telecommunications satellites manufacturing in Europe. *Industrial Marketing Management*, 43(2), 222–235.

Gast, J., Filser, M., Gundolf, K., & Kraus, S. (2015). Coopetition research: towards a better understanding of past trends and future directions. *International Journal of Entrepreneurship and Small Business*, 24(4), 492–521.

Gnyawali, D. R. & Park, B. J. R. (2009). Co-opetition and technological innovation in small and medium-sized enterprises: A multilevel conceptual model. *Journal of Small Business Management*, 47(3), 308–330.

Gnyawali, D. R. & Park, B. J. R. (2011). Co-opetition between giants: Collaboration with competitors for technological innovation. *Research Policy*, 40(5), 650–663.

Gregory, B. T., Harris, S. G., Armenakis, A. A., & Shook, C. L. (2009). Organizational culture and effectiveness: A study of values, attitudes, and organizational outcomes. *Journal of Business Research*, 62(7), 673–679.

Hatch, M. J. (1993). The dynamics of organizational culture. *Academy of Management Review*, 18(4), 657–693.

Hofstede, G. (1981). Culture and organizations. *International Studies of Management and Organizations*, 10(4): 15–41.

Iivari, J. & Huisman, M. (2007). The relationship between organizational culture and the deployment of systems development methodologies. *MIS Quarterly*, 31(1), 35–58.

Jarratt, D. & O'Neill, G. (2002). The effect of organisational culture on business-to-business relationship management practice and performance. *Australasian Marketing Journal*, 10(3), 21–40.

Jung, T., Scott, T., Davies, H. T., Bower, P., Whalley, D., McNally, R., & Mannion, R. (2009). Instruments for exploring organizational culture: A review of the literature. *Public Administration Review*, 69(6), 1087–1096.

Klimas, P. (2016). Organizational culture and coopetition: An exploratory study of the features, models and role in the Polish aviation industry. *Industrial Marketing Management*, 53, 91–102.

Liu, R. (2013). Cooperation, competition and coopetition in innovation communities. *Prometheus*, 31(2), 91–105.

Luo, X., Slotegraaf, R. J., & Pan, X. (2006). Cross-functional "coopetition": The simultaneous role of cooperation and competition within firms. *Journal of Marketing*, 70(2), 67–80.

Luo, Y. (2007). A coopetition perspective of global competition. *Journal of World Business*, 42(2), 129–144.

Maximini, D. (2015). *The Scrum Culture. Introducing Agile Methods in Organizations*. Switzerland: Springer International Publishing.

Naranjo-Valencia, J. C., Sanz Valle, R., & Jiménez Jiménez, D. (2010). Organizational culture as determinant of product innovation. *European Journal of Innovation Management*, 13(4), 466–480.

Naranjo-Valencia, J. C., Jiménez-Jiménez, D., & Sanz-Valle, R. (2011). Innovation or imitation? The role of organizational culture. *Management Decision*, 49(1), 55–72.

O'Donnell, C. (2012). This is not a software industry. In P. Zackariasson & T. L. Wilson (Eds), *The Video Game Industry Formation, Present State, and Future* (pp. 99–115). New York: Routledge.

Rijamampianina, R. & Carmichael, T. (2005). A framework for effective cross-cultural co-opetition between organisations. *Problems and Perspectives in Management*, 4, 92–103.

Ritala, P. (2012). Coopetition strategy: When is it successful? Empirical evidence on innovation and market performance. *British Journal of Management*, 23(3), 307–324.

Ritala, P. & Hurmelinna-Laukkanen, P. (2013). Incremental and radical innovation in coopetition—the role of absorptive capacity and appropriability. *Journal of Product Innovation Management*, 30(1), 154–169.

Ritala, P. & Tidström, A. (2014). Untangling the value-creation and value-appropriation elements of coopetition strategy: A longitudinal analysis on the firm and relational levels. *Scandinavian Journal of Management*, 30(4), 498–515.

Schein, E. H. (2010). *Organizational Culture and Leadership* (4th edition). San Francisco, CA: Jossey-Bass.

Srivastava, S. B. & Banaji, M. R. (2011). Culture, cognition, and collaborative networks in organizations. *American Sociological Review*, 76(2), 207–233.

Strese, S., Meuer, M. W., Flatten, T. C., & Brettel, M. (2016). Organizational antecedents of cross-functional coopetition: The impact of leadership and organizational structure on cross-functional coopetition. *Industrial Marketing Management*, 53, 42–55.

Xiao, Z. & Tsui, A. S. (2007). When brokers may not work: The cultural contingency of social capital in Chinese high-tech firms. *Administrative Science Quarterly*, 52, 1–31.

11

Coopetition and standardization

Anne Mione

Introduction

In this paper, we reveal how coopetition provides a new perspective on the standardization process. Standards are "a set of technical specifications adhered to by a producer, either tacitly or as a result of a formal agreement" (David & Greenstein, 1990). They perform different functions, such as defining products, ensuring compatibility, interoperability, guaranteeing safety, and reducing variety. The current world challenges for standards are considerable. They include ensuring food security for a growing population, building more accessible and smarter communities, protecting people's privacy, increasing cyber security and promoting economic development (ISO 2016 annual report). These challenges require knowledge about standardization, defined as the process of developing standards (understood as technical solutions that constitute market-dominant references).

Research has long differentiated standards according to two standardization processes: de facto standards are developed through market competition, and de jure standards are developed through committee negotiations. Thus, competition and cooperation are the fundamentals of standardization. Here, we explore how the introduction of the concept of coopetition, while perturbing this binary conception, offers a new view on the standardization process. We focus on the specific nature of the relationships between competitors who decide to cooperate in the standardization process. We aim to understand the strategic objectives of these coopetitors. A firm may shape and defend its own standard, ally and support a common standard, or adopt a hybrid position in searching for collaboration while seeking its own advantage. The concept of coopetition helps in understanding this situation. We suggest it throws new light on how firms manage this complex intertwinement between their individual interests and the collective mission for standards.

This focus leads us to disassemble the standardization process into three phases: pre-standardization, standardization, and post-standardization phases (Figure 11.1 below represents these three phases). The first phase describes a pre-standardization stadium; it presents a funnel to symbolize standardization as a movement that reduces variety. Among the diversity of techniques, devices, and solutions, only some will become standards as dominant solutions. Here, firms choose to compete, cooperate, or coopete to prepare a new standard emergence. In the contribution,

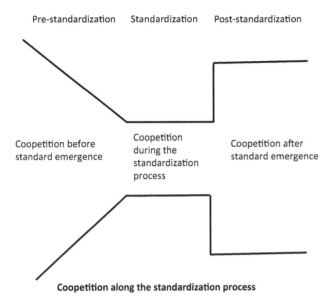

Pre-standardization   Standardization   Post-standardization

Coopetition before
standard emergence

Coopetition
during the
standardization
process

Coopetition after
standard emergence

Coopetition along the standardization process

Figure 11.1   Three loci of coopetition in the standardization process

we focus on coopetition strategies in this anticipatory state of a standard emergence. The second phase displays the standardization process. It represents as a rectangle to illustrate a confrontation between selected alternatives. The way sponsors support their standard against their rivals differs according to the context. In an institutional context, formal rules impose that rivals reach a consensus, which shapes specific strategies for competition, cooperation, and coopetition. In our contribution, we present research on coopetition in both market and institutional contexts. The third phase is post-standardization. We present a larger rectangle to illustrate a situation in which a standard has emerged and has largely diffused and gained dominance in the market. In this situation, the firms' strategies concern the adoption of the standard. They may choose to compete, cooperate, or coopete to conform to the dominant standard or to destabilize and propose a new standard. In the contribution, we show research on coopetition to conform and destabilize a standard.

The chapter is organized into two parts encapsulating these three phases. The first part presents the research on coopetition before standard emergence. We show how firms foster standardization in order to innovate, how setting standards is required for market innovation, why market stakeholders demand standards, and how a failure in coopetition slows innovation. The second part exposes research on coopetition during the standardization process and after standard emergence. We describe the de facto and de jure processes and show how coopetition differs in market or institutional contexts. We then present firms' strategies to conform or contest a standard and provide a new perspective considering standards to be a driver of coopetition.

Coopetition to foster standard emergence: The determining role of innovation

Research on coopetition has largely investigated how coopetition drives innovation. Research on standardization builds on the idea that innovation requires standardization. Standardization is required to commercialize a new product and create a new market; we present research showing that coopetition is in the best interests of standardization. To explore the relevance of coopetition to establishing new standards for creating a new market, we first propose analyzing the connection between innovation and standardization. We then discuss the two main mechanisms of standard emergence relative to competition and cooperation and introduce coopetition as a new perspective on standard-setting. The third section reveals the advantages and limits of coopetition as a relational strategy that seeks to establish standards that serve market innovation.

The relation between innovation and standardization is widely debated in the standardization literature. Standardization scholars are challenging the traditional perception of standards as obstructing innovation through their presentation of the "technology freezing" characteristic (Zoo et al., 2017). Considering the "innovation-standardization nexus," the authors recently reported different reasons that standardization can foster innovation. Initially, standards and standardization contribute to the creation and diffusion of innovation (Goluchowicz & Blind, 2011; Tassey, 2000). Standardization drives innovation when new standards impose requirements that lead firms to innovate. For example, the emission standards that regulate the car industry foster innovation to reduce CO_2 emissions. These regulatory standards specify the maximum emission rate authorized and plan the progressive reduction of CO_2 emissions over several years. The companies can anticipate and prepare to comply with the requirements; otherwise, they could be excluded from the market. Second, standardization facilitates the diffusion of innovation. Standards are a set of technical specifications and thus constitute a shared basis of advanced technological knowledge, condensed into an easily transferrable form for widespread adoption (Allen & Sriram, 2000). Standardization as a process of standard development offers critical opportunities to direct the focus of an emerging technology, which in turn facilitates the diffusion of innovation by increasing both economies of scale and network benefits (Swann, 2000). Blind (2002) also recognizes the significance of standardization as a diffusion channel of innovation. Third, standardization is considered an increasingly important tool to drive innovation that is often laden with complexity and uncertainty because of its ability to connect and coordinate the innovation process. Notably, Blind & Gauch (2009) show how different types of standards facilitate innovation in particular stages of the R&D process. Blind (2013) identifies four types of standards (variety reduction, minimum quality, compatibility, and information) and their effects on innovation. Variety reduction standards, by defining the specifications of products and services and reducing the variety of products, help firms attain economies of scale and critical mass for market success. Minimum-quality standards reduce the uncertainty and risks originating from the circulation of inferior goods in the market, thus building consumer trust in new, innovative products. This outcome leads to reduced transaction costs for a broader diffusion. Compatibility standards are central to achieving network externalities and avoiding lock-ins in old technologies. Information standards, by providing a common understanding of technological knowledge among standards users, reduce transaction costs and facilitate trade. In sum, the current body of literature recognizes a positive interplay between innovation and standardization (Zoo et al., 2017). This interplay can be specified as two specific mechanisms according to the competitive nature of the standardization process.

Coopetition as a strategy to foster innovation through standardization

Below, we specifically examine the advantages and limits of coopetition as a strategy to foster the development of a new product or market through standardization. We expose four case analyses in which coopetition succeeded or failed to set new standards for commercializing new products.

Coopetition as a required strategy to set standards for creating new markets

Coopetition constitutes a performant strategy to establish the institutional rules for creating a new market. Based on 300 questionnaires on standardization and interviews of the marketing directors of firms participating in the French Standard Development Organization (SDO), we empirically validated that companies chose to engage in normalization because they clearly identified the ability of norms to create new markets. We observed that leaders and innovators in the technology sector are more active in the development of standards. These businesses must cooperate because consensus is needed to establish institutional standards; at the same time, however, they compete with each other to promote their own technology and support the standard that is most beneficial to them. Thus, coopetition to establish norms appears to be a required phase of entrepreneurship strategy (Mione, 2009).

Coopetition as a strategy required by market stakeholders

A case analysis of the geosynthetics market, observing the innovation and standardization phases, showed the performance of coopetition in the early phase of development and a slowdown in the later phases of development (Mione, 2015). In this case analysis, the collective development of the market coexists with the individual interest of benefiting from the expertise of the different specialists. Cooperating facilitates competition as competitors obtain information on technical expertise; however, at that point in time, the development of the pie appears to be of greater importance than protecting the piece of the pie. Specifically, the development of the pie pre-empts the development of any part of the pie. For geosynthetics, the situation is more sensitive. Coopetition is not merely a market-development strategy; it is required by the users. Public works enterprises require reliable technical references, particularly with respect to new technology. Technical standards are these references, which are reliable precisely because they are the result of a process that involves all the players in the market. Therefore, coopetition can be a necessity for market development. For example, to develop an electronic document format, the market demanded de jure standards, and Microsoft was therefore required to engage in coopetition (Yami et al., 2015).

Coopetition failure as a breaker of innovation

The development of standards were fruitful to build new markets, but once markets were created, the development of standards became conflictual. The resurgence of competition in standardization drastically reduced the number of standards issued. When the market is developed, positions are defended. Each market has its own representation, conception, and methods. The interest in developing the global market is less collectively shared.

Coopetition is a complex strategy because it requires competitors to share a common vision of market development. A case analysis exploring standardization strategies to develop nonconventional material (bamboo and dried earth) for the Brazilian market (Mione, 2014, 2015) reported the same findings. Again, the stakeholders confirmed the need for standards to reduce information asymmetry and support market structures. In this case, we observed a failure in the development of common standards, which is due to the inability to agree upon a common vision. Social neoinstitutionalists show that battles over standards are based on wars between values, emphasizing the degree to which the contribution to the definition of standards constitutes the exercise of power to support specific representations.

We identified conflicts between contradictory registers of legitimacy (Suchman, 1995) in different situations of standard emergence (non-conventional material; Mione, 2014, 2015): the sustainable management of forests (Mione & Leroy, 2013) and geosynthetics (Mione, 2009, 2015). Because standardization requires legitimacy, coopetition in standardization constitutes a specific challenge; competition between values is barely addressed or resolved and generally leads to the failure of standardization. However, we can observe cases where coopetition enabled surpassing political opposition; this occurred when Microsoft achieved ISO standards as a result of its subtle management of coopetition (Yami et al., 2015).

Coopetition within the standardization process

Two modes of standard emergence: De facto and de jure standardization

The traditional literature on standardization states that competition and cooperation produce different types of standards. Specifically, standards are set through two main mechanisms: markets and committees (Farrell & Saloner, 1988; Funk & Methe. 2001). In this view, market–issued standards, also called "de facto" standards, emerge through competition, whereas committee–issued standards, also called "de jure" standards, are produced by the convergence of stakeholders through negotiation. Figures 11.2 and 11.3 below represent the two processes by which standards emerge.

A de facto standard spontaneously emerges from the market. Most firms adopt a technology that becomes a standard. A de jure standard is voluntarily defined in committees at the non-market level; this occurs when there is a need to create institutional rules to organize the market. SDOs gather a market's stakeholders and impose formal and consensual rules to establish formal standards. The consensual dimension requires at least enough cooperation to gather around a table and participate in the standard development.

However, this traditional view has been challenged by the introduction of a more complex understanding of the competitive relationship. Below, we show how the literature on de facto and de jure standards has progressively considered the hybrid nature of a competitive relationship and the introduction of coopetition.

Coopetition in de facto and de jure standardization

Competition is the dominant relational mode in de facto standardization. Much of the standard-ization literature has focused on de facto standards (Gawer & Cusumano, 2002; Schilling, 1998;

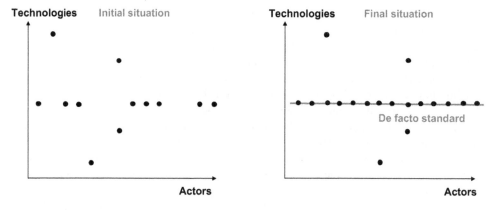

Figure 11.2 De facto standardization: the emergence of a standard through market competition

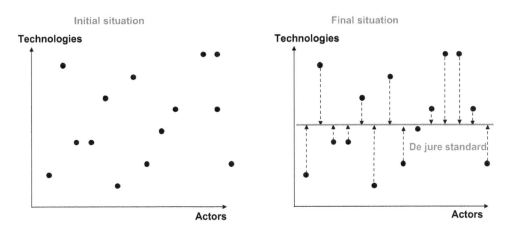

Figure 11.3 De jure standardization: the emergence of a standard through committee cooperation

Shapiro & Varian, 1999; Sheremata, 2004) and has demonstrated the aggressiveness of competition. In this context, the literature has described the "winner-takes-all" principle (Shapiro & Varian, 1999), which signifies that war is fatal to the loser. He is destroyed and disappears, which is a relatively scarce occurrence in traditional competition. Network effects explain this phenomenon, which provides a definite advantage to the survivor and assigns all benefits to the dominant player. Although there are certain limitations to this standardization movement, certain wars and battles remain famous because of the fatality issue (VHS/Betamax). However, a standards war requires allies, and Shapiro and Varian (1999) have long established that firms must ally with competitors to win a standards battle. This situation has been described as a coalition or a strategic alliance rather than as coopetition. However, Garud et al. (2002), who studied the standardization of Java sponsored by Sun Microsystems, noted that this process involved "coopetition." Gnyawali and Park (2011) referred specifically to coopetition in the context of innovation in the video industry. Direct references to coopetition to describe specific standards wars have recently occurred in various contexts, such as accounting (Fernandez & Pierrot, 2016), traceability (Allamano-Kessler et al., 2016) and the video industry (Allamano-Kessler & Mione, 2017). The de jure context offers more opportunities to identify coopetition because cooperation is clearly imposed by third actors in institutional contexts.

De jure standardization creates conditions in which competitors meet and collaborate. The research has examined how SDOs can resolve coordination problems. Comparing the relative performance of market competition versus committee coordination in forming standards, Farrell & Saloner (1988) find that although committees take longer to achieve a consensus than markets, committees tend to do better. Farrell (1996) emphasizes the advantage of achieving consensus and the benefits of avoiding a costly standards war. Other scholarship in this stream highlights firms' systematic venue preferences (Lehr, 1992; Lerner & Tirole, 2006) and the role that multiple competing standards organizations play in coordinating rule development (Genschel, 1997). Another stream of research has observed competitive relations during the standardization process. Oshri & Weeber (2006) noted that the two relational modes (competition and cooperation) can coexist at different stages of the development of a de facto or de jure standard. The researchers showed that at each stage of the development of a standard, actors choose among pure relational modes, cooperation or competition, or different levels of the hybrid mode. This approach had previously been developed in numerous works (Axelrod et al., 1995; De Laat, 1999) and shows the interest in deepening the knowledge of relational modes (cooperation and competition as "pure mode" and coopetition as "hybrid mode") at the emergence of a formal standard. Observing the de jure process, Yami et al. (2015) showed the subtle management of coopetition implemented by Microsoft for a document format. Microsoft alternated different relational modes in the coopetition situation within the AFNOR (French: SDO) and used coopetition as a means to maintain market control.

Research also shows that participating in committees develops the social capital of the engineers serving in these forums (Dokko & Rosenkopf, 2010; Riillo, 2013) and provides opportunities to make alliances (Rosenkopf et al., 2001; Benmeziane et Mione, 2015; Mione and Benmeziane, 2017; Waguespack & Fleming, 2009). Thus, de jure standardization creates the conditions for installing coopetition as a situation (Mione, 2009). In this context, coopetition constitutes a strategy to gain influence and control in the standard definition (Benzemiane & Mione, 2016). Realizing a quantitative study on data gathered from the European Cooperation for Space Standardization (ECSS) over the 1999–2014 period, Benmeziane & Mione (2016) show how coopetition is a performant strategy to obtain a strategic position within the SDO and to occupy a position to influence standard-shaping.

Coopetition to destabilize a dominant standard

Coopetition may serve strategies to destabilize a standard. We observe many situations where firms or organizations, instead of adopting the standard, choose to create a rival one. In sustainable management, the emergence and development of the Forest Stewardship Council (FSC) standard on sustainable forest management triggered the development of a rival standard (PEFC, first named Pan European Forest Certification and then called Program for the Endorsement of Forest Certification) (Mione & Leroy, 2013). In the context of electronic document formats, Microsoft would not conform to the ISO open-format standard and engaged in the ISO standardization process to define a new standard based on its own draft, OOXML (Yami et al., 2015). American and European universities have designed their own new ranking to destabilize the dominant Shanghai ranking. In these different situations, firms and organizations contest the order settled by the standard and offer an alternative. The choice not to conform and to engage in competition is based on three reasons. The first is that conforming adds weight to the standard; indeed, network effects apply to the standard (Mione, 2009). This is not only the case for interface standards that enable technical compatibility between networks. We support the idea that standards gain their structuring force on the market due to the network externality benefits (Katz & Shapiro, 1985). Only when they constitute a common reference will standards be an advantage for their users. The success of the ISO 9000 standard relates to this effect; firms choose this certification because of its widespread adoption and the more adopters, the more attraction to new users (Mione, 2009). For this reason, firms may refuse to conform to a specific standard because they do not want to contribute to its development through their own adoption and because to some extent this choice may influence followers. Creating, developing, and sustaining a rival standard is an attempt to interrupt the network effect that beneficiates to the dominant standard.

Second, firms and organizations may refuse to conform to a standard because they do not adhere to its value. Standards, however technical, define the behavioral rule that allows respecting values (Mione, 2009). In the sustainable management certification (Mione & Leroy, 2013), in geosynthetics (Mione, 2009), and for bamboos (Mione, 2015), we showed that rivals used different legitimacy registries, and that the battle of standards revealed a conflict between values.

Third, the decision not to conform and to instead propose an alternative may be due to the decision to control and shape instead of adapt to environment. Defining the "new game strategy," Buaron (1981: 27–8) is explicit about the advantage of shaping the environment:

> The successfull new-game strategist measures every strategic move by its impact on his relative competitive position. He knows that the first rule of gaining or sustaining an advantage over the competitors is to control the conditions of the game … So rather than waiting for the battle to come to him, he aims to choose the field and determine the manner and timing of the conflict. Continually weighing his company's strengths, vulnerabilities and resources against the competition, he is prepared to decide where to compete, how to compete and when to compete.
>
> *(Buaron, 1981: 27–8)*

More recently, D'Aveni (1995) showed that strategy is necessarily proactive, creating and perturbing the environment instead of admitting and adapting to it. Coopetition is required to install a standard battle and decide to settle new rules because standard definition requires allies. In this situation, the destabilization of the precedent order and the building of a new environment constitutes a driver for coopetition.

Standardization as a driver of coopetition

Standardization may also constitute an external driver of coopetition. In previous sections, we have reviewed research on standard-setting as a driver of coopetition. Another perspective explores standards as an external driver to coopetition. This is the case when firms decide to coopete in order to gain access to resources enabling them to conform to the standard. In an exploratory approach, Laifa and Mione (2012) considered how regulatory emission standards led firms to coopetition.

Bengtsson and Raza-Ullah (2016) have recently considered different levels of drivers triggering coopetition. The Gnyawali and Park (2009) model comprises the structuring foundation for the examination of drivers. This model offers the first dynamic coopetition conceptualization to feature the role of the drivers and integrates industry, organizational, and dyadic relational factors. Standards do not appear in this model. However, standards requirements may induce technological convergence and high R&D costs, which are elements beyond the three elements that describe the industry-level factors. New perspectives show that standard requirements impose new conditions that either authorize or forbid the product's entry into the market, thus exerting environmental pressure that favors coopetition. The institutional environment has been identified as a driver of coopetition (Mariani, 2007). The perspective of coopetition being either forced on or constrained by the environment is developed by Czakon and Czernek (2016), who add institutional, competitive, and customer pressure as exogenous drivers of coopetition. Finally, Bengtsson and Raza-Ullah (2016) proposed the inclusion of industrial characteristics, technological demands, and influential stakeholders as external drivers. We suggest considering standards as an external driver for coopetition.

However, standard-setting also constitutes a strategy that can drive coopetition. As noted by Overmars (2016), the intention to establish industry standards may induce coopetition because access to partners' broad capabilities can come in very handy when competing to win new product and technology battles (Hamel et al., 1989). Therefore, Overmars (2016) observes that one reason that companies can decide to collaborate with competitors is arguably their willingness to set industry standards (Overmars, 2016). In our view, standardization constitutes a driver of coopetition in two distinct situations: when competitors ally to settle a new standard and when competitors cooperate to share resources and innovate in order to be able to satisfy the requirements imposed by a new standard.

Conclusion

These insights lead to several recommendations for new research in this field. The first is to advocate the use of the coopetition concept to better understand standardization and firms' perspectives on their engagement in standardization. We suggest that standardization constitutes an ideal locus to explore coopetition from a strategic and managerial perspective. In standardization, coopetition is not exclusively a matter of simultaneous competition and cooperation on different levels, such as the market and non-market levels. Battling and partnership are simultaneously based on the standard definition. Partners fight and, at the same time, attempt to establish consensus; this is why the negotiation process is one emblematic locus of coopetition. In addition, de facto and de jure standards should not be differentiated as competitive or cooperative. De facto standardization requires collaboration and committee-issued standards also compete within the standardization process and in the market as soon as they are published; only through market competition will they gain dominance. Also, standardization can be seen as a pre-competition phase. However, in the research presented here, both phenomena, i.e., innovation and standardization, were intertwined. Finally, the standardization process is complex and requires overcoming apparent paradoxes. The concept of coopetition throws new light on the standardization process because it reconciles the antagonism between competition and cooperation. Such lenses are now required to better understand the complexity of the standardization process. We suggest starting with coopetition as a method of selecting standards that enable market innovation and, more generally, a market's smooth functioning.

References

Allamano-Kessler, R. & Mione, A. (2017). Coopetition to win a format battle; coo-standardization in the video industry. *22nd EURAS annual conference*, 28–30 June, Berlin.

Allamano-Kessler, R., Mione, A., & Larroque, L. (2016). Fatal competition, peaceful coexistence or active coopetition between traceability standards in the distribution channel? *21st EURAS annual conference*, June 29–July 1, Montpellier.

Allen, R. H. & Sriram, R. D. (2000). The role of standards in innovation. *Technological Forecasting and Social Change*, 64(2–3): 171–181.

Axelrod, R., Mitchell, W., Thomas, R. E., Bennett, D. S., & Bruderer, E. (1995). Coalition formation in standard-setting alliances. *Management Science*, 41(9), 1493–1508.

Bengtsson, M. & Raza-Ullah, T. (2016). A systematic review of research on coopetition: Toward a systematic level of understanding. *Industrial Marketing Management*, 57, 23–39.

Benmeziane, K. & Mione, A (2016). Coopetition to gain influence, leadership and control on Standard Setting Organization. *21st EURAS annual conference*, June 29–July 1, Montpellier.

Benzemiane, K. & Mione, A. (2015). Participating in standard setting organizations to build equity strategic alliances. *20th EURAS Annual Conference*, June 22–24, Copenhagen.

Blind, K. (2002). Driving forces for standardization at standardization development organizations. *Applied Economics*, 34, 1985–1998.

Blind, K. & Gauch, S. (2009). Research and standardisation in nanotechnology: evidence from Germany. *The Journal of Technology Transfer*, 34, 320–342.

Blind, K. (2013). The impact of standardization and standards on innovation. Compendium of evidence on innovation policy intervention. *Nesta Working Paper Series* (13/15), Manchester.

Buaron, R. (1981). New game strategy. *The Mac Kinsey Quarterly*, 12 (spring): 24–40.

Czakon, W. & Czernek, K. (2016). The role of trust-building mechanisms in entering network coopetition: The case of tourism networks in Poland. *Industrial Marketing Management*, 57, 64–74.

D'Aveni, R. (1995). *Hypercompétition*. Paris: Vuibert.

David, P.A. & Greenstein, S. (1990). *The Economics of Compatibility standards: An Introduction to Recent Research. Economics of Innovation and New Technology*, June, Stanford University.

De Laat, P. B. (1999). Systemic innovation and the virtues of going virtual: The case of the digital video Disc. *Technology Analysis and Strategic Management*, 11(2), 159–180

Dokko, G. & Rosenkopf, L. (2010). Social capital for hire? Mobility of technical professionals and firm influence in wireless standards committees. *Organization Science*, 21(3), 677–695.

Farrell, J. (1996). *Choosing the rules for formal standardization*. Working Paper, University of California at Berkeley. https://eml.berkeley.edu/~farrell/ftp/choosing.pdf.

Farrell, J. & Saloner, G. (1988). Coordination through committees and markets. *Rand Journal of Economics*, 19(2), 235–252.

Fernandez, A.-S. & Pierrot, F. (2016). The consequences of a third party decision on coopetition strategies; the case of the International Accounting Standard-Setting Process. *International Journal of Standardization Research*, 14(2), 1–19.

Funk, J. L. & Methe, D.T. (2001), Market and committee-based mechanisms in the creation and diffusion of global industry standards: the case of mobile communication. *Research Policy*, 30, 589–610.

Garud, R., Jain, S. & Kumaraswamy, A. (2002). Orchestrating institutional process for technology sponsorship: The case of Sun Microsystems and Java. *Academy of Management Journal*, 45 (1), 196–214.

Gawer, A. & Cusumano, M. (2002). *Platform Leadership: How Intel, Microsoft, and Cisco Drive Industry Innovation*. Harvard: Harvard Business School Press.

Genschel, P. (1997). How fragmentation can improve co-ordination: Setting standards in international telecommunications. *Organization Studies*, 18(4), 603–622.

Gnyawali, D. & Park, B. (2009). Co-opetition and technological innovation in small and medium-sized enterprises: A multilevel conceptual model. *Journal of Small Business Management*, 47(3), 308–330.

Gnyawali, D. & Park, B. J. (2011). Coopetition between giants: collaboration with competitors for technological innovation. *Research Policy*, 40(5), 650–663.

Goluchowicz, K. & Blind, K. (2011). Identification of future fields of standardisation: an explorative good idea? An example in practice. *British Journal of Management*, 23 (4), 532–560.

Hamel, G., Doz, Y., & Prahalad, C. K. (1989). Collaborate with your competitors and win. *Harvard Business Review*, January–February, 133–139.

ISO (International Standard Organization, also called International Organisation for Standardization). (2016). Annual report www.iso.org/publication/PUB100385.html.

Katz, M. & Shapiro, C. (1985). Network externalities competition and compatibility. *American Economic Review*, 75(3): 424–440.

Laifa, R. & Mione, A. (2012). Technical standards as drivers of coopetition, EIASM *Workshop on coopetition strategy*, September 12–14, Katowice, Poland.

Lehr, W. (1992). *The political economies of voluntary standard setting*. PhD Thesis, Stanford University.

Lerner, J. & Tirole, J. (2006). A model of forum shopping. *American Economy Review*, 96(4), 1091–1113.

Mariani, M. (2007). Coopetition as an emergent strategy: empirical evidence from an Italian consortium of opera house. *International Studies of Management and Organization*, 37(2), 87–126.

Mione, A. (2009). When entrepreneurship requires coopetition: The need for norms to create a market. *International Journal of Entrepreneurship and Small Business*, 8(1), 92–109.

Mione, A. (2014). Standard questions in developing a new market; the lessons from non-conventional materials. Key Engineering materials. *Trans Tech Publications*, 600, 413–418.

Mione, A. (2015). The value of intangibles in situation of innovation; Questions raised by the standards' case. *Journal of Innovation, Economics and Management*, 17(2), 49–68.

Mione, A. & Leroy, M. (2013). Décisions stratégiques dans la rivalité entre standards de qualité: le cas de la certification forestière. *Management International*, 17(2), 84–104.

Mione, A. & Benmeziane, K. (2017). Relational strategies in standard setting organizations; when alliances in standard shaping leads to alliances on the market. 17th EURAM annual conference, *21–24 June, Glasgow.*

Oshri, I. & Weeber, C. (2006). Cooperation and competition standards-setting activities in the digitization era: The case of wireless information devices. *Technology Analysis and Strategic Management*, 18(2), 265–283.

Overmars, C. (2016). *Factors that drive coopetition and exploration of potential supply-based drivers to coopetition*. University of Twente, 1st July.

Riillo, C. (2013). Profiles and motivations of standardization players. *International Journal of IT Standard and Standardization*, 11(2), 17–33.

Rosenkopf, L., Metiu, A., & George, V. (2001). From the bottom up? Technical committee activity and alliance formation. *Administrative Science Quarterly*, 46(4), 748–772.

Schilling, M. (1998). Technological lockout: an integrative model of the economic and strategic factors driving technology success and failure. *Academy of Management Review*, 23(2), 267–284.

Shapiro, C. & Varian, H. R. (1999). The art of standards war. *California Management Review*, 41(2), 8–32.

Sheremata, W. A. (2004). Competing through innovation in network markets: strategies for challengers. *Academy of Management Review*, 29, 359–377.

Suchman, M. (1995). Managing legitimacy: strategic and institutional approaches, *Academy of Management Review*, 20(3), 571–610.

Swann, G. M. P. (2000). *The Economics of Standardization: Final Report for Standards and Technical Regulations Directorate*. Department of Trade and Industry.

Tassey, G. (2000). Standardization in technology-based markets. *Research Policy*, (29), 587–602.

Waguespack, D. M. & Fleming, L. (2009). Scanning the commons? Evidence on the benefits to startups of participation in open standards development. *Management Science*, 55 (2), 210–223.

Yami, S., Chappert, H., & Mione, A. (2015). Strategic Relational sequences; Microsoft's coopetitive game in the OOXML standardization process. *M@n@gement*, 5(18), 330–356.

Zoo, H., de Vries, H. J., & Lee, H. (2017). Interplay of innovation and standardization: Exploring the relevance in developing countries. *Technological Forecasting and Social Change* (118), 334–348.

12

Coopetition and game theory[1]

Mahito Okura and David Carfi

Introduction

Many standard textbooks in microeconomic theory contain explanations of game theory, as it is a prominent section in microeconomics. However, there is one critical difference between game theory and traditional microeconomic theory. Traditional microeconomic theories, such as the perfect competition model, primarily focus on situations in which the decisions of one player (consumer and firm) never relate to the decisions of other players. However, this might not reflect in the real world. For example, the decision to lower prices in one supermarket might lead to decisions to lower prices in other supermarkets. In other words, one decision closely relates to other decisions. One attractive aspect of game theory is its ability to investigate such situations.

Although it is well-known that game-theoretical models are useful for analyzing various situations and markets, game theory is seldom used to investigate coopetitive situations. Coopetition studies have a long history. It has been more than twenty years since Brandenburger and Nalebuff (1996) published their pioneering study on coopetition; however, only a small number of studies have built game-theoretical models for investigating coopetition, such as Dearden and Lilien (2001), Okura (2007, 2008, 2009), Ngo and Okura (2008), Carfi and Schiliro (2012), Biondi and Giannoccolo (2012), Ohkita and Okura (2014), Arthanari et al. (2015), and Baglieri, Carfi, and Dagnino (2016).

There are three potential reasons why a game-theoretical model is seldom used in coopetition studies. First, most studies on coopetition are related to management rather than to economics. Moreover, game theory uses mathematical (and seemingly complex) models and equations based on (applied) microeconomics. Second, an important aim of many coopetition studies is to bring sophistication to the concept of coopetition and coopetition-related terms, such as value net. However, game theory seems unsuitable for this task. Third, case-study methods in coopetition studies are only moving towards quantitative methods as a common practice. These quantitative methods are based on observing situations and do not lend themselves readily to the game-theoretical model, which is mainly based on qualitative methods.

From this standpoint, the purpose of this study is to describe the advantages of game theory and how to use game-theoretical models in coopetition studies. To bridge the gap between coopetition studies and game-theoretical models, we describe the relationship between coopetition studies and game theory. Subsequently, we introduce the game-theoretical model of coopetition that appeared in the study by Okura (2009).

Game theory in coopetition studies

It is very important to understand that the infrequent use of game-theoretical models in coopetition studies does not imply that game theory is not useful for studies on the subject. For example, Brandenburger and Nalebuff (1996: 5–8) argued that game theory is useful for understanding coopetitive situations.[2] Lado et al. (1997: 113) argued that game theory can explain behavior in the context of inter-firm relationships. Clarke-Hill et al. (2003) and Gnyawali and Park (2009) explained a game theory approach in coopetition situation.[3] Okura (2007) explained the advantages of using game theory in coopetition studies. Pesamaa and Eriksson (2010) explained the usefulness of game theory for investigating actors' interdependent decisions. Rodrigues et al. (2011) applied game theory to investigating strategic coopetition. Ghobadi and D'Ambra (2011) summarized the characteristics, strengths, and limitations of using game theory in coopetition studies. Bengtsson and Kock (2014) pointed out that game theory is one of the research perspectives in coopetition studies. The game-theoretical models created by several studies enable research in several directions, such as insurance (Okura, 2007, 2009), green economy (Carfi & Schiliro, 2012), supply chain (Arthanari, Carfi, & Musolino, 2015), and R&D alliance (Baglieri et al., 2016).

Advantages of using game theory in coopetition studies[4]

There are three advantages to using game theory in coopetition studies.

The first advantage is that game theory is a very suitable methodology for analyzing inter-firm relationships because it can shed light on situations in which individual action significantly affects the payoffs of others (Shy, 1995: 11). Inter-firm relationships are a necessary condition to realize coopetition because coopetition is one of the situations that demonstrates a relationship among multiple firms. From this viewpoint, the market structures and conditions that are treated in both coopetition studies and game theory are very similar.

The second advantage is that game theory can easily depict coopetitive situations by isolating the cooperative and competitive aspects of coopetition using multiple stages. Coopetitive situation has a tendency to be complex because at least two aspects (competitive and cooperative aspects) appear simultaneously. Thus, both cooperative and competitive decisions, which have a close relationship, must be investigated. Game theory can also depict this situation and derive equilibrium stage by stage. In other words, multiple and complex relationships that consist of coopetition can be discomposed and analyzed.

The third advantage is that game theory is very rigorous and provides sophisticated solutions and equilibrium concepts. The discussions in game theory mainly consist of mathematical equations that are more objective expressions than verbal descriptions. Furthermore, the logical procedure of mathematical method is more formal than verbal description. For example, it is well-known that deriving first-order condition in an objective function is a typical way of discovering the optimal strategy. We insist, then, that results from game theory are very reliable; these results can be easily generalized, even if the focus of the analysis is specified. However, we also observe that game theory is not always the best methodology. Owing to the limitation in computation, the game theory model might contain some variables. However, the analysis in the game theory model might be insufficient to understand the actual situation, when neglected variables are critical for such explanation.

Representation of cooperation and competition in game theory

Suppose that a boy and a girl want to see a movie as a couple, and they have two choices, *Mission Impossible* (movie M) or *Pirates of the Caribbean* (movie P). Although the boy prefers to see movie M and the girl prefers to see movie P, both want to see a movie together. Thus, the boy's (girl's) preferences, in order, are as follows: see movie M (movie P) together, see movie P (movie M) together, see movie M (movie P) alone, and see movie P (movie M) alone. This game-theoretical situation is represented by the 2×2 matrix in Figure 12.1, referred to as Example 1 hereafter. In Figure 12.1, the pair of values in each cell (from left to right) represents the payoffs of the boy and girl, respectively. The matrix illustrates the players (the boy and girl), the strategies (movies M and P), and the payoffs (the values).

If the boy and girl simultaneously choose a movie, which one do they see? In other words, what is the outcome? This depends on the equilibrium, which is an important concept in game theory. In this game, the standard equilibrium concept used is the Nash equilibrium. As per this concept, "no player can profitably deviate, given the actions of the other players" (Osborne & Rubinstein, 1994: 15). Given this definition, the Nash equilibrium outcomes are "see movie M together" and "see movie P together." Although both outcomes cause the boy or girl to complain (for example, if "see movie M together" is the outcome, then the girl might complain), there is no alternative outcome that is better for both. In other words, this situation is somewhat competitive because either the boy or the girl can achieve the first best outcome. Then, a game such as that in Example 1 is sometimes termed the "battle of the sexes" (see, for example, Gibbons, 1992: 11).

Next, a slightly different situation can be considered. Suppose that the girl also prefers to see movie M instead of movie P. This implies that both the boy and girl want to see movie M. How does the Nash equilibrium change? To investigate this situation, we use the matrix in Figure 12.2, referred to as Example 2 hereafter.

Since the girl's preferences differ between Examples 1 and 2, her payoffs also differ. In this case, the Nash equilibrium outcomes are "see movie M together" and "see movie P together." Thus, although the girl's payoffs differ, the Nash equilibrium is the same in Examples 1 and 2. However, it is obvious that both the boy and girl prefer "see movie M together" to "see movie P together." Hence, if "see movie P together" were to be the outcome, both the boy and girl could do better by changing their strategies. However, "see movie P together" also constitutes the Nash equilibrium because both the boy and girl prefer to see a movie together.

One way of ensuring that the outcome is "see movie M together" or to rule out "see movie P together" is to introduce a coordinator to arrange the strategies. For example, suppose that a friend

	Girl	
	Movie M	Movie P
Boy Movie M	5,3	2,0
Boy Movie P	0,2	3,5

Figure 12.1 The battle of the sexes

	Girl	
	Movie M	Movie P
Movie M	5,5	2,0
Movie P	0,2	3,3

Figure 12.2 The coordination game

	Firm B	
	High	Low
High	4,4	1,5
Low	5,1	2,2

Figure 12.3 The Prisoner's Dilemma

of the boy and girl plays the role of the coordinator. In this situation, by indicating what strategies are desirable, the coordinator can ensure that the best outcome ("see movie M together") prevails. It denotes that the coordinator can ensure that cooperation between the boy and girl improves both their payoffs. In other words, this situation is somewhat cooperative because both boy and girl can achieve the first best outcome with the help of the coordinator. Subsequently, because it highlights the importance of coordination between players, a game such as that in Example 2 is sometimes termed a "coordination game" (for example, Osborne & Rubinstein, 1994: 16).

In Example 2, although an undesirable outcome constitutes the Nash equilibrium, a desirable outcome might emerge even in the absence of a coordinator. However, it is possible for an undesirable outcome to constitute a unique Nash equilibrium. In other words, a desirable outcome never emerges in the absence of a coordinator. To analyze such a situation, we introduce a different example, referred to hereafter as Example 3. Suppose that two firms, A and B, sell identical products to consumers. Firms choose between "high price" and "low price." Firm A's (B's) first preference is that firm A (B) chooses "low price" and firm B (A) chooses "high price." This would give firm A (B) a competitive advantage and higher profits. Firm A's second preference is that both firms choose "high price." Its third preference is that both firms choose "low price." The worst preference of firm A (B) is that firm A (B) chooses "high price" and firm B (A) chooses "low price," in which case many consumers would buy the product from firm B (A). The Example 3 is illustrated by the matrix in Figure 12.3, wherein the pair of values in each cell (left to right) represent firm A's and firm B's payoffs, respectively.

In Example 3, a unique Nash equilibrium is achieved when "both firms choose low price." It is obvious that a better outcome is realized when "both firms choose high price" than when "both firms choose low price." However, unlike in Example 2, the Nash equilibrium is not achieved when "both firms choose high price." Hence, in Example 3, a desirable outcome cannot emerge from voluntary actions. In this case, a third party acting as a coordinator might produce a desirable outcome.

It is noticed that the coordination required in Example 3 differs from that required in Example 2. In Example 2, the desirable outcome ("see movie M together") constitutes the Nash equilibrium. Thus, the coordinator simply informs the boy and girl of the best strategy. Contrarily, in Example 3, the desirable outcome ("both firms choose high price") is not a Nash equilibrium. Thus, even if the coordinator informs both firms of the desirable strategy, either of the firms will want to deviate from it because the desirable strategy will not be the best strategy for each individual firm. Either rules and incentive mechanisms or both will be needed to prevent such deviation. In summary, cooperation is more difficult in Example 3 than in Example 2. Labeling "both firms choose high price" and "both firms choose low price" as "cooperation" and "competition," respectively, clarifies why cooperation is more difficult to achieve in Example 3. The game in Example 3 is the well-known "Prisoner's Dilemma," in which a desirable outcome does not necessarily emerge even if the players pursue their preferred strategies.

Finally, for a later discussion on coopetition, we summarize these three results in terms of cooperation. In Example 1, there is no room to coordinate each choice because an outcome in which both the boy and girl are better off does not exist. In Example 2, a coordinator might change to an outcome in which both the boy and girl are better off. However, it may be possible to obtain the best outcome without the coordinator because it will also be a Nash equilibrium. Thus, there might be no room to coordinate each choice. In Example 3, the best outcome is never realized without a coordinator. Thus, a coordinator is surely needed for realizing the best outcome. From this perspective, we find that introducing a coordinator is critical for realizing cooperation in the case of the Prisoner's Dilemma.

The representation of coopetition in game theory

In many coopetitive situations, players such as individuals and firms choose their strategies sequentially, which gives rise to multiple types of strategies. For example, suppose that firms choose product quality and price. Firms normally choose quality before choosing price. Moreover, the quality level chosen in the first stage is arguably related to the subsequent pricing decision. Game theory can also be used during the analysis of sequential choice structures.[5] In addition to the players, strategies, and payoffs, a set of moves must be included. In the above example, quality choice is the first move and pricing is the second.

To illustrate the sequential moves, we incorporate sequential moves into Example 1. We introduce a "ladies-first rule," which allows the girl to choose first, instead of allowing the boy and girl to choose their strategies simultaneously. To determine the outcome in this situation, we must apply an appropriate equilibrium concept. In the terminology of game theory, it is referred to as the subgame-perfect equilibrium. Simply put, the subgame-perfect equilibrium is the Nash equilibrium in which the strategies of players represent a Nash equilibrium in each "subgame" of the original game. The subgame-perfect equilibrium can be derived by computing the Nash equilibrium at each sequential move. In game theory, it is standard practice to determine the subgame-perfect equilibrium by using "backward induction." According to the explanation in Fudenberg and Tirole (1991: 68–69), backward induction "is to start by solving for the optimal choice of the last mover for each possible situation he might face, and then work backward to compute the optimal choice for the player before." In the price–quality example, this involves analyzing the pricing decision first, although price is chosen second.

The application of backward induction to Example 1 with the ladies-first rule reveals that the unique subgame-perfect equilibrium is achieved when they choose to "see movie P together." The introduction of sequential moves into Example 1 eliminates one Nash equilibrium of the game ("see movie M together") because the girl is the first mover and she can decide which movie the couple sees together.

The sequential game represents a useful way of analyzing coopetitive situations because players choose multiple kinds of strategies and some (or all) of these strategies have decision orderings and relationships. To explain how coopetitive situations can be analyzed, we use Example 4, which is based on the research by Okura (2009).

Suppose that two insurance firms, A and B, play a two-stage game. In the first stage, both insurance firms decide whether to disclose the information about their policyholders for preventing insurance fraud. Such disclosure reduces insurance fraud in the insurance market and increases the benefits of both firms. Thus, the decision in the first stage may be cooperative as well as competitive. In the second stage, both insurance firms choose the quantities of insurance products. An increase in the quantities of insurance products in a rival insurance firm leads to a decrease in a firm's own quantities of insurance products. Thus, the decision in the second stage is surely competitive.

By backward induction, we first investigate the second stage. The amount of insurance in each insurance firm depends on the decisions made during the first stage. Thus, we must consider the second stage in all possible situations. In this game, there are four possible situations, that is, "both firms disclose information," "firm A discloses information and firm B does not disclose information," "firm A does not disclose information and firm B discloses information," and "both firms do not disclose information." It is obvious that the situations in "both firms disclose information" and "both firms do not disclose information" depict the lowest and highest amounts of insurance, respectively. In accordance with the amount of insurance, each insurance firm chooses a different quantity of insurance under the competitive insurance market. Subsequently, we derive the equilibrium quantity of insurance in the four possible situations by simple microeconomic theory.

After finishing the analysis in the second stage, we proceed to investigate the first stage. In the first stage, each insurance firm chooses whether to disclose its information. Subsequently, we depict that situation in a 2×2 matrix in Figure 12.4.[6]

It is evident that a unique subgame-perfect equilibrium is achieved when "both firms choose no disclosure," while it is undoubtedly better for "both firms to choose disclosure." Such disclosure would reduce insurance fraud and benefit both firms. However, benefits from a disclosure affect not only the firm that chooses disclosure but also the firm that chooses not to disclose. Thus, this gives each firm an incentive to free-ride by not disclosing. Such an undesirable outcome can be resolved by coordinating firms' decisions during the first stage. In addition, we observe that this result is maintained even when the number of insurance firms is more than two, because we can interpret "firm A" as "representative firm" and "firm B" as "other firms" in the model in Okura (2009).

		Firm B	
		Disclose	Not disclose
Firm A	Disclose	6,6	1,8
	Not disclose	8,1	2,2

Figure 12.4 The disclosure game

This result can explain the need for an information-exchange system such as the Life Insurance Network Center (LINC) in the life insurance market in Japan. The LINC compels all life insurance firms to disclose information. Thus, it can avoid realizing any undesirable outcomes. Finally, we know that cooperation and competition are realized in the first and second stages, respectively, and then a coopetitive situation is generated.

Example 4 shows that a game can combine cooperative and competitive elements and it can be analyzed stage by stage. Even if cooperative and competitive aspects are related, game theory facilitates formal derivation of results by using techniques such as backward induction.

Concluding remarks

In this study, we discussed the advantages of game theory and how game-theoretical models can be utilized in coopetition studies. Subsequently, we bridged the gap between coopetition studies and game-theoretical models. Our contribution is twofold. First, we explained the advantages of using game theory in coopetition studies. The advantages of game theory are: 1) it is a suitable methodology for analyzing inter-firm relationships; 2) it can discompose a coopetitive situation stage by stage; and 3) it can give very rigorous, reliable, and general results. Second, we showed the manner in which the game-theoretical model can be used in coopetition studies. We introduced the model used in Okura (2009), which depicted information-disclosing strategies to prevent insurance fraud. From the model's results, we understand that insurance firms cannot realize the best solution in a competitive insurance market; however, they can achieve this through a coordinator. In actuality, the Life Insurance Network Center becomes a coordinator, leading to cooperative information disclosure in the coopetitive insurance market. We imply that game theory can explain perspectives of actual coopetitive situations. For example, in this study, we introduced the model used in Okura (2009) for showing insurance firms' coopetitive information-disclosing strategies, in which all players are better off.

Many researchers in game theory are interested in analyzing coopetitive situations. Furthermore, the introduction of game-theoretical models in coopetition studies should foster collaboration among researchers in management and economics. The collaboration can formalize the choices of players and show policy implications. In addition, game theory can explain various situations by changing the settings and/or assumptions. Then, using game theory models, it is possible to compare many situations. In other words, we can compare situations in two countries or firms and understand how to achieve coopetition, what types of coopetition appear, whether coopetition is socially desirable, and so on. Ultimately, we believe that the study of coopetition within game theory has a wide variety of promising research agendas.

Notes

1 This article is a revised version of our article published in the *Journal of Applied Economic Sciences* 9(3) (Fall 2014): 457–468. This work was supported by JSPS KAKENHI Grant Number JP15K03727 (Mahito Okura).
2 Stein (2010: 257) mentioned that Brandenburger & Nalebuff (1996) "explain 'co-opetition' as an approach that intends to explain competition and cooperation in business networks in the spirit of game theory."
3 However, Clarke-Hill et al. (2003) used both co-operation and competition instead of coopetition.
4 This section is greatly indebted to the research by Okura (2007).
5 To simplify the explanation of sequential games, we omit strict definitions and proofs. For details of such definitions and proofs, see, for example, Gibbons (1992: Chapter 2).
6 Okura (2009) mathematically computed whether to disclose information. However, for simplicity, we represent the numerical example in Figure 12.4.

References

Arthanari, T., Carfi, D., & Musolino, F. (2015). Game theoretic modeling of horizontal supply chain coopetition among growers. *International Game Theory Review*, 17(02), 1540013.

Baglieri, D., Carfi, D., & Dagnino, G. B. (2016). Asymmetric R&D alliances in the biopharmaceutical industry: A multi-stage coopetitive approach. *International Studies of Management & Organization*, 46(2–3), 179–201.

Bengtsson, M. & Kock, S. (2014). Coopetition—Quo vadis? Past accomplishments and future challenges. *Industrial Marketing Management*, 43(2), 180–188.

Biondi, Y. & Giannoccolo, P. (2012). Complementarities and coopetition in presence of intangible resources: Industrial economic and regulatory implications. *Journal of Strategy and Management*, 5(4), 437–449.

Brandenburger, A. M. & Nalebuff, B. J. (1996). *Co-opetition*. New York: Doubleday.

Carfi, D. & Schiliro, D. (2012). A coopetitive model for the green economy. *Economic Modelling*, 29(4), 1215–1219.

Clarke-Hill, C., Li, H., & Davies, B. (2003). The paradox of co-operation and competition in strategic alliances: Towards a multi-paradigm approach. *Management Research News*, 26(1), 1–20.

Dearden, J. A. & Lilien, G. L. (2001). Advertising coopetition: Who pays? who gains? in M. R. Baye & J. P. Nelson (Eds), *Advertising and differentiated products*. Amsterdam: Elsevier.

Fudenberg, D. & Tirole, J. (1991). *Game Theory*. Cambridge, MA: MIT Press.

Ghobadi, S. & D'Ambra, J. (2011). Coopetitive knowledge sharing: An analytical review of literature. *Electronic Journal of Knowledge Management*, 9(4), 307–317.

Gibbons, R. (1992). *Game Theory for Applied Economists.* New Jersey: Princeton University Press.

Gnyawali, D. R. & Park, B. J. R. (2009). Co-opetition and technological innovation in small and medium-sized enterprises: A multilevel conceptual model. *Journal of Small Business Management*, 47(3), 308–330.

Lado, A. A., Boyd, N. G., & Hanlon, S. C. (1997). Competition, cooperation, and the search from economic rents: A syncretic model. *Academy of Management Review*, 22(1), 110–141.

Ngo, D. D. & Okura, M. (2008). Coopetition in a mixed duopoly market. *Economics Bulletin*, 12(20), 1–9.

Ohkita, K. & Okura, M. (2014). Coopetition and coordinated investment: Protecting Japanese video games' intellectual property rights. *International Journal of Business Environment*, 6(1), 92–105.

Okura, M. (2007). Coopetitive strategies of Japanese insurance firms: A game-theory approach. *International Studies of Management and Organization*, 37(2), 53–69.

Okura, M. (2008). Why isn't the accident information shared? A coopetition perspective. *Management Research*, 6(3), 219–225.

Okura, M. (2009). Coopetitive strategies to limit the insurance fraud problem in Japan. In G. B. Dagnino & E. Rocco (Eds), *Coopetition Strategy: Theory, Experiments and Cases*. London: Routledge.

Osborne, M. J. & Rubinstein, A. (1994). *A Course in Game Theory*. Cambridge, MA: MIT Press.

Pesamaa, O. & Eriksson, P. E. (2010). Coopetition among nature-based tourism firms: Competition at local level and cooperation at destination level. in S. Yami, S. Castaldo, G. B. Dagnino & F. Le Roy (Eds), *Coopetition: Winning Strategies for the 21st Century*. Massachusetts: Edward Elgar Publishing.

Rodrigues, F., Souza V., & Leitao, J. (2011). Strategic coopetition of global brands: A game theory approach to 'Nike + iPod Sport Kit' co-branding. *International Journal of Entrepreneurial Venturing*, 3(4), 435–455.

Shy, O. (1995). *Industrial Organization: Theory and Applications*. Cambridge, MA: MIT Press.

Stein, H. D. (2010). Literature overview on the field of co-opetition. *Verslas: Teorija ir Praktika*, 11(3), 256–265.

Part III

Coopetition tensions and management

13

Coopetitive tensions

Annika Tidström

Introduction

Coopetition consists of the paradox of cooperation and competition, which by definition can be seen as opposites. *Cooperation* means swimming or sinking together, while *competition* means that if one party swims the other party sinks and vice versa. The paradoxical nature of coopetition is naturally coupled with tension. It is a matter of preserving the competitive advantage of the focal company, and simultaneously sharing resources with another company. This tension is related to the balancing of cooperation and competition and, during the last decade, coopetition researchers have shown an increasing interest in studying tension in coopetition. The understanding of tension in coopetition is important from both a theoretical and managerial perspective and the research in this area is relatively nascent.

Defining tension in coopetition

First, it is important to know what we mean by coopetitive tensions. There is no common way of defining tension in coopetition. Many different concepts, such as conflict, disagreement, and friction, have been used in research related to coopetitive tensions. Sometimes conflict and tension are used interchangeably, although there is a difference in their meaning. According to Wilhelm (2011: 664) there is "an inherent tension between cooperation and competition … literature defines this tension as coopetition." In accordance with this view, tensions are integral to coopetition. Coopetition researchers (Fernandez et al., 2014; Le Roy & Fernandez, 2015) view tension as a natural incompatibility and one related to the paradox of cooperation and competition. Tension between cooperation and competition in coopetition can be seen as a prerequisite for, or as a cause of, conflict. It has been stated that "tensions create conflicts within firms" (Le Roy & Fernandez, 2015: 5). Tensions are more long-term and abstract than conflict, which is short-term and situation-specific (Tidström, 2014). The concepts of tensions and conflicts in coopetition are illustrated in Figure 13.1.

Coopetitive tensions may consequently be viewed either from the more general perspective of balancing cooperation and competition, or by exploring situations of conflict or incompatibility between firms involved in coopetition. In order to obtain a thorough understanding of

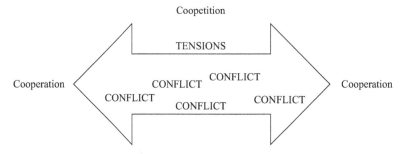

Figure 13.1 Tensions and conflict in coopetition

how to manage coopetition, it may be beneficial to focus on specific situations of incompatibility or conflict, as these often resemble tension on a more general level. However, it is sometimes difficult to draw a clear line between tension and conflict in coopetition. A tension concerning the division of cooperation and competition may be reflected in a conflict situation related to opportunistic behavior, or how much knowledge to share and what to keep secret. Moreover, conflicts in coopetition are related to each other, and may together reflect a tension. Accordingly, literature on conflict and conflict management is applicable when exploring tension. When aiming to understand tension, the first step is to identify what causes tension and what topics of tension exist.

Cause and topic of tension

The terms *cause* and *topic* of tension in coopetition are often used interchangeably, although there is a difference between them. A cause of tension is related to an issue or issues influencing the rise of a tension or conflict. As far as a cause of tension is concerned, it is possible to say that on the most abstract level, it is the coopetition paradox that causes tension. Moreover, it has been shown that a conflict in coopetition can trigger and be the cause of another conflict. Coopetition research distinguishes between silent or implicit, and articulated or explicit conflicts. In coopetitive business relationships, several conflicts may be silent, for example, hidden priorities, divergent economic interests, and different strategies, goals, and approaches (e.g., Fernandez et al., 2014; Gnyawali et al., 2016). It is possible to say that coopetitive conflicts may be caused by almost anything, and that a precise cause can be difficult to identify. Therefore, it is more reasonable to focus on the type or topic of conflict, which represents the issue or issues that the conflict is essentially about.

As far as the topic of tension is concerned, role tension is stressed in many coopetition studies (Bengtsson & Kock, 2000; Raza-Ullah, Bengtsson, & Kock, 2014). Role tension is related to the simultaneous existence of cooperation and competition. It might, for example, concern a situation when a manager perceives a cooperative and personal relationship with a manager from another company, while the firms are simultaneously competing for the same customers. A role tension may also involve incompatibility in dividing cooperative and competitive activities. The management of role tension is critical at both the organizational and relationship levels.

Another type of tension is related to opportunism, where the sharing of resources and activities can create an opportunistic situation, where one of the parties exploits a weaker party's interest (Fernandez & Chiambaretto, 2016; Osarenkhoe, 2010). Cooperation can impede a firm's operations by enabling the competitor first to obtain sight of, and then to imitate, the firm's core competences (Lado, Boyd, & Hanlon, 1997). This is a typical conflict in cooperation between competitors, and it is also often a critical conflict, as it may undermine the competitive advantage of one of the firms. However, topics of tensions in coopetition may also involve more general business relationship issues such as delays in deliveries from one company to the other, or the terms and modes of cooperation (Tidström, 2014). These types of tensions are often not as critical and intense as tensions related to opportunism.

There is little research on cause and type of tension, as most research focuses on the management of tension. Moreover, sometimes a similar issue may cause tension while on another occasion it may be the topic of tension. Increased communication and clear rules and agreements could perhaps reduce tension in coopetition. There are, however, some options available for managing tensions, and those are outlined below.

Managing tension in coopetition

As far as tension management in coopetition is concerned, coopetition research tends to view tensions as something that should be managed to deliver a desired and beneficial outcome. It is possible to distinguish between three streams of research concerning tension management: the underlying issues, separation/integration logic, and conflict management styles. These are summarized in Table 13.1 and further elaborated below.

The first stream of coopetition research (e.g., Tidström, 2014) stresses the importance of underlying issues to tensions. Underlying issues can be related to the compatibility of companies'

Table 13.1 Research on tension management

Streams of Research	Focus	Contributions	Limitations
Underlying issues	Compatibility and incompatibility of company-related issues such as goals and commitment	Influences the techniques of tensions management	Cannot be applied for managing tensions as such
Separation/ integration	Managing conflicts/tensions by separation and/or integrating cooperation and competition	Recognizes that separation and integration can be used on different levels	Views tensions and conflicts as manageable from a company level, without considering different options around using a technique or combining techniques on a certain level
Conflict management styles	Comprises the following styles for conflict management: collaboration, competition, compromise, accommodation, and avoidance	Focuses on an individual level and recognizes that various styles are used in various types of coopetitive relationships	Offers a one-sided perspective in only recognizing one party involved in a conflict

goals, visions, background, and size. These issues may influence both the style and success of tension management. For example, if both companies share a similar culture and background, and have a concurrent understanding of how value should be provided for the shared customer, the companies may be more likely to succeed in tension management. Another underlying issue that has been stressed is commitment: Morris et al. (2007) found that commitment concerns the perception that the other party is dedicated to strengthening both its own position and the relationship's position in the market. Moreover, commitment means that each party bears responsibility for the goals and activities that contribute to relationship outcomes. According to Morris et al. (2007), under-commitment by one of the parties will diminish the performance of both parties, but especially the party with the greater level of commitment. In a coopetitive business relationship, it is important that the companies are committed from the very start of the cooperation. If the goals for the cooperation are clearly set and the parties are committed to their tasks and to meeting their goals, it is far less likely that tension will arise than if the parties are not. The underlying issues for tension management are not similar to different techniques for tension management, but they serve as influential background issues in the success or failure of tension management.

Coopetition scholars often use a separation/integration logic as a way of managing tension in coopetition (e.g., Fernandez & Chiambaretto, 2016). The separation/integration logic was originally developed as a way of managing coopetition, but more recently it has been used in relation to the management of tension between cooperation and competition in coopetition. The separation logic implies that cooperation and competition, or more specifically, cooperative and competitive activities, are separated inside the company in order to avoid tension (Bengtsson & Kock, 2000; Seran et al., 2016). On the other hand, the integration logic means that cooperation and competition are integrated for tension management. The approach is based on the idea of the importance of individuals developing a coopetitive mindset and integrating cooperation and competition (Seran et al., 2016). There are studies showing support for the use of a separation logic and there are also studies supporting an integration logic. Most of these studies stress the value of using one of these logics over time and throughout the relationship between the firms involved in the particular coopetition. Scholars favoring integration criticize the separation logic on the grounds that it can itself be a source of tension (Seran et al., 2016). It has been argued that a combination of separation and integration would lead to the efficient management of coopetitive tension (Fernandez et al., 2014; Seran et al., 2016). It has been suggested that separation should be related to an organizational level, and integration to an individual level (Le Roy & Fernandez, 2015), which indicates the importance of relating different managing techniques to different levels.

A third stream of research (Raza-Ullah et al., 2014; Tidström, 2014) is influenced by the classic conflict management styles presented by Thomas and Kilmann (1974): collaboration, competition, compromise, avoidance, and accommodation. Tidström (2014) found that in inter-competitor cooperation, the styles most often applied were competition and avoidance, whereas the study found no evidence of the use of accommodation and compromise. However, a recent study of coopetition between a buyer and a seller, that is, vertical coopetition (Rajala & Tidström, 2016) found that the use of a collaborative style was most typical, and there were also situations when both accommodation and compromise were applied. Based on these findings it is possible to say that the nature of the coopetitive relationship, that is, whether it is vertical or horizontal, tends to influence the applied tension management styles.

The latest research on the management of tension in coopetition shows that the management occurs on different levels. Moreover, the same conflict or tension can be managed differently on distinct levels (Rajala & Tidström, 2016). For example, a team of individuals within one firm might apply a cooperative style when negotiating with representatives from the other firm, but simultaneously a compromising style may be employed on a relational level in meetings between the companies. However, there can also be differences in styles of tension management on the same level. For example, at the firm level, one of the firms might employ a competitive style, while the other employs an accommodating style.

Most coopetition research applies a *management* or *managerial* approach, and stresses the importance of managing coopetition and coopetitive tension. Naturally, a management approach is appealing from the perspective of business managers involved in coopetitive business relationships. However, the management option reflects a deliberate and strategic choice and activity. It is related to the single firm or the dyad, and the consequences of actions are considered predictable. This approach stems from traditional literature within strategic management. According to another, somewhat different, perspective, it is seen as more reasonable to cope with coopetition and tension in coopetition than to manage it. The coping perspective has its roots in business network research, according to which a business relationship influences and is influenced by other business relationships. Therefore, it is hard to manage, as a firm cannot influence the activities of, for example, its suppliers' suppliers, although those very activities may influence tension in relationships involving the firm. Coping represents a more dynamic and emergent perspective.

To sum up, it is possible to say that there are many ways to manage coopetitive tension. First, it is worth being aware of underlying issues that can influence the management of conflict. Second, an appropriate mix of separation/integration logic within different activities may be applied. However, the separation/integration logic is best suited to managing tension related to the paradox of cooperation and competition. The separation/integration logic seems to be well-suited for the strategic, predictable, and more long-term management of tension. When managing more emergent situations of incompatibility in coopetition, more fine-grained management styles are appropriate. The different management styles available are more aligned with coping with tension or conflict, rather than managing it. The three perspectives on tension management could be combined by identifying influential underlying issues affecting tensions, and thereafter aiming to prevent negative tensions by separating and/or integrating cooperative and competitive activities. Situations of conflict could then be managed using different kinds of management styles in separated and integrated activities. Moreover, it would be important to investigate combining tension management with the outcome of tension.

The outcome of tension

It is common to view coopetitive tension as negative, rather than as something positive. Tension per se is by definition negative as it is related to incompatibility. This is also the case in research on conflict within organizations as well as between organizations within a distribution channel. Examples of positive outcomes of conflict include the discovery of new and better ideas and processes, improved quality, and enhanced efficiency.

With regard to coopetition research, there are studies (e.g., Vaaland & Håkansson, 2003) outlining both negative and positive outcomes of conflict. Vaaland and Håkansson (2003) present conflict in business relationships as dysfunctional, or as a disease that disrupts. In the worst case, a negative outcome of a conflict may lead to termination of a coopetitive business relationship, which is often considered undesirable. However, the outcome of conflict in coopetition can also be positive; it might, for example, enhance creativity and innovation (Vaaland & Håkansson, 2003). A recent study on tension in vertical coopetition found no tensions that produced a wholly negative outcome for all parties (Rajala & Tidström, 2016). In other words, all conflict outcomes were positive for at least one of the parties involved. Moreover, there are studies showing that the outcome of a conflict in coopetition may be mutually positive, mutually negative, or mixed, meaning that it is positive for one of the parties and negative for the other (Tidström, 2014). Moreover, it may be possible to identify a neutral outcome, which implies that the outcome does not in any way concern any of the parties involved.

There are a few studies of outcomes, particularly on the benefits of tension in coopetition (e.g., Bengtsson et al., 2010). It is clear, however, that the outcome of a conflict can influence another conflict (Rajala & Tidström, 2016). Recent research also shows that the outcome of a tension may be different on different levels; for example, the outcome may be negative on the firm level owing to a reduction in revenue, while simultaneously being positive on a relational level owing to it giving rise to new and improved terms of cooperation.

Novel perspectives on coopetitive tension

Research on coopetitive tension highlights some important perspectives that should be acknowledged. First, tensions in coopetition should be analyzed from a multilevel perspective. Second, coopetitive tensions can be viewed from a practice perspective, by focusing on the practices and activities of the practitioners directly or indirectly involved. Third, it is worth considering a dynamic perspective on tensions, as no event in a business relationships occurs in isolation, but is instead influenced by past events, and will influence future events. These three perspectives are discussed in more detail below.

Research has traditionally viewed tension in coopetitive business relationships from the perspective of the organization or the relationship; however, there have been calls for coopetition to be studied from a multilevel perspective (e.g., Bengtsson & Kock, 2000, 2014; Gnyawali et al., 2016; Tidström & Rajala, 2016) following current research finding that coopetitive tensions can occur on multiple levels (Dorn, Schweiger, & Albers, 2016; Fernandez et al., 2014; Rajala & Tidström, 2016). According to the multilevel perspective, activities on one level influence and are influenced by activities on other levels. Therefore, it is important to view all issues of tension from the perspective of multiple levels, which means adopting a macro, meso, or micro level of analysis. The macro level represents the network level, or the external environment or context that influences and is influenced by a coopetitive business relationship. This level may comprise customers, suppliers, competitors, and governmental regulations. From a methodological perspective, this level can be studied by applying qualitative approaches, including the analysis of written documents related to the external environment. Another method for analyzing this level is to do so indirectly through respondents from the studied firms. The meso level can be divided into relationship and organizational levels; the relationship level concerns the interaction between the companies involved in coopetition, while the organizational or firm level relates to activities within one of these firms. The meso level can be empirically studied, for example, by applying single- or multiple-case study research including qualitative or quantitative methods. Current research often uses qualitative methods, whereas research applying quantitative methods is scarce.

The micro level constitutes individuals or groups of individuals within the firms. The micro level has recently attracted increased interest in coopetition research, especially in studies applying a practice perspective on coopetition. In a recent study, Lundgren-Henriksson and Kock (2016) apply a practice perspective and focus particularly on the individual level, and stress the importance of recognizing individuals in coopetition. Research focusing on this level of analysis could apply a qualitative research approach such as ethnography, discourse, or narrative analysis.

The practice perspective stems from the strategy-as-practice approach, which arose from a critique of the traditional view of considering strategy as something a company has. Instead, the practice approach focuses on the micro-foundations of strategizing, and highlights what individuals do and say. In terms of coopetition from a practice perspective, the focus would be on the activities or praxis of individuals as practitioners, and how those activities happen in practice. Research on coopetitive tensions could benefit from studying tensions from a practice perspective, by recognizing individual activities such as what is said and done. Individuals and relationships between individuals can be considered the starting point for coopetitive tensions between firms. In order to be able to understand the macro foundations of coopetitive tensions we need to start analyzing tensions at the grassroots level.

It is also a matter of fact that business relationships are dynamic rather than static. By definition, conflicts are also dynamic, in that they include a cause, a topic, an outcome, and management. Moreover, the outcome of a conflict may trigger other conflicts, and the intensity of a conflict can change over time. However, much of the research on tension in coopetition is conducted from a more static point of view; for example, when studying different types of tension or the management of tension. There are only a few recent studies that explore tensions from a dynamic perspective by recognizing types of tension in light of the outcomes of tension, or how the management of tension relates to its outcome.

Concluding remarks

This chapter presents some insights into coopetitive tensions that also can be seen as situations of conflict. However, there are still many gaps in our knowledge and suggestions for future research on coopetitive tensions are presented in Table 13.2 and described below.

Most research on tensions in coopetition focus on dyadic horizontal relationships, that is, cooperation between competitors. There is a lack of studies on tension within vertical coopetitive relationships between buyers and sellers, and of research on triads or groups of firms engaged in coopetition. Moreover, coopetition research is often based on large companies within the ITC sector, which suggests a need for more research within SMEs and other types of industries and business sectors. There is also a need to distinguish between levels of cooperation and competition and the nature of tensions. It has been argued that strong cooperation together with weak competition involves weak tensions with an outcome of limited dynamics, and that, in contrast, strong competition and weak cooperation involves strong tensions with potential benefits (Bengtsson et al., 2010).

Table 13.2 Current and future research on coopetitive tensions

Area of Research	Current Research	Future Research
Relationship type	Horizontal relationships	Vertical relationships
Size of companies	Large companies	SMEs
Concepts	Either tensions or conflicts	Interrelatedness of tensions and conflicts
Level of analysis	Single-level	Multiple levels
Focus	Organizations	Individuals
Tension management	Predictable and controllable	Unsure and emergent
Time	Coopetitive tensions as static	Coopetitive tensions as dynamic

Although there is a vast amount of current research on coopetitive tension, there remain many issues within this field that should be explored in the near future. First, on a conceptual level, there is a need to thoroughly explore the interrelatedness of coopetitive tensions and coopetitive conflicts. Special attention should be paid to exploring the interface between tension and conflict. Second, there is a need to explore elements of tensions on different levels and how they are related over time. The traditional relational- or organizational-level focus would need to be shifted down to the levels of individuals and groups of individuals and their activities in situations of conflict. It is through the activities of individuals that coopetition originates, exists, and develops. Moreover, we need to recognize that coopetitive tensions are dynamic and emergent, and that they may be hard to deliberately manage on a corporate level.

As far as coopetitive tensions are concerned, from a managerial perspective it is worth focusing on the initial phases of the coopetitive business relationship. In this phase, the terms of the relationship are established and joint goals agreed upon. If the companies are of the same size, and share the same opinion on how value is created, fewer negative tension may arise. Moreover, it is important to continuously balance cooperative and competitive activities, and to have a clear and well-communicated strategy of what to share and what to withhold. On a relational level, it may be worth using a collaborative style for tension management, with an outcome that is positive on multiple levels.

References

Bengtsson, M., Eriksson, J., & Wincent, J. (2010). Co-opetition dynamics – an outline for further inquiry. *Competitiveness Review: An International Business Journal*, 20(2), 194–214.

Bengtsson, M. & Kock, S. (2000). "Coopetition" in business networks—to cooperate and compete simultaneously. *Industrial Marketing Management*, 29(5), 411–426.

Bengtsson, M. & Kock, S. (2014). Coopetition – quo vadis? Past accomplishments and future challenges. *Industrial Marketing Management*, 43, 180–188.

Dorn, S., Schweiger, B., & Albers, S. (2016). Levels, phases and themes of coopetition: A systematic literature review and research agenda. *European Management Journal*, 34(5), 484–500.

Fernandez, A.-S. & Chiambaretto, P. (2016). Managing tensions related to information in coopetition. *Industrial Marketing Management*, 53, 66–76.

Fernandez, A.-S., Le Roy, F., & Gnyawali, D. R. (2014). Sources and management of tension in co-opetition case evidence from telecommunications satellites manufacturing in Europe. *Industrial Marketing Management*, 43(2), 222–235.

Gnyawali, D. R., Madhavan, R., He, J., & Bengtsson, M. (2016). The competition–cooperation paradox in inter-firm relationships: A conceptual framework. *Industrial Marketing Management*, 53, 7–18.

Lado, A. A., Boyd, N. G., & Hanlon, S. C. (1997). Competition, cooperation, and the search for economic rents: A syncretic model. *Academy of Management Review*, 22(1), 110–141.

Le Roy, F. & Fernandez, A. S. (2015). Managing coopetitive tensions at the working-group Level: The rise of the coopetitive project team. *British Journal of Management*, 26(4), 671–688.

Lundgren-Henriksson, E. L. & Kock, S. (2016). Coopetition in a headwind – The interplay of sensemaking, sensegiving, and middle managerial emotional response in coopetitive strategic change development. *Industrial Marketing Management*, 58, 20–34.

Morris, M., Kocak, A., & Özer, A. (2007). Coopetition as a small business strategy: Implications for performance. *Journal of Small Business Strategy*, 18(1), 35–55.

Osarenkhoe, A. (2010). A coopetition strategy – a study of inter-firm dynamics between competition and cooperation. *Business Strategy Series*, 11(6), 343–362.

Raza-Ullah, T., Bengtsson, M., & Kock, S. (2014). The coopetition paradox and tension in coopetition at multiple levels. *Industrial Marketing Management*, 43(2), 189–198.

Seran, T., Pellegrin-Boucher, E., & Gurau, C. (2016). The management of coopetitive tensions within multi-unit organizations. *Industrial Marketing Management*, 53, 31–41.

Rajala, A. & Tidström, A. (2016, August). A multilevel perspective on conflict management in vertical coopetition. *Paper presented at the 32nd Annual IMP Conference, Poznan, Poland*.

Thomas, K. & Kilmann, R. (1974). *Thomas-Kilmann Conflict Mode Instrument*. Tuxedo: Xicon.

Tidström, A. (2014). Managing tensions in coopetition. *Industrial Marketing Management*, 43(2), 261–271.

Tidström, A. & Rajala, A. (2016). Coopetition strategy as interrelated praxis and practices on multiple levels. *Industrial Marketing Management*, 58, 35–44.

Vaaland, T. & Håkansson, H. (2003). Exploring interorganizational conflict in complex projects. *Industrial Marketing Management*, 32(2), 127–138.

Wilhelm, M. (2011). Managing coopetition through horizontal supply chain relations: Linking dyadic and network levels of analysis. *Journal of Operations Management*, 29(8), 663–676.

14

Managing tensions related to information in coopetition

Anne-Sophie Fernandez and Paul Chiambaretto

Introduction

Coopetition researchers show that strategies create tensions at different levels (Fernandez et al., 2014; Tidström, 2014). These paradoxical tensions caused by the simultaneous combination of cooperation and competition are called coopetitive tensions. Previous studies have noted the different coopetitive tensions, proposing an understanding of the tensions and designing typologies (Fernandez et al., 2014; Tidström, 2014). Among the multiple tensions created in coopetition relationships, much attention has been paid to the value creation/value appropriation dilemma (Ritala & Hurmelinna-Laukkanen, 2009; Ritala & Tidström, 2014) at the expense of other types of coopetitive tensions. However, one critical tension in coopetitive relationships is linked to the management of information. Coopetitors must share information to achieve their common project – the collaborative objective – but they must also protect the same information to avoid its transfer to the partner – the competitive objective. This chapter focuses on this specific tension.

Building on previous research, we consider the management of coopetition to be the key success factor of any coopetitive relationship (Le Roy & Czakon, 2016). Several management principles have been highlighted: the separation principle (Bengtsson & Kock, 2000) at the organizational level, the co-management principle (Le Roy & Fernandez, 2015), or the arbitration principle (Pellegrin-Boucher et al., in press) at the team level, and the integration principle at the individual level (Chen, 2008). These principles can be combined to manage coopetitive tensions as a whole. However, we have little information regarding how these principles are concretely implemented to manage each type of coopetitive tension and, more particularly, how these principles can be implemented to manage tensions due to information in coopetitive relationships. The questions addressed in this chapter are as follows: how do coopetitors manage the tensions related to information? Do they implement separation, co-management, arbitration, or integration principles, and how do they do so?

This chapter is dedicated to the management of tensions due to information in coopetitive projects. After explaining the issues related to information management, we present the insights into this question and provide a research agenda on information management in coopetition.

Tensions related to information in coopetitive projects

Bengtsson and Kock (2014: 182) define coopetition as "a paradoxical relationship between two or more actors simultaneously involved in cooperative and competitive interactions, regardless of whether their relationship is horizontal or vertical." The combination of collaborative and competitive behaviors makes it indeed a paradoxical strategy that contributes to the emergence of tensions at various levels, including inter-organizational, intra-organizational, and inter-individual levels (Bengtsson & Kock, 2000; Czakon, 2010; Fernandez et al., 2014; Le Roy & Fernandez, 2015; Luo et al., 2006; Padula & Dagnino, 2007).

Coopetitive tensions are even more important at the project level because the implementation of coopetition strategies requires employees from competing parent firms to work together (Fernandez et al., 2014; Gnyawali & Park, 2011). The project level is thus relevant to an understanding of how intra-organizational tensions are managed. Among the numerous coopetitive tensions at the project level, the tension between sharing and protecting information is critical (Baruch & Lin, 2012; Fernandez et al., 2014; Fernandez & Chiambaretto, 2016; Levy et al., 2003).

The partners in an alliance can easily learn from one another, especially if they are competitors (Baruch & Lin, 2012; Capaldo & Petruzzelli, 2014; Lane & Lubatkin, 1998). Although partners must share information and knowledge to achieve the common goal of the collaboration (Dyer & Singh, 1998; Gnyawali & Park, 2011; Mention, 2011), each partner must also protect the strategic core of its knowledge from its competitor because partners that operate in the same industry must develop unique skills (Baruch & Lin, 2012; Baumard, 2010; Hoffmann et al., 2010; Ritala et al., 2015). Information that is shared within a common collaborative project potentially could be used in a different market in which the partners compete. In brief, the competing partner could benefit by appropriating the shared information (Hurmelinna-Laukkanen & Olander, 2014). Building on the work of Saxton and Dollinger (2004), we define the appropriability of information as the extent to which an organization could incorporate such information into its own products or markets. In inter-organizational relationships, firms must share resources while remaining wary of the risk that a partner may use these shared resources for other products or markets. This risk, or the "appropriability hazard" (Oxley, 1997), is stronger when partners are competitors because the appropriated resources might be used to develop products that could compete in the future with the focal firm's products (Ritala et al., 2009; Ritala & Tidström, 2014). In a coopetitive project in which partners could utilize shared information for their own purposes, the risk of opportunism and appropriation is particularly high (Baruch & Lin, 2012; Bouncken & Kraus, 2013; Hurmelinna-Laukkanen & Olander, 2014; Ritala & Hurmelinna-Laukkanen, 2009, 2013).

Thus, we define tensions related to information in a coopetitive project as the difference between a firm's need to share information to ensure the success of the common project and its need to limit information sharing to avoid informational spillover into other markets.

Managing information: A key success factor of coopetitive projects

Empirical studies on the impact of coopetition on performance (and innovation more precisely) have yielded mixed results. To explain these contrasting results, several authors have highlighted the role of information and knowledge management as a moderator between coopetition and innovation. For instance, Bouncken and Kraus (2013) found that sharing knowledge with and learning from a partner foster a positive impact of coopetition on innovation performance. In the same vein, Estrada and colleagues (2016) indicated that coopetition has a positive effect on product innovation performance only when internal knowledge-sharing mechanisms and formal knowledge protection mechanisms are present. Taken together, these contributions suggest that managing coopetition, and more precisely managing tensions related to information in coopetition, is essential (Bengtsson et al., 2016; Le Roy & Czakon, 2016; Park et al., 2014).

Managing coopetition is a pervasive research question, and recent research has identified several principles for successful management (Fernandez & Chiambaretto, 2016; Fernandez et al., 2014; Fernandez, Le Roy, & Chiambaretto, in press; Le Roy & Fernandez, 2015; Pellegrin-Boucher, Le Roy, & Gurău, in press; Seran et al., 2016; Tidström, 2014). The first principle, separation, advocates a functional, temporal, or spatial separation of the management of competition and the management of collaboration (Bengtsson & Kock, 2000; Herzog, 2010; Poole & Van de Ven, 1989). The second principle, integration, encourages individuals to transcend paradoxes (Chen, 2008; Farjoun, 2010; Luo et al., 2006; Oliver, 2004). Managers involved in coopetition must develop a coopetitive mindset to internalize the paradoxical nature of coopetition and to efficiently manage the related tensions (Chen, 2008; Gnyawali & Park, 2011; Luo et al., 2006; Raza-Ullah et al., 2014). Finally, the co-management principle states that firms can implement specific project structures in which they replicate managerial positions to manage potential tensions between the partners (Le Roy & Fernandez, 2015).

Beyond the principles used to manage coopetition, recent studies have investigated the organizational structures implemented by coopetitors to pursue common innovation projects. Le Roy and Fernandez (2015) highlight the creation of a common project team—the coopetitive-project-team—created by coopetitors to achieve their common project. More recently, Fernandez et al. (forthcoming) suggest that coopetitors can choose between two organizational structures—the coopetitive project team or the separated project team—depending on the nature of the innovation. The authors explain that each structure allows more or less information-sharing with competitors, but they do not examine how the information is shared, protected, and managed within the different organizational structures.

To sum up, only a few empirical contributions have gone beyond theoretical principles and identified the real stakes involved when managing coopetitive tensions at the project level (Fernandez et al., 2014; Fernandez, Le Roy, & Chiambaretto, forthcoming; Le Roy & Fernandez, 2015). Previous studies mainly address coopetitive tensions as a whole and do not investigate specific tensions in detail. The only contribution entirely dedicated to the information protection/ sharing dilemma is made by Fernandez and Chiambaretto (2016).

Managing information in coopetitive projects depending on the nature of the information

Because managing coopetition is the key success factor in coopetition, information management is the key success factor in coopetitive projects. The question becomes how to solve the dilemma between protecting and sharing information in coopetitive projects. Fernandez and Chiambaretto (2016) propose an answer to this question depending on the nature of the information and introduce two essential characteristics of a piece of information: its criticality and its appropriability. Depending on these two characteristics, the management of information in a coopetitive project can differ. Thus, we successively present the two characteristics: information criticality and information appropriability.

Information is critical if it is important or essential to a project's success (Pfeffer & Salancik, 1978). In a coopetitive project, certain information must be shared to avoid the failure of the common project (Baumard, 2010). Information that is critical to the success of the project should

Table 14.1 Management of different types of information

Criticality Appropriability	Critical	Non-critical
Appropriable	Protection and sharing	Protection
Non-appropriable	Sharing	Sharing

thus be shared, whereas non-critical information should be protected. To address information criticality, formal and informal control mechanisms can be used to separate critical from non-critical information, thereby ensuring that critical information is shared within the coopetitive project and that non-critical information is protected.

However, critical information can be appropriable or non-appropriable (Bengtsson et al., 2003; Das & Teng, 1998; Kumar, 2010). The risk of appropriation is higher in collaborations between competitors than in alliances between non-competitors (Hurmelinna-Laukkanen & Olander, 2014; Un et al., 2010). Non-appropriable critical information can be shared between coopetitors with low risk because the partner is unable to use the information for other projects (Padula & Dagnino, 2007; Un et al., 2010). However, appropriable critical information should, paradoxically, be both shared (for the project's success) and protected (to limit the long-term risk that a coopetitor will use this information for competing projects) (see Table 14.1). This situation is most important. How can coopetitors simultaneously protect and share the same information? Firms must answer this question to preserve their survival and to achieve goals of the common project.

Control mechanisms to manage information in coopetitive projects

To manage tensions related to information, the majority of firms rely on control mechanisms to foster the success of a common project while limiting the risk of opportunism (Das & Teng, 2001). Following Das and Teng (2001), control mechanisms are defined as a set of formal and informal rules designed to control the behavior of the partners and of the alliance *per se*. Control mechanisms are implemented to facilitate interactions between partners while limiting the risk of opportunism. Fostering cooperation between partners improves the partnership's "performance benefits" (i.e., the prospect of achieving the strategic goals of the alliance given the full compliance of all partners) (Das & Teng, 1996, 1998). However, control mechanisms should also minimize "relational risks" related to the level of each partner's commitment to the joint venture.

Control mechanisms may assume several forms. Formal control mechanisms may include contracts that define rules and penalties related to the information shared between coopetitors. Formal control mechanisms can also refer to formal procedures or structures to support the strategies of firms (Das & Teng, 1998, Lee & Cavusgil, 2006; Poppo & Zenger, 2002). Conversely, informal control mechanisms can be used to make decisions on a daily basis and to complement formal control mechanisms (Hurmelinna-Laukkanen & Olander, 2014; Ritala et al., 2009). For instance, to help determine whether a particular type of information should be shared to enhance a common project's short-term success or withheld to protect the parent firm's long-term success, managers must develop daily procedures and routines for categorizing information (Bouncken, 2011; Bouty, 2000). These informal control mechanisms, such as trust or reputation (Gulati, 1995; Lui & Ngo, 2004; Polidoro et al., 2011; Reuer & Ariño, 2007), also play a central role in the relational view of alliance governance and are not specific to the coopetition context.

However, several studies assert that formal and informal control mechanisms do not work separately and must be combined to manage tensions between partners and to increase alliance performance (De Man & Roijakkers, 2009; Faems et al., 2008; Lee & Cavusgil, 2006, Poppo & Zenger, 2002; Reuer & Ariño, 2007). In the specific case of coopetitive projects, we can assume that firms also combine formal and informal control mechanisms to manage tensions related to information.

The question of how formal and informal control mechanisms can allow the simultaneous sharing and protecting of appropriable critical information in coopetitive projects remains unanswered (Table 14.1). Depending on the information criticality and appropriability, firms will decide to protect (non-critical information), to share (non-appropriable and critical), or to protect and share (appropriable and critical information) the piece of information.

Solving the information protection/sharing dilemma: Insights from the space industry

In their recent contribution, Fernandez and Chiambaretto (2016) demonstrate how firms can solve the information protection/sharing dilemma in a coopetitive context, examining the manufacturing of telecommunication satellites. Two European competitors (ADS and TAS) have developed several common innovation projects such as Yahsat. With a global value of 1.8 billion dollars, Yahsat has become the most important space project in the world. The alliance between the ADS and TAS was driven by the presence of a common American competitor and by the high level of risk associated with Yahsat. To achieve the project goal, TAS and ADS pooled technological, financial, and human resources into a common project team. Yahsat thus represents an interesting case for studying the management of tensions related to information in coopetitive projects.

To highlight the nature of the information protection/sharing dilemma, they first reveal the existence of two types of informational tensions: financial and technical information. With regard to financial information, the authors show that ADS and TAS needed to agree on a common price before meeting with the client. To establish a suitable common price, the partners needed to share information about their respective margins and internal cost structures. However, this type of information is highly appropriable. The sharing of information related to margins or internal costs could expose either firm to a substantial risk in terms of future projects. Indeed, each firm would know its partner's competitive advantage, and this knowledge would distort future competition.

The second illustration of informational tension relates to technical information. Yahsat was a technically challenging project, and neither TAS nor ADS possessed the competencies and resources to undertake the project alone. Thus, the sharing of technical information between both partners was essential to the achievement of the project. However, the technical information shared within the project could have been appropriated and used to improve either partner's own products. Consequently, team members needed to share critical technical information to ensure the progress of the project while protecting appropriable technical information.

Regarding the management of tensions related to information, the authors showed that firms combined formal and informal control mechanisms to manage tensions related to information in the coopetitive project. The information system (IS) was designed to provide a formal control mechanism for the team, whereas project managers developed informal control mechanisms to manage informational tensions on a daily basis. These results confirmed that both separation (formal control mechanism) and integration (informal control mechanism) must be combined to efficiently manage coopetitive tensions (Fernandez et al., 2014; Pellegrin-Boucher et al., 2013). More precisely, they reveal that the use of formal and informal control mechanisms is related to the nature of the information: its appropriability and criticality (Baumard, 2010; Hurmelinna-Laukkanen & Olander, 2014; Kumar, 2010).

The common IS represented formal control mechanisms used to separate critical information (for the client at the corporate level and for the project at the project level) from non-critical information. Critical information was shared with the client or within the project, whereas non-critical information was protected from the coopetitor. The common IS also allowed the coopetitors to simultaneously share critical information (to ensure the project's success) and protect non-critical information (to preserve each parent firm's competitiveness). The implementation of these formal control mechanisms reflects the separation principle, i.e., the need to separate cooperative and competitive activities (Bengtsson & Kock, 2000).

Nevertheless, critical information shared through the common IS could become highly appropriable, and both parent firms face a high risk of opportunism. Because the common IS was insufficient to address this risk, additional informal control mechanisms were necessary. Project managers were responsible for assessing the level of appropriability hazard (Oxley, 1997). Critical and non-appropriable information could be shared with low risk because non-appropriable information could not be used outside of the project for other technologies, markets, or products (Bengtsson et al., 2003). Conversely, appropriable and critical information should by definition be shared to achieve the project, and protected because the information could be transferred and used by one firm at the expense of the other. To resolve this issue, project managers decided to transform the appropriable information into non-appropriable information. They asked to share data in aggregate form to successfully cooperate at the project level while remaining careful about potential leaks. For instance, project managers shared technical solutions but did not explain the steps that led to these solutions. To reduce the probability of reverse engineering, no details or calculation methods were provided. The same strategy was used for financial information. The only financial data shared between ADS and TAS were factory sale prices, which have little value without details regarding the firms' internal cost structures. Project managers' abilities to simultaneously share and protect information show that they have integrated the coopetition paradox. This result is consistent with the principle of integration highlighted in the coopetition management literature. Project managers have developed a coopetitive mindset and the capacity to transcend the paradox in a coopetitive context (Chen, 2008; Farjoun, 2010; Luo et al., 2006; Oliver, 2004).

To sum up, Fernandez and Chiambaretto (2016) have shown that firms can solve the information protection/sharing dilemma in coopetitive projects by combining formal and informal control mechanisms. In accordance with broader studies on principles to manage coopetition (Fernandez et al., 2014; Le Roy & Fernandez, 2015; Pellegrin-Boucher, Le Roy, & Gurău, forthcoming), coopetitors combine separation and integration principles to manage tensions due to information in coopetition.

Limitations of current contributions and research agenda

This chapter focuses on the management of a critical tension in coopetitive relationships: the tension due to information sharing/protecting between coopetitors. As previously explained, the success of coopetition depends on its management (Le Roy & Czakon, 2016). However, very little research has been designed to address this specific issue.

Only one study addressed the management of information in coopetitive projects. Fernandez and Chiambaretto (2016) distinguished different situations depending on the nature—critical and appropriable—of the information. The management of information in a coopetitive project is critical when the information is both critical and appropriable. The authors showed that coopetitors should combine formal control mechanisms, such as the design of specific information systems, with informal control mechanisms, such as the decisions of project managers, to manage critical and appropriable information in coopetitive projects. This result is consistent with previous research recommending the implementation of a combination of separation and integration principles to efficiently manage coopetition (Fernandez et al., 2014; Le Roy & Fernandez, 2015; Pellegrin-Boucher, Le Roy, & Gurău, forthcoming). The study of Chiambaretto and Fernandez (2016) represents a strong insight into the literature and encourages future studies to delve deeper and further. Future research could build on their work to address new research questions.

One line of research could further examine the control mechanisms highlighted in previous studies, examining the information systems used by coopetitors to manage critical and appropriable information. How is the information system built? What occurs to the information system at the end of the project? Researchers could also explore other control mechanisms or project managers used by firms to manage information in coopetitive projects.

A second perspective concerns innovation projects with multiple partners. How is critical and appropriable information managed in coopetitive projects involving more than two partners? Do they use the same control mechanisms? How is the information managed between competitors in open innovation or in open-source contexts? Do they share everything?

A third perspective concerns the nature of informational tension. Fernandez and Chiambaretto (2016) only considered two characteristics of the information (criticality and appropriability). Could we expect different findings depending on different types of information? The findings obtained here are illustrated in a R&D project. Does the informational tension differ depending on the project type? In addition, further investigation is necessary regarding marketing or selling coopetitive projects. How do coopetitors manage information related to their customers? Do they share or protect all the databases?

Finally, the management of information in coopetition relationships could be studied from a more longitudinal perspective. What occurs to the shared or protected information once the common project is achieved? What occurs when critical and appropriable information has been leaked? In addition, it would be interesting to consider whether information can be perishable. Thus, the value of certain information could be high at the beginning of the project but have no value at the end.

To conclude, we believe that the management of information in coopetitive relationships is a nascent research topic but a critical issue for coopetitors. Further investigation is absolutely necessary; thus, we encourage scholars to pay further attention to this exciting research question.

References

Baruch, Y. & Lin, C.-P. (2012). All for one, one for all: Coopetition and virtual team performance. *Technological Forecasting and Social Change*, 79(6), 1155–1168.

Baumard, P. (2010). Learning in coopetitive environments. In S. Yami, S. Castaldo, G. B. Dagnino, & F. Le Roy (Eds), *Coopetition: Winning Strategies for the 21st Century*. Cheltenham: Edward Elgar.

Bengtsson, M., Hinttu, S., & Kock, S. (2003). Relationships of cooperation and competition between competitors. Présenté à 19th Annual IMP Conference, Lugano.

Bengtsson, M. & Kock, S. (2000). "Coopetition" in business networks—to cooperate and compete simultaneously. *Industrial Marketing Management*, 29(5), 411–426.

Bengtsson, M. & Kock, S. (2014). Coopetition—Quo vadis? Past accomplishments and future challenges. *Industrial Marketing Management*, 43(2), 180–188.

Bengtsson, M., Raza-Ullah, T., & Vanyushyn, V. (2016). The coopetition paradox and tension: The moderating role of coopetition capability. *Industrial Marketing Management*, 53, 19–30.

Bouncken, R. B. (2011). Innovation by operating practices in project alliances – when size matters. *British Journal of Management*, 22(4), 586–608.

Bouncken, R. B. & Kraus, S. (2013). Innovation in knowledge-intensive industries: The double-edged sword of coopetition. *Journal of Business Research*, 66(10), 2060–2070.

Bouty, I. (2000). Interpersonal and interaction influences on informal resource exchanges between R&D researchers across organizational boundaries. *Academy of Management Journal*, 43(1), 50–65.

Capaldo, A. & Petruzzelli, A. M. (2014). Partner geographic and organizational proximity and the innovative performance of knowledge-creating alliances. *European Management Review*, 11(1), 63–84.

Chen, M.-J. (2008). Reconceptualizing the competition—cooperation relationship a transparadox perspective. *Journal of Management Inquiry*, 17(4), 288–304.

Chiambaretto, P. & Fernandez, A.-S. (2016). The evolution of coopetitive and collaborative alliances in an alliance portfolio: The Air France case. *Industrial Marketing Management*, 57, 75–85.

Czakon, W. (2010). Emerging coopetition: An empirical investigation of coopetition as inter-organizational relationship instability. In S. Yami, S. Castaldo, G. B. Dagnino, & F. Le Roy (Eds), *Coopetition: Winning Strategies for the 21st Century*. Cheltenham: Edward Elgar.

Das, T. K. & Teng, B.-S. (1996). Risk types and inter-firm alliance structures. *Journal of Management Studies*, 33(6), 827–843.

Das, T. K. & Teng, B.-S. (1998). Between trust and control: Developing confidence in partner cooperation in alliances. *Academy of Management Review*, 23(3), 491–512.

Das, T. K. & Teng, B.-S. (2001). Trust, control, and risk in strategic alliances: an integrated framework. *Organization Studies*, 22(2), 251–283.

De Man, A.-P. & Roijakkers, N. (2009). Alliance governance: balancing control and trust in dealing with risk. *Long Range Planning*, 42(1), 75–95.

Dyer, J. H. & Singh, H. (1998). The relational view: cooperative strategy and sources of interorganizational competitive advantage. *Academy of Management Review*, 23(4), 660–679.

Estrada, I., Faems, D., & de Faria, P. (2016). Coopetition and product innovation performance: The role of internal knowledge sharing mechanisms and formal knowledge protection mechanisms. *Industrial Marketing Management*, 53, 56–65.

Faems, D., Janssens, M., Madhok, A., & Looy, B.V. (2008). Toward an integrative perspective on alliance governance: connecting contract design, trust dynamics, and contract application. *Academy of Management Journal*, 51(6), 1053–1078.

Farjoun, M. (2010). Beyond dualism: Stability and change as a duality. *Academy of Management Review*, 35(2), 202–225.

Fernandez, A.-S. & Chiambaretto, P. (2016). Managing tensions related to information in coopetition. *Industrial Marketing Management*, 53, 66–76.

Fernandez, A.-S., Le Roy, F., & Chiambaretto, P. (in press). Implementing the right project structure to achieve coopetitive innovation projects. *Long Range Planning*. https://doi.org/10.1016/j.lrp.2017.07.009.

Fernandez, A.-S., Le Roy, F., & Gnyawali, D. R. (2014). Sources and management of tension in co-opetition case evidence from telecommunications satellites manufacturing in Europe. *Industrial Marketing Management*, 43(2), 222–235.

Gnyawali, D. R. & Park, B.-J. (2011). Co-opetition between giants: Collaboration with competitors for technological innovation. *Research Policy*, 40(5), 650–663.

Gulati, R. (1995). Does familiarity breed trust? The implications of repeated ties for contractual choice in alliances. *Academy of Management Journal*, 38(1), 85–112.

Herzog, T. (2010). Strategic management of coopetitive relationships in CoPS-related industries. In S. Yami, S. Castaldo, G. B. Dagnino, & F. Le Roy (Eds), *Coopetition: Winning Strategies for the 21st Century*. Cheltenham: Edward Elgar.

Hoffmann, W. H., Neumann, K., & Speckbacher, G. (2010). The effect of interorganizational trust on make-or-cooperate decisions: Disentangling opportunism-dependent and opportunism-independent effects of trust. *European Management Review*, 7(2), 101–115.

Hurmelinna-Laukkanen, P. & Olander, H. (2014). Coping with rivals' absorptive capacity in innovation activities. *Technovation*, 34(1), 3–11.

Kumar, M.V. S. (2010). Differential gains between partners in joint ventures: role of resource appropriation and private benefits. *Organization Science*, 21(1), 232–248.

Lane, P. J. & Lubatkin, M. (1998). Relative absorptive capacity and interorganizational learning. *Strategic Management Journal*, 19(5), 461–477.

Le Roy, F. & Czakon, W. (2016). Managing coopetition: the missing link between strategy and performance. *Industrial Marketing Management*, 53, 3–6.

Le Roy, F. & Fernandez, A.-S. (2015). Managing coopetitive tensions at the working-group level: the rise of the coopetitive project team. *British Journal of Management*, 26(4), 671–688.

Lee, Y. & Cavusgil, S. T. (2006). Enhancing alliance performance: The effects of contractual-based versus relational-based governance. *Journal of Business Research*, 59(8), 896–905.

Levy, M., Loebbecke, C., & Powell, P. (2003). SMEs, co-opetition and knowledge sharing: the role of information systems. *European Journal of Information Systems*, 12(1), 3–17.

Lui, S. S. & Ngo, H.-Y. (2004). The role of trust and contractual safeguards on cooperation in non-equity alliances. *Journal of Management*, 30(4), 471–485.

Luo, X., Slotegraaf, R. J., & Pan, X. (2006). Cross-functional "coopetition": the simultaneous role of cooperation and competition within firms. *Journal of Marketing*, 70(2), 67–80.

Mention, A.-L. (2011). Co-operation and co-opetition as open innovation practices in the service sector: Which influence on innovation novelty? *Technovation*, 31(1), 44–53.

Oliver, A. L. (2004). On the duality of competition and collaboration: network-based knowledge relations in the biotechnology industry. *Scandinavian Journal of Management*, 20(1–2), 151–171.

Oxley, J. E. (1997). Appropriability hazards and governance in strategic alliances: A transaction cost approach. *The Journal of Law, Economics, and Organization*, 13(2), 387–409.

Padula, G. & Dagnino, G. (2007). Untangling the rise of coopetition: The intrusion of competition in a cooperative game structure. *International Studies of Management and Organization*, 37(2), 32–52.

Park, B.-J. (Robert), Srivastava, M. K., & Gnyawali, D. R. (2014). Walking the tight rope of coopetition: Impact of competition and cooperation intensities and balance on firm innovation performance. *Industrial Marketing Management*, 43(2), 210–221.

Pellegrin-Boucher, E., Le Roy, F., & Gurău, C. (in press). Managing selling coopetition: A case study of the ERP industry. *European Management Review*.

Pellegrin-Boucher, E., Le Roy, F., & Gurău, C. (2013). Coopetitive strategies in the ICT sector: Typology and stability. *Technology Analysis & Strategic Management*, 25(1), 71–89.

Pfeffer, J. & Salancik, G. (1978). *The External Control of Organizations: A Resource Dependence Perspective*. New York: Harper & Row.

Polidoro, F., Ahuja, G., & Mitchell, W. (2011). When the social structure overshadows competitive incentives: The effects of network embeddedness on joint venture dissolution. *Academy of Management Journal*, 54(1), 203–223.

Poole, M. S. & Van de Ven, A. H. (1989). Using paradox to build management and organization theories. *The Academy of Management Review*, 14(4), 562.

Poppo, L. & Zenger, T. (2002). Do formal contracts and relational governance function as substitutes or complements? *Strategic Management Journal*, 23(8), 707–725.

Raza-Ullah, T., Bengtsson, M., & Kock, S. (2014). The coopetition paradox and tension in coopetition at multiple levels. *Industrial Marketing Management*, 43(2), 189–198.

Reuer, J. J. & Ariño, A. (2007). Strategic alliance contracts: dimensions and determinants of contractual complexity. *Strategic Management Journal*, 28(3), 313–330.

Ritala, P. & Hurmelinna-Laukkanen, P. (2009). What's in it for me? Creating and appropriating value in innovation-related coopetition. *Technovation*, 29(12), 819–828.

Ritala, P. & Hurmelinna-Laukkanen, P. (2013). Incremental and radical innovation in coopetition—the role of absorptive capacity and appropriability. *Journal of Product Innovation Management*, 30(1), 154–169.

Ritala, P., Hurmelinna-Laukkanen, P., & Blomqvist, K. (2009). Tug of war in innovation – coopetitive service development. *International Journal of Services Technology and Management*, 12(3), 255–272.

Ritala, P., Olander, H., Michailova, S., & Husted, K. (2015). Knowledge sharing, knowledge leaking and relative innovation performance: An empirical study. *Technovation*, 35, 22–31.

Ritala, P. & Tidström, A. (2014). Untangling the value-creation and value-appropriation elements of coopetition strategy: A longitudinal analysis on the firm and relational levels. *Scandinavian Journal of Management*, 30(4), 498–515.

Saxton, T. & Dollinger, M. (2004). Target reputation and appropriability: picking and deploying resources in acquisitions. *Journal of Management*, 30(1), 123–147.

Seran, T., Pellegrin-Boucher, E., & Gurau, C. (2016). The management of coopetitive tensions within multi-unit organizations. *Industrial Marketing Management*, 53, 31–41.

Tidström, A. (2014). Managing tensions in coopetition. *Industrial Marketing Management*, 43(2), 261–271.

Un, C. A., Cuervo-Cazurra, A., & Asakawa, K. (2010). R&D collaborations and product innovation. *Journal of Product Innovation Management*, 27(5), 673–689.

15

Knowledge management in coopetition

Isabel Estrada

Introduction

Coopetition, which implies the concurrent presence of cooperation and competition (Brandenburger & Nalebuff, 1996), is central to innovation. Firms face increasing pressure to cooperate in the innovation arena with other organizations with whom they compete fiercely in the marketplace (e.g., Gnyawali & Park, 2011; Le Roy & Czakon, 2016). The global automotive industry provides a good example of this. Leading carmakers such as Toyota and BMW are getting together to develop components that are so complex and costly (e.g., fuel-cell technology) that could not be easily developed by one firm on its own.[1] This chapter focuses on this form of coopetition: collaborative agreements between competing firms to jointly develop an innovation-oriented project, such as research and development (R&D), co-development of technologies, processes and/or products, etc.

In these coopetition settings, knowledge management is center stage (e.g., Fernandez & Chiamabretto, 2016; Ritala et al., 2015; Tsai, 2002). While the potential advantages of cooperating with competitors are evident (e.g., access to complementary knowledge), realizing these advantages requires intense knowledge sharing (Dussauge et al., 2000), which has been described as a "double-edged sword": a firm's core knowledge might end up reinforcing its competitor's market position (Bouncken & Kraus, 2013). Therefore, firms collaborating with competitors face a salient tension between knowledge sharing and knowledge protection (e.g., Estrada et al., 2016). Firms need to enforce the exchange of knowledge relevant to the joint project, while making sure that competitors will neither misuse that knowledge (Walter et al., 2015), nor accidentally access other valuable knowledge (Oxley & Sampson, 2004). Since knowledge is core to innovation, it is crucial to deal with the knowledge sharing–knowledge protection tension when working with competitors on innovation (e.g., Estrada et al., 2016; Ritala et al., 2015).

Against this backdrop, this chapter aims to review our current understanding of knowledge management issues in coopetition and propose some directions for future research on the phenomenon. The chapter's structure is as follows. First, the knowledge sharing–knowledge protection tension in coopetition is discussed. Second, an overview of recent research on knowledge management in coopetition is presented. Next, this literature is critically discussed, highlighting key research gaps and opportunities for future research. The chapter finishes with a short conclusion.

Coopetition and the knowledge sharing–knowledge protection tension[2]

As widely noted in the literature (e.g., Estrada et al., 2016; Ritala & Hurmelinna-Laukkanen, 2013), two important frameworks to study coopetition are the resource-based view of the firm (RBV[3]; Makadok, 2001) and transaction costs economics (TCE; Williamson, 1991). On the one hand, the RBV highlights that coopetition is an important strategy for value generation (Dussage et al., 2000). Coopetitors can possess mutually complementary resources, and normally use similar production processes and technology (Kim & Parkhe, 2009); this situation may smooth the process of bringing together their capabilities, generating fertile ground for synergies and innovation (Dussauge et al., 2000; Yan et al., 2017). On the other hand, TCE suggests that cooperating with competing firms encompasses hazards of value appropriation (e.g., García-Canal et al., 2008). Since coopetitors are market rivals, they could use a joint project to strengthen their market position vis- à-vis one another (Hamel, 1991). Furthermore, rivalry may contaminate and eventually take over the alliance (Park & Russo, 1996). Also, one party could take advantage by misappropriating resources of the other firm or of the alliance to opportunistically boost its own competitive position (Walter et al., 2015).

While both frameworks surely provide central ideas, coopetition arguably brings about both opportunities and hazards (Das & Teng, 2003; Dussauge et al., 2000). From this viewpoint, it is suggested that these two perspectives are complementary rather than competing (e.g., Castañer et al., 2014). Hence, the tension between value creation and value appropriation, idiosyncratic to the phenomenon of coopetition (Brandenburger & Nalebuff, 1996), is brought to the fore. In innovation settings, this tension finds its highest expression in the knowledge sharing–knowledge protection tension (e.g., Estrada et al., 2016; Ritala et al., 2015).

Coopetitors need to work closely with one another to effectively pool their knowledge and capitalize on their joint innovation options (Dussauge et al., 2000). Close interaction enables partnering firms to become familiar with each other's organizations; yet, in coopetition, this exposure may be problematic (Das & Teng, 2003); competitors may have opportunity, motivation, and ability to assimilate core knowledge from each other (Argote et al., 2003; Estrada et al., 2016). Thus, firms working with competitors incur salient risks of misuse and unintended leakage of information (e.g., Oxley & Sampson, 2004).

In a nutshell, firms seeking to profit from the innovation opportunities offered by coopetition (Yan et al., 2017) cannot escape the danger of giving away core knowledge to competitors (e.g., Castañer et al., 2014; Dussage et al., 2000). To the extent that these knowledge-related tensions impact the governance and outcomes of innovation agreements between competitors, knowledge management is crucial to these strategies (Fernandez & Chiambaretto, 2016; Ritala & Hurmelinna-Laukkanen, 2013).

The literature on knowledge management in coopetition: An overview

Table 15.1 summarizes examples of recent contributions relevant for the phenomenon of knowledge management in coopetition. Studies in this literature[4] can be classified into two main streams of research, depending on their main level of analysis (i.e., inter-organizational and intra-organizational). In this chapter, studies in these two streams are referred to, respectively, as relationship-level and firm-level studies.

Below, each stream is reviewed; afterwards, an overview of key insights is presented, bringing contributions from relationship-level and firm-level studies together, as well as from some recent studies that address both levels of analysis.

Table 15.1 Examples of relevant studies for the field of knowledge management in coopetition

Study	Foci of Analysis*		Purpose	Setting	Key Findings
	R	F			
Baum et al. (2000)	✓		To analyze the impact of the network composition of start-up companies on the performance achieved in the first stages after founding.	Start-ups in the Canadian biotechnology industry, founded between 1991 and 1996.	Startups that ally with established potential competitors typically exhibit lower initial performance. The impact of alliances with potential competitors varies with relative market scope and the competitor's innovative capabilities. For example, start-ups show better initial performance when they have relatively broader scope than their rivals.
Oxley & Sampson (2004)	✓		To analyze under which conditions alliance scope is used as a governance mechanism (to enable knowledge sharing while preventing knowledge leakages) in R&D alliances.	International R&D alliances formed by at least one firm in telecommunications equipment and/or electronics industries.	In R&D alliances, partners are less likely to select a broad alliance scope when: the overlap between their end-product markets is high (due to direct competition), and the overlap between their technology domains is low (due to lack of absorptive capacity). Partners are more likely to choose broad alliance scope when: all partners in the alliance are industry laggards, and the alliance is structured as an equity joint venture (and vice versa).
Enberg (2012)	✓		To analyze how knowledge integration can be managed in R&D projects between competitors.	Case study of Future Combat Air System (FCAS) project, a R&D project between five competing firms in five different countries.	Knowledge integration needs project management mechanisms like planning and process specification that foster shared understanding of the project. These mechanisms, while supporting knowledge integration, allow the partners to clearly demarcate what knowledge can be shared and to structure their face-to-face communication accordingly. Decision making should be a project team activity. Problem solving should be an individual activity to lessen unwanted knowledge leakages.

(continued)

Table 15.1 (Cont.)

Study	Foci of Analysis* R	F	Purpose	Setting	Key Findings
Ho & Ganesan (2013)	✓		To analyze under which conditions suppliers in coopetitive partnerships engage in mutual knowledge sharing.	Scenario experiment and survey study on firms in three technology-based industries (optics, automotive, and computing).	Under high customer participation and anticipated customer value, knowledge base compatibility between suppliers in coopetition increases knowledge sharing. If customer participation is high but customer value is low, knowledge base compatibility decreases knowledge sharing.
Ritala & Hurmelinna-Laukkanen (2013)		✓	To analyze the effects of a firm's potential absorptive capacity (PACAP) and appropriability regime on coopetition innovation outcomes.	Finnish firms in multiple industries involved in collaborative innovation with competitors.	PACAP positively affects incremental innovation. Appropriability regime is relevant for incremental and radical innovation. There is a positive interaction between PACAP and appropriability regime, which may be especially relevant for radical innovation.
Castañer et al. (2014)		✓	To analyze the performance implications of governance mode and governance fit in make-or-ally decisions.	Product innovation decisions (autonomous governance versus horizontal collaboration) in the aircraft industry.	Horizontal collaboration has a combination advantage and a governance disadvantage. It allows for higher market sales but also higher time to market than autonomous governance. Horizontal collaboration can yield superior performance when it fits the firm's resource endowment with respect to the product's resource requirements (e.g., firms lack the required resources for that product).
Walter et al. (2015)	✓		To analyze the effects of formalization and communication quality on perceived opportunism in R&D alliances between competitors.	German technology ventures in multiple industries involved in R&D alliances with competing incumbents.	The higher the degree of formalization (communication quality) in the relationship, the stronger (weaker) the perceptions of opportunistic behavior. The effect of formalization is more pronounced for knowledge appropriation than for other opportunism forms (strategic manipulation).

Reference			Objective	Method/Sample	Findings
Ritala & Tidström (2014)	✓	✓	To analyze value creation and value appropriation in coopetition networks, distinguishing between firm-level and relational-level strategies of the involved coopetitors.	Longitudinal in-depth case study of a coopetitive network formed by four Finnish manufacturing firms.	Participating firms held value-creation (collaborative versus competitive) and value-appropriation (positive-sum versus zero-sum) objectives at both firm and relational levels. Objectives at these two levels exhibited different levels of alignment, and tended to evolve over time. Hence, different value-creation and value-appropriation approaches could be identified across the network life cycle, eliciting different relational and firm strategies (e.g., firm-level strategy; value-creation approaches: "consistent coopetitive approach," "purely collaborative approach," and "fading interest").
Le Roy & Fernandez (2015)	✓		To analyze how coopetition tensions are managed at the working-group level (i.e., project team).	Longitudinal in-depth case study of a coopetitive project between two manufacturing firms in the aerospace industry.	To deal with tensions, the competitors combined integration-separation at two levels. They created a project team structure, purposefully separated from the other operations of the firms. At the working-group level, they applied the integration principle via "co-management" of the project.
Pahnke et al. (2015)		✓	To analyze the impact of indirect ties to competitors (via shared venture capitalist partners) on the innovation performance of entrepreneurial firms.	Firms in the medical device industry (minimally invasive surgical sector).	The number of indirect competitor ties has a negative effect on innovation, which is stronger when the focal firm-shared investor tie (i) is older, (ii) implies less commitment, and (iii) is formed at a higher geographic distance, in respect to the competitor-shared investor tie.
Bengtsson et al. (2016)	✓		To analyze the relationships between coopetition paradox, external tension, and internal tension, and the role of coopetition capability herein.	Swedish firms active in multiple industries.	The extent of coopetition paradox (cooperation intensity-competition intensity) positively affects how managers perceive external tensions, which in turn shapes their perception of internal tensions. Coopetition capability exerts a moderating effect on the coopetition paradox-external tension relationship: firms with strong coopetition capability show a tendency to describe a moderate degree of external tension (regardless of the extent of coopetition paradox).

(continued)

Table 15.1 (Cont.)

Study	Foci of Analysis*		Purpose	Setting	Key Findings
	R	F			
Bouncken et al. (2016)	✓		To analyze the relationship between alliance governance and coopetition intensity in product innovation alliances.	Vertical alliances formed by firms in the European medical device industry with major operations in Germany.	Alliance governance and coopetition intensity collectively impact product innovativeness in vertical innovation alliances. There is a negative (positive) interaction effect between singular transactional (relational) governance and coopetition intensity on product innovativeness. There is a positive interaction effect between plural governance (i.e., relational and transactional governance are jointly applied) and coopetition intensity on product innovativeness.
Estrada et al. (2016)		✓	To analyze the relationship between technological collaboration with competitors and firms' product innovation performance, examining the role of internal knowledge sharing and formal knowledge protection mechanisms herein.	Flemish manufacturing firms involved in technological collaboration with competitors.	When firms implement simultaneously (i) knowledge sharing mechanisms and (ii) knowledge protection mechanisms, collaboration with competitors has a positive impact on a focal firm's product innovation performance.
Fernandez & Chiambaretto (2016)	✓		To analyze how information-related tensions can be effectively managed in coopetition settings.	Longitudinal in-depth case study of a coopetitive project between two manufacturing firms in the aerospace industry.	The coopetitors faced tensions regarding financial and technical information, which they managed through combining formal and informal control mechanisms. They distinguished between critical and non-critical information and acted accordingly. They use formal control mechanisms (e.g., common information system) to share critical information. Then, the managers found informal ways to safely share critical information with one another (e.g., disguising details about cost structures).

* In this column, studies are classified as relationship-level studies (R) and/or firm-level studies (F), depending on their main level of analysis (i.e., inter-organizational and/or intra-organizational).

Knowledge management in coopetition (i): Relationship-level studies

The first stream of research focuses on the inter-organizational level, adopting the coopetitors' relationship as the main unit of analysis. A basic premise here is that the coopetitors' capability to manage the knowledge sharing–knowledge protection tension is determined by how they structure and orchestrate their relationship (e.g., Walter et al., 2015).

Within this stream, a first set of papers emphasizes the role of macro-structural aspects of collaborative agreements between competitors (e.g., Baum et al., 2000; Oxley & Sampson, 2004). When opportunism hazards are high, as occurs in coopetition, firms may tend to select protective governance structures such as joint ventures (e.g., García-Canal et al., 2008). Oxley and Sampson (2004) highlight alliance scope as an alternative mechanism to orchestrate knowledge exchange in R&D alliances while mitigating unintended information leakages. These authors conclude, amongst other things, that when partners are direct competitors in the market, they tend to limit their exposure by setting narrow scope agreements (i.e., they collaborate only on R&D activities). Other alliance structural characteristics, such as the alliance resource configuration (e.g., Baum et al., 2000; Ho & Ganesan, 2013), have been identified as relevant factors for the knowledge sharing–knowledge protection tension. For example, Baum et al. (2000) stress that although allying with competitors causes severe risks for start-ups due to the potential loss of proprietary information, these risks can be mitigated by prudently selecting coopetitors. To boost learning opportunities while lessening learning race risk, start-ups could select coopetitors with a relatively narrower market domain.

A second set of papers zooms in on the organization of the relationship itself, focusing on micro-structural aspects of coopetition (e.g., Bouncken et al., 2016; Enberg, 2012; Walter et al., 2015). These studies highlight more specific mechanisms adopted by competitors to structure, monitor, govern, and manage their collaborative agreements. For example, studying R&D alliances between competitors, Walter et al. (2015) analyze the effects of formalization and communication quality on perceived opportunism (e.g., the likelihood of knowledge misappropriation). They find that high communication quality mitigates opportunism perceptions, while formalization has the opposite effect. Enberg (2012) studies a R&D project between multiple competing firms in the aerospace industry and shows that to facilitate healthy knowledge integration, coopetitors should implement project management mechanisms (e.g., planning and process specification) that demarcate what knowledge can be shared and structure face-to-face discussions accordingly.

Overall, these relationship-level studies show that macro- and micro-structural aspects of relationships between coopetitors play an important role in managing the knowledge sharing–knowledge protection tension. Thus, the management of knowledge-related tensions is different for different coopetition relationships.

Knowledge management in coopetition (ii): Firm-level studies

This second stream of research examines the management of knowledge-related coopetition tensions at the intra-organizational level of analysis, thereby adopting a focal firm perspective (e.g., Pahnke et al., 2015; Ritala & Hurmelinna-Laukkanen, 2013). A core tenet in these papers is that a focal firm's ability to manage coopetition tensions is contingent on a variety of firm-level factors. Within this collection of literature, some papers underline the role of macro-organizational aspects, such as the firm's resource profile (e.g., Castañer et al., 2014) or network composition (e.g., Pahnke et al., 2015). For example, Pahnke et al. (2015) stress that, for entrepreneurial firms, sharing a venture capitalist partner with a competitor involves the serious threat that core knowledge spills over to that competitor. Their analyses suggest that firms could mitigate information outflows through, for example, minimizing the indirect ties to competitors via shared investors. Other studies offer a close-up view of the role of firm-level factors in managing knowledge-related dilemmas, focusing on fine-grained organizational aspects (e.g., Estrada et al., 2016; Ritala & Hurmelinna-Laukkanen, 2013). For example, Ritala and Hurmelinna-Laukkanen (2013) suggest that a firm's potential absorptive capacity and appropriability regime influence its ability to balance knowledge sharing and knowledge protection in coopetition settings. Potential absorptive capacity is crucial to learning from competitors, while a suitable appropriability regime guarantees safe knowledge transfer. Complementing this evidence, Estrada et al. (2016) stress two complementary organizational mechanisms: internal knowledge sharing (i.e., incentives for employees to internally share knowledge) and formal knowledge protection (e.g., patents). Knowledge sharing mechanisms bridge the gap between potential and realized absorptive capacity, enabling the combination of the competitors' and focal firm's knowledge; knowledge protection mechanisms demarcate knowledge limits, attenuating the risk that competitors inadvertently access core knowledge.

Together, these firm-level studies indicate that macro and micro intra-organizational characteristics are crucial to a firm's ability to manage knowledge-related tensions in coopetition. Thus, firms' capabilities to manage these tensions are heterogeneous.

Knowledge management in coopetition (iii): Key insights

Bringing together lessons generated by relationship-level and firm-level studies, it can be concluded that management of the knowledge sharing–knowledge protection tension is context-specific and firm-specific, in that it differs both across relationships and firms. Thus, two coopetitors' capability to effectively exchange knowledge depends on the overall structure of their alliance (e.g., governance form and scope) but also on the specific management mechanisms they implement to govern their relationship (e.g., formalization, communication quality). Also, a focal firm's ability to manage these coopetition tensions has to do with its overall alliance strategy (e.g., criteria used to select direct and indirect ties to competitors) and how well equipped the firm is to deal with these tensions (e.g., absorptive capacity, knowledge protection mechanisms). Therefore, both the inter-organizational and intra-organizational dimensions of knowledge management are key to dealing with knowledge-related tensions in coopetition.

Furthermore, some recent studies that conduct both relational and firm-level analyses suggest that the inter- and intra-organizational dimensions of knowledge management in coopetition may be highly interrelated. Based on the longitudinal study of a coopetition network, Ritala and Tidström (2014) reveal how coopetitors may follow different and dynamic value-creation and value-appropriation strategies on both firm and relationship levels. Other papers examining coopetition tensions in R&D alliances in general (i.e., not necessarily among competitors), also show that management solutions adopted at different levels can play out in balancing these tensions (e.g., Cassiman et al., 2009). More recently, some studies have started examining coopetition capabilities, highlighting both relational and firm-level implications (e.g., Bengtsson et al., 2016). Building on earlier work on coopetition (e.g., Gnyawali & Park, 2011) and the ambidexterity literature, Bengtsson et al. (2016) argue that coopetition implies relationship-level tensions (e.g., top managers face conflicts between knowledge sharing and protection), which in turn trigger firm-level tensions (e.g., employees do not understand managers' decisions). These authors conclude that coopetition capabilities aid managers' efforts to mitigate the relational coopetition paradox and bring employees on board, smoothing tensions within their organization.

To sum up, studies addressing the phenomenon from relationship-level and/or firm-level perspectives have suggested a range of mechanisms that coopetitors, individually and/or collectively, can implement to effectively orchestrate their agreements. Despite these remarkable contributions, this literature also presents some important gaps and limitations. The following section elaborates these issues and presents some promising avenues to further develop this research field.

Knowledge management in coopetition: Research gaps and agenda

Foci of analysis: Inter-organizational versus intra-organizational

As discussed, the majority of existing studies examine the management of the knowledge sharing–knowledge protection tension either focusing on the coopetitors' relationship or adopting a focal firm perspective. This tendency to embrace an almost one-sided focus of analysis (i.e., either inter-organizational or intra-organizational) still represents a central limitation of existing research. Coopetition scholars increasingly support this claim (e.g., Bengtsson et al., 2016; Fernandez et al., 2014).

Recent studies developing a more integrative approach (e.g., Bengtsson et al., 2016; Ritala & Tidström, 2014), have begun to show how important it is to account for the inter-organizational and intra-organizational levels to explaining knowledge management in coopetition. It is suggested that knowledge-related coopetition tensions may have implications on both levels simultaneously (Fernandez et al., 2014); thus, additional integrative studies are needed. Scholars should turn their attention towards the connections between relational and firm-level facets of knowledge management strategies in coopetition. Besides researching further the topic of coopetition capabilities (e.g., Bengtsson et al., 2016), an interesting path for future work could be to examine firm-level mechanisms that can act as bridges between the inter-organizational and intra-organizational aspects of knowledge management strategies. For example, it would be interesting to explore the role of firms' innovation committees or central innovation offices (e.g., Bianchi et al., 2015). While these mechanisms clearly focus on the internal organization of innovation activities, they might also facilitate the management of knowledge-related coopetition tensions in the long term (e.g., demarcating what is core knowledge within the overall innovation strategy of the firm).

Number of coopetitors: Dyadic versus multi-partner coopetition settings

Multi-partner agreements are commonplace coopetition strategies (e.g., Bengtsson & Kock, 2000; Browning et al., 1995). In the presence of multiple coopetitors, knowledge issues become even more salient (Das & Teng, 2002; Li et al., 2012). Yet, in coopetition research the majority of attention is paid to dyadic settings; a relatively smaller number of studies focus on multi-party coopetition (e.g., Enberg, 2012; Ritala & Tidström, 2014); furthermore, these studies mostly analyze coopetition issues without devoting too much attention to the specificities of multi-partner agreements. In other streams of the alliance literature, scholars do highlight the idiosyncratic nature of multi-partner alliances (e.g., Das & Teng, 2002; Thorgren et al., 2011), which can have a significant impact on knowledge-related issues (Li et al., 2012). These studies argue that interaction between two partners is fundamentally different from interaction in a larger group, because these settings involve differing ways for resource exchange and reciprocity (c.f. Das & Teng, 2002; Li et al., 2012; Thorgren et al., 2011). In dyadic agreements, the two partners bilaterally exchange resources and have bilateral reciprocity expectations (i.e., regarding one another). In multi-partner agreements we could find bilateral interaction between a given pair of partners but also generalized exchanges and reciprocity among all the partners (i.e., partners give to and expect to receive back from the alliance as a whole). This co-occurrence of bilateral and generalized interaction makes knowledge exchange notably complex. For example, in generalized exchanges it is challenging to monitor each party's behavior while the threat of undesirable knowledge leakage rises steeply (e.g., Li et al., 2012) because multiple parties have access to and could potentially misuse alliance knowledge. Thus, knowledge-related tensions may be aggravated in the presence of multiple coopetitors. Taking these ideas together, cross-fertilization between research on coopetition and multi-partner alliances seems very promising. For example, Das and Teng (2002) propose "social sanctions" as a key social control mechanism in multi-partner alliances. It could be interesting to explore the role of social sanctions in knowledge management strategies for multi-party coopetition.

Coopetition and the firm's alliance portfolio

Firms increasingly collaborate concurrently with different partners, thus building and maintaining portfolios of alliances (e.g., Sarkar et al., 2009). However, coopetition research tends to study coopetition agreements without specifically examining them as being part of firms' alliance portfolios—for two recent exceptions, see Chiambaretto and Fernandez (2016) and Park et al. (2014). Adopting an alliance portfolio perspective is relevant because alliances are interdependent (i.e., the effects of an alliance may depend on other alliances in the portfolio). Consequently, firms should design alliance portfolio management strategies (Faems et al., 2012) where formal and informal communication can play a crucial role (e.g., Sarkar et al., 2009). What are the implications of knowledge-related coopetition tensions for the management of alliance portfolios? Can these tensions contaminate other alliances in the portfolio? As suggested by the recent study by Park et al. (2014), it is relevant to systematically examine these questions. For example, Faems et al. (2012) propose two approaches to manage alliance portfolios: "standardization" (i.e., all alliances are managed using the same procedures) and "customization" (i.e., the firm tailors its management procedures to each type of partner). Future work could examine which approach is more effective to manage knowledge across the firm's alliance portfolio in the presence of coopetition. This line of research resembles the separation–integration dilemma stressed by some coopetition scholars (e.g., Le Roy & Fernandez, 2015), but proposes to extend its investigation to the alliance portfolio level.

Conclusion

Competitors working together in innovation-oriented projects face a fundamental tension between knowledge sharing and knowledge protection. Therefore, knowledge management strategies are center stage in these coopetition settings. This chapter has presented a discussion of existing research on the topic, offering suggestions for further development of the field. From this discussion, three themes have been identified as key areas that merit further scholarly effort: the connections between inter- and intra-organizational aspects of knowledge management in coopetition; the management of knowledge-related tensions in multi-partner settings; and the implications of these tensions for knowledge management within alliance portfolios.

Notes

1   For example, see www.nytimes.com/2013/07/03/business/for-gm-and-honda-a-fuel-cell-partnership.html.
2   For a more comprehensive development of this topic, the reader is referred to Estrada et al. (2016).

3 RBV is used here as a broad term including the capabilities-based and knowledge-based views of the firm.
4 This review is meant to be illustrative rather than exhaustive. For more elaborate reviews of the coopetition literature, see, for example, Bengtsson and Raza-Ullah (2016) and Dorn, Schweiger, and Albers (2016).

References

Argote, L., McEvily, B., & Reagans, R. (2003). Managing knowledge in organizations: An integrative framework and review of emerging themes. *Management Science*, 49(4), 571–582.

Baum, J. A., Calabrese, T., & Silverman, B. S. (2000). Don't go it alone: Alliance network composition and startups' performance in Canadian biotechnology. *Strategic Management Journal*, 267–294.

Bengtsson, M. & Kock, S. (2000). "Coopetition" in business networks—to cooperate and compete simultaneously. *Industrial Marketing Management*, 29(5), 411–426.

Bengtsson, M. & Raza-Ullah, T. (2016). A systematic review of research on coopetition: Toward a multilevel understanding. *Industrial Marketing Management*, 57, 23–39.

Bengtsson, M., Raza-Ullah, T., & Vanyushyn, V. (2016). The coopetition paradox and tension: The moderating role of coopetition capability. *Industrial Marketing Management*, 53, 19–30.

Bianchi, M., Croce, A., Dell'Era, C., Di Benedetto, C. A., & Frattini, F. (2015). Organizing for inbound open innovation: How external consultants and a dedicated R&D unit influence product innovation performance. *Journal of Product Innovation Management*, 33 (4), 492–510.

Bouncken, R. B. & Kraus, S. (2013). Innovation in knowledge-intensive industries: The double-edged sword of coopetition. *Journal of Business Research*, 66(10), 2060–2070.

Bouncken, R. B., Clauß, T., & Fredrich, V. (2016). Product innovation through coopetition in alliances: Singular or plural governance? *Industrial Marketing Management*, 53, 77–90.

Brandenburger, A. M. & Nalebuff, B. F. (1996). *Coopetition*. London: Harper Collins.

Browning, L. D., Beyer, J. M., & Shetler, J. C. (1995). Building cooperation in a competitive industry: SEMATECH and the semiconductor industry. *Academy of Management Journal*, 38(1), 113–151.

Cassiman, B., Di Guardo, M. C., & Valentini, G. (2009). Organising R&D projects to profit from innovation: Insights from co-opetition. *Long Range Planning*, 42(2), 216–233.

Castañer, X., Mulotte, L., Garrette, B., & Dussauge, P. (2014). Governance mode vs. governance fit: Performance implications of make-or-ally choices for product innovation in the worldwide aircraft industry, 1942–2000. *Strategic Management Journal*, 35(9), 1386–1397.

Chiambaretto, P. & Fernandez, A.-S. (2016). The evolution of coopetitive and collaborative alliances in an alliance portfolio: the Air France case. *Industrial Marketing Management*, 57, 75–85.

Das, T. K. & Teng, B. S. (2002). Alliance constellations: A social exchange perspective. *Academy of Management Review*, 27(3), 445–456.

Das, T. K. & Teng, B. S. (2003). Partner analysis and alliance performance. *Scandinavian Journal of Management*, 19(3), 279–308.

Dorn, S., Schweiger, B., & Albers, S. (2016). Levels, phases and themes of coopetition: A systematic literature review and research agenda. *European Management Journal*, 34(5), 484–500.

Dussauge, P., Garrette, B., & Mitchell, W. (2000). Learning from competing partners: outcomes and durations of scale and link alliances in Europe, North America and Asia. *Strategic Management Journal*, 21(2), 99–126.

Enberg, C. (2012). Enabling knowledge integration in coopetitive R&D projects—The management of conflicting logics. *International Journal of Project Management*, 30(7), 771–780.

Estrada, I., Faems, D., & de Faria, P. (2016). Coopetition and product innovation performance: The role of internal knowledge sharing mechanisms and formal knowledge protection mechanisms. *Industrial Marketing Management*, 53, 56–65.

Faems, D., Janssens, M., & Neyens, I. (2012). Alliance portfolios and innovation performance: connecting structural and managerial perspectives. *Group & Organization Management*, 37(2), 241–268.

Fernandez, A.-S. & Chiambaretto, P. (2016). Managing tensions related to information in coopetition. *Industrial Marketing Management*, 53, 66–76.

Fernandez, A.-S., Le Roy, F., & Gnyawali, D. R. (2014). Sources and management of tension in co-opetition case evidence from telecommunications satellites manufacturing in Europe. *Industrial Marketing Management*, 43(2), 222–235.

García-Canal, E., Valdés-Llaneza, A., & Sánchez-Lorda, P. (2008). Technological flows and choice of joint ventures in technology alliances. *Research Policy*, 37(1), 97–114.

Gnyawali, D. R. & Park, B. (2011). Coopetition between giants: Collaboration with competitors for technological innovation. *Research Policy*, 40, 650–63.

Hamel, G. (1991). Competition for competence and inter-partner learning within international strategic alliances. *Strategic Management Journal*, 12, 83–103.

Ho, H. & Ganesan, S. (2013). Does knowledge base compatibility help or hurt knowledge sharing between suppliers in coopetition? The role of customer participation. *Journal of Marketing*, 77(6), 91–107.

Kim, J. & Parkhe, A. (2009). Competing and cooperating similarity in global strategic alliances: an exploratory examination. *British Journal of Management*, 20(3), 363–376.

Le Roy, F. & Czakon, W. (2016). Managing coopetition: The missing link between strategy and performance. *Industrial Marketing Management*, 53, 3–6.

Le Roy, F. & Fernandez, A. S. (2015). Managing coopetitive tensions at the working-group level: The rise of the coopetitive project team. *British Journal of Management*, 26(4), 671–688.

Li, D., Eden, L., Hitt, M. A., Ireland, R. D., & Garrett, R. P. (2012). Governance in multilateral R&D alliances. *Organization Science*, 23(4), 1191–1210.

Makadok, R. (2001). Toward a synthesis of the resource-based and dynamic-capability views of rent creation. *Strategic Management Journal*, 22(5), 387–401.

Oxley, J. E. & Sampson, R. C. (2004). The scope and governance of international R&D alliances. *Strategic Management Journal*, 25(8–9), 723–749.

Pahnke, E. C., McDonald, R., Wang, D., & Hallen, B. (2015). Exposed: Venture capital, competitor ties, and entrepreneurial innovation. *Academy of Management Journal*, 58(5), 1334–1360.

Park, S. & M. Russo (1996). When competition eclipses cooperation: An event history analysis of joint venture failure. *Management Science,* 42(6), 875–890.

Park, B. J., Srivastava, M. K., & Gnyawali, D. R. (2014). Impact of coopetition in the alliance portfolio and coopetition experience on firm innovation. *Technology Analysis & Strategic Management*, 26(8), 893–907.

Ritala, P. & Hurmelinna-Laukkanen, P. (2013). Incremental and radical innovation in coopetition—The role of absorptive capacity and appropriability. *Journal of Product Innovation Management*, 30(1), 154–169.

Ritala, P., Olander, H., Michailova, S., & Husted, K. (2015). Knowledge sharing, knowledge leaking and relative innovation performance: An empirical study. *Technovation*, 35, 22–31.

Ritala, P. & Tidström, A. (2014). Untangling the value-creation and value-appropriation elements of coopetition strategy: A longitudinal analysis on the firm and relational levels. *Scandinavian Journal of Management*, 30(4), 498–515.

Sarkar, M. B., Aulakh, P. S., & Madhok, A. (2009). Process capabilities and value generation in alliance portfolios. *Organization Science*, 20(3), 583–600.

Thorgren, S., Wincent, J., & Eriksson, J. (2011). Too small or too large to trust your partners in multipartner alliances? The role of effort in initiating generalized exchanges. *Scandinavian Journal of Management*, 27(1), 99–112.

Tsai, W. (2002). Social structure of "coopetition" within a multiunit organization: Coordination, competition, and intraorganizational knowledge sharing. *Organization Science*, 13(2), 179–190.

Walter, S. G., Walter, A., & Müller, D. (2015). Formalization, communication quality, and opportunistic behavior in R&D alliances between competitors. *Journal of Product Innovation Management*, 32(6), 954–970.

Williamson, O. E. (1991). Comparative economic organization: The analysis of discrete structural alternatives. *Administrative Science Quarterly*, 36, 269–296.

Yan, Y., Faems, D., & Dong, J. (2017). Technological performance impacts of the overlaps with coopetitors. *Academy of Management Proceedings* (Vol. 2017, No. 1, p. 14395).

16

Making sense of coopetition sensemaking

Eva-Lena Lundgren-Henriksson and Sören Kock

Introduction

Coopetition scholars have in recent years begun to recognize complexities at the individual level, which is becoming particularly evident in studies dealing with coopetition tensions and paradoxes (Bengtsson et al., 2016; Le Roy & Fernandez, 2015; Raza-Ullah et al., 2014), as well as activities, processes, and practices (Dahl et al., 2016; Lundgren-Henriksson & Kock, 2016a, 2016b; Tidström & Rajala, 2016). A consensus is starting to spread that successful coopetition strategies start with successful tension management, which is supported by the fact that both the emerging practice and paradox approaches begin with individual coping.

It is not surprising that both approaches are rapidly rising in coopetition research, as the essence of coopetition lies in its complexity, duality, and the contradictory logics of interaction, at multiple levels of analysis. Scholars have therefore understood that, particularly for individuals dealing with this simultaneity in practice, tensions are experienced, for example, as role ambiguity (Bengtsson & Kock, 2000) and emotional ambivalence (Raza-Ullah et al., 2014). Therefore, coopetition requires the creation of new frames by managers (Mariani, 2007) and employees (Stadtler & Van Wassenhove, 2016) that can be realized in practice.

This chapter looks to the future and sets out to demonstrate a stronger connection between the coopetition paradox and sensemaking approaches. The sensemaking perspective captures the ongoing individual and collective processes of organizing, communicating, and creating and re-creating the meaning of the world (Maitlis & Christianson, 2014; Weick, 1995). It also incorporates a dimension of politics (Maitlis & Christianson, 2014; Maitlis & Sonenshein, 2010) that defines sensegiving as activities related to the preferred influencing of others' views of reality (Gioia & Chittipeddi, 1991). In other words, sensemaking becomes a cognitive and social tool for dealing with ongoing uncertainty and ambiguity while providing legitimacy for actions and interactions.

The coopetition paradox has become particularly interesting from a socio-psychological perspective. By applying the sensemaking perspective to coopetition, recent studies show that employees differ in their abilities to combine and deploy cooperative and competitive frames (Lundgren-Henriksson & Kock, 2016b; Stadtler & Van Wassenhove, 2016). These studies demonstrate the major potential of the perspective to open the black box of the coopetition paradox by delving deeper into individuals' thoughts, a largely underexplored research area (Le Roy & Fernandez, 2015). Despite its potential to reveal both individual and collective coping with uncertainty and ambiguity, the use of the sensemaking perspective in coopetition research has been rare. The research agenda offered here invites researchers to correct this deficiency.

The chapter is organized as follows. A brief review of the prior research on the coopetition paradox and the individual level is followed by notes on the use of case studies to examine sensemaking. We then discuss potential future avenues for coopetition sensemaking research and conclude with an overview of how the sensemaking perspective can be methodologically implemented within the coopetition research field.

The coopetition paradox at the individual level

Individuals at lower organizational levels have commonly been portrayed as recipients of coopetition tensions (Bengtsson et al., 2016; Raza-Ullah et al., 2014) that are transferred from top management engagement in inter-organizational interaction (Bengtsson et al., 2016; Fernandez et al., 2014; Raza-Ullah et al., 2014). The coopetition paradox thus exists due to simultaneous cooperation and competition between organizations, manifested through felt tensions, which stem from the difficulties in managing the opposing interaction logics (Bengtsson et al., 2016).

The dominant discourse concerning the management of coopetition tensions has revolved around the principles of separation and integration. The separation principle embraces the assumption that individuals deal with only one interaction logic at a time, meaning cooperation and competition are separated into different activities and times (Bengtsson & Kock, 2000). Recent research, however, shows that, particularly at lower organizational levels, individuals are able to internalize the coopetition paradox (Fernandez et al., 2014; Le Roy & Fernandez, 2015). From a cognitive perspective, managing tensions should therefore be approached as the ability to think paradoxically (Bengtsson et al., 2016; Gnyawali et al., 2016). In other words, the development of paradoxical frames indicates an employee's understanding of when to use a cooperative or a competitive frame, or both (Stadtler & Van Wassenhove, 2016). This presents an opening for the deeper integration of the sensemaking perspective into coopetition research.

By examining the coopetition paradox from a sensemaking perspective, the management of coopetition tensions shifts from the organizational level to the individual and group levels. Making sense of coopetition, i.e., dealing with the paradox, implies the creation of a coopetition frame—the combination of cooperative and competitive frames—by individuals (Lundgren-Henriksson & Kock, 2016a; Stadtler & Van Wassenhove, 2016). Shared coopetition frames mean the understanding and acceptance of simultaneous cooperation and competition between individuals at the intra- and/or inter-organizational levels, and enable the integration of coopetition activities and practices into daily working life (Lundgren-Henriksson & Kock, 2016b). We also acknowledge coopetition sensegiving as an equally important process in creating new frames, that is, the influence practised by individuals or groups, at the intra- or inter-organizational levels, to steer the dominant view of coopetition in a certain direction.

Using case studies to investigate sensemaking: The Finnish media industry case

Qualitative research and particularly in-depth case studies are valuable in studying sensemaking, as they enable multiple data collection methods by the researcher to closely follow how and why individuals think, feel or act (Eriksson & Kovalainen, 2008). This reasoning was the starting point for our studies on coopetition from a sensemaking perspective (Lundgren-Henriksson & Kock, 2016a, 2016b), which are based on the same data set and address coopetition as a strategic change. In other words, integrating coopetition into the daily working lives of managers at different levels was treated as a cognitive re-orientation of existing interpretative schemes (Gioia & Chittipeddi, 1991: 444), i.e., a new way of thinking and acting.

The case study follows the emergence of a particular collaboration between three organizations in the Finnish media industry that had a history of fierce competition. As they are part of a rapidly changing industry, the changes created possibilities for increased cooperation between the parties and forced cooperation. Managers and employees had to create new understandings regarding competitors becoming coopetitors, changing their roles individually and collectively.

In total, twenty-eight interviews were conducted over two years, closely following how the coopetition initiative unfolded from its formulation to its implementation phases in 2013 and 2014, from the perspectives of both higher- and lower-level managers. In practice, cooperation encompassed sharing journalistic material between the three organizations, contradicting the profession's business concepts that call for competitive thinking and uniqueness. By combining interviews with observation, texts, and artefacts, a holistic understanding of the challenges presented to the individuals involved in implementing coopetition in practice, and how they individually and collectively tried to cope with these, was enabled. In particular, the in-depth interviews allowed us to investigate how individuals worked out a new routine for implementing external material into the daily production of newspapers, while sharing their own material, as well as how they felt about taking part in inter-organizational meetings and establishing contact with other inter-organizational groups so that coopetition would continue on a permanent basis, which had not existed before. Examples from the case study will serve as foundations for the development of the arguments presented below.

How the sensemaking perspective can assist an increased understanding of the coopetition paradox: A future research agenda

The sensemaking perspective calls for a new research agenda in coopetition research. The importance of the perspective becomes evident when considering the outcomes, such as the development of a coopetition mindset. The mindset can be approached as accepting and understanding the paradox, and that understanding then forms the foundation for being able to make and shape coopetition in practice (Gnyawali et al., 2016). If a mindset is shared by managers and employees across an organization, the chances of successful strategy implementation and development naturally increase. However, the development of the mindset becomes complicated with respect to the interplay between the individual and collective levels in their own firm and in their partnering organizations, which we discuss next.

We posit that sensemaking cannot be addressed solely as an organizational construct, rather, we need to investigate sensemaking in relation to a number of interrelated elements across different actor levels (cf. Balogun et al., 2014). It should be noted that in this chapter we draw particularly on the strategy-as-practice stream of sensemaking studies that deals with implementing strategic change (Balogun & Johnson, 2005; Gioia & Chittipeddi, 1991). We have chosen discourse (Balogun et al., 2014; Vaara, 2010) and emotions (Cornelissen et al., 2014; Liu & Maitlis, 2014) as the most promising elements for coopetition sensemaking research, due to their interrelatedness and roles in influencing participation in strategy. In addition, even though the case findings show that managers differed in their frame creation *within* the management levels, the discussion treats the coopetition frames as becoming *shared* within a specific actor level. Inspired by advances made by sensemaking

Table 16.1 Summary of discourse and emotions, implications for the creation of coopetition frames, and future research agenda

	Assumptions on the Strategy-as-practice Approach	*Implications for Coopetition Frame Creation*	*Future Research Agenda*
Discourse	How strategies are talked about/ framed influences how sense is made, i.e., how strategy participation is legitimized	Both formal and informal talk may have enabling or hindering effects in terms of developing coopetition frames	What is the role of discourse in the construction of coopetition frames at top, middle, and lower employee levels? Are there differences, and if so, why? How are discourses connected at different levels and what is the effect on the creation of shared frames? How and why do managers and employees use particular discourses to influence the creation of shared frames?
Emotions	Positive emotions (felt and expressed) aid sensemaking, negative emotions (felt and expressed) impede sensemaking; emotions are contagious	The creation of shared coopetition frames is contingent on emotional dynamics	What is the role of felt and expressed emotions in the creation of coopetition frames? How do emotional dynamics (individual and collective emotions) influence the creation of shared coopetition frames? How are emotional dynamics connected between organizational actor levels? What is the effect on the shared creation of coopetition frames in an organization?

scholars and our case study findings, we have developed a framework for adopting a sensemaking perspective on coopetition (Figure 16.1). A summary is presented in Table 16.1.

Discourse

The discursive stream in strategy-as-practice studies posits that the way in which strategies are visualized and communicated in organizations can promote and provide legitimacy for participation in implementing strategy, but it can also have a hindering effect. In other words, talk in all forms has a powerful effect on how sense is made (Balogun et al., 2014; Weick et al., 2005). Applied to coopetition, this would imply that both the formal and informal use of discourse would either aid or hinder the development and deployment of coopetition frames.

The case study findings tell us that the sense produced by the coopetition strategy in inter-organizational meetings between top managers and in intra-organizational interaction between top managers and lower-level employees, as well as between other employees, differed greatly. The reason is to be found in discourse—how the coopetition strategy was talked about and portrayed differently at inter- and intra-organizational levels (Lundgren-Henriksson & Kock, 2016a, 2016b). In inter-organizational meetings between top managers, the tone of the discussions was highly positive, an enthusiasm prevailed, and a shared view of the future was created—coopetition was an opportunity. The findings also indicate that key managers used this enthusiasm in their sensegiving efforts, driven by personal incentives to realize coopetition. Hence, the coopetition frame was largely shared in the organizations at top management levels.

When engaging in sensegiving processes in their home organizations, key managers also tried to transfer this enthusiasm throughout their organizations. However, it became evident that these efforts had mixed results because *alternative and contradicting discourses* existed in parallel at lower organizational levels. Through talk at lower levels, another image of the coopetition initiative was communicated—c-oopetition as a threat to present and future organizational identity. In opposition to the discourse prevailing at higher management levels, it provided legitimacy for *not* participating in the implementation of the coopetition strategy.

However, the role of the external context must also be taken into account here (see the dotted arrows in Figure 16.1). Top managers were very much involved in creating the prevailing industry discourse together with industry consultants to promote participation in the coopetition strategy, whereas lower-level employees tried to match the industry discourse with the ways the strategy was portrayed and talked about *inside* the organizations. Clearly, there were difficulties with fitting these two ways of talking about the strategy together—as a future possibility versus a threat—and this proved detrimental to lower-level actors in the development of new frames. Hence, coopetition frames were not shared throughout organizations.

All the case examples highlight the crucial role of talk at the intra- and inter-organizational levels in coopetition frame creation, as well as the major *differences* between organizational levels. Most importantly, they create new questions to be tackled in future research. In all, there are no guarantees that the intended discourse produced and used by top managers will be the dominant discourse in an organization (Rouleau & Balogun, 2011). First, the influence from sensegiving at lower organizational levels on top management sensemaking (dashed arrows in Figure 16.1), i.e., the down-middle-top communication and discourse (Maitlis & Sonenshein, 2010), requires attention to understand how top managers' emerging understandings of coopetition are continuously challenged and developed (Gioia & Chittipeddi, 1991). Lower-level managers and employees might *deliberately* challenge top managers' views on coopetition, possibly leading to fragmentation within and across top management levels in their frame creation. Reasons might also exist to portray coopetition in a certain manner within a particular actor level to influence the overall sense made (solid arrows in Figure 16.1). Future research could hence investigate how sensegiving is executed in practice by an actor group, and discuss how coopetition is talked about and framed, and the rationale behind it.

Evidently, the everyday struggle of implementing coopetition in practice, and the resolution processes, differs between top managers and lower-level employees (Le Roy & Fernandez, 2015). To understand how coopetition frames are developed, maintained, and re-developed, research needs to delve into *how* and *why* coopetition is discussed, legitimized or not, and debated at different actor levels. In the case study, top managers assembled at formal inter-organizational meetings to discuss the future of the industry and emerging forms of coopetition, whereas lower-level managers and employees discussed technicalities and implementation issues. The emerging future was also touched upon at these levels, but in more informal ways colored by speculation and rumor (Balogun et al., 2014) at both intra- and inter-organizational levels, largely creating skepticism and complexity in making sense of coopetition. Both top managers and lower-level employees might engage in inter-organizational exchange (dotted arrows in Figure 16.1), yet, as the examples above testify, coopetition may be portrayed differently. A question for the future is, thus, to what degree do talk and framing at an inter-organizational level influence the creation of a coopetition frame, compared to talk within an organization?

Emotions and discourse

In order to delve even deeper into understanding how individuals create coopetition frames, emotions need to be connected with how coopetition is discussed and framed. The discussion has already shown that discourse differs at inter- and intra-organizational levels, and we will now show the same can apply to emotions. It is important to acknowledge emotions, since *felt and expressed emotions through talk and communication* in different forms have the power to re-inforce or impede sensemaking (Liu & Maitlis, 2014; Maitlis & Sonenshein, 2010). For our discussion here, the distinction between individual and collective emotions, i.e., emotional dynamics (Liu & Maitlis, 2014), is particularly interesting. The linkage between emotions and discourse (Brundin & Liu, 2015) suggests the sensegiving of particular managers or employees, where a specific position or attitude expressed in an emotional manner has the potential to influence the *collective emotional state* towards coopetition in an organization. Furthermore, it is important to emphasize that emotions are *contagious* (Cornelissen et al., 2014).

Emotions in coopetition research have been discussed in terms of the coopetition paradox. Tensions stem from individuals evaluating the benefits and drawbacks of coopeting, thus grasping both positive and negative emotions; the former connected to mutuality in terms of cooperation, the latter to a fear of the negative implications of coopeting for the individual or organization (Raza-Ullah et al., 2014). The discussion here centers on how emotions towards coopetition can become shared within and across actor levels, and their effect on the creation of a shared coopetition frame. Based on the case findings, we emphasize in particular the influence of negative emotions, such as anxiety and fear (Maitlis & Sonenshein, 2010).

Positive emotions reinforce sensemaking, become an aiding tool, and can enable the matching of cooperative and competitive frames. On the other hand, negatively oriented emotions can do the opposite and become contagious. Since coopetition encompasses interactions at both inter- and intra-organizational levels, the case study findings show that the sense produced at each level is influenced by, but also influences, other levels. In a worst-case scenario, then, this could mean that negativity and skepticism spread throughout an organization, hindering the sensemaking of individuals that might not otherwise have experienced those emotions. Negative or positive emotions, expressed through talk and speech for any particular reason in an organization, have a powerful effect on the felt emotions of individuals and subsequently on the sense made (boxes on the arrows in Figure 16.1).

The findings clearly show that the *affective dimension* had an influencing effect on the ability of managers to develop a coopetition frame. The shared positivity expressed in the inter-organizational meetings towards future forms of coopetition aided the development of high expectations concerning the future development of the relationship. Future research should therefore dig deeper into investigating emotions at the individual and collective levels, both in terms of felt and expressed emotions. For example, even though *expressed* emotions within a particular actor level are shared, variations might exist in individually *felt* emotions, potentially causing ambiguity for the individual. In this sense, dealing with contradictory individually felt and collectively expressed emotions introduces new perspectives on the coopetition paradox. Another issue to be tackled is whether managers and employees express what they really feel concerning coopetition, how they do that, and what the collective consequences are for the creation of coopetition frames. Thus, future research questions may ask: can expressed positive, negative, or confused emotions be linked to the success or failure of collective decision-making (Liu & Maitlis, 2014), such as in top management meetings where coopetition is discussed and debated?

Since the collective level in terms of coopetition also includes actor levels in the partnering organizations, *expected versus unexpected emotions* becomes a valid issue to be explored in the

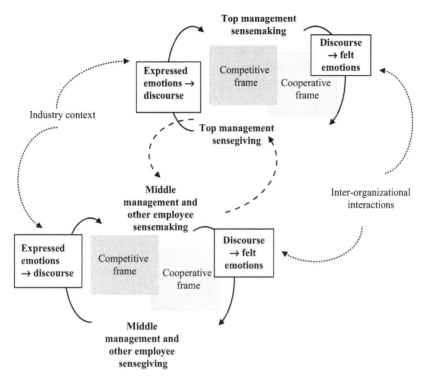

Figure 16.1 Coopetition frame creation, discourse, and emotions at multiple levels

future. For example, due to the different natures of intra- and inter-organizational interactions at higher and lower organizational levels, there are no guarantees that the actual experienced emotions of employees will match with top management's *expectations of employees' emotions*. The findings showed that skeptical views at lower organizational levels clearly stood in contradiction to the expected emotional response desired by top managers, resulting in top managers struggling to make sense of and doubting the emerging collective frame. Thus, a future research question might ask: how and why are emotions at different organizational levels connected and what is their influence on sensemaking in the organization?

Last, we wish to emphasize that adopting a sensemaking perspective on coopetition should be guided by the aim to shed light on the pluralism of views, emotions, and talk, i.e., the complexity of managing a strategy where ongoing parallel yet interconnected processes of sensemaking exist. Only then can the creation of a shared coopetition frame be comprehensively understood. Thus, we now turn to how the sensemaking perspective can be methodologically implemented in coopetition research.

How to implement the sensemaking perspective in coopetition research

In order to conduct an in-depth investigation on the creation of coopetition frames by individuals, the common methods for both data collection and analysis in coopetition research have to be re-evaluated. To explore how coopetition is made sense of at intra- and inter-organizational levels, future research must adopt techniques that allow movement closer to social interaction and meaning creation processes, such as ethnography (Eriksson & Kovalainen, 2008). Ethnographic methods also create the potential for more studies on sensemaking and materiality (Balogun et al., 2014), such as how the use of PowerPoints and different kinds of material tools and artefacts in both formal and informal meetings—where coopetition is discussed and debated—can influence how sense is made. To develop a holistic understanding, both higher and lower organizational actor levels should be incorporated, since sense differs between actor levels (Weick et al., 2005). In addition, future research could embrace narrative research and discourse analysis (Vaara, 2010) in examining how individuals participate in executing coopetition strategies, since these methodological choices strive to understand how legitimacy is socially and culturally produced and reproduced.

Sensemaking occurs through continuous cycles of cognition and action (Gioia & Chittipeddi, 1991), and is therefore not a static concept. Therefore, when following how managers and employees make sense of coopetition, a longer time frame should be adopted. Case studies have been popular in coopetition research where interviews seem to be the number-one choice for data collection. When exploring sensemaking through interviews, researchers must remember that it spans different temporal states—past-present-future (Gioia & Chittipeddi, 1991; Weick et al., 2005)—which is something that should help form the base for interviews.

However, in examining sensemaking, researchers must move beyond interviews as the number-one empirical data source and seek triangulation with other ethnographic-inspired methods, such as observation of top management inter- or intra-organizational meetings and everyday talk on the shop floor where coopetition plans are put into practice or abandoned. This becomes particularly evident when dealing with felt and expressed emotions, thus creating a new role for the coopetition researcher and calling for more longitudinal research to closely examine how coopetition develops—preferably by becoming a member of the studied organization or group—so as to glean viewpoints from the researched individuals (Eriksson & Kovalainen, 2008).

Concluding words

The aim of this chapter was to illustrate the benefits of a tighter integration of the sensemaking perspective into the coopetition paradox discussion, and to open new research avenues into investigating how actors at different levels make sense of coopetition. It is suggested that a sensemaking perspective on coopetition shifts the focus from the organizational management of tensions, including the principles of separation and integration, to psychological and social management by individuals. In other words, the perspective calls for alternative and complementary ways to manage the coopetition paradox, namely discursive use and framing, as well as sensitivity to the influencing role of emotional dynamics on strategy participation.

Managers can learn from the sensemaking perspective that shared perspectives on coopetition strategy are hard to accomplish across actor levels and over time. To understand how sense is generated in different ways, and how that results in unintended effects for strategy development, its discursive use in varying forms has to be investigated within all sections of the organization. In addition, top managers should bear in mind that managing employee emotions (Huy, 2002) regarding coopetition might prove difficult. Thus, the discussion on sensemaking and emotions calls for an investigation of managers' abilities to sense and manage collective emotions so that coopetition frames can become shared throughout an organization.

References

Balogun, J., Jacobs, C., Jarzabkowski, P., Mantere, S., & Vaara, E. (2014). Placing strategy discourse in context: Sociomateriality, sensemaking, and power. *Journal of Management Studies*, 51(2), 175–201.

Balogun, J. & Johnson, G. (2005). From intended strategies to unintended outcomes: the impact of change recipient sensemaking. *Organization Studies*, 26(11), 1573–1601.

Bengtsson, M. & Kock, S. (2000). "Coopetition" in business networks – to cooperate and compete simultaneously. *Industrial Marketing Management*, 29, 411–426.

Bengtsson, M., Raza-Ullah, T., & Vanyushyn, V. (2016). The coopetition paradox and tensions: The moderating role of coopetition capability. *Industrial Marketing Management*, 53, 19–30.

Brundin, E. & Liu, F. (2015). The role of emotions in strategizing. In Golsorkhi, D., Rouleau, L., Seidl, D., & Vaara, E. (Eds), *Cambridge handbook of strategy as practice* (2nd ed.) (pp. 632–646). Cambridge: Cambridge University Press.

Cornelissen, J. P., Mantere, S., & Vaara, E. (2014). The contraction of meaning: The combined effect of communication, emotions, and materiality on sensemaking in the Stockwell shooting. *Journal of Management Studies*, 51(5), 699–736.

Dahl, J., Kock, S., & Lundgren-Henriksson, E.-L. (2016). Conceptualizing coopetition strategy as practice: A multilevel interpretative framework. *International Studies of Management and Organization*, 46(2–3), 94–109.

Eriksson, P. & Kovalainen, A. (2008). *Qualitative Methods in Business Research*. London: Sage.

Fernandez, A.-S., Le Roy, F., & Gnyawali, D. R. (2014). Sources and management of tension in coopetition – Case evidence from telecommunications satellites manufacturing in Europe. *Industrial Marketing Management*, 43(2), 222–235.

Gioia, D. A. & Chittipeddi, K. (1991). Sensemaking and sensegiving in strategic change initiation. *Strategic Management Journal*, 12, 433–448.

Gnyawali, D. R., Madhavan, R., He, Y., & Bengtsson, M. (2016). The competition-cooperation paradox in inter-firm relationships: A conceptual framework. *Industrial Marketing Management*, 53, 7–18.

Huy, Q. N. (2002). Emotional balancing of organizational continuity and radical change: The contribution of middle managers. *Administrative Science Quarterly*, 47(1), 31–69.

Le Roy, F. & Fernandez, A.-S. (2015). Managing coopetitive tensions at the working-group level: The rise of the coopetitive project team. *British Journal of Management*, 26, 671–688.

Liu, F. & Maitlis, S. (2014). Emotional dynamics and strategizing processes: A study of strategic conversations in top team meetings. *Journal of Management Studies*, 51(2), 202–234.

Lundgren-Henriksson, E.-L. & Kock, S. (2016a). A sensemaking perspective on coopetition. *Industrial Marketing Management*, 57, 97–108.

Lundgren-Henriksson, E.-L. & Kock, S. (2016b). Coopetition in a headwind – The interplay of sensemaking, sensegiving, and middle managerial emotional response in coopetitive strategic change development. *Industrial Marketing Management*, 58, 20–34.

Maitlis, S. & Christianson, M. (2014). Sensemaking in organizations: Taking stock and moving forward. *The Academy of Management Annals*, 8(1), 57–125.

Maitlis, S. & Sonenshein, S. (2010). Sensemaking in crisis and change: Inspiration and insights from Weick (1988). *Journal of Management Studies*, 47(3), 551–580.

Mariani, M. M. (2007). Coopetition as an emergent strategy: Empirical evidence from an Italian consortium of opera houses. *International Studies of Management and Organization*, 37(2), 97–126.

Raza-Ullah, T., Bengtsson, M., & Kock, S. (2014). The coopetition paradox and tension in coopetition at multiple levels. *Industrial Marketing Management*, 43(2), 189–198.

Rouleau, L. & Balogun, J. (2011). Middle managers, strategic sensemaking, and discursive competence. *Journal of Management Studies*, 48(5), 953–983.

Stadtler, L. & Van Wassenhove, L. N. (2016). Coopetition as a paradox: Integrative approaches in a multi-company, cross-sector partnership. *Organization Studies*, 37(5), 655–685.

Tidström, A. & Rajala, A. (2016). Coopetition strategy as interrelated praxis and practices on multiple levels. *Industrial Marketing Management*, 58, 35–44.

Vaara, E. (2010). Taking the linguistic turn seriously: Strategy as a multifaceted and interdiscursive phenomenon. In Baum, J. A. C. & Lampel, J. (Eds), *The Globalization of Strategy* (Advances in Strategic Management, Volume 27) (pp. 29–50). Bingley, UK: Emerald Group Publishing Limited.

Weick, K. E. (1995). *Sensemaking in Organizations*. Thousand Oaks, CA: Sage.

Weick, K. E., Sutcliffe, K. M., & Obstfeld, D. (2005). Organizing and the process of sensemaking. *Organization Science*, 16(4), 409–421.

17

The rise of the coopetitive project team

Anne-Sophie Fernandez and Frédéric Le Roy

Introduction

The management of coopetitive tensions has become a critical issue in coopetitive success (Le Roy & Czakon, 2016; Le Roy et al., 2017). Previous studies have highlighted two contradictory principles for managing coopetition: the separation principle and the integration principle (Bengtsson & Kock, 2000; Fernandez et al., 2014; Fernandez & Chiambaretto, 2016; Le Roy & Fernandez, 2015; Pellegrin-Boucher et al., 2018). Whereas the separation principle relates to the organizational level, the integration principle relates to the individual level. However, the adoption of a coopetition strategy forces employees from both parent firms to work together (Fernandez et al., 2014; Gnyawali & Park, 2011). Although previous studies on coopetition management have paid less attention to the working-group level, it is critical to understanding how coopetitors work together, how they organize their daily work to achieve a common goal, how they select worker locations, how they are structured and coordinated, etc. (Fernandez et al., 2018).

Thus, the aim of this chapter is to understand how coopetition is managed at the working-group level. We highlight an original mode of organization: the coopetitive project team. We define the coopetitive project team as the pooling of human, financial, and technological resources from two coopetitors in a common and unique project team separated from both parent firms and fully dedicated to a common goal. The design and primary features of the coopetitive project team are analyzed. The coopetitive project team is governed by a mixed structure that is equally shared by both partners to preserve the partnership equity. Key managerial functions are duplicated (two individuals from both companies) without any hierarchical relationship. Project managers act as masters of coopetition by integrating the coopetition paradox and managing related tensions at the working-group level.

Both separation and integration principles are used to build the coopetitive project team. The separation principle is used to separate the coopetitive project team from both parent firms. The coopetitive project team is dedicated to collaboration, whereas the parent firms remain in competition. However, within the coopetitive project team, the competitive dimension is not excluded. According to the integration principle, project managers must internalize the duality of competition and collaboration and must behave accordingly in their daily work.

The implementation of both principles of separation and integration is not sufficient to manage coopetition at the working-group level. We show that firms must establish a bi-cephalous governance structure and a dual management committee. This organizational structure corresponds to a new principle known as the co-management principle (Le Roy & Fernandez, 2015), which is essential for the success of coopetition. Without this co-management, workers from both competitive firms will be unable to complete their common project.

Coopetition management

Coopetition is by definition a paradoxical relationship (Raza-Ullah et al., 2014; Tidström, 2014). The management of paradoxical tensions is a pervasive research question in organizational theories (Lewis, 2000; Smith & Lewis, 2011). Two contradictory approaches to managing paradoxical tensions are frequently debated. The first approach recommends paradox resolution by splitting opposite forces (Poole & Van de Ven, 1989). The second approach suggests that splitting creates vicious cycles. Therefore, scholars who support the second approach recommend accepting the paradox at both the individual and organizational levels. Once the paradox is accepted, a resolution strategy should be implemented (Tse, 2013).

Smith and Lewis (2011) do not oppose splitting and integration strategies but suggest combining them in a strategy of resolution. Combined with acceptance at both the organizational and the individual levels, the resolution strategy enables companies to benefit from the management of paradoxical tensions and to improve their sustainability (Smith & Lewis, 2011) and innovation (Tse, 2013) capabilities.

The pioneers of coopetition management literature, consistent with the paradox-solving approach through splitting, explain that "individuals cannot cooperate and compete with each other simultaneous(ly), and therefore the two logics of interactions need to be separated" (Bengtsson & Kock, 2000: 423). Thus, the management of collaboration and the management of competition should be split to manage coopetitive tensions (Bengtsson & Kock, 2000; Dowling et al., 1996; Herzog, 2010). The separation can be functional, temporal, or spatial. Partners can cooperate on one dimension of the value chain (i.e., R&D) while competing on another dimension (i.e., marketing activities).

However, other scholars note that the separation principle appears to be inefficient because it creates new internal tensions within the organization and integration issues for individuals (Chen, 2008; Oshri & Weeber, 2006). In the example cited above, a conflict can arise between the departments. Thus, it becomes very important to seek other solutions to manage coopetition. As noted by Wong and Tjosvold (2010), inter-individual relationships and personal interactions strongly contribute to coopetition management in a win-win way. To encourage these inter-individual relationships and personal interactions, an integration principle is highly recommended (Chen, 2008; Oshri & Weeber, 2006).

The integration principle is consistent with the acceptance of paradoxes (Lewis, 2000; Luscher & Lewis, 2008; Smith & Lewis, 2011), which allows individuals to understand their roles in a paradoxical context and to behave accordingly, following both logics simultaneously. Thus, the challenge for managers is to simultaneously manage collaboration and competition to optimize the benefits of coopetition (Luo, 2007). Instead of reducing competition or collaboration, firms would rather maintain them in a balance (Clarke-Hill et al., 2003).

The literature review highlights two primary but opposing principles for managing coopetitive tensions. In the separation approach, individuals are unable to integrate the coopetition duality. Consequently, to address coopetitive tensions, an appropriate organization design separates collaboration from competition. Conversely, in the integration approach, individuals can integrate coopetition duality into their daily activities. Thus, managing coopetition relies on the development of individuals' capacity for paradox integration (Bengtsson et al., 2016; Gnyawali et al., 2016).

Recent studies highlight the possible combination of both principles to efficiently manage coopetitive tensions (Fernandez et al., 2014; Fernandez & Chiambaretto, 2016; Le Roy &Fernandez, 2015; Pellegrin et al., 2018; Séran et al., 2016). Because the separation principle creates internal tensions within firms, a principle of integration at the individual level is recommended to manage them. This principle relies on individuals' capabilities to understand other roles.

However, assuming that the integration principle requires the development of cognitive capabilities to understand the dual logic of coopetition, we wonder whether this principle is realistic for all individuals. This question is even more appropriate at the working-group level. Indeed, the implementation of a coopetition strategy requires employees from both parent firms to work together (Fernandez et al., 2014; Gnyawali & Park, 2011). Unfortunately, we have little evidence about how coopetitors organize, structure, and coordinate their daily work to achieve their common goal.

To address this question, we conducted an in-depth case study within the most important and the most competitive sector of the space industry: the manufacturing of telecommunications satellites. We focus on an innovation programme called Yahsat that is jointly developed by the two European competitors, Thales and Airbus, who follow a coopetition strategy. The case uniquely represents a situation in which two firms engage in coopetition, examining the organizations and their relationships to provide deep insights regarding the management of coopetition. The common project team established by Thales and Airbus to conduct the program represents a unique case for investigating in-depth coopetitive tensions at the working-group level.

The formation of the coopetitive project team

Airbus and Thales are organized by projects. The organizational design for their common projects depends on the innovativeness of the project. When the project is an incremental innovation, Airbus and Thales use a simple organizational design. When the project is a radical innovation, they use a more complex organizational design that we named the coopetitive project team.

For low-innovation, low-risk, and low-cost projects, firms do not design a complex organization. In such projects, there is no need to combine similar and complementary knowledge to create new capabilities. Knowledge sharing remains limited to interfaces (project coordination), thus reducing the risk of plunder and unintended spillover. A simple organizational design allows the achievement of low-innovation projects while protecting the core knowledge of the firm against the opportunism of its coopetitors.

For highly innovative, risky, and costly projects, it makes sense to adopt a more complex organizational design. A specific team is fully dedicated to the project. The project team has its own technological, human, and financial resources dedicated to achieving a clear objective. The project is governed by a "project management office" (PMO) composed of a project manager and several deputies.

The project manager plays a critical role. He manages the time schedules and the technical performance as per the client's requirements. He is also responsible for team composition. Relationships between the project manager and the team members are functional rather than hierarchical. Team members depend on the technical departments allocated to the program. At the end of the program, they are transferred to another project.

When working together on very innovative projects, Airbus and Thales establish this organization to achieve their goal. They pool human resources into a mixed project team to create and exploit positive synergies from both the exploration and exploitation processes. Because the resources come from competing firms, tensions can arise within the team. The existence of coopetitive tensions allows us to name this specific organization a coopetitive project team. We define the coopetitive project team as an organizational mode that results from the pooling of technological, financial, and human resources between two competing firms that is fully dedicated to achieving a common goal within a specific time limit.

The coopetitive project team differs from traditional collaborative project teams because of the simultaneous expression of collaboration and competition within the team. Although they must collaborate, team members remain members of their parent firms. They defend their firm's interests while collaborating. They also know that collaboration is temporary and that they will have to compete for the next program. For these reasons, collaboration and competition occur simultaneously at the project team level. Thales and Airbus deliberately internalize the coopetitive tensions and their management within the coopetitive project team and, more precisely, within the PMO. To efficiently manage coopetition, the coopetitive project team is independent and allows the establishment of appropriate managerial tools.

The coopetitive project team: A dual design

The duality of the coopetitive project team governance structure

In the early stage of the program, tensions arise regarding leadership and the need to define the prime contractor. To manage these leadership tensions, the governance structure should reflect the power equity between Airbus and Thales. Several scenarios are possible. In the first scenario, a project manager from one parent firm could be appointed to coordinate and manage the entire program. He alone would independently make all the decisions for the program. The relationships between the project manager and deputies would be hierarchical. Tensions within the team would be expected to increase. To avoid leadership tensions, Airbus and Thales adopted an Integrated Overall Control (IOC) approach based on a mixed PMO composed of individuals from both companies (Figure 17.1).

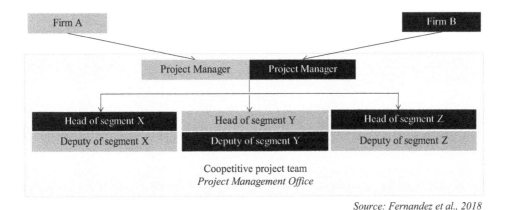

Source: Fernandez et al., 2018

Figure 17.1   The coopetitive project team organizational design

In the PMO, key managerial functions are duplicated and equally shared by Thales and Airbus: two project managers, two management controllers, two satellite managers, etc. A manager from Airbus or Thales and a deputy from the other company head each industrial segment. The duplication process reflects the equity between Airbus and Thales at the segment level. Without a hierarchical relationship, both managers have the same power in the decision-making process. Even if Airbus has been appointed as the agent, Airbus is not allowed to negotiate alone with the client. The negotiation process between the partners is permanent to ensure consensus between Airbus and Thales. This process suffers from a lack of flexibility and is slower and more difficult to implement than a regular program is. High levels of tension appear, especially during technically difficult phases, when each manager recommends a solution that is advantageous for its parent firm. However, the double loop in the decision-making process increases the legitimacy of the decision for all team members. Engineers accept a decision from their own project manager more easily than they accept one from the competing project manager.

The duplication in the governance structure of the coopetitive project team could be considered a waste of resources, but it is a requirement for financial reporting. The results from Yahsat should be established for each partner and presented to top management.

The duality of the coopetitive project team management committee

Autonomous from their parent firms, project managers and segment heads are in charge of managing tensions at the program level. When tensions are efficiently managed at the segment level, project managers are not involved. When conflict persists, project managers must intervene. When project managers do not agree on how to manage the tension, they refer to the formal procedure as defined in the partnership agreement, which involves a mixed steering committee (two Thales PMO members, two Airbus PMO members, heads of the business unit, and top managers from Airbus and Thales). When the mixed steering committee does not succeed, the procedure requires the involvement of executives from Thales and Airbus. This situation has never occurred in Yahsat.

In spite of the absence of hierarchy, project managers must control their respective work. The double control is essential to ensure each firm of the quality of work performed by the partner. Project managers also manage information within the team to manage tensions between sharing and protecting information. When Yahsat requires information, it is shared without any transfer of property right. In spite of its complexity, the dual governance structure allows the tandem project managers to integrate the ambiguity of coopetition and thus to manage tensions and potential conflicts.

Coopetitive project team operations

The coopetitive project team co-location

The geographical proximity of the subsidiaries of Thales and Airbus in the Toulouse area (South of France) facilitates the collaboration between firms and individuals. The coopetitive project team is co-located in Toulouse to facilitate the access of individuals to their parent firms.

To facilitate team members' interactions, Airbus and Thales decided to co-locate the coopetitive project team within the Airbus plant in a building that is exclusively dedicated to coopetitive programs, separated from the rest of the company by wire netting. The building is not freely accessible and, reciprocally, coopetitive project team members do not have access to Airbus. Within the team, a real melting pot occurs among individuals. For example, office doors do not mention the name of a team member's parent firm, to avoid distinctions between Thales and Airbus members.

The coopetitive project team co-location illustrates the principle of spatial integration in coopetition. Tensions between competition and collaboration are simultaneously managed at the same location. However, co-location could have an unintended effect. Over the years, team members may develop their own identity and feel disconnected from their parent firm. Their colleagues could perceive them as traitors because they work with a competitor.

The coopetitive project team composition

Yahsat is technically and relationally challenging because of the coopetition context. Thus, the team-building process is very important. Project managers require individuals with both technical and relational skills, but such resources are scarce. In the Telecom Business Unit, each project manager writes a checklist of the technical competencies that are required for Yahsat. He then looks for these competencies among individuals who hold specific relational skills that were developed through previous collaborative experiences. This assumption explains why the majority of Airbus Yahsat team members were members of a previous military telecommunications program, "Skynet." Junior managers are highly qualified but lack the experience to manage the coopetition context. The paradoxical situation is difficult to handle for individuals, primarily because of the tensions related to information management.

Whereas in traditional projects technical skills are the most important, in coopetition, relational skills are as important as technical in guaranteeing the success of the project team. To succeed, an individual should be able to integrate the paradoxical context, i.e., to cooperate with their competitors while defending the interests of the parent firm.

The project manager

In Yahsat, both project managers are among the best engineers but also hold specific managerial capacities that allow them to defend their project under all circumstances. These capacities allow the project managers to develop a coopetitive mind-set and to integrate the coopetition paradox. They understand the benefits of collaborating with a competitor as well as the risks of this collaboration. Because they are convinced of the strategic choice of coopetition, they are able to base their internal communication on the benefits of Yahsat for companies and individuals.

Considering the project manager's strategic role, choosing the appropriate person is highly critical for the companies. The assignment process is informal. The companies' career management policies do not account for the involvement of individuals in coopetitive programs. Some individuals find the coopetition context crippling and pressuring, whereas others find it creative, challenging, and inspiring. The project managers' motivation, commitment, and devotion represent key factors in the success of Yahsat.

Project managers manage tensions at the project team level, avoiding the propagation of conflict to the rest of the organization. They ensure the progress of Yahsat, regardless of the tensions and potential conflicts. For instance, during interfaces, project managers must manage the risks of transfers and imitation. They have the power to prohibit information transfers that are required by their top management and to allow information transfers prohibited by their top management. Project managers appear as the keystone of coopetition, balancing collaborative and competitive tensions to avoid conflicts and contribute to the program's success.

Conclusion

The question of organizational design is a key issue for the success of coopetition. For low-innovation, low-risk, and low-cost projects, firms use a simple organizational design. Conversely, for highly innovative, costly, and risky projects, firms design a coopetitive project team. This team is (1) spatially separated—co-located in a dedicated space and separated from both parent firms; (2) functionally separated—autonomous and resource-independent; and (3) temporally separated—respecting its own planning. According to the separation principle (Bengtsson & Kock, 2000; Dowling et al., 1996; Herzog, 2010), this organizational separation between competition and cooperation is necessary to manage coopetition.

However, the coopetitive project team design is insufficient for the daily management of all coopetitive tensions. In line with integration scholars (Chen, 2008; Das & Teng, 2000; Oshri & Weeber, 2006), our research highlights the necessity of individual integration for coopetition management. The project's progress relies primarily on the project managers. They must contain coopetitive tensions at the team level, avoiding the spread of tensions within the parent firms. Project managers are innovative people with the specific abilities (i.e., a combination of expertise and relational competencies) to create tools to manage daily tensions. They can be considered masters of coopetition. Their cognitive capabilities allow them to integrate the paradox, and this paradox integration allows them to manage coopetitive tensions. Project managers are decision-makers—they make all the decisions for the project—but they are also risk-takers—they can make decisions in contradiction with their internal policies.

Nevertheless, integration cannot be fully achieved by all members of the coopetitive project team. The integration of the paradox requires high cognitive capabilities that are difficult to acquire and develop for employees. Thus, employees involved in coopetition can behave either too competitively or too cooperatively. Consequently, a co-management principle is required at the working-group level to encourage balanced behaviors between collaboration and competition.

In dyadic coopetition, the co-management principle relies on both the bicephalous governance structure and the dual management committee. The managerial duplication in the governance structure reflects the equity of the partnership and is a key factor in the program's success. The co-management committee is entrusted with managing coopetitive tensions. Because individuals involved in a coopetitive project team refuse directives from a project manager from a competing firm, the co-management approach legitimizes the leadership of each firm and enhances collaboration among team members. Moreover, this duplication increases the control of each partner in the sharing process. Thus, co-management increases the confidence of team members and the probability of the program's success.

Finally, our research illustrates a combination of the separation principle (Bengtsson & Kock, 2000; Herzog, 2010) and the integration principle (Chen, 2008; Oshri & Weeber, 2006) with the co-management principle. Coopetitors have deliberately created a coopetitive project team that is (1) separated from the rest of the organization, (2) governed by a dual-governance structure and a co-management committee, and (3) managed on a daily basis by a project manager who has previously integrated the duality of coopetition. The coopetitive project team can be considered to be a managerial innovation to manage tensions and conflicts in a paradoxical context such as coopetition. To sum up, the efficient management of coopetitive tensions relies on the implementation of a separation principle at the organizational level, a co-management principle at the working-group level, and an integration principle at the individual level (Figure 17.2).

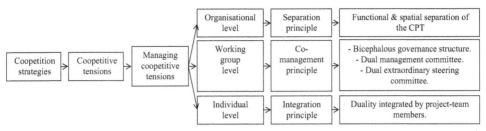

Figure 17.2 Managing coopetition by coopetitive project team

A research agenda on the coopetitive project team

The coopetitive project team is a fascinating research topic. Future research could explore several directions. The first direction consists of delving deeper into the coopetitive project team structure, as highlighted in this research. For instance, specific research could aim to better understand the role of the project manager or to further investigate the daily interactions between team members and their implications on knowledge sharing/protection. Who decides to share critical information, and how is the decision made? Do coopetitive project teams have specific information systems? We have noted the essential role of project managers in running coopetitive project teams. Senior managers appear to be more qualified than young ones. Further research could examine the manager profiles required to govern coopetitive project teams. Could companies train their managers to govern coopetitive project teams? How could they learn to govern coopetitive project teams? Further attention is also required to understand how information is managed within the coopetitive project team. A second research direction concerns the emergence of the coopetitive project team; how has this organizational structure emerged? Does the coopetitive project team result from learning processes or from previous collaborative experiences? Does the learning come from individuals or from firms? Do the coopetitive capabilities necessary to implement coopetition strategies belong to individuals or to companies? Another perspective could determine how the coopetitive project team structure could be used when coopetition involves more than two firms. Would firms use the same structure and the same mechanisms? As underscored by these questions, we believe that the coopetitive project team represents a strong opportunity for future research.

References

Bengtsson, M. & Kock, S. (2000). "Coopetition" in business networks—to cooperate and compete simultaneously. *Industrial Marketing Management*, 29, 5, 411–426.

Bengtsson, M., Raza-Ullah, T., & Vanyushyn, V. (2016). The coopetition paradox and tension: The moderating role of coopetition capability. *Industrial Marketing Management*, 53, 19–30.

Chen, M.-J. (2008). Reconceptualizing the competition-cooperation relationship: A transparadox perspective. *Journal of Management Inquiry*, 17, 4, 288–304.

Clarke-Hill, C., Li, H., & Davies, B. (2003). The paradox of co-operation and competition in strategic alliances: towards a multi-paradigm approach. *Management Research News*, 26, 1, 1–20.

Das, T. K. & Teng, B. S. (2000). A resource-based theory of strategic alliances. *Journal of Management*, 26(1), 31–61.

Dowling, M. J., Roering, W. D., Carlin, B. A., & Wisnieski, J. (1996). Multifaceted relationships under coopetition: Description and theory. *Journal of Management Inquiry*, 5, 2, 155–167.

Fernandez, A.-S., Le Roy, F., & Chiambaretto, P. (2018). Implementing the right project structure to achieve coopetitive innovation projects. *Long Range Planning*, 51, 2, 384–405.

Fernandez, A.-S., Le Roy, F., Gnyawali, D. (2014). Sources and management of tension in coopetition case evidence from telecommunications satellites manufacturing in Europe. *Industrial Marketing Management*, 43, 2, 222–235.

Gnyawali, D. R. & Park B.-J. (2011). Co-opetition between giants: Collaboration with competitors for technological innovation. *Research Policy*, 40, 5, 650–663.

Gnyawali, D. R., Madhavan, R., He, J., & Bengtsson, M. (2016). The competition–cooperation paradox in inter-firm relationships: A conceptual framework. *Industrial Marketing Management*, 53, February 2016, 7–18.

Herzog, T. (2010). Strategic Management of coopetitive relationships in CoPS – related industries. In S. Yami, S. Castaldo, G. B. Dagnino, and F. Le Roy (Eds), *Coopetition: Winning Strategies for the 21st Century*, pp. 200–216. Cheltenham: Edward Elgar.

Le Roy, F. & Czakon, W. (2016). Managing coopetition: the missing link between strategy and performance. *Industrial Marketing Management*, 53, 3–6.

Le Roy, F. & Fernandez, A.-S. (2015). Managing coopetitive tensions at the working-group level: The rise of the Coopetitive Project Team. *British Journal of Management*, 26, 671–688.

Le Roy, F., Fernandez, A.-S., & Chiambaretto, P. (2017). Managing coopetition in knowledge-based industries. In S. Sindakis and P. Theodorou (Eds), *Global Opportunities for Entrepreneurial Growth: Coopetition and Knowledge Dynamics within and across Firms*. Bingley, UK: Emerald Publishing Limited.

Le Roy, F., Robert, M., & Lasch, F. (2016). Choosing the best partner for product innovation: Talking to the enemy or to a friend? *International Studies of Management Organisation*, 46, 2–3, 136–158.

Le Roy, F. & Sanou, F. H. (2014). Does coopetition strategy improve market performance: An empirical study in the mobile phone industry. *Journal of Economics and Management*, 17, 63–94.

Lewis, M. (2000). Exploring paradox: Toward a more comprehensive guide. *Academy of Management Review*, 25, 4, 760–776.

Luo, Y. (2007). A coopetition perspective of global competition. *Journal of World Business*, 42, 2, 129–144.

Luscher, L. & Lewis, M. (2008). Organizational change and managerial sensemaking: Working through paradox. *Academy of Management Journal*, 51, 2, 221–240.

Oshri, I. & Weeber, C. (2006). Cooperation and competition standards-settings activities in the digitization area: The case of wireless information devices. *Technology Analysis & Strategic Management*, 18, 2, 265–283.

Pellegrin-Boucher, E., Le Roy, F., & Gurau, C. (2013). Coopetitive strategies in the ICT sector: typology and stability. *Technology Analysis & Strategic Management*, 25, 1, 71–89.

Pellegrin-Boucher, E., Le Roy, F., & Gurau, C. (2018). Managing Selling Coopetition: a case study of the ERP industry. *European Management Review*, 15, 1, 37–56.

Poole, M. S. & Van de Ven, A. (1989). Using paradox to build management and organizational theory. *Academy of Management Review*, 14, 4, 562–578.

Raza-Ullah, T., Bengtsson, M., & Kock, S. (2014). The coopetition paradox and tension in coopetition at multiple levels. *Industrial Marketing Management*, 43, 189–198.

Sanou, H., Le Roy, F., & Gnyawali, D. (2016). How does centrality in coopetition network matter? Empirical investigation in the mobile telephone industry. *British Journal of Management*, 27, 143–160.

Seran, T., Pellegrin-Boucher, E., & Gurau, C. (2016). The management of coopetitive tensions within multi-unit organizations. *Industrial Marketing Management*, 53, 31–41.

Smith, W. K. & Lewis, M. (2011). Toward a theory of paradox: a dynamic equilibrium model of organizing. *Academy of Management Review*, 36, 2, 381–403.

Tidström, A. (2014). Managing tensions in coopetition. *Industrial Marketing Management*, 43, 261–271.

Tse, T. (2013). Paradox resolution: A means to achieve strategic innovation. *European Management Journal*, 31, 6, 682–696.

Wong, A. & Tjosvold, D. (2010). *Guanxi* and conflict management for effective partnering with competitors in China. *British Journal of Management*, 21, 3, 772–788.

18

Coopetition capability

What is it?

Tatbeeq Raza-Ullah, Maria Bengtsson, and Vladimir Vanyushyn

Introduction

How can firms manage alliances with competitors (i.e., coopetition relationships) to create superior value? It is obvious that alliance management in general is both complex and challenging, especially when considering the high rate of alliance failure (Lunnan & Haugland, 2008; Park & Ungsson, 2001). Alliance capability is therefore crucial for the creation of value together with others, which, in turn, is a source of competitive advantage (Anand & Khanna, 2000; Ireland et al., 2002). Research on alliance capability has explored its several important dimensions, such as coordination, communication, bonding (in terms of the extent of interpersonal liking between partnering firms), and learning (Schreiner et al., 2009; Wang & Rajagopalan, 2015). Other dimensions include relational governance, inter-organizational capabilities (Zollo et al., 2002), relational capital, and integrative conflict management (Kale et al., 2000). All these capabilities serve to create a conducive environment for achieving beneficial outcomes. However, as many alliances between competitors are prone to fail due to the complex, paradoxical, and challenging nature of such relationships, we argue that besides general components of alliance capability, firms also require specific and complementary coopetition capability.

We propose that an essential precursor to the development of alliance capabilities is senior managers' ability to deal with paradoxical tensions embedded in and emerging from the very nature of the coopetition paradox inherent in alliances between competitors. It is not enough to have the capability to create conditions that favor cooperation, because competition activities also happen concurrently. Firms therefore need coopetition capability to enable them to work with the paradoxical contradictions inherent in such alliances (Bengtsson et al., 2016; Raza-Ullah, 2017a, b). In this chapter, we first discuss the paradoxical nature of the coopetitive relationship, the tension involved, as well as how tensions affect coopetitive alliance performance. Based on such understanding of alliances that involve coopetition, we thereafter propose the concept of coopetition capability and further develop the concept along the three dimensions: analytical, balancing, and emotional. We conclude with a discussion on the boundaries of coopetition capability as an additional dimension of a firm's overall alliance capability and outline directions for future research.

Coopetition in horizontal alliances

Coopetition is paradoxical

Coopetition relationships between firms are unique because they embody the paradox of simultaneous cooperation and competition (Bengtsson & Raza-Ullah, 2017; Fernandez et al., 2014; Raza-Ullah et al., 2014). Whereas cooperation is about creating a bigger pie, obtaining mutual gains, and moving toward a positive-sum game, competition includes maximizing private gains, behaving opportunistically, and commencing a zero-sum approach (Das & Teng, 2000). The pursuit of such contradictory yet interrelated logics of interactions simultaneously makes coopetition a complex, emotion-laden, and managerially challenging paradoxical phenomenon. Researchers note that despite the proliferation of coopetition relationships, above fifty percent of all collaborative arrangements between competitors fail (Harbison & Pekar, 1998), which further highlights the inherent complexity of coopetition and thus draws attention to the need to properly manage coopetition relationships.

The first step to manage coopetition is to understand its paradoxical nature as well as the underlying mechanisms and processes that influence performance. Coopetition research has already proposed a two-continua approach to understand coopetition's paradoxical nature. Such an approach can be expressed on a 2x2 grid with cooperation (ranging from low to high) on the vertical and competition (ranging from low to high) on the horizontal axis (Bengtsson et al., 2010). Further, coopetition is in its most managerially challenging form when both cooperation and competition are high (i.e., strong paradox). Alternatively, when either competition or cooperation largely overrides the other, the paradox as such would be weak (Bengtsson & Raza-Ullah, 2017). Moreover, coopetition researchers argue for the *both/and* nature of the coopetition paradox, which suggests that *both* cooperation *and* competition are pursued simultaneously. Thus, cooperating for a certain time period in which firms do not compete, or competing in another period without collaboration at the same time, would either mean cooperation or competition in isolation and not coopetition (Luo, 2007).

Paradoxical tension resulting from coopetition

The coopetition paradox consists of several, often intertwined, contradictions. The most commonly noted contradictions are value creation versus value capture (Lavie, 2007), knowledge sharing versus knowledge leakage (Ritala et al., 2015), and getting close versus keeping distance (Gnyawali et al., 2016). As the coopetition paradox becomes salient, it is cognitively and emotionally experienced by the actors engaged with the inherent contradictions. Managers' experience of the contradictions and the resultant cognitions and emotions creates what Raza-Ullah (2017b) names as experienced paradoxical tension. As the actors, and particularly senior managers, are often entangled with such contradictions, they find difficulty in both cognitively and emotionally dealing with the simultaneous contradictory demands. For example, on one hand managers need to ensure that knowledge is shared with the other firm to solve a joint problem or develop a new product. However, on the other hand, managers are very much concerned about the unintended leakage of important knowledge to the partner, which may cause harm to the focal firm in terms of, for instance, losing competitive advantage. Especially when the paradox is strong and the need to both cooperate and compete is intense, managers feel cognitively torn between the contradictory demands of what to share and what not to share, and thus experience high tension.

The contradictory conditions in coopetition also give rise to a blend of positive and negative emotions, which further exacerbate the level of experienced paradoxical tension. For instance, whereas positive emotions are felt when actors appraise coopetition as beneficial for their firm, negative emotions may arise when managers find that the partner is very opportunistic or attempts to steal sensitive knowledge (Raza-Ullah, 2017b). As actors become exposed to multiple contradictions in coopetition, they feel torn between several conflicting impulses and thus experience emotional ambivalence (Raza-Ullah et al., 2014). The individual cognitive resources to deal with the cognitive and emotional overloads created by a strong coopetition paradox become scarce as managers are required to attend to multiple, simultaneous, and intensely conflicting demands. Paradoxical tension therefore builds up when managers find it difficult to pursue the contradictory demands simultaneously and feel stretched between opposite directions with clashing cognitions and ambivalent emotions—all of which affect alliance performance.

Performance implications

Recent studies on coopetition have found that coopetition is a double-edged sword (Bouncken & Kraus, 2013) such that it can impact the performance outcomes both positively and negatively (e.g., Ritala & Sainio, 2014). We argue that coopetitive tension is the underlying mechanism that, if not managed appropriately, negatively associates coopetition with performance. Particularly when the coopetition paradox is strong and creates high tension, the likelihood of reduced performance (both in terms of focal firm performance and joint alliance performance) is high. This is in line with recent empirical studies that show that a strong paradox is associated with high tension (Bengtsson et al., 2016) and high tension in turn leads to lower performance. It is further suggested that a moderate level of tension is likely to positively influence performance, and therefore tension to an optimum level must exist to fuel performance (Bengtsson & Raza-Ullah, 2017). Studies have also found that a high degree of emotional ambivalence is related to lower levels of performance (Raza-Ullah, 2017a). Overall, there is substantial evidence suggesting that moderate levels of tensions, as opposed to low or high ones, are associated with positive effects on alliance performance.

What is coopetition capability?

Owing to coopetition's unique paradoxical nature, recent research has begun to evaluate the appropriate skill-set needed to manage coopetition and the resultant coopetitive tension. For example, scholars have proposed that both separation and integration strategies (Fernandez et al., 2014) as well as a combination of formal and informal control mechanisms for information sharing (Fernandez & Chiambaretto, 2016) are needed. Moreover, comprehensive frameworks of coopetition suggest that firms need to possess analytical and balancing capabilities to manage the paradox and tension in coopetition relationships (Gnyawali et al., 2016). Conceptual and theoretical work further suggests that in addition to the analytical and balancing capabilities, firms also need ambivalence management capability that could help managers deal with their emotional ambivalence (Bengtsson & Raza-Ullah, 2017). Earlier research has defined coopetition capability as "the ability to think paradoxically and to initiate processes that help firms attain and maintain a moderate level of tension, irrespective of the strength of the paradox." (Bengtsson et al., 2016: 22). Fundamentally, we propose that coopetition capability moderates the relationship between coopetition paradox and the resultant tension in such a way that firms with high levels of coopetition capability will report a moderate level of external tension irrespective of the strength of the paradox. Combining these insights, we suggest that coopetition capability has three main components—analytical, emotional, and balancing. Below we unpack

Table 18.1 Coopetition capability: Different dimensions, what they consist of and result in

Coopetition Capability	Consists of...	Results in...
Analytical capability	Paradoxical thinking; coopetition mind-set	An understanding of why, how, and when coopetition is needed
Balancing capability	Routines and processes (both ostensive and performative)	Separation and integration of the simultaneous contradictory demands; a repertoire of alternative strategies; reconfiguration of activities to balance the paradox
Emotional capability	Acceptance of ambivalent emotions; regulation of emotions through deep acting and surface acting	Creativity, accuracy in judgments, and superior performance; signaling assertiveness

these dimensions and formulate explicit expectations regarding the effects of each dimension on coopetitive tension, illustrated in Table 18.1.

Analytical dimension

The analytical dimension refers to the paradoxical thinking and mindset of senior managers that enables firms to see the constructive nature of contradictory forces (Smith & Tushman, 2005) inherent in the coopetition paradox. It helps in "exploring the tension in a creative way that captures both extremes" (Eisenhardt, 2000: 703), rather than focusing either on the cooperative or the competitive dimensions of coopetition. Managers with paradoxical thinking tend to be adept at developing a clear, precise, and unified understanding of the paradoxical situation. Such paradoxical mental frames create a lens through which managers constantly scan the business environment, assess potential opportunities and threats, and identify if there is a need to cooperate with a competitor. This is critical because coopetition may not always be needed, and many times firms can benefit by establishing pure collaborative relationships with partner firms. Moreover, analytical capability enables firms to recognize the suitable areas of cooperation with a particular competitor. In sum, the analytical dimension enables firms to understand why, how, and when it is beneficial to both cooperate and compete.

Balancing dimension

The balancing dimension includes the development and utilization of routines that help integrate, organize, and balance the simultaneous contradictory demands effectively. With such routines and processes in place, managers can perform multiple and inconsistent roles and tasks, as well as lessen the intensity of excessive cognitive overloads caused by tension and emotional ambivalence (Raza-Ullah, 2017a). One example of routines could be related to knowledge sharing. As mentioned earlier, when the demand of knowledge sharing is high, the risks of opportunism and transfer of important and sensitive knowledge also become high. Routines in this kind of scenarios would help boundary spanners to filter the right information, so that the only information shared with the other firm is that which is intended to be shared. Unintended leakage of knowledge may hurt the focal firm. Indeed, coopetition studies have found a negative impact of knowledge leakage on the positive relationship between knowledge sharing and the focal firm's innovation performance (Ritala et al., 2015).

As coopetitive relationships are dynamic and change over time, the routines developed to pursue conflicting demands cannot be rigid in nature. Rather, they embody both the ostensive and the performative aspects (Feldman & Pentland, 2003). The ostensive aspects (e.g., abstract standard operating procedures) assist the focal firm, for instance, to assign contrasting agendas to two separate units at the lower levels. As such, one unit is only involved in cooperation with the competitor firm, whereas another is focused entirely on competitive issues. Such structural differentiation allows firms to restrict the development of tension and emotional ambivalence at the lower levels, which is important because lower-level employees usually lack the analytical skills and cognitive frames to juxtapose paradoxical agendas (Bengtsson et al., 2016). The performative aspect (e.g., improvisation of existing routines, and accommodation of variations) further helps to tackle the varying intensities of cooperation and competition in the relationship. More precisely, it provides the flexibility to senior managers to improvise the routines in particular time periods and circumstances according to the situation (Raza-Ullah, 2017a). Doing so enables firms to develop a repertoire of alternative strategies, reconfigure activities, and meet the changing demands (Gibson & Birkinshaw, 2004) of coopetitive relationships. Further, managers are also able to change the scope and content of coopetitive relationships to balance the paradox without jeopardizing the common objectives.

The performative parts of routines are also helpful for senior managers in terms of integration because the dual structures eventually have to be integrated at the top level such that the ongoing tension is fostered in a creative way and its positive energy is tapped (e.g., Gibson & Birkinshaw, 2004; Smith & Tushman, 2005). Both the ostensive and the performative routines develop into capabilities that provide the basic infrastructure to firms through which managers are able to manage their own tension and ambivalent emotions. As a result, firms become more capable of pursuing contradictory demands simultaneously, as well as balancing them over time.

Emotional dimension

The emotional dimension is about managing emotional ambivalence. Drawing from emotion literature, particularly that related to emotional intelligence (Mayer et al., 2004) and emotional regulation (Hochschild, 1983), it has been defined as the ability to accept and regulate emotional ambivalence and its negative effects (Bengtsson & Raza-Ullah, 2017). Acceptance refers to embracing both the positive and the negative emotions in order to have a fuller understanding and more balanced view of the situation. Felt emotions provide cues or information to managers about the particular situations that they are in, which in turn guide them to think and act in ways that lead to synergistic outcomes. For instance, research has shown that people tend to interpret their experience of emotional ambivalence as a signal that they are in an unusual environment, which prompts them to collect more information to identify associations between unrelated stimuli, and therefore leads to increased creativity and superior performance (Fong, 2006). As emotional ambivalence is considered unpleasant and discomforting, a general response tendency is to either avoid it completely or to tip toward the preferred emotion to relieve the agony of ambivalence (van Harreveld et al., 2009). Yet, doing so leads to a biased and partial view of the situation (Pratt & Doucet, 2000), which negatively affects creativity, accuracy in judgements, and superior performance (cf. Raza-Ullah, 2017b). The acceptance of ambivalent emotions is thus an important first step geared toward managing it.

Regulation involves controlling the expression of emotional ambivalence to the partner, as well as decreasing the felt discomfort that conflicting emotions create within a person. Two different strategies can be used to regulate emotions—surface acting and deep acting. Surface acting consists of the outward display of emotions that are actually not felt (Grandey, 2000). As experiencing extreme emotional ambivalence may lead to paralysis, powerlessness, and delays in decision making, experimental research has shown that such cues are read by the partner firm as submissiveness, which in turn excites the partner to dominate the focal firm (Rothman, 2011). Research further suggests that this will hurt the achievement of joint long-term performance goals (Raza-Ullah, 2017b). Thus, surface acting in context of coopetition is especially important for firms to sustain superior gains.

Finally, deep acting is about experiencing those emotions that need to be displayed. In other words, the emotions that are felt, are displayed (Grandey, 2000). As the feeling of ambivalent emotions is part and parcel of managers' life in coopetition contexts, deep acting becomes a necessity because surface acting on a long-term basis may produce burnout signs such as depersonalization, emotional exhaustion, and diminished personal accomplishment (Cordes & Dougherty, 1993). For deep acting, managers may need to do reappraisals to modify their inner feelings about a situation. Taken together, these three dimensions of coopetition capability jointly produce balance in the relationship and help managers to experience moderate levels of tension, which are needed to enhance performance outcomes (Raza-Ullah, 2017b).

Discussion and venues for future research

In this chapter, we propose that coopetition capability is a component of the broader alliance capability (Wang & Rajagopalan, 2015). Given that coopetitive relationships are inherently paradoxical, tensions are bound to emerge in alliances between competitors due to contradicting dualities, demands, or logics of interactions pursued simultaneously. We seek to enhance the alliance capability debate by introducing a specific capability, referred to as coopetition capability, which enables senior managers to maintain the moderate level of such tensions, shown to be optimal for alliance performance. Partitioned into analytical, balancing, and emotional dimensions, such capability is distinct from generic alliance capability that relates to various aspects of the alliance management process, such as coordination, communication, bonding, and learning. In contrast to these capabilities, coopetition capability reflects managers' ability to handle paradoxical demands and thus underlies a firm's ability to further develop relational governance and integrative conflict management approaches. Handling paradoxical demands requires developing a clear, precise, and unified understanding of the paradoxical situation, performing multiple and inconsistent roles and tasks via the development of routines, and accepting and regulating emotional ambivalence and its negative effects—abilities addressed in the analytical, balancing, and emotional dimensions of coopetition capability, respectively.

The inclusion of coopetition capability into alliance capabilities will thus enhance the explanatory power of the models that focus on alliance outcomes. While an early exploratory empirical examination of the effects of analytical and balancing dimensions on tensions (Bengtsson et al., 2016) confirmed the distinctiveness and proposed effects, much work is needed in refining the coopetition capability measures in terms of increasing its applicability at various stages of an alliance life cycle, relevance to specific alliance contexts, and accounting for the broader effects on organizational members.

Although we propose that firms with higher levels of coopetition capability are able to reap superior outcomes in an already-established alliance via maintaining tensions at the performance-optimizing level, understanding the pre-formation phase—the choice of alliance partner—can be a fruitful direction for developing the coopetition capability concept further. Identifying and selecting the right firm at the right time for coopetition remains the core concern for successful coopetition outcomes. Selection of a competitor-partner with a short-term orientation when the focal firm has a long-term orientation, for instance, would be a mismatch, which in turn would likely result in a premature dissolution of the coopetition relationship (cf. Das & Teng, 2000). Managers with a superior understanding of when and why it is beneficial to cooperate and compete and with the ability to develop alternative strategies to manage both cooperation and competition are likely to both identify potential collaborators and negotiate terms of alliance agreement in such a way as to gain most from their ability to handle paradoxical tensions at the post-formation stage.

Furthermore, while we develop the concept of coopetition capability within a horizontal alliance setting—alliances with industry firms—coopetition capability may also prove useful when forming vertical alliances with firms within the value chain, and when studying private-public partnerships. Zhang et al. (2010: 78) argue that coopetition "is not limited to horizontal alliances but is contained in any type of alliances," but the nature of contradictory demands can be different. For example, in university-industry alliances contradictions due to varying levels of market focus and value definition among partners may exist (Hall et al., 2003), hence the capability to manage such contradictory demands might include additional components within analytical, balancing, and emotional dimensions.

Finally, we centered the development of the capability construct at the inter-organizational level and focused on capability's effect on tensions that emerge in inter-firm relationships on the senior management level. The effects of coopetition capability can be expected to be broader than that. Besides the tension that transpires at the top management level, tension can also spill over into the organization at lower levels. Senior managers that are able to maintain moderate levels of tensions are likely to be able to more effectively communicate the rationales of the alliance to employees in the organization, thus reducing the potential of internal tensions emergence within an organization that can manifest themselves in conflicting opinions, uncertainty about the value of the alliance, negligence in interaction with the partner, and ambivalent emotional state.

References

Anand, B. N. & Khanna, T. (2000). Do firms learn to create value? The case of alliances. *Strategic Management Journal*, 21(3), 295–315.

Bengtsson, M., Eriksson, J., & Wincent, J. (2010). Co-opetition dynamics-an outline for further inquiry. *Competitiveness Review*, 20(2), 194–214.

Bengtsson, M. & Raza-Ullah, T. (2017). Paradox at an inter-firm level: a coopetition lens. In W. Smith, M. Lewis, P. Jarzabkowski, & A. Langley (Eds), *Oxford Handbook of Organizational Paradox* (pp. 296–314). Oxford: Oxford University Press.

Bengtsson, M., Raza-Ullah, T., & Vanyushyn, V. (2016). The coopetition paradox and tension: The moderating role of coopetition capability. *Industrial Marketing Management*, 53, 19–30.

Bouncken, R. B. & Kraus, S. (2013). Innovation in knowledge-intensive industries: The double-edged sword of coopetition. *Journal of Business Research*, 66(10), 2060–2070.

Cordes, C. L. & Dougherty, T. W. (1993). A review and an integration of research on job burnout. *The Academy of Management Review*, 18(4), 621–656.

Das, T. K. & Teng, B.-S. (2000). Instabilities of strategic alliances: An internal tensions perspective. *Organization Science*, 11(1), 77–101.

Eisenhardt, K. M. (2000). Paradox, spirals, ambivalence: The new language of change and pluralism. *Academy of Management Review*, 25(4), 703–705.

Feldman, M. S. & Pentland, B. T. (2003). Reconceptualizing organizational routines as a source of flexibility and change. *Administrative Science Quarterly*, 48(1), 94–118.

Fernandez, A.-S. & Chiambaretto, P. (2016). Managing tensions related to information in coopetition. *Industrial Marketing Management*, 53, 66–76.

Fernandez, A. S., Le Roy, F., & Gnyawali, D. R. (2014). Sources and management of tension in co-opetition case evidence from telecommunications satellites manufacturing in Europe. *Industrial Marketing Management*, 43(2), 222–235.

Fong, C. T. (2006). The effects of emotional ambivalence on creativity. *Academy of Management Journal*, 49(5), 1016–1030.

Gibson, C. B. & Birkinshaw, J. (2004). The antecedents, consequences, and mediating role of organizational ambidexterity. *Academy of Management Journal*, 47(2), 209–226.

Gnyawali, D. R., Madhavan, R., He, J., & Bengtsson, M. (2016). The competition–cooperation paradox in inter-firm relationships: A conceptual framework. *Industrial Marketing Management*, 53, 7–18.

Grandey, A. A. (2000). Emotional regulation in the workplace: A new way to conceptualize emotional labor. *Journal of Occupational Health Psychology*, 5(1), 95–110.

Harbison, J. R. & Pekar, P. (1998). *Smart Alliances: A Practical Guide to Repeatable Success*. San Francisco: Jossey-Bass.

Hall, B. H., Link, A. N., & Scott, J. T. (2003). Universities as research partners. *Review of Economics and Statistics*, 85(2), 485–491.

Hochschild, A. R. (1983). *The Managed Heart*. Berkeley: University of California Press.

Ireland, R. D., Hitt, M. A., & Vaidyanath, D. (2002). Alliance management as a source of competitive advantage. *Journal of Management*, 28(3), 413–446.

Kale, H., Singh, H., & Perlmutter, H. (2000). Learning and protection proprietary assets in strategic alliances: Building relational capital. *Strategic Management Journal*, 21(3): 217–237.

Lavie, D. (2007). Alliance portfolios and firm performance: A study of value creation and appropriation in the US software industry. *Strategic Management Journal*, 28(12), 1187–1212.

Lunnan, R. & Haugland, S. (2008). Predicting and measuring alliance performance: A multidimensional analysis. *Strategic Management Journal*, 29(5), 545–556.

Luo, Y. D. (2007). A coopetition perspective of global competition. *Journal of World Business*, 42(2), 129–144.

Mayer, J. D., Salovey, P., & Caruso, D. R. (2004). Emotional intelligence: Theory, findings and implications. *Psychological Inquiry*, 15(3), 197–215.

Park, S. H. & Ungson, G. R. (2001). Interfirm rivalry and managerial complexity: A conceptual framework of alliance failure. *Organization Science*, 12, 37–53.

Pratt, M. G. & Doucet, L. (2000). Ambivalent feelings in organizational relationships. In S. Fineman (Ed.), *Emotion in Organizations*, Vol. II: 204–226. London: SAGE Publications Ltd.

Raza-Ullah, T. (2017a). *Emotions…Really? The Role of Emotional Ambivalence in Coopetition Alliances*. Paper presented at the 77th Annual Meeting of the Academy of Management, Atlanta.

Raza-Ullah, T. (2017b). *A theory of experienced paradoxical tension in co-opetitive alliances*. (Doctoral dissertation), Umeå University, Umeå. Retrieved from http://urn.kb.se/resolve?urn=urn:nbn:se:umu:diva-138385, Diva database. (0346–8291).

Raza-Ullah, T., Bengtsson, M., & Kock, S. (2014). The coopetition paradox and tension in coopetition at multiple levels. *Industrial Marketing Management*, 43, 189–198.

Ritala, P., Olander, H., Michailova, S., & Husted, K. (2015). Knowledge sharing, knowledge leaking and relative innovation performance: An empirical study. *Technovation*, 35, 22–31.

Ritala, P. & Sainio, L. M. (2014). Coopetition for radical innovation: technology, market and business-model perspectives. *Technology Analysis & Strategic Management*, 26(2), 155–169.

Rothman, N. B. (2011). Steering sheep: How expressed emotional ambivalence elicits dominance in interdependent decision making contexts. *Organizational Behavior and Human Decision Processes*, 116(1), 66–82.

Schreiner, M., Kale, P., & Corsten, D. (2009). What really is alliance management capability and how does it impact alliance outcomes and success? *Strategic Management Journal*, 30(13), 1395–1419.

Smith, W. K. & Tushman, M. L. (2005). Managing strategic contradictions: A top management model for managing innovation streams. *Organization Science*, 16(5), 522–536.

van Harreveld, F., van der Pligt, J., & de Liver, Y. N. (2009). The agony of ambivalence and ways to resolve it: Introducing the MAID model. *Personality and Social Psychology Review*, 13(1), 45–61.

Wang, Y. & Rajagopalan, N. (2015). Alliance capabilities: review and research agenda. *Journal of Management*, 41(1), 236–260.

Zhang, H. S., Shu, C. L., Jiang, X., & Malter, A. J. (2010). Managing knowledge for innovation: the role of cooperation, competition, and alliance nationality. *Journal of International Marketing*, 18(4), 74–94.

Zollo, M., Reuer, J. J., & Singh, H. (2002). Interorganizational routines and performance in strategic alliances. *Organization Science*, 13(6), 701–713.

19

A multi-level perspective on managing coopetition

Stefanie Dorn and Sascha Albers

Introduction

The initial contributions to coopetition research have primarily emphasized the potential positive outcomes of combining cooperative and competitive elements in a relationship (see, e.g., Brandenburger & Nalebuff, 1996). Simultaneously, the potential risks of doing this have also been increasingly acknowledged. For example, cooperating with a rival involves high risks of knowledge transfer as the obtained knowledge by a rival partner may result in a direct disadvantage for a focal firm (Das & Teng, 2000; Khanna et al., 1998). Coopetitive relationships can thus give rise to various tensions. Empirical studies on coopetitive relationships have, among other things, examined the tensions between value creation and appropriation (Fernandez et al., 2014), or information sharing versus protection (Fernandez & Chiambaretto, 2016). Due to these tensions, it is suggested that coopetition relationships require specific ways of managing. Only via these specific approaches to managing relationships could conflicts be avoided (Tidström, 2014) that might disrupt the relationship and lead to it missing the relationship's goal.

Consequently, recent contributions on coopetition have shed more light on the specific management challenges, instruments, and outcomes of such relationships across various levels of analysis (Le Roy & Czakon, 2016). While some studies have focused exclusively on the individual level and the traits or characteristics that an organization's members need in order to cope with coopetition, others have adopted a firm-level perspective and looked at structures, mechanisms, and their effectiveness. Such foci are crucial for a still-nascent field such as coopetition management, where there remains a need to gain in-depth insights to spawn and substantiate constructs (Gnyawali & Song, 2016).

In this chapter, we draw attention to the interdependencies between three different levels of analysis: the individual level, the inter-firm level, and the industry level. All of these levels are interconnected and the characteristics of one level influence how the other levels of a coopetitive relationship function (Chiambaretto & Dumez, 2016; Dahl et al., 2016).

We start by consolidating the knowledge on specific management parameters at the different levels of coopetitive relationships. We then highlight the connections that potentially exist between these levels and how they are relevant for managing coopetition. We finally illustrate the promises of a multi-level approach to coopetition by a current empirical study in the event industry before concluding.

The level of the individual in coopetitive relationships

Following Dahl and colleagues (2016), coopetition can be understood as a strategy that depends on the actions and interactions of individuals (see also Jarzabkowski et al., 2007; Vaara & Whittington, 2012; Whittington, 2006). Consequently, the way in which coopetitive relationships work is highly influenced by the traits and ways of interacting of the involved individuals (Dahl et al., 2016; Stadtler & Van Wassenhove, 2016).

The individual level plays a crucial role in coopetition research, since most of the tensions that have been studied are cognitive, manifest in the minds of individual organization members. For example, the need to share and protect information at the same time results in a tension that affects employees directly (Fernandez & Chiambaretto, 2016). Stadtler and Van Wassenhove (2016) suggested that specific individual capabilities play a crucial role in the success of a coopetitive strategy, as individuals need to be able to handle cooperative and competitive interactions simultaneously. Other studies have implicitly assumed that individuals are not able to integrate both cooperation and competition at the same time (Bengtsson & Kock, 2000), which necessitates structural solutions. As such, an empirical study by Raza-Ullah and colleagues (2014) showed that individuals may become uneasy when partnering with a competitor; while some of them prefer to engage in the cooperative activities, they also feel forced to exploit the partner and therefore engage in competition. These paradoxical demands related to their tasks can create a state of emotional ambivalence (Raza-Ullah et al., 2014).

Studies on coopetition have advocated that, in order to withstand the tensions triggered by simultaneously cooperating and competing, individuals must develop a coopetitive mindset (Fernandez & Chiambaretto, 2016; Le Roy & Fernandez, 2015; Oliver, 2004; Seran et al., 2016). Such a mindset is created by organizational learning and building routines (Lundgren-Henriksson & Kock, 2016; Seran et al., 2016). The current body of literature lacks an in-depth investigation into coopetitive mindsets. However, Le Roy and Fernandez (2015) suggest that, within their specific empirical context, project managers have developed such a mindset: "They understood the benefits of collaborating with a competitor as well as the risks due to this collaboration" (Le Roy & Fernandez, 2015: 681).

Other studies have emphasized the concrete capabilities and activities at the individual level (e.g., Raza-Ullah et al., 2014; Stadtler & Van Wassenhove, 2016). For example, it has been found that employees who work in a coopetitive relationship may, in certain contexts, be able to prioritize cooperative and competitive activities (Stadtler & Van Wassenhove, 2016). Individuals can integrate the companies' goals with those of the cooperation, and therefore undertake actions that are conducive to achieving these goals (Stadtler & Van Wassenhove, 2016). In doing so, the employees "demarcate" the cooperative and competitive logics and, counter-intuitively, are able to act upon both at the same time (Stadtler & Van Wassenhove, 2016).

The inter-firm level of a coopetitive relationship

The discussion of coopetition management at the inter-organizational level usually focuses on cooperative agreements between competitors. Therefore, coopetition management depends on the governance structure that the partners agree upon. At the outset of their relationship, the partnering rivals determine the structure as well as the rules and guidelines, which they act upon during the ongoing relationship. Two broader issues have garnered attention with respect to coopetition management: (1) targeted efforts to establish a balance between cooperation and competition (e.g., Park et al., 2014); and (2) an active approach to managing coopetitive tensions (e.g., Fernandez & Chiambaretto, 2016). Scholars have specifically discussed the following facets in these domains.

The first aspect comprises formal issues. More specifically, a bandwidth of forms of coopetitive relationships have been investigated, including more rigid forms such as equity partnerships and loose forms such as oral agreements (Dorn et al., 2016; Hung & Chang, 2012). Another formal issue relates to the allocation of tasks and responsibilities. For example, it has been found that a clear assignment of the rival partners' tasks and responsibilities may be conducive to cooperation and prevent the risks that stem from competition between the firms (Faems et al., 2010).

Second, the coopetition literature discusses three generic structural options regarding the allocation of cooperative and competitive tasks: separation (e.g., Bengtsson & Kock, 2000), integration (e.g., Chen, 2008), and hybrid versions combining both logics (e.g., Fernandez et al., 2014). Separation refers, for example, to a segregation of teams and personnel of cooperative and competitive task domains, as it implicitly assumes that individuals are incapable of dealing with the paradoxical tensions resulting from coopetition (Bengtsson & Kock, 2000; Herzog, 2010; Raza-Ullah et al., 2014). By contrast, integration emphasizes the enhanced creativity and learning potential created by a closeness to the partner, thereby promoting the integration of cooperative and competitive domains. This implies the development of a certain culture or the employment of individuals with certain experience and capabilities (Bouncken & Kraus, 2013; Chen, 2008; Oshri & Weeber, 2006; Stadtler & Van Wassenhove, 2016). As such, it becomes apparent that the structure and design of the coopetitive partnership and the individual level are highly interdependent.

Third, the literature on coopetition has acknowledged the importance of informal coordinating mechanisms within the partnership (Fernandez & Chiambaretto, 2016). Mutual adjustment while performing the tasks is necessary in order to develop routines and structured actions (Nickerson & Zenger, 2002). Trust is crucial for coopetition as well, since without trust it is barely possible to effectively and efficiently cooperate with a partner (Ring & van de Ven, 1992; Tidström, 2014).

Finally, theorizing has started on a potential coopetition capability at the organizational level (Bengtsson et al., 2016). Bengtsson and colleagues (2016: 28) stated that such a coopetition capability builds "the ability to think paradoxically and to initiate processes that help firms attain and maintain a moderate level of tension, irrespective of the paradox intensity level." They linked coopetition capability to the balancing of contradictions or to understanding when to enter a coopetitive relationship or developing alternatives (Bengtsson et al., 2016: 23). Moreover, they related coopetition capability to managers' attention and ability to handle coopetitive tensions (Bengtsson et al., 2016: 28). This reiterates the close link between the individual and inter-firm levels.

The industry context of the coopetitive relationship

The structure and characteristics of a market or industry can have a relevant influence on how coopetitive relationships function. For example, coopetition between firms has been studied in various highly dynamic contexts, such as high-technology sectors (Bouncken & Fredrich, 2012; Gnyawali & Park, 2011); industries that are highly consolidated and mature (Bonel & Rocco, 2007; Gnyawali, 2006; Lechner & Dowling, 2003); or in markets that pressure firms to set standards and are therefore at an earlier stage (Gnyawali & Park, 2011; Oshri & Weeber, 2006).

More generally, the competitive and cooperative behavior of firms is influenced by the way in which it is socially and economically embedded (Granovetter, 1985; Uzzi, 1997). Therefore, the competitive structure of the industry plays a crucial role. For example, firms may meet each other in several arenas, such as at different regional or product markets (Yu & Cannella, 2013) or various industry coalitions (Albers, 2017). Some empirical studies have shown that these competitive interdependencies may yield a state of "tacit collusion" (Ketchen et al., 2004); this may influence if and how competitors cooperate, as opportunistic behavior is always viewed against the backdrop of the partners' future behavior on other markets (Baum & Korn, 1999; Stephan & Boeker, 2001).

While the above situation refers to the number of economic encounters, the quality of these encounters is interesting for coopetition management as well. For example, a high competitive intensity with regard to similar resources and market segments in which firms operate (Chen, 1996) may influence the characteristics of their coopetitive relationship and vice versa. While contributions on coopetition advocate that balanced (strong) cooperation and competition are advantageous (Park et al., 2014), increased competition between firms may lead to negative emotional responses by managers (Vuori & Huy, 2016), thus potentially amplifying coopetitive tensions. Hence, the competitive intensity can have a strong influence on how managers handle coopetitive relationships (Gnyawali & Park, 2011; Raza-Ullah et al., 2014).

With regard to social ties, it has been discussed how social capital (that is, beneficial relationships with third parties) emerges and influences the firms' actions (Chung et al., 2000). Since a major risk of coopetitive relationships consists of opportunistic behavior and its relatively severe consequences for the other party, such social ties can present additional safeguards (Lui & Ngo, 2005; Parkhe, 1993). Acting opportunistically could reduce the firm's (access to) social capital. This, in turn, may influence how firms choose their form of agreement; failure to recognize their embeddedness or its mechanisms adequately could lead coopeting partners to deploy more rigid safeguards.

Table 19.1 summarizes and gives an overview of the selected approaches to coopetition management on the three levels of analysis. In the next section, we will briefly present the highlights from an empirical study that created a multi-level model and sheds light on the interdependencies between these levels.

Table 19.1 Summary of concepts for managing coopetition at multiple levels

Individual Level	Inter-firm Level	Industry Level
Developing coopetitive mindsets (Gnyawali & Park, 2009; Le Roy & Fernandez, 2015; Lundgren-Henriksson & Kock, 2016) integrating the companies' and the cooperation's goals (Le Roy & Fernandez, 2015; Stadtler & Van Wassenhove, 2016) Deploying demarcating behavior (Stadtler & Van Wassenhove, 2016) prioritizing cooperation or competition depending on the context (Stadtler & Van Wassenhove, 2016)	– Formal mechanisms: – allocation of tasks and responsibilities (Faems et al., 2010) – structure of the partnership (Hung & Chang, 2012) – integration or separation of cooperative and competitive domains (Bengtsson & Kock, 2000; Stadtler & Van Wassenhove, 2016) Informal mechanisms: – emphasizing the project manager role (Fernandez & Chiambaretto, 2016) – developing trust (Tidström, 2014) – developing a distinct organizational culture (Chen, 2008) – developing a coopetition capability (Bengtsson et al., 2016)	Considering the economic interdependencies: – number of encounters, such as multimarket contact (Yu & Cannella, 2013) – quality of encounters, such as competitive intensity between the firms (Gnyawali & Park, 2011; Park et al., 2014) – considering the social interdependencies (Chung et al., 2000; Granovetter, 1985; Parkhe, 1993)

Connecting different levels of analysis: Insights from coopetition in the trade fair industry

A recent study from the German trade fair industry specified the interdependencies between the different levels of a coopetitive relationship (Dorn, 2017). That empirical study focused on two distinct cooperative agreements between competing trade fair companies and was based on over twenty interviews with informants from different hierarchical levels, archival data, and on-site observations.

The German trade fair industry provides an interesting setting in which to study coopetition, as overcapacities, mature trade show topics and formats, and new international market entrants have led competition to increase dramatically. However, more and more trade show organizers have teamed up—despite being fierce rivals—in order to jointly cope with the industry's challenges. The trade fair organizers under investigation own venues and organize a variety of trade shows throughout the year, most of which are large international trade fairs.

In both of the studied cases, two competing trade show organizers joined forces by organizing a joint event. This close form of cooperating is especially critical, as trade fairs are an intangible service and the result of the cooperation does not become apparent until the day of the event itself. Jointly organizing an event also makes it necessary to work closely with the competitor and exchange information on areas such as marketing strategies, customer acquisition (in this context, the exhibitors and visitors), and technical aspects at the event site.

The study identified the aspects that make the relationships between the competitors work, and most of these aspects overlap across different levels of the coopetitive agreements. As such, the coopetitive relationships both have a certain formal frame, albeit a relatively loose one (case 1: oral agreement; case 2: a simple contract without a clear definition of roles and duties) and, in both cases, the companies refrained from a detailed contract. This was surprising considering that coopetition is connected to opportunism and comparatively high risks of knowledge transfer (Das & Teng, 2000; Yami & Nemeh, 2014). Additionally, coopetition can involve tensions on the level of the employee (Bengtsson et al., 2016; Fernandez et al., 2014) and loose formal guidelines could promote uncertainty regarding task allocation, thereby amplifying these tensions (Tidström, 2009).

The above-mentioned study (Dorn, 2017) drew on organizational embeddedness to explain these rather loose forms of agreement. It provides the following key insights. First, the informants stated that they considered the industry to be a close family. Specifically, persons from all hierarchical levels exhibited certain links to rival companies. For example, some of the employees and managers have worked with their competitors before. Moreover, frequent meetings and social events in the scope of the industry's associations' activities ensured that the firms' representatives met each other on different occasions throughout each year. There, they exchanged relevant knowledge and discussed recent trends and issues. Additionally, all of the firms exhibit multiple vertical business connections and have competitive encounters in various markets; thus, there is a high economic interdependence. Consequently, a potential explanation for the rather loose formal structures can be sought in the social and economic embeddedness that ensure that the firms will not exploit the others and behave opportunistically, as they might thereby lose access to social capital (Gnyawali & Madhavan, 2001).

The rather loose formal structure also gave rise to another important aspect: informal interaction mechanisms between firms (see Fernandez & Chiambaretto, 2016). These loose structures enabled the cooperation team to create a trusting atmosphere and to increase cooperation (Dorn, 2017). The project managers were free to communicate to the team and promoted the pursuit of a mutual goal with the competitor, applying certain gestures that established an equal footing between their firm and the partner (Dorn, 2017). For example, they let the representative of the competitor appear in press meetings and granted them visibility, which increased trust (Dorn, 2017). The informants reported that if the structure had been more rigid and formal, they would not have been as free in their decision making. Therefore, this empowerment seems crucial for effectively working with a competitor.

The study also revealed that deploying such demanding informal mechanisms requires that individuals "overcome" the tensions created by simultaneous cooperation and competition. The developed conceptual model shows how individuals handled certain forms of dissent with high pragmatism and appeared to adopt a long-term perspective that ultimately prevented certain tensions from escalating into conflicts. Similar to the study of Stadtler and Van Wassenhove (2016), the present study also highlights that individuals might sometimes blind out competition and focus on cooperative tasks. Regarding the communication, a high transparency and ability to accept criticism in a constructive way seems very important for overcoming tension.

Overall, the study by Dorn (2017) shows how the different levels of a coopetitive relationship are intertwined. It also promotes a more holistic perspective on such partnerships, as individual capabilities or the relationship structure alone may not always fully explain why and how coopetition can work.

Conclusion

Coopetition is characterized by the multifaceted interdependencies between the actors involved, which are reflected at the different levels in a coopetitive relationship. This chapter has aimed to shed light on the interdependencies between these different levels of analysis— the individual level, the inter-firm level, and the industry level. We started by sketching the current state of the literature and consolidated managerial approaches to handling coopetition for each level. We then presented an empirical study that illustrates the interdependencies between these levels.

From a multi-level perspective, there are ample opportunities for future research on coopetition. For example, the interdependence between the characteristics of the partnership at the inter-firm level and its influence on the individual level and vice versa would benefit from future investigation. As the trade fair study shows, a loose structure in terms of flexible contracts or oral agreements may foster the deployment of informal mechanisms as individuals can independently develop their own approaches and tools to cope with coopetitive tensions. However, the exact facilitators, inhibitors, and consequences of this effect are not yet explored. Longitudinal case studies could help to clarify if and under which circumstances there are also negative influences on the individuals if a coopetitive relationship's structures are relatively loose. In doing so, we also suggest more studies to incorporate the characteristics and structure of the industry in their theorizing. As highlighted before, the social or economic embeddedness and the competitive intensity might influence the firms' and employees' behavior and therefore could explain how and why firms and the individuals behave in certain ways within a coopetitive relationship. From a practitioner perspective, the issue of coopetition capabilities at the firm level and coopetitive mindsets at the individual level is of special interest.

It is our hope that this chapter will contribute to a clearer understanding of coopetition and its multifaceted nature. Practitioners should be aware that decisions at one level of analysis might require considerations at other levels. This is especially important when designing a cooperative partnership with a competitor and assigning or hiring individuals who work within such potentially tension-laden relationships.

References

Albers, S. (2017). Competition Dynamics of Alliance Networks. In T. K. Das (Ed.), *Managing Alliance Portfolios and Networks* (pp. 91–110). Charlotte: Information Age Publishing.

Baum, J. a. C. & Korn, H. J. (1999). Dynamics of Dyadic Competative Interaction. *Academy of Management Journal*, 278(20), 251–278.

Bengtsson, M. & Kock, S. (2000). "Coopetition" in Business Networks—to Cooperate and Compete Simultaneously. *Industrial Marketing Management*, 29(5), 411–426.

Bengtsson, M., Raza-Ullah, T., & Vanyushyn, V. (2016). The Coopetition Paradox and Tension: The Moderating Role of Coopetition Capability. *Industrial Marketing Management*, 53, 19–30.

Bonel, E. & Rocco, E. (2007). Coopeting to Survive; Surviving Coopetition. *International Studies of Management and Organization*, 37(2), 70–96.

Bouncken, R. B. & Fredrich, V. (2012). Coopetition: Performance Implications and Management Antecedents. *International Journal of Innovation Management*, 16(5), 1–28.

Bouncken, R. B. & Kraus, S. (2013). Innovation in Knowledge-Intensive Industries: The Double-Edged Sword of Coopetition. *Journal of Business Research*, 66(10), 2060–2070.

Brandenburger, A. M. & Nalebuff, B. J. (1996). *Co-opetition*. New York: Doubleday.

Chen, M.-J. (1996). Competitor Analysis and Interfirm Rivalry: Toward a Theoretical Integration. *Academy of Management Review*, 21(1), 100–134.

Chen, M.-J. (2008). Reconceptualizing the Competition-Cooperation Relationship: A Transparadox Perspective. *Journal of Management Inquiry*, 17(4), 288–304.

Chiambaretto, P. & Dumez, H. (2016). Toward a Typology of Coopetition: A Multilevel Approach. *International Studies of Management and Organization*, 46(3), 110–129.

Chung, S., Singh, H., & Lee, K. (2000). Complementarity, Status Similarity and Social Capital as Drivers of Alliance Formation. *Strategic Management Journal*, 21(1), 1–22.

Dahl, J., Kock, S., & Lundgren-Henriksson, E.-L. (2016). Conceptualizing Coopetition Strategy as Practice: A Multilevel Interpretative Framework. *International Studies of Management & Organization*, 46(2–3), 94–109.

Das, T. K. & Teng, B.-S. (2000). Instabilities of Strategic Alliances: An Internal Tensions Perspective. *Organization Science*, 11(1), 77–101.

Dorn, S. (2017). Teaming Up With a Rival: A Conceptual Multi-Level Model of Inter-Firm Coopetition. In *Essays on Coopetition – Conceptualization, Management, and Dynamics of a Paradoxical Relationship* (pp. 72–122). Cologne: University of Cologne.

Dorn, S., Schweiger, B., & Albers, S. (2016). Levels, Phases and Themes of Coopetition: A Systematic Literature Review and Research Agenda. *European Management Journal*, 34(2016), 484–500.

Faems, D., Janssens, M., & Van Looy, B. (2010). Managing the Co-operation-Competition Dilemma in R&D Alliances: A Multiple Case Study in the Advanced Materials Industry. *Creativity & Innovation Management*, 19(1), 3–22.

Fernandez, A.-S., & Chiambaretto, P. (2016). Managing Tensions Related to Information in Coopetition. *Industrial Marketing Management*, 53, 1–11.

Fernandez, A.-S., Le Roy, F., & Gnyawali, D. R. (2014). Sources and Management of Tension in Co-opetition Case Evidence from Telecommunications Satellites Manufacturing in Europe. *Industrial Marketing Management*, 43(2), 222–235.

Gnyawali, D. R. (2006). Impact of Co-Opetition on Firm Competitive Behavior: An Empirical Examination. *Journal of Management*, 32(4), 507–530.

Gnyawali, D. R. & Madhavan, R. (2001). Cooperative Networks and Competitive Cooperative Networks Dynamics: A Structural Embeddedness Perspective. *Academy of Management Review*, 26(3), 431–445.

Gnyawali, D. R. & Park, B.-J. (2009). Co-opetition and Technological Innovation in Small and Medium-Sized Enterprises: A Multilevel Conceptual Model. *Journal of Small Business Management*, 47(3), 308–330.

Gnyawali, D. R. & Park, B.-J. (2011). Co-opetition Between Giants: Collaboration With Competitors for Technological Innovation. *Research Policy*, 40(5), 650–663.

Gnyawali, D. R. & Song, Y. (2016). Pursuit of Rigor in Research: Illustration From Coopetition Literature. *Industrial Marketing Management*, 57, 12–22.

Granovetter, M. (1985). Economic Action and Social Structure: The Problem of Embeddedness. *American Journal of Sociology*, 91(3), 481–510.

Herzog, T. (2010). Strategic management of coopetitive relationships in CoPS-related industries. In *Coopetition: Winning Strategies for the 21st Century*, Yami, S., Castaldo, S., Dagnino, G. B., Le Roy, F. (Eds). Cheltenham, UK; Northampton, MA: Edward Elgar.

Hung, S. & Chang, C. (2012). A Co-opetition Perspective of Technology Alliance Governance Modes. *Technology Analysis & Strategic Management*, 24(7), 679–696.

Jarzabkowski, P., Balogun, J., & Seidl, D. (2007). Strategizing: The Challenges of a Practice Perspective. *Human Relations*, 60(1), 5–27.

Ketchen, D. J., Snow, C. C., & Hoover, V. L. (2004). Research on Competitive Dynamics: Recent Accomplishments and Future Challenges. *Journal of Management*, 30(6), 779–804.

Khanna, T., Gulati, R., & Nohria, N. (1998). The Dynamics of Learning Alliances: Competition, Cooperation, and Relative Scope. *Strategic Management Journal*, 19(3), 193–210.

Le Roy, F. & Czakon, W. (2016). Managing Coopetition: The Missing Link Between Strategy and Performance. *Industrial Marketing Management*, 53, 3–6.

Le Roy, F. & Fernandez, A.-S. (2015). Managing Coopetitive Tensions at the Working-group Level: The Rise of the Coopetitive Project Team. *British Journal of Management*, 26(4), 671–688.

Lechner, C. & Dowling, M. (2003). Firm Networks: External Relationships as Sources for the Growth and Competitiveness of Entrepreneurial Firms. *Entrepreneurship & Regional Development*, 15(1), 1–26.

Lui, S. S. & Ngo, H. (2005). An Action Pattern Model of Inter-Firm Cooperation. *Journal of Management Studies*, 42(6), 1123–1153.

Lundgren-Henriksson, E. L. & Kock, S. (2016). Coopetition in a Headwind – The Interplay of Sensemaking, Sensegiving, and Middle Managerial Emotional Response in Coopetitive Strategic Change Development. *Industrial Marketing Management*, 58, 20–34.

Nickerson, J. A. & Zenger, T. R. (2002). Being Efficiently Fickle. A Dynamic Theory of Organizational Choice. *Organization Science*, 13(5), 547–566.

Oliver, A. L. (2004). On the Duality of Competition and Collaboration: Network-based Knowledge Relations in the Biotechnology Industry. *Scandinavian Journal of Management*, 20(1–2), 151–171.

Oshri, I. & Weeber, C. (2006). Cooperation and Competition Standards-Setting Activities in the Digitization Era: The Case of Wireless Information Devices. *Technology Analysis & Strategic Management*, 18(2), 265–283.

Park, B.-J., Srivastava, M. K., & Gnyawali, D. R. (2014). Walking the Tight Rope of Coopetition: Impact of Competition and Cooperation Intensities and Balance on Firm Innovation Performance. *Industrial Marketing Management*, 43(2), 210–221.

Parkhe, A. (1993). Strategic Alliance Structuring: a Game Theoretic and Transaction Cost Examination of Interfirm Cooperation. *Academy of Management Journal*, 36(4), 794–829.

Raza-Ullah, T., Bengtsson, M., & Kock, S. (2014). The Coopetition Paradox and Tension in Coopetition at Multiple Levels. *Industrial Marketing Management*, 43(2), 189–198.

Ring, P. S., & van de Ven, A. H. (1992). Structuring Cooperative Relationships Between Organizations. *Strategic Management Journal*, 13(7), 483–498.

Seran, T., Pellegrin-Boucher, E., & Gurau, C. (2016). The Management of Coopetitive Tensions Within Multi-Unit Organizations. *Industrial Marketing Management*, 53, 31–41.

Stadtler, L. & Van Wassenhove, L. N. (2016). Coopetition as a Paradox: Integrative Approaches in a Multi-Company, Cross-Sector Partnership. *Organization Studies*, 37(5), 655–685.

Stephan, J. & Boeker, W. (2001). Getting to Multimarket Competition: How Multimarket Contact Affects Firms' Market Entry Decisions. *Multiunit Organization and Multimarket Strategy*, 18, 229–261.

Tidström, A. (2009). Causes of Conflict in Intercompetitor Cooperation. *Journal of Business & Industrial Marketing*, 24(7), 506–518.

Tidström, A. (2014). Managing Tensions in Coopetition. *Industrial Marketing Management*, 43(2), 261–271.

Uzzi, B. (1997). Social Structure and Competition in Interfirm Networks: The Paradox of Embeddedness. *Administrative Science Quarterly*, 42(1), 35–67.

Vaara, E. & Whittington, R. (2012). Strategy-as-Practice: Taking Social Practices Seriously. *The Academy of Management Annals*, 6(1), 285–336.

Vuori, T. O. & Huy, Q. N. (2016). Distributed Attention and Shared Emotions in the Innovation Process: How Nokia Lost the Smartphone Battle. *Administrative Science Quarterly*, 61(1), 9–51.

Whittington, R. (2006). Completing the Practice Turn in Strategy. *Organization Studies*, 27(5), 613–634.

Yami, S. & Nemeh, A. (2014). Organizing Coopetition for Innovation: The Case of Wireless Telecommunication Sector in Europe. *Industrial Marketing Management*, 43(2), 250–260.

Yu, T. & Cannella, A. A. J. (2013). A Comprehensive Review of Multimarket Competition Research. *Journal of Management*, 39(1), 76–109.

Part IV
Coopetition at different levels

20

Coopetiting with an irreconcilable asymmetric disadvantage

Philippe Baumard

Introduction

In a participative economy, coopetiting has become a dominant logic. Swift and aggressive new entrants have regularly destabilized established markets through constant recombination of assets and value chains to an unprecedented extent. Situations where several businesses cooperate and compete simultaneously have become so common that citing the concept's founding authors (Burt, 1983; Brandenburger & Nalebuff, 1996; Dowling et al., 1996) could be perceived as an act of unnecessary deference.

There is, however, a particular situation where mastering the rules of coopetition is a matter of survival for both partners: when a start-up and large corporation venture together to coproduce a disruptive innovation. In this chapter, we investigate why and how small innovative entrepreneurial firms and large corporate incumbents face irreconcilable differences when they engage in partnership to nurture a disruptive innovation. Observations and findings are derived from the first-hand experience of running several of these partnerships in the 2012–2017 period with large corporate firms from various industries. As we unveil the sources of irreconcilable asymmetries in such ventures, we discuss strategies that may improve the performance of such asymmetric ventures.

The purpose of innovation ventures between small entrepreneurial firms and large corporate incumbents is to leverage the specific assets of each party in order to create a dualistic innovation. The large firm contributes its industrial know-how, its market access and experience, and its mastery of the regulation and certification processes; in other words, all the determinants of success that are the outcomes of accumulation processes that are not yet available for the small firm. On the other hand, the small entrepreneurial firm may contribute its talent in exploring new boundaries, its creative combination of unexpected uses of technology, and its higher flexibility and acceptance of risks. In such partnerships, the mismatch of scale between the partners creates dramatic levels of asymmetry.

Irreconcilable asymmetries

An irreconcilable agreement is defined as a set of terms that cannot be brought into harmony or adjustment; hence, deemed as incompatible and beyond repair. This adjective is used as it usually signals the end of cooperation where efforts have been made by both parties and have eventually led to both parties implacably opposed to and unable to compromise. Georg Simmel, in his *Sociology of Conflict*, proposed a grounded theory of such a dynamic: both parties enter a tunnel of rational disagreements that progressively escalate to stakes that cannot be rationally conciliated. In such situations, both parties may not be at fault. Simmel (1903) suggested that both parties enter a state of mutual despite, which generates two separate and irreconcilable grounds outside of any rational realm. As Simmel noted:

> The misconception that the one factor tears down what the other builds up, and that what at last remains is the result of subtracting the one from the other (while in reality it is much rather to be regarded as the addition of one to the other) doubtless springs from the equivocal sense of the concept of unity.
>
> *(Simmel, 1903: 491)*

Such situations are commonly known as irremediable or irretrievable breakdown. The disagreement cannot be resolved because it concerns the *raison d'être* of the unity, and this unity cannot be summarized in a set of reconciliations of bearable asymmetries.

The same logic applies to a venture between two firms that cooperate on a mutual project, but are inherently competitors. The *raison d'être* of the venture encompasses both distinctive *raisons d'être* of the coopetitive partners (Bouncken et al., 2017). This problem has been seen in the literature mainly as a resource-based view issue, suggesting that the small gains of each partner's idiosyncratic resources may escalate into the erosion of one firm's idiosyncratic asset (Bouncken et al., 2017; Fernandez & Chiambaretto, 2016). Simmel's approach to the concept of unity defies such a conception. As Simmel stated:

> We describe as unity the agreement and the conjunction of social elements in contrast with their distinctions, separations, disharmonies. We also use the term unity, however, for the total synthesis of the persons, energies, and forms in a group, in which the final wholeness is made up, not merely of those factors which are unifying in the narrower sense, but also of those which are, in the narrower sense, dualistic.
>
> *(Simmel, 1903: 492)*

Inferring from Simmel, some resources may be subject to a phenomenon of escalation, while others are, *by essence*, dualistic: such resources do not exist outside of the realm of the cooperation. For instance, in most proofs of concept (POC) sought by start-ups with large incumbents, the large industrial firm would provide the real-life data that are required to demonstrate the algorithmic capability of the small firm's innovation. The data themselves will not generate a disruptive algorithmic function. The algorithm alone, without a series of tests, demonstrations, and validations, will hardly turn into an innovation. In that sense, a proof of concept is a dualistic asset. It increases the value of the small firm's assets by demonstrating its real-life capability, while offering the large incumbent a new medium of transformation of its informational assets. A dualistic asset is therefore composed of antagonistic components: on one hand, the small entrepreneurial firm does not wish to share its algorithm, which is the essence of its valuation and market value. On the other hand, the large firm does not wish to share its industrial knowledge, which constitutes the core of its rent, a barrier to entry to its market, proprietary information, and contributes to its status (Gnyawali & Madhavan, 2001).

Dualistic assets can become problematic when the technology is not mature, not yet articulated, and prone to causal ambiguities concerning its intellectual property. Such a situation is typical of start-ups. If a start-up may be able to finance a few patent filings, it does not stand the comparison with the intellectual property department of a large incumbent. While a micro-entity may benefit from micro-enterprise status, for instance in the United States, the real cost of holding intellectual property rights is loosely called to the price of its annuities. Filing a sound patent requires intellectual property experts who can contribute to a better redaction of a firm's claims. It also requires following the evolution of the art as to file a new patent as the firm's technology evolves, or as it becomes obsolete. On the other hand, large incumbents are accustomed to umbrella patenting strategies, i.e., patenting an array of innovations that cover all causal ambiguities related to the technological field, so as to display a strong intellectual property front in case of a disagreement. Large firms also possess strong incentive programs to encourage their engineers, in a much larger number than the small innovative firm, leading to irreconcilable asymmetries in terms of intellectual property. The small entrepreneurial firm is knowledgeable of such a mismatch that it can mitigate through secrecy; but if the large incumbent cannot verify the claims of the start-up, and, incidentally, look at the code, the dualistic asset development is likely to turn into a duel that the start-up is bound to lose.

Mind games and asymmetric spillovers: Chasing the butterflies

The motivation of the large corporate incumbent is precisely to seek voluntarily or involuntary spillovers from the disruptive small entrant. Exchange of technological information and know-how typically take place on a bilateral and reciprocal basis, leading to symmetric spillovers (Spence, 1984; d'Aspremont & Jacquemin, 1988). But in the matter of spillovers, size matters counter-intuitively. A wise assumption would suggest that the smaller firm would benefit to a larger extent from a spillover from a large firm it is partnering with (Rosen, 1991). The size of the cup, however, does not determine the size of the spillover. Large firms accumulate expensive learning experiences from alliances, joint ventures, and joint During these experiences, they learn that cooperating with competitors could be prone to dangerous mind games, potentially involving hidden agendas (Burt, 1983; Sheppard, 1995). A large incumbent may be genuinely interested in the disruptive innovation of a small start-up. It may also seek to investigate a potential disruption, with the intent of preemption, dissuasion, interdiction, or predation. Accordingly, with more experience in managing secrecy when dealing with coopetitors, a large incumbent interacting with a small start-up may be more astute and more prepared in the avoidance of unintentional spillovers.

Large firms are engaged in thorough exploitation of their knowledge rents. Because such rents are tightly intertwined with the security of their market positions, large firms will tend to further as much as they can a rent exploitation strategy. This phenomenon has been identified by Tirole (1988) as the "replacement effect," suggesting that a large firm takes the risk of disrupting its own presence on the market by over-investing in research and development. Monopolists replace themselves when they innovate. Consequently, aggressive new entrants may invest more in R&D than large defensive incumbents because large firms would make rational choices when it comes to supporting new patents that would be too self-disruptive (Reinganum, 1983).

Industrial economists, however, overlook the fact that monopolistic rents are merely theoretical. As Rosen (1991: 412) states: "the impact of market position on R&D strategy depends on how the new technology introduced by an innovation interacts with a firm's pre-R&D technology. The innovations most commonly modeled in the literature assume that an innovation replaces (substitutes for) existing technology." The large incumbent is likely to see the small start-up as a provider of an innovation that would add onto or complement its own technology, while keeping in mind that it may well hold the potential of disrupting its rent. For the large incumbent, despite its asymmetric disadvantage, the outcome of the innovation venture is *unknown.* The reasonable bet for the large firm is to consider itself in a *pre-innovation* market, i.e., to try to cannibalize a potentially disruptive start-up before it crystallizes into a revolutionary innovation (Reinganum, 1983).

However, as Katz & Shapiro (1987) suggested, in a two-firm patent race, the winner is always the pre-innovation leader with the highest R&D intensity. In a coopetitive agreement between a large incumbent and a small start-up, the small entrepreneurial firm is likely to be the one with the highest R&D investment ratio, despite the irreconcilable asymmetry of size of the two partners. Accordingly, a counter-intuitive hypothesis is that the large firm has more to gain from information and know-how spillovers than the large incumbent. Moreover, as de Bondt & Henriques noted (1995: 657), "some firms may be less able to absorb other firms' innovative ideas, not because they themselves are unable to be innovative but rather because of either an unwillingness or an inability to learn."

Large firms try to circumvent this disadvantage when coopeting with small start-ups by making sure that their personnel have access to specific training regarding the technology. This training typically consists of asking the small start-up to provide education to employees of the large firm that can absorb the disruptive know-how. Large incumbents may also seek to hire employees from the start-up in a pre-emptive move, claiming that this rather aggressive move is justified by a gentleman's agreement furthering a stronger bridge between the two asymmetric firms. In some fields, such as artificial intelligence, very large incumbents may engage in a systematic hunt for talent by over-investing in their initial headhunting as to preempt the global expert workforce. In these coopetitive games, all players are not equal. When a worldwide incumbent in the field of artificial intelligence hires a co-founder of a small disruptive start-up, the outcome is an irremediable breakdown for the small start-up.

Powerful incumbents may have an interest in decelerating the emergence of a disruptive technology; either by forcing a technically inefficient dominant technology that they control, or by making sure that an efficient technology does not reach the market (Abrahamson & Fombrun, 1992). Such incumbents can "forge the iron cage" to an extent that constitutes an irreconcilable asymmetry for a small new entrant. Accordingly, small innovative entrepreneurial firms entering a coopetitive agreement need to interlock their founders' commitment through restrictive term sheets, which protect the firm's foundation from aggressive incumbents. Small entrepreneurial firms cannot compete with the level of remuneration offered by their large competitors. In some industries, such as applied artificial intelligence and computer security, the salaries offered by the corporate incumbents can be three times the wages a start-up can afford. Start-up compensation systems are based on high-risk, high-gain expectations; i.e., founding members expect their sacrifice in terms of income to be further compensated by exit gains, when the company grows, or when they can hold stock options in a highly valuable firm. Most small innovative firms are butterflies: colorful creations "that flit from one success to another, and almost no one will be surprised if (they) metamorphose into something more ordinary. Some butterflies might chose to live longer at the cost of less beauty; others might risk their lives to attain more beauty" (Starbuck, 1993: 917). Butterflies are rarely capable of pack behavior. Shareholder's commitment to the firm is usually their weak spot: as the promises of a shiny future become uncertain, butterflies may accelerate their metamorphosis into former serial entrepreneurs seeking a comfortable position in a venture capital firm, or in the soft realms of a corporate life.

Appropriability hazards and critical assets

The table, below, summarizes the various asymmetries encountered by small innovative firms (start-ups) and large incumbents entering a coopetitive innovation venture. Reconcilable assets are constituents allowing a rational mitigation in a situation of coopetition. For instance, start-up founders may accept opening their firm's capital to the cooperating competitor. By giving a minority share to the large incumbent, the start-up would expect to lower the expectation of a future frontal competition, reassuring the large incumbent of their commitment to the course of action, while benefiting from a gain in status. Similarly, an early licensing strategy, from the start-up to the large incumbent, may signal to the large corporate partner a willingness to consider the venture as a priority for the small firm. A commitment from the start-up to a discounted price for the incumbent when the technology reaches the market may also signal to the corporate partner that the invention will not disrupt its market presence, as it will gain an early and discounted access to the technology before it reaches the market. Reconcilable assets, in short, can mitigate the "appropriability hazard" (Oxley, 1997). A well-crafted term sheet may compensate the uncertainty surrounding the appropriation of the invention, by offering a privilege of access, pricing, and early market entry (see Table 20.1, top-left corner).

Likewise, a large incumbent may compromise on several assets involved in innovation coopetition in order to reduce the asymmetry, and gain the trust and commitment of the start-up. In early stages, gaining corporate references is critical for young start-ups seeking market recognition or trying to raise their attractiveness for potential investors. A large firm may accept being mentioned as a partner of the small firm to fulfill this purpose. The incumbent may also grant the start-up with a supplier position in an emerging value chain, or, incidentally, make the promise of the emergence of such a value chain. A privilege data access under a non-disclosure agreement may also reassure the start-up that secure access to vital data will be maintained throughout the coopetitive venture. Some incumbents also grant access to their pool of expertise, either in R&D or close to the market, which is a guarantee for the start-up that it will not have to renegotiate access to a precious expertise when needed (see bottom-left corner of Table 20.1).

Irreconcilable assets (second column) are core capabilities that cannot be compromised or jeopardized as they are key to the survival of the firm. In an extremely asymmetric coopetition, irreconcilable assets are at the center of every decision. For instance, a small innovative firm depending on the secrecy of its algorithms will take every guarantee against an accidental spillover of its mathematical formulas. This may include imposing end-to-end encryption on its development servers, its GitHubs, its internal messaging system, forbidding external communication

Table 20.1 Reconcilable assets and irreconcilable asymmetries in a start-up: Incumbent coopetition

	Reconcilable Assets	Irreconcilable Assets (Non-negotiable)	Irreconcilable Asymmetries	Dualistic Assets
Start-up	Capital (seeding) Patent (licensing) Pricing (discount) Minority control	*Raison d'être* Founders Secret of invention Capital control	Intellectual property (disadvantage) R&D intensity (*advantage*) Human capital (*disadvantage*)	Proof of concepts Co-generated code Embedded component
Corporate incumbent	Status (piggy back) Market access Data access Expertise access	Historical rent Critical patent Direct competition Exploited rents contributing to core revenues	Market security (both) Sheer size (advantage) Forging the iron cage (advantage) Learning absorption (disadvantage)	Patent race *Raison d'être* of the joint venture

or publication unveiling its algorithms—even for research purposes—obfuscating its code, and protecting its algorithms through patenting, when possible, or through strictly enforced secrecy. But the secret of invention is not the sole irreconcilable asset of a start-up. The unity of its founders is far more critical, as small innovative firms are under the constant pressure of large incumbents in their field "headhunting" exceptional talents.

We identified four irreconcilable assets that start-ups are unlikely to compromise in a coopetitive innovation venture with a large incumbent: its *raison d'être*, its founders' unity, its secret of invention, and its capital control. Likewise, the large incumbent partnering with a small start-up may protect its own irreconcilable assets. Although its coopetitor might be small in size, its invention may still be highly disruptive if it ends in the hands of a major competitor. Accordingly, most large incumbents that we encountered would deter direct competition by explicitly naming the competitor that needs to be kept at large from knowing the details of the coopetitive venture. These informal recommendations, however, never reach the term sheet, as they would compromise a fair competition in the market, and more importantly, could be perceived as an overly aggressive move towards competitors. Incumbent's critical patents are also listed as "proprietary knowledge" both in the term sheets and in actual contractual documents. In doing so, the large incumbent clearly indicates that both its historical rents and its critical patent cannot be compromised by the coopetitive innovation venture.

The third column (Table 20.1) summarizes the irreconcilable asymmetries that we discussed earlier in this chapter. Irreconcilable asymmetries are core capabilities that are unbalanced between the two coopetitors while offering and will remain so throughout the venture, from start to finish. They constitute a threat for both parties as most traditional strategies to mitigate their negative effects on the coopetitive agreement will be ineffective. They cannot be spatially, functionally, or geographically separated (Dowling et al., 1996; Herzog, 2010). They cannot be integrated as the sheer asymmetries in size, scope, ownership, and power prevent the enactment of any equilibrium. The start-up founder cannot integrate competition and collaboration, favoring the incumbent, by accepting to compromise on a dimension already critically asymmetric. Likewise, despite its small size and its relative insignificance on the market, the large incumbent cannot jeopardize its core capabilities by giving excessive privilege and access to the small start-up. Irreconcilable asymmetries stand outside of the scope of humanely acceptable ambidexterity. Even if the rabbit trusts the lion, it is very unlikely to accept to nap in its mouth; reversely, even if the lion has nothing to fear of the rabbit, it is quite unlikely that it will surrender the keys of its iron cage.

There is absolutely no individual ambidexterity that could alleviate the sheer mismatch of scale between those coopetitors, as suggested by Chen (2008) or Das & Teng (1998). As Das and Teng noted:

> Having explicit goals in strategic alliances is not always possible, or even desirable. Partner firms often cannot agree on goals for the alliance that will effectively serve their respective interests. Moreover, given information asymmetry and the presence of hidden agendas, partner firms often have to tolerate a certain degree of goal ambiguity.
>
> *(Das & Teng, 1998: 506).*

In the collective pursuit of disruptive innovation between a small firm with the potential to disrupt its giant partner, and a giant incumbent that has the genuine capability of crushing its smaller partner, the question of a potential hidden agenda is outside the scope. Clearly, the large firm seeks to take advantage of unintentional spillovers from its young partner. It is here to learn about a possible technological disruption, which is as much a threat as an opportunity.

The objective of the small innovative firm is to access a sustainable market that will ensure steady growth. With an irreconcilable asymmetric disadvantage, the small firm's interest is to gain its partner's trust, to avoid any hidden agenda, and to display as few goal ambiguities as possible.

Overcoming the tensions in coopetition between start-ups and large incumbents

Based on our observations, we identified seven irreconcilable asymmetries that may play a central role in the success or failure of asymmetric innovation coopetitive ventures: intellectual property, R&D intensity, human capital, market security, organizational size, institutional power, and learning absorption (see Table 20.1, third column). Intellectual property is a disadvantageous and irreconcilable asymmetry for the start-up. As we discussed earlier, a start-up does not have the financial means to enter into a long and financially exhausting litigation process. At best, a start-up entering into an asymmetric coopetitive agreement with a large incumbent may secure a patent for each of its core inventive components on its core-targeted markets. In the hypothesis that the small firm did not raise an exceptional amount of seeding, first-round, or second-round capital, it will adequately protect its core inventions in its home market and maybe in a few markets of interest. However scarce and fragile a start-up intellectual property portfolio may be, it constitutes its main barrier, with secrecy, against external predators.

In a situation of tremendous external resource dependency (Pfeffer & Salancik, 1978), a start-up has little control over its environment. Even if it comes with a technological breakthrough, it will have to face the many interlock and cooptation mechanisms that protect incumbent markets (Burt, 1983) without the possibility of buffering environmental pressure, hoping to escape failure (Sheppard, 1995). A strategy to deter predatory behavior may involve opposing secrecy techniques that protect the invention, without compromising or revealing its core components (Baumard, 2010); but, practically, such counter-measures are ineffective when dealing with a large incumbent that could forbid market access when intellectual property is at stake. In that particular matter, our observations corroborate Fernandez & Chiambaretto's findings (2016): the most efficient mechanisms to prevent tensions related to critical information sharing in an asymmetric coopetition are informal control mechanisms.

The inner quality of these asymmetries is their presence *ex ante* and *ex post* of the collaboration. With very few exceptions, the mismatch of scale between the start-up and the corporate incumbent is likely to persist long after the cooperation. Such irreconcilable asymmetries have the property of "contradictory yet interrelated elements that exist simultaneously and persist over time" (Smith & Lewis, 2011: 382). Our experience suggests that successful asymmetric ventures rely on the early acceptance of the production of a dualistic asset: acknowledging the irreconcilable and permanent nature of the asymmetry, encouraging the internal patent race, identifying as early as possible the boundaries of background and foreground intellectual property, nurturing and preserving learning absorption mechanisms on both sides.

The study of paradoxical tensions in coopetitive ventures has been at the core of the existing literature, to the extent of sometimes exaggerating the phenomenon to justify its study. Indeed, literature that advocates that coopetitive ventures are more peaceful that frontal R&D competition are scarce. Our observations suggest that the difficulties in asymmetric R&D coopetition may not be related to the paradoxical nature of the organizational interaction, but rather by the irremediable asymmetries that they may carry.

Future research and directions

Dualistic assets trigger an intense rivalry between coopetitors while guaranteeing the *raison d'être* of the cooperation between competitors. The irreconcilable asymmetry they generate cannot be resolved by mitigation of spillovers, market sharing, or rational foreground IP sharing. In our observations of start-ups cooperating with very large incumbents, most start-ups would avoid confrontations through secrecy, reduced disclosure, and eventually through free-riding the emerging benefits of the cooperation. Future research should focus on understanding these dualistic situations where rivalry cannot be resolved by displacement or competitive agreements. Our findings suggest that informal control mechanisms (Fernandez & Chiambaretto, 2016) are inefficient when facing extremely asymmetric situations: an extensive benevolence on either side is very unlikely to reduce this category of asymmetries as they are tightly intertwined with the *raison d'être* of both players. Such situations are much more common than the literature suggests. They encourage discretion, discourage transparency and mutual loyalty, and have a deteriorating effect on innovation as both players need to accommodate a technological and commercial no-man's land at the heart of their communal venture. Dueling is inescapable. The question is how two or several coopetitive players can pursue internal dueling while displaying a consistent and sustainable communal front on the market they address.

References

Abrahamson, E. & Fombrun, C. J. (1992). Forging The Iron Cage: Interorganizational Networks And The Production Of Macro-Culture. *Journal of Management Studies*, 29, 2, 175–194.

Astley, W. G. & Fombrun, C. J. (1983). Collective Strategy: Social Ecology of Organizational Environments. *Academy of Management Review*, 8, 4, 576–587.

Baumard, P. (2010). Learning in Coopetitive Environments. In S. Yami, S. Castaldo, G. B. Dagnino, & F. Le Roy (Eds), *Coopetition: Winning Strategies for the 21st Century*. Cheltenham: Edward Elgar.

Bondt, R. D. & Henriques, I. (1995). Strategic Investment with Asymmetric Spillovers. *The Canadian Journal of Economics*, 28, 3, 656–674.

Bouncken, R. B., Fredrich, V., Ritala, P., & Kraus, S. (2017). Coopetition in New Product Development Alliances: Advantages and Tensions for Incremental and Radical Innovation. *British Journal of Management*, Early View, 1–20.

Bouncken, R. B., Gast, J., Kraus, S., & Bogers, M. (2015). Coopetition: A Systematic Review, Synthesis, and Future Research Directions. *Review of Managerial Science*, 9, 3, 577–601.

Brandenburger, A. M. & Nalebuff, B. J. (1996). *Co-Opetition*. New York: Doubleday.

Burt, R. S. (1983), *Corporate Profits And Cooptation: Networks Of Market Constraints And Directorate Ties In The American Economy*. New York: Academic Press.

Chen, M.-J. (2008). Reconceptualizing the Competition—Cooperation Relationship: A Transparadox Perspective. *Journal of Management Inquiry*, 17(4), 288–304.

d'Aspremont, C. & Jacquemin, A. (1988). Cooperative and Non-cooperative R&D in Duopoly with Spillovers. *American Economic Review*, 78, 1133–1137.

Das, T. K. & Teng, B.-S. (1998). Between Trust and Control: Developing Confidence in Partner Cooperation in Alliances. *Academy of Management Review*, 23(3), 491–512.

Dowling, M. J., Roering, W. D., Carlin, B. A., & Wisnieski, J. (1996). Multifaceted Relationships under Coopetition Description and Theory. *Journal of Management Inquiry*, 5(2), 155–167.

Downs George W., Jr. & Mohr, L. B. (1976). Conceptual Issues in the Study of Innovation. *Administrative Science Quarterly*, 21, 4, 700–714.

Fernandez, A.-S. & Chiambaretto, P. (2016). Managing Tensions Related to Information in Coopetition. *Industrial Marketing Management*, 53, 66–76.

Gnyawali, D. R. & Madhavan, R. (2001). Cooperative Networks and Competitive Dynamics: A Structural Embeddedness Perspective. *Academy of Management Review*, 26, 3, 431–445.

Gnyawali, D. R. & Madhavan, R. (2001). Cooperative Networks and Competitive Dynamics: A Structural Embeddedness Perspective. *Academy of Management Review*, 26, 3, 431–445.

Herzog, T. (2010). Strategic Management of Coopetitive Relationships In CoPS-related Industries. In S. Yami, S. Castaldo, G. B. Dagnino, & F. Le Roy (Eds), *Coopetition: Winning Strategies for the 21st Century*. Cheltenham: Edward Elgar.

Katz, M. L. & Shapiro, C. (1987). R&D Rivalry with Licensing or Imitation. *American Economic Review*, 77, 402–420.

Oxley, J. E. (1997). Appropriability Hazards and Governance in Strategic Alliances: A Transaction Cost Approach. *Journal of Law, Economics, and Organization*, 13(2), 387–409.

Pfeffer, J. & Salancik, G. R. (1978). *The External Control of Organizations. A Resource Dependence Perspective*. New York: Harper and Row.

Reinganum, J. (1983). Uncertain Innovation and the Persistence of Monopoly. *American Economic Review*, 83, 741–748.

Rosen, R. J. (1991). Research and Development with Asymmetric Firm Sizes. *Rand Journal of Economics*, 22, 411–429.

Sheppard, J. P. (1995). A Resource Dependenc Approach to Organizational Failure. *Social Science Research*, 24, 28–62.

Simmel, G. (1904). The Sociology of Conflict: II. *American Journal of Sociology*, 672–689.

Simmel, G. (1903). The Sociology of Conflict: I. *American Journal of Sociology*, 490–525.

Smith, W. K. & Lewis, M. W. (2011). Toward a Theory of Paradox: A Dynamic Equilibrium Model of Organizing. *Academy of Management Review*, 36(2), 381–403.

Spence, A. M. (1984). Cost Reduction, Competition, and Industry Performance. *Econometrica*, 52, 101–121.

Starbuck, W. H. (1993). Keeping a Butterfly and an Elephant in a House of Cards: The Elements of Exceptional Success. *Journal of Management Studies*, 30, 6, 885–921.

Tirole, J. (1988). The Theory of Industrial Organization. Cambridge: The MIT Press

21

Coopetitive portfolios
A review and research agenda

Paul Chiambaretto and Anne-Sophie Fernandez

Introduction

Over the past decade, a significant amount of research has been published on alliance portfolios, i.e., a firm's collection of direct alliances with partners (Lavie, 2007). Alliance portfolios have been investigated through different theoretical lenses and have shed new light on various concepts (Gomes et al., 2016; Wang & Rajagopalan, 2015; Wassmer, 2010). Nevertheless, alliance portfolios remain clearly under-investigated in the coopetition the literature. In this chapter, we focus our attention on coopetitive portfolios that we define as alliance portfolios that include alliances with competitors. To do so, we first detail the specificities of alliance portfolios and explain why it is important to investigate coopetition at the portfolio level. Second, we provide a review of the rare contributions in the coopetition literature that have adopted a portfolio perspective. Third, we provide a set of directions for future research to examine coopetition at the portfolio level.

The importance of reasoning at the portfolio level

Adopting an intermediate position between the dyad and the network, contributions on alliance portfolios investigate how a focal firm establishes and manages its network of direct alliances (Greve et al., 2014).

As Wassmer (2010) explains, the traditional approach to understanding alliance portfolios is additive logic (also called cumulative logic). Because it is increasingly difficult for firms to conduct purely individual strategies to be innovative, they must cooperate with partners to access specific resources or knowledge they do not own internally (Dyer & Singh, 1998). In fact, as they attempt to access additional resources, firms multiply their alliances and find themselves at the centre of a real alliance portfolio (Wassmer, 2010) or innovation network (Chesbrough, 2006). Following this approach, alliance portfolios are studied as the outcome of an additive process, in which the portfolio of alliances is the result of a series of individual alliance decisions (Bae & Gargiulo, 2004; Lavie & Miller, 2008). However, managing alliance portfolios in this way raises several concerns because the focal firm cannot have a coherent overview of its partnerships and tends to consider each new alliance as an independent event. This lack of hindsight leads some authors to characterize this behavior as "myopic" (Wassmer et al., 2010).

Conversely, the voluntary approach requires a shift in the level of analysis from the alliance level to the portfolio level. This change implies considering the synergies and conflicts that may exist between the different alliances in a firm's alliance portfolios. Concerning synergies, several studies have shown the relevance of simultaneously managing several alliances. Developing multiple alliances provides access to more resources (George et al., 2001) that can help develop unique resource combinations (Wassmer & Dussauge, 2011, 2012) or generate economies of scale (Lavie & Miller, 2008). Similarly, complementarities in terms of technologies or products can be developed if the focal firm adopts a strategy at the portfolio level (Asgari, Singh, & Mitchell, in press). If there were only synergies, firms would continue to increase their alliance portfolios. However, the reality is more complex. In the late 1990s, Gulati (1998) observed that the addition of a new partner or alliance creates redundancies with already-existing alliances and thus generates conflicts in the alliance portfolio (even if he did not use this word). Potentially, each new alliance could create negative repercussions on the other alliances in the portfolio. The greater the redundancy is with pre-existing alliances, the more significant the destruction of value for the focal firm (Vassolo et al., 2004; Wassmer & Dussauge, 2012). However, certain partners present higher degrees of redundancy and therefore deserve careful consideration before being integrated into a portfolio. Park et al. (2015) emphasized that the addition of a new partner that would compete with a pre-existing partner or with the focal firm might be a source of instability and thus destroy value at the level of the entire portfolio.

For the focal firm, the challenge lies in the firm's ability to determine the best composition or configuration of its alliance portfolio to maximize synergies while limiting conflicts and redundancies (Parise & Casher, 2003; Wassmer, 2010).

Alliance portfolios and coopetition: An under-investigated topic

A strong emphasis of coopetition at the dyadic and network levels

In recent years, several reviews of the coopetition literature have been conducted (Bengtsson & Kock, 2014; Bengtsson et al., 2016; Czakon et al., 2014; Dorn et al., 2016). Among the topics and themes investigated by these reviews, the level of analysis of coopetition relationships is presented as a critical issue. All of these reviews note that the vast majority (more than fifty percent) of contributions analyze coopetition at the dyadic or alliance level. This result is not surprising and seems consistent with the first definitions of coopetition, which considered it a "dyadic and paradoxical relationship" (Bengtsson & Kock, 2000). Furthermore, in these first contributions, the emphasis was placed on describing and understanding the phenomenon of coopetition. Researchers consequently began with the simplest cases of coopetition (dyadic agreement) before increasing their degree of complexity (Chiambaretto & Dumez, 2016).

Nevertheless, from the early stages of the development of a coopetition theory, some contributions have highlighted the existence of coopetition at the network level (Dagnino & Padula, 2002). These scholars underline the possibility of coopetitive settings with multiple partners or within ecosystems (Czakon & Czernek, 2016; Gueguen, 2009; Ritala et al., 2013; Sanou et al., 2016; Yami & Nemeh, 2014). These network-level contributions represent approximately twenty-five percent of the coopetition-related publications.

Consequently, we can clearly state that the majority of coopetition studies have focused either on dyadic relationships or on multiple/network relationships. Interactions between coopetition and other types of alliances entered into by the focal firms remain neglected. It is critical to simultaneously consider different types of alliances—cooperative and coopetitive—to understand how they interact with each other in alliance portfolios. An emerging set of contributions have begun to address these issues.

Existing contributions studying coopetition at the portfolio level

The first articles combining coopetition and alliance portfolios did not really mention the concept of coopetition. They mainly took into account the existence of competitors in the alliance portfolio of the firm. In this respect, Belderbos and colleagues (2006) studied the potential complementarity or substitutability of competitors with other partners in an alliance portfolio and their respective impact on productivity growth. Their analysis reveals that competitors and customers can be complementary such that firms should combine these two types of partners in their alliance portfolios to create synergies and foster productivity growth. Conversely, competitors and universities are substitutes, and therefore combining them in an alliance portfolio could actually do more harm than good.

In the same vein, Wassmer and Dussauge (2011, 2012) suggested that when a focal firm selects a new partner, it must avoid choosing a partner whose resources generate too much overlap with its own resources or with the resources of its pre-existing partners. Otherwise, the addition of this partner will negatively affect the focal firm's market value. Without mentioning coopetition, these authors clearly show that the degree of competition of the new partner with the focal firm or with the pre-existing partners is crucial when selecting a new partner.

In parallel, a limited group of scholars has initiated a deliberate analysis of coopetition at the portfolio level. Various complementary perspectives have been adopted.

Wu and colleagues (2010) used the literature on triads to understand how a focal firm can drive two competitors to collaborate together. Because the alliance portfolio literature is deeply grounded in the literature on triad dynamics (Gulati & Gargiulo, 1999; Madhavan et al., 2004), the researchers highlight how focal firms can become a sponsor and invite partners (that are in competition) to work together to create a unique value proposition.

A second set of contributions has examined the impact of coopetition on innovation. Because the relationship between coopetition and innovation is not clearly supported by empirical studies, two contributions changed the perspective adopted and switched to the portfolio level. More precisely, they encourage consideration of the share of coopetition in the alliance portfolio (i.e., the percentage of alliances signed with a competitor) to investigate its impact on the innovation performance of the focal firm. Ritala (2012) showed that there is no direct relationship between the degree of coopetition in an alliance portfolio and innovation and highlights the existence of various moderating variables. Park and colleagues (2014) extended the thread even further, indicating that the relationship between the percentage of coopetitive alliances in a portfolio and innovation has an inverted-U shape. In other words, they highlighted the existence of an optimal level of coopetition in a portfolio that maximizes innovation performance. This relationship is complex and positively moderated by the level of coopetition experienced by the focal firm. The key conclusions of Park and colleagues' (2014) model are presented in Figure 21.1.

Their contribution is particularly interesting because it raises the question of a pro-active management and structuring of the alliance portfolio (Castro & Roldán, 2015; Hoffmann, 2007; Lavie & Singh, 2012). This issue is also true in coopetitive portfolios. Bengtsson and Kock (2014) noted that

> firms interact with many other firms, and these interactions affect the coopetitive relationship over time. Furthermore, firms move in and out of relationships, and reconfigure their portfolio of relationships or alliances.

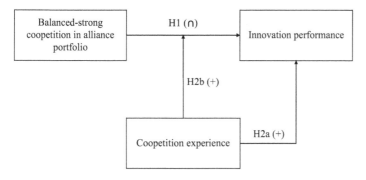

Source: Adapted from Park et al. (2014)

Figure 21.1   The link between alliance portfolio composition and innovation performance

However, the drivers of these reconfigurations remain unclear.

The contribution of Chiambaretto and Fernandez (2016) aims precisely to answer this call by investigating the different configurations of coopetitive portfolios and the drivers of the share of coopetitive agreements in alliance portfolios. Focusing on the air transport industry and providing a longitudinal analysis of Air France's alliance portfolio over a twelve-year period, they analyze the role of the environmental conditions on the configuration of the alliance portfolio. Building on the resource dependence theory (RDT), they show that when the environment is characterized by a high level of market uncertainty, firms tend to rely more on coopetition than on traditional alliances. Furthermore, when market uncertainty is high, firms tend to rely more on horizontal agreements than vertical ones. However, as soon as market uncertainty decreases, firms replace their coopetitive agreements with collaborative alliances and rely more on vertical agreements. Figure 21.2 illustrates their main conclusions.

To sum up, as shown in Table 21.1, only a limited amount of research has combined the coopetition and alliance portfolio literatures. We believe that there is significant potential for crossing these two concepts, so we provide directions for future research in the following section.

Directions for future research on coopetitive portfolios

In this section, we propose a research agenda for scholars interested in examining coopetitive portfolios. Three main research avenues require further investigation: the drivers and configurations of coopetitive portfolios; the management of coopetitive portfolios; and the performance outcomes of coopetitive portfolios.

Drivers and configurations of coopetitive portfolios

A rich body of literature has investigated the drivers of coopetition strategies. This literature has not only identified why firms adopt coopetition, but has also determined under which circumstances coopetition displays a higher performance than other relational modes. However, if theoretical models (Bengtsson & Kock, 2000; Brandenburger & Nalebuff, 1996; Lado et al., 1997) predict that coopetition should generate added value and superior performance than other relational models (cooperative or competitive), empirical studies suggest that this is true only in specific circumstances. Ritala (2012) found that market uncertainty and network

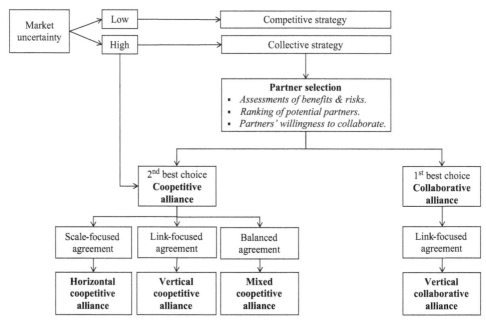

Figure 21.2   The role of market uncertainty in the configuration of coopetitive portfolios

Table 21.1 Summary of the existing literature on coopetitive portfolios

Research Article	Key Idea of the Study	Use the Term Coopetition
Belderbos et al. (2006)	Studies the potential complementarity or substitutability of competitors with other partners in an alliance portfolio and their respective impact on productivity growth	No
Wassmer and Dussauge (2011, 2012)	Shows that adding a firm presenting a high degree of competition with the focal firm or with the existing firms in the alliance portfolio can negatively affect the focal firm's market value	No
Wu et al. (2010)	Uses the literature on triads to understand how a focal firm can drive two competitors to collaborate together and create a unique value proposition	Yes
Ritala (2012)	Shows that there is no direct relationship between the degree of coopetition in an alliance portfolio and innovation	Yes
Park et al. (2014)	Reveals that the relationship between the percentage of coopetitive alliances in a portfolio and innovation has an inverted-U shape	Yes
Chiambaretto and Fernandez (2016)	Investigates different configurations of coopetitive portfolios and highlights uncertainty as a driver of the share of coopetitive agreements in alliance portfolios	Yes

externalities strengthen the positive impact of coopetition on innovation and performance. Ritala and Hurmelinna-Laukkanen (2013) also showed how absorptive capacity and appropriability strengthen or moderate the impact of coopetition on innovation. Wu (2014) proposed the existence of a bell-shaped curve between the level of coopetition and product innovation. More recently, Sanou and colleagues (2016) showed that centrality in a coopetitive network positively affects market performance. Finally, Le Roy and colleagues (2016) revealed that coopetition has a positive impact on product innovation when the parties are geographically distant.

Because most firms have an entire line of products that must be addressed (Teece, 1982) and because each product is associated with specific market conditions, it makes sense for firms to rely on different relational modes (individual, collaborative, or coopetitive). The combination of these different relational modes characterizes the configuration of a firm's alliance portfolio. It is thus important to understand the drivers of a low, moderate, or strong share of coopetition in an alliance portfolio. Are the drivers related to the focal firm's characteristics, such as its alliance and/or coopetition experience? Are the drivers related to the industry (or industries) in which the focal firm is present?

Furthermore, as in many contributions dedicated to alliance portfolios, it is important to analyze the configuration and structure of coopetitive portfolios. This implies investigating various dimensions such as the size of the coopetitive portfolio or its diversity. There are indeed different types of coopetition (Chiambaretto & Dumez, 2016; Chiambaretto & Fernandez, 2016; Dorn et al., 2016), and applying the concept of alliance portfolio diversity (Bruyaka & Durand, 2012; Duysters et al., 2012) to coopetitive portfolios could yield interesting results. In addition, it demands understanding of the mechanisms through which the synergies or conflicts between agreements in a coopetitive portfolio actually work.

Finally, a vast number of contributions focus on the evolution of alliance portfolios, but very few studies examine the evolution of coopetitive portfolios. In line with Chiambaretto and Fernandez (2016), we invite future scholars to investigate the evolution of coopetitive portfolios over time. From an initial perspective, a firm's alliance portfolio co-evolves with its strategy to reduce the effects of environmental uncertainty and change (Dittrich et al., 2007; Hoffmann, 2007; Ozcan & Eisenhardt, 2009; Lavie & Singh, 2012). While Chiambaretto and Fernandez's (2016) contribution aligns with this co-evolutionary approach, another set of contributions has linked alliance portfolio evolution to firm growth, highlighting how the changing needs of a firm affect the evolution of its alliances during the firm's life cycle (Hite & Hesterly, 2001; Maurer & Ebers, 2006; Rindova et al., 2012). Following these two approaches, additional research is needed to understand how coopetitive portfolios evolve over time. Is the share of coopetition in alliance portfolios defined by the focal firm's life cycle or by its environment? Do different types of uncertainty (market, technological, financial) lead to different configurations of coopetitive portfolios? What main reconfiguration and structuring actions can be implemented in a coopetitive portfolio? Because this research avenue requires the identification of new mechanisms or drivers, we expect case studies (especially longitudinal ones) to be particularly relevant.

The management of coopetitive portfolios

Along with the first articles on alliance portfolios, questions regarding their management have arisen. A stream of literature dedicated to "alliance capabilities," that is, the ability of firms to create and capture value through alliances (Anand & Khanna, 2000; Wang & Rajagopalan, 2015), already existed. However, this literature focused its attention on the dyadic level and neglected the interactions between the alliances highlighted by the literature on alliance portfolios. Few studies explored the management of alliance portfolios. Following the first contribution from Hoffmann

(2005), Heimeriks and Duysters (2007) were the first to deploy the concept of alliance capacity across the entire portfolio, although they did not really define the concept. The first definition of "alliance portfolio management capability" was provided by Sarkar and colleagues (2009), who characterized it as "organizational processes to proactively pursue alliance formation opportunities, engage in relational governance, and coordinate knowledge and strategies across the portfolio" (Sarkar et al., 2009: 583). It is essentially the third task (coordinating at the portfolio level) that characterizes the specificity of this capability. In a recent contribution, Castro and Roldán (2015,: 64) insist on this dimension and define this capacity as "the competence to develop alliance portfolio strategies, to establish a management system and coordinate the portfolio as a whole, facilitating the transfer and combination of resources between the actors."

In parallel to these contributions, several studies emerged on the management of coopetition (Bengtsson et al., 2016; Fernandez & Chiambaretto, 2016; Fernandez et al., 2014; Fernandez, Le Roy, & Chiambaretto, forthcoming; Le Roy & Fernandez, 2015; Tidström, 2014). These contributions aimed at understanding how firms can manage the tensions generated by coopetition strategies. In this vein, two key contributions began to address the question of "coopetition capability." First, Gnyawali and Park (2011) identified three main capabilities that are critical to managing coopetition. Whereas the first two capabilities—coopetition experience and executive mindset—enable firms to handle conflicts and tensions, the third—superior and complementary resources—helps firms to develop their relationship in a more balanced way. The second contribution, by Bengtsson et al. (2016: 22) clearly defines coopetition capability as "the ability to think paradoxically and to initiate processes that help firms attain and maintain a moderate level of tension, irrespective of the strength of the paradox."

However, no research has attempted to combine the management of coopetition and alliance portfolios. In their review and research agenda on coopetition, Dorn et al. (2016) invite researchers to "look at coopetitive alliance-portfolio management capabilities." Working on alliance portfolio management capabilities requires drawing lessons from both the alliance portfolio and coopetition management literatures. Several questions can be raised: to what extent is it similar to the management of traditional alliance portfolios? Is the management of coopetitive portfolios a sub-case of the management of alliance portfolios or does it require specific tools? Are these tools the same as those that are used to manage coopetition at the dyadic level? In-depth case studies and analyses of larger databases could provide insights regarding these questions.

Performance implications of coopetitive portfolios

Over the past decade, a significant amount of research has been dedicated to the link between alliance portfolio configurations and performance (Castro & Roldán, 2015; Lee et al., 2014; Wassmer et al., 2017). These contributions have shown that it is not the size of the portfolio that matters, but rather its configuration and management (Neyens & Faems, 2013; Wassmer, 2010). However, despite the seminal contributions provided by Ritala (2012) and Park and colleagues (2014), to the best of our knowledge, no other contributions have examined the performance of coopetitive portfolios.

To address the performance of coopetitive portfolios, several directions can be followed. A first path would be to investigate the existence of an optimal size or optimal composition of the portfolio that maximizes the focal firm's performance. Additional studies investigating coopetitive portfolio diversity could also bring interesting insights (Lee et al., 2014). Because the focal firm's performance can be measured in different ways, it would be highly relevant to diversify the types of performance examined. Previous contributions regarding the performance of coopetition have measured innovation performance (Bouncken & Kraus, 2013), financial performance (Luo et al., 2007), stock market reaction (Wu et al., 2015), and market performance (Ritala, 2012). Extensions of these contributions at the portfolio level would enrich the debate regarding the performance of coopetitive strategies.

Nevertheless, because the link between coopetition and performance is not a direct one, it is very unlikely that it will be different for coopetitive portfolios. Thus, it is essential to integrate moderating variables in the analyses. In the two contributions that have investigated coopetitive portfolios and performance, two types of moderating variables have been used: variables regarding the characteristics of the industry (Ritala, 2012) and the coopetition experience (Park et al., 2014). However, many other firm-specific, partner-specific, and industry-specific variables could be studied. Furthermore, in the rich literature regarding the performance of alliance portfolios, the majority of recent contributions have noted the key role of alliance portfolio management in performance (Castro & Roldán, 2015; Cui & O'Connor, 2012; Neyens & Faems, 2013; Schilke & Goerzen, 2010). Because several contributions have highlighted this management role in the performance of coopetition strategies (Le Roy & Czakon, 2016), we expect that coopetitive alliance portfolio management capabilities may also be important in explaining the performance of coopetitive portfolios.

We encourage further research to develop these future contributions on the performance of coopetitive portfolios. Future studies could address questions regarding the diversity or the optimal configuration of a coopetitive portfolio. To do so, we would expect the creation of specific databases that integrate the type of partner (competitor or not) and the type of agreement (structure, objective, etc.).

In a nutshell, with the joint development of two complementary streams of literature regarding coopetition and alliance portfolios, it is surprising that only a limited amount of research has combined these two concepts to study coopetitive portfolios. As coopetitive portfolios are a very promising research topic, we have provided various directions for researchers from both fields to pursue on this topic.

References

Anand, B. N. & Khanna, T. (2000). Do Firms Learn to Create Value? The Case of Alliances. *Strategic Management Journal*, 21(3), 295–315.

Asgari, N., Singh, K., & Mitchell, W. (in press). Alliance Portfolio Reconfiguration Following a Technological Discontinuity. *Strategic Management Journal*, n/a–n/a. https://doi.org/10.1002/smj.2554.

Bae, J. & Gargiulo, M. (2004). Partner Substitutability, Alliance Network Structure and Firm Profitability in the Telecommunications Industry. *Academy of Management Journal*, 47(6), 843–859.

Belderbos, R., Carree, M., & Lokshin, B. (2006). Complementarity in R&D Cooperation Strategies. *Review of Industrial Organization*, 28(4), 401–426.

Bengtsson, M. & Kock, S. (2000). "Coopetition" in Business Networks—to Cooperate and Compete Simultaneously. *Industrial Marketing Management*, 29(5), 411–426.

Bengtsson, M. & Kock, S. (2014). Coopetition—Quo Vadis? Past Accomplishments and Future Challenges. *Industrial Marketing Management*, 43(2), 180–188.

Bengtsson, M., Kock, S., Lundgren-Henriksson, E.-L., & Näsholm, M. H. (2016). Coopetition Research in Theory and Practice: Growing New Theoretical, Empirical, and Methodological Domains. *Industrial Marketing Management*, 57, 4–11.

Bengtsson, M., Raza-Ullah, T., & Vanyushyn, V. (2016). The Coopetition Paradox and Tension: The Moderating Role of Coopetition Capability. *Industrial Marketing Management*, 53, 19–30.

Bouncken, R. B. & Kraus, S. (2013). Innovation in Knowledge-intensive Industries: The Double-edged Sword of Coopetition. *Journal of Business Research*, 66(10), 2060–2070.

Brandenburger, A. M. & Nalebuff, B. J. (1996). *Co-Opetition: A Revolutionary Mindset That Redefines Competition and Cooperation* (Vol. 121). New York: Doubleday.

Bruyaka, O. & Durand, R. (2012). Sell-off or Shut-down? Alliance Portfolio Diversity and Two Types of High-tech Firms' Exit. *Strategic Organization*, 10(1), 7–30.

Castro, I. & Roldán, J. L. (2015). Alliance Portfolio Management: Dimensions and Performance. *European Management Review*, 12(2), 63–81.

Chesbrough, H. W. (2006). *Open Innovation: The New Imperative for Creating and Profiting from Technology*. Cambridge, MA: Harvard Business Press.

Chiambaretto, P. & Dumez, H. (2016). Towards a Typology of Coopetition: A Multilevel Approach. *International Studies of Management & Organization*, 46(2–3), 110–129.

Chiambaretto, P. & Fernandez, A.-S. (2016). The Evolution of Coopetitive and Collaborative Alliances in an Alliance Portfolio: The Air France Case. *Industrial Marketing Management*, 57, 75–85.

Cui, A. S. & O'Connor, G. (2012). Alliance Portfolio Resource Diversity and Firm Innovation. *Journal of Marketing*, 76(4), 24–43.

Czakon, W. & Czernek, K. (2016). The Role of Trust-building Mechanisms in Entering into Network Coopetition: The Case of Tourism Networks in Poland. *Industrial Marketing Management*, 57, 64–74.

Czakon, W., Mucha-Kuś, K., & Rogalski, M. (2014). Coopetition Research Landscape – a Systematic Literature Review 1997–2010. *Journal of Economics & Management*, 17, 122–150.

Dagnino, G. B. & Padula, G. (2002). Coopetition Strategy – A New Kind of Interfirm Dynamics for Value Creation. In *EURAM – The European Academy of Management Conference*. May 9–11, Stockholm.

Dittrich, K., Duysters, G., & de Man, A.-P. (2007). Strategic Repositioning by Means of Alliance Networks: The Case of IBM. *Research Policy*, 36(10), 1496–1511.

Dorn, S., Schweiger, B., & Albers, S. (2016). Levels, Phases and Themes of Coopetition: A Systematic Literature Review and Research Agenda. *European Management Journal*, 34(5), 484–500.

Duysters, G., Heimeriks, K. H., Lokshin, B., Meijer, E., & Sabidussi, A. (2012). Do Firms Learn to Manage Alliance Portfolio Diversity? The Diversity-Performance Relationship and the Moderating Effects of Experience and Capability. *European Management Review*, 9(3), 139–152.

Dyer, J. H. & Singh, H. (1998). The Relational View: Cooperative Strategy and Sources of Interorganizational Competitive Advantage. *Academy of Management Review*, 23(4), 660–679.

Fernandez, A.-S. & Chiambaretto, P. (2016). Managing Tensions Related to Information in Coopetition. *Industrial Marketing Management*, 53, 66–76.

Fernandez, A.-S., Le Roy, F., & Chiambaretto, P. (in press). Implementing the Right Project Structure to Achieve Coopetitive Innovation Projects. *Long Range Planning*. https://doi.org/10.1016/j.lrp.2017.07.009.

Fernandez, A.-S., Le Roy, F., & Gnyawali, D. R. (2014). Sources and Management of Tension in Co-opetition Case Evidence from Telecommunications Satellites Manufacturing in Europe. *Industrial Marketing Management*, 43(2), 222–235.

George, G., Zahra, S. A., Wheatley, K. K., & Khan, R. (2001). The Effects of Alliance Portfolio Characteristics and Absorptive Capacity on Performance: A Study of Biotechnology Firms. *The Journal of High Technology Management Research*, 12(2), 205–226.

Gnyawali, D. R. & Park, B.-J. (2011). Co-opetition Between Giants: Collaboration with Competitors for Technological Innovation. *Research Policy*, 40(5), 650–663.

Gomes, E., Barnes, B. R., & Mahmood, T. (2016). A 22-year Review of Strategic Alliance Research in the Leading Management Journals. *International Business Review*, 25(1, Part A), 15–27.

Greve, H. R., Rowley, T., & Shipilov, A. (2014). *Network Advantage: How to Unlock Value From Your Alliances and Partnerships* (1 edition). San Francisco, CA: Jossey-Bass.

Gueguen, G. (2009). Coopetition and Business Ecosystems in the Information Technology Sector: The Example of Intelligent Mobile Terminals. *International Journal of Entrepreneurship and Small Business*, 8(1), 135–153.

Gulati, R. (1998). Alliances and Networks. *Strategic Management Journal*, 19(4), 293–317.

Gulati, R. & Gargiulo, M. (1999). Where do Interorganizational Networks Come From? *American Journal of Sociology*, 104(5), 1439–1493.

Heimeriks, K. H. & Duysters, G. (2007). Alliance Capability as a Mediator Between Experience and Alliance Performance: An Empirical Investigation into the Alliance Capability Development Process★. *Journal of Management Studies*, 44(1), 25–49.

Hite, J. M. & Hesterly, W. S. (2001). The Evolution of Firm Networks: From Emergence to Early Growth of the Firm. *Strategic Management Journal*, 22(3), 275–286.

Hoffmann, W. H. (2005). How to Manage a Portfolio of Alliances. *Long Range Planning*, 38(2), 121–143.

Hoffmann, W. H. (2007). Strategies for Managing a Portfolio of Alliances. *Strategic Management Journal*, 28(8), 827–856.

Lado, A. A., Boyd, N. G., & Hanlon, S. C. (1997). Competition, Cooperation, and the Search for Economic Rents: A Syncretic Model. *Academy of Management Review*, 22(1), 110–141.

Lavie, D. (2007). Alliance Portfolios and Firm Performance: A Study of Value Creation and Appropriation in the U.S. Software Industry. *Strategic Management Journal*, 28(12), 1187–1212.

Lavie, D. & Miller, S. R. (2008). Alliance Portfolio Internationalization and Firm Performance. *Organization Science*, 19(4), 623–646.

Lavie, D. & Singh, H. (2012). The Evolution of Alliance Portfolios: The Case of Unisys. *Industrial and Corporate Change*, 21(3), 763–809.

Le Roy, F. & Czakon, W. (2016). Managing Coopetition: The Missing Link Between Strategy and Performance. *Industrial Marketing Management*, 53, 3–6.

Le Roy, F. & Fernandez, A.-S. (2015). Managing Coopetitive Tensions at the Working-group Level: The Rise of the Coopetitive Project Team. *British Journal of Management*, 26(4), 671–688.

Le Roy, F., Robert, M., & Lasch, F. (2016). Choosing the Best Partner for Product Innovation: Talking to the Enemy or to a Friend? *International Studies of Management and Organization*, 46(2), 136–158.

Lee, D. (Don), Kirkpatrick-Husk, K., & Madhavan, R. (2014). Diversity in Alliance Portfolios and Performance Outcomes: A Meta-Analysis. *Journal of Management*.

Luo, X., Rindfleisch, A., & Tse, D. K. (2007). Working with Rivals: The Impact of Competitor Alliances on Financial Performance. *Journal of Marketing Research*, 44(1), 73–83.

Madhavan, R., Gnyawali, D. R., & He, J. (2004). Two's Company, Three's a Crowd? Triads in Cooperative-Competitive Networks. *Academy of Management Journal*, 47(6), 918–927.

Maurer, I. & Ebers, M. (2006). Dynamics of Social Capital and Their Performance Implications: Lessons from Biotechnology Start-ups. *Administrative Science Quarterly*, 51(2), 262–292.

Neyens, I. & Faems, D. (2013). Exploring the Impact of Alliance Portfolio Management Design on Alliance Portfolio Performance. *Managerial and Decision Economics*, 34(3–5), 347–361.

Ozcan, P. & Eisenhardt, K. (2009). Origin of Alliance Portfolios: Entrepreneurs, Network Strategies, and Firm Performance. *The Academy of Management Journal*, 52(2), 246–279.

Parise, S. & Casher, A. (2003). Alliance Portfolios: Designing and Managing your Network of Business-partner Relationships. *Academy of Management Executive*, 17(4), 25–39.

Park, B.-J. (Robert), Srivastava, M. K., & Gnyawali, D. R. (2014). Impact of Coopetition in the Alliance Portfolio and Coopetition Experience on Firm Innovation. *Technology Analysis & Strategic Management*, 26(8), 893–907.

Park, G., Kim, M. J., & Kang, J. (2015). Competitive Embeddedness: The Impact of Competitive Relations Among a Firm's Current Alliance Partners on its New Alliance Formations. *International Business Review*, 24(2), 196–208.

Rindova, V. P., Yeow, A., Martins, L. L., & Faraj, S. (2012). Partnering Portfolios, Value-creation Logics, and Growth Trajectories: A Comparison of Yahoo and Google (1995 to 2007). *Strategic Entrepreneurship Journal*, 6(2), 133–151.

Ritala, P. (2012). Coopetition Strategy—When is it Successful? Empirical Evidence on Innovation and Market Performance. *British Journal of Management*, 23(3), 307–324.

Ritala, P., Agouridas, V., Assimakopoulos, D., & Gies, O. (2013). Value Creation and Capture Mechanisms in Innovation Ecosystems: A Comparative Case Study. *International Journal of Technology Management*, 63(3–4), 244–267.

Ritala, P. & Hurmelinna-Laukkanen, P. (2013). Incremental and Radical Innovation in Coopetition—The Role of Absorptive Capacity and Appropriability. *Journal of Product Innovation Management*, 30(1), 154–169.

Sanou, F. H., Le Roy, F., & Gnyawali, D. R. (2016). How Does Centrality in Coopetition Networks Matter? An Empirical Investigation in the Mobile Telephone Industry. *British Journal of Management*, 27(1), 143–160.

Sarkar, M., Aulakh, P. S., & Madhok, A. (2009). Process Capabilities and Value Generation in Alliance Portfolios. *Organization Science*, 20(3), 583–600.

Schilke, O. & Goerzen, A. (2010). Alliance Management Capability: An Investigation of the Construct and Its Measurement. *Journal of Management*, 36(5), 1192–1219.

Teece, D. J. (1982). Towards an Economic Theory of the Multiproduct Firm. *Journal of Economic Behaviour & Organization*, 3(1), 39–63.

Tidström, A. (2014). Managing Tensions in Coopetition. *Industrial Marketing Management*, 43(2), 261–271.

Vassolo, R. S., Anand, J., & Folta, T. B. (2004). Non-additivity in Portfolios of Exploration Activities: A Real Options-based Analysis of Equity Alliances in Biotechnology. *Strategic Management Journal*, 25(11), 1045–1061.

Wang, Y. & Rajagopalan, N. (2015). Alliance Capabilities Review and Research Agenda. *Journal of Management*, 41(1), 236–260.

Wassmer, U. (2010). Alliance Portfolios: A Review and Research Agenda. *Journal of Management*, 36(1), 141–171.

Wassmer, U. & Dussauge, P. (2011). Value Creation in Alliance Portfolios: The Benefits and Costs of Network Resource Interdependencies. *European Management Review*, 8(1), 47–64.

Wassmer, U. & Dussauge, P. (2012). Network Resource Stocks and Flows: How do Alliance Portfolios Affect the Value of New Alliance Formations? *Strategic Management Journal*, 33(7), 871–883.

Wassmer, U., Dussauge, P., & Planellas, M. (2010). How to Manage Alliances Better Than One at a Time. *MIT Sloan Management Review*, 51(3), 77–84.

Wassmer, U., Li, S., & Madhok, A. (2017). Resource Ambidexterity Through Alliance Portfolios and Firm Performance. *Strategic Management Journal*, 38(2), 384–394.

Wu, J. (2014). Cooperation with Competitors and Product Innovation: Moderating Effects of Technological Capability and Alliances with Universities. *Industrial Marketing Management*, 43(2), 199–209.

Wu, Q., Luo, X., Slotegraaf, R. J., & Aspara, J. (2015). Sleeping with Competitors: The Impact of NPD Phases on Stock Market Reactions to Horizontal Collaboration. *Journal of the Academy of Marketing Science*, 43(4), 490–511.

Wu, Z., Choi, T. Y., & Rungtusanatham, M. J. (2010). Supplier–Supplier Relationships in Buyer–Supplier Triads: Implications for Supplier Performance. *Journal of Operations Management*, 28(2), 115–123.

Yami, S. & Nemeh, A. (2014). Organizing Coopetition for Innovation: The Case of Wireless Telecommunication Sector in Europe. *Industrial Marketing Management*, 43(2), 250–260.

22

Coopetition and group dynamics

Aleksios Gotsopoulos

Introduction

Coopetition, the involvement of two or more organizations in interactions that are simultaneously cooperative and competitive in nature (Bengtsson & Kock, 2014: 14; Brandenburger & Nalebuff, 1997), has come to occupy a central position in modern business practice and research. In an ever faster-changing technological and market environment, organizations' ability to tap into the resources and the expertise of other organizations or to pool together resources in order to benefit from scale economies and increased bargaining power has become key to their sustained success.

The majority of research on coopetition has focused on coopetition between pairs of organizations (Davis, 2016). Individual organizations might maintain elaborate networks of coopetitors (Ahuja, 2000) and such networks might demonstrate considerable levels of overlap and closure (Coleman, 1988); yet, the unit of analysis generally remains that of the coopetitive dyad—the pair of organizations that simultaneously compete and cooperate (Gimeno, 2004; Ahuja et al., 2009).

Coopetition, however, also occurs in groups that involve multiple members. In such groups, members are invested in a common cause, but at the same time compete against some or all other organizations in the group (Das & Teng, 2002; Fonti et al., 2017; Zeng & Chen, 2003), and/or against other groups or organizations outside the focal group (Gnyawali & Park, 2009). The presence of multiple members in a group can alter the dynamics of coopetition materially, accentuating both the expected benefits and the potential problems. Coopetitive groups can differ significantly from coopetitive dyads on the basis of coopetition, the scope and the duration of the coopetitive relationship, the dynamics of partner selection, and the form and function of monitoring mechanisms. The dynamics and the function of such multi-party coopetitive groups are the focus of this chapter.

Coopetitive groups

Organizations form coopetitive relationships in order to gain access to their partners' resources (Gulati, 1995) and strengthen themselves vis-à-vis competitors (Gimeno, 2004). Because multi-member coopetitive groups are generally larger than coopetitive dyads, they promise access to more diverse resources and can offer significant competitive advantages to their members (Morris et al., 2007). Such advantages can be particularly pronounced when individual group members are small or when markets are characterized by heightened uncertainty.

In this vein, Fonti et al. (2017) analyzed the case of a diverse, forty-member coopetitive group that included universities, firms, and government agencies, and aimed at technological innovation. As each group member contributed to the common goal in ways that reflected their individual expertise, the size and the diversity of the group created significant complementarities among members' contributions and increased the group's innovation potential considerably. Similarly, Cusumano et al. (1992) highlight how, under the conditions of high market uncertainty that characterized the early VCR industry, the sizeable and diverse coopetitive group that formed around JVC played a crucial role in establishing VHS as the dominant technological design in the industry and enhanced group members' competitiveness.

When coopetitive groups form among organizations of the same type, expected benefits are associated more with size than with access to diverse resources. Large organizational size has been associated with lower failure rates, as it enhances both the legitimacy and the competitive strength of organizations (Dobrev & Carroll, 2003; Haveman, 1993). Coopetitive groups of similar organizations offer member organizations many of the benefits of large size, while still allowing them to maintain their independence and flexibility. Membership in a coopetitive group allows even small members to benefit from scale economies and increased bargaining power vis-à-vis buyers and suppliers (Morris et al., 2007). Fine-grained information sharing among members reduces duplication efforts (Gnyawali & Park, 2011) and eases adaptation to environmental change (Kraatz, 1998). Perhaps most importantly, coopetitive groups allow member organizations to pool together their resources. Sharing slack resources buffers individual members from environmental shocks and helps them to better withstand temporary disruptions (Uzzi, 1997). At the same time, as group members join forces, they become better able to launch competitive attacks against other groups or individual organizations, and to withstand similar attacks that emanate from outside the focal group (Gnyawali & Madhavan, 2001).

Challenges of coopeting in groups

Despite the promise of significant advantages that coopetitive groups hold over more limited, dyadic coopetitive relationships, their potential benefits appear to remain untapped much more often than those of dyadic relationships (Davis, 2016; Fonti et al., 2017). This is because the same factors that create a greater potential for advantages also accentuate problems of opportunism and free-riding that are generally endemic to coopetitive relationships.

In coopetitive groups that comprise heterogeneous members, the expectations and behavior of different types of members are often governed by different institutional logics (Jones et al., 2012). If the social norms that prescribe expectations regarding cooperative behavior, accepted levels of in-group competition, and schemes of benefit appropriation differ significantly among types of organizations, incentive misalignment and confusion occur (Fonti et al., 2017). As expectations of appropriate behavior conflict, member organizations are likely to withhold effort or defect, causing the group to dissolve or, at a minimum, underperform (Gulati et al., 2012).

Even in coopetitive groups that are more homogeneous, the sheer presence of multiple members increases the risk of conflict and mistrust almost exponentially. Multi-party relationships require each party to enact multiple partner-specific roles simultaneously (Simmel, 1950). When the diverse or even conflicting expectations of different parties are not met, or when one or some parties feel even just temporarily excluded from collaborative interactions, mistrust ensues (Davis, 2016).

The increasing tendency to mistrust one's partners as a group grows larger is not entirely misplaced. Organizations in coopetitive groups face a constant challenge of optimizing the allocation of limited resources between individual priorities and collective goals. Even though a stronger collective benefits all members, any individual organization might have a strong incentive to free-ride on others' contributions and redirect its own resources toward individual goals (McCarter et al., 2011). Such tendencies are accentuated as a coopetitive group grows larger; group size makes it more difficult to monitor and accurately assess the contributions of each individual member, and increases the incentives to act opportunistically (Zeng & Chen, 2003). Even if an organization wishes to cooperate, however, the sheer expectation that others will behave opportunistically can lead it to engage in *defensive defection* (McCarter et al., 2011); it might defect first and withhold effort toward the collective goal in order to avoid being labeled a "sucker" (Fonti et al., 2017; Gulati et al., 2012).

Despite their numerous potential advantages then, large coopetitive groups are often difficult to manage. As monitoring becomes more difficult with size, and as conflicting priorities or norms of interaction diminish trust, large groups are at constant risk of breaking up or fragmenting. The smaller-in-size, but more cohesive small worlds of fewer-in-number and similar-in-type organizations that might result from such fragmentation (Baum et al., 2003) are perhaps more functional; however, given their more limited size and scope they generally also lack the potential that brought larger groups together in the first place.

Monitoring mechanisms and formal sanctions

The significant benefits that coopetitive groups promise but often fail to deliver increase the need for effective governance mechanisms that will keep opportunistic behavior in check. Contracts that specify each member's contributions to the group and sanctions for those that fail to meet their obligations are, perhaps, the most straightforward of such mechanisms, and have been studied extensively (Williamson, 1991). Compared to dyads, larger coopetitive groups are better able to enforce contracts and apply sanctions on deviants. This is because both the severity and the credibility of sanctions depend crucially on whether the benefits that the enforcer(s) receive(s) from applying the sanctions are sufficient to compensate for the costs of sanctioning (Das & Teng, 2002; see also Coleman, 1990). Because in groups the costs of the sanctioning activities are shared across multiple members, the sanctioning capacity increases and the threat of sanctions becomes more credible.

The higher credibility of sanctions, however, does not address the increasing difficulty of detecting defectors as a group grows larger. As a group grows in size, interactions among group members become increasingly complex; assessing individual contributions accurately becomes problematic (Zeng & Chen, 2003) and any form of contract becomes incomplete, as even the most elaborate contracts fail to plan for all contingencies in an increasingly complex web of interactions (Fonti et al., 2017; Williamson, 1991). Formal sanctions become correspondingly irrelevant, if no breach of contract can be established. Rather unsurprisingly then, in larger coopetitive groups formal contracts do not constitute a particularly effective governance mechanism, but are rather better suited to offer guidance and complement other forms of governance (Poppo & Zenger, 2002).

Rational relational mechanisms of governance

In complex exchanges that are characterized by uncertainty and/or a difficulty of measuring contributions and performance, relational forms of governance appear to fare better than formal contracts (Dyer & Singh, 1998; Poppo & Zenger, 2002). Not relying on formally specified obligations and sanctions, but rather on fine-grained information exchange, flexibility, and shared norms, relational mechanisms are superior at dealing with the unforeseen circumstances that arise in complex, multi-member interactions.

Prior literature distinguishes between relational governance mechanisms with rational origins, in which expectations of future benefits encourage actors to cooperate in the present, and those with socially derived, normative underpinnings that can lead to cooperative behavior even in the absence of economic benefits (Poppo & Zenger, 2002; Uzzi, 1997). Among the relational governance mechanisms that have rational origins, reputation is, perhaps, the most significant. In groups where ties among members are characterized by a high degree of redundancy and closure (Burt, 1992; Coleman, 1990), focal organization A can learn about the behavior of organization B vicariously from organization C. As structural embeddedness increases, reputation becomes an asset (Granovetter, 1985; Gulati, 1995); establishing a reputation as trustworthy in its dealings with organization C allows organization B not only to benefit from an ongoing relationship with C, but also to develop a relationship with C's partner, organization A. In contrast, being labeled as an opportunist by C jeopardizes B's relationship not only with C, but with all of C's partners as well, and might cause B to be ostracized from the group. Notably, because reputation depends on partners' common understanding of what constitutes appropriate behavior in a coopetitive setting, a negative reputation and the resulting sanctions do not depend on formally proving violation of contract, but on a more nebulous and thus easier-to-establish breach of trust.

Relational governance mechanisms such as reputation address some of the problems that formal contracts cannot fully account for. Especially as closure increases, so does the probability that opportunistic behavior will be detected and penalized (Coleman, 1990). Such mechanisms, however, do not change the motives of organizations' behavior, which remain focused on the maximization of individual benefits. If the short-term benefits of opportunistic behavior are higher than the long-term costs, or if the end-game is in sight, organizations still have an incentive to behave opportunistically. In such cases, rational relational governance mechanisms fall apart: loss of reputation or the threat of expulsion from the group lose their effectiveness as sanctioning mechanisms, and defection becomes the dominant strategy (Murninghan, 1994; see also Uzzi, 1997).

Social relational mechanisms of governance and the emergence of group identity

Formal contracts and rational relational mechanisms attempt to enforce cooperation by increasing the economic costs of defection. However, by focusing group members' attention solely on the economic consequences of defection, they enforce a calculative approach to coopetition that encourages members to exploit loopholes, if doing so is possible, and to behave opportunistically, if detection can be avoided (McCarter et al., 2011). This becomes an increasingly pressing problem as groups grow in size; increasing complexity renders contracts incomplete, whereas relational mechanisms that are based on a rational cost-benefit analysis do little to prevent organizations from "self-interest seeking with guile" (Williamson, 1979) when doing so becomes easier.

Because of the shortcomings that characterize formal monitoring mechanisms and rational incentives, in larger coopetitive groups effective governance has to hinge more on members' voluntary prosocial behavior. Prosocial behavior—that is, an actor's willingness to accept sacrifices in order to assist her peers—requires a significant change in an actor's motives so that considerable value is placed on the well-being of the group. Granovetter (1985) attributes this kind of behavior that departs from neoclassical profit maximization to actors' desire "to derive pleasure from the social interaction that accompanies" their business interaction. As the continuation of such interaction presupposes the well-being on one's partner(s), the success of the partner(s) becomes a goal in its own right. Rather than attempting to take advantage of a weak or faltering partner (Ahuja, 2000), organizations might therefore volunteer resources and assistance, even if payback is uncertain both in time and type (Uzzi, 1997).

Essentially, prosocial behavior emanates from a sense of common fate that bounds together actors facing common threats (Portes & Sensenbrenner, 1993). In other words, altruism most often reflects an explicit or implicit understanding that stronger peers strengthen the aggregate group and thus, in the long-run, benefit the focal actor too (Audia & Rider, 2010; Uzzi, 1997). Yet, while the origins of prosocial behavior might be inherently rational, over time identification with the group becomes internalized. Because threats are perceived as originating from outside the focal group, often in the form of competition from a salient outgroup, they vividly highlight the distinction between members and non-members. A shared group identity quickly emerges to stress a sense of "we-ness" and clearly define the in-group in opposition to the out-group (Ingram & Yue, 2008; Portes & Sensenbrenner, 1993; see also Rao et al., 2003).

Identification with the group redefines members' priorities. The well-being of the collective becomes an important goal in its own right, even if it requires material sacrifices that might jeopardize the maximization of individual benefits. In some cases, the collective goal might assume such symbolic value that it takes precedence over an actor's more instrumental, individual goals; the *hedonic* benefits of contributing toward the group's success might more than compensate for the required sacrifices (Gottschalg & Zollo, 2007; Willer, 2009).

In other words, as group identity and collective goals are internalized, prosocial behavior becomes voluntary. The role of any form of monitoring mechanism correspondingly recedes, to the extent that such mechanisms are often fully absent in coopetitive groups that display a high degree of cognitive embeddedness (Uzzi, 1997). This absence of monitoring mechanisms is indeed meant to reinforce the moral rather than contractual nature of members' obligations. As norms of prosocial behavior become internalized, members abstain from opportunism not because of a threat of external sanctions, but because engaging in such behavior would damage their self-image (Gulati et al., 2012; McCarter et al., 2011).

Technically, the lack of monitoring mechanisms increases the risk that some members of the group will take advantage of others' trust and behave opportunistically (Coleman, 1988; Granovetter, 1985). In practice, however, the emergence of a shared identity and macroculture that emphasizes solidarity and moral integrity in business dealings has been found to keep the occurrence of malfeasance particularly rare (Carnevali, 2011; Das & Teng, 2002; Granovetter, 1985). As a result, when monitoring is inherently problematic—as it is in sizeable coopetitive groups—reliance on relational governance mechanisms that nurture and stress a shared group culture and identity might be the only viable option, yet an option that can be highly efficient.

Group size and the choice of group members

Previous research on coopetition has noted that strategic interdependencies and complementary resources maximize the potential of coopetitive relationships (Fonti et al., 2017; Gulati, 1995). In contrast, coopetition among organizations that are too similar and compete directly can lead to incentive misalignment, as coopetitors attempt to pursue private benefits at the cost of common benefits (Gimeno, 2004).

In sizeable coopetitive groups, however, these dynamics might be flipped. Organizations that come from diverse sectors or are otherwise significantly different (e.g., research universities versus profit-oriented firms) tend to abide by different and potentially conflicting institutional logics (Jones et al., 2012). As diversity increases, convergence on a shared group identity and macroculture becomes harder or altogether impossible, and might thus deprive sizeable coopetitive groups from the only effective governance mechanism available. Despite the significant potential benefits of resource complementarities, then, in larger groups diversity is more likely to cause conflict and fragmentation that precludes the realization of benefits (Fonti et al., 2017).

The crucial importance of shared macroculture implies that, to be successful, sizeable coopetitive groups have to display high levels of homogeneity (Audia & Rider, 2010; Carnevali, 2011). In contrast to arm's-length coopetitive relationships where homogeneity accentuates direct competition (Gimeno, 2004), in coopetitive groups with strong, shared identity, relations among members tend to be more commensalistic. Because competitive threats are framed as emanating from outside the group, solidarity characterizes interactions in-group, and competitive efforts are directed primarily against the out-group (Ingram & Yue, 2008).

The need to maintain a shared group identity that breeds trust and voluntary prosocial behavior also determines how group members are selected. Membership may require a direct referral or be a matter of birthright. Coopetitive groups that rely on a shared identity often emerge around a specific locale and rely on ethnic bonds or otherwise dense and overlapping network ties; the Modena knitwear industry (Lazerson, 1995), the Providence jewelers (Carnevali, 2011), or New York's Jewish diamond merchants (Coleman, 1988) provide some well-known examples. Strong identification with the locale or the ethnic group fosters a sense of common fate, facilitates enforceable trust, and reinforces a strong group identity that might exist independently of and even predate the business relationship (Audia & Rider, 2010; Portes & Sensenbrenner, 1993; Uzzi, 1997). In such groups, specialization and the development of strategic interdependencies among members might occur after the coopetitive relationship has started, rather than act as a prerequisite for its formation (Khanna & Rivkin, 2006).

In a similar vein, the need to maintain a strong group identity might impose limits on group size. Trust and goodwill in a group depend crucially on the strength of ties among members (Zeng & Chen, 2003). As a group grows larger, the number of ties that any focal organization needs to maintain grows exponentially, and can quickly become prohibitively taxing in terms of time and effort (Ahuja, 2000). While dropping some redundant ties might not cause a significant loss of information (Burt, 1992), it still increases the social distance among partners and can quickly diminish prosocial behavior (Baldassarri, 2015). As a result, a group whose success relies on a shared identity and the voluntary prosocial behavior of its members is likely to experience an upper threshold of size. As growth beyond such a threshold weakens the group's identity, it puts governance through moral suasion at risk, and can cause the group to underperform or fragment (Baum et al., 2003).

Conclusion

Despite the recently rich stream of literature on coopetition, coopetitive groups remain rather understudied and poorly understood. Because of their larger size and their ability to bring together numerous and diverse partners, coopetitive groups hold significantly higher potential than dyads. However, because size also accentuates problems of opportunism and free-riding that are inherent to coopetitive relationships, groups fail to achieve their potential much more often than dyads do (Fonti et al., 2017). The inadequacy of formal contracts and monitoring mechanisms as effective governance structures in the case of coopetitive groups implies that such

Table 22.1 A comparative analysis of governance mechanisms in the case of coopetitive groups

	Formal Contracts	*Rational Relational Mechanisms (e.g., reputation)*	*Normative Relational Mechanisms (e.g., internalized norms of behavior)*
Basis of compliance	Contract specifies partners' obligations and sanctions for deviants	Compliance is voluntary, based on a rational cost/benefit analysis of compliance versus deviance. Costs and benefits are not limited to the current period and partner(s), but also have to do with one's ability to form coopetitive relationships in future periods and/or with other partners	Compliance is voluntary, based on internalized values and principles of what constitutes appropriate behavior. Because group members value the group's well-being as a significant goal, they behave in a prosocial way, even if doing so requires sacrifices in terms of individual performance
Advantages	Simplicity: obligations and sanctions are well-defined	Reputation and trust require that an organization not only adhere to the letter of an agreement, but also demonstrate goodwill toward (a) partner(s). As a result, reputation constitutes a governance mechanism better suited than contracts to dealing with the unforeseen contingencies that emerge in complex relationships	When compliance and prosocial behavior are voluntary, monitoring mechanisms and sanctions become largely unnecessary. Because monitoring is inherently difficult in sizeable coopetitive groups that are characterized by complex interactions, normative relational mechanisms that promote voluntary compliance fare better than any other forms of governance mechanisms in sizeable groups
Disadvantages/ challenges	In sizeable coopetitive groups, contracts fail to account for all possible contingencies; as the web of interactions among members grows increasingly complex and as individual behavior becomes difficult to monitor, contracts lose their effectiveness	Rational relational mechanisms of governance do not change the underlying motives of group members' behavior, which remains focused on maximizing individual performance. A member is still expected to behave opportunistically, if she expects to get away with it, or if the endgame is in sight	The need to maintain a strong, shared group identity that is a prerequisite for voluntary prosocial behavior can pose constraints on diversity and group size. Conflicting institutional logics or size above a threshold can cause a group to fragment and fail to achieve its potential

groups need to rely much more on relational mechanisms that foster the emergence of a shared group identity and internalized values that promote members' voluntary prosocial behavior.

This phenomenon of (cognitive) embeddedness, puzzling as it is from a neoclassical point of view, has been studied in its own right and has augmented significantly our understanding of the role that trust, a shared macroculture, and a common identity play in economic transactions (Baum et al., 2003; Granovetter, 1985; Uzzi, 1996). Despite the importance of perceived common adversity in driving potential direct competitors to coalesce and cooperate, however, the origins and limits of such cooperation, as well as the circumstances under which it occurs, remain rather unclear. Geography and ethnic bonds are often evoked as explanations (Portes & Sensenbrenner, 1993; Uzzi, 1996), yet their role is likely less important in the case of larger and more mobile organizations or in today's more interconnected world, where common values rather than spatial collocation might drive coopetitive behavior (Weber et al., 2008). Literature on social movements that coalesce around a common goal and often compete against other groups with conflicting goals might offer some insights (Rao et., 2000), yet it tends to focus predominantly on individuals who often pursue symbolic rather than profit-oriented goals. Research on coopetitive coalitions that form at the early stages of new industries to promote competing perceptions of the industry (Grodal et al., 2015; see also Weber et al., 2008) perhaps takes a step further. This stream of literature, however, is still at its very early stages and does not address the occurrence and performance of embedded coopetitive groups in more mature industries.

In conclusion, coopetitive groups, their types, formation, and performance, as well as the governance mechanisms that can maximize their potential are topics significantly less understood than coopetitive dyads and their dynamics. Overall, effective coopetitive groups seem to be more prevalent in young industries and to form among small organizations that share strong bonds based on ethnic ties, similar location, or investment in a common cause. To what extent effective coopetitive groups can also form among larger organizations or in industries that are older is less clear. Better understanding the dynamics of coopetitive groups is important, however, given the increasing prevalence of coopetition in modern business. From a managerial perspective, a lack of better understanding of coopetitive groups and their dynamics is likely to limit the use and effectiveness of coopetition as a strategy. From a theoretical perspective, coopetition blurs the boundaries between individual organizations and the larger coopetitive groups they belong to, complicating the analysis of a number of related phenomena and calling for more research to be conducted in this field (Gotsopoulos & Pitsakis, 2017).

References

Ahuja, G. (2000). The duality of collaboration: inducements and opportunities in the formation of interfirm linkages. *Strategic Management Journal*, 21: 317–343.

Ahuja, G., Polidoro, F. Jr., & Mitchell, W. (2009). Structural homophily or social asymmetry? The formation of alliances by poorly embedded firms. *Strategic Management Journal*, 30: 941–958.

Audia, P. G. & Rider, C. I. (2010). Close, but not the same: locally headquartered organizations and agglomeration economies in a declining industry. *Research Policy*, 39: 360–374.

Baldassarri, D. (2015). Cooperative networks: altruism, group solidarity, reciprocity, and sanctioning in Ugandan producer organizations. *American Journal of Sociology*, 121: 355–395.

Baum, J. A. C., Shipilov, A. V., & Rowley T. J. (2003). Where do small worlds come from? *Industrial and Corporate Change*, 12: 697–725.

Bengtsson, M. & Kock, S. (2014). Coopetition—quo vadis? Past accomplishments and future challenges. *Industrial Marketing Management*, 43: 180–188.

Brandenburger, A. M. & Nalebuff, B. J. (1997). *Co-opetition*. New York: Bantam Doubleday Dell Publishing Group Inc.

Burt, R. S. (1992). *Structural Holes*. Cambridge, MA: Harvard University Press.

Carnevali, F. (2011). Social capital and trade associations in America, c. 1860–1914: a microhistory approach. *Economic History Review*, 64: 905–928.

Coleman, J. S. (1988). Social capital in the creation of human capital. *American Journal of Sociology*, 94: S95–S120.

Coleman, J. S. (1990). *Foundations of Social Theory*. Cambridge, MA: Harvard University Press.

Cusumano, M. A., Mylonadis, Y., & Rosenbloom, R. S. (1992). Strategic maneuvering and mass-market dynamics: the triumph of VHS over Beta. *The Business History Review*, 66: 51–94.

Das, T. K. & Teng, B.-S. (2002). Alliance constellations: a social exchange perspective. *Academy of Management Review*, 27: 445–456.

Davis, J. P. (2016). The group dynamics of interorganizational relationships: collaborating with multiple partners in innovation ecosystems. *Administrative Science Quarterly*, 61: 621–661.

Dobrev, S. D. & Carroll, G.R. (2003). Size (and competition) among organizations: modeling scale-based selection among automobile producers in four major countries, 1885–1981. *Strategic Management Journal*, 24: 541–558.

Dyer, J. H. & Singh H. (1998). The relational view: cooperative strategy and sources of interorganizational competitive advantage. *Academy of Management Review*, 23: 660–679.

Fonti, F., Maoret, M., & Whitbred, R. (2017). Free-riding in multi-party alliances: the role of perceived alliance effectiveness and peers' collaboration in a research consortium. *Strategic Management Journal*, 38: 363–383.

Gimeno, J. (2004). Competition within and between networks: the contingent effect of competitive embeddedness on alliance formation. *Academy of Management Journal*, 47: 820–842.

Gnyawali, D. R. & Madhavan, R. (2001). Cooperative networks and competitive dynamics: a structural embeddedness perspective. *Academy of Management Review*, 26: 431–445.

Gnyawali, D. R. & Park, B.-J. (2009). Co-opetition and technological innovation in small and medium-sized enterprises: a multilevel conceptual model. *Journal of Small Business Management*, 47: 308–330.

Gnyawali, D. R. & Park B.-J. (2011). Co-opetition between giants: collaboration with competitors for technological innovation. *Research Policy*, 40: 650–663.

Gotsopoulos, A. & Pitsakis, K. (2017). Coopetitive groups in aggregate populations: the emergence of UK university spinoffs as an organizational form. Sungkyunkwan University working paper.

Gottschalg, O. & Zollo, M. (2007). Interest alignment and competitive advantage. *Academy of Management Review*, 32: 418–437.

Granovetter, M. (1985). Economic action and social structure: the problem of embeddedness. *American Journal of Sociology*, 91: 481–510.

Grodal, S., Gotsopoulos, A., & Suarez, F. F. (2015). The co-evolution of categories and designs during industry Emergence. *Academy of Management Review*, 40: 423–445.

Gulati, R. (1995). Social structure and alliance formation patterns: a longitudinal analysis. *Administrative Science Quarterly*, 40: 619–652.

Gulati, R., Wohlgezogen, F., & Zhelyazkov, P. (2012). The two facets of collaboration: cooperation and coordination in strategic alliances. *Academy of Management Annals*, 6: 531–583.

Haveman, H. A. (1993). Follow the leader: mimetic isomorphism and entry into new markets. *Administrative Science Quarterly*, 38: 593–627.

Ingram, P. & Yue, L. Q. (2008). Structure, affect and identity as bases of organizational competition and cooperation. *Academy of Management Annals*, 2: 275–303.

Jones, C., Maoret, M., Massa, F. G., & Svejenova, S. (2012). Rebels with a cause: formation, contestation, and expansion of the de novo category "modern architecture". *Organization Science*, 23: 1523–1545.

Khanna, T. & Rivkin, J. W. (2006). Interorganizational ties and business group boundaries: evidence from an emerging economy. *Organization Science*, 333–352.

Kraatz, M. S. (1998). Learning by association? Interorganizational networks and adaptation to environmental change. *Academy of Management Journal*, 41: 621–643.

Lazerson, M. (1995). A new phoenix? Modern putting-out in the Modena knitwear industry. *Administrative Science Quarterly*, 40: 34–59.

McCarter, M. W., Mahoney, J. T., & Northcraft, G. B. (2011). Testing the waters: using collective real options to manage the social dilemma of strategic alliances. *Academy of Management Review*, 36: 621–640.

Morris, M. H., Koçak, A., & Özer, A. (2007). Coopetition as a small business strategy: implications for performance. *Journal of Small Business Strategy*, 18: 35–55.

Murninghan, K. J. (1994). Game theory and organizational behavior. *Research in Organizational Behavior*, 16: 83–123.

Poppo, L. & Zenger, T. (2002). Do formal contracts and relational governance function as substitutes or complements? *Strategic Management Journal*, 23: 707–725.

Portes, A. & Sensenbrenner, J. (1993). Embeddedness and immigration: notes on the social determinants of economic action. *American Journal of Sociology*, 98: 1320–1350.

Rao, H., Monin, P., & Durand, R. (2003). Institutional change in Toque Ville: nouvelle cuisine as an identity movement in French gastronomy. *American Journal of Sociology* 108: 795–843.

Rao, H., Morrill, C., & Zald, M. N. (2000). Power plays: how social movements and collective action create new organizational forms. *Research in Organizational Behavior*, 22: 237–282.

Simmel, G. (1950). *The Sociology of Georg Simmel*. K. H. Wolff, trans. Glencoe, IL: Free Press.

Uzzi, B. (1996). The sources and consequences of embeddedness for the economic performance of organizations: the network effect. *American Sociological Review*, 61: 674–698.

Uzzi, B. (1997). Social structure and competition in interfirm networks: the paradox of embeddedness. *Administrative Science Quarterly*, 42: 35–67.

Weber, K., Heinze, K. L., & DeSoucey, M. (2008). Forage for thought: mobilizing codes in the movement for grass-fed meat and dairy products. *Administrative Science Quarterly*, 53: 529–567.

Willer, R. (2009). Groups reward individual sacrifice: the status solution to the collective action problem. *American Sociological Review*, 74: 23–43.

Williamson, O. E. (1979). Transaction-cost economics: the governance of contractual relations. *Journal of Law and Economics*, 22: 233–261.

Williamson, O. (1991). Comparative economic organization: the analysis of discrete structural alternatives. *Administrative Science Quarterly*, 36: 269–296.

Zeng, M. & Chen, X.-P. (2003). Achieving cooperation in multiparty alliances: a social dilemma approach to partnership management. *Academy of Management Review*, 28: 587–605.

23

Coopetition and ecosystems

The case of Amazon.com

Alain Wegmann, Paavo Ritala, Gorica Tapandjieva,
and Arash Golnam

Introduction

In the mid-1990s, Brandenburger and Nalebuff (1995, 1996) defined coopetition as a win-win strategy among the company, its suppliers, its customers, its substitutors, and its complementors. This seminal definition focuses on the parallel nature of substitutive/competitive and collaborative relationships. Later, a distinct literature on *coopetition* emerged; the focus was on how firms organize into relationships and networks in which they simultaneously collaborate and compete in their pursuit to create and appropriate value (Bengtsson & Kock, 2000; Ritala & Hurmelinna-Laukkanen, 2009).

Recently, the coopetition literature has become increasingly interested in how collaboration and competition coincide in multi-actor networks and systems. Examples include studies on how individual firms build business models and platforms that involve collaboration with competitors (Ritala et al., 2014), how firms organize into competing multi-actor coalitions including coopetitors (Carayannis & Alexander, 2001; Gueguen, 2009), and how coopetition affects industry evolution and dynamics (Basole et al., 2015; Choi et al., 2010; Rusko, 2011).

Coopetition is therefore integrally linked with another relevant concept in contemporary strategy—*business and innovation ecosystems*. The ecosystem literature focuses on the systems of actors who create value together over a shared context, purpose, or value proposition (e.g., Adner, 2017; Moore, 1993, 2013), and on the efforts to lead and manage such ecosystems (Iansiti & Levien, 2004; Ritala et al., 2013; Rohrbeck et al., 2009; Williamson & De Meyer, 2012). Ecosystems involve actors who represent inter-organizational networks, but they also span across different industries (Moore, 1993), as well as involve individual customers and other market and institutional actors, thus providing a broad level of analysis that explains the connectivity of contemporary markets (Lusch et al., 2016; Tsujimoto et al., 2017; Vargo & Lusch, 2011). In addition, there is a rapidly developing discussion on *platform ecosystems* that enable different market actors—including competitors—to jointly create value via interacting through digital platforms (e.g., Ceccagnoli et al., 2012; Eloranta & Turunen, 2016; Gawer, 2014; Gawer & Cusumano, 2008; Ondrus et al., 2015; Thomas et al., 2014).

Although the literature of ecosystems and platforms has acknowledged the relevance of coopetitive interactions and dynamics (Basole et al., 2015; Gueguen, 2009; Ondrus et al., 2015;

Ritala et al., 2013), it lacks a systematic means to understanding *how different actors in ecosystems perceive the coopetitive dynamics, and how this can be modeled.* To this end, we build on systemic enterprise architecture methodology (SEAM), as it helps us to examine business activities from various perspectives in a systems context (Wegmann, 2003). We use the example of Amazon.com (later: "Amazon") and its ecosystem to illustrate these issues.

Conceptual background: Ecosystems, coopetition, and the SEAM approach

The literature on business and innovation ecosystems is still nascent, and conceptual and boundary issues are continuously debated (Oh et al., 2016; Ritala & Almpanopoulou, 2017). An emerging consensus is beginning to surface over the key components and approaches (for reviews and discussion, see, e.g., Aarikka-Stenroos & Ritala, 2017; Järvi & Kortelainen, 2017; Tsujimoto et al., 2017; Valkokari, 2015). Recently, strategy and management scholars have begun viewing ecosystem as a distinct theoretical construct (Adner, 2017; Lusch et al., 2016).

Adner (2017) provides the following definition, upon which we base also our approach: "The ecosystem is defined by the alignment structure of the multilateral set of partners that need to interact in order for a focal value proposition to materialize". The ecosystem is typically built around a focal firm, product, or platform, which creates a shared context for the value creation and structure for the ecosystem actors (Adner, 2017; Eloranta & Turunen, 2016; Thomas et al., 2014).

This definition helps us to not only identify the boundaries of the ecosystem but also the relevant actors and their interconnections. In this definition, the "focal value proposition" is an important determinant around which ecosystems can be viewed as a "structure." This enables us to adopt actor-specific perspectives of the ecosystem, typically that of the focal actor. Furthermore, Adner (2017) proposes an ecosystem strategy: "the way in which a focal firm approaches the alignment of partners and secures its role in a competitive ecosystem". Together, these definitions can be used for understanding strategies of coopetitive ecosystems.

We focus on coopetition in an ecosystems context that relates to the interdependence and co-existence of competitive and collaborative relationships within the ecosystem. Our illustrative analysis is based on Amazon, a prime example of coopetition strategies with a diverse amount of ecosystem actors. Coopetition perspectives in the Amazon case have been previously documented from the business model and platform perspective by Ritala et al. (2014), as well as from a value network perspective (Golnam et al., 2014). We take these discussions further, as we examine both the overall view of coopetition in ecosystems and the different actor perspectives. For instance, an ecosystem leader might be willing to orchestrate competitive and collaborative interactions within its ecosystem, whereas, for some actors, coopetition in ecosystems is a given condition that these actors must accept.

Our approach further develops the concept of ValueMap (Golnam et al., 2013) that was developed as part of method called SEAM (Wegmann, 2003). SEAM is a method used to model service offerings and service implementation; the offering delivers the value for the customer, and the implementation is the means for providing this value. SEAM was originally developed for analyzing and designing business and IT alignment and their related value creation. However, given its universal applicability and recent extensions (Golnam et al., 2013), it can also be used understand how an ecosystem's leader and partners can collaborate to bring value to their customers. This background helps us study ecosystems with a clearly identified leader or platform, as in the mainstream strategy literature. We adopt a more overarching system lens. In particular, we examine the *ecosystem configurations* from an overall perspective and from the perspectives of different actors in the ecosystem.

Example and principles of the modeling approach

We base our discussion on a concrete example, as examples are important for embodying theories (Barsalou, 2008). Using the example of product sales of Amazon, we analyze the structure of the Amazon's coopetitive ecosystem and make explicit how each actor perceives collaboration and competition. This extends the ecosystem literature, which typically adopts a focal-actor-centric view (e.g., Ritala et al., 2013; Rohrbeck et al., 2009; Williamson and De Meyer, 2012). It also contributes to the coopetition literature by providing lenses for analyzing coopetition strategy from an ecosystem perspective.

SEAM was designed to illustrate a situation with precision and concreteness; it creates diagrams more detailed than those typically used in management studies. In our example, *precise* means that we can understand the specific responsibility of each actor. *Concrete* means that we can understand who or what, in the perceived reality, is represented by each model element. This is based on the principle that models can be abstract and precise at the same time (D'Souza & Wills, 1998).

We present an example of Amazon selling alkaline batteries (e.g., a pack of eight AA batteries). It illustrates the Amazon Marketplace—a website that allows Amazon and many other partners to do e-commerce in a coopetitive manner. Amazon is the leader of the Marketplace and provides the technological platform to manage the collaboration. We consider five actors: Energizer, the battery producer; BestDeal, one particular third-party seller; Paul King, a customer; and Amazon as the ecosystem and platform leader. We also discuss the case in which Amazon itself also sells Energizer batteries, and the case in which Amazon sells batteries branded Amazon Basics (hypothetically produced by Energizer for Amazon). These examples are interesting as there are relatively few roles (producer, seller, customer, ecosystem leader) but various companies fulfilling these roles. Furthermore, the large number of similar competitive actors makes the ecosystem highly coopetitive.

Figure 23.1 represents the ecosystem by using the notation proposed by Adner (2017). The figure provides a baseline illustration of the interaction between the four key ecosystem roles: battery producer, seller, ecosystem-platform provider (Amazon.com), and end customer. The dashed lines indicate that all actors can communicate to the end customer. Although we can understand the basic ecosystem value-proposition rationale through this view, it should be extended to cover the broader ecosystem logic, the competitive and collaborative relational interdependencies and, eventually, to explain the role of coopetition. For instance, as we do not know which company fulfills which role, it is difficult to perceive the complexity of the ecosystem (e.g., the fact that Amazon can compete with the sellers). Coopetition is not yet visible either, as we see only one actor for each role.

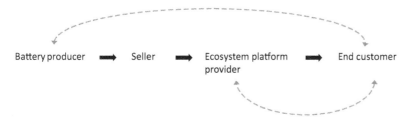

Figure 23.1   Amazon ecosystem using Adner (2017) representation

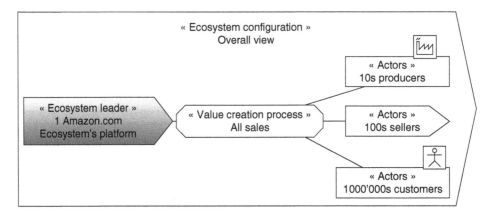

Figure 23.2 Ecosystem configuration—all actors represented (SEAM notation)

In Figure 23.1, there is an implicit product flow: the batteries "flow" from the producers to the customers. In a coopetitive ecosystem, this is still the baseline logic. To represent the coopetitive roles within the ecosystem in more detail, it is necessary to make explicit the number of actors of each category and thus further elaborate the above-described baseline model. Here, we use the SEAM method for this purpose, as it enables an examination of both the overall systems view and the actor-specific perspectives.

To understand multiple perspectives of the ecosystem, we need to understand the value each actor gains by their participation in it. Therefore, it is useful to analyze its collaborations and responsibilities, moving away from the linear baseline logic described earlier. We also develop separate models by using concrete labels and actor names, as it helps to understand the motivation of each actor.

Figure 23.2 shows the Amazon coopetitive ecosystem from a *super observer viewpoint*, examining the overall ecosystem configuration. The next three figures represent the Amazon coopetitive ecosystem, from four different viewpoints. Figure 23.3 shows the view of the seller; Figure 23.4 shows the view of the producer; and Figure 23.5 shows the view of the consumer. Using these models, we illustrate how the value is created for the actors in each role and how they perceive their role in a coopetitive ecosystem.

In all figures, we provide an order of magnitude for the number of each kind of actor. In this example, there are tens of producers, hundreds of sellers and millions of customers. Only one platform exists that provides the connectivity for these actors (by the definition of an ecosystem as a structure). These numbers are one of the important specificities of this ecosystem. Coopetition occurs between actors with the same role. For example, there are hundreds of sellers. These sellers compete; i.e., they are substitutors. They can also be complementors by selling complementary products (e.g., battery testers). Amazon organizes the interactions between the actors and brings to the sellers and producers millions of customers.

In Figure 23.2, it is possible to already see the essence of coopetition. The collaboration between these roles, however, is shown abstractly. It is only when we model the interaction from the viewpoint of one specific actor that the behavior is represented precisely.

In Figure 23.3, we focus on the view of *one* seller: BestDeal.

In our scenario, the logistics are managed by Amazon. The seller buys in volume from the battery manufacturer; a few palettes are delivered to Amazon, who then manages the thousands of individual shipments to the customers. The seller is responsible for the sales transaction to the customers (mostly setting the price and accepting/monitoring the customers' orders).

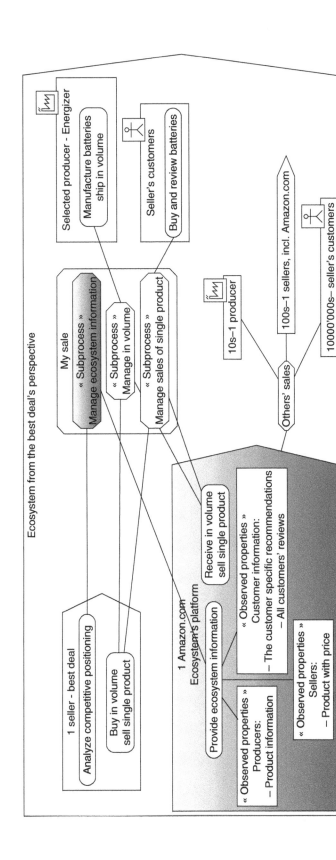

Figure 23.3 Seller's perspective (SEAM notation)

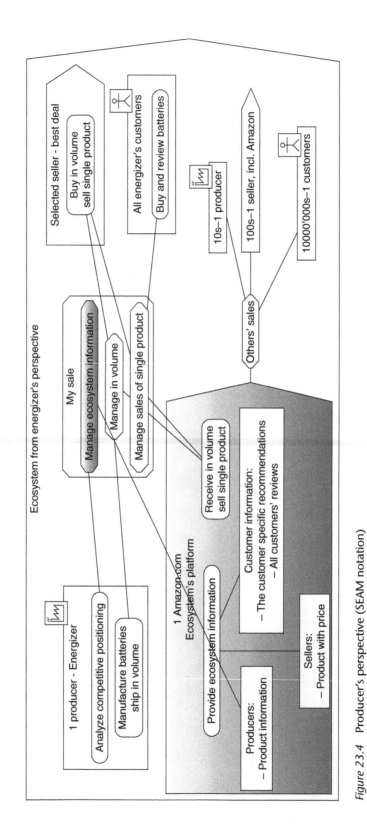

Figure 23.4   Producer's perspective (SEAM notation)

The coopetitive positioning is explained as follows. First, to sell batteries, BestDeal competes with hundreds of other sellers but it can also collaborate with other sellers to sell complementary products. Note that BestDeal also competes with a special competitor: the internal unit of Amazon that sells batteries (either branded as Energizer, or branded as Amazon Basics). In Figure 23.3, the actor named "100–1 Sellers incl. Amazon" represents all the sellers (except BestDeal) and includes Amazon's retail unit that sells against BestDeal. Amazon, in the role of the seller, is considered a separate entity from the Amazon ecosystem leader. If needed, we can make explicit the potential conflict of interest by showing a link between Amazon as ecosystem leader and Amazon as seller. Note that in the current implementation of the Marketplace, Amazon sellers usually do not appear explicitly on the website. So, for the consumer, there is no visible difference between the platform and the seller. This gives an advantage to Amazon's internal sales' function, compared to its competitors. Despite this disadvantage, the independent sellers still choose to be present on the platform in order to access the millions of potential customers.

By their simultaneous presence on the Marketplace's platform, the sellers complement each other's offerings; this contributes to retaining existing consumers and attracting new ones, which is a condition of success for the Marketplace.

The interest of the sellers is access to the large number of pre-existing customers. The Marketplace was created about six years after Amazon's inception (1994). In 2000, Amazon had twenty million customers. Hence the sellers' market shares are likely to be larger, compared to those of online sellers in an open market. This is probably why the Marketplace attracts mostly relatively small and lesser-known sellers. Amazon also provides the infrastructure for managing and accessing these customers (product selection and ordering, shipment logistic, payment logistic, etc.). This reduces the barrier of entry for the sellers and reduces their risks.

Another benefit provided by Amazon to the sellers is the ecosystem's information. The sellers can find precise information about their buyers and can find aggregate information on all customers (e.g., ecosystem share), and on individual customers (i.e., product reviews). For instance, the seller might acquire its ranking among other vendors, possibly where its price is compared to the competitors; and it can obtain information on all the battery providers. To adjust their coopetition strategy within the ecosystem, such information is useful for the individual sellers.

Overall, we can state that Marketplace is intrinsically coopetitive. It is similar to the "physical" market, with the difference that—by being virtual—customers worldwide can be accessed by one seller. Thus, by cohabiting the Marketplace together, with the help of the platform leader, the sellers can reach a huge market in which even a small market share provides lucrative opportunities.

In Figure 23.4, we focus on the view of the producer. The producer is also in a coopetitive situation, as it co-exists with other battery producers. As for the seller, the Marketplace is interesting due to its size as it significantly outweighs the downside of the competition. For the battery producer, who is one step further from the customer, the Marketplace might appear as yet another marketing channel. Hence, the coopetitive aspects for the customer are less critical than for the seller.

Last, we focus on one customer (Figure 23.5)—labeled here as Paul King (ideally, we should represent a "concrete" person; this helps us keep in mind that the ecosystem needs to create "concrete" values for "concrete" people). The consumer appreciates the diversity of the battery sellers and producers; he manages this diversity through the information provided by the ecosystem leader.

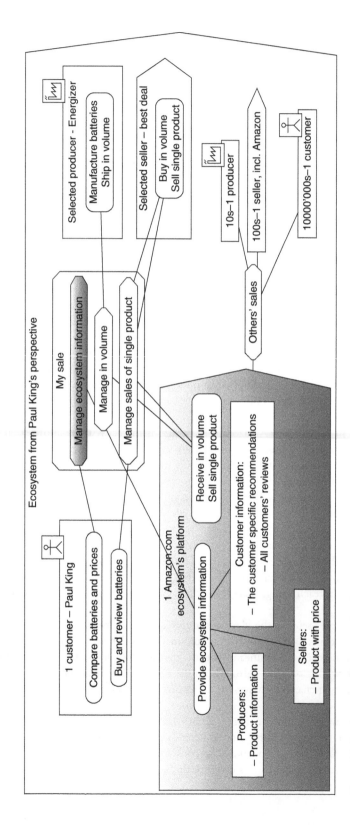

Figure 23.5 Consumer's perspective (SEAM notation)

Discussion and implications

This chapter has provided a brief overview of the role of coopetition in ecosystems, using Amazon ecosystem strategy as an empirical illustration. In doing so, we have provided several scholarly and practical implications to both coopetition and ecosystems research streams.

Implications for researchers

First, we have illustrated how to build the impetus for partners to join a coopetitive ecosystem. Between 1994 and 2000, by developing the sale of approximately ten product categories, Amazon created a customer base of about twenty million customers worldwide. They did not hesitate to share this customer base with the other sellers, who are also their direct competitors. The millions of customers, together with the pre-built Amazon infrastructure to access them, were the compelling impetus that made sellers and producers join the Marketplace, which enabled the creation of a successful long-term coopetition strategy (for further discussion, see also Ritala et al., 2014). These implications show the prominence of an ecosystem as a concept for the analysis of coopetitive interdependencies, thus furthering research on coopetition in ecosystems and networks.

Second, our results lead us to propose an alternative approach to the definition and analysis of an ecosystem. Adner (2017) defines the ecosystem as "the alignment structure of the multilateral set of partners that need to interact in order for *a focal value proposition* to materialize." We have shown that the Marketplace was and continues to be possible because all actors gain value from the market. Hence, ecosystems can also be seen from a more overarching, external, and configurational perspective: "the alignment structure of the multilateral set of partners that need to interact in order for *both joint and actor-specific value propositions* to materialize". This means that in addition to the focal value-proposition perspective, ecosystems could also be analyzed as systems that enable stakeholder-specific value propositions. Furthermore, analysis of broad-spanning platform ecosystems such as Amazon Marketplace might require viewing ecosystem linkages beyond the immediate structure, or in other words, "affiliations" (cf. Adner, 2017). Such loosely coupled ecosystem actors (such as individual or prospective customers) might be affiliated to the ecosystem merely via shared logic (Autio & Thomas, 2014).

Third, our analysis enable us to better understand the concept of an ecosystem strategy, i.e., "the way in which a focal firm approaches the alignment of partners and secures its role in a competitive ecosystem" (Adner, 2017). In particular, we have examined the perspective of both focal actors and peripheral actors. The Amazon platform provides an infrastructure that, for small and mid-size sellers and producers, dramatically reduces the cost and risks of e-commerce. It provides all services for managing the goods and insures the financial and information flow, information on the ecosystem, and access to millions of customers. Thus, Amazon has clearly defined and secured the roles of all players in the ecosystem. These issues provide a better understanding of how focal actors can act as ecosystem leaders and platform providers by ensuring value creation for both focal and peripheral actors (Eloranta & Turunen, 2016; Iansiti & Levien, 2004; Williamson & De Meyer, 2012).

Implications for practitioners

When designing an ecosystem, the ecosystem leader needs to identify how to attract its partners/competitors and how to attract their collaborative inputs. This requires designing how each actor contributes to the overall ecosystem, what value it receives, and how the actors compete. This calls for defining precisely the role of each actor and understanding what resources (e.g., information) are possessed by whom, and where such resources are needed. All of the above is what is usually called the ecosystem governance or design. The diagrams presented in this study provide a set of useful tools for designing these aspects.

In our case, the power of attraction of Amazon was its large customer base and the convenient access to the Amazon platform connecting all actors. Before being an ecosystem leader, Amazon already had a large customer base. To sustain its growth Amazon decided to give access to its customer base to its competitors. To access Amazon's customer base was so compelling that almost no external seller or producer could resist collaborating, despite the inherent competition with Amazon and the open competition with the other partners. At that point, Amazon became the leader of a new ecosystem. The internal business units of Amazon (who were selling and possibly producing products) became competitors with their new partners.

To analyze the motivation of each actor for joining the ecosystem, we propose the following design process. First the ecosystem designer (i.e., Amazon in our case) needs to identify all potential actors in the ecosystem and analyze how they would collaborate and compete (Golnam et al., 2014). For each actor, the designer needs to identify its motivation (Regev & Wegmann, 2004). To do so, it analyzes each actor's strategic goal (e.g., to stay in business, to broaden the market, to diversify). Knowing the strategic goals, it is possible to analyze what each actor perceives in its environment (e.g., e-commerce growth), how it evaluates this perception (e.g., absolute necessity to become an e-commerce actor), and the resulting tactical goals (e.g., becoming member of the Amazon ecosystem) (Regev et al., 2011). From this analysis, it is possible to assess what each actor provides and what value it receives from being in the ecosystem (Golnam et al., 2013). Using the same technique, it is possible to further specify the functionality of the Amazon platform and of other systems that will support the ecosystem.

On the other hand, due to the special nature of our case, it is also important to recognize that not all ecosystem leaders can create designs that are as compelling to other actors. Therefore, ecosystem strategy and coopetitive interactions require careful assessment, where different actors' roles, motivations, resources, and interdependencies are taken into account. The tools introduced in this chapter could be helpful in identifying these and other aspects.

Coopetition and ecosystems: Future research agenda

There are many interesting research trajectories in the intersection of coopetition and ecosystems literatures, which we briefly iterate here.

First, the *dynamics* of competition and collaboration change a lot when the examination is brought to the level of ecosystem. In dyadic coopetition relationships, competition often influences collaboration in one way or another, and vice-versa. In networked contexts, competition and collaboration affect each other as well. However, they do not always interact, as they might also merely co-exist, due to the multiplicity of within-network linkages between actors (see, e.g., Bengtsson & Kock, 2000; Ritala & Tidström, 2014). In an ecosystem context, these dynamics are much more complex, scalable, and sometimes subject to network effects. For instance, in platform ecosystems (such as in our Amazon Marketplace case) benefits of competitor involvement on one side of the platform (here, the third-party seller side) provides both supply-side network effects and cross-side, indirect network effects that benefit individual customers. This shows how ecosystem contexts might generate substantial benefits of coopetition, beyond the typical logic examined in coopetition studies. Future studies on coopetition and ecosystems could look at these and other types of mechanisms of how collaboration and competition interact and how their benefits can be scaled in ecosystems and platforms.

Second, future studies on *coopetition strategy* could explore the special features of ecosystem context further. A well-known argument in the coopetition literature is that involving competitors in value creation provides possibilities for increasing the size of the "pie," and thus all actors are able to capture more value in the end (Brandenburger & Nalebuff, 1996; Ritala & Hurmelinna-Laukkanen, 2009). In an ecosystem context, the boundaries of inquiry are broader and multiple industries are often involved (Moore, 1993; Williamson & De Meyer, 2012). Thus, it might be that some competitors are involved in capturing the value, while some merely participate in the value creation aspect, and eventually end up capturing value from different markets. Future studies could examine how the ecosystem context influences coopetition strategy by providing more alternatives and mechanisms for both deliberate and emergent value creation and capture dynamics.

Third, longitudinal research designs could look into how coopetition (or lack of it) affects *ecosystem emergence, evolution, and decline*. Coopetition has been noted as being influential in industrial evolution and competitiveness (Choi et al., 2010; Rusko, 2011). Similarly, for ecosystems, coopetition might play a role in improving the legitimacy and breadth of new ecosystems, as well as affecting their evolution over time (for better or worse). These types of issues provide fertile ground for research integrating coopetition and ecosystem perspectives.

Conclusion

Coopetition research has provided a lot of knowledge of competitive and collaborative interaction in alliance and network contexts, while ecosystem context has remained less explored. As a remedy, we have discussed the role of coopetition in ecosystems, and reviewed the contributions in this field. We also utilized Amazon and its Marketplace platform as an example to illustrate the ecosystem strategy and coopetition from a multi-actor perspective. Using a visual modeling method, SEAM, we illustrated how Amazon is able to create value for itself and other stakeholders by making clear choices of how to design the structure, platform, and interactions in the ecosystem. Overall, we can conclude that coopetition is an integral phenomenon in the ecosystem context, given the importance of competitive and collaborative actors, and their interdependencies in the ecosystem.

References

Aarikka-Stenroos, L. & Ritala, P. (2017) Network management in the era of ecosystems: Systematic review and management framework. *Industrial Marketing Management*.

Adner, R. (2017). Ecosystem as structure an actionable construct for strategy. *Journal of Management*, 43(1), 39–58.

Autio, E. & Thomas, L. (2014). Innovation ecosystems: Implications for innovation management. In M. Dodgson, N. Philips, & D. M. Gann (Eds), *The Oxford Handbook of Innovation Management* (pp. 204–228). Oxford: Oxford University Press.

Barsalou, L. (2008). Grounded cognition, *Annual Review of Psychology*, 59, 617–645.

Basole, R. C., Park, H., & Barnett, B. C. (2015). Coopetition and convergence in the ICT ecosystem. *Telecommunications Policy*, 39(7), 537–552.

Bengtsson, M. & Kock, S. (2000). "Coopetition" in business networks—to cooperate and compete simultaneously. *Industrial Marketing Management*, 29(5), 411–426.

Brandenburger, A. M. & Nalebuff, B. J. (1995). The right game: Use game theory to shape strategy. *Harvard Business Review*, 73(4), 57–71.

Brandenburger, A. M. & Nalebuff, B. J. (1996). *Co-opetition*. New York: Doubleday.

Carayannis, E. G. & Alexander, J. (2001). Virtual, wireless mannah: a co-opetitive analysis of the broadband satellite industry. *Technovation*, 21(12), 759–766.

Ceccagnoli, M., Forman, C., Huang, P., & Wu, D. J. (2012). Cocreation of value in a platform ecosystem: The case of enterprise software. *MIS Quarterly*, 36(1), 263–290.

Choi, P., Garcia, R., & Friedrich, C. (2010). The drivers for collective horizontal coopetition: a case study of screwcap initiatives in the international wine industry. *International Journal of Strategic Business Alliances*, 1(3), 271–290.

D'Souza, D. F. & Wills, A. C. (1998). *Objects, Components, and Frameworks with UML: The Catalysis(SM) Approach*. Addison-Wesley Professional, 1 edition.

Eloranta, V. & Turunen, T. (2016). Platforms in service-driven manufacturing: Leveraging complexity by connecting, sharing, and integrating. *Industrial Marketing Management*, 55, 178–186.

Gawer, A. & Cusumano, M. A. (2008). How companies become platform leaders. *MIT Sloan Management Review*, 49(2), 28–35.

Gawer, A. (2014). Bridging differing perspectives on technological platforms: Toward an integrative framework. *Research Policy*, 43(7), 1239–1249.

Golnam, A., Ritala, P., & Wegmann, A. (2014). Coopetition within and between value networks—a typology and a modelling framework. *International Journal of Business Environment*, 5, 6(1), 47–68.

Golnam, A., Viswanathan, V., Moser, C. I., & Ritala, P. (2013). Value map: A diagnostic framework to improve value creation and capture in service systems. In *Proceedings of the Third International Symposium on Business Modeling and Software Design*, Noordwijkerhout, the Netherlands, July 8–10, 2013.

Gueguen, G. (2009). Coopetition and business ecosystems in the information technology sector: the example of Intelligent Mobile Terminals. *International Journal of Entrepreneurship and Small Business*, 8(1), 135–153.

Iansiti, M. & Levien, R. (2004). Strategy as ecology. *Harvard Business Review*, 82(3), 68–81.

Järvi, K. & Kortelainen, S. (2017). Taking stock on empirical research on business ecosystems: A literature review. *International Journal of Business and Systems Research*, 11(3), 215–228.

Lusch, R. F., Vargo, S. L., & Gustafsson, A. (2016). Fostering a trans-disciplinary perspectives of service ecosystems. *Journal of Business Research*, 69(8), 2957–2963.

Moore, J. F. (1993). Predators and prey: A new ecology of competition. *Harvard Business Review*, 71(3), 75–83.

Moore, J. F. (2013). *Shared purpose: A thousand business ecosystems, a worldwide connected community, and the future.* Available online: www.arm.com/files/pdf/Shared_Purpose.pdf.

Ondrus, J., Gannamaneni, A., & Lyytinen, K. (2015). The impact of openness on the market potential of multi-sided platforms: a case study of mobile payment platforms. *Journal of Information Technology*, 30(3), 260–275.

Oh, D. S., Phillips, F., Park, S., & Lee, E. (2016). Innovation ecosystems: A critical examination. *Technovation*, 54, 1–6.

Regev, G. & Wegmann, A. (2004). Defining early IT system requirements with regulation principles: the lightswitch approach. *Requirements Engineering Conference*, 2004. Proceedings. 12th IEEE International (pp. 144–153). Kyoto, Japan, September 6–10, 2004.

Regev, G., Hayard, O., & Wegmann, A. (2011). Service systems and value modeling from an appreciative system perspective. In: Snene, M., Ralyté, J., & Morin, J. H. (Eds), *Exploring Services Science*. IESS 2011. *Lecture Notes in Business Information Processing*, 82, 146–157. Berlin, Heidelberg: Springer.

Ritala, P., Agouridas, V., Assimakopoulos, D., & Gies, O. (2013). Value creation and capture mechanisms in innovation ecosystems: a comparative case study. *International Journal of Technology Management*, 63(3–4), 244–267.

Ritala, P. & Almpanopoulou, A. (2017). In defense of "eco" in innovation ecosystem. *Technovation*, 60–61, 39–42.

Ritala, P., Golnam, A., & Wegmann, A. (2014). Coopetition-based business models: The case of Amazon.com. *Industrial Marketing Management*, 43(2), 236–249.

Ritala, P. & Hurmelinna-Laukkanen, P. (2009). What's in it for me? Creating and appropriating value in innovation-related coopetition. *Technovation*, 29(12), 819–828.

Ritala, P. & Tidström, A. (2014). Untangling the value-creation and value-appropriation elements of coopetition strategy: A longitudinal analysis on the firm and relational levels. *Scandinavian Journal of Management*, 30(4), 498–515.

Rohrbeck, R., Hölzle, K., & Gemünden, H. G. (2009). Opening up for competitive advantage – How Deutsche Telekom creates an open innovation ecosystem. *R&D Management*, 39(4), 420–430.

Rusko, R. (2011). Exploring the concept of coopetition: A typology for the strategic moves of the Finnish forest industry. *Industrial Marketing Management*, 40(2), 311–320.

Thomas, L. D., Autio, E., & Gann, D. M. (2014). Architectural leverage: putting platforms in context. *Academy of Management Perspectives*, 28(2), 198–219.

Tsujimoto, M., Kajikawa, Y., Tomita, J., & Matsumoto, Y. (2017). A review of the ecosystem concept—Towards coherent ecosystem design. *Technological Forecasting and Social Change*.

Valkokari, K. (2015) Business, innovation, and knowledge ecosystems: How they differ and how to survive and thrive within them. *Technology Innovation Management Review*, 5(8), 17–24.

Vargo, S. L. & Lusch, R. F. (2011). It's all B2B... and beyond: Toward a systems perspective of the market. *Industrial Marketing Management*, 40(2), 181–187.

Wegmann, A. (2003). On the Systemic Enterprise Architecture Methodology (SEAM). *Proceedings of the 5th International Conference on Enterprise Information Systems*, pp. 483–490. Angers, France, April 23–26, 2003.

Williamson, P. J. & De Meyer, A. (2012). Ecosystem advantage. *California Management Review*, 55(1), 24–46.

24

Patterns of coopetition in meta-organizations

Jamal Eddine Azzam and Héloïse Berkowitz

Introduction

Coopetition, as a concept, suggests that firms address uncertainty by adopting strategies simultaneously combining cooperation and competition (Bengtsson & Kock, 2000; Brandenburger & Nalebuff, 1996; Yami et al., 2010). Such paradoxical strategies pursue various objectives, such as conducting precompetitive R&D, introducing new technological standards, opening new markets, and developing complex products. This perspective in strategic management addresses managerial concerns about when and how to cooperate with competitors to create and capture value. This chapter argues that coopetition in the highly competitive and protected domain of intellectual property permits the solving of complex problems such as anti-common problems or trolling and value destruction by non-practising entities. Patent pools are independent organizations through which more than three members (firms, research centers, universities, etc.) agree to license their patents to each other and to any third parties. These devices aim to solve, at least partly, the coopetition tensions of intellectual property, but relatively little is known about the resulting internal and external dynamics of coopetition at the level of patent pools.

This chapter develops an organizational approach to analyze how competing firms cooperate to collectively address patent-related concerns. To do so, we study meta-organizations in the field of patents (Berkowitz & Bor, 2017). Meta-organizations are organizations in which members are themselves organizations, and they aim to collectively control external organizations and to influence the surrounding environment (Ahrne & Brunsson, 2008; Berkowitz & Dumez, 2016; Gulati et al., 2012). As such, meta-organizations constitute a device through which organizations avoid uncertainty and create negotiated environments (Cyert & March, 1963). Only a few studies have focused on coopetition and meta-organizations (Chiambaretto & Dumez, 2016). In addition, little research has thoroughly examined how coopetition can take shape at the inter-organizational level and in both market and non-market environments. This chapter aims to better understand such coopetition dynamics in meta-organizations by studying intellectual property arrangements such as patent pools.

We show that patent pools and other forms of patenting arrangements, as meta-organizations, follow different patterns of coopetition in market and non-market environments, with three objectives: 1) creating value; 2) appropriating value; and 3) preserving created value for members.

We contribute to the meta-organization literature by making explicit some of the conditions of valuable coopetition (Berkowitz & Dumez, 2016). Further, we clarify how and why competitors cooperate on patents and open a new avenue for research on coopetition to explore its stakes beyond dyadic value creation–value appropriation.

This chapter is organized as follows. It first describes coopetition tensions that exist in intellectual property. We then show the relevance of analyzing patent pools as meta-organizations and the governance mechanisms that are developed to reduce tensions. Finally, we discuss the resulting patterns of coopetition in market and non-market environments.

Coopetition tensions in the domain of patents

The literature on coopetition highlights drivers, tensions, processes and outcomes of such strategic behaviors at different levels and in different empirical settings (for a review, see Bengtsson & Kock, 2014; Gnyawali & Song, 2016). Patents represent a strategic resource based on the right to exclude others from using technological inventions (Ayerbe & Chanal, 2010; Hall, 1992; Hsu & Ziedonis, 2013). Clarifying how competing firms cooperate on patents adds another piece to the puzzle of implementing a coopetition strategy (Cassiman et al., 2009; Faems et al., 2010; Fernandez et al., 2014; Seran et al. 2016). Furthermore, exploring coopetition in a context such as intellectual property could enhance the understanding of patent strategies and their patterns. We aim to contribute to the coopetition field by exploring how and why competitors cooperate on patents.

The anti-commons problem in intellectual property

Many technology-based sectors such as biotechnology, consumer electronic, semiconductor, and telecommunications are characterized by a multi-invention setting where independent actors such as individual inventors, universities, and firms develop and patent technological components that form the final products (Hall & Ziedonis, 2001; Hobday et al., 2000; Somaya et al., 2011). In such settings, firms must address the problem of patent fragmentation or patent thicket, which is "an overlapping set of patent rights requiring that those seeking to commercialize new technology obtain licenses from multiple patentees" (Shapiro, 2000: 119). This problem of patent blocking creates what Heller and Eisenberg (1998: 698) described as an anti-commons tragedy "when multiple owners each have a right to exclude others from a scarce resource and no one has an effective privilege of use." In other words, the multiplication of blocking patents could lead to the underuse of a technology. This occurs when those wanting to use and build on a technology must address the challenging and expensive task of acquiring licenses from multiple patent-holders (Somaya et al., 2011).

The problem of patent blocking concerns not only firms wanting to use the technology but also its developers or promoters. Indeed, their individual and parallel investments in R&D lead them to have a limited number of all patents required for secured-market operation. This is particularly the case for standardized technologies, as epitomized by the Blu-Ray video. This standard was introduced in 2006 and was developed by more than twenty independent (and competing) companies individually holding a (small) part of all the related patents.

The problem of trolling and value destruction by non-practising entities

Patent "trolls" or patent "sharks" are "corporations that seek to generate supra-normal returns on patent-protected technology through the suing of inadvertent infringers in one-shot trials"

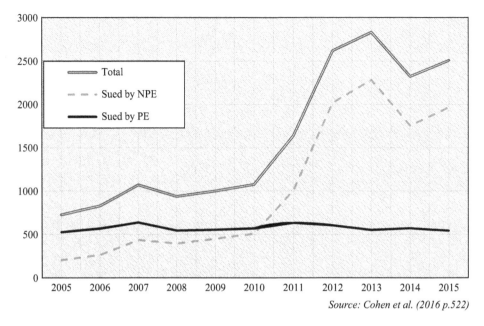

Source: Cohen et al. (2016 p.522)

Figure 24.1 Patent litigation against publicly traded firms between 2005 and 2015 in the US

(Reitzig et al., 2010: 948). They are non-practising entities (NPEs) in the sense that they do not invest in R&D activities and do not develop or commercialize products. Rather, NPEs exploit information asymmetries in markets and acquire patents from financially distressed actors (start-ups, individual inventors, or universities) to trigger profitable hold-up situations (Pénin, 2012). Their targets for infringement lawsuits and royalty extraction are practising entities, that is, firms with market-related activities and investments, sued either individually (for instance, RIM by NTP) or more often collectively (for example, Acacia against manufacturers of healthcare information technologies) (Tucker, 2014). Figure 24.1 reflects the evolution of patent litigation against publicly traded firms in the US.[1]

For firms, trolling is a major threat. A deputy general counsel for patents at Google who recently experienced litigation by NPEs[2] explains that

> patent owners sell patents for numerous reasons (such as the need to raise money or changes in a company's business direction). Unfortunately, the usual patent marketplace can sometimes be challenging, especially for smaller participants who sometimes end up working with patent trolls. Then bad things happen, like lawsuits, lots of wasted effort, and generally bad karma.

Bessen and Meurer (2014) estimated that the tax on innovation exerted by NPEs, that is, the direct cost to defendants' firms, was $29 billion in 2011, and they found that much of this tax falls on small and medium-sized companies.[3]

Other empirical evidence shows the negative impacts of lawsuits by NPEs on innovation by firms and their investments in R&D. Bessen et al. (2011) found that defendants have lost over half-a-trillion dollars from 1990 to 2010 and over $83 billion per year between 2007 and 2010, which is the equivalent of more than one-fourth of US industrial R&D spending each year.

In the case of small firms, Smeets (2014) identified an evident negative impact (2.6–4.7%) of patent litigation on subsequent R&D intensity. More recently, Cohen et al. (2016) analyzed data on patent litigation in the US between 2005 and 2015 and found that firms on average reduce their R&D investment by more than 25% after settling with NPEs. Other evidence shows the negative impact of patent litigation by NPEs on incremental innovations. Tucker (2014) analyzed the case of the healthcare information technology "PACS[4]" and identified a one-third decline in sales that was not the result of a suppression of demand by hospitals. Rather, hospitals' demand for the improvement of imaging IT solutions was unsatisfied during the period of litigation between the NPE and the sued firms. This resulted in lower incremental product innovation. Overall, these studies show that NPEs' opportunistic, predatory behavior negatively impacts sued firms and hinders innovation without increasing small-inventor activity. Hence, from both managerial and public welfare points of view, NPEs represent a serious threat due to the cost of their actions and the detrimental effects on innovation.

We have highlighted several tensions relative to coopetition in intellectual property. We now consider why it is relevant to analyze these dimensions at the level of the meta-organization.

Meta-organizations as a relevant level of analysis

Chiambaretto and Dumez (2016) showed that meta-organizations in the airline industry allowed the development of multi-level coopetition strategies. In the intellectual property domain, setting up meta-organizations also emerges as an efficient collective strategy to address coopetition tensions and concerns. Therefore, we argue that meta-organizations are a relevant level of analysis of coopetition in intellectual property as well.

Patent pools as coopetitive meta-organizations

Indeed, an effective strategy to address the problem of patent fragmentation and blocking is the aggregation of patents related to a technological standard in a meta-organization. The objective of such a strategy is to make the patents essential to a standard available to all its potential adopters. Such aggregation takes the form of patent pools. Patent pools are independent organizations through which more than three members (firms, research centers, universities, etc.) agree to license their patents to each other and to any third parties (den Uijl et al., 2013; Layne-Farrar & Lerner, 2011; Lerner et al., 2007; Lerner & Tirole, 2004). In that sense, patent pools constitute coopetitive meta-organizations, i.e., formal associations of competitors that develop both cooperative and competitive strategies. Patent pools have been used to promote many technological standards, such as Blu-Ray, MPEG, and MVC. Table 24.1 provides some examples of patent pools. They operate as one-stop shopping to bundle many complementary patents essential to a specific technological standard and owned by many independent actors. The latter commit to licensing all their patents essential to the technological standard promoted through the pool and to not taking any action to subvert such commitment. The pool's licensees can be the other patent holders but could also be non-patent holders, whether they are incumbents, new entrants, large players, or small ones. Then, collected royalties are shared among patent holders depending on their contribution to the pool.

Patent pools are based on cooperation to promote the use of technological standards. This can be at a global level, such as MPEG2 for the video compression used in DVD players and recorders, TVs, personal computers, or game machines, or at a regional level, such as ARIB-Uldage for Japanese Digital Broadcasting. In some cases, different competing patent pools can emerge. This is the case for the Blu-Ray video standard around which two patent pools have

Table 24.1 Examples of patent pools and their characteristics

	ARIB-Uldage	MVC	MPEG2	One-Blue	PremierBD
Technological field	Digital broadcasting receivers and digital broadcasting services in Japan	Digital video coding standard	Video and image compression and decompression technology	Blu-Ray video technologies	
Members holding patents in the pool	Dolby; Fujitsu; Hitachi; INFOCITY; JVC KENWOOD; KDDI; LG; Mitsubishi; NEC; NHK Engineering System; Nippon Hoso Kyokai; Orange; TDF SAS; Panasonic; Pioneer; Sanyo; Sharp; Sony; Nippon Hoso Kyokai; Columbia University; Thomson/Technicolor; Toshiba	Dolby; Electronics and Telecommunications Research Institute; Fraunhofer-Gesellschaft zur Foerderung der angewandten Forschung e.V.; Fujitsu; GE Video Compression; Hitachi; HP; Koninklijke KPN N.V.; LG; Mitsubishi; Nippon Telegraph and Telephone; NTT DOCOMO; Panasonic; Siemens; Sony; Tagivan II; Columbia University; Thomson/Technicolor	Alcatel Lucent; ARRIS Technology; British Telecommunications; Canon; CIF Licensing; Cisco Technology; Fujitsu; GE Technology; HP; JVC Kenwood; KDDI; Philips; LG; Multimedia Patent Trust; Nippon Telegraph & Telephone; Orange; Panasonic; Robert Bosch; Samsung; Sanyo; Sharp; Sony; The Columbia University; Thomson/Technicolor; Toshiba	Dell Computer; Hitachi; HP; JVC Kenwood; LG; Panasonic; Philips; Pioneer; Sharp; Samsung; Sony; Taiyo Yuden; Yamaha	Columbia University; Disney; Mitsubishi; Technicolor; Toshiba
Number of patents	641	1145	1080	7600	3612
Number of licenses	302	41	1164	73	47

(Source: adapted from Ayerbe and Azzam, 2015; Uijl et al., 2013.)

developed: One-Blue by Sony and its allies and PremierBD by Toshiba and its partners. Whatever their number in a given field, patent pools sustain cooperation between firms through the grant-back clause implying that all participants (patent holders and licensees) commit to licensing back patents of any improvement related to the standard (Lerner et al., 2007; Lerner & Tirole, 2004).

However, patent pools may experience internal competition between patent holders who seek to achieve both economic and strategic goals.[5] One can observe in Table 24.1 that most patent holders are competitors in their respective markets. These actors join pools for common access to patents and hence ensure their ability to develop and commercialize products. Members also try to collectively compete against alternative technological standards. However, patent holders are interested in the royalties that patent pools generate. For this reason, they try to enhance their power by integrating more and more patents. Indeed, the share of royalties is based, in many patent pools, on the number of essential patents integrated (Layne-Farrar & Lerner, 2011). Figure 24.2 shows the distribution of patent ownership in two patent pools related to the Blu-Ray video standard.

Competition within patent pools concerns not only patent ownership and patent insertion but also the determination of royalties. Patent holders are not homogeneous; some are companies with market operations (vertically integrated firms), while others are without market activities, such as universities, research institutes, or firms specialized in R&D. Royalties (from pools) are the main source of revenue for this second group of patent holders. Vertically integrated firms must apply for licenses and pay royalties when they decide to join patent pools, notably when their products use the pool's patents.

Finally, the licensing terms of patent pools can induce another form of competition between patent holders. Indeed, patent pools with complementary patents allow members to engage in independent licensing (Lerner et al., 2007; Lerner & Tirole, 2004). This clause implies that patent holders are free to license their individual pooled patents for an unrelated use without sharing related revenues with other pool members. Indeed, patented inventions could be used in multiple fields, as is the case for technologies related to the MPEG2 standard for digital video compression, also used in products such as DVDs and high-definition television (Lerner et al., 2007). Hence, the agreement states that the "MPEG-2 Licensor will grant MPEGLA a nonexclusive license under its Essential Patents, while retaining the right to license them independently for any purpose, including for making MPEG-2-compliant products."[6] In turn, this rule represents a window for more competition to generate additional income by licensing the same patents in another field and hence to outperform the other patent holders (Ayerbe and Azzam, 2015).

Organizational mechanisms in a coopetitive meta-organization

Coopetitive meta-organizations may develop specific features as a response to patent trolling. Indeed, companies' concerns over predation by NPEs and the associated risk of value destruction lead some firms to take initiatives to make information about existing patents, technology value, and patent transactions available and transparent. The objective is to identify potential NPEs and inhibit their opportunistic behavior.

The LOT Network (License on Transfer) was created in June 2014 at the initiative of Google, three other large companies (Canon, Dropbox, and SAP) and two start-ups (Asana and Newegg) from the information and technology sectors. The LOT Network is a non-profit organization aiming to solve the trolling problem and to reduce litigation risk by NPE litigation. The LOT Network permits the immunizing of more than 600,000 worldwide patents owned by approximately 100 member companies and other actors, such as NGOs. Among these companies, several are direct competitors in their respective sectors, such as CBS, Netflix, and Showtime in media; Amazon and

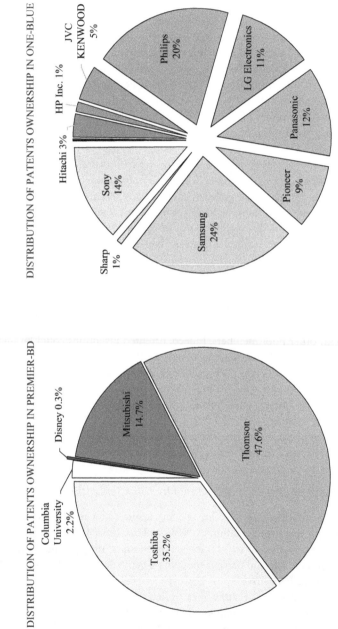

Figure 24.2 Distribution of patent ownership for two competing pools

Google in Internet-related services; SAS and SAP in software development; Canon, GoPro, Lenovo, and Mundo Reader in consumer electronic devices; and Subaru, Daimler, Ford, General Motors, Honda, Hyundai, Kia, Mazda, and Nissan in automotive. The common purpose of these companies is to trace patent transactions and changes in patent ownership to anticipate NPE predation strategies. In doing so, operating companies can focus their attention and resources on innovation and product development, as the director of IP development at Hyundai Motor[7] explains:

> by joining the LOT Network, we will use this opportunity to focus more on R&D rather than using resources to fight against unnecessary lawsuits from NPEs. I hope this will help the automobile industry build healthier environment for its customers.

The operating mode of LOT is that companies deliberately decide to join the network and submit their patents. Once a company joins the network, it maintains ownership of the submitted patents. However, the network *a priori* commits to give licenses to all other members when it sells one (or more) of these patents to a third-party actor (that is not a member of LOT) with more than fifty percent of revenues generated through patent assertion.[8] Hence, LOT member companies own a potential license on all the submitted patents to use them as immunity against any intimidation for patent infringement by an NPE. At the same time, companies keep ownership of their patent as well as the freedom to use them for other purposes (assert, license, or cross-license), as a senior VP and chief IP counsel at SAP[9] explains:

> the structure of the LOT Network helps protect innovative patent owners from unwarranted litigation, without stifling valid, beneficial uses of patents … As long as a company owns their patent they retain all their rights to it.

Furthermore, LOT is open to all companies seeking immunization against NPE predation, even if they do not own patents.

LOT aims to generate a network effect to attract more innovative companies (large companies or start-ups) and to become more attractive for other potential participants. At the end of 2017, LOT attracted more than 100 companies from various sectors (automotive, banking, computer, electronic, IT, media, retailing, etc.). To achieve this, LOT applies an adjusted membership fee depending on each member company's annual revenues (from $1,500 a year for companies with less than $10 million in revenue to $20,000 a year for companies with revenue greater than $1 billion). After the creation of LOT in 2014, some members have sold certain patents to other outside players, including NPEs, but none of the other members has been attacked for violation of these patents.

Lessons learned: Criss-crossing patterns of coopetition inside and outside meta-organizations

Meta-organizations in the patent field raise interesting and complex issues of coopetition at different levels, as Chiambaretto and Dumez (2016) noted for the airline industry. First, at the internal level, by bringing together competitors in a formal organization, in our case patent pools and the LOT Network, meta-organizations aim to increase cooperation among certain types of actors. Different benefits may result from gathering in such coopetitive meta-organizations, as we synthesize in Table 24.2. However, simultaneously, meta-organizations may result in unfair, opportunistic internal strategies among members (e.g., hiding patents).

Such coopetitive meta-organizations achieve three kinds of objectives. First, they may facilitate value creation for member companies through technological standard diffusion and cost

Table 24.2 Meta-organizations' objectives in different cases of patent pools

	MPEG 2	LOT Network
Benefits from the Meta-organization	Value creation Value appropriation	Created value preservation

Table 24.3 Coopetitive dimensions of market and non-market strategies in patent pools

	Market Environment	Non-market Environment
MPEG2	Competition (on prices, products, innovations, etc.)	Cooperation (sharing patents) Competition (increasing patent shares to earn more royalties)
LOT Network	Competition (on prices, products, innovation, etc.)	Cooperation to prevent opportunistic behaviors

reduction of negotiation to access key patents. In addition, they permit value appropriation thanks to royalties. Finally, some meta-organizations (e.g., LOT Network) even allow members to preserve created value by developing mechanisms to prevent opportunistic behaviors. However, there can be cases where the meta-organization itself enters into conflict with one of its members, as we showed in the case of the MPEG2. This occurs when a member develops its own strategy, discarding collectively defined rules at the meta-organizational level. These results contribute to the literature on meta-organizations by identifying conditions under which coopetition may be valuable or deterrent (Berkowitz & Dumez, 2016).

Second, at the external level, meta-organizations create a coherent group of actors who may enter into competition with other meta-organizations. In patent pools, meta-organizational competition addresses imposing standards. Competition now occurs among groups of cooperating competitors. In that sense, meta-organizations' development triggers a shift in the coopetition's gravity center that may exist at the industry level: gravity moves from player-to-player coopetition to internal and external meta-organizational coopetition in patent pools.

Patent pools are a rare case where the meta-organization facilitates market strategies through cooperation among competitors in a non-market environment (see Table 24.3). This case brings interesting insights regarding tensions related to coopetition. The literature stresses separation mechanisms to manage coopetition-related tensions, i.e., cooperating in a specific field (domain or activity) and competing in another field (Bengtsson & Kock, 2000; Fernandez & Chiambaretto, 2016; Seran et al., 2016). The concept of the meta-organization shows how tension between cooperation and competition can persist despite this separation. Indeed, patent pools are created by organizations that compete in a market environment to cooperate in a nonmarket environment. However, these organizations continue to compete to capture value within meta-organizations despite the cooperative orientation.

The coexistence of cooperation and competition within meta-organizations adds to the competition between member organizations in the market environment through price and/ or product strategies. In addition to this coopetition within meta-organization, we have shown earlier that standards wars may add yet another layer of competition among meta-organizations. Highlighting these criss-crossing patterns of coopetition resulting from the establishment of meta-organizations is the main contribution of our chapter.

Conclusion

In this chapter, we analyzed and discussed collective intellectual property arrangements as examples of coopetitive meta-organizations, i.e., formal associations of competitors that develop both cooperative and competitive strategies. In the case of intellectual property, coopetition occurs both within and outside of meta-organizations. Patent pools and other arrangements such as the LOT Network indeed constitute a meta-organizational response to two major concerns in the field of intellectual property: anti-commons and trolling. However, meta-organizations may result in unfair, opportunistic internal strategies among members (e.g., hiding patents). Meta-organizations also contribute to increased competition outside of their membership through standard wars that oppose certain meta-organizations.

Our chapter highlights that these meta-organizations follow different patterns of coopetition in market and non-market environments. These meta-organizations have three objectives: 1) creating value; 2) appropriating value; and 3) preserving created value for members. Such meta-organizations' development results in a shift in coopetition. From industry coopetition, it moves to coopetition between the member and the meta-organization (when individual strategy conflicts with collective strategy) or, above all, to coopetition across meta-organizations (in standards wars).

In the field of intellectual property, patterns of coopetition appear to be multi-level (organizational, meta-organizational), multi-dimensional (market and non-market), and criss-crossing. Further investigating these criss-crossing patterns of coopetition could provide a better understanding of both the optimization of patenting strategies and the efficient governance of patent pools. Studying coopetition in or through meta-organizations is an emerging and promising venue of research (Berkowitz & Bor, 2017; Chiambaretto & Dumez, 2016). Future research could further investigate the links between forms of meta-organizations (membership, sector, governance mechanisms) and coopetition patterns across patent pools, for instance, using qualitative comparative analysis.

Another fruitful path would involve modeling the optimal meta-organization membership for companies. Studying firms' membership as a portfolio of meta-organizations would allow for the analysis of the costs and benefits of such strategies, as well as the synergies that can exist among meta-organizations and further the understanding of patenting strategies. Further, it would be interesting to analyze how members derive value from this membership and which organizational capabilities they build on to do so. This would contribute to ongoing research efforts to better understand the management of co-opetition (Bengtsson et al., 2016; Fernandez et al., 2014; Le Roy & Czakon, 2016).

Last, an interesting venue for research entails investigating the impacts and dynamics of eco-responsible patent pools. The Eco-Patent Commons is an organization established by private companies and administered by the World Business Council for Sustainable Development (WBCSD). Its objective is to diffuse "green" patents. The Eco-Patent Commons aims to make available (without royalties), to all participant and non-participant companies, patents related to technologies for energy conservation and efficiency, pollution prevention, materials reduction, and increased recycling ability. Beyond securing the use of environment-friendly technologies, the pool also aims to provide an open platform for collaboration among competitors for a cross-fertilization of sustainability-related technological competencies. In-depth case studies of this pool and its members would pave the way to understanding the role of meta-organizations in the diffusion of eco-responsible practices and resulting forms of coopetition.

Notes

1　It is important to note that the problem of patent trolling is not specific to the American context, since other evidence in Europe shows that NPEs are responsible for approximately 10% of patent suits in the field in Germany (between 2000 and 2008) and 11% in the UK (between 2000 and 2010) (Love, Helmers, & McDonagh, 2014).

2　In 2012, Google was the target of lawsuits by two NPEs (SimpleAir and Vringo) claiming the violation of their patents by two products developed by Google: the online advertising service Adwords and the operating system Android.

3　The only legal cost per defense (outside counsel, prior art search, jury consultants, etc.) is $420,000 for small and medium-sized firms and $1.52 million for large firms (Bessen & Meurer, 2014). Other elements such as negotiation and potential damages contribute to the total cost.

4　The PACS (picture archival and communications system) is a medical imaging technology used by hospitals for economic storage and used as an access facility for large amounts of data and images from multiple imaging devices. This lawsuit was launched by Hospital Systems Corporation, a subsidiary of Acacia, one of the largest patent-assertion companies, with 536 patents in 2011, against GE Healthcare, Fujifilm Medical Systems, Siemens Medical Solutions, Philips Electronics, and McKesson Corp.

5　We report only "fair" competitive behaviors here. However, other unfair behaviors exist, such as patent dissimulation to create a hold-up situation (see Lerner, Strojwas, & Tirole, 2007). In 2007, the administrator of the patent pool MPEG2 sued one of the pool's members, Alcatel-Lucent, for breach of contractual obligations. Indeed, Alcatel-Lucent transferred patents essential to the standard MPEG2 to a newly created company (Multimedia Patent Trust) to extract additional royalties and hence avoid the contractual commitment of placing essential patents in the patent pool.

6　www.justice.gov/archive/atr/public/busreview/215742.htm#N_11_.

7　www.businesswire.com/news/home/20160201005240/en/LOT-Network-Demonstrates-Rapid-Growth-Community-Battle.

8　"What's notable about LOT is that because each of our members agree to provide licenses to one another once a patent asset falls into the hands of a PAE (patent assertion entity), we've established a way to essentially immunize our community against PAE suits involving those assets" (Ken Seddon, CEO of LOT Network). www.ip-watch.org/2016/12/01/helping-patenters-sea-paes-interview-lot-networks-ken-seddon/.

9　http://au.pcmag.com/internet-products/13101/news/google-dropbox-more-team-up-to-battle-patent-trolls.

References

Ahrne, G. & Brunsson, N. (2008). *Meta-organizations*. Cheltenham, UK; Northampton, MA: Edward Elgar Publishing.

Ayerbe, C. & Azzam, J. E. (2015). Pratiques coopétitives dans l'Open Innovation: Les enseignements des patent pools/Coopetitive practices in Open Innovation: Lessons from patent pools. *Management International*, 19(2), 95–114.

Ayerbe, C. & Chanal, V. (2010). Droits de Propriété Intellectuelle et innovation ouverte: les apports de Henry Chesbrough/Intellectual Property rights and open innovation: contributions of Henry Chesbrough. *Management International*, 14(3), 99–104.

Bengtsson, M. & Kock, S. (2000). "Coopetition" in business Networks—to cooperate and compete simultaneously. *Industrial Marketing Management*, 29(5), 411–426.

Bengtsson, M. & Kock, S. (2014). Coopetition—Quo vadis? Past accomplishments and future challenges. *Industrial Marketing Management*, 43(2), 180–188.

Bengtsson, M., Raza-Ullah, T., & Vanyushyn, V. (2016). The coopetition paradox and tension: The moderating role of coopetition capability. *Industrial Marketing Management*, 53, 19–30.

Berkowitz, H. & Bor, S. (2017). Why meta-organizations matter: A response to Lawton et al. and Spillman. *Journal of Management Inquiry*, *OnlineFirst*. Retrieved from http://journals.sagepub.com/eprint/XYqEiCKF4JAWgVRPGeAS/full.

Berkowitz, H. & Dumez, H. (2016). The concept of meta-organization: Issues for management studies. *European Management Review*, 13(2), 149–156.

Bessen, J. E., Meurer, M. J., & Ford, J. L. (2011). The private and social costs of patent trolls. *Reputation*, 34(4), 26–35.

Bessen, J. & Meurer, M. J. (2014). The direct costs from NPE disputes. *Cornell Law Review*, 99(2), 387–424.

Brandenburger, A. & Nalebuff, B. (1996). *Co-opetition*. New York: Harper Collins Business.

Cassiman, B., Di Guardo, M. C., & Valentini, G. (2009). Organising R&D projects to profit from innovation: Insights from co-opetition. *Long Range Planning*, 42(2), 216–233.

Chiambaretto, P. & Dumez, H. (2016). Toward a typology of coopetition: A multilevel approach. *International Studies of Management & Organization*, 46(2–3), 110–129.

Cohen, L., Gurun, U. G., & Kominers, S. D. (2016). The growing problem of patent trolling. *Science*, 352(6285), 521–522.

Cyert, R. M. & March, J. G. (1963). *A Behavioral Theory of the Firm*. Englewood Cliffs, NJ: Prentice-Hall.

den Uijl, S., Bekkers, R., & de Vries, H. J. (2013). Managing intellectual property using patent pools. *California Management Review*, 55(4), 31–50.

Faems, D., Janssens, M., & Van Looy, B. (2010). Managing the co-operation–competition dilemma in R&D alliances: A multiple case study in the advanced materials industry. *Creativity and Innovation Management*, 19(1), 3–22.

Fernandez, A.-S. & Chiambaretto, P. (2016). Managing tensions related to information in coopetition. *Industrial Marketing Management*, 53, 66–76.

Fernandez, A.-S., Le Roy, F., & Gnyawali, D. R. (2014). Sources and management of tension in co-opetition case evidence from telecommunications satellites manufacturing in Europe. *Industrial Marketing Management*, 43(2), 222–235.

Gnyawali, D. R. & Song, Y. (2016). Pursuit of rigor in research: Illustration from coopetition literature. *Industrial Marketing Management*, 57, 12–22.

Gulati, R., Puranam, P., & Tushman, M. (2012). Meta-organization design: Rethinking design in interorganizational and community contexts. *Strategic Management Journal*, 33(6), 571–586.

Hall, B. H. & Ziedonis, R. H. (2001). The patent paradox revisited: an empirical study of patenting in the US semiconductor industry, 1979–1995. *RAND Journal of Economics*, 32(1), 101–128.

Hall, R. (1992). The strategic analysis of intangible resources. *Strategic Management Journal*, 13(2), 135–144.

Heller, M. A. & Eisenberg, R. S. (1998). Can patents deter innovation? The anticommons in biomedical research. *Science*, 280(5364), 698–701.

Hobday, M., Rush, H., & Tidd, J. (2000). Innovation in complex products and system. *Research Policy*, 29(7–8), 793–804.

Hsu, D. H. & Ziedonis, R. H. (2013). Resources as dual sources of advantage: Implications for valuing entrepreneurial-firm patents. *Strategic Management Journal*, 34(7), 761–781.

Layne-Farrar, A. & Lerner, J. (2011). To join or not to join: Examining patent pool participation and rent sharing rules. *International Journal of Industrial Organization*, 29(2), 294–303.

Le Roy, F. & Czakon, W. (2016). Managing coopetition: the missing link between strategy and performance. *Industrial Marketing Management*, 53, 3–6.

Lerner, J., Strojwas, M., & Tirole, J. (2007). The design of patent pools: The determinants of licensing rules. *The RAND Journal of Economics*, 38(3), 610–625.

Lerner, J. & Tirole, J. (2004). Efficient patent pools. *The American Economic Review*, 94(3), 691–711.

Love, B., Helmers, C., & McDonagh, L. (2014). Is there a patent troll problem in the UK? *Faculty Publications*. Retrieved from http://digitalcommons.law.scu.edu/facpubs/863.

Pénin, J. (2012). Strategic uses of patents in markets for technology: A story of fabless firms, brokers and trolls. *Journal of Economic Behavior & Organization*, 84(2), 633–641.

Reitzig, M., Henkel, J., & Schneider, F. (2010). Collateral damage for R&D manufacturers: how patent sharks operate in markets for technology. *Industrial and Corporate Change*, 19(3), 947–967.

Seran, T., Pellegrin-Boucher, E., & Gurau, C. (2016). The management of coopetitive tensions within multi-unit organizations. *Industrial Marketing Management*, 53, 31–41.

Shapiro, C. (2000). Navigating the patent thicket: Cross licenses, patent pools, and standard setting. *Innovation Policy and the Economy*, 1, 119–150.

Smeets, R. (2014). Does patent litigation reduce corporate R&D? an analysis of US public firms. *Working Paper, Rutgers University*. Available at: www.tilburguniversity.edu/upload/8f3507ab-df1f-46c5-89a4-e1855f171404_Main_Litigation.pdf.

Somaya, D., Teece, D., & Wakeman, S. (2011). Innovation in multi-invention contexts: Mapping solutions to technological and intellectual property complexity. *California Management Review*, 53(4), 47–79.

Tucker, C. E. (2014). Patent trolls and technology diffusion: The case of medical imaging. *Working Paper, Massachusetts Institute of Technology*. Available at SSRN: https://ssrn.com/abstract=1976593 or http://dx.doi.org/10.2139/ssrn.1976593.

Yami, S., Castaldo, S., Dagnino, G. B., & Le Roy, F. (2010). *Coopetition: Winning Strategies for the 21st Century*. Cheltenham, UK; Northampton, MA: Edward Elgar.

25

Visualizing coopetition
Multidimensional sequence analysis

Alain Jeunemaitre, Hervé Dumez, and Benjamin Lehiany

Introduction

Coopetition is an odd construct that links together two contrasting notions—competition and cooperation. The first calls to mind an individual struggle for particular gains. The second supports the idea of collective action to reach specific objectives. Coopetition is also ambiguous with respect to time: it refers both to simultaneity (competition and cooperation occurring at the same time) and to sequentiality (competitive processes succeeding cooperative processes). As such, coopetition may be said to be a multifaceted concept that can lead to multiple visual representations. The purpose of the present paper is to study this concept through these visualizations. As noted by Tufte (1990: 12), "The world is complex, dynamic, multidimensional; the paper is static, flat. How are we to represent the rich visual world of experience and measurement on mere flatland?"

It would be illusory to refer to all the possible ways of representing coopetition. There are many ways by which an account of a concept can be given through flatland visuals. Design tools are available, for example, to visualize dynamic and multidimensional data (see, for instance, Basole, 2014). In particular, they have been applied to topics related to social media coopetition, to visualize how firms cooperate and compete to attract public attention in media coverage (Sun et al., 2014). Rather than discussing which software may best provide for visualization, our focus is on templating coopetition through the ordering of visuals. Accordingly, the approach we have taken has been first to consider how visuals have been used in the literature on coopetition, and then to examine visuals regarding selected related topical words, namely *cooperation, competition, dynamics, sequence, dyadic, network, objectives, governance, value creation, industry, value creation, innovation, drivers, processes,* and *outcomes.* As a supplement to this, coopetition was crossed with these topical reference words *via* the internet, providing additional visuals through search engines such as Google Image. Finally, coopetition was also crossed with terms of visual representation, namely *decision trees, graphs, figures, templates, diagrams, tools, photos, tables, pictures, charts, drawings,* and *displays.*

To put the findings in order in the exercise of envisioning coopetition, three sections are proposed. First, views on coopetition are discussed, with a specific focus on the visual perspective. Second, a meta-table is presented, cataloging visuals on attributes of coopetition stemming from a literature review and search engine images. Coopetition is viewed as an interactive process occurring between and/or within firms, composed of a mixture of cooperative and/or competitive moves that may lead to added value for the firm. The interactive process itself may develop in different dimensions, i.e., relating to products, services, supply chain, research and development, etc. For this reason, the meta-table on generic forms of visuals highlights two facets of coopetition: static versus dynamic, and unidimensional versus multidimensional. Finally, from the meta-table, a synthetic visual template derived from dynamic/multidimensional coopetition is proposed and discussed.

Views on coopetition

Coopetition may be viewed as deriving from two possible starting points. In the first, a firm assesses its competitive environment and seeks opportunities to cooperate accordingly. Inversely, in the second, a firm assesses its resources, capabilities, and business network relationships, and seeks to cooperate accordingly. With this in mind, it is critical to consider affiliated evidence regarding industrial organization, emphasizing the competitive environment of the firm, as well as strategy, putting the focus on the idiosyncrasies of the firm, when considering both Michael Porter (1980) and Brandenburger and Nalebuff's (1996) *diamond* visuals on gaining competitive advantage.

Firm- versus industry-centric views on coopetition

In Porter's visual competitive advantage, strategy and rivalry depend on the conditions of supply and demand that co-exist with the scope of support within the industry, with the whole being inserted into a context of public regulatory policies. It focuses on the characteristics and profitability of the industry. Economic performance is related to the behavior of buyers and sellers as driven by industry structure. In other words, maximizing profit or gaining competitive advantage mainly pertains to the search for market power and is dependent on barriers to entry, monopoly, oligopoly, or atomistic markets, and contestability (Baumol et al., 1982). In so doing, strategic rent-seeking behavior may be seen as reducing strategic risk (Lado et al., 1997).

Under a similar *diamond* format, Brandenburger and Nalebuff (1996) and Dixit and Nalebuff (2008) propose examining competitive advantage from the inside view of the firm. Demand conditions become identified customers, supply/suppliers, competition/competitors, industry support/complements. It therefore defines an additional framework for strategists, the so-called PARTS structure game (with P standing for the number of competitive game players, A for company added value, R for rules of the game, T for tactics, S for scope of the businesses that are in opportunistic relationships with the players).

Thus, in a way the two different perspectives echo whether coopetition is looked at from either a player's (actor school of thought) or industry (activity school of thought) perspective (Bengtsson & Raza-Ullah, 2016), or, as pointed out by Grant (1991), coopetition must be seen as an inside-out process of strategy formulation. From the point of view of the firm, in terms of the industry, the concept proposes an alteration of the traditional interplay between market forces. Coopetition lies in between perfect competition and collusion. From the inside of the firm perspective, it introduces a rethinking of the dimensions of the supply and distribution channels of the business, products, services, supply chain, and R&D in interaction with competitors.

Sequential versus simultaneous views on coopetition

In support of the aforementioned *diamond,* Brandenburger and Nalebuff (1996) developed a dynamic game framework that visualizes coopetition as cooperative, followed by a competitive sequence. The "game of the business" illustrates, in a simplified version, a firm facing a competitor. According to payoffs in visual matrices, in a first phase the firm would increase the net creation of collective value through cooperation, and then in a second phase it would compete for apportionment of the added surplus. However, in this regard, there has been little investigation into the visualization of coopetition by means of matrices or by making use of game theory. Despite examples illustrating the interest in using game theory to rethink mutual interactions with competitors, the concept seems to have provided more insights than practical use for decision makers. The relevance of game theory itself in business strategy has been subject to skepticism (Shapiro, 1989).

At the same time, it should be noted that cooperation and competition within a game theory framework has been studied not only with respect to strategy but also in other social sciences and biology (Nowak, 2006). In particular, extended work on cooperation has incorporated network analysis (Axelrod and Amilton, 1981) and complex systems approaches (Axelrod, 1997), leading to additional visuals such as graphs on evolutionary dynamics (Allen et al., 2017).

Rather than from a game-theoretical perspective, the concept of coopetition has been increasingly examined as primarily nested in an assessment of the resources and dynamic capabilities of firms (Wernerfelt, 1984; Barney & Clark, 2007). As a result, Bengtsson and Kock (2000) have addressed a further issue of cooperation and competition, specifically as not occurring in succession but rather taking into consideration simultaneous strategic moves, leading to new coopetition visuals, which are discussed below. This approach has paved the way for an array of publications in academic journals. Over the past two decades, the number of publications in journals with ISI impact factors of above 0.5 has grown from two in 1996 to more than twenty in 2014 (Bengtsson & Raza-Ullah, 2016).

Thus, with the support of the game theory framework, coopetition thinking has provided both primary visuals and a synthesis of the resulting cooperative advantages, both concerning the economic environment and industry structure as well as the idiosyncratic resources of the firm.

Accordingly, a broad sweep on coopetition permits the elicitation of two properties of the concept: first, it is an interactive, dynamic process. Coopetition as the focus of game theory is about timely strategic moves that may occur in particular environments, with a possible succession of competition and cooperation phases. It may be looked upon as finite or infinite depending on the length of the period of time under consideration, with a start and an end as a transforming process in business strategy. Second, coopetition may also develop simultaneously on multiple business dimensions at the industry level (market segments, geographic location, etc.) and/or at the firm level (organizational units, products, value-chain activities, etc.). For instance, competitors may cooperate in R&D or infrastructure platforms while competing for products and services (Cassiman et al., 2009). Similarly, they may compete in one geographical market while simultaneously cooperating in another (Lehiany & Chiambaretto, 2014).

Exploring visuals

In consideration of the above coopetition properties, it is possible to explore the way coopetition can be illustrated. On the one hand, coopetition has been depicted in either unidimensional or multidimensional perspectives (Bengtsson et al., 2010). Drawing on graphs, typologies, matrices, continua, networks, chronologies, trees, and other forms, the unidimensional perspective aims at depicting the intensity (Bengtsson et al., 2010; Luo, 2005, 2007), nature (Dagnino & Padula, 2002), or dynamics of coopetition over a given dimension. The multidimensional perspective, in turn, builds on multidimensional figures and frameworks to illustrate the different areas in which coopetition takes place (Dumez & Jeunemaître, 2006a), the different levels of coopetition strategies (Dagnino & Padula, 2002), or the complex articulation between different components explaining coopetition (Bengtsson & Raza-Ullah, 2016). Unidimensional versus multidimensional perspectives represent then a first line of inquiry structuring the way coopetition can be conceptualized and illustrated.

On the other hand, the phenomenon of coopetition has been templated either from a static or dynamic perspective. Building on graphs, typologies, matrices, networks, and continua, the static perspective depicts coopetition in terms of the interactions between actors (see for instance Le Roy & Guillotreau, 2010; Hu, 2014; Wiener & Saunders, 2014), referring to the state of the relationship at a given moment. This perspective therefore assumes that coopetition is a particular, hybrid form of relationship in which competitive and cooperative components occur simultaneously (Bengtsson & Kock, 2000; Yami & Le Roy, 2010). In contrast, the dynamic perspective, building on chronologies, sequences, or decision trees, puts the stress on processes that structure coopetition over time (see Dumez & Jeunemaître, 2006b; Bengtsson et al., 2010; Lehiany & Chiambaretto, 2014). This perspective illustrates successive sequences or continuous timelines where two or more companies alternatively compete and cooperate.

From the above differentiating considerations—i.e., static versus dynamic, unidimensional versus multidimensional—a meta-table on coopetition visuals may then be proposed with pre-formatted templates stemming from the literature and from Google Image sources (see Table 25.1). In other words, using heterogeneous sources of data and information, reflecting upon generic pre-formatted visuals may help with a reading of the concept in a more consistent and uniform way (Dumez, 2016). The visuals presented below will not be commented on one by one, but rather only where they have significance.

Table 25.1 Meta-table on coopetition visuals

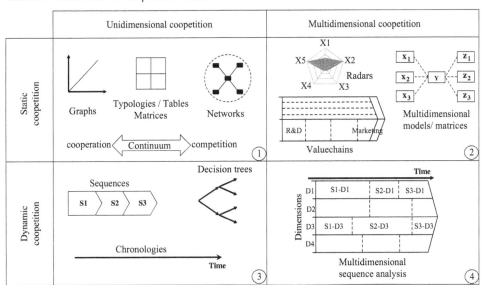

Static-unidimensional coopetition

In the upper-left part of the quadrant, coopetition is studied as a hybrid form of interaction. Competitive and cooperative components occur in a particular period of time and on a single dimension—a business, market segment, supply chain function, organizational division, or strategic level of analysis—under a defined mutual objective. For instance, Bengtsson and Kock (2000) summarize the balance between the extremes of the coopetitive continuum, which may result a in cooperation-dominated relationship, an equal relationship, or a competition-dominated relationship. Other qualitative visual typologies characterize coopetition as active or passive, with possible mixed flexible outcomes (Czakon & Rogalski, 2014). The interest of such visuals is to better apprehend the intensity of coopetition within a continuum between competition and cooperation and the rise of the coopetition concept in a game structure (Padula & Dagnino, 2007).

Also, visuals provide an account of the coopetitive environment and the underlying motives through the lenses of matrices or tables (Carfi & Musolino, 2015). For example, focusing on different possible levels of competition and cooperation, Luo (2007) typifies coopetitive situations as contending, adapting, isolating, or partnering. Is the situation governed by small or large global enterprises, and with a greater or lesser influence of foreign markets? Are coopetitive situations dispersing, networking, concentrating, or connecting (Luo, 2007)? This goes along with the motives for cooperation, which is another studied dimension, whether the main focus is added knowledge or economic value even if driven by rent-seeking strategic behavior. Motives may range from entering new markets, time savings, increases in bargaining power, gaining scale and scope, gaining qualified labor, access to new knowledge diversification, or costs savings. The motives may take place in environments driven by destructive creation, hyper-competition, competition, collusion, or monopoly.

The possible areas of cooperation or collaboration comprise another research dimension, concerning development, sharing of existing knowledge, infrastructure, certification and standards, or government policies. These are embodied in looking at governance models, including more or less formal agreements such as equity or non-equity alliances and pre-conditions for cooperation that may apply to production, or distribution and sales. Static visuals on one dimension permit the characterization of coopetition according to proxy qualitative or quantitative variables on an abscissa and ordered at the origin (Wiener & Saunders, 2014). Of course, as a strategic project, the stability of coopetition hinges on a shared cultural value dimension where profiles in partnerships may be driven by similarities, reputations, the strategic fit of coopetitors, relational risks by opportunism, or the appropriation of resources and/or competencies. Thus, the upper-left part of the quadrant enables visual constructs that focus on a static rationale for coopetition according to a chosen dimension and that provide insights into the coopetition balance of power (Velu, 2016).

Static-multidimensional coopetition

In the upper-right part of the quadrant, coopetition is studied as a static interaction on multiple dimensions. At a given time point, different market segments can be crossed with the intensity of cooperation within clusters of firms, for example, regarding co-investment and location (Arthanari and al., 2015). In the selected dimensions, the points at which cooperation and competition occur simultaneously can be identified, or how the creation and appropriation of the value of coopetition combines added knowledge with network effects (Ritala & Hurmelinna-Laukkanen, 2009) or for the intra-organization units of the firm (Tsai, 2002). For instance, through a value chain analysis, cooperation and competition occur simultaneously across different activities. Matrices, radar, or value-chain visuals may be appropriate for this purpose (Cassiman et al., 2009) or regarding types of coopetition governance in several dimensions (Bouncken & Fredrich, 2016).

Dynamic-unidimensional coopetition

The lower-left part of the quadrant addresses coopetition as an interactive process made up of successive phases of cooperation and competition occurring on a single dimension—a business, market segment, supply chain function, organizational division, or strategic level of analysis—under a possibly changing mutual objective. Coopetition develops over time through phases of competition and cooperation, as stated in the game theory perspective developed by Brandenburger and Nalebuff (1996). These phases may be expressed under different displays, concentrating on a given set of firms and an industry (Okura, 2007). A visual tree is a suitable generic pre-format for conveying coopetition decision making processes (Rodrigues et al., 2011), in conjunction with objectives and the environment. In particular, it questions whether a risk matrix may be worked out that crosses capacity and resource utilization with expected synergies and profits.

Dynamic-multidimensional coopetition

The lower-right part of the quadrant is typical of sequence analysis occurring on multiple dimensions—businesses or market segments, supply chain functions, or organizational divisions—under plausible changing mutual objectives. For instance, Dumez and Jeunemaitre (2006a) developed a multidimensional strategic sequence analysis that builds on three strategic dimensions: the market (strategies in prices, quantities, marketing, etc.), market boundaries (strategies aiming at redefining market boundaries and structure, such as mergers and acquisitions, product bundling, tying), and the non-market environment (lobbying, antitrust, corporate social responsibility; Baron, 1995), showing how companies may compete in one dimension while simultaneously cooperating in others. Other dynamic multidimensional models have been developed (Raza-Ullah et al., 2016), drawing, for instance, on the competition context (industrial, relational, and firm-specific factors) along with the coopetition paradox (cooperation versus competition) and tensions in coopetition (emotional ambivalence at the organizational and inter-organizational levels).

Visuals on the achievement of coopetition objectives suggest that the time scale is a determining factor of analysis. When viewed from complex systems mathematical figures, and considering the Matthew effect, coopetition as the learning curve accumulates advantage over time. As a result, evolutionary game systems indicate that the prevalence of long-term learning, together with random elements, preserves cooperative stability (Allen et al., 2017).

Proposing a visual template for studies on coopetition

The purpose of this section is not how to interpret and analyze coopetition, but rather to propose an intermediate tool that organizes collected raw material (quantitative and/or qualitative data) on cooperative processes with the analysis itself; in other words, it provides a visual framework template. The interest in such a framework is to help researchers collect the most relevant data on the process to be studied, in accordance with the appropriate issues to be raised.

Based on the previous section, the template (described in Figure 25.1) shall incorporate two properties of coopetition: that coopetition is a process and therefore requires a dynamic

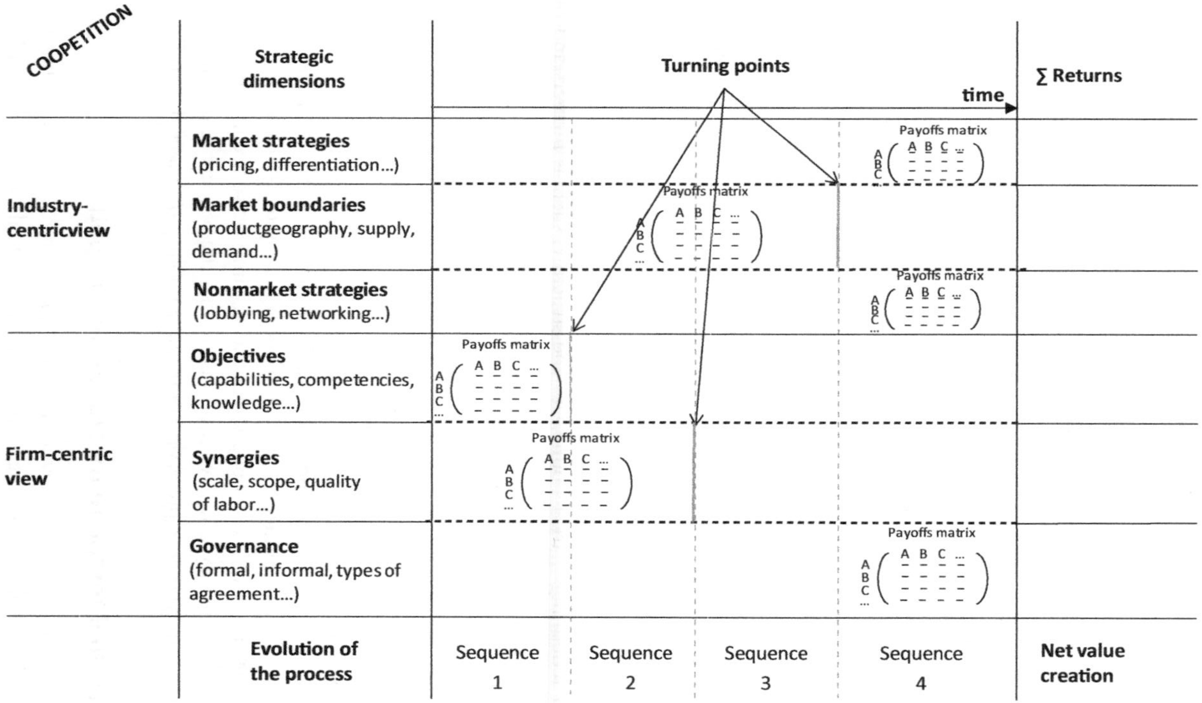

Figure 25.1 Coopetitive multidimensional sequence analysis

perspective, and the importance of including one or more dimensions of interaction. The template shall therefore be both chronological and multidimensional.

Describing the template

The first column refers to the different possible dimensions of coopetition. These dimensions can be categorized from the point of view of the market in which coopetition is to be played out (market, market boundaries, and non-market), as well as from the internal point of view of the firm (objectives, synergies, governance).

The second column provides a dynamic layout of the cooperative processes by sequences and by dimensions. The process is broken down into identified sequences that are separated by focal turning points. Each sequence is identified by a payoff matrix.

The third column expresses what is expected by the actors (Σ returns) and what has or has not been fulfilled (net value creation).

The template draws the researcher's attention to three fundamental elements. The coopetition process may thus be studied on different, clearly defined dimensions, for example, in order to identify the tensions between dimensions (Fernandez et al., 2014) that are inherent to the process. Put differently, if there is a change in the coopetition process, in which dimensions is the change accounted for?

The sequences of the coopetitive process (entry into the process, new sequence in an ongoing process) can be characterized by payoff matrices. Firms make assumptions about the predictable gains that they may achieve from cooperation with their competitors, as well as the gains that their competitors may achieve. During the process, valued matrices may change, either by evolution or by revolution. Then, turning points occur that trigger a move from one cooperative sequence to another.

Assessing coopetition outcomes

As there are turning points, it is necessary to distinguish between the *ex ante* point of view and the *ex post* point of view with respect to what was expected and what was fulfilled. A firm may decide to enter into a coopetition agreement with one or more competitors because it believes that it will achieve gains in the process and that competitors will make equal or lesser gains (but undoubtedly not higher). Matrix estimates are done *ex ante* before entry into the process. Once firms are involved, each periodically reviews the evolution of the estimates and looks at whether or not the expected gains have materialized and how the situation of the partners has developed. If the company understands that the gains it has received from coopetition are lower than those it had expected *ex ante* or that the gains of competitors are higher than anticipated, tensions may then appear in the coopetition process that could possibly lead to a turning point.

In the same way that the *ex ante* and *ex post* perspectives shall be isolated, it is also necessary to separate between the actors' and the researchers' points of view (Dumez, 2006b). Of course, in a process as complex as coopetition, which is easily unstable, involving many players and multiple dimensions, firms may be mistaken in assessing expected gains (theirs and those of their competitors) as to whether their evaluations fulfill (or not) their expectations. It is therefore crucial for the researcher to identify the possible cognitive biases of the actors (excessive optimism or pessimism, over- or under-reaction to particular events). Accordingly, the template invites the collection of accurate data in the construction of payoff matrices that may have led two or more companies to a coopetitive sequence regarding the key events driving a revision of the matrices, i.e., a turning point leading to a new sequence in the coopetition process. The issue is identifying the key dimension(s) that may have been causal in a turning point sequence change. To that end, it is likely that there is an interest in combining quantitative with qualitative analysis. When quantitative matrices are workable using plausible estimates, the analysis of returns and net value creation will be more rigorous. Nevertheless, qualitative assessment of the data can also constitute a major step towards rigorously analyzing the sequential process of coopetition. In order to gain access to these matrices, it is essential to carry out qualitative analyses (interviews with the actors involved, analysis of in-house documents, press articles) regarding how firms have *ex ante* anticipated their potential gains and those of their competitors as well as how they estimated gains or losses in the process, to complement and articulate with the quantitative analysis.

As mentioned above, the template is not intended to analyze coopetitive processes. For example, it does not in itself provide causal explanations. Instead, it helps to prepare this analysis: first, by identifying gaps in the collected material (do the data make it possible to *ex ante* reconstruct the expected payoff matrices of actors and their progress over time? How can the dynamics of the actors' thinking about their diminished or fulfilled expectations and about anticipated competitors' gains be reconstructed?); second, it helps to identify the critical dimensions and events that have structured the coopetition process (and, again, to identify gaps in the data to reconstruct critical events); finally, it helps in developing a narrative on the coopetition process from its inception (the expected gains by the different actors) and then with the delineated sequences. Narration renders the process intelligible (Abbott, 2001; Dumez & Jeunemaitre, 2006b) and represents a further step in the treatment of the empirical material, allowing a deeper level of analysis and interpretation.

Conclusion

Publications on coopetition make use of diagrams and figures, highlighting two important points. First, coopetition may be seen from an outside view of the firm—in the tradition of industrial economics—or from an internal one—in the tradition of the resource-based view of the firm. These two perspectives on coopetition have occasionally been viewed in opposition and as complimentary. Second, visuals illustrate that research on coopetition is structured by two dimensions: static versus dynamic and uni- versus multi-dimensional. On this basis, a multidimensional coopetition sequence analysis (MCSA) template has been put forward. It attempts to articulate internal and external views on cooperation, multidimensionality, and a sequential analysis of its dynamics. In itself, the template is not solely an analytical tool, but is rather intended to facilitate the theorizing of coopetitive processes.

References

Abbott, A. (2001). *Time Matters. On Theory and Method*. Chicago: University of Chicago Press.

Allen, B., Lippner, G., Chen, Y.-T., Fotouhi, B., Momeni, N., Yau, S.-T., & Nowak, M. A. (2017). Evolutionary dynamics on any population structure. *Nature,* 544(7649), 227–237.

Arthanari, T., Carfì, D., & Musolino, F. (2015). Game theoretic modeling of horizontal supply chain coopetition among growers. *International Game Theory Review*, 17(2).

Axelrod, R. (1997). *The Complexity of Cooperation: Agent-based Models of Competition and Collaboration*. Princeton, NJ: Princeton University Press.

Axelrod, R. & Hamilton, W. (1981). The evolution of cooperation. *Science*, 211(4489), 1390–1396.

Barney, J. B. & Clark, D. (2007). *Resource-based Theory, Creating and Sustaining Competitive Advantage*. New York: Oxford University Press.

Baron, D. P. (1995). Integrated strategy: market and nonmarket components. *California Management Review*, 37(2), 47–65.

Baron, D. P. (1996). *Business and Its Environment*. Upper Saddle River: Prentice Hall.

Basole, R. C. (2014). Visual business ecosystem intelligence: lessons from the field. *IEEE Computer Graphics and Applications*, 34(5), 26–34.

Bates, R. H., Greif, A., Levi, M., & Rosenthal, J.-L. (1998). *Analytic Narratives.* Princeton, NJ: Princeton University Press.

Baumol, W. J., Panzar, J. C., & Willig, R. D. (1982). *Contestable Markets and the Theory of Industry Structure.* New York: Harcourt Brace Jovanovich.

Bengtsson, M., Eriksson, J., & Wincent, J. (2010). Co-opetition dynamics – an outline for further inquiry. *Competitiveness Review: An International Business Journal*, 20(2), 194–214.

Bengtsson, M. & Kock, S. (2000). Coopetition in business networks-to cooperate and compete simultaneously. *Industrial Marketing Management*, 29(5), 411–426.

Bengtsson, M. & Kock, S. (2014). Coopetition—Quo vadis? Past accomplishments and future challenges. *Industrial Marketing Management*, 43(2), 180–188.

Bengtsson, M. & Raza-Ullah, T. (2016). A systematic review of research on coopetition: toward a multilevel understanding. *Industrial Marketing Management*, 57, 23–39.

Brandenburger, A. & Nalebuff, B. (1996). *Coopetition.* New York: Doubleday Publishing Group.

Bouncken, R. B. & Fredrich, V. (2016). Learning in coopetition: Alliance orientation, network size, and firm types. *Journal of Business Research*, 69(5), 1753–1758.

Carfì, D. & Musolino, F. (2015). A coopetitive-dynamical game model for currency markets stabilization. *Atti della Accademia Peloritana dei Pericolanti-Classe di Scienze Fisiche, Matematiche e Naturali*, 93(1), 1.

Cassiman, B., Di Guardo, M. C., & Valentini, G. (2009). Organising R&D projects to profit from innovation: Insights from co-opetition. *Long Range Planning*, 42(2), 216–233.

Chiambaretto, P. & Dumez, H. (2016). Toward a typology of coopetition: a multilevel approach. *International Studies of Management & Organization*, 46(2–3), 110–129.

Czakon, W. & Rogalski, M. (2014). Coopetition typology revisited–a behavioural approach. *International Journal of Business Environment*, 6(1), 28–46.

Dagnino, G. B. & Padula, G. (2002). Coopetition strategy. A new kind of interfirm dynamics for value creation. *Communication at EURAM second annual conference*, Stockholm, May 9–11, 2002.

Dixit, A. K. & Nalebuff, B. (2008). *The Art of Strategy: A Game Theorist's Guide to Success in Business and Life.* New York: WW Norton & Company.

Dumez, H. (2006). Why a special issue on methodology: Introduction. *European Management Review*, 3(1), 4–6.

Dumez, H. (2016). *Comprehensive Research: A Methodological and Epistemological Introduction to Qualitative Research.* Copenhagen: CBS Press

Dumez, H. & Jeunemaître, A. (2000). *Understanding and Regulating the Market at a Time of Globalization: The Case of the Cement Industry.* Basingstoke: Macmillan Press Ltd.

Dumez, H. & Jeunemaitre, A. (2006a). Multidimensional strategic sequences: A research programme proposal on coopetition. *2nd Workshop on Coopetition Strategy*, 2006, Milan, Italy.

Dumez, H. & Jeunemaitre, A. (2006b). Reviving narratives in economics and management: Towards an integrated perspective of modelling, statistical inference and narratives. *European Management Review*, 3(1), 32–43.

Esty, D. C. & Geradin, D. (Eds) (2001). Regulatory co-opetition. In *Regulatory Competition and Economic Integration: Comparative Perspectives* (chapter 2, pp. 30–47). Oxford: Oxford University Press.

Fernandez, A.-S., Le Roy, F., & Gnyawali, D. R. (2014). Sources and management of tension in co-opetition case evidence from telecommunications satellites manufacturing in Europe. *Industrial Marketing Management*, 43(2), 222–235.

Gnyawali, D. R. & Song, Y. (2016). Pursuit of rigor in research: Illustration from coopetition literature. *Industrial Marketing Management*, 57, 12–22.

Gnyawali, D. R., He, J., & Madhavan, R. (2006). Impact of co-opetition on firm competitive behavior: An empirical examination. *Journal of Management*, 32(4), 507–530.

Golnam, A., Ritala, P., & Wegmann, A. (2014). Coopetition within and between value networks–a typology and a modelling framework. *International Journal of Business Environment*, 6(1), 47–68.

Grant, R. M. (1991). The resource-based theory of competitive advantage: Implications for strategy formulation. *California Management Review*, 33(3), 114–135.

Hu, J. (2014). Bipartite consensus control of multiagent systems on coopetition networks. *Abstract and Applied Analysis*, article ID 689070, 9 pages.

Jorde, T. M. & Teece, D. J. (1990). Innovation and cooperation: implications for competition and antitrust. *The Journal of Economic Perspectives*, 4(3), 75–96.

Lado, A. A., Boyd, N. G., & Hanlon, S. C. (1997). Competition, cooperation, and the search for economic rents: a syncretic model. *Academy of Management Review*, 22(1), 110–141.

Lehiany, B. & Chiambaretto, P. (2014). SMAA: A framework for a sequential and multidimensional analysis of alliances. *Management international/International Management/Gestiòn Internacional*, 18, 85–105 (in French).

Le Roy, F. & Guilotreau, P. (2010). Successful strategies for challengers: competition or coopetition with dominant firms? in Yami, S., Castaldo, S., & Dagnino, G. B. (Eds), *Coopetition: Winning Strategies for the 21st Century* (chapter 12, pp. 238–255). Chelthenham: Edward Elgar.

Luo, Y. (2005). Toward coopetition within a multinational enterprise: a perspective from foreign subsidiaries. *Journal of World Business*, 40(1), 71–90. https://doi.org/10.1016/j.jwb.2004.10.006

Luo, Y. (2007). A coopetition perspective of global competition. *Journal of World Business*, 42(2), 129–144.

McWilliams, A. & Smart, D. L. (1993). Efficiency v. structure-conduct-performance: Implications for strategy research and practice. *Journal of Management*, 19(1), 63–78.

Nowak, M. A. (2006). Five rules for the evolution of cooperation. *Science*, 314(5805), 1560–1563.

Okura, M. (2007). Coopetitive strategies of Japanese insurance firms a game-theory approach. *International Studies of Management & Organization*, 37(2), 53–69.

Padula, G. & Dagnino, G. B. (2007). Untangling the rise of coopetition: the intrusion of competition in a cooperative game structure. *International Studies of Management & Organization*, 37(2), 32–52.

Porter, M. E. (1980). *Competitive Strategy: Techniques for Analyzing Industries and Competitors.* New York: Free Press.

Ritala, P. & Hurmelinna-Laukkanen, P. (2009). What's in it for me? Creating and appropriating value in innovation-related coopetition. *Technovation*, 29(12), 819–828.

Rodrigues, F., Souza, V., & Leitão, J. (2011). Strategic coopetition of global brands: a game theory approach to 'Nike+ iPod Sport Kit' co-branding. *International Journal of Entrepreneurial Venturing*, 3(4), 435–455.

Shapiro, C. (1989). The theory of business strategy. *The Rand Journal of Economics*, 20(1), 125–137.

Sun, G., Wu, Y., Liu, S., Peng, T. Q., Zhu, J. J., & Liang, R. (2014). EvoRiver: Visual analysis of topic coopetition on social media. *IEEE Transactions on Visualization and Computer Graphics*, 20(12), 1753–1762.

Tadelis, S. (2013). *Game Theory: An Introduction.* Princeton, NJ: Princeton University Press.

Teece, D. J., Pisano, G., & Shuen, A. (1997). Dynamic capabilities and strategic management. *Strategic Management Journal*, 18(7), 509–533.

Tsai, W. (2002). Social structure of "coopetition" within a multiunit organization: Coordination, competition, and intraorganizational knowledge sharing. *Organization Science*, 13(2), 179–190.

Tufte, E. R. (1990). Escaping flatland. In *Envisioning Information* (chapter 1, pp. 12–36). Cheshire, CT: Graphics Press LLC.

Velu, C. (2016). Evolutionary or revolutionary business model innovation through coopetition? The role of dominance in network markets. *Industrial Marketing Management*, 53 (February), 124–135.

Wernerfelt, B. (1984). A resource-based view of the firm. *Strategic Management Journal*, 5(2), 171–180.

Weiss, L. W. (1979). The structure-conduct-performance paradigm and antitrust. *University of Pennsylvania Law Review*, 127(4), 1104–1140.

Wiener, M. & Saunders, C. (2014). Forced coopetition in IT multi-sourcing. *The Journal of Strategic Information Systems*, 23(3), 210–225.

Part V

Coopetition outcomes
and implications

26

Challenges and merits of coopetitive innovation

Johanna Gast, Wolfgang Hora, Ricarda B. Bouncken,
and Sascha Kraus

Introduction

The term *coopetition* is a neologism of the words "coo(peration)" and "(com)petition" (Brandenburger & Nalebuff, 1996). Given that more than half of all cooperative relationships appear between firms within the same industry or competitors (Harbison et al., 1998), the concept of simultaneous cooperation and competition has been introduced to firms' strategy toolbox as an additional approach to reduce the gap between the traditional approaches of cooperation and competition (Roy & Yami, 2009). In the last two decades, the interest in coopetition has increased tremendously, due to today's complex, volatile, and dynamic environments (Bengtsson & Kock, 2014).

Since Brandenburger and Nalebuff's (1996) seminal contribution, rising academic attention to coopetition can be identified, mostly in the fields of management and business. Recent literature reviews have synthesized the state of the art of coopetition literature (Bengtsson & Kock, 2014; Bouncken et al., 2015; Gnyawali & Song, 2016) highlighting that coopetition is analyzed on the inter-firm level between two or more organizations (Bouncken & Kraus, 2013; Quintana-Garcia & Benavides-Velasco, 2004), the intra-firm level within firms and their business units (Luo et al., 2006; Tsai, 2002) as well at the network level (Peng & Bourne, 2009). Context-wise, a range of different settings are examined, including different industries and firm types. Most of the existing literature focuses on large enterprises in different industries such as high- and low-tech industries; few studies examine the role of coopetition for small- and medium-sized enterprises (SMEs) (Gast et al., 2015). Further, researchers applied a variety of methodological approaches, though the majority of the existing studies conducted qualitative research to arrive at an in-depth theoretical understanding of coopetition (Bouncken et al., 2015). Most of the quantitative studies are published within the last decade (Dorn et al., 2016).

A crucial finding of extant research is the fact that inter-organizational alliances and coopetition in particular play an important role in advancing firms' technological progress and innovative capabilities (Gnyawali & Park, 2011). The special implication of coopetition for innovation stems from the possibility to exchange relevant and complementary resources, capabilities, and knowledge through coopetitive relationships among competitors (Estrada et al., 2016). Since individual firms often do not possess all necessary resources and skills to innovate on their own (Parra-Requena et al., 2015), they typically do not innovate in a complete vacuum (Freel, 2003) but do so in cooperation with external partners. By means of partnerships with suppliers, customers, or even competitors, flows of resources, capacities, and knowledge are facilitated that can then induce mutual innovation development (Bouncken et al., 2015). Existing research even postulated that "the best partner for a firm in a strategic alliance is sometimes one of its strong competitors" (Gnyawali & Park, 2009: 312). Because rivals, generally, share similar contexts, threats, and opportunities and possess complementary resources that are relevant to the other party (Gnyawali & Park, 2009), they represent key sources of resources and knowledge, which may accelerate innovation. Therefore, various studies have attempted to examine the importance of coopetition for innovation (Ritala et al., 2016). Although many articles highlight the importance of coopetition for enhancing a firm's innovation capacity, research on the relationship between coopetition and innovation is still young and emerging.

To advance the present understanding in this field and to enable additional quantitative inquiries, an overview of the existing findings is necessary. To pave the way for a stronger elaboration on the linkages between coopetition and innovation, this chapter therefore reviews prior quantitative studies with respect to their insights into the coopetition and innovation relationship.

Review approach

To synthesize the literature across the domain of coopetition in innovation, this chapter represents the insights gained from a systematic, evidence-informed literature review (Tranfield et al., 2003). Table 26.1 presents the six electronic databases that were scanned for publications appearing in peer-reviewed academic business and management journals, omitting books, book chapters, discussion papers, and non-referred publications (Ordanini et al., 2008). We deliberately focused our systematic review approach on articles using the search items "co-opet*" or "coopet*" and "innov*" in the respective titles, abstracts, and/or keywords to identify scientific research, which links coopetition and innovation. Further, we concentrated on articles applying quantitative research to provide a summary of the previously tested relationships, variables used, and the respective findings. These selection criteria resulted in a final sample of seventeen scholarly articles.

Table 26.1 Systematic review approach

Databases	• ABI Inform/ProQuest • EBSCOhost/business source Premier • EconLit	• ScienceDirect • Web of Science • Wiley
Selection criteria	*Keywords*	"co-opet*" or "coopet*" AND "innov*" in titles, abstract, keywords
	Type of publication	Peer-reviewed articles in business and management journals
	Type of methodology	Quantitative research
	Timeframe	Published until 2017

State-of-the-art review of research on coopetition and innovation

A brief overview of the scope and breadth of existing research

Academic research exploring the relationship between coopetition and innovation through quantitative research methods is relatively young and emerging. Although the first academic article in this field using a quantitative approach was published in 2004, a slight uptrend can only be identified between 2011 and 2013, and from 2015 onwards (Figure 26.1). Overall, the slowly increasing number of publications per year is in accordance with the recent attention paid to coopetition and innovation in specific academic journals. Journals that published special issues on coopetition and, therefore, presented at least two articles on coopetition and innovation are *Industrial Marketing Management* (four articles); and *British Journal of Management*, *International Journal of Technology Management*, *Journal of Business Research*, and *Technovation* (each two articles). The remaining contributions are published in *International Journal of Production Economics*, *International Studies of Management Organisation*, *Journal of Product Innovation Management*, and *Journal of Service Management* (each one article). Regarding the analytical approaches applied in the reviewed studies, it is worth noting that regression and structural equation models (ten and six articles, respectively) are typically used to test the linkages between coopetition and innovation and other control variables.

Empirical insights on the linkages between coopetition and innovation

The rationale behind coopetition for innovation can be explained based on different theoretical frameworks, including transaction cost theory, game theory, and the resource- or capabilities-based view. According to transaction cost theory, coopetition represents a means to transmit tacit knowledge among firms, which is typically not easily shared and formalized due to its tacit nature (Quintana-Garcia & Benavides-Velasco, 2004). Additionally, however, coopetition is seen as a risky endeavor since knowledge spillovers endanger the protection of key knowledge, and incentives to act in an opportunistic way may undermine the potential benefits of coopetition (Estrada et al., 2016; Kraus et al., 2017; Quintana-Garcia & Benavides-Velasco, 2004).

Based on game theory, the cooperative interaction of coopetition is a way to increase the overall size of the business pie, while the competitive one means that each partner tries to compete for the largest share of the mutually enlarged pie (Brandenburger & Nalebuff, 1996). In fact,

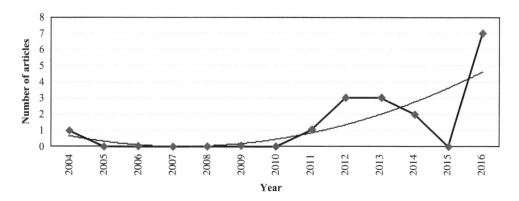

Figure 26.1 Chronological development of the number of scientific articles

game theory proposes that it is sometimes more beneficial to look for a win–win situation with a competitor than to act independently to outcompete the rival, as it can be very difficult or even impossible to beat and eliminate the competitor completely (Ritala, 2012; Quintana-Garcia & Benavides-Velasco, 2004).

Following the resource- or capabilities-based view, a competitive advantage stems from unique, valuable, inimitable, and non-substitutable resources and capabilities (Barney, 1991). Since competitors are likely to possess complementary resources, capabilities, and knowledge (Park et al., 2014), coopetition enables access to complementary, but not-yet-internalized resources and capabilities (Estrada et al., 2016; Mention, 2011). This may help coopetitors to create new resources and capabilities based on mutual development (Quintana-Garcia & Benavides-Velasco, 2004) and to generate a joint knowledge base using all partners' know-how, which can be beneficial for firms' market and innovation performance, as well as their technological diversity and innovation capacity (Ritala, 2012; Ritala & Hurmelinna-Laukkanen, 2013; Quintana-Garcia & Benavides-Velasco, 2004). When collaborating respectively, cooperating rivals face several ways to share, internalize, recombine, and develop supplementary and complementary resources and knowledge, which then can promote innovation (Estrada et al., 2016).

By exploring the role of coopetition for innovation, several prior studies claim a positive relationship between coopetition and innovation (e.g., Bouncken et al., 2016; Bouncken & Kraus, 2013; Estrada et al., 2016; Park et al., 2014; Ritala & Hurmelinna-Laukkanen, 2013). Findings suggest, for instance, that coopetition has a positive effect on radical and incremental innovation (Bouncken et al., 2017; Bouncken & Fredrich, 2012; Le Roy et al., 2016; Ratzmann et al., 2016; Ritala & Hurmelinna-Laukkanen, 2013) although the findings still tend to be rather ambiguous. On the one hand, coopetition may be more beneficial for radical than for incremental innovation (Bouncken & Fredrich, 2012). For radical innovations, which are particularly resource-demanding and seek to create completely novel products and services, research argues that collaboration between competitors can have positive implications, as coopetitors profit from a greater and more complementary set of resources, experiences, and knowledge, as well as additional risk-sharing possibilities (Bouncken & Fredrich, 2012; Bouncken & Kraus, 2013). On the other hand, however, radical innovations are found to be less frequent in coopetition than incremental innovations (Ritala & Hurmelinna-Laukkanen, 2013). When studying the different implications of coopetition for radical and incremental innovations, research also focusses on coopetition's effect on the different stages in incremental and radical innovation processes. Bouncken et al. (2017), for instance, find that coopetition is beneficial for early and later stages of incremental innovation. Yet in the case of radical innovation such benefits occur only in less-uncertain later stages.

Besides, coopetition can have a positive influence on new product development and introductions of product innovations (Bouncken et al., 2016; Estrada et al., 2016; Pereira & Leitão, 2016; Wu, 2014; Tomlinson & Fai, 2013; Quintana-Garcia & Benavides-Velasco, 2004). According to Wu (2014), coopetition has an inverted-U-shaped relationship with product innovation performance while Bouncken et al. (2016) and Estrada et al. (2016) emphasize that coopetition can improve product innovativeness or product innovation performance conditioned by the presence of transactional and relational governance mechanisms, or internal knowledge sharing and formal knowledge protection mechanisms, respectively. In contrast, Ritala and Hurmelinna-Laukkanen (2013) note that new product development is the least common type of coopetition. Additionally, Tomlinson and Fai (2013) report that coopetition has no significant effect on innovation in the context of SMEs. This last finding is particularly surprising, since SMEs may significantly benefit from coopetition given their limited access to resources, capabilities, and knowledge (Bouncken & Kraus, 2013; Gast et al., 2017; Quintana-Garcia & Benavides-Velasco, 2004).

Pereira and Leitão (2016) reveal that the acquisition of external knowledge positively affects product innovation in high-tech and medium-low-tech manufacturing firms. Coopetition can foster this effect even further, but it mainly depends on the coopeting firms' ability to detect and assimilate external sources. This ability, formally known as "absorptive capacity," is not only relevant for product innovations, but together with the firms' "appropriability regime," that is, how firms protect themselves from imitation, it enables incremental innovations of already-existing products or services (Ritala & Hurmelinna-Laukkanen, 2013). Moreover, appropriability regimes are crucial for radical innovations while absorptive capacity has no significant effect (Ritala & Hurmelinna-Laukkanen, 2013). The importance of absorptive capacity and appropriability regimes stems from the fact that cooperation with competitors comes along with the risks of knowledge leakage, imitation, and opportunism. That is why mechanisms are needed to protect core knowledge on the one hand, and to enable knowledge sharing and development on the other hand (Ritala & Hurmelinna-Laukkanen, 2013). In this line, governance mechanisms (Bouncken et al., 2016; Ratzmann et al., 2016; Steinicke et al., 2012) as well as knowledge sharing and protection mechanisms (Estrada et al., 2016) are crucial to improve product innovativeness through coopetition, as they can facilitate the positive effect of coopetition for innovation.

Different governance mechanisms play a key role in fostering innovativeness through coopetition. First, formal and relational governance help to promote coordination and mitigate opportunism among partners to create a setting necessary for innovation through coopetition (Steinicke et al., 2012). Second, product innovativeness benefits from coopetition when combined with transactional and relational governance mechanisms even to the extent that coopetition seems to have no direct positive effect on innovation when governance mechanisms are completely absent (Bouncken et al., 2016). Regarding knowledge sharing and protection mechanisms, Estrada et al. (2016) show that coopetition positively affects product innovation performance only when firms can internalize and recombine new knowledge while simultaneously assuring that their own knowledge is secured and not spilled over unintendedly. Hence, internal knowledge sharing mechanisms and formal knowledge protection mechanisms need to be present for coopetition to have a positive impact on firms' product innovation performance (Estrada et al., 2016). Additionally, trust, contractual complexity, and dependence determine the relationship between coopetition and innovation in the sense that different governance gestalts can foster or constrain breakthrough and incremental innovations (Ratzmann et al., 2016).

In more detail, Ratzmann et al. (2016) show that breakthrough innovations are promoted by gestalts including low contractual complexity and low trust; high contractual complexity and high dependence; and high contractual complexity, low dependence, and low trust; while they reveal that a gestalt of high contractual complexity, low dependence, and high trust restrains breakthrough innovations. In the case of incremental innovations, the authors find that innovation-fostering gestalts include low contractual complexity and high trust; high contract complexity and high dependence; and high contractual complexity, low dependence, and high trust. At the same time, they report that a gestalt of high contractual complexity, low dependence, and low trust constrains incremental innovations.

Next to these firm-internal factors that can determine the effectiveness of coopetition for innovation, external factors such as market uncertainty, network externalities, coopetition intensity (Ritala, 2012), technological uncertainty (Bouncken & Kraus, 2013), or the firms' position in a coopetitive network (Baierl et al., 2016) affect coopetition's implications for innovation. For example, coopetition is advantageous when market uncertainty, network externalities (Ritala, 2012), or technological uncertainty (Bouncken & Kraus, 2013) are high since cooperation among rivals can lead to risk- and cost-sharing opportunities, which are of crucial importance in these environments. Furthermore, a central position in a coopetitive network has a significant impact on innovativeness as it enables information flows and knowledge spillovers, which can result in a more diverse stock of information (Baierl et al., 2016). Moreover, research emphasizes that coopetition is an important strategy in innovation- and knowledge-intensive, dynamic, and complex industries that are confronted with short product life cycles, high R&D investments, and technological standards (Bouncken et al., 2017; Quintana-Garcia & Benavides-Velasco, 2004). In such dynamic and complex environments with high levels of market uncertainty and risks, coopetition represents an important strategy as it allows companies to catch up with the evolving technological progress and avert risks more easily (Bouncken & Kraus, 2013).

Another stream of research within the coopetition literature focuses on the balance between cooperative and competitive forces in coopetition. In the context of innovation, Park et al. (2014) highlight that balanced coopetition with moderately high cooperation and competition has a positive effect on innovation performance.

Since most of the studies analyzing the possible linkage between coopetition and innovation focus on manufacturing firms, Mention (2011) examines the influence of coopetition on innovation novelty in service firms. Interestingly, the author finds that exploiting information from competitors does not stimulate innovation novelty in service firms. Information sourcing from competitors supports an imitation strategy rather than the willingness to introduce new services to the market.

Table 26.2 presents an overview of the existing findings regarding the relationships between coopetition and innovation.

Conclusion and outlook for future research

Over the past two decades, an increasing number of studies has been published in the field of coopetition with the body of knowledge growing as a result. In sum, coopetition has become a well-accepted concept in research whereby the relationship between coopetition and innovation represents an intensively researched topic in this field. To advance future research on coopetition and its linkages with innovation, this chapter presents the insights gained from a systematic literature review of prior quantitative studies with a particular focus on their findings on the coopetition and innovation relationship.

To summarize, coopetition appears to be a beneficial strategy for firms to enhance their overall innovation performance, although differences can be identified for different types of innovations including radical, incremental, product, or process innovations. In addition, governance as well as knowledge sharing and protecting mechanisms are crucial measures that should be incorporated in coopetitive relationships to avoid opportunism among partners and to provide an environment favorable for innovativeness.

Since the reviewed studies partially show contradictory results, further empirical research is required to better validate constructs and variables, to approve already-analyzed relationships, to study new relationships, and to conduct research in different contexts. The latter can be achieved by not only focusing on certain types of innovation and certain organizational, industrial, or geographical settings, but by exploring the relationship between coopetition and innovation in broader contexts including different firm types—for example, SMEs, family firms, and start-ups—by analyzing different innovation types, including business model innovation (Bouncken & Fredrich, 2016), and by applying more cross-industry and cross-geography studies. Despite an extensive search for scholarly articles that conducted a quantitative approach, we only identified seventeen studies. Additional quantitative, experimental, and especially meta-analytic studies would facilitate the synthesis of existing findings and advance the understanding of the impact of coopetition on innovation, and vice versa, in more detail.

Table 26.2 Overview of findings on the linkages between coopetition and innovation

Study	Research Context	Links to Theoretical Lenses	Sample and Method	Coopetition Variable	Innovation Variable	Main Findings
Baierl et al., 2016	Effect of network attributes on corporate innovativeness in coopetitive corporate venture capital (CVC) networks	-	162 corporations engaged in CVC, linear regression	Centrality, subgroups, structural holes	Innovativeness	• Central position in a coopetitive network is beneficial for innovativeness, highlighting the importance of networking for the development of a coopetitive network position • Being a member of a restricted subgroup affects innovativeness negatively as it stops information flows and knowledge spillovers, leading to less diverse information • Structural holes have no direct effect on innovativeness
Bouncken & Fredrich, 2012	Effect of coopetition on competitive success, radical innovation and incremental innovation, and the role of trust and dependency	Transaction cost theory	469 German IT firms, structural equation modelling (SEM)	Alliance strategy, alliance function	Radical innovation, incremental innovation	• Coopetition improves radical innovation as critical knowledge is combined across partners • Coopetition is more beneficial for radical than for incremental innovation
Bouncken & Kraus, 2013	Effect of coopetition on revolutionary and radical innovation	-	830 German IT SMEs, SEM	Knowledge sharing, inlearning, uncertainty	Revolutionary innovation, radical innovation	• Coopetition affects revolutionary innovation negatively and radical innovation positively • Revolutionary innovation declines with greater coopetitive knowledge sharing • Greater uncertainty increases the effect of coopetition on revolutionary innovation

(*continued*)

Table 26.2 (Cont.)

Study	Research Context	Links to Theoretical Lenses	Sample and Method	Coopetition Variable	Innovation Variable	Main Findings
Bouncken et al., 2016	Effect of transactional and relational governance on product innovativeness in vertical alliances	Transaction cost theory	372 firms in the medical device industry with major operations in Germany, covariance-based SEM & latent moderated structural equations method	Transactional governance, relational governance	Product innovativeness	• If coopetition increases, greater transactional governance reduces product innovativeness • Coopetition benefits from plural governance • No direct positive effect of coopetition on innovation performance in the absence of governance
Bouncken et al., 2017	Effect of coopetition in different phases of NPD alliances and innovation outcomes	-	1,049 new product development (NPD) alliances in the German medical and machinery sectors, covariance-based SEM	Coopetition intensity in pre-launch phase, coopetition intensity in launch phase	Radical innovation, incremental innovation	• Increasing coopetition intensity affects incremental innovation positively • Obtained result changes when NPD alliance phases are separated • Benefits of coopetition intensity for incremental innovation hold for both pre-launch and launch phases of NPD alliances, while radical innovation only increases along coopetition intensity in the product launch phase of NPD alliances

Estrada et al., 2016	Role of knowledge sharing and protection mechanisms for the innovation performance of coopetition strategies	Transaction cost theory, capability-based view	627 manufacturing firms participating in fifth wave of the CIS Tobit regression	Competitor collaboration, internal knowledge sharing mechanism, formal knowledge protection mechanism	Product innovation performance	• Coopetition affects product innovation performance positively only if internal knowledge sharing mechanisms and formal knowledge protection mechanisms are implemented
Le Roy et al., 2016	Effect of cooperation strategies on radical and incremental product innovation	-	3,933 French firms participating in the fourth wave of the CIS, dichotomic logic model	Cooperation with competitors, cooperation with non-competitors	Radical product innovation, incremental product innovation	• Choice for a cooperation strategy is guided by three factors: the type of the cooperation partner (competitor or non-competitor), the type of innovation (radical or incremental), and in case of competitors, the location of the partners (national or international) • Cooperation with customers has the greatest impact on radical and incremental product innovation • Cooperation with universities affects radical and incremental product innovation positively • Cooperation with suppliers affects radical product innovation negatively and has no significant effect on incremental product innovation • International coopetition helps to achieve radical product innovation, especially for firms in North America and Europe

(continued)

Table 26.2 (Cont.)

Study	Research Context	Links to Theoretical Lenses	Sample and Method	Coopetition Variable	Innovation Variable	Main Findings
Mention, 2011	Effect of cooperation practices and use of information sources on innovation novelty	Transaction cost theory	1,052 Luxembourgish service firms participating in fourth wave of the Flemish Community Innovation Survey (CIS), logistic regression	Cooperation: science-based, market-based, coopetition, intra-group; information sources: science-based, market-based, from competitors, intra-group	Innovation novelty	• Exploiting information from competitors does not stimulate innovation novelty in service firms • Information sourcing from competitors supports imitation rather than the willingness to develop new services • Exploitation and assimilation of internal and external resources lead to a competitive advantage
Park et al., 2014	Effect of coopetition on firms' innovation performance	Transaction cost theory	Panel data (1990–2003) of 1,930 firms in semiconductor industry, negative binomial regression	Competition intensity, cooperation intensity	Coopetition-based innovation performance	• Benefits of cooperation-dominant coopetition are greater than competition-dominant coopetition • When competitive intensity increases to a certain degree, the benefits in the form of enhanced innovation performance increase as well • Balanced coopetition provides innovation benefits most effectively
Pereira & Leitão, 2016	Effect of absorptive capacity and coopetition on product innovation	-	4,912 Italian manufacturing firms and 3,660 Portuguese manufacturing firms, logit regression	Absorptive capacity enablers: external knowledge sourcing, internal R&D activities, employees' expertise;	Product innovation	• Effect of acquisition of external knowledge on product innovation is significantly positive for high-tech and medium-low-tech manufacturing firms

	Focus	Theory	Method/Sample	Coopetition relationships	Outcomes	Key findings
Quintana-Garcia & Benavides-Velasco, 2004	Effect of coopetition on innovative capability	Transaction cost theory, resource-based view, game theory	Panel study of 73 European biotechnology SMEs, linear regression and Poisson model	Cooperation with direct competitors, Cooperation only, competition	coopetition relationships: with home-based competitors, with competitors from abroad	• Coopetition affects product innovation positively but the strength of the effect depends on firms' absorptive capacity • No significant effect of coopetition relationships across geographical borders
					Technology diversity, product lines	• Coopetition is an important strategy for new product line developments • Coopetition helps to acquire new knowledge and skills from the partner as well as to create and access other capabilities through the intensive exploitation of existing ones • Coopetition positively affects technological diversity as partners get access to complementary resources
Ratzmann et al., 2016	Effect of dependence, trust, and contractual complexity on innovation in coopetition relationships		1,286 managers of IT firms PLS-SEM	Trust, contractual complexity, dependence	Breakthrough innovation, incremental innovation	• High levels of dependence enhance breakthrough and incremental innovations • Governance gestalts matter such that coopetition can foster or constrain breakthrough and incremental innovation

(continued)

Table 26.2 (Cont.)

Study	Research Context	Links to Theoretical Lenses	Sample and Method	Coopetition Variable	Innovation Variable	Main Findings
Ritala & Hurmelinna-Laukkanen, 2013	Effects of absorptive capacity and appropriability regime on the outcome of innovation in coopetition	Resource-based view	138 Finnish firms, multivariate multiple regression and multivariate analysis of covariance	Potential absorptive capacity, appropriability regime	Incremental innovation, radical Innovation	• Coopetition leads less frequently to radical than to incremental innovations • Standardization is most common type of coopetition; new product development is the least common • Firms' absorptive capacity and appropriability regimes are important elements when firms strive for innovation through coopetition • Absorptive capacity and appropriation enable incremental innovation • Appropriability regimes are relevant for radical innovation while absorptive capacity has no significant effect
Ritala, 2012	Effect of coopetition on firms' innovation and market performance	Resource-based view, game theory	209 Finnish firms, hierarchical regression	Coopetition alignment	Innovation performance	• Coopetition is beneficial for innovation performance • Coopetition is especially successful under high market uncertainty as risks and costs can be shared with competitors • When uncertainty is low, coopetition does not necessarily provide added value • Coopetition is successful under high network externalities, which is important in the innovation context

Author	Aim	Theory	Sample/Method	Variables	Dependent variable	Findings
Steinicke et al., 2012	Role of governance mechanisms in fostering innovativeness in service firms	-	225 German firms in the logistic industry SEM	Governance mechanisms: formalization, mutual influence, cultural similarity	Innovativeness	• Different forms of governance play a key role in fostering innovativeness • Formal and relational governance mechanisms help to promote coordination and hinder opportunism among partners • Relational governance is more important for service firms than formal governance while the latter is more important in manufacturing firms • 62% of the firms rely on contractual set-ups (oral agreements or written contracts)
Tomlinson & Fai, 2013	Effect of cooperative ties that enhance SME innovation	-	371 UK manufacturing SMEs, hierarchical multivariate regression	Cooperation buyers, cooperation suppliers, cooperation competitors	Product innovation, process innovation	• Cooperation with suppliers or buyers enhances product and process innovation • Coopetition has no significant impact on innovation for UK SMEs
Wu, 2014	Relationship between coopetition and product innovation	Game theory	1,499 Chinese firms, zero-inflated negative binomial regression	Technological capability, research collaboration	Product innovation	• Coopetition has an inverted-U-shaped relationship with firms' product innovation performance • Strong technological capability weakens the relationship between coopetition and product innovation • Cooperation with universities or research institutes negatively influences the link between coopetition and product innovation

Investigating how coopetition influences firms' innovation capabilities over a longer period of time could be another promising area of further research, as well as the role of management (Le Roy & Czakon, 2016) and coopetition capabilities (Bengtsson et al., 2016) for the implication of coopetition on innovation.

References

Baierl, R., Anokhin, S., & Grichnik, D. (2016). Coopetition in corporate venture capital: The relationship between network attributes, corporate innovativeness, and financial performance. *International Journal of Technology Management*, 71(1/2), 58–80.

Barney, J. (1991). Firm resources and sustained competitive advantage. *Journal of Management*, 17(1), 99–120.

Bengtsson, M. & Kock, S. (2014). Coopetition-Quo vadis? Past accomplishments and future challenges. *Industrial Marketing Management*, 43(2), 180–188.

Bengtsson, M., Raza-Ullah, T., & Vanyushyn, V. (2016). The coopetition paradox and tension: The moderating role of coopetition capability. *Industrial Marketing Management*, 53, 19–30.

Bouncken, R. B., Fredrich, V., Ritala, P., & Kraus, S. (2017). Coopetition in new product development alliances: Advantages and tensions for incremental and radical innovation *British Journal of Management*, forthcoming.

Bouncken, R. B., Gast, J., Kraus, S., & Bogers, M. (2015). Coopetition: A review, synthesis, and future research directions. *Review of Managerial Science*, 9(3), 577–601.

Bouncken, R. B. & Kraus, S. (2013). Innovation in knowledge-intensive industries: The double-edged sword of coopetition. *Journal of Business Research*, 66(10), 2060–2070.

Bouncken, R. B., Clauß, T., & Fredrich, V. (2016). Product innovation through coopetition in alliances: Singular or plural governance? *Industrial Marketing Management*, 53, 77–90.

Bouncken, R. B. & Fredrich, V. (2012). Coopetition: Performance implications and management antecedents. *International Journal of Innovation Management*, 16(5), 1–12.

Bouncken, R. B. & Fredrich, V. (2016). Business model innovation in alliances: Successful configurations. *Journal of Business Research*, 69(9), 3584–3590.

Brandenburger, A. & Nalebuff, B. (1996). *Co-opetition*. New York: Doubleday Publishing.

Dorn, S., Schweiger, B., & Albers, S. (2016). Levels, phases and themes of coopetition: A systematic literature review and research agenda. *European Management Journal*, 34(5), 484–500.

Estrada, I., Faems, D., & de Faria, P. (2016). Coopetition and product innovation performance: The role of internal knowledge sharing mechanisms and formal knowledge protection mechanisms. *Industrial Marketing Management*, 53, 56–65.

Freel, M. S. (2003). Sectoral patterns of small firm innovation, networking and proximity. *Research Policy*, 32(5), 751–770.

Gast, J., Filser, M., Gundolf, K., & Kraus, S. (2015). Coopetition research: Towards a better understanding of past trends and future directions. *International Journal of Entrepreneurship and Small Business*, 24(4), 492–521.

Gast, J., Kallmünzer, A., Kraus, S., Gundolf, K., & Arnold, J. (2017). Coopetition of small- and medium-sized family enterprises: Insights from an it business network. *International Journal of Entrepreneurship and Small Business* (in press).

Gnyawali, D. R. & Park, B.-J. R. (2011). Co-opetition between giants: Collaboration with competitors for technological innovation. *Research Policy*, 40(5), 650–663.

Gnyawali, D. R. & Park, B. (2009). Co-opetition and technological innovation in small and medium-sized enterprises: A multilevel conceptual model. *Journal of Small Business Management*, 47(3), 308–330.

Gnyawali, D. R. & Song, Y. (2016). Pursuit of rigor in research: Illustration from coopetition literature. *Industrial Marketing Management*, 57, 12–22.

Harbison, J. R., Pekar, P. P., & Stasior, W. F. (1998). *Smart Alliances: A Practical Guide to Repeatable Success*. San Francisco: Jossey-Bass.

Kraus, S., Meier, F., Niemand, T., Bouncken, R. B., & Ritala, P. (2017). In search for the ideal coopetition partner – An experimental study. *Review of Managerial Science* (in press).

Le Roy, F. & Czakon, W. (2016). Managing coopetition: the missing link between strategy and performance. *Industrial Marketing Management*, 53(1), 3–6.

Le Roy, F., Robert, M., & Lasch, F. (2016). Choosing the best partner for product innovation: Talking to the enemy or to a friend? *International Studies of Management and Organization*, 46(2–3), 136–158.

Luo, X., Slotegraaf, R. J., & Pan, X. (2006). Cross-functional "coopetition": The simultaneous role of cooperation and competition within firms. *Journal of Marketing*, 70(2), 67–80.

Mention, A.-L. (2011). Co-operation and co-opetition as open innovation practices in the service sector: Which influence on innovation novelty? *Technovation*, 31(1), 44–53.

Ordanini, A., Rubera, G., & DeFillippi, R. (2008). The many moods of inter-organizational imitation: A critical review. *International Journal of Management Reviews*, 10(4), 375–398.

Park, B., Srivastava, M. K., & Gnyawali, D. R. (2014). Walking the tight rope of coopetition: Impact of competition and cooperation intensities and balance on firm innovation performance. *Industrial Marketing Management*, 43(2), 210–221.

Parra-Requena, G., Ruiz-Ortega, M. J., García-Villaverde, P. M., & Rodrigo-Alarcón, J. (2015). The mediating role of knowledge acquisition on the relationship between external social capital and innovativeness. *European Management Review*, 12(3), 149–169.

Peng, T. J. A. & Bourne, M. (2009). The coexistence of competition and cooperation between networks: implications from two Taiwanese healthcare networks. *British Journal of Management*, 20(3), 377–400.

Pereira, D. & Leitão, J. (2016). Absorptive capacity, coopetition and generation of product innovation: contrasting Italian and Portuguese manufacturing firms. *International Journal of Technology Management*, 71(1–2), 10–37.

Quintana-Garcia, C. & Benavides-Velasco, C. A. (2004). Cooperation, competition, and innovative capability: a panel data of European dedicated biotechnology firms. *Technovation*, 24(12), 927–938.

Ratzmann, M., Gudergan, S. P., & Bouncken, R. (2016). Capturing heterogeneity and PLS-SEM prediction ability: Alliance governance and innovation. *Journal of Business Research*, 69(10), 4593–4603.

Ritala, P. (2012). Coopetition strategy: When is it successful? Empirical evidence on innovation and market performance. *British Journal of Management*, 23(3), 307–324.

Ritala, P. & Hurmelinna-Laukkanen, P. (2013). Incremental and radical innovation in coopetition: The role of absorptive capacity and appropriability. *Journal of Product Innovation Management*, 30(1), 154–169.

Ritala, P., Kraus, S., & Bouncken, R. (2016). Introduction to coopetition and innovation: Contemporary topics and future research opportunities. *International Journal of Technology Management*, 71(1–2), 1–9.

Roy, P. & Yami, S. (2009). Managing strategic innovation through coopetition. *International Journal of Entrepreneurship and Small Business*, 8(1), 61–73.

Steinicke, S., Marcus Wallenburg, C., & Schmoltzi, C. (2012). Governing for innovation in horizontal service cooperations. *Journal of Service Management*, 23(2), 279–302.

Tomlinson, P. R. & Fai, F. M. (2013). The nature of SME co-operation and innovation: A multi-scalar and multi-dimensional analysis. *International Journal of Production Economics*, 141(1), 316–326.

Tranfield, D., Denyer, D., & Smart, P. (2003). Towards a methodology for developing evidence-informed management knowledge by means of systematic review. *British Journal of Management*, 14(3), 207–222.

Tsai, W. (2002). Social structure of "coopetition" within a multiunit organization: Coordination, competition, and intraorganizational knowledge sharing. *Organization Science*, 13(2), 179–190.

Wu, J. (2014). Cooperation with competitors and product innovation: Moderatinng effects of technological capability and alliances with universities. *Industrial Marketing Management*, 43(2), 199–209.

27

Building a first-mover advantage from coopetition

André Nemeh

Introduction

Previous research highlighted the role of product innovation in sustaining firms' competitive advantage (Verona & Ravasi, 2003). A firm's strategy that accounts for how managers invest resources in new product development (NPD) initiatives has been mentioned as a factor that determines that success of NPD. However, the process by which firms manage their resources in order to have successful product launches has been minimally studied (Henard & McFadyen, 2012; Henard & Szymanski, 2001). To maintain and upgrade their resource bases, firms can proceed by using internal research and development (R&D) or by collaborating with external partners through research centers, suppliers, and competitors. While every type of relationship has its own advantages and disadvantages, collaboration with competitors or coopetition has been identified as the most challenging (Bengtsson & Kock, 2000 Das & Teng, 2000; Fernandez et al., 2014; Gnyawali & Park, 2011; Le Roy & Fernandez, 2015; Tidström, 2014). This difficulty of coopetition management stems from the paradoxical nature of coopetition. Firms need to share resources in order to increase value creation, but they must also protect the resources that constitute the source of their competitive advantage and their capacity to appropriate value from these resources (Dagnino & Padula, 2002; Ritala & Tidström, 2014).

Results of previous research on the impact of coopetition on NPD are mixed. Recently, Estrada and colleagues (2016) studied the reasons behind these mixed results and showed that firms that benefit from coopetitive NPDs have both formal knowledge sharing mechanisms (e.g., incentives to employees) and formal protection mechanisms (e.g., patents, trademarks, etc.). Both factors are related to how firms manage their resources. We believe that the different approaches of resources orchestration are a reason why some firms benefit more than others. The way firms manage their internal resources before and through coopetition is essential in determining the actual and future gains from collaboration.

Our research builds on the results of previous works and aims to understand the process of how firms maintain/build their resources in order to achieve a first-mover advantage from coopetition.

In the following sections, we review the literature on coopetition strategy and first-mover advantage before highlighting the role played by firm's resource orchestrating strategy in enabling FMA based on coopetitive NPD.

Literature review

Coopetition strategy: Motives, management, and impact

Coopetition is defined as "a paradoxical relationship that emerges when two or more rival firms cooperate in some activities, and at the same time compete with each other in other activities" (Bengtsson & Kock, 2000: 412). Research on coopetition can be separated into three groups, including its determinants, its implementation/management, and its impact and outcomes. As coopetition is a complex and multi-level phenomenon, focusing just on the process will give a myopic and incomplete vision and understanding. An understanding of rivals' motives to enter into coopetition, the resulting process of cooperative/competitive interactions, and its results and consequences will provide a complete coverage of the coopetitive relationship (Le Roy & Czakon, 2016).

Firms adopt this strategy in order to share risks/costs of R&D, to set industry standards, and to reduce time to market (Gnyawali & Park, 2009). In spite of all these positives, coopetition is a phenomenon full of tensions (Fernandez et al., 2014; Ritala et al., 2017) and the way these tensions are managed will determine the benefits of coopetition (Tidström, 2009, 2014). Existing research focuses on the sources, levels, and characteristics of tensions (Bengtsson & Kock, 2000; Fernandez et al., 2014; Raza-Ullah et al., 2014; Tidström, 2014). It proposes two methods to manage them: separation and integration. Recently, Le Roy & Fernandez (2015) proposed the coopetitive project team as an ideal way to handle these tensions by combining separation and integration principles (Fernandez, Le Roy, & Chiambaretto, in press).

With respect to coopetition benefits, the only criterion that we have to justify the effectiveness of this strategy for innovation is the increasing adoption of it by firms in high- and low-tech sectors. This indicator is insufficient to legitimize coopetition as a strategy for value creation, especially in the absence of real evidence on the relationship between coopetition and technological innovation. Different outcome variables were used to study the impacts of coopetition—including innovation type (radical or incremental)—or of the coopetition impact on innovative performance (new product introduction, speed of product introduction, etc.) (Gnyawali & Park, 2011; Park et al., 2014; Ritala & Hurmelinna-Laukkanen, 2009, 2013; Weber & Heidenreich, in press). Belderbos and colleagues (2004) showed a positive impact on innovative capacity of firms, while Nieto & Santamaría (2007) showed a negative one. Therefore, we have contradictory results on the impact of coopetition on technological innovation. These contradictory results mean that the process by which coopetition impacts innovation still needs more investigation and in-depth research.

Academia and professional media also show us that a win-win situation is not always the result of this type of collaboration and that asymmetric benefits between rival/partners may exist. In front of this situation, it is important to analyze how managers of competing firms choose to coopete and generate benefits from this paradoxical relationship. This is important since firms that don't achieve their objectives from coopetition will not just lose their contribution to the coopetitive project but sometimes will lose a whole market. In this chapter, we focus on the first-mover advantage as a coopetition outcome.

First-mover advantage: Definition, characteristics, and enablers

The first-mover advantage is defined in terms of the ability of a pioneering firm to earn positive economic profits (profits in excess of the cost of capital) (Lieberman & Montgomery, 1988).

From the previous definition, we see that in order for a firm to have a first-mover advantage, it has to (1) innovate rapidly to enter the market first, and (2) maintain this advantage.

The first part is related to the innovation speed, defined as the time elapsed between (a) the initial development (including the conception and definition of an innovation) and (b) the ultimate commercialization (which is the introduction of a new product into the marketplace) (Mansfield, 1988; Murmann, 1994; Vesey, 1991). The literature in this stream focuses on the factors that lead firms to quick innovations. This body of research distinguishes between two types. First, a firm's related factors include (a) strategic orientations (emphasis placed upon fast new product development), (b) scope-related strategic-orientation factors (the relative broadness of the project stream), and (c) individual/team factors (the presence of an influential product champion(s) and empowerment of the project team). Second, the external factors include the degree of technological uncertainty and complexity and how the firm manages its suppliers and R&D collaborations (Kessler & Chakrabarti, 1996).

The second part is related to the first-mover advantage enablers. Literature distinguishes between macro-, micro-, and firm-level FMA enablers (see Figure 27.1). At the macro level, Suarez & Lanzolla (2007) identify two environmental enablers: the pace of market evolution and pace of technological evolution. The pace of market evolution refers to the average market change, or the time elapsed between different product life cycle stages. The pace of techno-logical evolution refers to the average change in the level of technology performance, or the technology "S-curve" (Cooper & Schendel, 1976; Foster, 1986; Sahal, 1982). The authors study the impact of these two environmental enablers on the micro-level enablers, or what Lieberman and Montgomery (1988) call "isolating mechanisms." These authors distinguish among three different isolating mechanisms. The first is technology leadership, such as learning/experience effects and R&D patenting that gives a firm a technological edge over competitors (Gilbert & Newbery, 1982; Lilien & Yoon, 1990; Spence, 1977). Second, resource pre-emption is the cost advantage that arises from advanced appropriation of scarce input resources or economies of scale that are created from pre-emptive investments in the plant and equipment (Dixit, 1980;

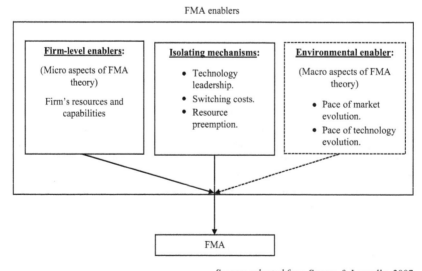

Source: adapted from Suarez & Lanzolla, 2007

Figure 27.1 First-mover advantage enablers

MacMillan, 1983; Prescott & Visscher, 1977). Third, switching costs arise from habit formation in buyers or from the installed-base effect in the presence of network effects (Carpenter & Nakamoto, 1989; Nelson, 1980; Schmalensee, 1982).

At the firm level, a firm's ability to derive FMA should be assessed "with reference to the competence and capabilities which new entrants have, relative to the competitors" (Teece et al., 1997: 529). Early followers and late entrants tend to deploy different skills and resources (Robinson et al., 1992). Some studies outline the substantial effect of a firm's history on the relationship between entry order and market performance (Carroll et al., 1996; Klepper, 2002). Research on FMA invites scholars to forge links with the resource-based view to design more sophisticated studies on the timing of market entry (Lieberman & Montgomery, 1998). This marriage between the two perspectives is based on the idea that the firm's resource base tends to influence the likelihood and timing of entry, but in ways that are complex and still poorly understood (Lieberman & Montgomery, 1998).

Resource orchestration strategy as an enabler of first-mover advantage from coopetition

High-tech industries are designated high-velocity environments. One of the coopetition virtues is accelerating the time to market (Gnyawali & Park, 2009). Therefore, coopetition is chosen to adapt to these environments. Until now, the role of coopetition in accelerating time to market was seen as equal for all partners. This meant that all partners that entered into coopetition would accelerate their time to market. Research on FMA or innovation speed (Kessler & Chakrabarti, 1996) contradicts this view and shows that competitors/partners will have different speeds of product introduction based on the external and internal factors mentioned above.

Henard & Szymanski (2001) organized the NPD activities into four broad categories: product, strategy, process, and marketplace. They indicated that one relatively under-researched area is strategy. This category is related to how firms manage and invest resources in NPD initiatives (Henard & McFadyen, 2012).

At the resource management level, Sirmon and colleagues (2011) highlight that achieving a competitive advantage entails optimally orchestrating and configuring firm resources and capabilities. Resource orchestration refers to "the comprehensive process of structuring, bundling, and leveraging the firm's resources with the purpose of creating value for customers and competitive advantages for the firm" (2011; 1392). In this regard, three mechanisms for resources orchestration are at play. First, structuring refers to the management of the firm's resource portfolio via acquisition, accumulation, or divesture. Second, bundling refers to the combining of firm resources to construct or alter capabilities. Third, leveraging refers to the application of a firm's capabilities to create value for customers and wealth for owners. This definition highlights the temporary nature of the competitive advantage in the sense that firms have to orchestrate their resources to implement strategies that help them achieve a series of temporary competitive advantages over time (Sirmon et al., 2010). The temporality of the competitive advantage relates to the velocity of the environment and the firm's life cycle stage (see Figure 27.2).

Thus, each firm has a perception of the environmental velocity that will lead to a timely evaluation at the industry level. This in turn leads the firm to set its agenda and priorities to orchestrate its resources according to this perception (McGrath et al., 1984). The time spent in developing these resources differs according to the complexity and the efforts required for their development (Pacheco-de-Almeida & Zemsky, 2007). In this regard, speed in developing resources is intrinsic and relates to multiple factors, such as corporate governance, low capital costs, and R&D intensity (Pacheco-de-Almeida et al., 2015). Therefore, each firm will manage its resources at different speeds.

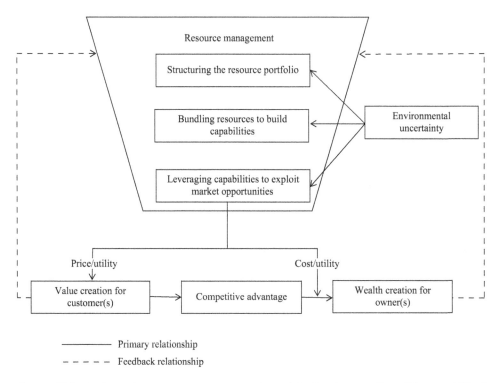

Figure 27.2 A dynamic resource management model of value creation (Sirmon, Hitt, & Ireland, 2007)

In coopetition, the way a firm manages its internal resources before and through collaboration is essential in determining the actual and future gains from such collaboration. The firm's situation will in turn determine the resource management conditions, mechanisms, and speed. Different resource orchestration approaches will lead to different levels of both formal knowledge sharing mechanisms (e.g., incentives to employees) and formal protection mechanisms (e.g., patents, trademarks, etc.). This will consequently lead to different learning speeds, different levels of protection of valuable resources (Estrada et al., 2016), and different speeds of product introduction from the coopetitive NPD project.

Firm's resources have to be ready to be bundled and combined with resources and knowledge absorbed from the coopetitive NPD to achieve the planned product introduction speed (Katila, 2002; Levin et al., 1987). Such coordination is vital in NPD projects that regroup suppliers and academia in general and in coopetitive projects since knowledge absorbed from competitors becomes increasingly obsolete with time, compared to the knowledge gained from other sources (Katila, 2002). This means that competitors' knowledge gained from coopetition has to be quickly integrated in order to benefit from it in NPD. Resource preparation benefits from competitors' knowledge and enhances formal protection mechanisms as a determinant of benefits from coopetition (Estrada et al., 2016). These protection mechanisms require time to be obtained and implemented (e.g., patents) (Manzini & Lazzarotti, 2016).

Theoretical implications and future research directions

At a theoretical level, with respect to the first-mover advantage research, the debate on how resource orchestration strategies play a vital role in determining innovation speed (Lieberman & Montgomery, 1998) remains open. Resources from acquisitions require more time to be appropriated and integrated into knowledge and competencies (Ranft, Lord, & Carolina, 2002). In this regard, Maritan & Peteraf (2011) assert that knowledge acquisition is important for innovation and the balance between acquisition and accumulation, which can be achieved through a well-conceived resource orchestration strategy. Market-oriented coopetition has to be pursued when firms have reduced technological uncertainty so they can evaluate their importance and consequently protect them. Future research can study if firms of different sizes with different resource stocks can achieve similar results using different resource orchestration strategies that challenge the positive effect of slack resources. This idea needs to be developed and compared with studies on a contingent view of slack (Lawson, 2001; Nohria & Gulati, 1996).

Moreover, the question of how to rapidly introduce products from coopetitive NPD is also posed. On one side, different resource orchestration strategies are implemented according to the speed objectives. However, in terms of accelerating innovation, coopetition is not a "magical" tool to boost the product development efforts of all the competitors involved, since only those that are ready for coopetition will obtain this advantage. Evaluating the impact of coopetition requires considering innovation speed in addition to traditional impact measurements such as innovation capacity (Gnyawali & Park, 2011; Ritala & Hurmelinna-Laukkanen, 2009, 2013) or competitive behavior (Gnyawali et al., 2006). To benefit from coopetition, firms must plan a rapid launch, diverse product applicability, or both. As Gnyawali and Park (2011) demonstrate, Sony introduced its flat screen to rapidly benefit from its internal development capability while Samsung was slower and integrated the results into a wider product portfolio, thereby gaining greater market share in the medium term.

Future research can analyze the relationship between resource orchestration approaches and FMA via a quantitative approach with a large sample. These studies could benefit from archival data (e.g., SDC platinum database) or they could be based on surveys. Data on product introduction time can be obtained from specialized databases or by extensive research in specialized press via databases such as Factiva.

We approached the relationship between coopetition and innovation speed via the lenses of the resource-based view (resource orchestration), since previous research highlighted the role of ambidexterity to achieve a competitive advantage (Tushman & O'Reilly, 1996). More precisely, firms that balance exploration and exploitation will achieve superior performance. Future research could analyze how different firm strategies balance exploration and exploitation, and organizational and human resources factors could lead to differences in terms of benefits from coopetition (Junni et al., 2013, 2015).

At a methodological level, an issue could be to go beyond the analysis of the organizational level to study the micro-foundations of resources in order to better understand the resource orchestration phenomenon. From the coopetition perspective and beyond the organizational and project team levels addressed here, industry and individual levels could be covered to clarify their impacts on coopetition outcomes.

At the managerial level, firms must choose how to manage their resources to achieve their speed objectives. Those pursuing fast product introductions must start structuring their resources earlier before entering into coopetition so that they can bundle their resources during coopetition and leverage those in terms of new products and services. This early preparation enables benefits from coopetition speed. This speed advantage is also achieved by astutely selecting the strategic activities and key technologies to produce within the firm (make, buy, or ally decision).

References

Belderbos, R., Carree, M., & Lokshin, B. (2004). Cooperative R&D and firm performance. *Research Policy*, 33(10), 1477–1492.

Bengtsson, M. & Kock, S. (2000). "Coopetition" in business Networks—to cooperate and compete simultaneously. *Industrial Marketing Management*, 29(5), 411–426.

Carpenter, G. S. & Nakamoto, K. (1989). Consumer preference formation and pioneering advantage. *Journal of Marketing Research*, 285–298.

Carroll, G. R., Bigelow, L. S., Seidel, M. D. L., & Tsai, L. B. (1996). The fates of de novo and de alio producers in the American automobile industry 1885–1981. *Strategic Management Journal*, 17(S1), 117–137.

Cooper, A. C. & Schendel, D. (1976). Strategic responses to technological threats. *Business Horizons*, 19(1), 61–69.

Dagnino, G. B. & Padula, G. (2002). Coopetition strategy: a new kind of interfirm dynamics for value creation. In *Innovative research in management, European Academy of Management (EURAM), second annual conference, Stockholm*.

Das, T. & Teng, B. (2000). A resource-based theory of strategic alliances. *Journal of Management*, 26(1), 31–61.

Dixit, A. (1980). The role of investment in entry-deterrence. *The Economic Journal*, 90(357), 95–106.

Estrada, I., Faems, D., & de Faria, P. (2016). Coopetition and product innovation performance: The role of internal knowledge sharing mechanisms and formal knowledge protection mechanisms. *Industrial Marketing Management*, 53, 56–65.

Fernandez, A.-S., Le Roy, F., & Chiambaretto, P. (in press). Implementing the right project structure to achieve coopetitive innovation projects. *Long Range Planning*.

Fernandez, A.-S., Le Roy, F., & Gnyawali, D. R. (2014). Sources and management of tension in co-opetition case evidence from telecommunications satellites manufacturing in Europe. *Industrial Marketing Management*, 43(2), 222–235.

Foster, R. N. (1986). Working the S-curve: assessing technological threats. *Research Management*, 29(4), 17–20.

Gilbert, R. J. & Newbery, D. M. (1982). Preemptive patenting and the persistence of monopoly. *The American Economic Review*, 514–526.

Gnyawali, D. R., He, J., & Madhavan, R. (2006). Impact of co-opetition on firm competitive behavior: An empirical examination. *Journal of Management*, 32(4), 507–530.

Gnyawali, D. R. & Park, B.-J. (2009). Co-opetition and technological innovation in small and medium-sized enterprises: A multilevel conceptual model. *Journal of Small Business Management*, 47(3), 308–330.

Gnyawali, D. & Park, B. (2011). Co-opetition between giants: collaboration with competitors for technological innovation. *Research Policy*, 40(5), 650–663.

Henard, D. H. & McFadyen, M. A. (2012). Resource dedication and new product performance: A resource-based view. *Journal of Product Innovation Management*, 29(2), 193–204.

Henard, D. H. & Szymanski, D. M. (2001). Why some new products are more successful than others. *Journal of Marketing Research*, 38(3), 362–375.

Junni, P., Sarala, R. M., Taras, V., & Tarba, S. Y. (2013). Organizational ambidexterity and performance: A meta-analysis. *The Academy of Management Perspectives*, 27(4), 299–312.

Junni, P., Sarala, R. M., Tarba, S. Y., Liu, Y., & Cooper, C. L. (2015). Guest editors' introduction: The role of human resources and organizational factors in ambidexterity. *Human Resource Management*, 54(S1).

Katila, R. (2002). New product search over time: past ideas in their prime? *Academy of Management Journal*, 45(5), 995–1010.

Kessler, E. H. & Chakrabarti, A. K. (1996). Innovation speed: A conceptual model of context, antecedents, and outcomes. *Academy of Management Review*, 21(4), 1143–1191.

Klepper, S. (2002). The capabilities of new firms and the evolution of the US automobile industry. *Industrial and Corporate Change*, 11(4), 645–666.

Lawson, M. B. (2001). In praise of slack: Time is of the essence. *The Academy of Management Executive*, 15(3), 125–135.

Le Roy, F. & Czakon, W. (2016). Managing coopetition: the missing link between strategy and performance. *Industrial Marketing Management*, 53, 3–6.

Le Roy, F. & Fernandez, A. S. (2015). Managing coopetitive tensions at the working-group level: The rise of the coopetitive project team. *British Journal of Management*, 26(4), 671–688.

Levin, R. C., Klevorick, A. K., Nelson, R. R., Winter, S. G., Gilbert, R., & Griliches, Z. (1987). Appropriating the returns from industrial research and development. *Brookings Papers on Economic Activity*, 1987(3), 783–831.

Lieberman, M. B. & Montgomery, D. B. (1988). First-mover advantages. *Strategic Management Journal*, 9(S1), 41–58.

Lieberman, M. B. & Montgomery, D. B. (1998). First-mover (dis)advantages: Retrospective and link with the resource-based view. *Strategic Management Journal*, 19(12), 1111–1125.

Lilien, G. L. & Yoon, E. (1990). The timing of competitive market entry: An exploratory study of new industrial products. *Management Science*, 36(5), 568–585.

MacMillan, I. C. (1983). Preemptive strategies. *Journal of Business Strategy*, 4(2), 16–26.

Mansfield, E. (1988). The speed and cost of industrial innovation in Japan and the United States: External vs. internal technology. *Management Science*, 34(10), 1157–1168.

Manzini, R. & Lazzarotti, V. (2016). Intellectual property protection mechanisms in collaborative new product development. *R&D Management*, 46(S2), 579–595.

Maritan, C. A. & Peteraf, M. A. (2011). Invited editorial: Building a bridge between resource acquisition and resource accumulation. *Journal of Management*, 37(5), 1374–1389.

McGrath, J. E., Kelly, J. R., & Machatka, D. E. (1984). The social psychology of time: Entrainment of behavior in social and organizational settings. *Applied Social Psychology Annual*.

Murmann, P. A. (1994). Expected development time reductions in the German mechanical engineering industry. *Journal of Product Innovation Management*, 11(3), 236–252.

Nelson, P. (1980). Comments on "The Economics of Consumer Information Acquisition". *The Journal of Business*, 53(3), S163–S165.

Nieto, M. J. & Santamaría, L. (2007). The importance of diverse collaborative networks for the novelty of product innovation. *Technovation*, 27(6), 367–377.

Nohria, N. & Gulati, R. (1996). Is slack good or bad for innovation? *Academy of Management Journal*, 39(5), 1245–1264.

Pacheco-de-Almeida, G. & Zemsky, P. (2007). The timing of resource development and sustainable competitive advantage. *Management Science*, 53(4), 651–666.

Pacheco-de-Almeida, G., Hawk, A., & Yeung, B. (2015). The right speed and its value. *Strategic Management Journal*, 36(2), 159–176.

Park, B. J., Srivastava, M. K., & Gnyawali, D. R. (2014). Impact of coopetition in the alliance portfolio and coopetition experience on firm innovation. *Technology Analysis & Strategic Management*, 26(8), 893–907.

Prescott, E. C. & Visscher, M. (1977). Sequential location among firms with foresight. *The Bell Journal of Economics*, 378–393.

Ranft, A. L. & Lord, M. D. (2002). Acquiring new technologies and capabilities: A grounded model of acquisition implementation. *Organization Science*, 13(4), 420–441.

Raza-Ullah, T., Bengtsson, M., & Kock, S. (2014). The coopetition paradox and tension in coopetition at multiple levels. *Industrial Marketing Management*, 43(2), 189–198.

Ritala, P. & Hurmelinna-Laukkanen, P. (2009). What's in it for me? Creating and appropriating value in innovation-related coopetition. *Technovation*, 29(12), 819–828.

Ritala, P. & Hurmelinna-Laukkanen, P. (2013). Incremental and radical innovation in coopetition—The role of absorptive capacity and appropriability. *Journal of Product Innovation Management*, 30(1), 154–169.

Ritala, P. & Tidström, A. (2014). Untangling the value-creation and value-appropriation elements of coopetition strategy: A longitudinal analysis on the firm and relational levels. *Scandinavian Journal of Management*, 30(4), 498–515.

Ritala, P., Huizingh, E., Almpanopoulou, A., & Wijbenga, P. (2017). Tensions in R&D networks: Implications for knowledge search and integration. *Technological Forecasting and Social Change*, 120, 311–322.

Robinson, W. T., Fornell, C., & Sullivan, M. (1992). Are market pioneers intrinsically stronger than later entrants? *Strategic Management Journal*, 13(8), 609–624.

Sahal, D. (1982). *The Transfer and Utilization of Technical knowledge*. New York: Free Press.

Schmalensee, R. (1982). Product differentiation advantages of pioneering brands. *The American Economic Review*, 72(3), 349–365.

Sirmon, D. G., Hitt, M. A., & Ireland, R. D. (2007). Managing firm resources in dynamic environments to create value: Looking inside the black box. *Academy of Management Review*, 32(1), 273–292.

Sirmon, D. G., Hitt, M. A., Arregle, J. L., & Campbell, J. T. (2010). The dynamic interplay of capability strengths and weaknesses: investigating the bases of temporary competitive advantage. *Strategic Management Journal*, 31(13), 1386–1409.

Sirmon, D. G., Hitt, M. A., Ireland, R. D., & Gilbert, B. A. (2011). Resource orchestration to create competitive advantage: Breadth, depth, and life cycle effects. *Journal of Management*, 37(5), 1390–1412.

Spence, A. M. (1977). Entry, capacity, investment and oligopolistic pricing. *The Bell Journal of Economics*, 534–544.

Suarez, F. F. & Lanzolla, G. (2007). The role of environmental dynamics in building a first mover advantage theory. *Academy of Management Review*, 32(2), 377–392.

Teece, D. J., Pisano, G., & Shuen, A. (1997). Dynamic capabilities and strategic management. *Strategic Management Journal*, 509–533.

Tidström, A. (2009). Causes of conflict in intercompetitor cooperation. *Journal of Business & Industrial Marketing*, 24(7), 506–518.

Tidström, A. (2014) Managing tensions in coopetition. *Industrial Marketing Management*, 43(2), 1–11.

Tushman, M. L. & O'Reilly III, C. A. (1996). Ambidextrous organizations: Managing evolutionary and revolutionary change. *California Management Review*, 38(4), 8–29.

Verona, G. & Ravasi, D. (2003). Unbundling dynamic capabilities: an exploratory study of continuous product innovation. *Industrial and Corporate Change*, 12(3), 577–606.

Vesey, J. T. (1991). The new competitors: they think in terms of "speed-to-market". *The Executive*, 5(2), 23–33.

Weber, B. & Heidenreich, S. (in press). When and with whom to cooperate? Investigating effects of cooperation stage and type on innovation capabilities and success. *Long Range Planning*.

28

Technology-based coopetition and intellectual property management

Marcus Holgersson

Introduction

Coopetition, i.e., collaboration between competitors, is challenging but potentially rewarding for the involved parties (Fernandez et al., 2014; Gnyawali & Park, 2011). In technology-based coopetition, competitors collaborate in order to advance technological development and/or to share innovation investments. *Technology-based coopetition* is here more specifically defined as a relationship between two or more actors that to some degree collaborate in inventing and developing technology, while competing on the related product and service markets. It is driven by factors such as shorter product life cycles, the convergence of technologies, and increasing innovation investments (Gnyawali & Park, 2009).

Apart from regulatory challenges, such as antitrust laws and regulations (Jorde & Teece, 1990), technology-based coopetition is related to several managerial challenges, such as technological risks, not-invented-here syndromes, opportunism, and more generally by tensions between collaboration and competition (Fernandez et al., 2014). These tensions have received much attention by extant research on coopetition (Cassiman et al., 2009; Ritala & Hurmelinna-Laukkanen, 2013). This literature has proposed to organizationally separate collaboration from competition within coopetition actors, since the logics of collaboration and competition are difficult to combine (Bengtsson & Kock, 2000).

One area of management that is particularly relevant in technology-based coopetition is intellectual property (IP) management. The balance between protecting and sharing technology, knowledge, and IP needs to be properly managed in order to succeed with coopetition (Ritala & Hurmelinna-Laukkanen, 2013), and in contrast to organizationally separating the logics of collaboration and competition, IP management can deal with collaboration and competition simultaneously.

This chapter introduces IP management in technology-based coopetition. It includes a general description of the role for IP management in competition and collaboration, as well as a framework for classifying IP relevant to coopetition. A key point is that the sharing of knowledge, technology, and IP in coopetition needs to be controlled. Controlled sharing, in turn, is accomplished by the use of intellectual property rights (IPRs) with associated licenses and license clauses.

The empirical examples relate to a specific type of coopetition that is identified and defined in the chapter, namely post-divestiture coopetition. Such coopetition may result from divestitures (divestments) and mergers and acquisitions (M&A) processes—for example, when a business unit of one large firm is sold to a competing large firm—while technological relationships are kept between the former owner and the business unit. Thus, the coopetition is a result of a disintegration process, where the disintegrated parties (competitors) keep collaborating to develop, maintain, and/or use several shared technologies (including technological platforms) or other resources or activities. More specifically, the chapter describes the case of Volvo Cars being divested from Ford Motor Company and acquired by Geely Holding Group, and the case of Saab Automobile being divested from General Motors (GM) and acquired by Spyker Cars. In both these cases the management of IP played significant roles.

IP management in competition and collaboration

IPRs are often viewed as means for decreasing competition and thereby for improving competitive advantage. IPRs include, for example, patents, copyrights, design rights, trademarks, and trade secret rights, and they make up "a family of temporary, restricted, and transferable or licensable rights to exclude others from commercializing someone's intellectual or intangible creations or inventions under certain conditions" (Granstrand & Holgersson, 2015). Since the legal role of the IPRs is to exclude others from commercializing the related propertized intellectual resources—i.e., the related IP—IPRs are often seen as tools for increasing monopolistic power and for avoiding competition on the market. Society's motives for having IPR systems vary across the different types of IPRs, but typically relate to incentivizing the creation and distribution of intellectual creations—such as technical inventions, music, art, and literature—and providing protection for creators and consumers.

A specific and especially important type of IPR in technology-based businesses is the patent. For a patent to be granted the underlying invention needs to be novel, sufficiently inventive, and useful/technically applicable. In exchange for the patent right the patentee provides financial payments to the national patent offices where patent protection is wanted as well as a detailed description of the invention that is published. With a patent, the inventor has the right to initiate litigation against infringers (i.e., an indirect right to exclude others from using its invention), and by that right limit/delay imitations of the patented invention. Patents are therefore important strategic tools for appropriating value from innovations, including new products, services, and processes (Granstrand, 1999).

Patents can typically last up to twenty years, and the relevant time window for technology-related IP management consequently consists of at least forty years. At each point in time IP management needs to consider up to twenty-year-old patents as well as new patents that may stay alive up to twenty years into the future. An alternative to patenting is the use of trade secrets (Arundel, 2001; Holgersson & Wallin, 2017). These may leak quickly but they may also be kept for a very long time (consider, for example, the recipe for Coca-Cola). Copyrights and trademarks may also last longer than twenty years, meaning that the time window for IP management more generally may extend well beyond forty years. This has implications for coopetition, since IPRs from times of pure competition or collaboration still need to be considered if the relationship transforms into coopetition.

Contrary to common belief, knowledge sharing is an important function of the patent system. As described above, the patentee needs to provide a detailed description of the invention when applying for a patent. This description is then published, so that everyone can learn from it, contributing to cumulative knowledge development over time. The collaborative function of patents extend beyond the mere publications, however. Much recent research has identified the role of patents for enabling R&D collaborations (Alexy et al., 2009; Granstrand & Holgersson, 2014; Hagedoorn & Zobel, 2015). Actually, research has shown that it is more important for firms to protect their technology with patents when engaged in R&D collaborations, or in other terms when involved in various forms of open innovation, than when employing a fully integrated strategy. This indicates that in order for firms to be willing to share their technologies with collaborators, they first want to be somewhat protected through patents (Holgersson & Granstrand, 2017). When sharing technologies with collaborators, firms expose themselves to opportunistic threats, which to some degree can be mitigated by protecting the technologies with patents, and by clearly outlining how the technologies may be used by collaborators in the related (license) contracts.

Coopetition combines the logics of collaboration and competition, and collaboration between competitors is related to even larger concerns about opportunism, as compared to collaboration between non-competitors (Ritala & Hurmelinna-Laukkanen, 2009). This may hamper the use of coopetition, limiting the related benefits. Therefore, IP management that balances and combines the logics of competition and collaboration has an important role to play in coopetition.

Relevant IP in coopetition

When managing IP in coopetition, several different categories of IP need to be considered. Four important categories, as described by Granstrand and Holgersson (2014), are outlined below (see Figure 28.1). These categories of IP (or technology or knowledge more generally) are relevant also in purely collaborative relationships, but they are even more important to properly manage in coopetition due to the larger risks for and consequences of opportunistic actions.

Imagine a simple case with two parties that compete on a product and/or service market. They are now about to start collaborating in the development of a technology in order to share innovation investments and/or advance technological developments in a faster/better way (i.e., they become technology-based coopetitors). When initiating the collaboration, both parties may have available IP that is relevant for the collaboration to build upon. This category of IP is called *background IP*, and initially they have to agree upon how each party's background IP can be used by the other party. The second category of IP is called *foreground IP*. This includes IP that is in some sense jointly developed as part of the collaboration. The parties need to agree upon how the foreground IP can be used by the different parties. For example, they might decide that one of them is allowed to commercialize products based on the IP in some specific markets while the other is allowed to commercialize products based on the IP in all other markets (e.g., Bez et al., 2016), or they might agree that both parties are allowed to use all foreground IP for any purposes.

The third category of IP is called *sideground IP* and includes IP that is relevant for the collaboration but developed outside the collaboration by one of the parties while the collaboration is still ongoing. The fourth category of IP is called *postground IP* and includes IP that is relevant for the collaboration but developed after the collaboration has ended by one of the parties.

Sideground and postground IP are closely related to the concept of knowledge/technology spillovers (Arora et al., 2016; Jaffe, 1986). One competitor may, for example, learn about the other competitor's background IP from their joint collaboration, and develop complements or substitutes to the technologies, products, and/or services of its competitor. Consequently, there is a tension for each competitor between, on the one hand, enabling foreground IP and value-enhancing sideground and postground IP (from both competitors) through a joint collaboration, and, on the other hand, risking increased competition due to substitute technologies, products, and/or services from the competitor.

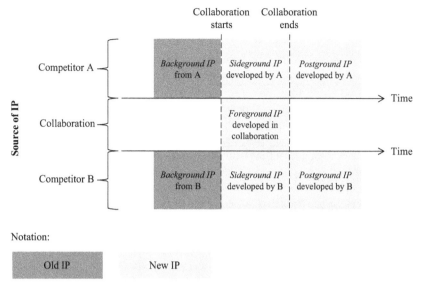

Source: Adapted from Granstrand & Holgersson, 2014

Figure 28.1   IP categories relevant for coopetition

Sideground and postground IP may, for example, include complementary components or improvements of jointly developed technologies. It is then important for coopetitors to ensure accessibility to such sideground and postground IP developed by the other party, since the future value and relative competitiveness of their background and foreground IP might otherwise be severely limited, and the other party may enjoy a strengthened competitive position due to its exclusive position in improvements, complements, and/or substitutes.

Substitutes turned out to play a major role in a case presented by Granstrand and Holgersson (2014), involving a small firm with strong capabilities in research and development (R&D) and a large firm with a strong position in complementary assets (Teece, 1986), including production and marketing. In such a setup, in which the small firm is dependent upon the capabilities of its partner for commercialization, the large firm can learn from the small R&D firm and the development of foreground IP, and develop substitutes to it. In the end, the large firm can choose to commercialize its own substitute sideground IP instead of the joint foreground IP, and in that way appropriate more value, while the small firm is left without commercialization opportunities.[1] Challenges like these may be especially severe for small firms in coopetition with large firms (Alvarez & Barney, 2001), or in other types of relationships with unbalanced bargaining power.

The next section will provide an introduction to how license agreements can be set up to mitigate these kinds of tensions. By structuring the IP portfolio according to the different types of IP above, and matching it with different types of licenses, the logics of collaboration and competition can be combined to enable well-functioning coopetition, enabling access to IP while at the same time limiting and establishing boundaries for the use of it.[2]

License contracting in technology-based coopetition

When two or more competitors start to collaborate, the background and foreground IP is related to a set of available and future IPRs, respectively, with ownership distributed across the coopetitors. Licenses are required to give coopetitors access to the foreground IP and the required background IP, and the license clauses stipulate how, where, and when each actor can commercially use the IPRs of the other(s). Consequently, proprietary technologies can be protected with patents or other IPRs while simultaneously being shared with partners, mixing open and closed innovation strategies (Chesbrough, 2003; Holgersson & Granstrand, 2017) and managing the tension between collaboration and competition.

Clever licensing can be used to turn the risks and threats related to exposing background IP to competitors into an opportunity. Different license clauses can be combined to obtain a good balance between collaboration in technology development and competition on product and service markets within the technology-based coopetitive relationship. *Field-of-use clauses* can be used to specify for which fields of use a specific technology or other type of IP can be used by the licensee (the actor who licenses from the IP owner). For example, two coopetitors within the automotive industry may agree that both of them are free to use the foreground IP from a project on electric vehicles (EVs) in any type of vehicle, including internal combustion engine (ICE) or hybrid vehicles, but that the background IP of each party can only be used specifically in EVs by the other party. In that way each party avoids its background IP ending up in all vehicles produced by the other party, which would have led to reduced differentiation and increased competition on the ICE market. Thus, the agreement improves the innovativeness of the coopetitors within the EV business, while allowing for competition on the EV market. Similarly, the license contracts can specify on which *geographic markets* the licensee can use the licensed IP, during which *time period* this right is valid, and whether or not the licensee has the *exclusive right* in various fields of use and/or geographic markets.

The license agreements may also include other types of clauses, such as change-of-technology clauses and change-of-control clauses. *Change-of-technology clauses* relate to changes in the object of the license (i.e., the licensed IP). These include *assign-back clauses*, which stipulate "that the licensee must transfer ownership of any improvements it makes to the licensed technology back to the licensor," *grant-back clauses*, which stipulate "that the licensee must license any improvements it makes to the licensed technology back to the licensor," and *grant-forward clauses*, which stipulate "that the licensor must offer the licensee a license on any improvements of the licensed technology made by the licensor" (Granstrand & Holgersson, 2014: 23). These types of clauses are especially useful for dealing with sideground and postground IP, reducing the risks associated with these, as discussed above. In the case with the EV project above, adding grant-back and grant-forward clauses to the agreement may, for example, ensure that postground IP related to improvements of the foreground technologies developed in the collaboration will be accessible for both parties.

Change-of-control clauses relate to changes in the subject of the license (i.e., the licensee), and stipulate "that the licensor has the right to terminate the license agreement in case of a change of ownership of the licensee" (Granstrand & Holgersson, 2014). These are useful for a party to ensure that IP that is licensed to a coopetitor does not eventually end up in the hands of a third party through an acquisition of the coopetitor, potentially increasing competition.

Finally, *up-front royalty payments* and/or *termination clauses* can be designed to incentivize the commercialization of foreground IP rather than sideground or postground substitutes (Granstrand & Holgersson, 2014). *Royalties* and payment schemes (including up-front and running royalties) are more generally included to compensate for possible imbalances between the different coopetitors with regards to the value of background IP brought into the collaboration and/or with regards to the amount of investments the different parties make to contribute to foreground IP. Antitrust issues, especially relating to illegal market division, need to be considered when making all of the above agreements.

Coopetition in M&As and divestitures: Post-divestiture coopetition

One type of coopetition that to date has received limited attention relates to M&A and divestiture processes. This type of *post-divestiture coopetition* includes a selling firm that has divested a business unit (BU) and sold it to an acquiring firm. The relationship consists of competitive elements between the selling firm and the acquirer (including the acquired BU) as well as of collaborative elements connected to interdependences between the BU and the remaining businesses in the selling firm.

Consider a firm consisting of several business units, in between which there are interdependences that may, for example, include joint supplier agreements, a shared technology base/platform, and/or joint distribution channels. If that firm would sell one of its business units to a competing firm, that focal business unit (BU) would typically remain interdependent and in collaboration with the other business units within the selling firm, at least throughout a transition period, while at the same time becoming part of a competing business. This process is illustrated in Figure 28.2.

The requirements for an M&A and divestiture process to lead to post-divestiture coopetition are: (1) that there is collaboration between the selling firm and the BU, typically due to complementarities between the activities and/or resources of the BU and the remaining businesses in the selling firm, including background IP in the selling firm that the BU is dependent upon, and vice versa; and (2) that the selling firm is competing with the acquirer and/or with the BU after the transaction stage, typically with substitutes on product and/or service markets. After the transaction, the selling firm and the BU keeps collaborating due to interdependencies in background IP—for example, leading to improvements of a shared technology, i.e., leading to foreground IP.

The coopetition stage may eventually move back to a pure competition stage—for example, if the BU changes to a technological platform that is independent of the selling firm. However, the element of collaboration may also increase over time, essentially extending the stage of coopetition in time—for example, if the shared technology platform of the selling firm and the BU is increasingly used and improved throughout other businesses of the acquirer after integrating the BU.

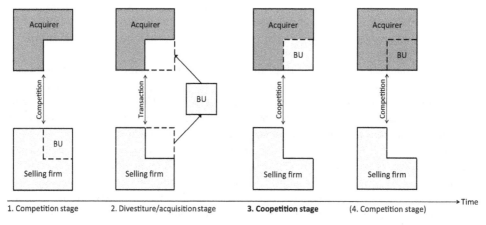

Figure 28.2 Development of post-divestiture coopetition in the divestiture process of a business unit (BU) from a selling firm to a competing acquirer (same shade of gray indicates complementary resources and/or activities)

Cases from the automotive industry

The case of Ford divesting Volvo Cars and selling it to Geely in 2010 can illustrate the development of post-divestiture coopetition. IP management was then especially challenging, and important, due to the large technological overlaps and interdependences across business units.

Around 2008/2009, Ford initiated the divestiture process of Volvo and eventually sold it to Geely. At the time of transaction, all of Volvo's cars were based on technologies and platforms that were shared with other car models within the Ford group. In the transaction stage, i.e., when the agreements surrounding the deal were to be created, the parties needed first to agree to which unit (Volvo or Ford) that each IPR was to be kept/transferred in connection to the transaction, and, second, to agree how each IPR could be used by the other party. In other terms, the parties needed to disassemble the portfolio of background IP to ensure that both Volvo's and Ford's businesses could continue after the transaction (Granstrand & Holgersson, 2013). Such portfolios may consist of up to twenty-year-old patents, as argued above (and even older IPRs of other types), making it a challenging task to disassemble them, as illustrated by the following quote:

> An external lawyer said that she had never seen anything like this [in terms of the number and comprehensiveness of IP contracts] ... We had busloads of consultants and lawyers coming here each week to handle the separation.
>
> *(Paul Welander, Senior Vice President, Volvo Cars)*

At the center of this process were considerations of how to collaborate in the continued use of the shared technologies and platforms (background IP), how to make and deal with improvements of these (foreground IP), and how and where to compete with products based on the shared technologies and platforms.

After the transaction, Volvo developed new technologies and platforms that were independent of Ford's technologies, meaning that the interdependences and collaborative elements of the coopetition between Ford and Volvo decreased over time. As Volvo's product lines kept undergoing generation shifts, the element of collaboration kept decreasing as the background and foreground IP became obsolete. Roughly a decade after the divestiture, all of Volvo's product lines were based on independent platforms, moving the relationship from a stage of coopetition to a purely competitive stage, as illustrated in Figure 28.2. The length of the coopetition stage is thus related to the frequency of product, service, or process generation shifts, to which degree new generations build on previous ones, and the remaining lifetime of the related IPRs.

The development of post-divestiture coopetition does not always start with a stage of competition between the selling firm and the acquirer (cf. stage 1 in Figure 28.2). The coopetition may result from competition between the selling firm and the BU, while the other business units of the acquirer do not compete with the selling firm. The case of GM divesting Saab and selling it to Spyker can illustrate this, again also illustrating the important role of IP management.

As a result of the financial crisis in 2008 and the subsequent downturn on the automotive market, GM divested Saab and sold it to Spyker in 2010. Spyker is a Dutch sports car manufacturer and not really a competitor to GM before acquiring Saab. The deal included supplier agreements and licenses to GM technologies (background IP), which Saab needed to commercialize its cars. Saab had just introduced the new 2010 Saab 9–5, which was built on the Epsilon II platform, which in turn was shared with other GM models. The relationship thus included elements of collaboration in supply and technologies and elements of competition on product markets.

In this case, change-of-control clauses played an important role for how GM controlled and limited the competition. Spyker wanted the Chinese firms Pang Da and Youngman to invest in Saab in order to strengthen its finances and improve its access to the Chinese market. However, the agreements between GM and Saab included change-of-control clauses that gave GM the right to cancel them if a sufficient share of Saab's ownership changed, and GM expressed its intention to execute this right given the risk for increased competition on the Chinese market if Saab would come under Chinese ownership:

> GM would not be able to support a change in the ownership of Saab which could negatively impact GM's existing relationships in China or otherwise adversely affect GM's interests worldwide.
>
> *(James Cain, Spokesman, GM)*

Saab and Spyker were essentially caught in a catch-22. Additional financing was needed to continue the operations, while such financing would lead to the termination of the necessary agreements that gave Saab access to GM's background IP, in turn stopping operations. This situation eventually became too challenging, and Saab filed for bankruptcy in late 2011.

The cases of Volvo and Saab exemplify how IP management is necessary in post-divestiture and technology-based coopetition to enable collaboration in and access to background and foreground IP that is distributed across coopetitors. The cases also exemplify how IP management can be used by coopetitors to effectively control and limit competition. Thus, IP management provides tools for combining collaboration and competition in coopetition.

Conclusions and avenues for future research

This chapter has hopefully contributed to a nuanced view of IP in coopetition. Intuition often says that IP mainly deals with protection and proprietary strategies, but this chapter shows that such protection is also an enabler of collaboration. When controlling competitive threats through IP management, firms may be more open to collaborating with their competitors. Thus, IP management may combine the logics of collaboration and competition, which contrasts the previous coopetition literature, in which a separation between these logics has been proposed (e.g., Bengtsson & Kock, 2000). There are several avenues for future research, and a few of these follow below.

First, future research should further the analysis of how IP management and contracting, including different license clauses, can be used to combine the logics of collaboration and competition. Although the cases in this chapter basically illustrate dyads, IP management can also facilitate coopetition between large numbers of firms, for example, through standard-setting and licensing regulations (e.g., Holgersson et al., 2018). Again, this is an area for additional research, since formal contracting is likely to become more important when the number of coopetitors increases.

Second, social relationships and trust may play an important role for managing, controlling, and sharing IP, technology, and knowledge in coopetition. Explicit contracting is incomplete (Grossman & Hart, 1986), and it should be complemented with implicit contracting through social relationships, norms, and trust to fully function. This may be especially challenging when the partners are competitors. The use and benefits of implicit contracting of knowledge, technology, and IP in coopetition, and its interaction with explicit contracting, therefore need to be better understood.

Third, both explicit and implicit contracting relate to the framework of relevant IP in coopetition in Figure 28.1. This framework can be broadened to include not only IP, but also technology and knowledge more generally. Analyzing coopetition with this model is useful, and it raises a number of questions for coopetition research more generally. How much of background knowledge and IP should be included in a collaboration, and how can agreements and organizational set-ups help to control it? How do pure collaborative relationships aimed at enhancing joint development of foreground knowledge/IP need to be adapted when the collaborators are also competitors? What are the risks with knowledge spillovers and sideground/postground IP, and how can the risks be turned into opportunities?

Fourth, the chapter has introduced the concept of post-divestiture coopetition. As M&As and divestitures increase in both frequency and size (Carlton & Perloff, 2005), post-divestiture coopetition becomes increasingly common and important for firms to manage, not least in industries where different business units build on shared technology platforms. Extant coopetition research has, if at all, mainly considered M&As and divestitures as consequences of and alternatives to coopetition (e.g., Dowling et al., 1996). This chapter identifies M&As and divestitures also as causes of coopetition. Post-divestiture coopetition is often especially complex, due to the close interdependences between the coopetitors. As such, it deserves more attention, both in its own right and as an extreme case for understanding other types of coopetition.

Consequently, the coopetition research area may have much to learn from, and teach to, the research areas of IP management and divestitures and M&As. Needless to say, research is often highly competitive. These three research areas, however, have much to gain from some coopetition.

Notes

1   In fact, this logic may turn a purely collaborative relationship into coopetition and eventually pure competition between two former collaborators competing with substitute foreground and sideground IP.
2   Typically, direct joint ownership of IPRs is not recommended, for various reasons (Granstrand & Holgersson, 2013). If the foreground IP should be jointly owned by the coopetitors they may set up an IP-holding joint venture that takes full ownership to the IP, while the holding company is jointly owned by the coopetitors. More commonly, however, collaborators and coopetitors use license contracting to ensure accessibility to IP for the involved parties, and this is in focus here.

References

Alexy, O., Criscuolo, P., & Salter, A. (2009). Does IP strategy have to cripple open innovation? *MIT Sloan Management Review*, 51(1), 71–77.

Alvarez, S. A. & Barney, J. B. (2001). How entrepreneurial firms can benefit from alliances with large partners. *The Academy of Management Executive*, 15(1), 139–148.

Arora, A., Athreye, S., & Huang, C. (2016). The paradox of openness revisited: Collaborative innovation and patenting by UK innovators. *Research Policy*, 45(7), 1352–1361.

Arundel, A. (2001). The relative effectiveness of patents and secrecy for appropriation. *Research Policy*, 30(4), 611–624.

Bengtsson, M. & Kock, S. (2000). "Coopetition" in business networks—to cooperate and compete simultaneously. *Industrial Marketing Management*, 29(5), 411–426.

Bez, M., Le Roy, F., Gnyawali, D. R., & Dameron, S. (2016). *Open Innovation between competitors: A 100 billion dollars case study in the pharmaceutical industry*. Paper presented at the 3rd World Open Innovation Conference, Barcelona, Spain.

Carlton, D. W. & Perloff, J. M. (2005). *Modern Industrial Organization* (4th ed.). Boston: Pearson Education.

Cassiman, B., Di Guardo, M. C., & Valentini, G. (2009). Organising R&D projects to profit from innovation: Insights from co-opetition. *Long Range Planning*, 42(2), 216–233.

Chesbrough, H. W. (2003). *Open Innovation: The New Imperative for Creating and Profiting from Technology*. Boston, MA: Harvard Business School Press.

Dowling, M. J., Roering, W. D., Carlin, B. A., & Wisnieski, J. (1996). Multifaceted relationships under coopetition. *Journal of Management Inquiry*, 5(2), 155–167.

Fernandez, A.-S., Le Roy, F., & Gnyawali, D. R. (2014). Sources and management of tension in co-opetition case evidence from telecommunications satellites manufacturing in Europe. *Industrial Marketing Management*, 43(2), 222–235.

Gnyawali, D. R. & Park, B.-J. (2009). Co-opetition and technological innovation in small and medium-sized enterprises: A multilevel conceptual model. *Journal of Small Business Management*, 47(3), 308–330.

Gnyawali, D. R. & Park, B.-J. (2011). Co-opetition between giants: Collaboration with competitors for technological innovation. *Research Policy*, 40(5), 650–663.

Granstrand, O. (1999). *The Economics and Management of Intellectual Property: Towards Intellectual Capitalism*. Cheltenham: Edward Elgar Publishing.

Granstrand, O. & Holgersson, M. (2013). Managing the intellectual property disassembly problem. *California Management Review*, 55(4), 184–210.

Granstrand, O. & Holgersson, M. (2014). The challenge of closing open innovation: The intellectual property disassembly problem. *Research-Technology Management*, 57(5), 19–25.

Granstrand, O. & Holgersson, M. (2015). *Intellectual Property: The Wiley-Blackwell Encyclopedia of Consumption and Consumer Studies*, New York: Wiley.

Grossman, S. J. & Hart, O. D. (1986). The costs and benefits of ownership: A theory of vertical and lateral integration. *Journal of Political Economy*, 94(4), 691–719.

Hagedoorn, J. & Zobel, A.-K. (2015). The role of contracts and intellectual property rights in open innovation. *Technology Analysis & Strategic Management*, 27(9), 1050–1067.

Holgersson, M. & Granstrand, O. (2017). Patenting motives, technology strategies, and open innovation. *Management Decision*, 55(6), 1265–1284.

Holgersson, M. & Wallin, M. W. (2017). The patent management trichotomy: Patenting, publishing, and secrecy. *Management Decision*, 55(6), 1087–1099.

Holgersson, M., Granstrand, O., & Bogers, M. (2018). The evolution of intellectual property strategy in innovation ecosystems: Uncovering complementary and substitute appropriability regimes. *Long Range Planning*, 51(2), 303–319.

Jaffe, A. B. (1986). Technological opportunity and spillovers of R&D: Evidence from firms' patents, profits and market value. *American Economic Review*, 76(5), 984–999.

Jorde, T. M. & Teece, D. J. (1990). Innovation and Cooperation: Implications for competition and Antitrust. *Journal of Economic Perspectives*, 4(3), 75–96.

Ritala, P. & Hurmelinna-Laukkanen, P. (2009). What's in it for me? Creating and appropriating value in innovation-related coopetition. *Technovation*, 29(12), 819–828.

Ritala, P. & Hurmelinna-Laukkanen, P. (2013). Incremental and radical innovation in coopetition—the role of absorptive capacity and appropriability. *Journal of Product Innovation Management*, 30(1), 154–169.

Teece, D. J. (1986). Profiting from technological innovation: Implications for integration, collaboration, licensing and public policy. *Research Policy*, 15(6), 285–305.

29
Coopetition and market performance

Paavo Ritala

Introduction

Coopetition can be viewed as a specific type of relational logic beyond pure competition or collaboration, as it can combine the benefits of both (Chen & Miller, 2015; Lado et al., 1997). In this regard, coopetition has been portrayed as a paradoxical relational strategy (e.g., Gnyawali et al., 2016; Raza-Ullah et al., 2014), as, at first sight, collaborating with competitors seems to contradict the idea of the traditional competitive strategy. However, early coopetition literature, as well as a wealth of examples from business practice, established that coopetition can provide benefits for the focal firm, as well as for its coopetitive partners. Thus, at best, a coopetition strategy allows firms to search for improved market performance outcomes not available through a competitive or collaborative strategy only. The reason is that markets are often evolving and growing and, often, there are many opportunities for competitors to collaborate in different parts of the value chain for efficiency and effectiveness reasons (for a discussion, see, e.g., Walley, 2007).

Market performance benefits via coopetition can be achieved by different means. For instance, some firms utilize coopetition to share resources and risks in research and development (R&D), manufacturing, or marketing (Choi et al., 2010; Gnyawali & Park, 2011; Ritala et al., 2017), therefore lowering the costs of the actors involved. Furthermore, some firms have been shown to utilize coopetition-based strategies and business models for global, scalable growth, as in the well-documented case of Amazon.com (Ritala et al., 2014). Finally, coopetition is often used for fighting over market shares, with different coalitions among competitors going head-to-head over customers, as in the case of global airline alliances (Chiambarretto et al., 2016).

This chapter provides an integrative review of the existing evidence for coopetition and market performance and provides insights into key mechanisms and contingencies, as well as practical examples. Here, the examination is delimited to the focal firm level, that is, how an individual firm can pursue improved market performance by collaborating with competitors. This question is fundamental for a firm's coopetition strategy, and the aim of this chapter is to provide a useful and accessible outlook on the field in this regard.

Markets, performance, and coopetition

Market performance has been defined as a firm's economic outcomes, relative to its competitors (Delaney & Huselid, 1996). To better understand what market performance means for coopetition strategy, several important points need to be discussed.

First, we need to define *markets* (the context within which performance is discussed), as well as *competitors* (the actors that compete over performance differentials in these markets). For the current analysis, markets refer to the overall products, services, institutions, and actors with shared features and, typically, a group of competitors has common features (Chen, 1996). To become successful in such markets, firm performance should ultimately be examined in a relative sense, against other *horizontal* market players, that is, competitors. However, industry and market boundaries are getting increasingly blurry and dynamic (Storbacka & Nenonen, 2011; Vargo & Lusch, 2011), which makes such assessment sometimes difficult, if not impossible. Therefore, for the purposes of this chapter, market performance is examined from the firm perspective (i.e., whether the firm can enhance its market performance through coopetition in general), as well as from the relative perspective (i.e., whether the firm can perform better than its horizontal competitors). Second, the *performance* component relates to the focal firm's financial and economic outcomes. These outcomes include cost and resource efficiency, profitability, and sales growth, as well as changes in market share (Delaney & Huselid, 1996). Assessing such performance outcomes is not straightforward, however, and feasible data is not always available.

Coopetition undoubtedly has a major potential to affect market performance. The coopetition literature at large has suggested that coopetition is a strategy that can positively affect focal firm performance, although this is subject to different contingencies and conditions (for reviews, see, e.g., Bouncken et al., 2015; Gast et al., 2015; Walley, 2007). However, the body of literature quantitatively assessing the effect of coopetition and market performance is very limited. It includes survey-based studies with perceptional assessment of overall market performance, which find that coopetition positively affects a firm's market performance under certain conditions (Bouncken & Fredrich, 2012; Ritala, 2012) or, alternatively, decreases the firm's market performance in international markets (Nakos et al., 2014). Studies using objective performance measures include Luo et al. (2007), who found a curvilinear relationship between the focal firm's coopetition involvement and its financial performance, measured with return on equity (ROE). Furthermore, Ritala et al. (2008) used return on assets (ROA) and found that global information and communications technology (ICT) firms' performance suffers if they have too many key competitors among their focal alliance portfolio but benefits if they have formed strategic alliances with many of their key competitors. Finally, Sanou et al. (2016) investigated the relative increase in the number of subscribers (i.e., market share) as an indicator of the positive effect of coopetition on market performance.

Given the scarce quantitative evidence for a direct coopetition–market performance link, it is fair to say that there is no overarching understanding of the variety of mechanisms and means in how and why coopetition affects the focal firm's market performance. Thus, the remainder of this chapter pursues to provide more understanding on this core issue in coopetition literature and practice.

Main benefits of coopetition for market performance

What follows is a short, integrative overview of the literature, which includes evidence, description, and implications between coopetition strategy and various types of market performance.

The related contingencies and contextual issues are discussed and illustrative examples are pinpointed.

This review builds on the previous categorization of the main motivations and benefits of coopetition developed in Ritala (2012) and Ritala et al. (2014). In particular, the main benefits of coopetition that drive a focal firm's market performance are divided into four categories: (1) resource efficiency; (2) market growth and development; (3) new market creation; and (4) competitive dynamics. These four categories are analyzed mostly from the focal firm's strategic perspective, that is, how the market performance in this particular category is facilitated by collaboration with competitors. Table 29.1 provides a comprehensive overview of the field in this regard, and the next sections briefly elaborate each of the four categories.[1]

The *resource efficiency* category involves concrete cost savings and profitability measures and implications. For instance, the literature provides much evidence of the benefits of coopetition for cost savings in upstream activities, such as R&D and manufacturing (Choi et al., 2010; Gnyawali & Park, 2011; Ritala et al., 2017), as well as downstream activities, such as delivery, logistics, branding, and marketing (Chiambaretto et al., 2016; Kotzab & Teller, 2003; Teller et al., 2016). Furthermore, some studies have discussed specifics in terms of the types of resource efficiencies achieved. For instance, Peng et al. (2012) studied a broad range of measures related to productivity and performance in a Taiwanese supermarket network that utilized coopetition. They found that coopetition can improve a broad range of such measures over time, leading to improved quality and a reduction in various operational costs.

Market growth and development is a broad category, providing evidence of how coopetition improves market performance in terms of raising overall sales by broadening and developing the current markets (Gnyawali & Park, 2011; Peng et al., 2012). In general, coopetition especially allows market growth in contexts where horizontally aligned firms can utilize their own or shared interfaces and platforms in pursuing larger markets (Basole et al., 2015; Gueguen, 2009; Ritala et al., 2014). Coopetition can also help improve the overall conditions and legitimacy of industries, including social and environmental aspects (Volschenk et al., 2016). Furthermore, the benefits of coopetition are both local and international. The former often refers to geographically co-located activities (see Teller et al., 2016) that help competitors improve the market conditions and customer access, for instance. In doing so, coopetition helps the participating firms access their partners' customer bases, as well as benefit from sharing of brands and marketing efforts (Chiambaretto & Dumez, 2016; Chiambaretto et al., 2016; Czernek & Czakon, 2016; Wang, 2008). International growth via coopetition initiatives has also been observed across many studies. It is well-known that coopetition allows established players to enter new foreign markets by collaborating with local rivals (Chiambaretto & Fernandez, 2016). Furthermore, Vanyushyn et al. (2009) and Kock et al. (2010) suggested that coopetition is a feasible strategy especially for resource-constrained small- and medium-sized enterprises (SMEs) for pursuing international opportunities and thus gaining new market share.

New market creation involves particular benefits of coopetition that relate to joint infrastructures, relationships, resources, and capabilities shared among the horizontal players. First, coopetition helps in creating new markets and industries through the development of shared technological infrastructures, platforms, and standards (Christ & Slowak, 2009; Ondrus et al., 2015; Ritala et al., 2009). They help particularly in the emergence of new technical solutions or product families, where coopetition ensures that enough horizontal participation is involved in the new market creation (such as Blu-Ray, Mobile TV, or mobile payments, as discussed in the previous references). Second, coopetition helps to build legitimacy for new market creation by providing customers more variety (Ritala & Hurmelinna-Laukkanen, 2009; Wang and Xie, 2011), and a related broader potential customer base. Finally, coopetition helps to create new market niches

Table 29.1 Coopetition and market performance: Overview of the research field

	Resource Efficiency	Market Growth and Development	New Market Creation	Competitive Dynamics
Main mechanisms	Resource and risk sharing in pre-competitive activities (Gnyawali & Park, 2011; Gwynne, 2009); productivity, cost efficiency, quality, and safety improvements (Kotzab & Oum et al., 2004; Peng et al., 2012; Rusko, 2011; Kotzab & Teller, 2003); improved resource utilization via cross-selling and co-branding (Chiambaretto et al., 2016; Lindström & Polsa, 2016; Oum et al., 2004)	Growth of sales in current markets (Gnyawali & Park, 2011; Peng et al., 2012); developing the common market legitimacy via social and environmental initiatives (Volchenk et al., 2016); geographic market expansion and internationalization (Chiambaretto & Fernandez, 2016; Kock et al., 2010; Vanyushyn et al., 2009); product-market expansion (Ansari et al., 2016; Garrette et al., 2009)	Set-up of technological infrastructures, platforms, and standards among horizontal actors to create traction and legitimacy for new markets (Christ & Slowak, 2009; Ondrus et al., 2015; Ritala et al., 2009; Vanhaverbeke & Noordehaven, 2001; Wang & Xie, 2011); creation of customer appeal through a variety of choices in a particular category (Ritala & Hurmelinna-Laukkanen, 2009)	Central position in coopetitive network increases the competitive abilities of the focal firm (Gnyawali et al., 2006; Ritala et al., 2017; Sanou et al., 2016); focal firm market share growth (Gnyawali & Park, 2011); increase in joint competitiveness of coopetitors against the rest of the field (Choi et al., 2010; Fernandez et al., 2014; Oxley et al., 2009)
Indicators and measures used	Inventory, operating, purchasing, and delivery costs (Peng et al., 2012); productivity, measured by overall outputs divided by overall inputs (Oum et al., 2004)	Sales growth rate, number of customer visits (Peng et al., 2012), store performance (Teller et al., 2016); market share: number of subscribers and the average increase (Sanou et al., 2016)	New product launches (Garrette et al., 2009); installed user base (Wang & Xie, 2011)	Volume of competitive actions (Gnyawali et al., 2006; Sanou et al., 2016); stock market reactions to competitors' shares outside the coopetition agreement (Oxley et al., 2009)
Contingencies and contextual issues	Coopetition pays off especially when there is a lot of market uncertainty, allowing risks and costs to be shared among horizontal actors (Gnyawali & Park, 2011; Gwynne, 2009; Ritala, 2012);	Firms can grow markets faster in industries where joint platforms, standards, and interfaces among competitors are available (Basole et al., 2015: Carayannis & Alexander, 2001; Christ & Slowak, 2009; Gueguen, 2009; Mione, 2009; Ritala et al., 2014; Wang & Xie, 2011);	Creating a new market category via coopetition relationships with the incumbents (Ansari et al., 2016); the number and variety of supporting firms of a new technology/market is appreciated by customers (Ritala & Hurmelinna-Laukkanen, 2009; Wang & Xie, 2011)	Coopetition improves the firm's tendency to engage in competitive actions (Gnyawali et al., 2006; Sanou et al., 2016); coopetition announcements reduce the value of other horizontal actors outside the alliance (Oxley et al., 2009);

	industry infrastructures, standards, and associations provide accessible contexts through which competitors can coordinate resource efficiency improvements (Mione, 2009; Spiegel, 2005)	coopetition in internationalization is a source of opportunities (Kock et al., 2010; Vanyushyn et al., 2009) but might also reduce export market performance (Nakos et al., 2014); agglomeration effects from geographic co-location help to increase competitors' performance (Czernek & Czakon, 2016; Teller et al., 2016; Wang, 2008)		when coopetition negatively affects the bargaining power of industry's customers and suppliers, there are potential antitrust problems (Gnyawali, 2008; Jorde & Teece, 1990)
Illustrative industry examples	Joint R&D and production facilities between Sony and Samsung to reduce costs and share risks (Gnyawali & Park, 2011); code-sharing alliances between airlines (Chiambaretto et al., 2016; Oum et al., 2004); joint marketing campaigns between small ICT firms (Lindström & Polsa, 2016)	Amazon.com was able to grow its share of global e-commerce markets by providing access to competitors to its sales and web platforms (Ritala et al., 2014); retail and service sector stores enjoy agglomeration benefits by being closely located and providing customers improved access to a variety of products and services (Teller et al., 2016)	Blu-Ray and HD-DVD standards battled for new market dominance (Christ & Slowak, 2009); firms were able to create markets for new services in the US TiVo ecosystem by creating coopetition relationships with incumbent broadcasting sector actors (Ansari et al., 2016)	New Zealand and Australian wine industry competitors collaborated on screwcap technology in order to attain global competitiveness (Choi et al., 2010); collaboration by regional competitors Thales Alenia Space and Astrium in order to improve global competitiveness (Fernandez et al., 2014)

and categories as it allows new entrants to integrate their ideas with the horizontal incumbent players. For instance, Ansari et al. (2016) showed how coopetition strategy allowed new entrants to collaborate with industry incumbents in cable TV markets and therefore to penetrate the markets with new offerings (i.e., TiVo services).

Competitive dynamics approaches have provided a lot of evidence of the interplay of the competitive and collaborative aspects of coopetition. This evidence includes studies assessing how firms have been able to affect their competitiveness and market shares via utilizing coopetition alliances (Gnyawali & Park, 2011). Furthermore, studies have shown how coopetition helps the actors involved increase their relative competitiveness against their industrial peers (Choi et al., 2010; Fernandez et al., 2014; Oxley et al., 2009). For instance, Gnyawali et al. (2006) suggested that the centrality in coopetitive alliance networks increases the focal firm's tendency to engage in competitive actions, with a reduced risk of encountering aggressive counter-reactions (see also Sanou et al., 2016). Indeed, central firms in networks with coopetitive relationships can utilize their bargaining power to reduce the risks and increase the benefits of coopetition (e.g., Ritala et al., 2017). Finally, some researchers have expressed a cautious note in that coopetition can also lead to collusive behavior in cases when competition is subdued, or the bargaining power of customers or suppliers is reduced (Bengtsson et al., 2010; Gnyawali et al., 2008; Jorde & Teece, 1990).

Future research opportunities in coopetition and market performance

Based on this chapter, it is evident that we already know a lot about coopetition and market performance. However, there are still many opportunities for further research. In this section, some of the pressing research gaps and future research opportunities are discussed.

The first future research opportunity is related to pursuing more objectivity and rigor in *the methods and measurement of the market performance outcomes of coopetition*. Overall, it is evident that our understanding of coopetition and market performance relies mostly on case-based evidence, and very few quantitative studies have examined market performance using objective measures. These benefits could be examined at the firm level, such as in Luo et al. (2007). However, firm performance itself is affected by many different issues; thus, it is not a surprise that such measurement is rarely available or observable. Thus, the literature could also pursue the quantification of the coopetition benefits more directly. One good attempt is documented in Peng et al. (2012), where various indicators are tracked and linked to coopetition initiatives. Future research could provide a more detailed tracking of the performance benefits of coopetition relationships within the firm's alliance portfolio and contrast them against other types of alliances such as non-competitive or vertical alliances (this is done in some coopetition and innovation studies, such as Quintana-Garcia & Benavides-Velasco, 2004). Furthermore, studies could explicate how coopetition affects focal firm performance via different direct measures, such as how much revenue coopetition initiatives have generated or the types of resource efficiencies achieved. In all of the research designs, it would be important to specify how coopetition strategy in particular—as opposed to "regular" alliance strategy—has benefited market performance.

Second, interfirm collaboration—as well as coopetition—is increasingly being organized via *technological platforms and related ecosystems* (Cennamo & Santalo, 2013). Therefore, it would be relevant to further examine how firms scale their business by interacting with their competitors through connectivity provided by modern platform-based models. Existing coopetition literature has shown some indication of how platform leadership allows companies to reap profits by involving competitors in their growing ecosystems (Ondrus et al., 2015; Ritala et al., 2014), but more evidence would be useful.

Third, future studies could dig deeper into the *competitive dynamics implications* of coopetition strategy. There is evidence for how competitors can collaborate in order to make themselves more competitive in regional and global competition (Choi et al., 2010; Gnyawali & Park, 2011; Ritala et al., 2017), and that coopetition allows firms to pursue competitive strategies more effectively (Gnyawali et al., 2006) and subsequently improve their market performance (Sanou et al., 2016). However, our understanding in this field is still scant. More studies could be conducted that examine the dynamics of competition, collaboration, and coopetition in markets, and how these dynamics between different relationships affect focal firm performance, as well as the relative market share of actors involved. Further research could also be dedicated to the potential antitrust and collusion implications of coopetition, which remain underexplored, despite earlier conceptual discussions and calls for further research (for discussion, see, e.g., Bengtsson et al., 2010; Gnyawali et al., 2008; Jorde & Teece, 1990).

Conclusion

This chapter has provided an integrative outlook on the state-of-the-art evidence of coopetition and market performance. This includes examination of the mechanisms, indicators, and contingencies related to the market performance benefits of coopetition in four categories: (1) resource efficiency; (2) market growth and development; (3) new market creation; and (4) competitive dynamics. Overall, as this review demonstrates, coopetition research has already provided a compelling account of potential market performance benefits. However, there is a lot more to be done to understand the specific antecedents, contingencies, and outcomes. The increasing research interest in coopetition and contributions using different methods will hopefully provide much more evidence in this regard.

Note

1 This review excludes some of the previously mentioned quantitative studies measuring market performance with generic performance measures (e.g., Luo et al., 2007; Ritala, 2008, 2012; Bouncken and Fredrich, 2012) because they cannot be categorized in any particular stream.

References

Ansari, S. S., Garud, R., & Kumaraswamy, A. (2016). The disruptor's dilemma: TiVo and the US television ecosystem. *Strategic Management Journal*, 37(9), 1829–1853.

Basole, R. C., Park, H., & Barnett, B. C. (2015). Coopetition and convergence in the ICT ecosystem. *Telecommunications Policy*, 39(7), 537–552.

Bengtsson, M., Eriksson, J., & Wincent, J. (2010). Co-opetition dynamics–an outline for further inquiry. *Competitiveness Review: An International Business Journal*, 20(2), 194–214.

Bouncken, R. B., Gast, J., Kraus, S., & Bogers, M. (2015). Coopetition: a systematic review, synthesis, and future research directions. *Review of Managerial Science*, 9(3), 577–601.

Bouncken, R. B. & Fredrich, V. (2012). Coopetition: performance implications and management antecedents. *International Journal of Innovation Management*, 16(05), 1250028.

Garrette, B., Castañer, X., & Dussauge, P. (2009). Horizontal alliances as an alternative to autonomous production: Product expansion mode choice in the worldwide aircraft industry 1945–2000. *Strategic Management Journal*, 30(8), 885–894.

Carayannis, E. G. & Alexander, J. (2001). Virtual, wireless mannah: a co-opetitive analysis of the broadband satellite industry. *Technovation*, 21(12), 759–766.

Cennamo, C. & Santalo, J. (2013). Platform competition: Strategic trade-offs in platform markets. *Strategic Management Journal*, 34(11), 1331–1350.

Chen, M. J. (1996). Competitor analysis and interfirm rivalry: Toward a theoretical integration. *Academy of Management Review*, 21(1), 100–134.

Chen, M. J. & Miller, D. (2015). Reconceptualizing competitive dynamics: A multidimensional framework. *Strategic Management Journal*, 36(5), 758–775.

Chiambaretto, P., Gurău, C., & Le Roy, F. (2016). Coopetitive branding: Definition, typology, benefits and risks. *Industrial Marketing Management*, 57, 86–96.

Chiambaretto, P. & Dumez, H. (2016). Toward a typology of coopetition: a multilevel approach. *International Studies of Management & Organization*, 46(2–3), 110–129.

Chiambaretto, P. & Fernandez, A.-S. (2016). The evolution of coopetitive and collaborative alliances in an alliance portfolio: the Air France case. *Industrial Marketing Management*, 57, 75–85.

Choi, P., Garcia, R., & Friedrich, C. (2010). The drivers for collective horizontal coopetition: a case study of screwcap initiatives in the international wine industry. *International Journal of Strategic Business Alliances*, 1(3), 271–290.

Christ, J. & Slowak, A. (2009). Why Blu-Ray vs. HD-DVD is not VHS vs. Betamax: the co-evolution of standard-setting consortia. *FZID Discussion Papers*, 05/2009.

Czernek, K. & Czakon, W. (2016). Trust-building processes in tourist coopetition: The case of a Polish region. *Tourism Management*, 52, 380–394.

Delaney, J. T. & Huselid, M. A. (1996). The impact of human resource management practices on perceptions of organizational performance. *Academy of Management Journal*, 39(4), 949–969.

Fernandez, A.-S., Le Roy, F., & Gnyawali, D. R. (2014). Sources and management of tension in co-opetition case evidence from telecommunications satellites manufacturing in Europe. *Industrial Marketing Management*, 43(2), 222–235.

Gast, J., Filser, M., Gundolf, K., & Kraus, S. (2015). Coopetition research: towards a better understanding of past trends and future directions. *International Journal of Entrepreneurship and Small Business*, 24(4), 492–521.

Gnyawali, D. R., He, J., & Madhavan, R. (2006). Impact of co-opetition on firm competitive behavior: An empirical examination. *Journal of Management*, 32(4), 507–530.

Gnyawali, D. R., He, J., & Madhavan, R. (2008). Co-opetition: Promises and challenges. In Wankel, C. (Ed.), *21st Century Management: A Reference Handbook*. Thousand Oaks, CA: SAGE.

Gnyawali, D. R. & Park, B. J. R. (2011). Co-opetition between giants: Collaboration with competitors for technological innovation. *Research Policy*, 40(5), 650–663.

Gnyawali, D. R., Madhavan, R., He, J., & Bengtsson, M. (2016). The competition–cooperation paradox in inter-firm relationships: A conceptual framework. *Industrial Marketing Management*, 53, 7–18.

Gueguen, G. (2009). Coopetition and business ecosystems in the information technology sector: the example of Intelligent Mobile Terminals. *International Journal of Entrepreneurship and Small Business*, 8(1), 135–153.

Gwynne, P. (2009). Automakers hope "coopetition" will map route to future sales. *Research Technology Management*, 52(2), 2.

Jorde, T. M. & Teece, D. J. (1990). Innovation and cooperation: implications for competition and antitrust. *The Journal of Economic Perspectives*, 4(3), 75–96.

Kock, S., Nisuls, J., & Söderqvist, A. (2010). Co-opetition: a source of international opportunities in Finnish SMEs. *Competitiveness Review: An International Business Journal*, 20(2), 111–125.

Kotzab, H. & Teller, C. (2003). Value-adding partnerships and co-opetition models in the grocery industry. *International Journal of Physical Distribution & Logistics Management*, 33(3), 268–281.

Lado, A. A., Boyd, N. G., & Hanlon, S. C. (1997). Competition, cooperation, and the search for economic rents: a syncretic model. *Academy of Management Review*, 22(1), 110–141.

Lindström, T. & Polsa, P. (2016). Coopetition close to the customer—A case study of a small business network. *Industrial Marketing Management*, 53, 207–215.

Luo, X., Rindfleisch, A., & Tse, D. K. (2007). Working with rivals: The impact of competitor alliances on financial performance. *Journal of Marketing Research*, 44(1), 73–83.

Mione, A. (2009). When entrepreneurship requires coopetition: the need for standards in the creation of a market. *International Journal of Entrepreneurship and Small Business*, 8(1), 92–109.

Nakos, G., Brouthers, K. D., & Dimitratos, P. (2014). International alliances with competitors and non-competitors: The disparate impact on SME international performance. *Strategic Entrepreneurship Journal*, 8(2), 167–182.

Oum, T. H., Park, J.-H., Kim, K., & Yu, C. (2004). The effect of horizontal alliances on firm productivity and profitability: Evidence from the global airline industry. *Journal of Business Research*, 57(8), 844–853.

Ondrus, J., Gannamaneni, A., & Lyytinen, K. (2015). The impact of openness on the market potential of multi-sided platforms: a case study of mobile payment platforms. *Journal of Information Technology*, 30(3), 260–275.

Oxley, J. E., Sampson, R. C., & Silverman, B. S. (2009). Arms race of détente? How interfirm alliance announcements change the stock market valuation of rivals. *Management Science*, 55(8), 1321–1337.

Peng, T. J. A., Pike, S., Yang, J. C. H., & Roos, G. (2012). Is cooperation with competitors a good idea? An example in practice. *British Journal of Management*, 23(4), 532–560.

Quintana-Garcia, C. & Benavides-Velasco, C. A. (2004). Cooperation, competition, and innovative capability: a panel data of European dedicated biotechnology firms. *Technovation*, 24(12), 927–938.

Raza-Ullah, T., Bengtsson, M., & Kock, S. (2014). The coopetition paradox and tension in coopetition at multiple levels. *Industrial Marketing Management*, 43(2), 189–198.

Ritala, P., Hallikas, J., & Sissonen, H. (2008). The effect of strategic alliances between key competitors on firm performance. *Management Research: Journal of the Iberoamerican Academy of Management*, 6(3), 179–187.

Ritala, P. & Hurmelinna-Laukkanen, P. (2009). What's in it for me? Creating and appropriating value in innovation-related coopetition. *Technovation*, 29(12), 819–828.

Ritala, P., Hurmelinna-Laukkanen, P., & Blomqvist, K. (2009). Tug of war in innovation—Coopetitive service development. *International Journal of Services, Technology and Management*, 12(3), 255–272.

Ritala, P. (2012). Coopetition strategy—when is it successful? Empirical evidence on innovation and market performance. *British Journal of Management*, 23(3), 307–324.

Ritala, P., Golnam, A., & Wegmann, A. (2014). Coopetition-based business models: The case of Amazon.com. *Industrial Marketing Management*, 43(2), 236–249.

Ritala, P., Huizingh, E., Almpanopoulou, A., & Wijbenga, P. (2017). Tensions in R&D networks: Implications for knowledge search and integration. *Technological Forecasting and Social Change*, 120, 311–322.

Rusko, R. (2011). Exploring the concept of coopetition: A typology for the strategic moves of the Finnish forest industry. *Industrial Marketing Management*, 40(2), 311–320.

Sanou, F. H., Le Roy, F., & Gnyawali, D. R. (2016). How does centrality in coopetition networks matter? An empirical investigation in the mobile telephone industry. *British Journal of Management*, 27(1), 143–160.

Spiegel, M. (2005). Coopetition in the telecommunications industry. In Crew, M. A. & Spiegel, M. (Eds), *Obtaining the Best from Regulation and Competition*. Boston, MA: Kluwer Academic.

Storbacka, K. & Nenonen, S. (2011). Scripting markets: From value propositions to market propositions. *Industrial Marketing Management*, 40(2), 255–266.

Teller, C., Alexander, A., & Floh, A. (2016). The impact of competition and cooperation on the performance of a retail agglomeration and its stores. *Industrial Marketing Management*, 52, 6–17.

Vanhaverbeke, W. & Noordehaven, N. G. (2001). Competition between alliance blocks: The case of the RISC microprocessor technology. *Organization Studies*, 22(1), 1–30.

Vanyushyn, V., Holmlund, M., & Kock, S. (2009). Cooperation with competitors and internationalization: Evidence from the west coast of Finland. *Journal of Euromarketing*, 18(2), 89–100.

Vargo, S. L. & Lusch, R. F. (2011). It's all B2B… and beyond: Toward a systems perspective of the market. *Industrial Marketing Management*, 40(2), 181–187.

Volschenk, J., Ungerer, M., & Smit, E. (2016). Creation and appropriation of socio-environmental value in coopetition. *Industrial Marketing Management*, 57, 109–118.

Walley, K. (2007). Coopetition: an introduction to the subject and an agenda for research. *International Studies of Management & Organization*, 37(2), 11–31.

Wang, Y. (2008). Collaborative destination marketing understanding the dynamic process. *Journal of Travel Research*, 47(2), 151–166.

Wang, Q. & Xie, J. (2011). Will consumers be willing to pay more when your competitors adopt your technology? The impacts of the supporting-firm base in markets with network effects. *Journal of Marketing*, 75(5), 1–17.

30

The value implications of coopetition

Jako Volschenk

Introduction

Coopetition is often expressed using an analogy of a pie that is increased in size to benefit all (win-win), rather than fighting to increase the size of your own slice at the expense of others (win-lose). How we think of value impacts how we view the increasing size.

In 2010, a wine bottling company asked me to investigate to what extent they could recover empty wine bottles for reuse through reverse logistics. The company was mostly interested in the cost-saving benefit that they could achieve through such an initiative. Being an environmentalist, I was also aware that such an initiative would have ecological benefits, such as less waste in landfills and reduced carbon emissions. However, it was also clear that the company would not be able to do this on their own and that such an initiative would have to be driven at an industry level in order to be successful. Furthermore, not only would the value created by such an initiative benefit the incumbent company as well as other firms, but the initiative would also benefit society in both economic and environmental terms. However, the coopetition literature at the time was lacking words to accurately describe the creation and appropriation of value by such an initiative.

First, when looking at the available coopetition theory at that time, I soon realised that the literature then focused mostly (if not only) on value captured between and within coopeting firms (Ritala & Tidström, 2014). Whilst there was sufficient literature about value appropriation in the coopetition and collaboration bodies of literature, these typically did not consider a wider stakeholder view of value (see Dagnino & Padula, 2002; Dyer et al., 2008; Ritala & Hurmelinna-Laukkanen, 2009; Ritala & Tidström, 2014; Park et al., 2014).

Second, coopetition literature (Dagnino & Padula, 2002; Dyer et al., 2008; Janssen et al., 2013; Khanna et al., 1998) mostly described value as economic or knowledge value, with little acknowledgement of other forms of value. For instance, not much was said about the social and environmental value that may be created when firms work together.

Research on the value aspect of coopetition is still limited, at both theoretical and empirical levels (Ritala & Tidström, 2014). As such, our understanding is constrained by the "incomplete conceptualization and measurement of value and by scant characterization of the different patterns of stakeholder value appropriation" (Garcia-Castro & Aguilera, 2014). With an increased focus on sustainability, governance and reporting, describing and understanding value is all the more important.

This chapter proposes how we can look differently at coopetition-related value, and in the process become better at articulating the creation and appropriation of such value.

This chapter consist of broadly three value-related conversations surrounding coopetition.

- Section 2 of the chapter deals with the value appropriation view, i.e., who is able to capture the value that is created in coopetition.
- Section 3 provides an overview of the kind of value that can be generated in coopetition.
- Section 4 combines these two views of value into an integrated typology of value creation and appropriation referred to as the coopetition value matrix or CVM.

Expanding the value appropriation view

Stakeholder theory

For a long time, the interests of shareholders have been considered to be the most important obligation for companies (Freeman & Reed, 1983: 48). However, there is also a long history of authors (Barnard, 1938; Berle & Means, 1932) who opposed this view. Barnard (1938: 89) maintained that the role of companies is to serve society, and that the executive's role is to instil a sense of moral purpose in the company.

Fortunately, managers do not make decisions based solely on their own interests, but also consider the wider socio-economic impacts (Lado et al., 1997). Socio-economists have argued that the decisions of managers are embedded in social systems (Granovetter, 1985), implying that a broader stakeholder view (Freeman, 2010) of value is not only warranted, but also desirable. In fact, not considering the wider implications of coopetitive actions is sub-optimal (Freeman, 2010; Harrison & Wicks, 2013; Hart & Milstein, 2003) as it could potentially destroy or create value for society, and for the companies.

Neither the natural environment nor competitors are considered extremely prominent in the stakeholder literature (Ambler & Wilson, 1995: 4; Driscoll & Starik, 2004). Some (for instance, Ambler & Wilson, 1995) have argued that there is little practical use to acknowledging competitors as stakeholders of each other. Notwithstanding, in the context of coopetition, competitors co-create value and should therefore be regarded as stakeholders. Furthermore, the position of civil society is unclear and ill-defined (Lépineux, 2005).

Stakeholders are any groups or individuals who can impact or who may be impacted by the achievement of the objectives of an organization (Freeman & Reed, 1983). This could include public interest groups, the government, competitors, employees, customers, as well as the natural (or ecological) environment (Freeman & Reed, 1983). Some authors (such as Carroll & Buchholtz, 2012) also include the general public and civic groups in the definition.

Public benefit

One of the core principles of coopetition is that it requires a mutual benefit for the coopeting parties (Czakon et al., 2016). The total benefit that can be generated through an alliance is often defined as *the sum of **common benefits** and **private benefits*** (Dyer et al., 2008; Ritala & Tidström, 2014). Dyer et al. (2008) maintained that coopetition initiatives are most stable when common benefits and private benefits are high. This chapter suggests that we measure not only the value that is created for the coopeting parties, but also consider the public benefit (or cost).

Public goods, like the fresh air and oxygen provided by a forest (Pigou, 1937), are characterized by non-rivalrous consumption and non-excludability (Bannock et al., 2003). But environmental goods are often common goods, meaning that it is rivalrous (unlike public goods), but non-excludable (like public goods). The best example would be fish stock. Noone can be excluded from fishing, but catching a fish means that it is unavailable to the next person, i.e., it is rivalrous (Ostrom, 1990). Volschenk et al. (2016) used the broader term of "public benefit" to describe benefits that accrue to society, whether these are excludable or not.

A typology of value appropriation

We can therefore define four levels of benefit, namely: (i) common benefits; (ii) privately captured common benefits; (iii) private benefits; and (iii) public benefits. To illustrate the different classifications of value (Table 30.1), I will use four examples of coopetition.

The first example shows the application of the theory in the luxury hotel industry (1a–c), the second is that of a shared logistics network between furniture companies (2a–d), the third relates to joint R&D in the auto industry (3a–d), and the fourth deals with the benefits of fishing companies collectively protecting the fish resource in their control (4a–d).

The first two examples illustrate economic value (from respectively increased revenues and reduced costs), the third illustrates knowledge value, and the fourth shows an example with little short-term economic or knowledge value for the coopetitors. How the value is appropriated by the different parties indicates different dynamics based on different contexts.

The common value (1a–4a) generated can be appropriated in positive-sum logic (2b and 3b) or zero-sum logic (1b and 4b). But in the first three examples it is also possible for private value to be generated outside of the coopetition boundaries. In the case of the joint logistics and joint R&D examples, the private benefits (2c and 3c) are based on product-related boundaries, while the zero-sum benefit in the case of the luxury hotel group (1c) is based on geographic boundaries.

Three of the examples (2, 3, and 4) generate public goods in the form of reduced emissions (2d and 3d), reduced resource consumption (3d), and increased biodiversity (4di). But example 4 also delivers a common good in the form of increased fishing resources (4dii).

The increased typology in Table 30.1 provides us with the capacity to describe the dynamics of value appropriation. However, in combination with the appropriation of value, it is also necessary for us to understand the nature of the value that we create.

Expanding the value creation view

Value creation versus value destruction

When considering the practice of working with your competitor, it is also necessary to distinguish coopetition from collusion. Practically, one can view coopetition and collusion as, respectively, the virtuous and non-virtuous sides of the same phenomenon. Walley (2007) argued that the two should be considered separate and that coopetition implies that companies collaborate not only for their own benefit, but also for the benefit of the consumer. Such collaboration creates "win-win-win" situations. On the other hand, when the consumer is penalized in any way, then collusion is occurring (Walley, 2007). Lado et al. (1997) argued that syncretic rent-seeking behavior (i.e., coopetition) is far from competition-destroying collusion, but instead enhances competitiveness in a market through innovation and cost reductions beyond what competition can provide.

Table 30.1 A typology of value appropriation

	Positive-sum	Zero-sum
Common benefit: value that is generated as a result of the coopetition relationship in positive-sum logic (Ritala & Tidström, 2014; Park et al., 2014; Rai, 2013), and accrues collectively to the coopetitors in relation to some level of contribution in the initiative (Janssen et al., 2013: 2). When such value is captured by one coopetitor, it leads to the second classification, namely privately captured common benefit	**1a)** The aggregate increase in revenue generated by competing luxury hotels from joint destination marketing (see Wang, 2008) aimed at attracting more tourists to Cape Town **2a)** The total cost saving generated from a joint logistics network in which competing furniture companies use the same distribution channel (see Janssen et al., 2013) **3a)** The total intellectual capital generated from joint R&D by auto-manufacturers (e.g., Toyota & PSA Peugeot Citroen in their research around city transport) **4a)** Firms ensure long-term profitability by preventing over-exploitation of the fishing resource	
Privately captured common benefit: value that accrues to a particular coopetitor from the collective value generated in the coopetition relationship. The process of appropriation of value can happen in positive-sum or zero-sum logic (Ritala & Tidström, 2014)	**2b)** The cost reduction enjoyed by a furniture company as a result of a joint logistics network. The fact that it may experience a cost reduction does not prevent its competitor(s) from enjoying a similar cost reduction **3b)** The increase in intellectual capital of a particular auto manufacturer (e.g., PSA Peugeot Citroen) generated from joint R&D. What it learns from the initiative does not prevent Toyota from also gaining knowledge and both may gain the same knowledge	**1b)** The revenue accruing to a particular luxury hotel in Cape Town as a result of joint destination marketing (with other luxury hotels). Each tourist it attracts means one fewer customer for other hotels in Cape Town **4b)** The revenue accruing to a fishing company as a result of sustained fishing resources
Private benefit: value that a firm can capture unilaterally through acquiring knowledge or resources from its partners and applying it outside the boundaries of the coopetition initiative (Khanna et al., 1998; Dyer et al., 2008: 138; Ritala & Tidström, 2014; Dagnino & Padula, 2002: 42; Park et al., 2014). Such value can be captured in differentiating (positive-sum) logic (Ritala & Tidström, 2014) or zero-sum logic (Rai, 2013)	**2c)** The revenue generated by a company that sells both furniture and interior design products when it uses a joint distribution channel with other furniture companies that do not sell interior design products **3c)** The value of intellectual capital that an auto company (PSA Peugeot Citroen) can apply in its motorcycle plant, while its competitor (Toyota) does not operate in that market (and is not able to capture such value)	**1c)** The revenue generated by a luxury hotel group that is present in Cape Town when it is able to refer a guest to its branch in Paris, while at least one of its competitors has a branch there

(*continued*)

Table 30.1 (Cont.)

	Positive-sum	Zero-sum
Public benefit: value that accrues to society (Pigou, 1937). In order to be considered public goods, the benefits should be non-rivalrous and non-excludable (Bannock et al., 2003)	**2d)** Because of the shared logistics network, the companies are (hypothetically) able to lower their carbon footprint. Lower air pollution is a public good **3d)** The product of the joint R&D could be vehicles that pollute less, or that are less resource intensive to produce. These benefits are public goods **4di)** The protection of biodiversity is a public good	**4dii)** The increased fishing resource is a common good, meaning that it is rivalrous and excludable. The natural resource increases due to the protection it enjoys, and any member of society (including companies) can capture the benefit

It is this exploration of value that forces us to think about the type of value that we create. Historically, coopetition literature showed a propensity to focus on economic and knowledge value. Narrowing the construct of value to only economic value has been criticized on the grounds that it could obscure aspects of value that extend beyond profit and economic return (Harrison & Wicks, 2013; Hausman & McPherson, 2006).

The six capitals

The six capitals model is a typology of value that is particularly helpful in expressing the kind of value that we create or destroy (International Integrated Reporting Council (IIRC), 2013). The term "capital" is used to describe any store of value that can be used in the production of goods and services. Value creation therefore describes the act of increasing one or more of the six capitals. Needless to say, the total stock of value does not necessarily remain constant over time.

All organizations depend on the six capitals (Table 30.2) in order to produce goods and services. They do so by consuming, enhancing, modifying, or affecting the capitals in its quest to create financial or other forms of capital. For instance, when a firm spends money to train staff, the assumption would be that the increase in human capital exceeds the decrease in financial capital. In turn, the firm hopes that increased human capital would lead to cost efficiencies, i.e., an increase in financial capital.

Table 30.2, to a large extent, considers only the kind of value that we create, and not to whom that value is allocated. Natural capital in particular can be problematic. Natural capital also includes the value of eco-system services that nature provides, such as

- food, water, and fuel
- regulating processes such as flood and disease regulation
- an assimilative function in absorbing pollution

These three points are indicative of an anthropocentric view of value, i.e., nature only has value while it is perceived so by humans. But nature also has value when there is noone to observe (Rolston, 1986).

Volschenk et al. (2016) argued that coopetition creates *socio-environmental* value. Socio-environmental value includes both anthropocentric value (i.e., humans as the central being in

Table 30.2 Descriptions of the six capitals

Financial capital	The pool of funds that an organization has access to, i.e., it would include debt, equity, or another source. Financial capital is used to acquire other forms of capital, or emanates from the exchange of other forms of capital
Manufactured capital	Human-created, product-orientated equipment and tools, including buildings. However, manufactured capital can extend outside the firm to also include roads and other public infrastructure (IIRC, 2013)
Intellectual capital	Knowledge-based assets, including R&D competencies, tacit knowledge, processes, and intellectual property. Intellectual capital creates shareholder value by combining material, financial, and human resources.
Human capital	People's competencies, capabilities, and experience, as well as their motivation to innovate. Human capital includes people's ability to lead, manage, and collaborate.
Social capital	Institutions and relationships established within and between organizations, communities, stakeholders, and other networks to enhance individual and collective well-being. Social and relationship capital includes broader interpretations, such as the ability to exchange information and the organization's licence to operate.
Natural capital	Natural capital consists of both renewable and non-renewable environmental stocks

the universe) (Hattingh, 2009) and intrinsic value (Rolston, 1986), but excludes value that is rivalrous, i.e., value that can be captured by companies as common or private benefit. Socio-environmental benefits are thus best described as *the sum of intrinsic ecological value and benefits that accrue to society because of environmental improvements* (Volschenk et al., 2016).

An integrated view of value creation and appropriation

The coopetition value matrix

Sections 2 and 3 of this chapter portrayed value creation and appropriation as two independent constructs. Combining value creation and appropriation into a single typology enables the conceptual disaggregation of value to illustrate how the total created value is appropriated to coopetitors and other stakeholders (Volschenk, 2016).

The coopetition value matrix (CVM) (Table 30.3) is a typology of value that addresses the gap in the literature as identified by Garcia-Castro and Aguilera (2014) and Ritala and Tidström (2014) by:

- improving the articulation of value creation;
- improving the articulation of value appropriation;
- allowing a better understanding of the dynamics of the two processes;
- allowing a better understanding of how different manifestations of value interact; and
- allowing the articulation of potential opportunities for increased value creation or appropriation

The CVM illustrates extensions of the existing literature by suggesting the addition of *privately captured common benefit* and *public benefit* to the nomenclature of value appropriation (left-hand

Table 30.3 The coopetition value matrix

		Value Creation					
		Financial Capital	Manufactured Capital	Intellectual Capital	Human Capital	Social Capital	Natural Capital
Value appropriation	Common	Increased funds or access to funds as a result of the coopetition relationship in positive-sum logic (Ritala & Tidström, 2014; Park et al., 2014; Rai, 2013), including increased revenue or lower expenses	A positive-sum logic (Ritala & Tidström, 2014; Park et al., 2014; Rai, 2013) increase in collective stock of human-created, product-orientated equipment and tools, including buildings	A positive-sum logic (Ritala & Tidström, 2014; Park et al., 2014; Rai, 2013) increase in the collective knowledge stock of the coopetitors as a result of the coopetition relationship	A positive-sum logic (Ritala & Tidström, 2014; Park et al., 2014; Rai, 2013) increase in the collective stock of people's competencies, capabilities, and experiences the coopetition partners have access to.	A positive-sum logic (Ritala & Tidström, 2014; Park et al., 2014; Rai, 2013) increase in the collective stock of institutions and relationships that the coopetition partners gain, including goodwill	A positive-sum logic (Ritala & Tidström, 2014; Park et al., 2014; Rai, 2013) increase in access to natural capital as a result of the coopetitive relationship
	Privately captured common	The component of funds captured by any particular firm from the benefit created within the coopetition initiative. The appropriation can follow either positive or zero-sum logic (Ritala & Tidström, 2014)	A positive-sum logic increase in the manufactured capital of any particular firm (Steinmo & Jakobsen, 2013) that relates to the objectives of the coopetitive initiatives	A positive-sum logic increase in the knowledge stock of any particular firm (Steinmo & Jakobsen, 2013) that relates to the objectives of the coopetitive initiatives	A positive-sum logic increase in the human capital of any particular firm (Steinmo & Jakobsen, 2013) that relates to the objectives of the coopetitive initiatives	A positive-sum logic increase in the social capital of any particular firm (Steinmo & Jakobsen, 2013) that relates to the objectives of the coopetitive initiatives	The component of natural capital captured by a firm from the benefit created within the coopetition initiative. The appropriation can follow either positive or zero-sum logic (Ritala & Tidström, 2014), depending on whether the resource is a common or public good

Private	Funds generated by a firm outside of the coopetition relationship from skills or resources acquired inside the coopetition relationship (Khanna et al., 1998; Dyer et al., 2008: 138; Ritala & Tidström, 2014; Dagnino & Padula, 2007: 42; Park et al., 2014). The appropriation can follow either a positive (Ritala & Tidström, 2014) or zero-sum logic (Rai, 2013)	A positive-sum or zero-sum logic increase in the manufactured capital outside of the coopetitive relationship, but based on knowledge that was acquired inside the coopetitive relationship. Based on different backgrounds and different experiences, firms may learn different things (Steinmo & Jakobsen, 2013: 3)	A positive-sum logic increase in the knowledge stock of a firm that has value outside of the coopetitive relationship, but based on knowledge that was acquired inside the coopetitive relationship. Based on different backgrounds and different experiences, firms may learn different things (Steinmo & Jakobsen, 2013: 3)	A positive-sum logic increase in the human capital stock of a firm that has value outside of the coopetitive relationship, but based on competencies that were acquired inside the coopetitive relationship.	A positive-sum logic increase in the social capital stock of a firm that has value outside of the coopetitive relationship, but based on the coopetitive relationship	Natural capital captured by a firm outside of the coopetition initiative, but which can be linked to the initiative. The appropriation can follow either positive or zero-sum logic (Ritala & Tidström, 2014), depending on whether the resource is a common or public good
Public	Socio-economic value: economic value accruing to society as a result of the coopetitive relationship. The appropriation follows positive-sum logic	Public infrastructure: an increase in the collective stock of human-created, product-orientated equipment and tools, including buildings and public infrastructure, that society has access to. The appropriation follows positive-sum logic	Public knowledge: an increase in the knowledge stock in society (i.e., public knowledge) as a result of the coopetitive activities or relationship. The appropriation follows positive-sum logic	A positive-sum increase in the collective stock of society's competencies, capabilities and experiences as a result of the coopetition initiative	Social cohesion: a positive-sum logic (Ritala & Tidström, 2014; Park et al., 2014; Rai, 2013) increase in the collective stock of institutions and relationships that society gains as a result of the coopetition initiative	Socio-environmental value: an increase in environmental value expressed as the utility for society, or as intrinsic value. Such value can, for instance, derive from protecting a species of fauna or flora, reducing resource intensity or reducing waste. The appropriation follows positive-sum logic

vertical column), while also incorporating the six capitals into the value creation view (the top row of the CVM).

As the rows proceed downwards in the matrix, the benefit moves further away from the coopetition relationship. Also, as the rows proceed from left to right, the value becomes more abstract/indirect in nature. By implication, the CVM suggests that socio-environmental value is the most abstract and indirect in nature (Volschenk, 2016).

Conclusion

This chapter provides an overview of the most recent discourse around value in coopetition initiatives by incorporating stakeholder theory and the six capitals model into an integrated typology (CVM). The CVM allows us to map value from coopetition, as well as study the systemic flow of value. The CVM therefore provides a convenient diagnostic tool.

The CVM allows us to look at initiatives such as the example of an industry drive to reuse wine bottles, and understand who stands to benefit, in what ways they benefit, and where more value can be created. The CVM also allows us to study the dynamic links between different cells in the matrix (Volschenk, 2016), meaning that we can intentionally grow value in one cell of the CVM via another cell.

References

Ambler, T. & Wilson, A. (1995). Problems of stakeholder theory. *Business Ethics: A European Review*, 4(1), 30–35.

Bannock, G., Baxter, R., & Davis, E. (2003). *The Penguin Dictionary of Economics*. 7th edition. London: Penguin Books Ltd.

Barnard, C. (1938). *The Function of the Executive*. Cambridge, MA: Harvard University Press.

Berle, A. & Means, G. (1932). *The Modern Corporation and Private Property*. New York: Commerce Clearing House.

Carroll, A. B. & Buchholtz, A. K. (2012). *Business and Society: Ethics and Stakeholder Management*. 8th edition. Mason, OH: South-Western, Cengage Learning.

Czakon, W., Mucha-Kuś, K., & Sołtysik, M. (2016). Coopetition strategy – What is in it for all? A study of common benefits in the Polish energy balancing market. *International Studies of Management & Organization*, 46(2–3), 179–201.

Dagnino, G. B. & Padula, G. (2002). *Coopetition strategy: A new kind of interfirm dynamic for value creation*. Paper presented at The European Academy of Management, Second annual conference, Stockholm, Sweden, May 9–11.

Driscoll, C. & Starik, M. (2004). The primordial stakeholder: Advancing the conceptual consideration of stakeholder status for the natural environment. *Journal of Business Ethics*, 49(1), 55–73.

Dyer, J. H., Singh, H., & Kale, P. (2008). Splitting the pie: Rent distribution in alliances and networks. *Managerial and Decision Economics*, 29(2–3), 137–148.

Freeman, R. E. & Reed, D. L. (1983). Stockholders and stakeholders: A new perspective on corporate governance. *California Management Review*, XXV(3), 88–106.

Freeman, R. E. (2010). *Strategic Management: A Stakeholder Approach*. Cambridge: Cambridge University Press.

Garcia-Castro, R. & Aguilera, R. V. (2014). Incremental value creation and appropriation in a world with multiple stakeholders. *Strategic Management Journal*, 1 April. [Online] Available: doi: 10.1002/smj.2241.

Granovetter, M. (1985). Economic action and social structure: The problem of embeddedness. *American Journal of Sociology*, 91(3), 481–510.

Harrison, J. & Wicks, A. (2013). Stakeholder theory, value, and firm performance. *Business Ethics Quarterly*, 23(1), 97–124.

Hart, S. L. & Milstein, M. B. (2003). Creating sustainable value. *Academy of Management Executive*, 17(2), 56–69.

Hattingh, J. (2009). Environmental ethics. Climate change and arctic sustainable development: Scientific, social, cultural and educational challenges. UNESCO International Experts Meeting, March 3–6,

Monaco. [Online] Available: www.unesco.org/ csi/LINKS/monaco-abstracts/Hattingh_Keynote_abstract_MonacoUNESCOarctic.pdf.

Hausman, D. H. & McPherson, M. (2006). *Economic Analysis, Moral Philosophy and Public Policy.* 2nd edition. Cambridge, UK: Cambridge University Press.

International Integrated Reporting Council (IIRC). (2013). *Capitals: Background Paper for <IR>.* [Online] Available: http://integratedreporting.org/wp-content/uploads/2013/03/IR-Background-Paper-Capitals.pdf.

Janssen, G., De Man, A., & Quak, H. (2013). *Fairness and value appropriation in logistics alliances: A case-study approach.* Proceedings of the 24th POMS Annual Meeting, Denver, Colorado, USA. [Online] Available: www.pomsmeetings.org/ConfProceedings/043/FullPapers/FullPaper_files/043-0632.pdf.

Khanna, T. R., Gulati, R., & Nohria, N. (1998). The dynamics of learning alliances: Competition, cooperation and relative scope. *Strategic Management Journal,* 19(3), 193–210.

Lado, A., Boyd, N., & Hanlon, S. (1997). Competition, cooperation and the search for economic rents: A syncretic model. *Academy of Management Review,* 22(1), 110–141.

Lépineux, F. (2005). Stakeholder theory, society and social cohesion. *Corporate Governance: The International Journal of Business and Society,* 5(2), 99–110.

Ostrom, E. (1990). *Governing the Commons: The Evolution of Institutions for Collective Action.* Cambridge, UK: Cambridge University Press.

Park, B.-J. R., Srivastava, M. K., & Gnyawali, D. R. (2014). Walking the tight rope of coopetition: Impact of competition and cooperation intensities and balance on firm innovation performance. *Industrial Marketing Management,* 43(2), 210–221.

Pigou, A. (1937). *The Economics of Welfare.* 4th edition. London: MacMillan & Co.

Ritala, P. & Hurmelinna-Laukkanen, P. (2009). What's in it for me? Creating and appropriating value in innovation-related coopetition. *Technovation,* 29(12), 819–828.

Ritala, P. & Tidström, A. (2014). Untangling the value-creation and value-appropriation elements of coopetition strategy: A longitudinal analysis on the firm and relational levels. *Scandinavian Journal of Management,* 30(4), 498–515.

Rai, R. (2013). A coopetition-based approach to value creation in interfirm alliances: Construction of a measure and examination of its psychometric properties. *Journal of Management.* [Online] Available: doi 10.1177/0149206313515525.

Rolston, H. (1986). The preservation of natural value in the solar system. Hargrove, E. (Ed.), *Beyond Spaceship Earth: Environmental Ethics and the Solar System.* San Francisco, CA: Sierra Club Books.

Steinmo, M. & Jakobsen, S. (2013). *Greening an Industry through coopetition: The role of proximity in an R&D alliance to create environmental innovations.* 35th DRUID Celebration Conference, Barcelona, Spain, June 17–19. [Online] Available: http://druid8.sit.aau.dk/acc_papers/b96ih3sjlnsyeu96apnq04skphpy.pdf.

Volschenk, J. (2016). *An Investigation into Environmental Coopetition in the South African Wine Industry.* PhD dissertation, University of Stellenbosch, Stellenbosch, South Africa.

Volschenk, J., Ungerer, M., & Smit, E. (2016). Creation and appropriation of socio-environmental value in coopetition. *Industrial Marketing Management.* [Online] Available: http://dx.doi.org/10.1016/j.indmarman.2016.05.026.

Walley, K. (2007). Coopetition: An introduction to the subject and an agenda for research. *International Studies of Management and Organization,* 37(2), 11–31.

Wang, Y. (2008). Collaborative destination marketing: Understanding the dynamic process. *Journal of Travel Research,* 47(2), 151–166.

31

Coopetition and business models

Chander Velu

Introduction

Studies have shown that firms are increasingly cooperating and competing at the same time in order to create competitive advantage and, hence, deliver superior returns (Bouncken & Kraus, 2013; Brandenburger & Nalebuff, 1995; Ritala et al., 2014; Rusko, 2014). Such simultaneous collaborative and competitive activities have been termed *coopetition* (Bengtsson & Kock, 2014; Yami et al., 2010). Business models are a key concept in providing an understanding of how firms can affect the mechanism of value creation and capture within a coopetition setting (Ritala et al., 2014; Velu, 2017).

Business models are a form of activity system that connects the internal perspective of the firm, such as resources and routines, with the external perspective, such as partners, markets, and customers, and therefore articulates how the firm goes to market to implement the strategy (Baden-Fuller & Haefliger, 2013; Zott & Amit, 2010; Zott et al., 2011). Business models can be seen as complex systems with components that connect the customer value proposition, how value is created, the means of value capture, and the partners in the value network. Figure 31.1 provides a summary of the key components of a business model based on the four Vs—value proposition, value creation, value capture, and value network. Coopetition entails when and how the value network is formed between competing firms in order to develop and deliver the value proposition. Coopetition might involve the design of new business models in order to align the customer value proposition with how value is created and captured (Velu & Stiles, 2013; Velu, 2017). New business model design might require reactivating—changing the set of activities; relinking—changing the linkage between activities; repartitioning—changing the boundaries of the focal firm; or relocating—changing the location in which activities are performed (Dos Santos et al., 2015).

Coopetition has been shown to be valuable from a demand perspective such as improving the value proposition to the customer. Examples of coopetition from a demand perspective include airline alliances such as that between Oneworld and Start Alliance, where firms form a global network in order to broaden their flight connectivity and provide customers with more convenient travel options (Fan et al., 2001). Studies have shown that the degree of market uncertainty drives the incentive for firms in the airline industry to cooperate, which can be in the form of horizontal coopetition between firms in the same market, vertical coopetition representing a supplier–retailer relationship,

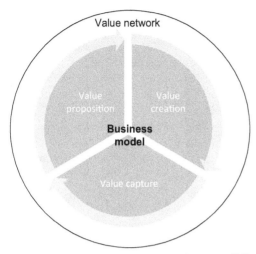

Source: Adapted from Velu, C; BMI Research Programme (2018)

Figure 31.1 Components of the business model

or both (Chiambaretto & Dumez, 2016; Chiambaretto & Fernandez, 2016). Coopetition has also been valuable from a supply perspective, such as the more efficient management of the supply chain. An example of coopetition from a supply perspective is the manufacturing alliance whereby Samsung supplies components for the Apple iPhone but both firms compete in the smartphone consumer market (Vergara, 2012). In addition, coopetition is also possible in order for firms to improve their ability for innovativeness. An example of this is the coopetition among biotechnology firms in order to increase technology diversity and new product development (Quintana-García & Benavides-Velasco, 2004). These forms of coopetition often involve a re-design of the business model of the firms. This chapter will illustrate the business model design issues by examining three cases in the bond trading market, book retailing, and the television markets, respectively, in order to draw some key implications from a business model perspective.

Case vignettes

The rationale for coopetition-based business models could be to increase the size of the current market, to create new markets, or to increase efficiency in resource utilization in order to help improve the firms' competitive position (Ritala et al., 2014). In this section we will examine three cases in order to provide the rationale for coopetition. In the first case, we examine the coopetition behavior among investment banks in the bond trading market in order to establish when firms might innovate their business model in an evolutionary or revolutionary manner, and the motivation behind these choices. In the second case, we examine the development of an e-commerce platform by Amazon in the book retailing industry. In the third case, we examine coopetition in sharing research and development activities between Samsung Electronics and the Sharp Corporation to develop the LCD television market.

Electronic trading and bond markets

The reasons for firms to adopt a coopetition strategy could be either defensive or offensive (Velu, 2017). The defensive reason could entail protecting an existing business model through evolutionary innovation. An offensive reason could entail major changes in the competitive land-scape by changing the business model through revolutionary innovation. We discuss how firms adopt coopetition strategies in network markets over time in order to respond to new tech-nology, through either evolutionary or revolutionary business model innovation.[1]

Network markets are markets that display network externalities. In network markets the utility to each customer of adopting a firm's proposition increases with an increase in the total number of customers who have adopted the proposition (Farrell & Saloner, 1986; Katz & Shapiro, 1985). The dynamics of customer adoption of a new proposition and dis-adoption of an old proposition will affect the resource base of the firm in terms of market share. The rate of adoption and dis-adoption tends to follow an S-shaped or reverse-S-shaped curve, whereby they are initially slow, then accelerate, and then finally slow down again. Therefore, such changes in market shares over time might influence firms to adopt coopetition as a strategy to create com-petitive advantage. We discuss how the changing nature of the customer base motivates firms to adopt coopetition strategies to help innovate their business models.

The US bond market was the largest securities market in the world, with over $17 trillion in bonds outstanding at the end of the year 2000. The bond industry has primary and secondary markets. In the primary market, government agencies and corporations issue new securities to raise funds. In the secondary market, institutional investors (such as asset-management firms and pension funds) buy and sell these securities to optimize the returns on their portfolios. The market was highly concentrated, with the top ten banks having approximately 94–98 percent of the market share between them.

Back in 1995 bond trading was done through the banks, acting as intermediaries between buyers and sellers via telephone calls. The dealer banks earned revenues via the difference between the bid–ask spread (buy and sell prices). They assumed some risks by holding an inven-tory of bonds, as they might not be able to match the buy and sell orders exactly at any one point in time. The holding of inventory needed capital from the banks. Such a process was relatively slow and inefficient. The advent of the Internet provided the basis for a more transparent market. Two possible business models emerged. The first is an evolutionary business model innovation whereby the role of the banks as an intermediary remains the same but the process is transferred to an electronic trading platform rather than a telephone-based system. Prices and inventory levels are posted by the trading parties on the platform to enable trading. The second business model involves a revolutionary model that disintermediates the dealer banks as market-making intermediaries. The dealer banks' role changes from being an intermediary to a credit guarantor in order to enable trading directly between buyers and sellers on an electronic platform. This enables investors as buyers and sellers to trade directly with one another in order to reduce costs and improve the timeliness of trades being completed. The bank earns revenues from charging a fee for the role as a credit guarantor. In this model, banks can reduce the amount of economic risk capital set aside for market-making compared to the telephone-based business model, as their role as market-making intermediaries becomes redundant and there is no need to hold inventories of bonds.

Following the advent of the Internet, in 1999 a new entrant launched RevolTrade, a revolu-tionary version of the business model, which aimed to disintermediate the banks. RevolTrade was able to price the bond cheaper for customers as a result of the new business model having no inventory positions. Initially, the banks did not respond, as the new entrant had not changed the market shares of the banks dramatically. However, a few months after its launch, RevolTrade was beginning to take market share away from the less-dominant banks (the banks with rela-tively smaller market shares). The reason for this was that with smaller market shares customers were less likely to benefit significantly from the network effects compared to customers of the dominant banks (with relatively larger market shares). In early 2000, in response to RevolTrade, a group of less-dominant banks decided to form a consortium, Begonia, and launched an evolutionary business model using an electronic trading platform. The consortium of less-dominant banks had a market share between them of 19.4 percent. The less-dominant banks adopted a coopetition strategy as a defensive mechanism. However, once they adopted the evolutionary business model, the rate of customer attrition from the dominant banks started to accelerate, due to the reverse-S-shaped dis-adoption dynamics, as they were losing customers to the new entrants, as well as to Begonia. In response, in 2001 a group of dominant banks with market shares of 46 percent joined forces to launch a revolutionary business model, Orchid. Orchid effectively disintermediated the role of the banks as intermediaries and enabled the amount of capital required to be reduced by approximately 75 percent. This enabled the dominant banks to change the game dramatically, as merely copying the less-dominant bank consortium would not be helpful to create competitive advantage for them. The dominant banks adopted a coopetition strategy as an offensive mechanism, but only after the less-dominant banks had adopted a more defensive strategy first. In summary, we can draw two conclusions. First, in network markets, as a defensive mechanism to protect their existing business model, the less-dominant firms tend to engage in coopetition by innovating their business models in an evolutionary manner before the dominant firms. Second, in network markets, as an offensive strategy to alter the existing business model, the dominant firms will tend to engage in coopetition by innovating their business models in a revolutionary manner after the less-dominant firms. In drawing these conclusions, we provide a more nuanced insight and build on the study by Ritala and Sainio (2014), which demonstrated that increased technological coopetition contributes positively to business model radicalness.

Electronic book retailing

Platform-based business models are becoming increasingly prevalent in the digital economy. Platforms can be a collection of resources such as technologies, knowledge, or skills that enable intermediaries to facilitate an exchange between actors in a market place (Thomas et al., 2014; Velu, 2015). Such platform-based intermediaries might leverage the resources of other competing firms in order to enhance the value of the platform and, hence, increase the transaction flow of exchanges. We discuss the case of Amazon, which adopted such a platform-based approach.[2]

Amazon began as an online bookseller in July 1995. The business model of Amazon was disruptive to the traditional bricks-and-mortar booksellers for several reasons. Amazon was able to provide a wider assortment of books, to price them just as competitively, and with distribution available all the time and promotion based on online reviews, all of which provide a more compelling proposition than the traditional retail model. After three years, Amazon started diversifying its platform to sell other products such as music and electronic consumer goods. Amazon soon recognized that leveraging its processes, infrastructure, and brand through its platform provides a great opportunity to expand the market and create superior competitive advantage. Such a strategy might require working with competitors. In order to implement such a coopetition-based strategy, Amazon launched a third-party marketplace, Amazon Marketplace, in November 2000. Competitors of any size could list and sell their books (and other products) alongside Amazon's own propositions by leveraging Amazon's e-commerce platform and customer base. This enabled Amazon to implement its "single store strategy," whereby Amazon becomes the place of choice for customers to buy either new or used books from Amazon or its competitors by comparing them on a single page. Amazon provided automated tools to third-party retailers to migrate their catalogs of new and used books to the Amazon web page. Moreover, other supplier information was also readily accessible by the customer, such as supplier ratings, shipping costs, and returns policies.

Amazon's decision to cooperate with competitors was not straightforward, as there was a significant amount of resistance from within the firm. For example, there were concerns that allowing competitors to list books alongside Amazon could imply that Amazon could be undercut on price all the time. However, Amazon's business model was in doubt by mid-2000, and this was reflected in the stock price, which fell by two-thirds in mid-2000 and by 80 percent by the end of that year. Amazon Marketplace was partly a response to such a loss in confidence by the investor community about Amazon. Among other relevant initiatives, Amazon Marketplace enabled the firm to offset operating expenses while increasing sales. The marginal cost of enabling competitors to list their products on Amazon.com was negligible, but Amazon earned commissions and subscription fees. Moreover, Amazon needed to hold less inventory of its own. In summary, Amazon built a platform-based business model by linking competitors' activities with its own in order to leverage the combined resources and provide a compelling customer value proposition. The platform-based business model enabled Amazon to reduce costs by holding less inventory of its own while earning revenues from commissions on third-party sales. Third-party sales via Amazon.com accounted for 20 and 35 percent of North American sales by 2002 and 2010, respectively. Coopetition-based strategy enabled the combination of increased sales and reduced costs, contributing considerably to Amazon's profitability and, hence, competitive position.

Flat-screen LCD televisions

Coopetition strategies could be motivated by the need to innovate products in order to stay ahead of other competitors and potential new entrants that leverage new technologies (Jorde & Teece, 1990). Coopetition among competitors might provide access to complementary knowledge and resources in a timely manner. Such coopetition among competitor firms might result in improved technological standards in the industry and also impact more widely on other participating firms in the industry. We discuss developments in the flat-panel television industry, where product life cycles are very short, capital investment is very large, and product range is broad.[3]

Samsung Electronics and Sony Corporations were longtime rivals, as they competed over many products in the electronics industry. However, they decided to cooperate in the development of the liquid crystal display (LCD) flat-panel TV market by establishing an R&D collaboration in 2003. The initial commitment from both firms was $1 billion each to develop the seventh-generation LCD TV. This commitment was tripled for the eighth-generation technology a few years later.

In order to better understand what prompted two large rival firms to cooperate in the LCD market it would be instructive to review developments in the TV market. The cathode ray tube (CRT) was the main form of TV technology for a long time but was replaced by the flat-panel television. The main technologies in flat-panel TV were LCD and plasma display panels (PDP). However, there were also a number of other technologies, such as electroluminescent display (ELD), light-emitting diode (LED), and organic light-emitting diode (OLED). Both Sony and Samsung were unable to develop the technology themselves for LCD TV as a result of the compressed nature of the timescale for the rate of development in new TV-based technologies. Sony was the leader in the CRT TV market. Samsung was a leader in LCD panel production but was not the largest LCD TV maker. Each firm had unique capabilities that the other firm needed in order to build and establish the standards in flat-screen TV and to dominate that market. Samsung brought strengths in LCD technology, while Sony contributed complementary skills in high-quality standards in technology and product quality with brand recognition in television, respectively. Both firms also cross-licensed their patents, with 11,000 patents from Samsung and 13,000 from Sony, respectively.

Sony launched the Bravia series within one year of establishing the joint R&D collaboration with Samsung, following suit with the Bordeaux series. By 2008 Samsung and Sony were ranked first and second, respectively, in the TV market, which was a considerable improvement from their position as fourth and third, respectively, before the R&D collaboration. In summary, Samsung and Sony redesigned their business models through repartitioning their upstream activities by sharing R&D resources. The cooperation of Samsung and Sony in upstream R&D activities enabled them to compete effectively in the downstream TV market by enabling the firms to create quality flat-screen LCD TVs. Table 31.1 provides a summary of the three coopetition-based business models.

Discussion

Competitors are increasingly cooperating among themselves in order to create superior competitive advantage. Such a coopetition strategy provides the basis for extending the conventional strategy literature through the positioning school or the resource-based view. The business model provides a valid lens through which to articulate more clearly why the network of firms is an important element in the process of value creation and value capture. There are several reasons for such coopetition, which can be viewed from a market or resources perspective (Ritala, 2012). First, firms might have a desire to protect their existing share of the market, increase the size of the current market, or create totally new markets. Second, firms might want to access resources that they do not possess, use fewer resources, or use their existing resources more efficiently. These motivations are aimed at improving performance through competitive advantage from existing business or at growth through innovation.

We have discussed a number of cases in this chapter in relation to firms adopting a coopetition strategy in order to create superior competitive advantage. In the first case, we examined how demand-side network externalities in the US bond trading market influenced incumbent firms of different levels of dominance to innovate their business models, in either an evolutionary or a revolutionary manner, in order either to protect their existing market or to create new markets, respectively. In the second case, we examined the electronic book retailing market, whereby Amazon created the Amazon Marketplace and allowed competitors to sell books on the same platform as a basis for creating a larger market and benefiting from scale economies by reducing its unit cost base. This enabled Amazon Marketplace to reduce costs, sharing its platform infrastructure and, hence, to hold less inventory while earning revenues from commissions from third-party sales, which helped to improve its bottom line. The basis of coopetition is the platform-based business model, whereby resources and the brand of Amazon are leveraged by competitors to gain access to customers for their products. In the third case, we examined coopetition between two large rival incumbents, Samsung and Sony, in order to access each other's complementary resources and, hence, enable innovation in the newly evolving LCD TV market. The basis of coopetition is the outsourcing of the upstream R&D activities via a joint initiative of both firms, with a view to competing in the downstream product market. The sharing of knowledge resources enables faster product development. These cases emphasize the importance of business model innovation in enabling implementation of the coopetition strategy. The case vignettes illustrate how the business model design could vary depending on how the

Table 31.1 Comparison of coopetition-based business models

	Value Proposition	Value Creation	Value Capture	Value Network	Rationale for Coopetition
Electronic trading and bond markets – revolutionary business model innovation	Enable direct trading between investors in order to reduce costs and improve timeliness of trades	Banks provide credit guarantee for the trades	Banks charge a fee for acting as credit guarantor	Dominant banks cooperating in order to change the structure of the market in a revolutionary manner	Help to innovate the business model to create a new market
Electronic book retailing – Amazon Marketplace	Enable customers to buy either new or used books from Amazon or its competitors by comparing them on a single page	Consolidating Amazon and third-party books on a single store page and providing comparisons of ratings, shipping costs, and returns policy	Amazon earns the margin on its own inventory and charges a commission on the sale of third-party products	Cooperate with competitors by enabling them to list books on the Amazon Marketplace website	Reduce costs by holding less inventory, while earning revenues from commissions on third-party sales
Flat-screen LCD televisions	Improved quality of flat-screen LCD televisions	Cross-licensed patents	Sony and Samsung were able to launch and sell their own brand of flat-screen televisions	Repartitioning upstream activities by sharing R&D resources	Sharing specialized resources enables faster product development

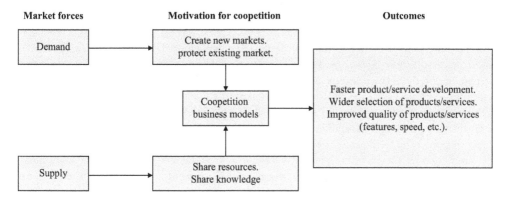

Figure 31.2 Framework for coopetition-based business models

objectives of the market-demand-based or supply-based considerations drive the motivation for coopetition. Demand-based considerations could include the motivation to create new markets to protect an existing market. Supply-based considerations could include the motivation to share resources or knowledge assets. We develop a framework as one of the key contributions to summarize the findings from this chapter in Figure 31.2.

There are a number of open research issues in relation to business models and coopetition. These can be grouped into three categories, namely, risk management of business models, innovation-driven business model design, and inter-temporal business model design. The first open research issue relates to how risk needs to be shared between parties within a coopetition arrangement. The business model design will influence how risks are shared between the different parties so that there are sufficient incentives for them to work together despite being competitors. The framework of the design of the business model needs to incorporate elements of which aspects to centralize or decentralize, as well as how to coordinate the activities of the firms. Such a business model design would need to factor in information management so that the right information were available to the parties concerned to make the decision, while minimizing conflicts of interest.

The second area where further research is needed is the design of coopetition-based business models that stimulate innovation. Often competitor firms might come together because the pace of change in the markets and technologies is too fast for each firm to innovate quickly enough and to remain competitive. Therefore, bringing resources together to help the innovation process is a key element of the coopetition strategy. However, it is not clear how the value created would be captured by the relevant parties as new propositions are developed. By the very definition of such innovation, it would not be possible to define all the means of sharing the value upfront. Therefore, an appropriate business model design that provides sufficient incentives for innovation so that each party can capture value appropriately needs further investigation.

The third area of research is the further contribution to the debate about how strategy influences structure, and vice versa. In particular, it would be helpful to conduct further longitudinal research on how coopetition-based business models might influence the strategy formulation of the firms involved and, hence, as a result influence the design of future business models. In particular, among the issues that require further investigation are the following questions: would firms that have adopted coopetition-based business models in the past adopt further coopetition-based business models in the future, and, if so, how would they go about designing them?

Conclusion

Coopetition is increasingly becoming the approach that is adopted by competing firms in order to create competitive advantage. The reason for coopetition could be defensive or offensive, depending on the relative threats and opportunities. Often the basis for coopetition is to grow existing, or create new, markets, to share resources in fast-changing environments in order to achieve efficiency, and also to enhance innovation capabilities. Coopetition requires the ability of firms to design, implement, and manage new business models. This chapter provides an overview of some cases to illustrate the rationale for coopetition-based business model design. The research in coopetition and business model design is very much at a nascent stage, with much more still to investigate regarding how, when, and why business model innovation is required for coopetition-based strategies to contribute in order to create competitive advantage.

Notes

1 This case example is drawn from Velu, C. (2016).
2 This case example is drawn from Ritala, Golnam, & Wegmann (2014).
3 This case example is drawn from Gnyawali & Park (2011).

References

Baden-Fuller, C. & Haefliger, S. (2013). Business models and technological innovations. *Long-Range Planning*, 46(6), 419–426.

Bengtsson, M. & Kock, S. (2014). Coopetition – Quo vadis? Past accomplishment and future challenges. *Industrial Marketing Management*, 43(2), 180–188.

Bouncken, R. & Kraus, S. (2013). Innovation in knowledge intensive industries: The double edge sword of coopetition. *Journal of Business Research*, 66(1), 2060–2070.

Brandenburger, A. & Nalebuff, B. J. (1995). The right game: Use game theory to shape strategy. *Harvard Business Review*, 73(4), 57–71.

Chiambaretto, P. & Fernandez, A. S. (2016). The evolution of coopetitive and collaborative alliances in an alliance portfolio: The Air France case. *Industrial Marketing Management*, 57, 75–85.

Chiambaretto, P. & Dumez, H. (2016). Towards a typology of coopetition: A multilevel approach. *International Studies of Management and Organization*, 46, 110–129.

Dos Santos, J., Spector, B., & Van Der Heyden, L. (2015). Towards a theory of business model change. In N. Foss, & T. Saebi (Eds), *Business Model Innovation: The Organizational Dimension*. Oxford: Oxford University Press.

Fan, T., Vigeant-Langlois, L., Geissler, C., Bosler, B., & Wilmking, J. (2001). Evolution of global airline strategic alliance and consolidation in the twenty-first century. *Journal of Air Transport Management*, 7(6), 349–360.

Farrell, J. & Saloner, G. (1986). Installed base and compatibility: Innovation, product preannouncements and predation. *American Economic Review*, 76 (December): 940–955.

Gnyawali, D. R. & Park, B. J. (2011). Co-opetition between giants: Collaboration with competitors for technological innovation. *Research Policy*, 40(5), 650–663.

Jorde, T. M. & Teece, D. J. (1990). Innovation and cooperation: Implications for competition and antitrust. *The Journal of Economic Perspective*, 4(3), 75–96.

Katz, M. L. & Shapiro, C. (1985). Network externalities, competition and compatibility. *American Economic Review*, 75(3), 424–440.

Quintana-García, C. & Benavides-Velasco, C. A. (2004). Cooperation, competition, and innovative capability: A panel data of european dedicated biotechnology firms. *Technovation*, 24(12), 927–938.

Ritala, P. (2012) Coopetition Strategy – when is it successful? Empirical evidence on innovation and market performance. *British Journal of Management*, 23, 307–324.

Ritala, P., & Sainio, L. M. (2014). Coopetition for radical innovation: Technology, market and business model perspective. *Technology Analysis and Strategic Management*, 26(2), 155–169.

Ritala, P., Golnam, A., & Wegmann, A. (2014). Coopetition-based business models: The case of Amazon. com. *Industrial Marketing Management*, 43(2), 236–249.

Rusko, R. (2014). Mapping the perspectives of coopetition and technology-based networks: A case of smartphones. *Industrial Marketing Management*, 43(5), 801–802.

Thomas, L., Autio, E, & Gann, D. (2014). Architectural leverage: Putting platform in context. *Academy of Management Perspectives*, 28(2), 198–219.

Velu, C. (2015). Knowledge management capabilities of lead firms in innovation ecosystems. *AMS Review*, 5(3–4), 123–141.

Velu, C. (2016). Evolutionary or revolutionary business model innovation through coopetition? The role of dominance in network markets. *Industrial Marketing Management*, 53, 124–135.

Velu, C. (2017). A systems perspective on business model evolution: the case of an agricultural informational service provider in india. *Long Range Planning*, 50(5), 603–620.

Velu, C. (2018). BMI Research Programme, Mimeo, Institute for Manufacturing, Department of Engineering, University of Cambridge.

Velu, C. & Stiles, P. (2013). Managing decision-making and cannibalization for parallel business models. *Long Range Planning*, 46(6), 443–458.

Vergara, R. A. G. (2012). Samsung Electronics and Apple, Inc.: A study in contrast in vertical integration in the 21st century. *American International Journal of Contemporary Research*, 2(9), 77-81.

Yami, S., Castaldo, S., Dagnino, G. B., & Le Roy, F. (2010). *Coopetition: Winning Strategies for the 21st Century*. Cheltenham: Edward Elgar.

Zott, C. & Amit. R. (2010). Business model design: An activity system perspective. *Long Range Planning*, 43(2–3) 216–226.

Zott, C., Amit, R., & Massa, L. (2011). The business model: Recent developments and future research. *Journal of Management*, 37, 1019–1042.

Part VI
Coopetition beyond strategy

32

Coopetition and the dynamic capabilities framework

David J. Teece

Introduction

Although the term "coopetition" became common in business only after the release of a 1996 book with that title (Brandenburger & Nalebuff, 1996), the activities it describes have a much longer history.[1] In 1936, for example, two vertically integrated oil companies, Standard Oil of California (renamed Chevron in 1984) and the Texas Company (Texaco), created a joint venture that would use Standard's huge Middle East oil reserves to feed (directly or through crude oil exchanges) Texaco's international refining and retailing operations. The joint venture, eventually known as Caltex, was perhaps the largest joint venture in business history and lasted until the parent companies merged in 2001. Yet, throughout the life of Caltex (a brand name that remains common in the Asia-Pacific region), its two owners continued to compete in the United States under their respective brands, Chevron and Texaco. This example demonstrates the viability of certain coopetition arrangements—despite their inherent tensions.

Cooperative arrangements among competing firms have become more common as technology has become more widely dispersed both geographically and among firms. Whereas, thirty years ago, R&D excellence and commercialization capability resided in maybe fifty to 100 private corporations worldwide (e.g., IBM, TI, GE, Siemens, Roche, Exxon, Shell), today there are dozens of strong technology firms in almost every field, a steady stream of new enterprises, and the growing phenomenon of entry across traditional industry boundaries.

At the same time, technological challenges themselves, such as autonomous vehicles, have become too complex and cross-disciplinary for most stand-alone firms to have all the relevant capabilities in-house. This is amplified by the decline in the relative importance of in-house research departments, which many corporations have refocused more narrowly on commercial projects. The digitization of everything has likewise spurred requirements for collaboration among firms at different levels—and sometimes at the same level—in an industry.

Such arrangements are filled with risks and opportunities. Opportunities include low-cost access to valuable resources and a chance for insight into a rival's mindset. Risks include dependence on a rival and the peril of unintended knowledge leakage. The risks vary with the degrees of competition and cooperation in the relationship (Luo, 2007).

This chapter has two main goals. First, it will review and expand my previous work on coopetition. In the past, I wrote primarily about classic horizontal and vertical alliances. Today, it's also important to consider standards organizations and business ecosystems. While these forms are somewhat looser than formal alliances, they still require analysis and strategy in order to produce good results. The second goal is to integrate the notion of coopetition with the dynamic capabilities framework. Although I've written extensively about dynamic capabilities since their introduction, I have not yet explicitly addressed coopetition from a dynamic capabilities perspective.

Dyadic coopetition

Although the term "coopetition" didn't become well-known in economics and business strategy until the late 1990s, I and others were writing about these types of relationships earlier, particularly in the contexts of joint research activities and strategic alliances. In this section, I review my early writings on horizontal and vertical cooperation among pairs of current and potential rivals.

Horizontal coopetition

In the 1980s, I wrote a series of articles (including several co-authored with Tom Jorde) that made the case for cooperation benefitting competition. Then, in my 1992 article in the *Journal of Economic Behavior and Organization*, I summarized my arguments for the necessity of cooperation between rivals for the purpose of innovation. At the time, this was not accepted in the field of antitrust/competition policy. Looking up "cooperation" in textbooks from this period would lead to a discussion of cartels, and not much else. A nuanced appreciation of how cooperation could aid competition simply did not exist. However, in the US, the 1984 National Cooperative Research Act had opened the door for research consortia to reduce their risk of antitrust prosecution; but the limits were not clear, nor had the relaxation been extended to cooperation in manufacturing (Jorde & Teece, 1989), which finally came in 1993. Inter-firm cooperation for any number of purposes had of course been permitted and common, in Japan and elsewhere, for decades (Gerlach, 1992).

As Teece (1992) observed, horizontal collaboration among innovators can be important for defining technical standards, internalizing spillovers, sharing risk, and reducing unnecessary duplication of research effort. Shared research can range from an informal system of consultation to shared facilities. Some level of collaboration may also be needed in the case of systemic innovations requiring large-scale investments. Shipping containers, for example, required major changes to transportation equipment and port facilities before their full benefit could be realized.

The 1992 paper goes on to analyze the range of organizational arrangements for alliances that can be created to develop (and possibly also commercialize) new technologies. Horizontal alliances can include any of the following: technology swaps, joint R&D, restrictive technology licensing rights, equity investments, or co-marketing. The key element is that they involve some level of medium-term strategic coordination beyond what can be achieved through simple market transactions. The alliance mechanism, usually specified in a contract, allows the freer sharing of information and some degree of joint decision making (Mayer & Teece, 2008). As Hamel, Doz, and Prahalad (1989) emphasized, it is important to bring strategic intent to the relationship so that learning opportunities are not overlooked and technological secrets are not recklessly exposed. Classic contemporary alliances include civilian airline arrangements such as "Star Alliance" and "Oneworld" that involve joint marketing and codesharing of flights.[2]

Vertical coopetition

De Figueiredo and Teece (1996) considered a variant form of coopetition where a vertically integrated firm supplies a downstream competitor. This is common, in large part because a vertically integrated firm often needs to sell upstream parts to outside firms in order to operate at efficient scale and/or expose its in-house operation to market discipline. A prominent contemporary example is the relationship between Samsung and Apple. Although the two firms compete fiercely in the smartphone market and the courthouse, Samsung continues to sell Apple key components for the iPhone, such as the display. The one exception is the processor chip (manufactured to Apple's design), for which Apple was eventually able to find another suitable supplier after its dispute with Samsung intensified.

De Figueiredo and Teece (1996) identify three potential technological hazards that can develop in such relationships if appropriate safeguards aren't in place to protect against them. First, the integrated supplier can control the pacing of technology at the frontier, which affects the opportunities available to the downstream customer. Second, the integrated supplier may refuse to sell the most advanced inputs, at least in the quantity desired, to the downstream buyer. And, third, the downstream buyer may inadvertently reveal technical or market information to the integrated supplier that the supplier can use in its in-house downstream operation.

Safeguards that can prevent these hazards from making the arrangement untenable include the desire to maintain a valuable long-term relationship, the relative ease of substitution for either or both partners, and the financial size of the transactions involved. Nevertheless, the hazards are real. In the market for enterprise resource planning (ERP) software, ERP provider SAP began using database software from Oracle, the market leader, in 1989. Oracle learned so much about the ERP market from its work with SAP that Oracle entered the market in 1995. It became a strong competitor with SAP, but SAP continued to rely on Oracle database software (Pellegrin-Boucher et al., 2013).

As this example suggests, the hazards are sometimes unavoidable because of the dominant position of one of the firms. This is the case for small sellers in Amazon's Marketplace program. They can't do without the global exposure that Amazon's website can provide, but they operate under a constant threat that Amazon will move into their product categories.

Multi-sided coopetition

Since the 1990s, technologies have become more complex and interdependent. Coopetition, accordingly, has become a multi-sided affair because even two strong firms are unlikely to be adequate to develop and commercialize major innovations, such as wireless communications. Technical standards provide the agreed-on technology foundation that enables multi-sided commercial cooperation. Standards development organizations and business ecosystems are therefore increasingly the venues in which coopetition plays out.

Standards development

Standards have become ever-more important in the digital era as products that were once separate are more easily integrated or able to communicate in a common language. The digital revolution has abolished borders between telephones, music players, the web, TVs, cameras, and more. This in turn has pushed providers of content and services towards horizontal and vertical partnerships to leverage the power of business ecosystems, as discussed in the next sub-section.

Standards for complex enabling technologies such as 3G, 4G, and 5G communications require collaborative development if they are to provide full interoperability across ecosystems and industries. Standards enable modularization, which allows firms to specialize, developing complementary products that are certain to work through the standard interface (see Langlois & Robertson, 1992).

Standards development organizations (SDOs) provide a framework for horizontal and vertical cooperation among fierce rivals. While these multi-sided arrangements are looser than dyadic strategic alliances, they are nonetheless affected by similar strategic concerns. Firms in a standards development organization develop technologies that might benefit the standard. The technology, if selected by the SDO, is integrated with others into a formal standard specification then licensed to implementers.

As candidate technologies are submitted, experts at a standards development organization cooperatively evaluate competing possibilities with an eye toward producing the highest-performance result possible. One or more firms must usually take a leadership role in order to ensure that the standard includes all the necessary technologies for an end-to-end solution. Because various proposed technologies will often have different technical advantages, decisions may be influenced by commercial feasibility. Substantial testing may be required to ensure that implementation criteria are met.

Most SDOs consist of multiple working groups, each focused on specific technologies within the standard. The 5G standard, for example, encompasses numerous separate technologies covered by hundreds of patents owned by more than a dozen organizations, primarily global corporations such as Nokia and Qualcomm. Dozens of other firms who will be implementing the standard have a stake in the outcomes. Implementers are third-party beneficiaries of FRAND agreements between the SDO and those members that provide technology into the standard.[3] SDOs and regulatory bodies need to be alert to the proclivity of some implementers to free ride by bringing standard-based products to market while refusing to take licenses for the underlying patents.

Ecosystems

Horizontal and vertical coopetition also occurs when rival firms participate in a shared ecosystem. Ecosystems typically arise around a platform that provides some combination of hardware, software, standards, interfaces, and rules. In the digital world, platforms can be software-only, like Alphabet's Android operating system (OS), or they can be linked to hardware, like Apple's iPhone and iPad, which are tightly integrated with Apple's proprietary iOS software. The key is that companies and users can, jointly or separately, innovate and attract users far more productively with the platform than if they were to try to achieve the same goals without it.

The platform enables providers of complements to add value and, if they choose, interact with each other. When there is platform-to-platform competition, adoption and commercial success is likely a function of which platform can recruit the most (and the best) complementors. The viability of a platform-based ecosystem depends on continued innovation and maintenance of the platform by its owner(s) and a delicate balance of cooperation and competition among the providers of complements. Complementors each seek a profitable position within the ecosystem, as in the case of two video games on a smartphone.

In another twist, a relationship that seems complementary can turn into a variant of vertical coopetition if the platform owner decides to enter the market for one or more of the complements. Microsoft, for example, diversified into browsers, streaming media, and messaging applications that were already being provided on its Windows operating system by stand-alone firms (Teece, 2012). Although this raised Microsoft's costs, it prevented complementors from becoming large enough to exercise market power.

This can play out in reverse, with complementors moving from conflict to cooperation. Microsoft and Salesforce, for example, had sued each other over patent infringement claims in 2010 and demonstrated hostile relations at every turn until new Microsoft CEO Satya Nadella switched to a culture of cooperation. During his keynote appearance at a 2015 Salesforce conference, he underscored the need for embracing coopetition within and across ecosystems:

> Our customers are going to make choices that make the most sense for them ... They are going to use all these different applications and multiple platforms. It is incumbent upon us, especially those of us who are platform vendors to partner broadly to solve real pain points our customers have.
>
> *(cited in Miller, 2015)*

Coopetition and dynamic capabilities

Most studies of coopetition take the existence of the relationship as given. This bypasses the fundamental question of how a coopetitive arrangement and specific partners are selected from among the strategic options.

For the past two decades, one of the primary focuses of my research has been the elaboration of the dynamic capabilities framework. It encompasses the processes, analyses, and decisions that can generate coopetitive relationships. In this section, I briefly summarize the dynamic capabilities framework then draw out the linkages between the framework and coopetition.

The dynamic capabilities framework

A strategic management approach that can help to navigate contemporary business challenges like coopetition is the dynamic capabilities framework. One of the earliest definitions of dynamic capabilities was "the firm's ability to integrate, build, and reconfigure internal and external competences to address rapidly changing environments" (Teece et al., 1997: 516). That definition still applies, although the speed of change in the environment may be less relevant than the prevailing degree of uncertainty (Teece et al., 2016).

Although dynamic capabilities are limited by some scholars to replicable routines (e.g., Helfat & Winter, 2011), the more comprehensive capabilities framework, as described by Teece (2014), incorporates both routines and managerial decision-making, which allows for the inclusion of higher-level capabilities that I organize into sensing, seizing, and transforming. While some in the literature have treated these as strictly the result of managerial cognition and decision making (e.g., Helfat & Martin, 2015), they generally entail activities throughout the organization.

The dynamic capabilities framework also encompasses other elements, particularly strategy formation, which is separate from dynamic capabilities. A strategy can be defined as "actions that respond to a high-stakes challenge" (Rumelt, 2012: 6). Capabilities provide inputs to, and then help enact, the strategy. The framework also encompasses external actors including complementors, rival firms, and the institutions that regulate and/or interact with the focal organization.

It is often helpful to see capabilities from a hierarchical perspective. At the base lie ordinary capabilities, which consist of the processes that deploy people, facilities, and equipment to carry out the current business of the firm. They lend themselves to being measured and benchmarked, which also makes them easier for others to replicate. Since they are therefore unlikely to provide a unique advantage, strong ordinary capabilities need to be accessed, but not necessarily owned.

When operating in-house, ordinary capabilities allow a firm to achieve best-practice levels of efficiency, regardless of whether the current output plan is likely to be suitable in the future. The pursuit of high efficiency can thus deprive a company of the resilience needed to change promptly when the need arises. Efficiency should be balanced by measures to mitigate risk and an organizational culture that enables rapid improvisation.

The next level of the capability hierarchy consists of components of dynamic capabilities that I call "microfoundations" (Teece, 2007). They include processes for forming external partnerships or for developing new products. Microfoundations are elements of dynamic capabilities, and they allow the firm to integrate, reconfigure, add, or subtract resources, including ordinary capabilities (Eisenhardt & Martin, 2000). Moreover, they are sometimes unique to a company, as in the case of Cisco's distinctive competence in managing acquisitions (Mayer & Kenney, 2004). However, they resemble ordinary capabilities in that they are oriented toward following an existing plan and are relatively replicable by rivals.

Higher-level dynamic capabilities, along with strategy formation, generate a plan for the future and enable its implementation. They govern identification of the parameters for entering into a partnership and for setting the directions in which new products should be developed. These higher-level dynamic capabilities are difficult for rivals to copy because they arise from a company's unique history of competitive experiences, organizational learning, and managerial choices. When well-developed, they allow a firm to maintain continued (evolutionary) fitness vis-à-vis the external business environment and coherence among the elements of the system (Teece, 2017a).

The high-level capabilities can be grouped into three clusters of entrepreneurial activities that take place concurrently throughout the organization: sensing, seizing, and transforming. They encompass organizational processes as well as unique managerial decisions (Augier & Teece, 2009; Teece, 2012, 2016).

The activities for "sensing" and sensemaking include environmental scanning, which brings disorganized information and unstructured data from the external environment into the organization. Managers at various levels must generate and test hypotheses about latent consumer demand, technological possibilities, and other forces that affect the firm's future. In a firm with strong capabilities, relevant information finds its way to where it will be properly assessed and handled. The top management team combines and analyzes the data from internal and external sources to continuously monitor the firm's environment, prioritize problems, and identify new opportunities.

"Seizing" capabilities determine how quickly the organization can respond to significant opportunities and threats once they have been identified. The activities involved include investing to commercialize new technologies; identifying and deciding how to fill capability gaps; and designing (or updating) and implementing business models for various products and services (Teece, 2017).

"Transforming" capabilities are responsible for keeping the elements of the organizational system aligned both internally, externally, and with the strategy. These capabilities are most critical when a new business model involves a significant change to the organization's design or conflicts with an existing business model. Minor transformations must also be made periodically for a variety of reasons. Fostering an organizational culture that favors flexibility and experimentation, while challenging to bring about, can provide a solid foundation for quicker and easier transformations and, therefore, for future advantage.

Dynamic capabilities and coopetition

Coopetition involves critical issues of alignment and congruence. The dynamic capabilities approach, because of its general systems nature, highlights the importance of such factors (Teece, 2017a). In the absence of congruence, there is a real danger that coopetition will collapse, with undesirable outcomes. Strong dynamic capabilities are vital to planning and managing successful coopetition. This is clearly true in the case of a microfoundation capability such as alliance formation. This section will discuss the relationship of coopetition with sensing, seizing, and transforming.

Sensing capabilities are critical in at least two ways. In the first instance, they are important for helping to identify the most promising directions in which to expand or redirect the firm's activity. Then, within this new direction, they enable the firm to identify possible partners or comparators for missing capabilities, depending on whether the capability is to be developed in-house.

New initiatives almost always entail developing or acquiring new-to-the-company ordinary or microfoundation capabilities. Capability gaps are the "distance" separating the existing and the desired capabilities (Teece, 2017b). Capability distance can be calculated on at least three dimensions: (i) technical distance—how close the target technology is to the firm's existing knowledge base; (ii) market distance—how close the target customers are to the firm's existing customer base, in terms of willingness to pay, location, etc.; and (iii) business model distance— how suitable are the firm's existing cost structure, supply relationships, and revenue models for conducting the target activity.

Even recognizing the gaps in the first place can pose a challenge due to over-optimism about a new plan or other cognitive blinders. Often it is only after an organization falls short in one of its strategic initiatives that the true size of the gap(s) will be apparent. Management may have thought that a particular capability, such as supply chain management, was in place, only to discover that it was inadequate to the requirements of a new product or strategy.

Once a capability gap has been identified, the capabilities for seizing are engaged to calibrate and choose the best way to fill it. The greater the distance to be covered, the greater the cost in terms of time, effort, and expense if the capability is to be developed in-house. Making changes on all three dimensions at once constitutes a radical transformation for which the effort and attention required is more than the "sum" of the distances involved. With large gaps, especially when coupled with a narrow market window, some form of vertical or horizontal alliance may be the best choice.

Partnering is most desirable when a needed capability is available in a competitive supply market. In markets such as electronics assembly and back-office services, world-class capabilities can be accessed virtually at cost.

In many cases, however, potential suppliers have distinctive profiles, and the most attractive partner may also be an actual or potential competitor. In such cases, seizing capabilities can enable the focal firm to develop and manage the coopetitive relationship. After a relationship has been successfully established, care must be taken to limit technology leakage across the interface, to learn continuously from the partner, and to avoid becoming overly dependent.

Coopetition can, of course, be desirable for reasons other than bridging a specific capability gap. Examples include cases of cost-sharing and technological complementarity. Sensing and seizing capabilities are needed here, too, for judging technical trends and assessing the industrial landscape for potential allies.

Capabilities for transforming are needed to create an organizational conduit for analysis of, and learning from, the partner firm(s) so that the knowledge can be integrated and operationalized. Transforming capabilities are also exercised when coopetition takes a discrete organizational form such as a joint venture. The processes and managerial mindset required are similar to those for ambidexterity (O'Reilly & Tushman, 2008). Relevant assets must be aligned with the needs of the new unit; the unit must be ensured adequate resources and the correct balance between autonomy and integration with incumbent units; and incumbent units must be correctly reconfigured to compensate for any assets that were subtracted.

Conclusion

The conditions of knowledge dispersion and globalization that led to the emergence of the coopetition concept have only become more deeply entrenched in the business landscape over time. Coopetition takes many forms, from the dyadic alliances first analyzed by game theorists to looser interactions among the competing complementors in a business ecosystem.

The dynamic capabilities framework provides deep insights into the basis for coopetition and its implementation. The framework is broad and inclusive enough to allow the framing and assessment of the complex tradeoffs that coopetition entails. In a coopetition context, keeping capabilities and strategies aligned is challenging. But, so long as the strategic hazards are properly managed, coopetition can aid innovation and learning, and contribute to profitable outcomes.

Notes

Acknowledgement: I'm grateful to Greg Linden for very helpful comments and assistance.

1 Looking beyond the world of business, co-opetition can be traced back to at least the fifth century BC, when rival Greek city-states Athens and Sparta successfully joined forces to oppose a Persian invasion before eventually engaging in an all-out war against each other. The ancient proverb that "the enemy of my enemy is my friend" also suggests elements of a co-opetition model.
2 Star Alliance was founded in 1997 and today includes twenty-seven members. Oneworld was founded in 1999 and has thirteen members.
3 FRAND (fair, reasonable, and non-discriminatory terms) is the criterion that licensing terms are required to meet by many SDOs (Sherry, Teece, & Grindley, 2015).

References

Augier, M. & Teece, D. J. (2009). Dynamic capabilities and the role of managers in business strategy and economic performance. *Organization Science*, 20(2), 410–421.

Brandenburger, A. M. & Nalebuff, B. J. (1996). *Co-opetition*. New York: Doubleday.

De Figueiredo, J. M. & Teece, D. J. (1996). Mitigating procurement hazards in the context of innovation. *Industrial and Corporate Change*, 5(2), 537–559.

Eisenhardt, K. M. & Martin, J. A. (2000). Dynamic capabilities: what are they? *Strategic Management Journal*, 21(10/11), 1105–1121.

Gerlach, M. L. (1992). *Alliance Capitalism: The Social Organization of Japanese Business*. Berkeley, CA: University of California Press.

Hamel, G., Doz, Y. L., & Prahalad, C. K. (1989). Collaborate with your competitors and win. *Harvard Business Review*, 67(1), 133–139.

Helfat, C. E. & Martin, J. A. (2015). Dynamic managerial capabilities: Review and assessment of managerial impact on strategic change. *Journal of Management*, 41(5), 1281–1312.

Helfat, C. E. & Winter, S. G. (2011). Untangling dynamic and operational capabilities: Strategy for the (N) ever-changing world. *Strategic Management Journal*, 32(11), 1243–1250.

Jorde, T. M. & Teece, D. J. (1989). Competition and cooperation: Striking the right balance. *California Management Review*, 31(3), 25–37.

Langlois, R. N. & Robertson, P. L. (1992). Networks and innovation in a modular system: Lessons from the microcomputer and stereo component industries. *Research Policy*, 21(4), 297–313.

Luo, Y. (2007). A coopetition perspective of global competition. *Journal of World Business*, 42(2), 129–144.

Mayer, D. & Kenney, M. (2004). Economic action does not take place in a vacuum: Understanding Cisco's acquisition and development strategy. *Industry and Innovation*, 11(4), 299–325.

Mayer, K. J. & Teece, D. J. (2008). Unpacking strategic alliances: The structure and purpose of alliance versus supplier relationships. *Journal of Economic Behavior & Organization*, 66(1), 106–127.

Miller, R. (2015). Cooperation Is the new normal at Microsoft. techcrunch.com, Oct. 1. Available at https://techcrunch.com/2015/10/01/cooperation-is-the-new-normal-at-microsoft/.

O'Reilly, C. A. & Tushman, M. L. (2008). Ambidexterity as a dynamic capability: Resolving the innovator's dilemma. *Research in Organizational Behavior*, 28, 185–206.

Pellegrin-Boucher, E., Le Roy, F., & Gurău, C. (2013). Coopetitive strategies in the ICT sector: Typology and stability. *Technology Analysis & Strategic Management*, 25(1), 71–89.

Rumelt, R. P. (2012). Good strategy/bad strategy: The difference and why it matters. *Strategic Direction*, 28(8).

Sherry, E. F., Teece, D., & Grindley, P. (2015). FRAND commitments in theory and practice: A response to Lemley and Shapiro's "A simple approach." Tusher Center for the Management of Intellectual Capital, UC Berkeley, Working Paper No. 3. Available at http://innovation-archives.berkeley.edu/businessinnovation/documents/Tusher-Center-Working-Paper-3.pdf.

Teece, D. J. (1992). Competition, cooperation, and innovation: Organizational arrangements for regimes of rapid technological progress. *Journal of Economic Behavior & Organization*, 18(1), 1–25.

Teece, D. J. (2007). Explicating dynamic capabilities: The nature and microfoundations of (sustainable) enterprise performance. *Strategic Management Journal*, 28(13), 1319–1350.

Teece, D. J. (2012) Next-generation competition: New concepts for understanding how innovation shapes competition and policy in the digital economy. *Journal of Law, Economics, and Policy*, 9(1), 97–118.

Teece, D. J. (2014). The foundations of enterprise performance: dynamic and ordinary capabilities in an (economic) theory of firms. *Academy of Management Perspectives*, 28(4), 328–352.

Teece, D. J. (2016). Dynamic capabilities and entrepreneurial management in large organizations: Toward a theory of the (entrepreneurial) firm. *European Economic Review*, 86, 202–216.

Teece, D. J. (2017a). Dynamic capabilities as (workable) management systems theory. *Journal of Management and Organization*, forthcoming.

Teece, D. J. (2017b). Business models and dynamic capabilities. *Long Range Planning*. In press, https://doi.org/10.1016/j.lrp.2017.06.007.

Teece, D., Peteraf, M., & Leih, S. (2016). Dynamic capabilities and organizational agility. *California Management Review*, 58(4), 13–35.

Teece, D. J., Pisano, G., & Shuen, A. (1997). Dynamic capabilities and strategic management. *Strategic Management Journal*, 18(7), 509–533.

33

The emergence of coopetitive marketing

Călin Gurău, Paul Chiambaretto, and Frédéric Le Roy

Introduction

The concept of coopetition was initially developed in strategic management as a paradoxical paradigm that combines the advantages of competition with those of cooperation between two or more organizations (Bengtsson & Kock, 1999, 2000; Brandenburger & Nalebuff, 1996). Although the extant literature on coopetition focuses mainly on innovation, R&D, and production agreements, lately several studies have started to analyze and present coopetitive alliances in marketing, deconstructing the strategic and operational elements that can enhance their viability and performance. In comparison with the previous focus on strategic alliances, inter- and intra-organizational tensions, and coopetition management, the new research incorporates the market relationships and competitive advantages, paradoxically built by collaborating with a direct or indirect competitor.

Acknowledging the increasing importance of coopetitive strategies in marketing, this chapter attempts to provide: (a) a general definition of coopetitive marketing; (b) an analysis of the transition from coopetition towards coopetitive marketing; (c) a general review of the main research contributions in coopetitive marketing; and (d) a future research agenda that maps the existing knowledge gaps that represent opportunities for further research.

Defining coopetitive marketing

Traditionally, economic theory considered competition and collaboration as opposite inter-organizational situations. In their model of the inter-organizational relationship continuum, Easton et al. (1993) define five relational situations: conflict, competition, co-existence, cooperation and collusion. From a market regulation perspective, the dichotomy between competition and cooperation is fundamental to preserve market dynamics and competitive rivalry, which ultimately benefits the consumers.

The economic theories of oligopoly reveal that collusive strategies are usually more profitable than the competitive ones (Tirole, 1989). In addition, many extant studies have shown that coopetitive strategies allow firms to achieve more profits and competitive advantages than either a pure collaborative or competitive stance (Bengtsson & Kock, 1999, 2000; Brandenburger &

Nalebuff, 1996; Lado et al., 1997; Peng et al., 2012; Ritala, 2009). On the one hand, a competitive relationship stimulates technological and managerial innovations, increases market focus, and contributes to continuous improvements in work efficiency and effectiveness. On the other hand, collaboration enhances specialization and complementarity in the value added chain, leads to economies of scale and experience, and accelerates R&D and the overall time to market. Thus, organizations able to combine and sustain these two relational models will reap the specific benefits of both competition and cooperation (Bengtsson & Kock, 2014).

According to Bengtsson and Kock (2014) or Dorn et al. (2016), the main theoretical foundations of coopetition are based on the resource-based view, game theory, and social network theory. These theoretical associations demonstrate the complex and multi-level structure of coopetition (Pellegrin-Boucher et al., 2013); if the resource-based view is strongly rooted in the organizational perspective, game theory adds the elements of relationship negotiation and management, while social network theory enlarges the category of relevant stakeholders (Akpinar & Vincze, 2016), introducing a market perspective. Social network theory also associates coopetition with the newly developed paradigm of collaborative consumption, raising the question of competition versus cooperation between the participants to the sharing economy (Schor, 2015). Nevertheless, coopetition strategies represent a complex combination of advantages and challenges, derived from their paradoxical nature. The simultaneous co-existence of competition and cooperation relations between two or more organizations (or intra-organizational departments) results in tensions at inter-organizational, intra-organizational, and inter-individual levels (Fernandez et al., 2014; Fernandez & Chiambaretto, 2016; Tidström, 2014).

In parallel, drawing inspiration from the existing academic and professional literature (Kotler & Keller, 2012), we define marketing as the activities realized by an organization to identify, know, understand, and satisfy its target market in order to realize a profit on a long-term perspective. Closely associated with this definition are the four areas of marketing applications: product, price, distribution, and communication. The latest marketing definitions often adopt a multi-stakeholder perspective, contending that an organization has to create value for various categories of stakeholders (e.g., employees, consumers, investors, government, and the overall society) by incorporating in its strategy and objectives the principles of social corporate responsibility (Kotler & Keller, 2012).

Considering the specific characteristics of coopetition strategy, we can define *coopetitive marketing* as an inter-organizational paradoxical relationship between two or more organizations that are simultaneously in a situation of competition and cooperation, developed and managed in order to better satisfy the consumers/stakeholders targeted by these organizations and to obtain a profit on a long-term perspective. In comparison with the previous definitions of coopetition, the one we propose adds the clear direct purpose of creating better value for the customers/stakeholders and a derived objective of profitability, considered from a long-term, sustainable perspective.

Transitioning from coopetition to coopetitive marketing

Although it is considered primarily a strategic management topic, many seminal papers on coopetition have been published in marketing journals, such as the papers of Bengtsson and Kock (1999 and 2000), published, respectively, in the *Journal of Business and Industrial Marketing* and in *Industrial Marketing Management*. Recently, *Industrial Marketing Management* published two special issues dedicated to coopetition strategies. Finally, papers on coopetition have also been published in the *Journal of Marketing* (Luo et al., 2006), *Journal of Marketing Research* (Luo et al.,

2007), *Journal of Business Research* (Bouncken & Krauss, 2013), and in the *Journal of Product and Innovation Management* (Ritala & Hurmelinna-Laukkanen, 2013).

Quite paradoxically, despite being published in marketing journals, the extant literature on coopetition is rather skewed, comprising studies focusing mainly on coopetitive agreements touching innovation (Bouncken & Kraus, 2013; Fernandez et al., 2018; Gnyawali & Park, 2009, 2011), the R&D process (Bouncken et al., in press; Nemeh & Yami, 2016), or manufacturing (Ehrenmann & Reiss, 2012; Fernandez et al., 2014). Several contributions clearly indicate that the cooperative dimension of coopetition should indeed occur far from markets and far from customers (Bengtsson & Kock, 2000; Blomqvist et al., 2005; Walley, 2007). These studies conclude that the paradox generated by coopetition cannot be understood by customers; therefore, it must remain "hidden" from them (Bengtsson & Kock, 1999, 2000).

However, these assumptions were based on the limited number of studies describing and investigating, at that time, coopetitive agreements in marketing, commerce, or customer service. The observed reality supports the existence and need for a market-oriented coopetition (Robert et al., 2018), as the majority of inter-organizational agreements are realized at the marketing and commercial level. For example, research conducted by the Association of Strategic Alliance Professionals in 2009, highlights that forty-five percent of the total number of alliances is represented by co-marketing and commercial agreements, of which R&D and manufacturing-focused alliances represent only sixteen percent. These alliances involve either vertical supplier-client relationships, as well as, increasingly, horizontal cooperation between competing organizations. In addition, several recent contributions have highlighted the existence of coopetition in which the collaboration involves activities close to the market, such as marketing or retailing activities (Chiambaretto & Dumez, 2016; Chiambaretto et al., 2016; Lindström & Polsa, 2016; Rusko, 2011; Teller et al., 2016; Robert et al., 2018). Therefore, a stronger focus on coopetition agreements involving activities close to the market is needed.

The technological or production orientation of the existing coopetition research led to an excessive inward focus on the inter-organizational coopetition strategy, performance, and management, neglecting the impact of these agreements on customers, investors, or other categories of stakeholders. An intermediary step was made by the studies investigating the role of coopetition in supply chain functioning, performance, and coordination (Bakshi & Kleindorfer, 2009; Kwok & Lee, 2015; Lacoste, 2012; Wu et al., 2010). Because supply chain theory incorporates the inter-organizational and/or inter-departmental relationships that determine the whole range of activities, from raw materials extraction and provision to the sale and consumption of the final product on the market, these contributions can be understood as first steps towards including market research and stakeholder interests in the cooperative dimension of coopetition.

Another stream of coopetition literature considered the situation in which coopetition strategies involve, in addition to the main organizational actors, a third-party, such as a client, an institution, a union, or the government (Bengtsson & Kock, 2000; Castaldo et al., 2010; Depeyre & Dumez, 2010; Freel, 2003; Rindfleisch & Moorman, 2003; Wu et al., 2010). The findings of these studies provide a twofold perspective regarding the roles played by the third party in the initiation, development, facilitation, and management of the coopetitive relationship: first, the third party is considered a powerful initiator of a coopetition strategy (Depeyre & Dumez, 2010; Castaldo et al., 2010); second, the third party is often entrusted to manage collaboration in order to ensure the success of the coopetitive strategy (Bengtsson & Kock, 2000; Rindfleisch & Moorman, 2003). However, it is also possible that various third parties (i.e., stakeholders) have a different attitude and involvement in coopetitive relationships.

The progressive development of the empirical base of coopetition research has created new opportunities to describe, analyze, and model the implication of coopetition for final clients—either individual or organizational—and has reinforced the idea that coopetition agreements can also occur in marketing and commercial activities. On this preliminary basis, coopetition research has built several notable contributions to marketing knowledge in several different areas.

Contributions of the coopetition literature to marketing knowledge

To present the main contributions of the coopetition literature to marketing knowledge, we choose a typology related to the main areas of marketing theory and action: market research, product portfolio, product policy, pricing, distribution, communication, and branding.

Market research

Identifying and properly understanding the profile and the behavior of the targeted customer segment(s) represents one of the main challenges and objectives of the marketing function in any organization. As the data collected and processed about consumers and competitors represent the market intelligence of the firm, organizations usually conduct market research individually, carefully protecting the findings from competitors. Firms have good reasons to protect their market intelligence because this information represents the basis of developing and implementing their marketing-mix strategy at the product, price, distribution, and communication level (Baumard, 2010; Fernandez & Chiambaretto, 2016). However, in some cases, small and medium-sized enterprises from the same sector may decide to share the costs of market research, which has become an important source of organizational costs. Amabile and Gadille (2006) describe such a collaboration between several French mutual insurance companies (e.g., MAIF, MACIF) that decided to share their statistics of accidents in order to achieve a more complete vision regarding the overall market profile and evolution. This represents a classic case of coopetition, as these organizations collaborate in market research and information sharing but compete fiercely in developing and commercializing insurance products. A quite similar setting is described by Kotzab & Teller (2003) regarding the Austrian grocery industry, in which some competing firms exchange knowledge based on their market research. Finally, Okura (2008) suggested that although competing firms may achieve a win-win situation by sharing information about customers, they are usually reluctant to do so.

Product portfolio

In many consumer-oriented markets, directly competing products are often part of the product portfolio of the same organizational group, being produced and commercialized though different brand names by different departments or subsidiaries of the same corporation (e.g., in the cosmetics market, both Vichy and la Roche-Posay, two brands in direct competition, are produced and commercialized by L'Oreal). Tsai (2002) and Luo (2005) provide a detailed description of the main issues surrounding the production and commercialization of competing products within the same organization; in fact, by using a combination of synergy, collaboration, and competition, these groups succeed to reduce the costs of production and commercialization—by sharing the same manufacturing facilities and logistic channels while creating a fierce competition in marketing and sales. This strategy is often hidden to the customer, as competition inflates the attractiveness and the price of products that are often highly similar.

Product development

Some companies attempt to reduce the costs of product development by collaborating with direct competitors, either by exchanging licenses (e.g., cross-licensing agreements between Samsung and Nokia, and Samsung and Ericsson), by creating common product platforms (e.g., PSA Peugeot Citroen has collaborative agreements to share platforms with several partners, including Fiat, Mitsubishi, and Toyota), or by developing and adhering to the same set of technological standards (e.g., the standard setting group in industrial automation, which includes direct competitors (Slowak, 2008). A good example of product development coopetition is provided by Gnyawali and Park (2011) regarding the collaboration between Samsung and Sony to become leaders of the LCD television screen market. As a result of their cooperation, the two companies are using the same technology to manufacture LCD TV screens; however, the branding, packaging, pricing, distribution, and commercialization of the products manufactured by the two firms are highly competitive and confrontational.

Pricing

Although the marketing theory and practice indicate that pricing strategies are highly specific to the market offer of each company, there are situations when competitors can collaborate at the price level. Robert et al. (2018) provide a good example of pricing coopetition in the real estate sector: a series of independent French retail estate agencies created the *Fichier AMEPI* (the French equivalent of the Multiple Listing Systems (MLS) that exists in the US), allowing them to share the commercialization of retail estate offers provided. The retail estate listings shared in the MLS could be sold either by the mandated agency—in which case the agency gets the entire commission—or by a partner/competitor participating in the MLS, in which case the mandated agency shares half of the commission with the selling one. This arrangement system is beneficial for all the parties involved, as the study shows that the real estate goods shared in this coopetitive setting are usually sold faster and at a higher price through this system than though the classical one.

Distribution

The global development of the market demand for specific products and services puts a high pressure on the distribution costs of companies. To reduce these costs and achieve a maximum exposure of their own product or service, companies from a specific sector may partner in order to share distribution costs or channels, although they may compete directly for global market shares (Pellegrin-Boucher et al., 2018). An example of this strategy is found in code-sharing agreements between airlines. These agreements allow competing airlines to extend their distribution network by accessing the network distribution of their partner/competitor (Chiambaretto & Dumez, 2016; Chiambaretto & Fernandez, 2016). Another example are the coopetitive agreements realized by the three main competing producers of ERP applications—IBM, Oracle, and SAP—for joint marketing operations and commercialization (Pellegrin-Boucher et al., 2018). Finally, regarding the distribution, Teller et al. (2016) have shown that the co-location of competing stores in the same area tends to foster coopetition between them, and this strategy indirectly increases their performance.

Communication

The exponential increase in communication costs, or a monopoly situation regarding specific communication channels, may influence competing firms to share their efforts in order to create joint communication campaigns (Lee & Shen, 2009; Samu et al., 1999). Quite paradoxically, an increasing number of competing firms have decided to join their forces and communicate together (Lindström & Polsa, 2016). It is very often the case in the tourism industry in which the local firms (hotel, theme parks) compete locally but collaborate to communicate jointly for the destination to attract tourists in the region (Pesämaa & Eriksson, 2010; Wang & Krakover, 2008). This practice, called destination marketing, is a very rich research field to study coopetition strategies with a strong marketing orientation (Czernek & Czakon, 2016; Della Corte & Aria, 2016; Grängsjö, 2003; Kylanen & Rusko, 2011). In destination marketing, coopetition strategies are initiated based on the mutual need to attract customers in the region or city and deliver enhanced value to the customers. To study this particular instance of coopetition, researchers usually adopt a case study perspective (Czernek & Czakon, 2016; Kylanen & Rusko, 2011) and/or analyze the complex relationship within the local network of coopetitors using game theory (Wang & Krakover, 2008).

Branding

Although most coopetitive agreements and relationships are hidden from final customers, the phenomenon of coopetitive co-branding is fully visible for the entire market. Chiambaretto et al. (2016) provide a comprehensive definition and typology of co-branding between competitors that they coin *coopetitive branding*, illustrating various categories with relevant examples from the clothing market (Vans and Spitfire) or from the food industry (Milka and Daim). The advantage of these coopetitive agreements is to associate an organization's own brand name with the brand name of another highly recognized competitor, aiming to merge the separate consumer segments of the coopeting organizations into a larger market for the co-branded product. However, this strategy is not without risks, as the final consumer may feel betrayed and confused by this paradoxical association.

Future research agenda

The increasing penetration of marketing-related topics into the coopetitive literature signals the maturity phase of the coopetition paradigm and research. However, this is only the beginning regarding the combination of coopetition and marketing theories, as there is still much to be done. Although interesting, coopetitive marketing research is still fragmentary and anecdotal, lacking a level of abstraction that allows a balanced combination of quantitative and qualitative research.

As a future research agenda, we suggest several main areas of further development. The first one concerns the logical continuation of the existing research, developing knowledge into the main areas of marketing theory and practice while also attempting to develop integrative bridges between various application areas (see Table 33.1 for more details).

Nevertheless, other promising research directions beyond the ones studied so far should be investigated. First, the customer relationship marketing paradigm (Kumar, 2010; Reinartz et al., 2004) can also provide interesting insights into coopetitive strategies and processes, considering the competing partner as a client (or at least a stakeholder) that needs to be satisfied and preserved on a long-term basis. Second, the rapidly developing environment of the sharing economy, which blurs the differences between individuals and organizations and creates hybrid, spontaneous forms of business partnerships (Hamari et al., 2016; Walley, 2007; Zervas et al., in press), may provide interesting opportunities for coopetitive research, in terms of both theory development and application modeling. Investigating a coopetitive sharing economy could be a promising research avenue. Finally, building on the marketing literature that has used several indicators to evaluate the efficiency of marketing alliances, such as their impact on brand attitudes (Simonin & Ruth, 1998), product evaluations (Lee et al., 2013), purchase intentions (Helmig et al., 2007), and/or purchase behavior (Swaminathan et al., 2012), we think it is important to understand the impact of coopetition strategies with these indicators that are usually neglected in coopetition articles.

However, the cross-fertilization between marketing and coopetition research should not be limited only to specific research areas or market contexts but may also include the application of new research methodologies involving decision-making analysis, longitudinal studies, or quantitative surveys. In addition, we take this opportunity to call for more publications bridging the gap between strategic management and marketing to investigate coopetition strategies.

We summarize the current insights and future research perspectives on coopetitive marketing in Table 33.1.

The exponential development of the coopetition literature since its foundation in the late 1990s demonstrates the validity and the relevance of this paradigm for the present market and managerial landscape. This dynamism is to be continued in the future, diversifying the topics of research and connecting the loose ends into a synthetic theoretical paradigm that can be applied to various areas of management and marketing theory and practice.

Table 33.1 Insights and future research perspectives on coopetitive marketing

	Previous Insights	Example of Research Perspectives
Market research	• Joint market research practices between competitors	• Definition of the type of information shared or protected by competitors in a market research context
Product portfolio	• Cooperation on upstream phases between competing products in a product line of a single firm	• Analysis of the motivations to cooperate with other product managers
Product development	• Joint R&D between competitors with a strong competition for the commercialization	• Identification of tasks shared (or in competition) for the marketing development of new products
Pricing	• Analysis of the impact of coopetition practices on final prices	• Definition of different pricing strategies for coopetitors
Distribution	• Joint distribution of products of competing firms	• Analysis of various distribution channels or retailing strategies by coopetitors
Communication	• Joint communication and advertising campaigns between competing firms	• Identification of the type of communication messages (content, media, etc.) for joint communication
Branding	• Development of coopetitive branding practices	• Analysis of the determinants, management, and performance of coopetitive branding agreements
Relationship management	---	• Analysis of the relevance of customer relationship management practices to manage coopetitive relationships
Sharing economy	---	• Identification of potential similarities between the sharing economy practices and coopetitive behaviors
Marketing indicators	---	• Stronger use of marketing indicators and methods to assess the relevance of coopetition strategies for customers

References

Akpinar, M. & Vincze, Z. (2016). The dynamics of coopetition: A stakeholder view of the German automotive industry. *Industrial Marketing Management*, 57, 53–63.

Amabile, S. & Gadille, M. (2006). Coopération interentreprise, système d'information et attention organisationnelle. *Revue française de gestion*, 164, 97–118.

Bakshi, N. & Kleindorfer, P. (2009). Co-opetition and investment for supply-chain resilience. *Production and Operations Management*, 18(6), 583–603.

Baumard, P. (2010). Learning in coopetitive environments. In S. Yami, S. Castaldo, G. B. Dagnino, & F. Le Roy (Eds), *Coopetition: Winning Strategies for the 21st Century*. Cheltenham: Edward Elgar.

Bengtsson, M. & Kock, S. (1999). Cooperation and competition in relationships between competitors in business networks. *Journal of Business & Industrial Marketing*, 14(3), 178–194.

Bengtsson, M. & Kock, S. (2000). "Coopetition" in business networks—to cooperate and compete simultaneously. *Industrial Marketing Management*, 29(5), 411–426.

Bengtsson, M. & Kock, S. (2014). Coopetition—Quo vadis? Past accomplishments and future challenges. *Industrial Marketing Management*, 43(2), 180–188.

Blomqvist, K., Hurmelinna, P., & Seppänen, R. (2005). Playing the collaboration game right—balancing trust and contracting. *Technovation*, 25(5), 497–504.

Bouncken, R. B., Fredrich, V., Ritala, P., & Kraus, S. (in press). Coopetition in new product development alliances: advantages and tensions for incremental and radical innovation. *British Journal of Management*.

Bouncken, R. B. & Kraus, S. (2013). Innovation in knowledge-intensive industries: The double-edged sword of coopetition. *Journal of Business Research*, 66(10), 2060–2070.

Brandenburger, A. M. & Nalebuff, B. J. (1996). *Co-Opetition: A Revolutionary Mindset That Redefines Competition and Cooperation* (Vol. 121). New York: Doubleday.

Castaldo, S., Moellering, G., Grosso, M., & Zerbini, F. (2010). Exploring how third-party organizations facilitate co-opetition management in buyer–seller relationships. In S. Yami, S. Castaldo, G. B. Dagnino, & F. Le Roy (Eds), *Coopetition: Winning Strategies for the 21st Century*. Cheltenham: Edward Elgar.

Chiambaretto, P. & Dumez, H. (2016). Toward a typology of coopetition: a multilevel approach. *International Studies of Management & Organization*, 46(2–3), 110–129.

Chiambaretto, P. & Fernandez, A.-S. (2016). The evolution of coopetitive and collaborative alliances in an alliance portfolio: The Air France case. *Industrial Marketing Management*, 57,

Chiambaretto, P., Gurău, C., & Le Roy, F. (2016). Coopetitive branding: Definition, typology, benefits and risks. *Industrial Marketing Management*, 57, 86–96.

Czernek, K. & Czakon, W. (2016). Trust-building processes in tourist coopetition: The case of a Polish region. *Tourism Management*, 52, 380–394.

Della Corte, V. & Aria, M. (2016). Coopetition and sustainable competitive advantage. The case of tourist destinations. *Tourism Management*, 54, 524–540.

Depeyre, C. & Dumez, H. (2010). The role of architectural players in coopetition: the case of the US defense industry. In S. Yami, S. Castaldo, G. B. Dagnino, & F. Le Roy (Eds), *Coopetition: Winning Strategies for the 21st Century* (p. 124). Cheltenham: Edward Elgar.

Dorn, S., Schweiger, B., & Albers, S. (2016). Levels, phases and themes of coopetition: A systematic literature review and research agenda. *European Management Journal*, 34(5), 484–500.

Easton, G., Burell, G., Rotschild, R., & Shearman, C. (1993). *Managers and Competition*. Oxford: Blackwell Publishers.

Ehrenmann, F. & Reiss, M. (2012). Co-opetition as a facilitator of manufacturing competitiveness: opportunities and threats. In H. El Maraghi (Eds), *Enabling Manufacturing Competitiveness and Economic Sustainability*. Berlin: Springer.

Fernandez, A.-S. & Chiambaretto, P. (2016). Managing tensions related to information in coopetition. *Industrial Marketing Management*, 53, 66–76.

Fernandez, A.-S., Le Roy, F., & Gnyawali, D. R. (2014). Sources and management of tension in co-opetition case evidence from telecommunications satellites manufacturing in Europe. *Industrial Marketing Management*, 43(2), 222–235.

Fernandez, A.-S., Le Roy, F., & Chiambaretto, P. (2018). Implementing the right project structure to achieve coopetitive innovation projects. *Long Range Planning*, 51(2), 384–405.

Freel, M. S. (2003). Sectoral patterns of small firm innovation, networking and proximity. *Research Policy*, 32(5), 751–770.

Gnyawali, D. R. & Park, B.-J. (2009). Co-opetition and technological innovation in small and medium-sized enterprises: A multilevel conceptual model. *Journal of Small Business Management*, 47(3), 308–330.

Gnyawali, D. R. & Park, B.-J. (2011). Co-opetition between giants: Collaboration with competitors for technological innovation. *Research Policy*, 40(5), 650–663.

Grängsjö, Y. von F. (2003). Destination networking: Co-opetition in peripheral surroundings. *International Journal of Physical Distribution & Logistics Management*, 33(5), 427–448.

Hamari, J., Sjöklint, M., & Ukkonen, A. (2016). The sharing economy: Why people participate in collaborative consumption. *Journal of the Association for Information Science and Technology*, 67(9), 2047–2059.

Helmig, B., Huber, J.-A., & Leeflang, P. (2007). Explaining behavioural intentions toward co-branded products. *Journal of Marketing Management*, 23(3/4), 285–304.

Kotler, P. & Keller, K. L. (2012). *Marketing Management*. Paris: Pearson France.

Kotzab, H. & Teller, C. (2003). Value-adding partnerships and co-opetition models in the grocery industry. *International Journal of Physical Distribution & Logistics Management*, 33(3), 268–281.

Kumar, V. (2010). *Customer Relationship Management*. London: John Wiley & Sons, Ltd.

Kwok, J. J. M. & Lee, D.-Y. (2015). Coopetitive supply chain relationship model: application to the smartphone manufacturing network. *PLOS One*, 10(7), e0132844.

Kylänen, M. & Rusko, R. (2011). Unintentional coopetition in the service industries: The case of Pyhä-Luosto tourism destination in the Finnish Lapland. *European Management Journal*, 29(3), 193–205.

Lacoste, S. (2012). "Vertical coopetition": The key account perspective. *Industrial Marketing Management*, 41(4), 649–658.

Lado, A. A., Boyd, N. G., & Hanlon, S. C. (1997). Competition, cooperation, and the search for economic rents: A syncretic model. *Academy of Management Review*, 22(1), 110–141.

Lee, J. K., Lee, B.-K., & Lee, W.-N. (2013). Country-of-origin fit's effect on consumer product evaluation in cross-border strategic brand alliance. *Journal of Business Research*, 66(3), 354–363.

Lee, S. Y. & Shen, F. (2009). Joint advertising and brand congruity: Effects on memory and attitudes. *Journal of Promotion Management*, 15(4), 484–498.

Lindström, T. & Polsa, P. (2016). Coopetition close to the customer—A case study of a small business network. *Industrial Marketing Management*, 53, 207–215.

Luo, X., Rindfleisch, A., & Tse, D. K. (2007). Working with rivals: The impact of competitor alliances on financial performance. *Journal of Marketing Research*, 44(1), 73–83.

Luo, X., Slotegraaf, R. J., & Pan, X. (2006). Cross-functional "coopetition": The simultaneous role of cooperation and competition within firms. *Journal of Marketing*, 70(2), 67–80.

Luo, Y. (2005). Toward coopetition within a multinational enterprise: a perspective from foreign subsidiaries. *Journal of World Business*, 40(1), 71–90.

Nemeh, A. & Yami, S. (2016). The determinants of the emergence of coopetition strategy in R&D. *International Studies of Management & Organization*, 46(2–3), 159–178.

Okura, M. (2008). Why isn't the accident information shared? A coopetition perspective. *Management Research: Journal of the Iberoamerican Academy of Management*, 6(3), 219–225.

Pellegrin-Boucher, E., Le Roy, F., & Gurău, C. (2018). Managing selling coopetition: A case study of the ERP industry. *European Management Review*, 15(1), 37–56.

Pellegrin-Boucher, E., Le Roy, F., & Gurău, C. (2013). Coopetitive strategies in the ICT sector: typology and stability. *Technology Analysis & Strategic Management*, 25(1), 71–89.

Peng, T.-J. A., Pike, S., Yang, J. C.-H., & Roos, G. (2012). Is cooperation with competitors a good idea? An example in practice. *British Journal of Management*, 23(4), 532–560.

Pesämaa, O. & Eriksson, P.-E. (2010). Coopetition among nature-based tourism firms: Competition at local level and cooperation at destination level. In S. Yami, S. Castaldo, B. Dagnino, & F. Le Roy (Eds), *Coopetition: Winning Strategies for the 21st Century*. Cheltenham: Edward Elgar Publishing.

Reinartz, W., Krafft, M., & Hoyer, W. D. (2004). The customer relationship management process: Its measurement and impact on performance. *Journal of Marketing Research*, 41(3), 293–305.

Rindfleisch, A. & Moorman, C. (2003). Interfirm cooperation and customer orientation. *Journal of Marketing Research*, 40(4), 421–436.

Ritala, P. (2009). Is coopetition different from cooperation? The impact of market rivalry on value creation in alliances. *International Journal of Intellectual Property Management*, 3(1), 39–55.

Ritala, P. & Hurmelinna-Laukkanen, P. (2013). Incremental and radical innovation in coopetition—the role of absorptive capacity and appropriability. *Journal of Product Innovation Management*, 30(1), 154–169.

Robert, M., Chiambaretto, P., Mira, B., & Le Roy, F. (2018). Better, faster, stronger: The impact of market-oriented coopetition on product commercial performance. *M@n@gement*, 21(1), 574–610.

Rusko, R. (2011). Exploring the concept of coopetition: A typology for the strategic moves of the Finnish forest industry. *Industrial Marketing Management*, 40(2), 311–320.

Samu, S., Krishnan, H. S., & Smith, R. E. (1999). Using advertising alliances for new product introduction: Interactions between product complementarity and promotional strategies. *Journal of Marketing*, 63(1), 57–74.

Schor, J. (2015). Getting sharing right. *Contexts*, 14(1), 14–15.

Simonin, B. L. & Ruth, J. A. (1998). Is a company known by the company it keeps? Assessing the spillover effects of brand alliances on consumer brand attitudes. *JMR, Journal of Marketing Research*, 35(1), 30–42.

Slowak, A. (2008). Standard-setting capabilities in industrial automation: a collaborative process. *Journal of Innovation Economics & Management*, 2, 147–169.

Swaminathan, V., Reddy, S. K., & Dommer, S. L. (2012). Spillover effects of ingredient branded strategies on brand choice: A field study. *Marketing Letters*, 23(1), 237–251.

Teller, C., Alexander, A., & Floh, A. (2016). The impact of competition and cooperation on the performance of a retail agglomeration and its stores. *Industrial Marketing Management*, 52, 6–17.

Tidström, A. (2014). Managing tensions in coopetition. *Industrial Marketing Management*, 43(2), 261–271.

Tirole, J. (1989). *The Theory of Industrial Organization*. Cambridge: MIT Press.

Tsai, W. (2002). Social Structure of "coopetition" within a multiunit organization: Coordination, competition, and intraorganizational knowledge sharing. *Organization Science*, 13(2), 179–190.

Walley, K. (2007). Coopetition: An introduction to the subject and an agenda for research. *International Studies of Management and Organization*, 37(2), 11–31.

Wang, Y. & Krakover, S. (2008). Destination marketing: competition, cooperation or coopetition? *International Journal of Contemporary Hospitality Management*, 20(2), 126–141.

Wu, Z., Choi, T. Y., & Rungtusanatham, M. J. (2010). Supplier–supplier relationships in buyer–supplier–supplier triads: Implications for supplier performance. *Journal of Operations Management*, 28(2), 115–123.

Zervas, G., Proserpio, D., & Byers, J. W. (in press). The rise of the sharing economy: Estimating the impact of airbnb on the hotel industry. *Journal of Marketing Research*.

34

Management tools for inter-network coopetition[1]

Thuy Séran and Hervé Chappert

Introduction

Coopetition creates tensions that can be extremely strong and can jeopardize the effective pursuit of coopetition (Bonel & Rocco, 2007). Therefore, managing tensions is a critical task for coopetitive organizations and an essential condition for achieving performance (Bengtsson & Kock, 2014; Chen, 2008; Raza-Ullah et al., 2014). Within the strategy field, researchers of coopetition investigate management tools to provide solutions that will reduce coopetitive risks and tensions (Fernandez & Chiambaretto, 2016; Fernandez et al., 2014; Gnyawali & Madhavan, 2001; Luo, 2007; Peng & Bourne, 2009; Seran et al., 2016), while within the management accounting field, authors focus on studies of inter-organizational cooperation, which include coopetitive relationships (Dekker, 2016; Grafton & Mundy, 2016; Mouritsen & Thrane, 2006; van der Meer-Kooistra & Scapens, 2008). The purpose of this chapter is to combine management accounting and strategy approaches in a discussion about coopetition management.

A literature review is conducted that combines two theoretical corpuses. At an organizational level, a consensus exists between the two approaches, even though the authors may use different terms to explain how formal and informal controls are mobilized to manage coopetitive tensions. At a network level, coopetitive and management accounting literatures offer general management principles, but they do not converge to explain how control mechanisms contribute to coopetition success (Czakon et al., 2014). Accordingly, we focus our research on a network, and we propose an integrative management accounting framework that can be applied to manage network coopetitive tensions. This framework is illustrated by a detailed analysis of the coopetitive network governance within the banking industry.

Levels of coopetitive tensions

Given that coopetitive tensions may come from several sources, Fernandez et al. (2014) develop a multi-level conceptual framework to understand key drivers of tension in coopetition and key approaches to managing that tension. We propose to aggregate coopetitive tensions according to levels and sources involved to clarify the principles applied (Table 34.1).

Table 34.1 Coopetitive tensions and principles

Levels	Coopetitive Tensions			
	Personal	*Organizational level (dual-level analysis)*		*Network level*
	Inter-personal	*Intra-organizational*	*Inter-organizational*	*Intra- and inter- network*
Sources	Belonging to the parent firm and coopetitive identity	Allocation of resources and creation of appropriation of business unit value	Value creation and appropriation Knowledge sharing and learning	Resource and power asymmetry
Principles	Separation-integration and combining both separation and integration			Sponsorship or integration

At the individual level, partners face continual pressures to manage cooperative and competitive tensions that emerge from collaboration with competitors. Explicit and implicit strategic priorities may lead to different mindsets and behaviors with respect to managers (Fernandez et al., 2014) and, hence, belonging to opposing firms is a source of cognitive dissonance and psycho-cognitive stress for managers (Dekker, 2016; Seran et al., 2016).

At the intra-organizational level, units cooperate to simultaneously develop synergies and scale effects, while also competing for internal limited technological human and financial resources (Luo et al., 2006; Seran et al., 2016).

At the inter-organizational level, the first tension arises due to the confrontation between common value creation and private value appropriation (Gnyawali et al., 2012; Madhavan, 2012). A partner who increases his or her resources and competences so that they exceed those of his or her coopetitor will gain a competitive advantage in future competition. As a consequence, tensions may then appear when each partner attempts to capture the previously created value (Cassiman et al., 2009). The second conflict is due to the risks associated with the transfer of confidential information and the risks of technological imitation. Partners join strategic resources to achieve their goals (Gnyawali & Park, 2009). However, at the same time, they must protect their core competencies from their competitors. Sharing information with their competitors, in subtle ways over time, may introduce homogeneity into their products and reduce the distinctiveness of each firm (Grafton & Mundy, 2016). In some cases, regulatory risk could also be a source of tension, and when such tension appears, it is a particularly salient concern (Anderson et al., 2014). Indeed, any exchange of information between competitors exposes them to the risk of perceived or real collusion, and hence, potentially could result in their being subject to anti-competition legislation (Grafton & Mundy, 2016).

At the network level, competition intensifies as the life cycle advances toward maturity (Baum & Korn, 1996; Bettis & Hitt, 1995; Korn & Baum, 1999). Tensions are specific and more intense during this process given that members' interests may become more conflicted if the industry shrinks (Luo, 2007). The resources and power of each competitor structure the network and significantly influence coopetition (Ketchen et al., 2004).

While these principles appear meaningful conceptually, we know little about how to help a network manage the tensions in coopetition. Therefore, to deeply understand which mechanisms contribute to network coopetition success, we investigate an integrative management accounting framework and illustrate it using a banking industry case.

Banking inter-network coopetition

Cooperative banking, a part of the banking industry, is a perfect illustration of a network coopetitive case. In Europe, cooperative banking is an important economic sector that offers access to more than 71,000 bank agencies and employs approximately 850,000 people (EACB, 2017). BP-CE[2] is the third important cooperative banking network in France and is classified as one among the top thirty systemic banks in the world by the Financial Stability Board.

In the last few decades, coopetitive activities have become more frequent in the cooperative banking sector, for three reasons. The first is linked to the application of the 1984 Finance Act, which ended the privileges of cooperative banks, forcing them to diversify, acquire new skills, and make alliances with competitors through internal or external development. As a result, cooperative banks established coopetition within the same bank network or with competitor bank networks.

The second reason for the acceleration of the phenomenon of coopetition in the cooperative banking network is the impact of the international legal environment in the banking sector. To satisfy the criteria of prudential rules following the 2008 crisis, banks must now prove the viability of their business model, demonstrate their credit risk and their low risk of governance, and publish all relevant information (Bonomo et al., 2016).

The third reason is the digitalization of the banking sector, particularly considering that new entrants are major companies in information technology, e-retailing and media (Fintech). While these Fintech players are not yet competitors of banks, they offer targeted and more convenient services. Hence, corporate and investment banks, as well as retail banks, are now embracing coopetition by taking these Fintech players as news partners in their ecosystems.

In 2009, the Group Central Institution BP-CE founded a common board to manage the coopetitive activities of the two networks, BP and CE (Figure 34.1).

Their competitive and cooperative activities are summarized in Table 34.2. These two networks include regional banks, which are independent banks competing in the areas of sales activities. In these two networks, Caisse d'Epargne (CE) and Banque Populaire (BP), competitive activities account for 64.5% of the total net banking income (traditional retail and commercial banking activities) and are conducted by eighteen banks in the BP network and seventeen in the CE network.

Cooperative activities and coopetitive tensions

The cooperative activities of these two banking networks include a shared information system, three common management funds and the joint representation of external actors (customers, financial markets, government, financial regulators). These activities are monitored by two organizations, namely the IT group central institution and the group central institution.

IT system tensions

Some tensions are created by shared information technology systems (IT systems). Initially, both networks had their own information system, but in 2015 they decided to jointly manage a new shared information system. The objectives behind this collaboration in digitalizing their banking activities were mainly to reduce IT costs and time to market, and to consolidate their network expertise and competencies. While the IT Group Central Institution was created to manage this cooperative activity, once the integration strategy was defined and approved by the IT Group Central Institution, common strategy reduced the regional banks' bargaining powers

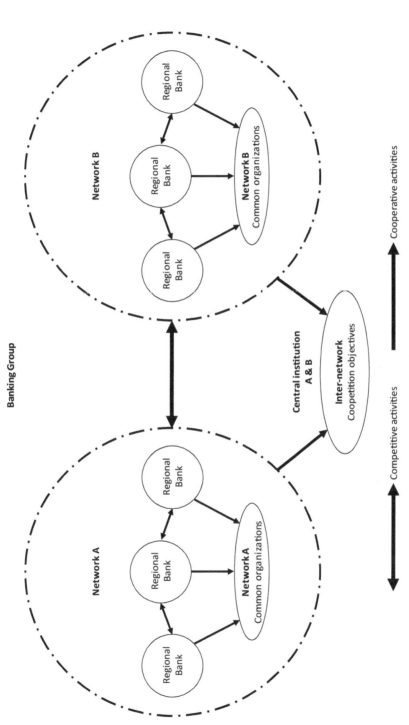

Figure 34.1 BP-CE cooperative and competitive activities

Table 34.2 Cooperative and competitive activities

Competitive activities (65% of net banking income)	Banking products sales
Cooperatives activities	Common information system management
	Regulatory risk management
	Networks representation activities

and freedom of choice. Consequently, tension appeared as banks compared the costs of their contributions to this common project to the gains in terms of knowledge and customer data.

Risk management tensions

Tensions could also be created by regulatory risk management. In addition to their own fund management system, the two networks created a second common governance board, namely the Group Central Institution, to manage global coopetitive strategies, mutual funds and prudential compliance. Thus, since 2009, the global network financial risk has been supported by a common fund, the Fonds de Garantie Mutuel (FGM), in which the BP network and the CE network have each deposited €180 million.

The objective of common funds is to ensure coherence, solvency, and liquidity for the two banking networks and their subsidiary, Natixis. Therefore, the operating rules regarding these common funds establish the terms and conditions for member contributions. Although these mechanisms were originally established under a mutualist reinsurance approach, this solidarity, perceived as the distinctive value of cooperatives, creates tensions. For Natixis, in past crises, the equity and liquidity of all the banks in the two networks were called upon to financially support Natixis' risky activities. This solidarity placed the two cooperative networks in a difficult situation and, as a consequence, their opening-up to the stock market resulted in tensions between the Group Central Institution and the listed subsidiary with all the banks in the two networks. Indeed, using of external capital considerably increase the cost of financing cooperatives and increase the need for profitability of their activities.

The Group Central Institution is also responsible for prudential consolidation, which is a consolidation of the financial risks and the performance of the two networks to fit financial prudential standards requirements. This financial consolidation brings together the balance sheets of the independent banks that belong to the two networks to offset the risks and performances of these banks. As the two banking networks include independent regional banks whose competitive advantages and individual risks depend strongly on the economy of the territory, they must engage in financial consolidation to compensate for the risks. However, the prudential consolidation creates tensions among the regional banks since the regional banks must provide more relevant information, such as financial statements, in accordance with prudential rules to avoid the exclusion of the network.

Networks representation tensions

At last, tensions could be created by networks representation activities. The Group Central Institution represents regional banks and negotiates and signs national and international agreements on their behalf. It also manages their interests and establishes coopetitive banking network strategy (Moody, 2016: 18). However, because conflict arises between cooperative and shareholder values due to the diversity of the two networks' property structures (Gnyawali & Madhavan, 2001), it is becoming increasingly more difficult for the Group Central Institution to ensure the cohesion of the network and defend mutualist values (democracy and solidarity). Furthermore, the tension between the BP and CE cooperative networks and Natixis is due to the shared common fund and the opposition in value between the network's actors, i.e., capitalist values for Natixis and cooperative values for the rest of the network. Cooperative network banks are owned and governed by their members such that each member clearly holds a vote in the democratic process in accordance with the one-person-one-vote democratic principle. The ideal cooperative bank seeks to maximize the benefits of its members (who are also customers) and maximize consumer bonuses. However, with respect to Natixis, even if it is a subsidiary of BP and CE, it has a shareholder logic whereby maximizing the rate of return on capital is, if not the exclusive, at least the dominant business objective.

Management accounting tools

To manage tensions within a coopetitive inter-network we have to understand the role of management accounting in a cooperative network. As summarized in Table 34.1, separation, integration, and combining are the three principles employed to manage tensions at the individual and organizational levels. At the network level, resources and power depend on centrality, property structure, and network density (Gnyawali & Madhavan, 2001), and two principles are identified to manage coopetitive tensions—sponsorship and integration (Luo, 2007). Sponsorship refers to the effort to "pacify the volatility of steep rivalry among competitors," to "establish collaborative opportunities and platforms for members to share complementary resources," and to "create more favorable conditions" such as "competitive pressures from new entrants and substitutes and bargaining power from suppliers and buyers or government policies and international treaties" (Luo, 2007). Luo (2007) shows that integration is an effort to put a firm's coopetition scheme under a unified and coordinated umbrella to better nurture the implementation of this global strategy to establish a well-coordinated coopetition program and prioritize the role played by each member.

While knowledge about principles is acknowledged, little is known about the tools to use. Management control mechanisms include a control system design that is based primarily on an information system used to share information and governance. Additionally, it encompasses performance measurement systems, such as goal setting, incentive systems, and performance monitoring, and involves process or behavioral control, social control, and informal control (Table 34.3). These control mechanisms must first be clarified from a perspective that will facilitate their use in a network with complex cooperative and competitive relationships.

At the organizational level, both coopetitive and management accounting literatures agree on the role of formal and informal control as tools to manage coopetitive tensions. Several studies have emphasized that formal and informal control mechanisms do not work separately and must be combined to manage tensions between partners and increase alliance performance (de Man & Roijakkers, 2009; Faems et al., 2008). Seran et al. (2016) provide an in-depth study of leading French banking institutions to unveil how formal and informal management helps individuals cope with coopetition tensions. Accordingly, their study develops the paradox integration thread of thinking through a scrutiny of various practices implemented to alleviate tensions. Fernandez & Chiambaretto (2016) suggest that the management of tensions related to information in coopetitive projects requires a combination of formal control mechanisms, i.e., information criticality, and informal control mechanisms, i.e., information appropriation, both of which are designed to foster the success of a common project while limiting the risk of opportunism (Das & Teng, 2001).

Table 34.3 Synthesis of management control mechanism and tools

Management control mechanisms	Tools
Inter-organizational management controls systems design	Design of tasks, information sharing, information technology
Performance measurement systems	Goal setting, incentive systems, performance monitoring, and executive rewards
Process controls	Rules, regulations, structures, job descriptions, reporting structures
Behavioral control, social control, informal control	Trust, socialization processes, values

At the network level, both coopetitive and management accounting insist on the role of formal contract and informal social mechanisms, such as trust, shared norms, implicit sanctions, and symbolic communication (Caglio & Ditillo, 2008; Dekker, 2016; Peng & Bourne, 2009). These mechanisms lead to increased cognitive salience of competitors as well as to mutual coordination. Indeed, formal contracts, which are often incomplete, are performed with other mechanisms, such as informal social control (Anderson et al., 2014). Informal self-enforcing agreements between firms, i.e., relational contracts, rely on a range of social and other relationship-based control mechanisms and are sustained by the expected value of the future relationship (Baker et al., 2002).

More specifically, a network, because of its lack of central authority, exercises control through the installation of a governance board that is characterized by joint authority, monitoring, and decision making (Dekker, 2004). This form of hierarchy, however, results in decision making and conflict resolution being subject to inter-firm communications and negotiations. In this sense, the design and implementation of management control is also subject to negotiation and approval by partners' executives. The management accounting resulting from these negotiations is a mix of mechanisms and practices that are meant to serve the interests of the various partners rather than those of a single firm. Another difference between the inter-firm and the intra-firm settings is the role of arbitrators in the event of relationship failures or conflicts. This role also results from the absence of a complete hierarchy, and thus adds other parties to the relationship that are not present within the firm (Dekker, 2016).

Although both the coopetitive and the management accounting literature propose tools to manage coopetitive tensions at the network level, there remains a lack of a comprehensive theoretical framework.

Simons (1995) developed a theoretical framework that aims to frame a strategic area, establish and create a strategy, develop opportunities and focus on managing multiple tensions. This framework links business strategy, including the alliance strategy, and system control management to balance tensions (Figure 34.2). Simons' framework includes four managerial control levers: (1) beliefs systems; (2) boundary systems; (3) diagnostic control systems; and (4) interactive control systems.

Cooperative strategic area

The beliefs control system is "the explicit set of organizational definitions that senior managers communicate formally and reinforce systematically to provide basic values, purpose, and direction." This formal communication style provides basic shared values and direction for

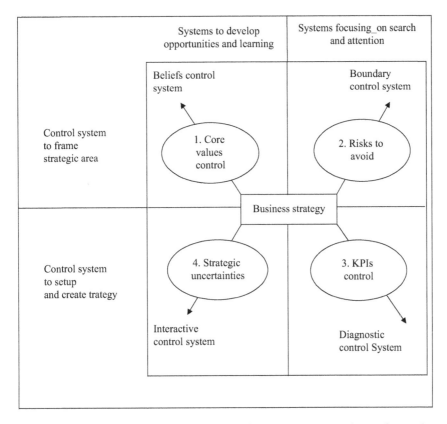

Figure 34.2 Interrelation levers of control with strategy, opportunity, and attention

inter-coopetitive networks and relies on relational contracting to establish credible commitments among firms (Grafton & Mundy, 2016). This system is presented as behavioral control, social control, and informal control in Table 34.3. Specifically, the Group Central Institution as a network representative organization makes extensive use of shared values, group norms, meetings, informal gatherings, partner selection, restricted access, and the threat of collective sanctions to manage various relational and decision risks associated with coopetitive activities. Dependence and repeated exchanges between partners can reduce opportunistic behaviors because any firm that operates against the norms of the group potentially faces the threat of being excluded from other collaborative activities critical to their survival as an independent bank.

The boundary control system is defined as "the acceptable domain of strategic activity for organizational participants, through communicating, implementing and enforcing codes of business conduct." As such, it outlines the acceptable domain of the banking business model, including credit risk and security, for inter-coopetitive networks and is presented in Table 34.3 as an inter-organizational management controls systems design. Concretely, the Group Central Institution oversees the global coopetitive activities of the two networks through the implementation of a three- to five-year strategic plan voted on by both banking networks and the strengthening of internal control. As part of its supervisory role, the Group Central Institution has the power to dismiss and replace the top managers from among the network members (e.g., regional banks) if they fail to comply with its directives or banking regulations. A strong internal merger has occurred in recent years within the regional banks of these networks, either for economy of scale or in the event that they were not sufficiently profitable.

Cooperative strategy

We propose to set up and create cooperative strategy through diagnostic and interactive control systems. The diagnostic control system is designed "to ensure the implementation of intended strategies and the achievement of planned outcomes, allowing the managers to monitor the activity of employees or partner's organizations through the review of critical performance coopetitive variables" and is represented by the performance measurement systems and process controls in Table 34.3. The system includes budget and reporting and allows feedback of coopetitive networks (Table 34.4).

The interactive control system is based on "the personal involvement and interest of managers in the critical elements of strategy design and implementation, creating an ongoing dialogue with subordinates and partners, and actively finding of best solutions for the identified problems" and controls inter-coopetitive networks with the use of formal tools in an interactive way. For example, the implementation of cost allocation control systems in the annual budget is managed via an interactive control system through the informal internal networks that are inter-related and embedded one in another (Seran et al., 2016). This control is effective because, on the one hand, cooperative banking networks are characterized by an information asymmetry between member-owners (shareholders) and managers that is much stronger than in conventional banking networks. The limitation of the ownership rights of the members and, in particular, the weak correlation between dividend and bank's performances, weakens their incentive to control the managers.

Table 34.4 Integrative management accounting framework for banking network coopetitive tensions management

Inter-network Coopetition Activities	Coopetitive Tensions	Control Mechanisms & Tools	Simons' Levers of Control
Common information system management	Tension created in IT activities management	Cost allocation and annual budget	Diagnostic and interactive control system
	Tension created by knowledge sharing	Specific governance structures through role and task sharing	Diagnostic and interactive control system
Regulatory risk management	Tension in the management of mutual funds and the joint subsidiaries taking more financial risks	Five-year strategic plan; internal audit control	Boundary control system
	Tensions created by comparing IT performance and IT risks between regional banks	Global network consolidated reporting/ IT—internal audit control	Diagnostic control system
Networks representation activities	Representation equilibrium between cooperative values and shareholder values	Decision system (equity, interdependence); democracy; solidarity	Beliefs control system; interactive control system

On the other hand, the dilution of control and the weak link between capital ownership and the composition of management bodies reinforce discretionary managerial power and organizational inefficiency that can include overstaffing, lack of penalties for incompetence, lack of motivation to reduce operating costs and improve productivity, excessive remuneration, existence of free cash flows and creation of high reserves (Akella & Greenbaum, 1988; Mayers & Smith, 1994). However, the discretionary power of regional banking managers is limited by the risk of being closed or merged by a collective decision and by the existence of an internal labor market in which managers must preserve their reputations (informal control system). These informational asymmetries favor the development of informal interactive control through the networks of senior executives.

Conclusions: Contributions and research agenda

Combining both coopetition and management accounting literatures is necessary to build an integrative management accounting framework for network coopetition. Simons (1995, 1999) posits that effective control is achieved by integrating the four levers of control, since "the power of these levers in implementing strategy does not lie in how each is used alone, but rather in how they complement each other when used together. The interplay of positive and negative forces creates a dynamic tension." Simons also states that beliefs and interactive controls create positive energy and that boundary and diagnostic controls create negative energy as they assess planned objectives. From our case study, this equilibrium produced good results in terms of cost and income synergies according to our financial data analysis from the beginning of the alliance to 2013. Moreover, financial performance also exhibited good results and risks were reduced. The performances were driven by boundary and diagnostic control systems, i.e., negative energy. However, these systems have some limits linked to the specificities of cooperative banks, which sometimes make them ineffective. Hence, they are completed with beliefs control systems and interactive control systems, i.e., positive energy. A perfect example of the interaction of beliefs and interactive control systems was demonstrated in the cooperative banking case presented above. Whereas management accounting literature contributes by advancing knowledge on the coopetition phenomenon by providing structured coopetitive management tools, management accounting is perceived as coopetitive strategic alignment by incorporating the tools as concrete actions and performance measurements. Concretely, the integrative framework proposed (Figure 34.3) as a management tool facilitates the achievement of the following four objectives: (1) frame the coopetitive strategy area using the definition of shared value to obtain commitment to the coopetitive purpose, i.e., belief system, and to design the network governance and risk management to stake out the territory, i.e., boundary system; (2) establish a strategy based on the performance measurement, i.e., diagnostic system, and create competition through the positioning of the uncertainty environment, i.e., interactive system; (3) focus on research based on the definition of risk domain; and (4) develop new opportunities and learning within the coopetitive network.

Conversely, coopetition enriches management accounting literature by developing emerging literature on the boundaries between intra-firm and inter-firm management accounting (Dekker, 2016) and on the horizontal relationships network among competitors. Moreover, coopetitive tensions appearing during the time span of the inter-firm management accounting literature consume the whole-time span of coopetition studies (Czakon et al., 2014). However, as these tensions remain under-examined in management accounting literature (Grafton & Mundy, 2016), the topic provides interesting opportunities for future studies.

First, the new institutionalist theory can be a paradoxical approach for coopetitive networks as their members may belong to a hybrid organization or a meta-organization that has different institutional logics.

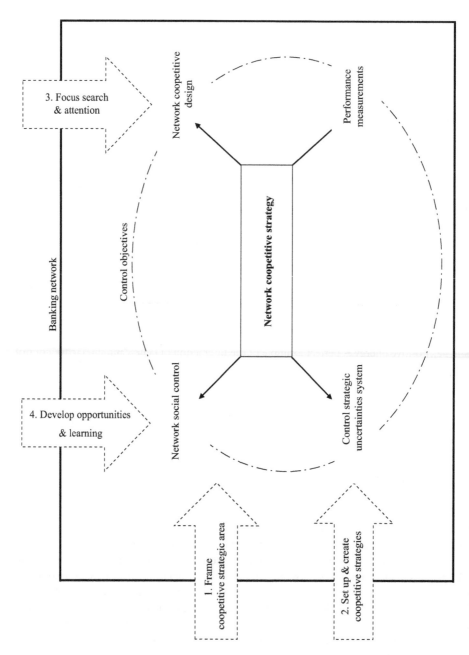

Figure 34.3 Integrative management control framework for a coopetitive network

Second, network-level or industry-level empirical studies are still few. This level of analysis takes into account market structure contingencies, ecosystem competition, and collective growth strategies. Tensions arising under these conditions are stronger in a coopetitive context because each individual defends his/her parent firm. While partner companies often agree on a collaborative strategy to be pursued jointly, they are also likely to pursue individual strategies that relate to their individual objectives. In particular, when a firm's private aspirations diverge from (or conflict with) the collaborative strategy, it results in competing tensions and greater complexity for alliance staff who are expected to act in the best interests of both parties. In fact, the role of the management control system is to balance the interests and decisions of boundary spanners with respect to the different objectives and strategies being pursued (Dekker, 2016). To investigate management control in the boundary organization through the boundary spanner, the boundary object concept may facilitate understanding how boundary spanner profiles and mechanisms must be mobilized for successful coopetition and why coopetition stabilizes over time.

Notes

1 Acknowledgments: we thank the IRCCF of Montréal (Canada) and the BPCE (France), particularly Mr Séran, Mr Grafouillère, and Mr Viguié, for their valuable contributions, which helped us to improve our research significantly. All errors and shortcomings remain the authors' responsibility.
2 Banque Populaire Caisse d'Epargne.

References

Akella, S. R. & Greenbaum, S. I. (1988). Savings and Loan ownership structure and expense-preference. *Journal of Banking and Finance*, 12, 419–437.

Anderson, S. W., Christ, M. H., Dekker, H. C., & Sedatole, K. L. (2014). The use of management controls to mitigate risk in strategic alliances: Field and survey evidence. *Journal of Management Accounting Research*, 26(1).

Baker, G., Gibbons, R., & Murphy, K. J. (2002). Relational contracts and the theory of the firm. *The Quarterly Journal of Economics*, 117(1), 39–84.

Baum, J. A. C. & Korn, H. J. (1996). Competitive dynamics of interfirm rivalry. *Academy of Management Journal*, 39(2), 255–291.

Bengtsson, M. & Kock, S. (2014). Coopetition—Quo vadis? Past accomplishments and future challenges. *Industrial Marketing Management*, 43(2), 180–188.

Bettis, R. A. & Hitt, M. A. (1995). The new competitive landscape. *Strategic Management Journal*, 16, 7–19.

Bonel, E. & Rocco, E. (2007). Coopeting to survive; surviving coopetition. *International Studies of Management & Organization*, 37(2), 70–96.

Bonomo, G., Schneider, S., Turchetti, P., & Vettori, M. (2016). *SREP: How Europe's banks can adapt to the new risk-based supervisory playbook.* New York: McKinsey & Company.

Caglio, A. & Ditillo, A. (2008). A review and discussion of management control in inter-firm relationships: Achievements and future directions. *Accounting, Organizations and Society*, 33, 865–898.

Cassiman, B., Di Guardo, M. C., & Valentini, G. (2009). Organising R&D projects to profit from innovation: Insights from co-opetition. *Long Range Planning*, 42, 216–233.

Chen, M.-J. (2008). Reconceptualizing the competition-cooperation relationship: a transparadox perspective. *Journal of Management Inquiry*, 20, 1–19.

Czakon, W., Mucha-Kus, K., & Rogalski, M. (2014). Coopetition research landscape – A systematic literature review 1997–2010. *Journal of Economics & Management*, 17, 122–150.

Das, T. K. & Teng, B.-S. (2001). A risk perception model of alliance structuring. *Journal of International Management*, 7, 1–29.

de Man, A.-P. & Roijakkers, N. (2009). Alliance governance: Balancing control and trust in dealing with risk. *Long Range Planning*, 42(1).

Dekker, H. C. (2004). Control of inter-organizational relationships: evidence on appropriation concerns and coordination requirements. *Accounting, Organizations and Society*, 29, 27–49.

Dekker, H. C. (2016). On the boundaries between intrafirm and interfirm management accounting research. *Management Accounting Research*, 31, 86–99.

EACB. (2017). *Co-operative Banks: Definition, Characteristics and Key figures – EACB*. European Association of Co-operative Banks.

Faems, D., Janssens, M., Madhok, A., & Van Looy, B. (2008). Toward an integrative perspective on alliance governance: Connecting contract design, trust dynamics, and contract application. *Academy of Management Journal*, 51(6),

Fernandez, A.-S. & Chiambaretto, P. (2016). Managing tensions related to information in coopetition. *Industrial Marketing Management*, 53, 66–76.

Fernandez, A.-S., Le Roy, F., & Gnyawali, D. R. (2014). Sources and management of tension in co-opetition case evidence from telecommunications satellites manufacturing in Europe. *Industrial Marketing Management*, 43(2), 222–235.

Gnyawali, D. R. & Madhavan, R. (2001). Cooperative networks and competitive dynamics: A structural embeddedness perspective. *Academy of Management Review*, 26(3), 431–445.

Gnyawali, D. R., Madhavan, R., He, J., & Bengtsson, M. (2012). Contradiction, dualities and tensions in cooperation and competition: A capability based framework. In *Annual meeting of the Academy of Management (AoM)*. Boston, MA.

Gnyawali, D. R. & Park, B. J. (2009). Co-opetition and technological innovation in small and medium-sized enterprises: A multilevel conceptual model. *Journal of Small Business Management*, 47(3), 308–330.

Grafton, J. & Mundy, J. (2016). Relational contracting and the myth of trust: control in a co-opetitive setting. *Management Accounting Research*, in press.

Ketchen Jr., D. J., Snow, C. C., & Hoover, V. L. (2004). Research on competitive dynamics: recent accomplishments and future challenges. *Journal of Management*, 30(6), 779–804.

Korn, H. J. & Baum, J. A. C. (1999). Chance, imitative, and strategic antecedents to multimarket contact. *Academy of Management Journal*, 42(2), 171–193.

Luo, X., Slotegraaf, R. J., & Pan, X. (2006). Cross-functional "coopetition": The simultaneous role of cooperation and competition within firms. *Journal of Marketing*, 70, 67–80.

Luo, Y. (2007). A coopetition perspective of global competition. *Journal of World Business*, 42, 129–144.

Mayers, D. & Smith, C. W. (1994). Managerial discretion, regulation, and stock insurer ownership structure. *The Journal of Risk and Insurance*, 61(4), 638–655.

Moody. (2016). *Company Profile: BPCE*. Moody's Investors Service.

Mouritsen, J. & Thrane, S. (2006). Accounting, network complementarities and the development of inter-organisational relations. *Accounting, Organizations and Society*, 31, 241–275.

Peng, T.-J. A. & Bourne, M. (2009). The coexistence of competition and cooperation between networks: Implications from two Taiwanese healthcare networks. *British Journal of Management*, 20, 377–400.

Raza-Ullah, T., Bengtsson, M., & Kock, S. (2014). The coopetition paradox and tension in coopetition at multiple levels. *Industrial Marketing Management*, 43(2), 189–198.

Seran, T., Pellegrin-Boucher, E., & Gurau, C. (2016). The management of coopetitive tensions within multi-unit organizations. *Industrial Marketing Management*, 53, 31–41.

Simons, R. (1995). Control in an age of empowerment. *Harvard Business Review*, 73 (March–April), 80–88.

Simons, R. (1999). How risky is your company? *Harvard Business Review*, 77, 85–95.

van der Meer-Kooistra, J. & Scapens, R. W. (2008). The governance of lateral relations between and within organisations. *Management Accounting Research*, 19, 365–384.

35

Vertical coopetition in buyer–supplier relations

Miriam Wilhelm

Introduction

The concept of coopetition has evolved in a distinct, rapidly growing stream of research that can occur within organizations (Luo et al., 2006; Tsai, 2002) or between firms (Chen, 2008; Yami et al., 2010). Most research to date has focused on the inter-organizational level, particularly horizontal coopetition, that evolves when two (or more) rivals cooperate (e.g. Bengtsson & Kock, 2000; Fernandez et al., 2014; Gnyawali & Park, 2011; Ritala, 2012). There is common agreement, however, that the concept of coopetition can be fruitfully applied to vertical relationships as well (Castaldo et al., 2010). Thus, researchers have recently started to focus on the internal tensions that evolve in interorganizational collaborations where the parties involved, such as a buyer and a supplier or seller, are not direct competitors by definition. Such a condition has been termed "vertical coopetition" (Lacoste, 2012; 2014).

Our understanding of vertical coopetition, as it arises in supply chains and networks, is still limited and research has only recently started to analyze how buying firms develop opposing types of relationships with their suppliers (e.g., Kim et al., 2013; Lechner et al., 2016; Wilhelm, 2011; Zerbini & Castaldo, 2007). Vertical coopetition can be said to differ from horizontal coopetition, as vertical relations often emerge out of a mutual interest to interact and are generally more stable than horizontal relations (Bengtsson & Kock, 2000; Zerbini & Castaldo, 2007). In principle, there are two conceivable scenarios that lead to vertical coopetition: (1) based on direct competition; (2) based on indirect competition between a buyer and a supplier.

(1) In some cases suppliers can become direct competitors in the buyer's market, which usually involves the vertical integration of downstream activities (Dowling et al., 1996; Lechner et al., 2016). For example, in the automotive industry this has occurred most prominently when system suppliers—often triggered by increased outsourcing by carmakers—take over the development and manufacturing of technologically sophisticated automotive parts that used to be the core competence of the carmakers, and start to compete with the in-house capacities of their customer. Sometimes this can involve the assembly of the whole car, especially in the case of the production of niche models. For example, system integrators like Magna and Pininfarina regularly compete with carmakers who can either decide to manufacture niche models in-house or to outsource them to system integrators. This can even culminate in threats of acquisition

(Pathak et al., 2014) as the spectacular case of Magna's almost-takeover of Chrysler in 2007 demonstrated (Wernle & Barkholz, 2007).

While this scenario could also be seen as a transition towards horizontal coopetition (as buyer and supplier compete on the same stage of the value chain now), the supplier often continues to deliver different components to the buyer, leading to a mixing of different logics and dynamics (see also Pellegrin-Boucher et al., 2013). Moreover, this horizontal form of competition in buyer–supplier relations is often temporary (i.e., the duration of a vehicle model project), and the buying firm can decide for the "make"-option again in the new vehicle model cycle. For example, the German carmaker Volkswagen regularly asks external suppliers to compete against its 100%-affiliated factories that are producing strategic parts such as transmissions, engines, and seats; for some models the in-house option is chosen, for others, the parts are outsourced.

(2) In the second scenario, buyer and seller collaborate but compete over shares of value creation and capturing. Relations are thus "multiplex," as they represent more than just a single feature (Zerbini & Castaldo, 2007: 944) and constitute a "new hybrid form of supplier relationship, which combines cooperation and price-competitive transactions" (Lacoste, 2012: 649). As this constellation is more prevalent in practice, it will be the focus of the following sections. Competition in vertical buyer–supplier relations is of a more indirect nature and evolves as a result of the embeddedness of such relations in a wider supplier network (Oliver, 2004; Wu et al., 2010). The tensions caused by this form of indirect competition can nevertheless be fierce.

Keeping to the example of the automotive industry, carmakers' ongoing vertical disintegration of activities has resulted in the formation of long-term collaborative relationships, at least with first-tier suppliers and some service providers who are providing technologically complex modules and systems (e.g., Dyer & Nobeoka, 2000; Sako, 2004). At the same time, the embeddedness of these dyadic relations in the context of supplier networks creates "tension and contradiction" (Sydow & Windeler, 1998: 280) due to parallel horizontal competition between suppliers in the network. Suppliers with similar technological competences regularly compete for the development and production of a specific part for the same project when the carmaker follows a dual or parallel sourcing strategy (Richardson, 1993; Wu & Choi, 2005). Moreover, the presence of "out-suppliers" (Robinson et al., 1967), i.e., suppliers that could potentially get an R&D and delivery contract, may further fuels competitive tensions. The respective existence of latent ties (Mariotti & Delbridge, 2012) can strengthen the power position of the buyer firm and increase its ability to capture a higher share of the value.

Similar to the case of horizontal coopetition, vertical coopetition, at its heart, holds the tension between value creation and value sharing. A buying firm and a supplier will only enter into a collaborative relationship if they are able to "extend the pie" through coordination efforts across organizational boundaries and differentiation efforts through idiosyncratic investments (Jap, 1999). For the automotive industry, the potential for value creation is highest in the early stages of the product development process, when carmaker and supplier pool their complementary technological capabilities to jointly develop the specifications of the vehicle in a way that reduces costs and/or adds further functionalities to the car. As suppliers possess more detailed knowledge of their parts, they can formulate functional specifics much more precisely; they can identify potentials for the standardization and simplification of parts construction for the use of alternative materials, and they can also recognize potentials for the parallel usage of a part in other models ("carry-over-parts") (Clark & Fujimoto, 1991). A rule of thumb in the industry states that seventy percent of the costs—and, thus, cost reduction potentials—are determined in the pre-development phase. Value appropriation typically occurs much later in the process, at the stage of series production, when economies of scale and specialization effects can be fully exploited. Tensions can surface in an early stage of the collaboration, however, during negotiations over prices or intellectual property rights. In order to enhance our understanding of this complex form of vertical coopetition in buyer–supplier relationships, we now turn to recent discussions in the supply chain management literature.

Coopetition in supply chain management

While a collaborative paradigm is still prevalent in the supply chain management literature today (Chen & Paulraj, 2004; Terpend & Krause, 2015), recently scholars have started to embrace the idea that the parallel existence of competition and cooperation must not necessarily be detrimental to the buyer–supplier relationship but can actually be desirable (Klein et al., 2007; Nair et al., 2011). Moreover, there is a growing recognition that relations that are "too cozy" can bring out "dark sides" such as the risk of increased supplier opportunism (Villena et al., 2011).

Coopetition in supply chain management has predominantly been analyzed from a structural perspective (Choi & Wu, 2009; Pathak et al., 2014). From such a perspective, cooperation is understood as the direct link between two companies, whereas the absence of a link between two companies suggests competition when at least one of the three conditions are met: (1) the two firms can supply a product of equivalent functionality; (2) the firms require similar scarce resources or input; or (3) the two firms have overlapping and complementary technology such that learning and value appropriation incentives exist (Pathak et al., 2014: 255). Competition between two suppliers is likely to affect relations that these suppliers have with the buyer as well. Thus, a structural perspective sharpens our understanding of competitive tensions in a buyer–supplier dyad that results from its embeddedness in a larger network with multiple and overlapping relational linkages (Wilhelm, 2011; Pathak et al. 2014).

A further characteristic of supplier networks in the automotive industry—and interorganizational networks more generally—is that one or more actors are typically able to exert more power over other network members due to their network centrality (Wasserman & Faust, 1994), organizational size (and concomitant resource control), and/or their ability to bridge structural holes (Burt, 1995). This "hub firm" role can be ascribed to the buying firm or original equipment manufacturer that "sets up the [supply] network, and takes a pro-active attitude in the care of it" (Jarillo, 1988: 32). A network led by a hub firm in this way is often referred to as a "strategic network" (e.g., Gulati et al., 2000; Jarillo, 1988; Sydow & Windeler, 1998). Due to its proximity to the end consumer, the hub firm has more power to determine market strategy and choose network partners than other network members. The repeated exchanges between a buying firm and various suppliers result in relatively stable relations that set the boundaries of the network, although the nature of each dyadic relation may, over time, change along the continuum of cooperation and competition (Sydow & Windeler, 1998).

Research in supply chain management has often highlighted the important role of these buying firms (Monczka et al., 1998; Pathak et al., 2014; Petersen et al., 2005; Richardson, 1993). Buyers—particularly in the automotive industry—exert influence on the selection and interaction of their immediate suppliers and, thereby, influence not only the direct link they have to selected suppliers, but also the indirect links to two or even more competing suppliers (Wilhelm, 2011; Wu et al., 2010). This does not mean that suppliers are completely without power and merely react to their customers' demands. Particularly mega-suppliers like Bosch or Denso, but also those component suppliers with strong technological capabilities, can play out their power positions by demanding higher prices for their stand-alone innovations, take advantage of the diminishing ability of carmakers to evaluate the real development and manufacturing costs for purchasing parts, or withdraw from the price-cutting game when they perceive the pressure as becoming too strong. Suppliers can also decide to initiate horizontal collaborations with each other in order to better serve their customer's request for global delivery of parts or share costs in R&D. At the same time, the horizontal cooperation between suppliers can help them to strengthen their bargaining position vis-à-vis their customer. In order to better understand how these actions can change the dynamics and outcomes of vertical coopetition, we argue for the need to expand our methodological scope and analyze the triadic relation between a buyer and two competing suppliers.

The triadic nature of vertical coopetition

Whereas buyer–supplier relations are typically conceptualized as dyadic relations, they are usually embedded in supply networks, which are more comprehensive, incorporating sets of individual and connected supply chains with links among them (Sturgeon et al., 2008).

Researchers have pointed to the importance of looking at the interactions between dyads that are embedded in the same network (Wu & Choi, 2005). Some have shown that a dyadic relational link between a buyer and a supplier operates differently when the buyer maintains additional dyadic relations to competing suppliers. In its most simplified form, the parallel dyadic relations a buying firm maintains with two suppliers can be depicted as a triad. Figure 35.1 illustrates different triadic constellations between a buyer and two suppliers that result in different forms of vertical coopetition.

Triad ABC (vertical coopetition with balanced competition)

Competition between supplier B and C, which typically results from overlapping product markets that these suppliers are active in, will affect relations between buying firm A and supplier B (and A and C, respectively). In this constellation, the buying firm interacts with each individual supplier independently and "serves as a router of information exchange between suppliers" (Choi et al., 2002: 122). Depending on the degree of resulting competition, the resulting A–B relationship will either be "balanced" (cooperation and competition are represented to equal degrees), predominantly competitive, or predominantly cooperative. While this constellation bears the highest potential of balanced coopetition, the realization of this potential depends on the ability of the buying firm A to manage each relationship with supplier B and C and with potential suppliers on the market (i.e., "out-suppliers"). For example, the buying firm could decide to

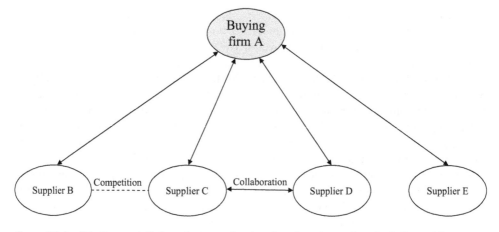

Figure 35.1   Triadic constellations between buying firm A and suppliers B, C, D, and E

strategically reveal cost or product-related information of supplier B to supplier C in order to stimulate competition between them. The active creation and encouragement of interdependencies between two suppliers, termed a "triadic sourcing strategy," can help buying firms to "nurture and benefit from cooperation and competition between two suppliers with partially overlapping capabilities" (Dubois & Fredriksson, 2008: 176). An over-stimulation of competition, however, could discourage suppliers from investing in improvement activities as they fear diminishing returns of efforts (Li & Wan, 2017).

Triad ACD (vertical coopetition with reduced competition)

If supplier C and D form a cooperative relationship, this can potentially harm the degree of competition in the network. Buying firms are often wary of the horizontal cooperation between their suppliers, as they fear the loss of bargaining power vis-à-vis their suppliers. In fact, cooperative relationships between suppliers can often stray into collusive practices. For instance, in several industries, such as airlines and steel, price increases and decreases occur in tandem (Choi et al., 2002: 122). Thus, formally supplier C and D are competitors (as they operate in the same product market) who have chosen to reduce their competitive actions vis-à-vis the buyer. In exceptional cases, however, induced cooperation between suppliers could lead to a higher degree of performance transparency among suppliers and, paradoxically, to a higher degree of network internal competition. This requires, however, the strong network governance from a skillful and powerful buying firm, as illustrated by the case of Toyota (see Wilhelm, 2011).

Triad ADE (cooperation with reduced competition)

Missing (cooperative or competitive) ties between supplier D and E indicate a monopolist position of supplier E. In this case, there is a lack of competition in the network leading to a situation where a supplier could dictate prices. In the automotive industry, the lack of alternative supply sources can occur for specific parts but is often only temporary, as carmakers are usually eager to develop alternative sources. For example, Toyota invested in the seat supplier Trim Masters to introduce competition to its existing seat supplier Johnson Control, keeping them motivated to improve and reduce costs (Liker, 2004). Later on, Toyota merged three of its group companies to form the new Toyota Boshoku, creating the fourth-largest global seat and interior supplier. However, the lack of alternative sources does not always need to reflect the actual market situation but can also arise from over-embeddedness with suppliers. The case of Nissan's near-bankruptcy at the end of the 1990s demonstrated that long-term, exclusive relations with suppliers can easily lead to inertia and a situation where market competitors are purposefully left outside the network, leading to detrimental performance consequences for the network (see also Stevens et al., 2015). This scenario clearly lacks competitive elements and is, technically speaking, not a type of vertical coopetition, but it is nevertheless included here to demonstrate the danger of a limited perspective that looks at each buyer–supplier dyad in isolation. Thus, even though the triadic perspective constitutes a simplification of the complexity of real-life supplier networks, it is a useful first step to think about the interrelationships between different dyadic relations that a buyer has with its suppliers and the resulting nature of vertical coopetition.

Vertical and horizontal coopetition in comparison

Whereas the above outlined the usefulness of a triadic perspective to better grasp the indirect nature of vertical coopetition, this section summarizes the distinct nature of the concept by contrasting it with horizontal coopetition (see Table 35.1).

Table 35.1 Horizontal and vertical coopetition compared

	Horizontal Coopetition	Vertical Coopetition
Strategic orientation	"cooperate to compete"	"compete to cooperate"
Nature of competition	direct	direct and indirect
Methodological scope	dyadic	triadic
Power relations	more symmetrical, i.e., collaboration between "giants"	more asymmetrical, i.e., buying firm as "hub firm"
Central tension	fights over shares of knowledge appropriation, patenting	fights over the degree of vertical integration
		fights over shares of margins, price negotiations

An important difference between horizontal and vertical coopetition can be found in the strategic orientation of the cooperating firms. Whereas a main motive for rivals to cooperate is to strengthen their competitive position against other rivals ("cooperate to compete"), the strategic orientation for vertical coopetition can be better described as "compete to cooperate": in order to qualify for a new project with their customer—and prove worthy as a collaboration partner—suppliers must compete against each other based on their ability to meet technical requirements, price targets, and quality performance. Moreover, competition between rivals will be of a more direct nature due to the overlap in product markets of the alliance partners, as opposed to a buyer and a supplier who are active at different stages of the value chain. Due to the embeddedness of the buyer–supplier dyad, competitive tensions arise from the indirect competition between suppliers, that can, however, be moderated by the active involvement of the buying firm (Wu et al., 2010). This also implies, however, that the buying firm has a higher ability to influence the dynamics within triadic constellations; and power asymmetries are more likely to be pronounced for vertical coopetition than for horizontal coopetition (e.g., Gnyawali & Park, 2011). Finally, although tensions between value creation and value sharing characterize both types of coopetition, the tension will surface in conflicts around shares of knowledge appropriation in the patent filing process (and sometimes unintended knowledge spillovers) between rivals, and the "fight over margins" between a buyer and a supplier.

Avenues for further research

This chapter applies recent discussion from the supply chain management literature on the phenomenon of vertical coopetition between a buyer and a supplier. While the current structural perspective in supply chain management, and the triadic level of analysis, has proved to be a valuable approach to analyze vertical coopetition, it also opens up several directions for further research.

First, our analysis of coopetition was restricted to the level of buying firms and their first-tier suppliers. Research in coopetition in supply networks indicates, however, that there can be "spillovers" for competitive tensions to the second-tier suppliers (Pathak et al., 2014). A single decision of a buyer to source from a particular supplier can lead to a cascading set of dissolutions of ties and the creation of structural holes. In this context, it would be interesting to extend the simplified depiction of vertical coopetition outlined here to embrace multiple tiers of the supply chain and analyze the coopetitive dynamics between tiers.

Future studies could also explore how the purposeful creation and closing of structural holes (e.g., Pathak et al., 2014; Wilhelm, 2011) creates different forms of competitive tensions. For example, a collaboration between two competing suppliers that was initiated by the buyer to exchange manufacturing knowledge would cause different competitive tensions based on performance differences (see also Wilhelm, 2011), rather than self-initiated R&D collaborations among suppliers that aim to strengthen their competitive positions vis-à-vis the buyer. Both forms of competition are likely to affect the buyer–supplier collaboration differently, calling for further, more systematic inquiries.

Finally, coopetition researchers have started to engage with the emerging paradox perspective from management studies (Schad et al., 2016; Smith et al., 2013) and have called for the understanding of coopetition through an explicit paradox lens (Bengtsson & Kock, 2014; Czakon & Fernandez, 2014). A paradox perspective with its focus on dynamics and processes might shed new light on how actors experience and respond to tensions that arise from structural coopetition. In this context, the importance of cognitive capabilities of individuals to respond to paradoxical tensions has been highlighted (Smith & Tushman, 2005) and named by Bengtsson et al. (2016) as "coopetition capabilities." We argue that due to the different dynamics of vertical coopetition and the expected power asymmetries between a buyer and a supplier, the nature of paradoxical tensions might differ and so might a buyer's and a supplier's responses and their required coopetition capabilities (see Wilhelm & Sydow, 2018). A paradox perspective could thus fruitfully complement the structural view outlined here to further explore these issues.

Conclusion

Vertical coopetition can be directly related to the recent debate on the "dark side of buyer-supplier relations" (Anderson & Jap, 2005; Fang et al., 2011; Kim & Choi, 2015; Noordhoff et al., 2011), which challenges the overall positive view on collaboration with suppliers in supply chain management theory and practice. This perspective highlights the necessity of having both relational and transactional mechanisms (Liu et al., 2009) in order to generate value and overcome the relational inertia that inhibits partners' capacity to meet changing market demands (Villena et al., 2011). This approach increasingly questions the cooperative–competitive dichotomy that is commonly used to describe buyer–supplier relationships (Sako & Helper, 1998; Wu & Choi, 2005). A more nuanced picture of the way cooperation and competition are intertwined in buyer–supplier relations could help to more adequately reflect the conflicting interests of buyers and suppliers. In this regard, the concept of vertical coopetition widens our perspective to understand buyer–supplier relations as triadic constellations and sensitizes managers of buying firms to the importance of not only managing dyadic relations with their suppliers but also urges them to think about the interrelationships between these relations in order to stimulate and adjust the desired degree of competition in the collaboration with suppliers.

References

Anderson, E. & Jap, S. D. (2005). The dark side of close relationships. *MIT Sloan Management Review*, 46(3), 75–82.

Bengtsson, M. & Kock, S. (2000). "Coopetition" in business networks—to cooperate and compete simultaneously. *Industrial Marketing Management*, 29(5), 411–426.

Bengtsson, M. & Kock, S. (2014). Coopetition—Quo vadis? Past accomplishments and future challenges. *Industrial Marketing Management*, 43(2), 180–188.

Bengtsson, M., Raza-Ullah, T., & Vanyushyn, V. (2016). The coopetition paradox and tension: The moderating role of coopetition capability. *Industrial Marketing Management*, 53, 19–30.

Burt, R. S. (1995). *Structural Holes: The Social Structure of Competition*. Boston: Harvard University Press.

Castaldo, S., Möllering, G., Grosso, M., & Zerbini, F. (2010). Exploring how third-party organizations facilitate coopetition management in buyer-seller relationships. In S. Yami, S. Castaldo, G. Dagnino, & F. Le Roy (Eds), *Coopetition: Winning Strategies for the 21st Century* (pp. 141–165.). Cheltenham: Edward Elgar Publishing.

Chen, I. J. & Paulraj, A. (2004). Towards a theory of supply chain management: the constructs and measurements. *Journal of Operations Management*, 22(2), 119–150.

Chen, M.-J. (2008). Reconceptualizing the competition–cooperation relationship: A transparadox perspective. *Journal of Management Inquiry*, 17(4), 288–304.

Choi, T.Y., Wu, Z., Ellram, L., & Koka, B. R. (2002). Supplier-supplier relationships and their implications for buyer-supplier relationships. *IEEE Transactions on Engineering Management*, 49(2), 119–130.

Clark, K. B. & Fujimoto, T. (1991). *Product Development Performance: Strategy, Organization, and Management in the World Auto Industry*. Boston: Harvard Business School Press.

Czakon, W. & Fernandez, A. (2014). Editorial–From paradox to practice: the rise of coopetition strategies. *International Journal of Business Environment*, 6(1), 1–10.

Dowling, M. J., Roering, W. D., Carlin, B. A., & Wisnieski, J. (1996). Multifaceted relationships under coopetition: Description and theory. *Journal of Management Inquiry*, 5(2), 155–167.

Dubois, A. & Fredriksson, P. (2008). Cooperating and competing in supply networks: Making sense of a triadic sourcing strategy. *Journal of Purchasing and Supply Management*, 14(3), 170–179.

Dyer, J. H. & Nobeoka, K. (2000). Creating and managing a high-performance knowledge-sharing network: The Toyota case. *Strategic Management Journal*, 21(21), 345–367.

Fang, S.-R., Chang, Y.-S., & Peng, Y.-C. (2011). Dark side of relationships: A tensions-based view. *Industrial Marketing Management*, 40(5), 774–784.

Fernandez, A. S., Ji, F. X., & Yami, S. (2014). Balancing exploration and exploitation tension in coopetition: the case of European space innovation programmes. *International Journal of Business Environment*, 6(1), 69.

Gnyawali, D. R. & Park, B.-J. (Robert). (2011). Co-opetition between giants: Collaboration with competitors for technological innovation. *Research Policy*, 40(5), 650–663.

Gulati, R., Nohria, N., & Zaheer, A. (2000). Strategic networks. *Strategic Management Journal*, 21(3), 203–215.

Jap, S. D. (1999). Pie-expansion efforts: Collaboration processes in buyer-supplier Relationships. *Journal of Marketing Research*, 36(4), 461–475.

Jarillo, J. C. (1988). On strategic networks. *Strategic Management Journal*, 9(1), 31–41.

Kim, S., Kim, N., Pae, J. H., & Yip, L. (2013). Cooperate "and" compete: coopetition strategy in retailer-supplier relationships. *Journal of Business & Industrial Marketing*, 28(4), 263–275.

Kim, Y. & Choi, T.Y. (2015). Deep, sticky, transient, and gracious: An expanded buyer-supplier relationship typology. *Journal of Supply Chain Management*, 51(3), 61–86.

Klein, R., Rai, A., & Straub, D. W. (2007). Competitive and cooperative positioning in supply chain logistics relationships. *Decision Sciences*, 38(4), 611–646.

Lacoste, S. (2012). "Vertical coopetition": The key account perspective. *Industrial Marketing Management*, 41(4), 649–658.

Lacoste, S. (2014). Coopetition and framework contracts in industrial customer-supplier relationships. *Qualitative Market Research: An International Journal*, 17(1), 43–57.

Lechner, C., Soppe, B., & Dowling, M. (2016). Vertical coopetition and the sales growth of young and small firms. *Journal of Small Business Management*, 54(1), 67–84.

Li, C. & Wan, Z. (2017) Supplier competition and cost improvement. *Management Science*. 63(8), 2460–2477.

Liker, J. K. (2004). *The Toyota Way*. New York: McGraw-Hill Education.

Liu, Y., Luo, Y., & Liu, T. (2009). Governing buyer–supplier relationships through transactional and relational mechanisms: Evidence from China. *Journal of Operations Management*, 27(4), 294–309.

Luo, X., Slotegraaf, R. J., & Pan, X. (2006). Cross-functional "coopetition": The simultaneous role of cooperation and competition within firms. *Journal of Marketing*, 70(2), 67–80.

Mariotti, F. & Delbridge, R. (2012). Overcoming network overload and redundancy in interorganizational networks: The roles of potential and latent ties. *Organization Science*, 23(2), 511–528.

Monczka, R. M., Petersen, K. J., Handfield, R. B., & Ragatz, G. L. (1998). Success factors in strategic supplier alliances: The buying company perspective. *Decision Sciences*, 29(3), 553–577.

Nair, A., Narasimhan, R., & Elliot, B. (2011). Coopetitive buyer-supplier relationship: An investigation of bargaining power, relational context, and investment strategies. *Decision Sciences*, 42(1), 93–127.

Noordhoff, C. S., Kyriakopoulos, K., Moorman, C., Pauwels, P., & Dellaert, B. G. (2011). The bright side and dark side of embedded ties in business-to-business innovation. *Journal of Marketing*, 75(5), 34–52.

Oliver, A. L. (2004). On the duality of competition and collaboration: network-based knowledge relations in the biotechnology industry. *Scandinavian Journal of Management*, 20(1–2), 151–171.

Pathak, S., Wu, Z., & Johnston, D. (2014). Towards a theory of co-opetition of supply networks. *Journal of Operations Management*, 32, (5), 254–267.

Pellegrin-Boucher, E., Le Roy, F., & Gurău, C. (2013). Coopetitive strategies in the ICT sector: typology and stability. *Technology Analysis & Strategic Management*, 25(1), 71–89.

Petersen, K. J., Handfield, R. B., & Ragatz, G. L. (2005). Supplier integration into new product development: Coordinating product, process and supply chain design. *Journal of Operations Management*, 23(3–4), 371–388.

Richardson, J. (1993). Parallel sourcing and supplier performance in the Japanese automobile industry. *Strategic Management Journal*, 14(5), 339–350.

Ritala, P. (2012). Coopetition strategy—when is it successful? Empirical evidence on innovation and market performance. *British Journal of Management*, 23(3), 307–324.

Robinson, P. J., Faris, C. W., & Wind, Y. (1967). *Industrial Buying and Creative Marketing*. Boston: Allyn & Bacon.

Sako, M. (2004). Supplier development at Honda, Nissan and Toyota: comparative case studies of organizational capability enhancement. *Industrial and Corporate Change*, 13(2), 281–308.

Sako, M. & Helper, S. (1998). Determinants of trust in supplier relations: Evidence from the automotive industry in Japan and the United States. *Journal of Economic Behavior & Organization*, 34(3), 387–417.

Schad, J., Lewis, M., & Raisch, S. (2016). Paradox research in management science: Looking back to move forward. *Academy of Management Annals*, 10(1), 5–64.

Smith, W., Gonin, M., & Besharov, M. (2013). Managing social-business tensions: A review and research agenda for social enterprise. *Business Ethics Quarterly*, 23(3), 407–442.

Smith, W. K. & Tushman, M. L. (2005). Managing strategic contradictions: A top management model for managing innovation streams. *Organization Science*, 16(5), 522–536.

Stevens, M., MacDuffie, J. P., & Helper, S. (2015). Reorienting and recalibrating inter-organizational relationships: Strategies for achieving optimal trust. *Organization Studies*, 36(9), 1237–1264.

Sturgeon, T., Van Biesebroeck, J., & Gereffi, G. (2008). Value chains, networks and clusters: reframing the global automotive industry. *Journal of Economic Geography*, 8(3), 297–321.

Sydow, J. & Windeler, A. (1998). Organizing and evaluating interfirm networks: A structurationist perspective on network processes and effectiveness. *Organization Science*, 9(3), 265–284.

Terpend, R. & Krause, D. R. (2015). Competition or cooperation? Promoting supplier performance with incentives under varying conditions of dependence. *Journal of Supply Chain Management*, 51(4), 29–53.

Tsai, W. (2002). Social structure of "coopetition" within a multiunit organization: Coordination, competition, and intraorganizational knowledge sharing. *Organization Science*, 13(2), 179–190.

Villena, V. H., Revilla, E., & Choi, T.Y. (2011). The dark side of buyer-supplier relationships: A social capital perspective. *Journal of Operations Management*, 29(6), 561–576.

Wasserman, S. & Faust, K. (1994). *Network Analysis: Methods and Applications*. Cambridge: Cambridge University Press.

Wernle, B. & Barkholz, D. (2007). Magna plots Chrysler's future. www.autonews.com/article/20070507/SUB/70504049/magna-plots-chryslers-future, accessed December 11, 2017.

Wilhelm, M. M. (2011). Managing coopetition through horizontal supply chain relations: Linking dyadic and network levels of analysis. *Journal of Operations Management*, 29(7–8), 663–676.

Wilhelm, M. & Sydow, J. (2018). Managing coopetition in supplier networks: A paradox perspective. *Journal of Supply Chain Management*, 54(3), 22–41.

Wu, Z. & Choi, T.Y. (2005). Supplier-supplier relationships in the buyer-supplier triad: Building theories from eight case studies. *Journal of Operations Management*, 24(1), 27–52.

Wu, Z., Choi, T. Y., & Rungtusanatham, M. J. (2010). Supplier-supplier relationships in buyer-supplier-supplier triads: Implications for supplier performance. *Journal of Operations Management*, 28(2), 115–123.

Yami, S., Castaldo, S., Dagnino, B., & Le Roy, F. (2010). *Coopetition: Winning Strategies for the 21st Century*. Cheltenham: Edward Elgar Publishing.

Zerbini, F. & Castaldo, S. (2007). Stay in or get out the Janus? The maintenance of multiplex relationships between buyers and sellers. *Industrial Marketing Management*, 36(7), 941–954.

36

Coopetition for SMEs

Malin H. Näsholm, Maria Bengtsson, and Marlene Johansson

Introduction

The business landscape, particularly in knowledge-intensive and technologically advanced markets, is changing as a result of disruptive innovations, increased complexity of the technologies and systems, and the fast-paced development of markets. Therefore, SMEs face a number of challenges, such as increasing research and development costs, high risk and uncertainty in new technological developments, and market entrance. Small and medium-sized enterprises usually lack resources and are therefore more dependent on other firms (BarNir & Smith, 2002; Gnyawali & Park, 2009); they often need to cooperate with competitors (Bengtsson & Kock, 2000) to meet these challenges.

> Small- and medium-sized enterprises (SMEs) are particularly vulnerable to environmental forces and may therefore seek to supplement their insufficient resources and reduce uncertainty by adopting coopetition strategies.
>
> *(Granata et al., 2016: 82)*

Coopetition can be a necessity for survival for these firms, as the citation above illustrates; however, it is also a risky strategy for them. On the one hand, it can be argued that SMEs benefit the most from coopetition; on the other hand, they are also the most vulnerable when cooperating with competing firms. This chapter addresses the question of what capabilities are needed for coopetition to be a successful strategy for SMEs.

It is important to acknowledge that SMEs have specific characteristics. These types of businesses are often defined as having few employees and limited turnover and market presence, referred to as the liabilities of smallness and newness (Hannan & Freeman, 1984; Stinchcombe, 1965). Therefore, SMEs engage in alliances with other firms as a strategy to strengthen their competitive position (Van Gils & Zwart, 2009). Alliances have been argued to be especially important for new and entrepreneurial firms, since partnering with other firms can provide capabilities that enhance their performance and reputation (Stuart et al., 1999) and help SMEs to overcome challenges of resource constraints and limited market presence (Morris et al., 2007). Most inter-firm relationships are coopetitive as they comprise elements of both cooperation and competition (Zhang et al., 2010), and firms have different roles, such as customer, supplier, or competitor, in relation to each other in different activities, depending on the specific project (Ross & Robertson, 2007). Pursuing coopetition may be a particularly relevant strategy for SMEs to overcome their vulnerabilities and liabilities of being small and new (Bengtsson & Johansson, 2014). Small and medium-sized enterprises may benefit the most from cooperating with competing firms because of the threat of larger competitors and resource constraints (Gnyawali & Park, 2009). Small firms can cooperate with each other to join forces against larger firms, or they can partner with larger competitors to integrate into dominating technological platforms and gain access to larger markets. As a firm grows, relationships with competitors can become even more important (Lechner & Dowling, 2003).

While cooperating with competitors can be a proactive and successful strategy, Thomason et al. (2013) suggest that it can often be less intentional for small firms and can emerge, for example, due to customer demands. This implies that SMEs can be forced to engage in coopetition and adopt this strategy out of the necessity to obtain the benefits available, or even to survive. Coopetition has been found to be challenging, risky, and filled with tension (cf. Das & Teng, 2000; Gnyawali & Park, 2009; Raza-Ullah et al., 2014). These risks may be even more important for smaller firms, and making the wrong choice about who to coopete with can be critical for a small firm (Morris et al., 2007; Baum et al., 2000). If an alliance fails, it could even threaten the existence of a small firm (Rosenbusch et al., 2011). Coopetitive relationships are particularly challenging for small firms allying with larger firms due to the power disparities and asymmetry between the partners. Yet reviews of coopetition (Bouncken et al., 2015; Gast et al., 2015) point to the entrepreneurship context (SMEs, family firms, and start-ups) as a fairly underexplored area in coopetition research.

In this chapter, we address the specificities of coopetition for SMEs, particularly when allying with larger firms. We examine the research within coopetition that has specifically focused on SMEs, and we outline the specific benefits and challenges of coopetition for SMEs.

Coopetition has been argued to require specific capabilities (Bengtsson et al., 2016; Gnyawali & Park, 2011) in addition to general alliance management capabilities. This chapter discusses what such coopetition capabilities would entail for SMEs, and, drawing on the specific challenges that SMEs face when coopeting, we argue that additional dimensions of alliance and alliance portfolio management capabilities are required.

Benefits of coopetition for SMEs

In coopetition research, the focus has mainly been on larger firms, and there are only a few that have specifically focused on the situation and circumstances of SMEs (Gnyawali & Park, 2009). The few studies focusing on SMEs have noted the importance of coopetition in varied contexts, such as professional football (Robert et al., 2009), accounting firms (Huang & Chu, 2015), and tourism (Della Corte & Aria, 2016; von Friedrichs Grängsjö, 2003). Researchers have listed numerous benefits of cooperating with competitors for SMEs. Alliances with competing firms have, for example, been argued to provide access to resources, facilitate entry to new markets (BarNir & Smith, 2002), increase speed in technology development (Gnyawali & Park, 2009), help SMEs to meet risks, gain economies of scale (Morris et al., 2007), reduce uncertainty, and enhance financial performance (Levy et al., 2003).

Innovation has been noted as a key motive for SMEs to coopete, driven by increasingly high R&D costs and short product life cycles in high-tech industries (Gnyawali & Park, 2009). Through collaboration with competing firms, small firms can develop technologies that they could not have done on their own, since they have limited resources to invest in research and development and to more rapidly bring them to market (Morris et al., 2007). Coopetition is also a way for SMEs to strengthen their internationalization (cf. Vanyushyn et al., 2009). Coopetitive relations can be a source of international opportunities for SMEs (Kock et al., 2010), and SMEs may be willing to collaborate with domestic competitors in international markets to acquire resources (Chetty & Wilson, 2003). Jankowska (2011) found that smaller firms were more optimistic about the benefits of coopetition for their internationalization.

Soppe et al. (2014) found that the majority of entrepreneurial firms that they studied choose to coopete with smaller or equally sized firms. For small firms, joining together in business groups or networks can be a strategy for competing with larger firms (Lechner & Leyronas, 2009; Lindström & Polsa, 2016). Lin and Zhang (2005) argue that forming networks, even with competing firms, is a crucial strategy for SMEs to survive in a highly competitive industry. For SMEs, it may be an important strategy to partner with a larger competitor due to its strong and competitive position within the industry. Bengtsson and Johansson (2014), for example, demonstrate that allying with large competitors enables small firms to maneuver in global business landscapes and grow to secure a position in the market.

Specific challenges for SMEs when coopeting

One of the defining characteristics of SMEs is that they are small and therefore have limited resources compared to larger firms. The lack of resources and skills is described as a liability of smallness (Baum et al., 2000; Hannan & Freeman, 1984), and it is difficult to gain access to capital to develop internally. In addition, what has been referred to as a liability of newness describes the potential difficulties that entrepreneurial firms face in establishing a foothold in either an existing or new market—since they, for example, lack a track record, customer references, and legitimacy (Aldrich & Auster, 1986; Bengtsson & Johansson, 2014; Stinchcombe, 1965). Many SMEs have limited markets, and they depend on a niche customer base and narrow product or service lines (Storey, 1994; Van Gils & Zwart, 2009). These liabilities make the risks involved in coopetition particularly important for SMEs, as failure would be critical for them (Morris et al., 2007). The liabilities of small firms also make them particularly vulnerable to environmental forces (Morris et al., 2007; Granata et al., 2016). For example, the implications of the global financial crisis have been severe for SMEs, and coopetition has been suggested as an appropriate business strategy for overcoming these challenges (Kossyva et al., 2015).

As previously stated, coopetitive relationships are particularly challenging for small firms allying with larger firms due to the power disparities and asymmetry between the partners. While power asymmetry and unequal access to resources may be reasons to form a coopetitive relationship, they may also be the cause of additional unilateral actions, an emerging coopetive component (Czakon, 2009). Casciaro and Piskorski (2005) highlight the risks of needing a partner's resources. There is a risk that the firm loses control of its partner or becomes too dependent on the partner (Gnyawali & Park, 2009). If the small firm becomes dependent on the partner for key resources, there is a potential for the partner to take advantage of this power (Chiambaretto, 2015). The small firm's ability to defend itself against the power of a large firm is low once the relationship has been established (Katila et al., 2008). Bengtsson and Johansson (2014) argue that large firms that assemble and develop integrated systems often use strategies to either lock in or lock out the SME from integrated horizontal value systems. The small firm can be locked out if the large firm develops its own solutions that outcompete those provided by the SME, or it can be locked in as a supplier within the large firm's own value chain.

Coopetition involves a number of risks, for example, unintentional knowledge leakage, imitation, opportunistic behavior of the partner, and loss of competitive advantage, which make it difficult to manage coopetition (Gnyawali & Park, 2009; Ritala & Hurmelinna-Laukkanen, 2009). Potential conflicts between partners and internal contradictions make alliances unstable and often unsuccessful (Das & Teng, 2000). In addition, coopetition, by its nature of simultaneously pursuing cooperation and competition between firms, involves a number of contradictory demands (such as knowledge sharing and protecting, and exploration and exploitation), which result in tensions at individual, organizational, and inter-organizational levels (Fernandez et al., 2014; Raza-Ullah et al., 2014). These inherent tensions make it difficult to manage coopetition (Fernandez et al., 2014; Gnyawali & Park, 2009). We argue that this tension could be particularly salient in SMEs because, with fewer employees, more of the employees would be involved in interaction with the coopetitor, which would mean that these individuals need to cope with these contradictory demands more directly (compared to larger firms, where competitive and collaborative activities could be more separate). On the other hand, in a smaller firm, more employees could have both better insight into the relation and a better understanding of why collaborating with a competing firm is necessary. The level of tension that an individual experiences is dependent on how involved he or she is in the coopetitive interaction and how much he or she interacts with the other firm (Näsholm & Bengtsson, 2014). Bengtsson et al. (2016) argue that the way in which top managers deal with this tension is important for how coopetition and tensions are perceived in the organization, and that the top managers could be more capable of handling the contradictory demands. However, in a small or new firm, the owner or manager may not have these capabilities or experience.

Capabilities needed by SMEs

Successful coopetition requires that partners are active and committed, and that they have the resources to be so (Lindström & Polsa, 2016). The time and additional costs that may be required to manage the relationship can offset the benefits of coopeting; however, with the flexibility of SMEs, coopetition can be less difficult to handle than for their larger, more rigid counterparts (Morris et al., 2007). For small firms, the owners or managers play a key role in the success of a coopetitive relationship, for example, in terms of their knowledge, social capital, perceptions (Thomason et al., 2013), and social networks (BarNir & Smith, 2002). Soppe et al. (2014) found that in small firms, coopetitive inter-firm relationships tended to be managed centrally, often directly by the CEO. Gnyawali and Park (2009; 2011) suggest that managers of SMES need coopetition experience, and they need to "develop a coopetition mindset" in order to meet the challenges of managing coopetitive alliances. Morris et al. (2007) and Thomason et al. (2013) suggest that for small businesses, successful coopetition is based on trust, mutual benefit, and commitment, and that they should develop policies and procedures to promote this. This view may be too harmonious, since a moderate level of tension and a balance between the cooperative and competitive aspects of the relationship have been found to be the most dynamic and ultimately beneficial (Bengtsson et al., 2010; Bengtsson et al., 2016). The tensions involved in coopeting should be seen as a source of competitive advantage, although managers need to handle them and prevent them from turning into conflicts (Fernandez et al., 2014). Bengtsson et al. (2016) argue that coopetition capability involves being able think paradoxically and to initiate processes that help firms to attain and maintain a moderate level of tension. In addition, the managers involved must also be able to deal with simultaneous conflicting emotions (Raza-Ullah et al., 2014). For small firms, the individuals' capabilities to manage coopetition and cope with paradoxical or contradictory demands would be more crucial, since larger firms have greater human resources.

To manage the risks involved in alliances and to improve alliance success, a number of tools have been identified, such as setting up specifically dedicated alliance units or managers, creating databases, using external experts, and setting up training programs for staff (Heimeriks et al., 2009). However, these types of investments can be too costly for SMEs that are more dependent on individual managers to have the knowledge and alliance management experience (Kale & Singh, 2009). With their liabilities and the higher stakes involved, it is particularly important for smaller firms to develop alliance capabilities in order to manage their alliances. Although research has addressed the way in which alliance management capabilities are developed, more research is needed regarding what these capabilities actually consist of and which capabilities are needed to manage a firm's entire portfolio of alliances (Schreiner et al., 2009; Wassmer, 2010).

Alliance management capabilities have been described as including dimensions of inter-organizational learning, alliance transformation, and inter-organizational coordination (Schilke & Goerzen, 2010). As described, due to the power asymmetry in alliances with larger partners, SMEs risk becoming locked into a larger firm's value chain or locked out of the market if they are not able to protect their unique offer and competitive advantage. To maintain their independence and avoid unwanted knowledge leakage, we argue that SMEs' alliance capabilities must involve an additional dimension of *guarding*, signifying an ability to both protect their own interests and keep their partners at an appropriate distance (Bengtsson et al., 2015).

To avoid becoming both too dependent on one partner and too vulnerable, SMEs need to develop a portfolio of alliances that can be used to balance and counter the asymmetry with larger firms (Bengtsson & Johansson, 2014). Kale and Singh (2009) argue that alliance *portfolio* management capability is distinct from alliance capability, and that there are additional advantages for SMEs to be gain by managing their alliances as a portfolio. Bengtsson et al. (2015) draw on case studies of high-tech SMEs and earlier studies of such capabilities (Kale & Singh, 2009; Schilke & Goerzen, 2010) to develop four dimensions of alliance portfolio management capability that SMEs specifically require. These dimensions take into consideration the specific challenges, tensions, and risks that SMEs face. They are named agility, balancing, portfolio proactiveness, and awareness (Bengtsson et al., 2015).

Agility signifies an SME's need for speed and flexibility, not only in configuring but also in reconfiguring its alliance portfolio to meet the strategic moves of alliance partners (Bengtsson et al., 2015). The balancing dimension signifies that it is not enough for SMEs to coordinate across alliances and resolve conflicts, as argued by Kale and Singh (2009), but that smaller firms need to be able to use competing alliances to counter the hostile moves of large partners. The dimension of portfolio proactiveness is specific to SMEs in that, for them, it is not only crucial to identify alliance opportunities, but also to be proactive at a portfolio level to predict competitive moves, take initiative to form new alliances, and terminate alliances that become a threat (Bengtsson et al., 2015). This is supported by Soppe et al. (2014), who found that entrepreneurial firms need to be ready and able to end a collaboration that could become harmful. Finally, for SMEs, an important capability is awareness: to continually analyze and be updated on developments in the market, to understand the changing relationships between different actors in their industry, and to understand the collaborative and competitive landscape (Bengtsson et al., 2015).

Conclusion

It has been argued that coopetition is becoming the dominant logic in some industries, and that SMEs need to integrate coopetition into the firm's daily routines and strategic thinking

(Baumard, 2009). The few studies within coopetition that have focused specifically on SMEs have demonstrated that there is much for small firms to gain by collaborating with competing firms. Furthermore, only a few studies have addressed the challenges of partnering with a larger firm due to the power asymmetry and dependency. For some SMEs, coopeting may be necessary for the firm's survival, and it can be a successful strategy to develop and grow. However, the liabilities of small firms also exaggerate make the risks involved, and failure could be fatal.

To make coopetition a strategy for success, SMEs require capabilities to manage the risks and tensions involved. Small and medium-sized enterprises are more dependent on their owners or managers, and more of their employees are directly involved in the coopetitive interaction. This makes the individuals' capabilities and experience more important for SMEs, which could be both a strength and a weakness in comparison to larger firms. Firms also need to develop their alliance portfolio management capabilities, since they need to navigate relationships and use them to remain independent. Therefore, small firms must keep their entire portfolio of alliances in mind to be proactive and balance their alliances, especially if they partner with larger firms. As discussed, due to the power asymmetry these relationships are particularly challenging and place additional demands on SMEs' capabilities.

Further empirical research is required regarding the specificities of small firms and the capabilities they need to make the most of their coopetitive strategies. Empirical studies focusing on coopetition relationships between small and large firms are lacking. It is important to further explore the effects of different forms of inter-firm asymmetries on an SME's ability to sustain such relationships. If SMEs choose to partner with a large firm in areas of less strategic importance for the partner, it might be less likely that the partner attempts to lock in or lock out the SME. Therefore, studies are needed with regard to the ways in which such dimensions are dealt with when partners are selected. Furthermore, studies are required that consider the different constellations of dyadic coopetitive relationships between SMEs and between SMEs and larger partners. In addition, further research could address coopetitive alliance portfolios, from the focal firm's perspective, and the capabilities needed to manage them. Additional research on both coopetition capabilities and alliance portfolio capabilities has been called for. Longitudinal in-depth studies are needed to further explore the dynamic interplay between different relationships and how they evolve over time to understand how SMEs can sustain themselves in dynamic and competitive industries.

References

Aldrich, H. & Auster, E. R. (1986). Even dwarfs started small: Liabilities of age and size and their strategic implications. *Research in Organizational Behavior*, 8, 165–186.

BarNir, A. & Smith, K. A. (2002). Interfirm alliances in the small business: The role of social networks. *Journal of Small Business Management*, 40(3), 219–232.

Baum, J. A., Calabrese, T., & Silverman, B. S. (2000). Don't go it alone: Alliance network composition and startups' performance in Canadian biotechnology. *Strategic Management Journal*, 21(3), 267.

Baumard, P. (2009). An asymmetric perspective on coopetitive strategies. *International Journal of Entrepreneurship and Small Business*, 8(1), 6–22.

Bengtsson, M., Eriksson, J., & Wincent, J. (2010). Co-opetition dynamics – an outline for further inquiry. *Competitiveness Review*, 20(2), 194–214.

Bengtsson, M. & Johansson, M. (2014). Managing coopetition to create opportunities for small firms. *International Small Business Journal*, 32 (4), 401–427.

Bengtsson, M., Johansson, M., & Näsholm, M. H. (2015) SMEs' alliance portfolio management capability: Strategies for dealing with larger partners. In Das, T. K. (Ed.), *Strategic Alliances for SME Development*, Information Age Publishing, 1–22.

Bengtsson, M. & Kock, S. (2000). Coopetition' in business networks, to cooperate and compete simultaneously. *Industrial Marketing Management*, 29(5), 411–426.

Bengtsson, M., Raza-Ullah, T., & Vanyushyn, V. (2016). The coopetition paradox and tension: The moderating role of coopetition capability. *Industrial Marketing Management*, 53, 19–30.

Bouncken, R. B., Gast, J., Kraus, S., & Bogers, M. (2015). Coopetition: a systematic review, synthesis, and future research directions. *Review of Managerial Science*, 9(3), 577–601.

Casciaro, T. & Piskorski, M. J. (2005). Power imbalance, mutual dependence, and constraint absorption: A closer look at resource dependence theory. *Administrative Science Quarterly*, 50(2), 167–199.

Chetty, S. K. & Wilson, H. I. (2003). Collaborating with competitors to acquire resources. *International Business Review*, 12(1), 61–81.

Chiambaretto, P. (2015). Resource dependence and power-balancing operations in strategic alliances: The role of market redefinition strategies. *M@n@gement*, 18(3), 205–223.

Czakon, W. (2009). Power asymmetries, flexibility and the propensity to coopete: an empirical investigation of SMEs' relationships with franchisors. *International Journal of Entrepreneurship and Small Business*, 8(1), 44–60.

Das, T. K. & Teng, B. S. (2000). Instabilities of strategic alliances: An internal tensions perspective. *Organization Science*, 11(1), 77–101.

Della Corte, V. & Aria, M. (2016). Coopetition and sustainable competitive advantage. The case of tourist destinations. *Tourism Management*, 54, 524–540.

Fernandez, A. S., Le Roy, F., & Gnyawali, D. R. (2014). Sources and management of tension in co-opetition case evidence from telecommunications satellites manufacturing in Europe. *Industrial Marketing Management*, 43(2), 222–235.

Gast, J., Filser, M., Gundolf, K., & Kraus, S. (2015). Coopetition research: towards a better understanding of past trends and future directions. *International Journal of Entrepreneurship and Small Business*, 24(4), 492–521.

Granata, J., Géraudel, M., Gundolf, K., Gast, J., & Marquès, P. (2016). Organisational innovation and coopetition between SMEs: a tertius strategies approach. *International Journal of Technology Management*, 71(1–2), 81–99.

Gnyawali, D. R. & Park, B.-J. R. (2009). Co-opetition and technological innovation in small and medium-sized enterprises: A multilevel conceptual model. *Journal of Small Business Management*, 47(3), 308–330.

Gnyawali, D. R. & Park, B.-J. R. (2011). Co-opetition between giants: Collaboration with competitors for technological innovation. *Research Policy*, 40(5), 650–663.

Hannan, M. T. & Freeman, J. (1984). Structural inertia and organizational change. *American Sociological Review*, 49(2), 149–164.

Heimeriks, K. H., Klijn, E., & Reuer, J. J. (2009). Building capabilities for alliance portfolios. *Long Range Planning*, 42(1), 96–114.

Huang, H. C. & Chu, W. (2015). Antecedents and consequences of co-opetition strategies in small and medium-sized accounting agencies. *Journal of Management & Organization*, 21(06), 812–834.

Jankowska, B. (2011). Implications of coopetition for international competitiveness and internationalization of firms: perspective of SME and large companies. *International Journal of Business and Management Studies*, 3(1), 49–58.

Kale, P. & Singh, H. (2009). Managing strategic alliances: What do we know now, and where do we go from here? *Academy of Management Perspectives*, 23(3), 45–62.

Katila, R., Rosenberger, J. D., & Eisenhardt, K. M. (2008). Swimming with sharks: Technology ventures, defense mechanisms and corporate relationships. *Administrative Science Quarterly*, 53, 295–332.

Kock, S., Nisuls, J., & Söderqvist, A. (2010). Co-opetition: a source of international opportunities in Finnish SMEs. *Competitiveness Review: An International Business Journal*, 20(2), 111–125.

Kossyva, D., Sarri, K., & Georgolpoulos, N. (2015). Co-opetition: a business strategy for SMEs in times of economic crisis. *South-Eastern Europe Journal of Economics*, 12(1).

Lechner, C. & Dowling, M. (2003). Firm networks: external relationships as sources for the growth and competitiveness of entrepreneurial firms. *Entrepreneurship & Regional Development*, 15(1), 1–26.

Lechner, C. & Leyronas, C. (2009). Small-business group formation as an entrepreneurial development model. *Entrepreneurship Theory and Practice*, 33(3), 645–667.

Levy, M., Loebbecke, C., & Powell, P. (2003). SMEs, co-opetition and knowledge sharing: the role of information systems. *European Journal of Information Systems*, 12(1), 3–17.

Lin, C.Y. Y. & Zhang, J. (2005). Changing structures of SME networks: lessons from the publishing industry in Taiwan. *Long Range Planning*, 38(2), 145–162.

Lindström, T. & Polsa, P. (2016). Coopetition close to the customer—A case study of a small business network. *Industrial Marketing Management*, 53, 207–215.

Morris, M. H., Koçak, A., & Özer, A. (2007). Coopetition as a small business strategy: implications for per-formance. *Journal of Small Business Strategy*, 18(1), 35.

Näsholm, M. H. & Bengtsson, M. (2014). A conceptual model of individual identifications in the context of coopetition. *International Journal of Business Environment 5*, 6(1), 11–27.

Raza-Ullah, T., Bengtsson, M., & Kock, S. (2014). The coopetition paradox and tension in coopetition at multiple levels. *Industrial Marketing Management*, 43(2), 189–198.

Ritala, P. & Hurmelinna-Laukkanen, P. (2009). What's in it for me? Creating and appropriating value in innovation-related coopetition. *Technovation*, 29(12), 819–828.

Robert, F., Marques, P., & Le Roy, F. (2009). Coopetition between SMEs: an empirical study of French pro-fessional football. *International Journal of Entrepreneurship and Small Business*, 8(1), 23–43.

Rosenbusch, N., Brinckmann, J., & Bausch, A. (2011). Is innovation always beneficial? A meta-analysis of the relationship between innovation and performance in SMEs. *Journal of business Venturing*, 26(4), 441–457.

Ross, W. T. & Robertson, D. C. (2007). Compound Relationships Between Firms. *Journal of Marketing*, 71(3), 108–123.

Schilke, O. & Goerzen, A. (2010). Alliance management capability: An investigation of the construct and its measurement. *Journal of Management*, 36(5), 1192–1219.

Schreiner, M., Kale, P., & Corsten, D. (2009). What really is alliance management capability and how does it impact alliance outcomes and success? *Strategic Management Journal*, 30(13), 1395–1419.

Soppe, B., Lechner, C., & Dowling, M. (2014). Vertical coopetition in entrepreneurial firms: theory and practice. *Journal of Small Business and Enterprise Development*, 21(4), 548–564.

Stinchcombe, A. L. (1965). Social Structure and Organizations. In: March, J. G. (Ed.), *Handbook of Organizations*. Chicago: Rand McNally & Company, 142–193.

Storey, D. J. (1994). *Understanding the Small Business Sector.* London: International Thomson Business Press.

Stuart, T. E., Hoang, H., & Hybels, R. C. (1999). Interorganizational endorsements and the performance of entrepreneurial ventures. *Administrative Science Quarterly*, 44(2), 315–349.

Thomason, S. J., Simendinger, E., & Kiernan, D. (2013). Several determinants of successful coopetition in small business. *Journal of Small Business & Entrepreneurship*, 26(1), 15–28.

Van Gils, A. & Zwart, P. S. (2009). Alliance formation motives in SMEs an explorative conjoint analysis study. *International Small Business Journal*, 27(1), 5–37.

Vanyushyn, V., Holmlund, M., & Kock, S. (2009). Cooperation with competitors and internationaliza-tion: Evidence from the west coast of Finland. *Journal of Euromarketing*, 18(2), 89–100.

von Friedrichs Grängsjö, Y. (2003). Destination networking: Co-opetition in peripheral surroundings. *International Journal of Physical Distribution & Logistics Management*, 33(5), 427–448.

Wassmer, U. (2010). Alliance portfolios: A review and research agenda. *Journal of Management*, 36(1), 141–171.

Zhang, H. S., Shu, C. L., Jiang, X., & Malter, A. J. (2010). Managing knowledge for innovation: The role of cooperation, competition, and alliance nationality. *Journal of International Marketing*, 18(4), 74–94.

37

Open coopetition

Frédéric Le Roy and Henry Chesbrough

Introduction

Open innovation between competitors is a growing area of interest for both researchers and practitioners. Many important industrial success stories began with competitors working together to achieve radical innovation. For instance, the innovative and successful Airbus A300 program was launched in the seventies through the collaborative effort of three European competitors (Sud Aviation, Hawker Siddeley Aviation, and Deutsche Aviation). This pooling enhanced knowledge-sharing among competitors and allowed the success of the Airbus Consortium to challenge Boeing worldwide. More recently, Samsung and Sony worked together to develop LCD technology and became the leaders in the flat-screen television market (Gnyawali & Park, 2011). Sanofi and Bristol-Myers Squibb collaborated to bring two blockbuster drugs successfully to market (Bez et al., 2016).

These examples of open innovation (OI) between competitors are conceptually interesting due to the massive financial investments required. For instance, in the satellite industry, Arabsat was the most important space program of the decade. The program, which is worth 1.8 billion dollars, was achieved by close collaboration between the two European competitors Airbus and Thales (Fernandez et al., 2014). In another instance, the European firm Sanofi and the American firm BMS invested billions of dollars to develop and jointly sell two drugs: Plavix and Aprovel. These examples are collaborations between direct competitors and involve tremendous sums of money. They deserve more attention than they have received to date from academic scholars because they raise interesting questions about innovation, collaboration, competition, and governance.

However, most previous scholars in open innovation do not consider the fact that the openness of innovation could be conducted with competitors. The OI literature has focused on the analysis of three core process: inbound flows (i.e., the importation of knowledge—buying), outbound flows (i.e., the exportation of knowledge—selling) (Dahlander & Gann, 2010), and "coupled innovation" (Piller & West, 2014). These three core processes are not differentiated on whether the source or the destination of the knowledge flow is a competitor.

Therefore, this chapter highlights how the three core processes of innovation should be organized and managed when the open innovation process concerns direct rivals. We seek to show how OI between competitors affects each of the three OI processes and leads to new potentially fruitful research areas. We also attempt to define a research program for OI involving full collaboration with competitors: the outside-in from a competitor, the inside-out to a competitor, and the coupled innovation process between competitors. We call this strategy open coopetition and use the OI and coopetition literature to highlight the main promising research avenues inspired by this new concept.

Open innovation definition and core processes

There are limits to the ability of vertical integration to achieve the scale and scope required for companies to achieve and sustain industry leadership in the twenty-first century. In areas such as cloud computing, artificial intelligence, and geo-mapping, achieving very high volume is vital for competitive success. As a result, opening the innovation process is occasionally a necessary form of organization for the emergence of technical innovation and economic performance (Cassiman & Veugelers, 2006; Chesbrough, 2003, 2006). Openness facilitates access to information regarding new customer needs and new production techniques from a much broader set of sources than traditional internal R&D. Therefore, by increasing firms' strategic flexibility and learning capacity, opening the innovation process becomes crucial for supporting innovation activity (Chesbrough, 2006). This openness helps manage complex coordination (i.e., situations that are difficult to manage with simple price systems) by avoiding dysfunctions sometimes associated with internal hierarchy (Belderbos et al., 2004).

Opening the innovation process is the main topic of scholars interested in open innovation (Chesbrough, 2003, 2006; Chesbrough & Brunswicker, 2014; West et al., 2014). Open innovation appears as a pervasive question for both practitioners and academics. Because useful knowledge is increasingly dispersed around the world in multiple industries and contexts, firms must open up their innovation processes to harness this wealth of knowledge. Such openness allows firms to foster their innovation process at a lower cost. Openness presents several advantages. Firms benefit from outside-in knowledge, resulting in better outcomes, faster time to market, and greater sharing of risk (Chesbrough, 2006). When firms pursue inside-out open innovation strategies, they can expect higher revenues from the commercialization of intellectual property rights and greater exploration of new markets and new business models to apply to those rights (Chesbrough, 2006).

The definition of open innovation has evolved over time. It began as "a paradigm that assumes that firms can and should use external ideas as well as internal ideas, and internal and external paths to market, as the firms look to advance their technology" (Chesbrough, 2003). The definition was subsequently refined to be the "use of purposive inflows and outflows of knowledge to accelerate internal innovation, and expand the markets for external use of innovation, respectively," (Chesbrough et al., 2006). More recently, it has been defined as "a distributed innovation process based on purposively managed knowledge flows across organizational boundaries, using pecuniary and non-pecuniary mechanisms in line with the organization's business model" (Chesbrough & Bogers, 2014). The business model of the firm dictates the knowledge to be brought into the firm and the knowledge that is allowed to go outside the firm. This business model creates value and captures a portion of the value to enable the firm to sustain its innovations over time (Chesbrough, 2010).

Three core processes of openness have been identified in the OI literature: the outside-in process, the inside-out process, and the coupled process (Gassman & Enkel, 2004).

- The outside-in process means that companies choose to integrate external knowledge in their innovation process. The ways of accomplishing this are numerous. Companies can in-license, purchase patents, purchase companies, etc. Chesbrough (2003) used the case of Cisco to show how a company can save costs by reducing internal R&D efforts and increase its knowledge by opening its innovation process to outside technology.
- The inside-out process means that companies externalize their knowledge to bring ideas into the market faster than could be done by internal development. Companies can out-license, sell IP, create spin-offs, etc. This process enables the creation of new sources of revenues in areas in which the company has not developed its products. Chesbrough (2003) used the case of Xerox to show how this company missed its chance to create revenues by failing to license out its non-core innovations.
- The third process is coupled innovation. This process allows companies to combine the outside-in and inside-out processes. The coupled process internalizes the knowledge of partners and externalizes a company's own knowledge to them. The coupled innovation process should extend deeper than technology internalization and externalization. Companies can choose to collaborate to create new knowledge together, and partners can be clients, suppliers, universities, companies in other industries, competitors, etc.

These three core processes are the pillars underlying open innovation research. The most investigated core process is the outside-in process. A significant amount of research has been dedicated to the question of using outside technology to lower costs and increase the efficiency of innovation processes. The inside-out process is less studied and perhaps the least used by companies. Many companies prefer to keep their patents inside and do not want them to be developed by other companies, thereby missing the revenues of licensing or selling their technology. The third process has been more frequently examined by open innovation and other types of scholars. This process should be a coupled outside-in and inside-out process, with licensing agreements or technology selling. In addition, it should be a broader process involving real cooperation between companies. In this case, this is not only a question of technology exchange by licensing agreement but also a question of creating new technology together. This is this last coupled innovation process that corresponds to collaboration with competitors for innovation.

Cooperation with a competitor for innovation

Collaboration with a competitor for innovation includes both a cooperative and a competitive relation between firms offering the same type of product for the same type of customers (Fernandez et al., 2014; Le Roy & Fernandez, 2015; Gnyawali & Madhavan, 2008). In an apparent paradox, cooperating with a competitor does not lead to lower levels of competition between coopetitive firms.

A variety of factors explain the development of coopetition strategies for innovation (Gnyawali and Park, 2009; Pellegrin-Boucher et al., 2013). The first relates to firms' objective of achieving critical mass against the background of a globalized economy to compensate for insufficient resources. This factor is particularly important in so-called digital industries, where high volumes of data are needed for analytics, for improving algorithms, and for spreading the resulting high fixed costs over more transactions. The second explanatory factor is technological in nature. It is increasingly difficult for a single firm to gather all the resources necessary to develop innovations in its industry. The ongoing growth of R&D budgets forces an increasing number of firms to pool their research. Coopetition enables firms to reach a critical R&D

budget size that is required for effective innovation programs. As a consequence, coopetition strategies have become crucial in industries affected by both globalization and technology.

Despite its importance, coopetition challenges intuition and common sense. Indeed, *a priori,* two competing firms have an interest in relying on their own resources and skills and particularly in not allowing their competitor to benefit from such resources and skills. However, collaboration between competitors is common in high-tech industries. How do we explain this anomaly? We suggest that the most interesting partner for a firm is the one that develops similar or highly complementary products (and frequently for the same consumers). Paradoxically, the more dangerous a competitor is, the more attractive it may be as a partner (Hamel, 1991; Hamel et al., 1989). From this perspective, the best partners are simultaneously potentially the most dangerous competitors (Hamel et al., 1989).

Cooperation with competitors differs from cooperation with non-competitors because partners face higher risks of technology imitation and entry into the target market for the innovation (Gnyawali & Park, 2011; Le Roy & Fernandez, 2015). This means that there are important potential disadvantages to collaboration between direct competitors that also must be considered, as one's intuition would suggest. The early work of Gary Hamel (1991) reminds us that many horizontal alliances are actually learning races between competitors. The winner is the competitor that learns the most first in this conception. Competitor alliances can become entangled in litigation between the parties. In other cases, alliances between competitors can initially be between equal partners, but subsequent events can tip the alliance toward one of the parties. In the worst case, collaborating with a competitor might not be the solution to competitiveness but instead might be the problem. Indeed, the real agenda of a competitor-partner might not be to create value together but rather to have direct access to coopetitor knowledge. The common innovative project acts as a lure, and the collaborative plan becomes a Trojan horse designed to plunder the partner's technology. Therefore, the outcome of collaborating with an aggressive competitor would be damaging for the collaborator. At the end of such collaboration, an overly naïve firm would be a firm without distinctive knowledge and, therefore, one without a competitive advantage.

Despite these high levels of risk, certain companies nonetheless widely collaborate with their competitors. As noted above, the most salient cases of this open coopetition arise when large investments are required to innovate. In such cases, the alternative may be even less attractive than coopetition. Going it alone without a competitor may doom the innovation project to insufficient resources or unacceptably high risks. With all the attendant risks that open coopetition involves, it may nonetheless be preferable to the counterfactual situation.

Knowledge-sharing is a necessary part of cooperation, and trust is an important vector in achieving effectiveness and cooperation performance. However, in the context of coopetition, tensions are higher, and trust and confidence are more difficult to establish (Fernandez et al., 2014). Appropriately defining a good knowledge absorption/protection balance and a level of trust renders coopetition more complex, risky, and presumably less efficient. We might thus expect a lower innovation performance for coopetition compared to cooperation among non-competitors. However, we find no agreement in the literature regarding this point.

The literature reveals contradictory findings. Some studies find negative (or no) effects of coopetition on innovation performance (for example, on the novelty of innovation, Nieto & Santamaria, 2007; Santamaria & Surroca, 2011), whereas others present a picture that is less negative or observe positive effects (Table 37.1). Kang & Kang (2010) describe an inverted-U-shaped relationship for R&D coopetition (for product innovation). A positive effect of coopetition is described for the innovation performance of a firm in general (Tomlinson, 2010) and labor productivity in particular (Belderbos et al., 2004). Focusing on intensity, Neyens et al. (2010)

suggest that continuous coopetition increases radical innovation performance and that discontinuous coopetition increases incremental innovation performance. Thus, the impact of opening the innovation process to competitors remains unclear.

A full research program on OI between competitors

Following the open innovation literature, opening the process of innovation to competitors should be done in three ways: outside-in from a competitor, inside-out to a competitor, and through a coupled innovation process. Therefore, we highlight how openness with a competitor affects these three core processes.

Outside-in from a competitor means using the knowledge of a competitor to develop one's own technology. This type of process has not been extensively studied in past research. It seems counter-intuitive for a company to use the technology of its competitor instead of developing its own technology.

Two basic situations should be distinguished: the outside-in process without collaboration and the outside-in process with collaboration. In the first situation, there is only knowledge flow without collaboration. For instance, a company uses a patent from a competitor or purchases technology from a competitor. To the best of our knowledge, there is no research on this topic. However, certain cases could be identified. For example, in the Chinese automotive industry, the Chinese company CRCC used licenses from the German company Siemens to develop its own technology (Meng, 2016). Research is needed to better understand this type of strategy. The Chinese company had to choose between the costs and risks of internal development and the opportunity to use the Siemens technology. Using the Siemens technology could decrease the time to market. However, this strategy hurts the past investments of CRCC. CRCC must change its core process, and the risk is the difficulty of being equally as good as Siemens, which could transfer its past technologies and maintain and advance the new one.

In the second situation, a company can use the knowledge of its competitor and collaborate with this competitor to create new knowledge. For example, in the *Enterprise Resource Planning* (ERP) industry, SAP used the Oracle database to develop its ERP; however, this could not be done without a close relationship. SAP had to collaborate with Oracle to obtain relevant databases. At the same time, SAP and Oracle were competing to sell their own ERP solutions (Pellegrin et al., 2013). The customer could make a choice between a pure Oracle solution and an Oracle–SAP solution. This situation appears very common in the TIC industry but is not frequently studied. The fundamental problem stems from the fact that the company must share its knowledge with its competitor-supplier to provide a better solution for the client. However, in doing so, the company opens its technology to its competitor-supplier, which creates the risk of plunder. Even if the supplier is not a strong competitor at the beginning, collaborating increases the overlap and creates an opportunity to enter the market.

The inside-out process is the mirror of the outside-in process. This type of process also has not been extensively studied in past research. It seems very counter-intuitive for a company to reveal its knowledge to a competitor. Two basic situations should also be distinguished: the inside-out process without collaboration and the inside-out process with collaboration. The process without collaboration is a strategy in which a company opens its knowledge to a competitor without collaborating with the competitor. For example, Siemens licensed its technology to CRCC. Siemens obtained revenues from this licensing and had access to the Chinese market. However, this strategy is risky. If the competitor-client is able to quickly imitate the technology, it could become a more dangerous rival in the market. Therefore, companies balance the opportunity to create new revenues with the risk of enforcing the competitor-client. In the Siemens case, the Chinese company rapidly imitated the Siemens technology and became a strong competitor in both the Chinese and the global market. Siemens never won a new call of tender in the Chinese market and now faces a competitor with similar technology and lower prices in the international market.

The inside-out process can also be performed with collaboration. A company can open its technology to a competitor-client and collaborate to improve the technology. For example, as previously shown, Oracle collaborated with SAP to sell its database to this competitor-client. By collaborating, Oracle increased its revenues from the database. However, Oracle gave provided SAP with access to its technology. SAP developed its own database, and now Oracle is no longer a provider for SAP. Therefore, a company must strike a balance between collaborating with a competitor-client to make money and protecting its knowledge ensure that this client will need it in the future. Regarding the other strategy, additional research is required to better understand the opportunity and risk involved in opening the innovation process to a competitor.

The third OI process is coupled innovation, a mix of the outside-in and inside-out processes. Two competitors could decide to open their innovation processes to each other. Two basic situations could be distinguished: the coupled process without collaboration and the coupled process with collaboration. The coupled process between competitors without collaboration has not been extensively studied in past research. This type of strategy is based on behavior, such as using the license from a competitor and simultaneously licensing to this competitor. To the best of our knowledge, there is no research to date on this topic. We suggest that this type of strategy creates a significant opportunity for both companies but also produces significant risks of technology imitation. Further research is needed to examine this strategy.

The coupled process could be extended to intensive collaboration between competitors to create new knowledge. Sony and Samsung together developed the LCD technology for flat screen television (Gnyawali & Park, 2011). Sony brought its own technology and patents in television to the collaboration, and Samsung came with its technology and patents in LCD technology. Together, they created new technologies and new patents. The companies shared the flat-screen and patent revenues. This strategy was very successful; they became the number-one and number-two companies in the market. LCD technology became the standard, replacing plasma technology in the flat-TV industry. Another interesting case is the collaboration of BMS and Sanofi in the drug industry (Bez et al., 2016). Sanofi discovered a new high-potential drug, but the costs and the risks of development were too high for this company. The firm also lacked access to the US market. Therefore, Sanofi decided to collaborate with a US competitor, BMS, to develop, produce, and commercialize the drug, sharing the patent for the final new drug. This strategy has been a great success for both companies.

The coupled process is full of strong incentives for competitors. On the one hand, they can decrease many of the costs and risks of innovation. One the other hand, they can combine their knowledge to co-create a new and efficient product. However, this strategy is also risky because the risk of plunder is very high. Therefore, OI between competitors can produce the best but also the worst. Additional research is required to determine under which conditions the coupled process between competitors creates high values for companies.

OI with competitors includes six different processes: outside-in from a competitor without collaboration, outside-in from a competitor with collaboration, inside-out to a competitor without collaboration, inside-out to a competitor with collaboration, the coupled process without collaboration, and the coupled process with collaboration. These six processes could be detailed for OI behaviors such as licensing and patents (see Tables 37.1 and 37.2). They could also be detailed for other OI behaviours.

Table 37.1 OI with competitor based on licensing

OI	Outside-in from a Competitor	Inside-out to a Competitor	Coupled Process with a Competitor
Without collaboration between competitors	Licensing-in from a competitor	Licensing-out to a competitor	Both licensing-in from a competitor and licensing-out to this competitor
With collaboration between competitors	Licensing-in from a competitor and collaborating with him to develop the technology	Licensing-out to a competitor and collaborating with him to develop the technology	Both licensing-in from a competitor and licensing-out to this competitor, and collaborating with him to develop the technology

Table 37.2 OI with competitor based on patents

OI	Outside-in from a Competitor	Inside-out to a Competitor	Coupled Process with a Competitor
Without collaboration between competitors	Buying patents from a competitor	Selling patents to a competitor	Both selling patents to a competitor and buying patents from this competitor
With collaboration between competitors	Buying patents from a competitor and collaborating with him to develop the technology	Selling patents to a competitor and collaborating with him to develop the technology	Both selling patents to a competitor and buying patents from this competitor, and/or collaborating with him to develop the technology

The majority of these processes have not been fully studied in past research on OI, particularly the outside-in and inside-out processes with competitors (without or with collaboration), even if these processes appear to be counter-intuitive and to challenge theory and practice. These processes, as well as the coupled innovation process, continue to provide new avenues for future studies.

A research program for "open coopetition"

The six processes of OI with competitors are future research fields. We focus here on the three processes with collaboration. The three processes without collaboration are clearly shown in the OI literature but do not concern coopetition. Indeed, coopetition involves collaboration. In the section, we focus on coopetitive OI with competitors, i.e., OI between competitors involving collaboration. We name this type of strategy "open coopetition."

We define open coopetition as OI between competitors including collaboration. Open coopetition includes licensing agreements and/or buying and selling patents when they involve collaboration. In open coopetition, patents or licenses are the explicit asset but are only the visible face of the iceberg. Collaboration exists to permit the exchange and sharing of more tacit knowledge. However, open coopetition also includes more complex elements than simply licensing and patenting, although these may be the most concrete, tangible elements to observe.

In open coopetition, companies should collaborate to define a technological standard, to build and develop a platform, to create and expand an ecosystem, etc. Open coopetition means that the basis of the relationship to innovate is simultaneously competitive and collaborative, from the perspective of creating an entirely new industry, business model, platform, ecosystem, etc. In this way, open coopetition extends the dyadic perspective of coopetition to a broader context of third parties, networks, and ecosystems.[1]

As open coopetition is a novel concept, we build on the OI and coopetition literature to highlight this type of strategy. Given the high risk of opportunism in opening innovation to a competitor, the OI and coopetition literature accepts the idea of "pre-competitive" collaboration in an upstream technology market, followed by competition downstream in the product market (Hunter and Stephens, 2010; Quintas and Guy, 1995). There is a clear separation of upstream activities based on collaboration and downstream activities based on competition. However, this point of view does not fully conform to company behaviour. Le Roy and Fernandez (2015) show the case of Airbus and Thales in the satellite industry. These two competitors collaborate to win certain calls for tender in the global market. When they win a call for tender, they collaborate to create the technology, to manufacture the satellite, and to supply the client. They share their knowledge on the project from upstream to downstream activities. This situation in which companies are coupled in both the upstream technology market and the downstream product market has not been extensively studied.

From this perspective, the research question examines the conflicting incentives in cooperating with direct competitors (and not only in a pre-competitive upstream market) in inside-out, outside-in, and coupled open innovation based on collaboration with a competitor. The basic assumptions are as follows. Coopetition for new products involves the sharing of resources and knowledge (Le Roy and Fernandez, 2015). By sharing their resources, firms have access to important economies of scale. The opportunity for new knowledge creation is very high. However, this is a risky strategy because there is significant opportunity for plunder. This risk of plunder is so high that conflict could damage the common work. The common project could fail and never end in the creation of a new product.

Unfortunately, the literature has not previously examined the performance implications of direct competitors engaging in inside-out, outside-in, and coupled open innovation based on collaboration with a competitor. We can theorize about several of those implications.

In a collaborative OI process with a competitor, there is repeated interaction between the competing firms over time, providing a repeated game set-up to the competitive behavior of firms. Under these conditions, more cooperation can be sustained over time than in single-shot games (Axelrod, 1984). A coupled competitor can credibly threaten to punish an overly aggressive partner's behavior by withholding her coupled contribution to the partner. Coopetition for innovation creates both a high potential for knowledge creation and a high risk of plunder. The more coopetitors open their knowledge, the higher the opportunity of creating new knowledge, and the higher the risk of plunder. As the number of coopetitors increases, the risks of free-riding or defecting by one of the parties also increase, while the ability to police behavior becomes more complex (Olson, 1991).

The central question is therefore to know how companies should be successful in inside-out, outside-in, and coupled open innovation processes based on collaboration with a competitor. The literature on OI highlights this question in several non-conclusive ways.

First, literature on open innovation highlights the general dilemma of opening the innovation process. As a general rule, companies face the paradox of openness, in which they must be open and collaborate with many partners and simultaneously must focus on the way to capture the value created together (Laursen and Salter, 2014) . One of the main risks of OI is the loss of internal assets (knowledge, resources, and technology). The challenge for a company is to find the right balance between opening its knowledge and protecting its core technologies (Henkel, 2006; Chesbrough and Brunswicker, 2014). In the same way, companies face the "disclosure paradox" regarding the costs of collaboration and the uncertainty of its outcome (Dahlander and Gann, 2010). Defining the explicit and tacit knowledge to share is a very difficult task when uncertainty about the outcome is high.

These OI paradoxes are even more intense when the partner is an industrial one and/or a competitor (Chiaroni et al., 2011). However, the OI literature does not provide sufficient focus on solving these paradoxes. For example, the question of IP relevance is ambiguous in the open innovation literature (Holgersson and Granstrand, forthcoming). For certain authors, the implementation of IP is a key point in securing the appropriation of profit (Henkel, 2006). IP are necessary to protect knowledge both in the early stage of collaboration (Huizingh, 2011) and in the exploitation stage (West and Gallagher, 2006). For other authors, however, IP implementation does not really solve the problem, but rather is a source of the problem (Mortara and Minshall, 2011). Indeed, IP strategy can be costly and can negatively affect the willingness to collaborate (Dahlander and Gann, 2010). Therefore, the question regarding the relevance of IP strategy in open innovation between competitors remains open.

Second, the OI literature examines the management of collaboration. As a general rule, managing the openness of innovation with partners is a difficult task (Enkel et al., 2009). The challenge is to establish a partnership in which the partners are close enough to collaborate, but far enough to create cross-fertilization with their different skills (Dahlander and Gann, 2010). In this perspective, competitors are potentially good partners. They have some similar but not fully analogous skills. Therefore, the potential for cross-fertilization is high. However, the OI literature suggests that the challenge begins once the partner has been selected. Once the partnership is launched, partners should try to turn the partnership to their own advantage (Dahlander and Gann, 2010) by exploiting asymmetric information and increasing their negotiation power to capture the majority of the collaboration's value. This opportunistic behavior could damage the effectiveness of the common project. If the partner is a competitor, the opportunism risk is higher and it might be difficult to have a fully collaborative relationship. As a general rule, the OI literature does not indicate how to solve these problems, especially when the partner is a competitor.

In conclusion, questions concerning the key success factors of open innovation based on collaboration with a competitor remain open. The questions include the following: which managerial tools do companies use to manage the open coopetition process? Are there specific organizational designs? What is the role of IP in the success of the open coopetition process? How is IP managed in the event of a discontinued collaboration? What are the incentives for being fully collaborative? Why are companies fair or unfair in the open coopetition process? What are the full benefits of this process? These research questions provide several avenues for future empirical and theoretical responses.

Note

1 This definition differs from that of Teixeira and Tingting (2014), in which open co-opetition is co-opetition with an open source.

References

Axelrod, R. (1984). *The Evolution of Cooperation*. New York: Basic Books.
Belderbos, R., Carree, M., & Lokshin, B. (2004). Cooperative R&D and firm performance. *Research Policy*, 33(10): 1477–1492.

Bez, M., Le Roy, F., Gnyawali, D., & Dameron, S. (2016), Open Innovation between competitors: A 100 billion dollars case study in the pharmaceutical industry, *3th World Open Innovation Conference*, Barcelona, Spain.

Cassiman, B. & Veugelers, R. (2006). In search of complementarity in innovation strategy: internal R&D and external knowledge acquisition. *Management Science,* 52: 68–82.

Chesbrough, H. (2003). *Open Innovation: The New Imperative for Creating and Profiting from Technology.* Boston: Harvard Business School Press Books.

Chesbrough, H. (2006). *Open Business Models: How to Thrive in the New Innovation Landscape.* Boston: Harvard Business School Press Books.

Chesbrough, H. (2010). Business Model Innovation: Opportunities and Barriers. *Long Range Planning,* 43(2), 354–363.

Chesbrough, H. (2012). Open Innovation. *Research Technology Management,* 55: 20–27.

Chesbrough, H. & Bogers, M. (2014). Explicating open innovation: Clarifying an emerging paradigm for understanding innovation. In H. Chesbrough, W. Vanhaverbeke, & J. West (Eds), *New Frontiers in Open Innovation*: 3–28. Oxford: Oxford University Press.

Chesbrough, H. & Brunswicker S. (2014). A fad or a phenomenon? The adoption of open innovation practices in large firms. *Research Technology Management,* 57: 16–25.

Chesbrough, H. W., Vanhaverbeke, W., & West, J. (2006). *Open Innovation: The New Imperative for Creating and Profiting from Technology.* Boston: Harvard Business School Press Books.

Chiaroni, D., Chiesa, V., & Frattini, F. (2010). Unravelling the process from closed to open innovation: Evidence from mature, asset-intensive industries. *R&D Management,* 40(3): 222–245.

Chiaroni, D., Chiesa, V., & Frattini, F. (2011). The open innovation journey: How firms dynamically implement the emerging innovation management paradigm. *Technovation,* 31(1), 34–43.

Dahlander, L. & Gann, D. M. (2010). How open is innovation? *Research Policy,* 39(6): 699–709.

Enkel, E., Gassmann, O., & Chesbrough, H. W. (2009). Open R & D and open innovation: exploring the phenomenon. *R&D Management,* 39(4): 311–316.

Fernandez A.-S., Le Roy, F., & Gnyawali, D. (2014). Sources and management of tension in coopetition case evidence from telecommunications satellites manufacturing in europe. *Industrial Marketing Management,* 43: 222–235.

Fey, C. F. & Birkinshaw, J. (2005). External sources of knowledge, governance mode, and R&D performance. *Journal of Management,* 31: 597–621.

Gassmann, O. & Enkel, E. (2004). Towards a theory of open innovation: three core process archetypes. *R&D Management Conference,* Taiwan.

Gnyawali, D. R., He, J., & Madhavan, R. (2008). Co-opetition: promises and challenges. In C. Wankel (Ed.), *21st Century Management*. Thousand Oaks, CA, 386–398.

Gnyawali, D. R. & Park, B.-J. (2009). Co-opetition and technological innovation in small and medium-sized enterprises: A multilevel conceptual model. *Journal of Small Business Management,* 47(3): 308–330.

Gnyawali, D. R. & Park, B. J. (2011). Co-opetition between giants: Collaboration with competitors for technological innovation. *Research Policy,* 40: 650–663.

Hamel, G. (1991). Competition for competence and inter-partner learning within international strategic alliances. *Strategic Management Journal,* 12: 83–104.

Hamel, G., Doz, Y., & Prahalad, C. K. (1989). Collaborate with your competitors and win. *Harvard Business Review,* 67: 133–139.

Henkel, J. (2006). Selective revealing in open innovation processes: The case of embedded Linux. *Research Policy,* 35(7): 953–969.

Hunter J. & Stephens S. (2010). Is open innovation the way forward for big pharma? *Nature Reviews Drug Discovery,* 9: 87–88.

Holgersson, M. & Granstrand, O. (forthcoming). Patenting motives, technology strategies, and open innovation, forthcoming in *Management Decision.*

Huizingh, E. K. (2011). Open innovation: State of the art and future perspectives. *Technovation,* 31(1): 2–9.

Kang, K. H., & Kang, J. (2010). Does partner type matter in R&D collaboration for product innovation? *Technology Analysis and Management,* 22 (8): 945–959.

Kwanghui, L., Chesbrough, H., & Yi, R. (2010). Open innovation and patterns of R&D competition. *International Journal of Technology Management,* 52: 295–321.

Laursen, K. & Salter, A. (2006). Open for innovation: The role of openness in explaining innovation performance among UK manufacturing firms. *Strategic Management Journal,* 27(2): 131–150.

Laursen, K. & Salter, A. J. (2014). The paradox of openness: Appropriability, external search and collaboration. *Research Policy*, 43(5), 867–878.

Le Roy, F. & Fernandez, A.-S. (2015). Managing coopetitive tensions at the working-group level: The rise of the Coopetitive Project Team. *British Journal of Management*, 26: 671–688.

Le Roy, F., Robert, M., & Lasch, F. (2016). Choosing the best partner for product innovation: Talking to the enemy or to a friend? *International Studies of Management Organisation*, 46.

Meng, D. (2016). Government's Role in Knowledge Absorption of High Speed Train Industry of China. *Open Innovation Seminar*, University of Berkeley, Berkeley.

Mortara, L. & Minshall, T. (2011). How do large multinational companies implement open innovation? *Technovation*, 31(10–11): 586–597.

Neyens, I., Faems, D., & Sels, L. (2010). The impact of continuous and discontinuousalliancestrategies on start-upinnovationperformance. *International Journal of Technology Management*, 52: 392–410.

Nieto, M. J. & Santamaria, L. (2007). The importance of diverse collaborative networks for the novelty of product innovation. *Technovation*, 27: 367–377.

Olson, M. (1991). *Strategy and Choice*. Boston: MIT Press.

Pellegrin-Boucher, E., Le Roy, F., & Gurau, C. (2013). Coopetitive strategies in the ICT sector: typology and stability. *Technology Analysis & Strategic Management*, 25(1): 71–89.

Piller, F. & West, J. (2014). Firm, user and innovation – an interactive model of open innovation. In Chesbrough, H., Wim Vanhaverbeke, W., & West, J. (Eds), *New Frontiers in Open Innovation*. Oxford: Oxford University Press, 29–49.

Quintas, P. & Guy, K. (1995). Collaborative, pre-competitive R&D andthe firm. *Research Policy*, 24(3): 325–348.

Ritala, P. & Hurmelinna-Laukkanen, P. (2009). What's in it for me? Creating and appropriating value in innovation related coopetition. *Technovation*, 29: 819–828.

Santamaria, L. & Surroca, J. (2011). Matching the goals and impacts of R&D collaboration. *European Management Review*, 8: 95–109.

Teixeira, J. & Tingting, L. (2014). Collaboration in the open-source arena: The WebKit case. ACM SIGMIS CPR 2014. 52nd ACM conference on Computers and people research. Singapore: ACM. pp. 121–129.

Tomlinson, P. R. (2010). Co-operative ties and innovation: some new evidence for UK manufacturing. *Research Policy*, 39: 762–775.

West, J. & Gallagher, S. (2006). Challenges of open innovation: The paradox of firm investment in open source software. *R&D Management*, 36(3): 319–331.

West, J., Salter, A., Vanhaverbeke, W., & Chesbrough, H. (2014). Open innovation: The next decade. *Research Policy*, 43(5): 805–811.

Index